Frommer's®

South Africa

7th Edition

by Pippa de Bruyn & Dr. Keith Bain

WILEY

John Wiley & Sons, Inc.

Travel
916.804
De
2011

Published by:

JOHN WILEY & SONS, INC.

111 River St.

Hoboken, NJ 07030-5774

ISBN 978-1-118-07478-7 (paper); ISBN 978-1-118-17618-4 (ebk); ISBN 978-1-118-17619-1 (ebk); ISBN 978-1-118-17620-7 (ebk)

Editor: Stephen Bassman
Production Editor: Erin Amick
Cartographer: Andrew Dolan
Photo Editor: Richard Fox
Production by Wiley Indianapolis Composition Services

Front cover photo: Leopard (Panthera pardus) resting in tree © WILDLIFE GmbH/Alamy Images
Back cover photo: Clifton Bay, Cape Town © Peter Adams Photography Ltd./Alamy Images

For information on our other products and services or to obtain technical support, please contact our Customer Care Department within the U.S. at 877/762-2974, outside the U.S. at 317/572-3993 or fax 317/572-4002.

Wiley also publishes its books in a variety of electronic formats. Some content that appears in print may not be available in electronic formats.

Manufactured in the United States of America

5 4 3 2 1

CONTENTS

13 PLANNING YOUR TRIP TO SOUTHERN AFRICA 440

LIST OF MAPS

ABOUT THE AUTHORS

Pippa de Bruyn was born in Durban, raised in Johannesburg, and has now settled in Cape Town. She is an award-winning journalist and is also a coauthor of *Frommer's India* and *Frommer's Kenya & Tanzania*. Cape-based **Keith Bain** is a coauthor of *Frommer's India, Frommer's Kenya & Tanzania, Frommer's Eastern Europe, Pauline Frommer's Italy,* and *Pauline Frommer's Ireland*. Both are founders of www.bestkeptshhh.com, which offers bespoke trips to Southern Africa, East Africa and India.

ACKNOWLEDGMENTS

Our heartfelt thanks to those in the industry whose hospitality and passion turn the grueling task of painstaking research into pleasure. You know who you are.

HOW TO CONTACT US

In researching this book, we discovered many wonderful places—hotels, restaurants, shops, and more. We're sure you'll find others. Please tell us about them, so we can share the information with your fellow travelers in upcoming editions. If you were disappointed with a recommendation, we'd love to know that, too. Please write to:

Frommer's South Africa, 7th Edition
John Wiley & Sons, Inc. • 111 River St. • Hoboken, NJ 07030-5774
frommersfeedback@wiley.com

ADVISORY & DISCLAIMER

Travel information can change quickly and unexpectedly, and we strongly advise you to confirm important details locally before traveling, including information on visas, health and safety, traffic and transport, accommodations, shopping, and eating out. We also encourage you to stay alert while traveling and to remain aware of your surroundings. Avoid civil disturbances, and keep a close eye on cameras, purses, wallets, and other valuables.

While we have endeavored to ensure that the information contained within this guide is accurate and up-to-date at the time of publication, we make no representations or warranties with respect to the accuracy or completeness of the contents of this work and specifically disclaim all warranties, including without limitation warranties of fitness for a particular purpose. We accept no responsibility or liability for any inaccuracy or errors or omissions, or for any inconvenience, loss, damage, costs, or expenses of any nature whatsoever incurred or suffered by anyone as a result of any advice or information contained in this guide.

The inclusion of a company, organization. or website in this guide as a service provider and/or potential source of further information does not mean that we endorse them or the information they provide. Be aware that information provided through some websites may be unreliable and can change without notice. Neither the publisher nor author shall be liable for any damages arising herefrom.

FROMMER'S STAR RATINGS, ICONS & ABBREVIATIONS

Every hotel, restaurant, and attraction listing in this guide has been ranked for quality, value, service, amenities, and special features using a **star-rating system.** In country, state, and regional guides, we also rate towns and regions to help you narrow down your choices and budget your time accordingly. Hotels and restaurants are rated on a scale of zero (recommended) to three stars (exceptional). Attractions, shopping, nightlife, towns, and regions are rated according to the following scale: zero stars (recommended), one star (highly recommended), two stars (very highly recommended), and three stars (must-see).

In addition to the star-rating system, we also use **eight feature icons** that point you to the great deals, in-the-know advice, and unique experiences that separate travelers from tourists. Throughout the book, look for:

special finds—those places only insiders know about

fun facts—details that make travelers more informed and their trips more fun

kids—best bets for kids and advice for the whole family

special moments—those experiences that memories are made of

overrated—places or experiences not worth your time or money

insider tips—great ways to save time and money

great values—where to get the best deals

warning—traveler's advisories are usually in effect

The following abbreviations are used for credit cards:

AE	American Express	DISC	Discover	V	Visa
DC	Diners Club	MC	MasterCard		

TRAVEL RESOURCES AT FROMMERS.COM

Frommer's travel resources don't end with this guide. Frommer's website, **www.frommers. com,** has travel information on more than 4,000 destinations. We update features regularly, giving you access to the most current trip-planning information and the best airfare, lodging, and car-rental bargains. You can also listen to podcasts, connect with other Frommers. com members through our active-reader forums, share your travel photos, read blogs from guidebook editors and fellow travelers, and much more.

THE BEST OF SOUTHERN AFRICA

P eople come to southern Africa to experience its bounty of natural beauty, to witness the fascinating array of wildlife species, still living as they have for millennia, and to soak up the sun. Few leave disappointed; in fact, as surveys taken after the 2010 World Cup proved, the destination exceeds visitor expectations. With its immensely varied terrain supporting a rich diversity of fauna and flora, the region offers a correspondingly diverse range of experiences, but the one constant is the hospitality of its people. Whether you're here on safari, on a self-drive tour through the vast hinterland, or simply want to lie on the beach or sample wine in one of the world's most beautiful cities, South Africa is ready to welcome you, and this chapter will help you experience the very best it has to offer.

unique SOUTHERN AFRICAN MOMENTS

o **Spotting Zebra Grazing on the Mountain from the Highway** (Cape Town): Zebra, wildebeest, and various antelope graze on Table Mountain's slopes, literally minutes from the city center. Look out for them from the highway as you drive in from the airport. See chapter 4.

o **Enjoying the Sunset and Moonrise from Table Mountain** (Cape Town): From this great vantage point, you can watch the sun sink into the Atlantic Ocean, turning the craggy Twelve Apostles a deep pink; then walk across the plateau to the lip and watch the city lights start to twinkle and take in the dusky outline of the hinterland mountains under a moonlit sky. See chapter 4.

o **Getting Caught Up in the Cape Minstrel Carnival** (Cape Town): Every new year, brightly dressed troops of "coloured" (the local term denoting mixed-race) men and children dance through the streets of Cape Town, singing to the quick-paced strum of banjos and the thump of drums. Inspired by American minstrels who came to the Cape in the late 1800s, the actual celebration dates from 1834, when slaves took to the streets to celebrate their liberation. See p. 40.

o **Watching Whales from the Whitest Sand Dunes** (Western Cape): At De Hoop Nature Reserve's Koppie Alleen, the massive white dunes stretch deep beneath the sea, turning its blue hue into a hypnotic turquoise. This is the perfect place to watch the southern right whales that come to breed off the Overberg Coast—said to offer the best land-based whale-watching in the world. See chapter 5.

o **Walking through Carpets of Flowers** (Northern Cape): In this annual miracle of almost spiritual proportions, the semi-arid and seemingly barren West Coast bursts into life after the first spring rains. More than 2,600 species of flowers literally carpet the Namaqualand plains for a few weeks before sinking back into the soil for another yearlong wait. See chapter 5.

o **Visiting the World's Largest Open-Air Galleries** (Western Cape and KwaZulu-Natal): The bushman (or San) paintings are one of South Africa's greatest cultural treasures and shed light on the lives, pressures, and trance experiences of Bushman shamans. Some 20,000 individual rock paintings have been recorded at 500 different cave and overhang sites between Royal Natal National Park and Bushman's Neck; one of them, Sebaayeni Cave, contains 1,146 individual paintings. Other prime sites include the main caves in Giant's Castle game reserve and Battle Cave in the Injasuti Valley. The Cederberg in the Western Cape is another treasure trove of paintings, easily accessed by overnighting at Bushmans Kloof reserve. See chapters 5 and 11.

o **Jiving with Jo'burg Jollers to the Sounds of Kwaito** (Gauteng): The best place to experience the melting pot of rainbow-nation culture, and to celebrate the emergence of a cohesive national identity, is on the dance floors, grooving to kwaito, South Africa's own homegrown version of house. Look for performances (or recordings) by Brothers of Peace (B.O.P.), Mandoza, Mafikizolo, Zola, M'Du, Mzekezeke, Kabelo, Mapaputsi, Bongo Maffin, or Mzambiya. See chapter 9.

o **Being Haughtily Ignored by a Leopard** (Kruger area, the North-West, Eastern Cape, and Botswana): Watching a languid leopard sprawled along a branch, often with a bloodied paw carelessly slung over her kill, is one of the great highlights of any safari. By far the most elusive of the Big 5, leopard sightings are far from guaranteed however. For the closest guarantee book a lodge in the Sabi Sand; if it's Mala Mala your chances are extremely high. See chapter 10.

o **Smelling Fresh Bush Air and the Wind in Your Hair** (Kruger area, the North-West, Eastern Cape, and Botswana): There's nothing quite like the smell of the bush at dawn, or the wind in your hair as you trundle along dirt tracks, birds flitting alongside you. Winter (May–Aug) is considered to be the best time of the year, as animals are the most visible. But be prepared: Rangers set off in their open-topped vehicles before dawn, when temperatures are barely above zero. See chapters 8, 10, 11, and 12.

o **Seeing the Zulu King's Reed Dance** (KwaZulu-Natal): Experience a centuries-old ethnic tradition as you join some 15,000 Zulus, many dressed in tribal gear, to watch virginal women dance for the Zulu prince Gideon, who would traditionally pick a wife here. See chapter 10.

o **Baptized by Victoria Falls** (Zimbabwe): You'll never forget the sight (or sometimes, just the sound) of more than 500 million liters (130 million gallons) of water a minute thundering into the Batoka Gorge, creating soaring rainbows and a mist of drenching spray. Be prepared to get thoroughly drenched. See chapter 11.

o **Rafting the Churning Waters of the Zambezi** (Victoria Falls, Zimbabwe): There is absolutely nothing like hearing this mighty river pound past, drowning the guides' last-minute instructions as you plunge into swirling white waters, the most challenging commercially run rapids in the world, with such fitting names as The Muncher and Boiling Pot. See chapter 11.

o **Drinking the Waters of the Delta** (Okavango Delta, Botswana): As you're poled along in your *mokoro* (dugout canoe), past palm-fringed islands and aquatic game, sample the crystal-clear waters of the delta. Scoop up a handful (keeping an eye out for crocs!) and take a sip. See chapter 12.

THE wildest ANIMAL ENCOUNTERS

o **Staring Down a Roaring Lion** (private game reserves in Kruger, the Madikwe, KZN, Eastern Cape, and Botswana): Tourists are notoriously hungry for shots of big cats, and if you spend 2 nights at one of the top private game reserves, you will certainly get close to lions, often on the first drive. If you're lucky, you'll be close when the king of the jungle makes his presence known: a spine-tingling 114-decibel roar that will make the entire vehicle shudder, and be heard 8km (5 miles) away. See chapters 8, 10, 11, and 12.

o **Trapped by a Leopard** (private game reserves in Kruger, the Madikwe, KZN, Eastern Cape, and Botswana): You may hole up in your room while a leopard gnaws its dinner outside your door at any of the private game-reserve lodges that are set in the bush. Animals roam freely in this environment, and if dinner happens to be on your patio, celebrate the fact that you're not it and plunder the minibar. See chapters 7, 9, 10, and 12.

o **Stalking a Rhino on Foot** (Kruger National Park, Hluhluwe-Umfolozi Reserve): Tracking rhino is no mean feat: They can smell humans up to 800m (2,624 ft.) away. Being on foot, with only the sounds of the bush and your beating heart as you crouch just meters from an animal as large as a tank, is exhilarating. For the best rhino-tracking experience, stay at Royal Malewane lodge, in the Thornybush game reserve adjoining Kruger, or **Plains Camp at Rhino Walking Safari** in southern Kruger. You will almost definitely track white rhino on the Bushman, Wolhuter, and Napi trails run by Kruger National Park, and the Umfolozi trails run by Hluhluwe-Umfolozi. See chapters 9 and 10.

o **Swimming with Penguins** (Boulders Beach, Cape Town): This is a beautiful place to swim; large boulders create natural swimming pools shared by the only land-breeding colony of jackass penguins. Watch them waddle and dive through the crystal-clear waters, which are slightly warmer than the Atlantic seaboard side—cold comfort, given how icy that is. See chapter 4.

o **Eyeballing a Great White Shark** (Cape Town, Hermanus, and Mossel Bay, Western Cape): Forget tawdry images of razor-toothed monsters chomping at metal bars—this is a riveting, myth-dispelling opportunity to get up close and personal with one of Earth's most ancient creatures, viewing great white sharks in their natural habitat. Most South African shark-cage diving companies adhere to a strict code of conduct, and many are involved in eco-research aimed at helping to save the endangered great white. Nowhere else on the planet can you get to the sharks with so little effort. See chapters 4, 5, and 6.

o **Watching Rare Turtles Nest** (Zululand, KwaZulu-Natal): In November and December, the female leatherback and loggerhead turtles leave the safety of the sea at night to lay their eggs above the high-tide mark on the northern beaches of KwaZulu-Natal. Two months later, hatchlings scramble out of their nests and make a run for the ocean. Only one or two out of every thousand survive to maturity and return to the exact same beach where they were born to produce the next generation. See chapter 10.

o **Avoiding a Territorial Hippo** (Victoria Falls, Okavango Delta, KwaZulu Natal): The upper reaches of the Zambezi and the Okavango Delta's watery channels are best explored by gliding along in a canoe (for the most authentic African safari, sign up for the 3-day Kanana Mokoro Trail and camp out on islands in the delta), but you're more than likely to meet a hippo this way. Always treat them with respect—despite a relatively docile appearance, they are Africa's most dangerous mammal; responsible for more deaths than crocodiles or lions. See chapters 10, 11, and 12.

THE best PRIVATE GAME LODGES & CAMPS

o **Kwandwe** (Eastern Cape): The Eastern Cape wilderness differs markedly from your romanticized notions of Africa. Characterized by its strange, rugged beauty, with alien-looking euphorbia trees standing sentinel on pretty arid plains. The best here, by far, is Kwandwe—miles from any major settlement, serene and magically untamed. With input from members of the local community, and some of the best rangers (adept at bringing to life the most intimate details of the bush), the reserve also offers a range superb of accommodations. See p. 264.

o **Singita** (Sabi Sands Reserve and Kruger National Park): The much-lauded Singita offers the most stylish (and photographed) game lodge experience in Africa, with a choice of four beautiful camps, from plush colonial (Ebony) to the last word in contemporary Afro-chic (Lebombo). Game-viewing is superlative, with top-notch rangers and a very personal approach. Add intelligent, discreet service, exquisite food, and a connoisseur's selection of wines (all included in the price), and you're assured an unforgettable stay. See p. 345.

o **Royal Malewane** (Thornybush Reserve, Limpopo Province): With privately situated suites that offer every luxury, this is all about deep relaxation, enhanced by what is generally considered the best bush spa in Africa. If you can bear to leave your private pool and viewing deck (or in-room lounge and fireplace), you'll find the on-foot tracking is the country's best. See p. 354.

o **Jamala** (Madikwe, South Africa): Our favorite lodge in malaria-free Madikwe, with sumptuous accommodation in five huge, privately located villas; superb, gentle staff; very hands-on personal attention from the owners; sublime cuisine; and an overall sense of decadence and generosity that has you feeling totally pampered and spoiled within 24 hours of arrival. See p. 359.

o **Phinda** (Zululand, KwaZulu-Natal): Showcasing a diversity of terrains (again, this being in subtropical Zululand, quite different from the stereotypical idea of the African bush) and extraordinary animal concentrations, this private sanctuary benefits from some of the country's classiest bush accommodations, some in glass-walled boxlike cottages that bring the surrounding forest or plain right into the bedroom. Guides are the very best in KZN, amenable to your every whim, and you can mix things up with scuba-diving among the coral reefs at nearby Mabibi or Sodwana, or witnessing the ancient turtles arriving on the shores of a nearby beach. See p. 389.

o **Selinda Camp** (Selinda Reserve, Botswana): This is one of our favorite camps in Africa, overlooking the Selinda Spillway (lesser known and more exclusive than the nearby Delta). Game-viewing is out of this world (including large numbers of predators, but rich in variety), but it's the personal service that really sets this lovely camp apart. See p. 437.

- **Eagle Island** (Okavango Delta, Botswana): An Orient Express camp, with all the luxury that implies. Set among the floodplains, the Fish Eagle Bar enjoys one of the best locations in Africa. See p. 429.
- **Nxabega Okavango Tented Camp** (Okavango Delta, Botswana): Offering Afro-chic style and luxury; attentive service; superb cuisine along with a superb location, this has the feel of an elegant vintage gentlemen's club—all very Hemingway meets Blixen. See p. 432.
- **Mombo Camp** (Moremi, Okavango, Botswana): At the confluence of two river systems, Mombo has long been regarded as one of the best game-viewing spots in Africa, attracting large numbers of plains game and their attendant predators; for game-viewing that's much on a par, but at a much friendlier price, take a look at sister camp **Duba Plains.** See p. 426.
- **Linyanti Bush Camp** (Chobe Enclave, Bostwana): On the edge of the Linyati marshes, this area sees huge concentrations of game in the winter months, and the only lodging option here is this intimate little camp. Personally run by owners Beks and Sophia, the camp offers understated luxury, superlative guiding, and exceptional value. See p. 436.
- **Jack's Camp** (Makgadikgadi Pans, Botswana): Desert reserves have a very special effect on the spirit, and these classic 1940s safari camps, situated under palm trees on the fringe of the pans, offer one of the most unusual experiences in Africa. (For a more luxurious desert lodge—we're talking swimming pools and top-end service—head for Tswalu, in the Kalahari.) See p. 439.

THE best FAMILY-FRIENDLY LODGES & CAMPS

- **Hlosi** (Amakhala Game Reserve): Amakhala may not be the best-stocked or best-located game reserve in the malaria-free Eastern Cape, but at high-end Hlosi, there's plenty to keep children entertained through out their stay. Besides a children's room stocked with books, toys and PS2 consoles, and cupboards filled with children's games in the family suites), all kinds of activities are offered (including a safe camp-out session with a ranger telling campfire stories while marshmallows are being roasted). See p. 264.
- **Morokuru Farm House** (Madikwe): With just three well-staffed villas on its own 2,000-plus-hectare (4,940-acre) private reserve abutting malaria-free Madikwe, exclusivity and privacy (there are never any other guests besides you and those you choose to accompany you) make this a great retreat for families seeking solitude to really reconnect. See p. 361.
- **Kirkman's Camp** (Sabi Sands): Game drives unexpectedly end up at "breakfast pizza" stations (replete with bottles of ice cold bubbly for parents), or you could round a corner to find someone waiting with ice cream in the middle of the bush. Rangers pitch their knowledge so that its interesting for adults yet age appropriate; ask for Lennox when you book, and your children will be devastated to say goodbye to a man who knows that the best way to teach is with laughter. See p. 347.
- **Londolozi** (Sabi Sands): The Vartys, who own and manage this camp, see it as a real priority to provide the sense of privilege they had as a family with regular

access to the bush. Their Lion Cubs Den is aimed at fostering bush knowledge among children, custom designed around each individual child's interests but offering a diverse array of activities from starting a fire with a couple of sticks and pancake cooking in a termite mound oven, to learning how to dive a Land Rover or wallowing in the mud. See p. 348.

○ **Mala Mala** (Sabi Sands): A more serious approach to bush education, with fabulous books carefully selected to be age appropriate. And then of course there's the game—the kids will see everything they ever dreamed of within the first day. It's large size and sprawling well-tended grounds also make for a more hotel-like experience; great for nervous little ones (or parents). See p. 349.

○ **Linyanti Ebony Camp** (Botswana): The most exciting family adventure ever: Just four tents, each offering understated luxury (flushing toilets; hot and cold running water); one of them a spacious family tent sleeping four. There's even the luxury of a small plunge pool. Best of all there's no age restriction (though be aware this is a malaria area). Very good value, too. See p. 436.

○ **Chitabe Letaba** (Delta): Another great option, **Chitabe Letaba** is only five en-suite tents, two with adjoining bedrooms suitable for families, each with wooden floors and metal-framed four-poster beds under a canopy of trees. See p. 428. For more Wilderness Safari child-friendly camps, see chapter 12.

THE best PARKS & NATURE RESERVES

○ **Table Mountain National Park** (Cape Town and Cape Peninsula, Western Cape): With so much natural, unfettered beauty so startlingly close to a major city, it's easy to forget that vast portions of the horn-shaped protruding peninsula that makes up Africa's most southwesterly point is actually a preserve, not only for an entire plant kingdom and free-roaming wild animals, but for some of the most splendid mountain and coastal scenery on the planet. You can easily see it by bike, car, or cableway—by why not hike from Table Mountain's Signal Hill all the way to Cape Point?—and discover that nature herself made Cape Town one of the world's favorite city destinations, and certainly Africa's most beautiful. See p. 110.

○ **De Hoop Nature Reserve** (Whale Coast, Western Cape): A magnificent coastal reserve featuring deserted beaches, interesting rock pools, beautiful *fynbos* (uniquely diverse shrublands), a wetland with more than 200 bird species, and a number of small game, but for many, the best reason to come here is because it offers some of the best land-based whale-watching in the world. See p. 181.

○ **Tsitsikamma National Park** (Garden Route, Western Cape): Stretching from Storms River Mouth to Nature's Valley, this coastline is best explored on foot via the 5-day Otter Trail. If the trail is full or you're pressed for time, take the 1km (½-mile) walk to the mouth, or complete the first day of the Otter Trail, which terminates at a beautiful waterfall. See p. 200.

○ **Kgalagadi (Kalahari) Transfrontier Park** (Botswana): This is one of the largest conservation areas in Africa—twice the size of Kruger—yet because of the long distances you need to travel to reach it, this desert reserve is seldom included in the first visitor's itinerary. Pity, for it is starkly beautiful, with red dunes, blond grasses, and sculptural camelthorn trees contrasting with cobalt-blue skies and supports the famed black-maned "Kalahari" lion, hyena, wild dog, and cheetah. See p. 416.

o **Addo Elephant National Park** (Eastern Cape): The main game-viewing area is compact, but this is the place to see elephant by the ton—the Addo herds are famously relaxed; you're also almost sure to see baggy-skinned babies up to mischief, chasing warthogs at the waterholes. Addo now extends from the edge of the Karoo to the coast. See p. 259.

o **Madikwe Game Reserve** (North-West): Rapidly gathering momentum as one of the country's most sought-after getaways, this 75,000-hectare (185,250-acre) malaria-free reserve offers highly diverse eco-zones, allowing it to support an unusual range of species—but mostly its famous for its wild dogs sightings. See p. 357.

o **Kruger National Park** (Mpumalanga and Limpopo Province): One of Africa's greatest game parks, with probably the best-developed infrastructure, Kruger is the most cost-effective, do-it-yourself way to go on safari. Most accommodations are very basic; there are however an increasing number of classy private concessions, where the finest lodgings are available—for a price. See p. 318.

o **iSimangaliso Wetland Park** (Zululand, KwaZulu-Natal): This World Heritage Site encompasses five distinct ecosystems, includes the croc-rich estuary, swamp and dune forests, and the Mkhuze savanna and offshore coral reefs. It is also close to Hluhluwe-Umfolozi, the province's largest Big 5 reserve. See p. 391.

o **uKhahlamba-Drakensberg Park** (KwaZulu-Natal): The Drakensberg in its entirety is spectacular, but if you have time to visit only one region, head north for the Amphitheatre. One of the most magnificent rock formations in Africa, it is also the source of South Africa's major rivers: the Vaal, the Orange, and the Tugela. Rolling grasslands, breathtaking views, and crystal-clear streams. See p. 395.

o **Moremi Game Reserve** (Botswana): No visit to Botswana would be complete without a trip to Moremi, which makes up much of the eastern shores of the delta and offers arguably the best game-viewing in southern Africa, though the more exclusive experiences are to be had on the many concessions that border the reserve. See p. 425.

THE best OUTDOOR ADVENTURES

o **Paragliding Off Lion's Head and Landing on Camps Bay Beach** (Cape Town): It's a breathtaking ride hovering high above Cape Town's ever-changing cityscape, the slopes of Table Mountain folded beneath your weightless feet. As you glide toward the white sands of Camps Bay, lapped by an endless expanse of ocean, you'll have time to admire the craggy cliffs of the Twelve Apostles. See p. 129.

o **Kayaking to Cape Point** (Cape Town): Kayaking is the most impressive way to view this towering outcrop, the southwestern-most point of Africa. It's also the ideal opportunity to explore the rugged cliffs that line the coastline, with numerous crevices and private coves on which to beach yourself. See p. 128.

o **Mountain Biking through the Knysna Forests** (Garden Route, Western Cape): Starting at the Garden of Eden, the 22km (14-mile) Harkerville Red Route is considered the most challenging in the country. Its steep, single-track slip paths take you past indigenous forests, silent plantations, and magnificent coastal fynbos. See p. 202.

o **Bungee Jumping off Bloukrans River Bridge** (Garden Route, Western Cape): Real daredevils do the highest bungee jump in the world in just their birthday suits, leaping 216m (708 ft.) and free-falling (not to mention screaming) for close to 7 seconds, but do it off Vic Falls Bridge and you bounce through a rainbow with incredible views of the thundering falls. See p. 199.

o **Surfing the Mighty Zambezi River** (Victoria Falls, Zimbabwe): Not content to merely raft down the Zambezi, adrenaline-seekers can plunge into the churning waters attached to a Boogie board and ride the 2- to 3m-high (6½–9¾-ft.) waves. See p. 408.

o **Riding with Wild Animals** (Okavango Delta, Botswana): You haven't lived until you've outraced a charging elephant on the back of your trusty steed. Experience Africa as a pioneer by taking a horse safari in the Delta, staying at the popular (and very luxurious) Macatoo Camp. See p. 423.

THE best SOUTH AFRICAN HISTORY STOPS

o **Apartheid Museum** (Johannesburg, Gauteng): Few other museums are able to achieve the emotional impact generated by this reminder of South Africa's ugly past. The collection of images, audiovisual presentations, and intimate tales of human suffering and triumph in the face of adversity is staggering; raw and vivid, the journey from oppression to democracy is powerfully evoked here. See p. 293.

o **Bo-Kaap** (Cape Town): This Cape Muslim area, replete with cobbled streets and quaint historical homes, was one of the few "nonwhite" areas to escape destruction during the apartheid era, despite its proximity to the city. This was where the first freed slaves lived in Georgian houses that still stand today, and it's believed that Afrikaans was first penned here—in Arabic script. See p. 118.

o **The Red Location Museum** (Port Elizabeth, Eastern Cape): This award-winning architectural wonder is made up of 12 individual, rusty, corrugated iron "memory boxes," filled with exhibits and narratives about local life and culture, and the community's contribution to the struggle against apartheid. See p. 255.

o **Origins Centre** (Johannesburg, Gauteng): For anyone interested in understanding the great genetic strand that purportedly binds all of humanity to a common African ancestor, this new museum is filled with clues, from little bits of sharpened rock to fascinating films depicting the shamanic trance rites of the nomadic San people. While the design and layout owes much to contemporary art galleries, this new attraction is a source of fairly hard-core academic knowledge, including DNA testing (at a price) that may provide you with a better idea of where your own ancestral roots may lie. See p. 298.

o **Cradle of Humankind** (Gauteng): Having shot to fame in 1947 with the discovery of a 2.5-million-year-old hominid skull, the region continues to produce fascinating finds about the origins of mankind. Tours with paleontologists introduce you to many intriguing aspects of human evolution, in an area that's remained unchanged for millions of years. See p. 282.

o **The Vukani Collection** (Eshowe, KwaZulu-Natal): While most Westerners head for the cultural villages to gain some insight into Zulu tribal customs and culture,

Vukani is where Zulu parents take their children. With the largest collection of Zulu artifacts in the world, this is a highly recommended excursion, particularly for those interested in crafts. Note that if you aren't venturing this far afield, the **Campbell Collection** in Durban is an alternative. See p. 386.

THE most authentic
CULINARY EXPERIENCES

○ **Preparing and Eating a Cape Malay Meal** (Cape Town): Typified by mild, sweet curries and stews, this cuisine is easy on the uninitiated palate. The most authentic restaurant is Biesmiellah, located in the Bo-Kaap in Cape Town, and many of the top restaurants in the Cape incorporate Cape Malay spicing in creative ways. Better still, join a "cooking safari," during which you cook alongside Bo-Kaap families in their own homes. Learn to roll roti and fold samosas, and then tuck into a gratifying home-cooked meal, featuring the results of your own labor. You'll leave having made friends with a community. See chapter 5.

○ **Tucking in to Boerekos** (Winelands): South Africa's countryside is dotted with small-town communities where traditional Afrikaner *boerekos* (farmers' food) is still a staple, although perhaps given a contemporary update in the manner of innovative 21st-century chefs (such as Chris Erasmus at Franschhoek's Pierneef à La Motte, who is revisiting a pre-British Cape cuisine). But if you want a spread of typical dishes, stop at Boschendal (btw. Stellenbosch and Franschhoek) for their old-fashioned buffet. See chapter 5.

○ **Piling your plate high with barbecue meat in the townships** (Cape Town): Take a Sunday Gospel Tour with Siviwe Mbinda's **Vamos** to experience community life not found in the Eurocentric beach enclaves; after the church service you finish up at Mzoli's, where you choose your meat from the butchery, which is then barbecued for you while DJs pump out loud electronic beats to the gregarious patrons. The place rocks on weekends. See chapter 5.

○ **Lunching in the Cape Vineyards** (Winelands): Set aside at least one afternoon to lunch in the Winelands overlooking vine-carpeted valleys. Recommended options include the lovely terraces at **Constantia Uitsig**, and **Catharina's** on the Constantia Wine Route; or **Overture** or **Delaire Graff** in Stellenbosch. See chapter 6.

○ **High Tea at the Colonial Nellie** (Cape Town): The Mount Nelson has been serving up the best high tea south of the equator for over a century. Luxuriate on sofas under chandeliers with plates piled high with sandwiches and cakes, to the sound of a tinkling pianist or fountain. A gracious colonial-era experience, it's a relative bargain at R160 a head. See p. 99.

○ **Eating with Your Fingers:** You'll find that the African staple *pap* (maize-meal prepared as a stiff porridge that resembles polenta) is best sampled by balling a bit in one hand and dipping the edge into a sauce. Try *umngqusho*—a stew made from maize kernels, sugar beans, chilies, and potatoes—said to be one of Nelson Mandela's favorites. You'll sample *pap* along with mountains of barbecued meat on a township tour in Cape Town, P.E., Durban, or Johannesburg (see chapters 5, 8, 9, and 11), or visit **amaZink,** just outside Stellenbosch in the Cape Winelands (p. 158).

o **Dining Under the Stars to the Sounds of the Bush** (private game reserves throughout southern Africa): There's nothing like fresh air to work up an appetite, unless it's the smell of sizzling food cooked over an open fire. Happily, dinners at private game reserves combine both more often than not. Weather permitting, meals are served in a *boma* (a reeded enclosure), or in the bush in riverbeds or under large trees. Armed rangers and/or massive fires keep predators at bay.

o **Chow a Bunny** (Durban): A Durban institution, the bunny chow is a hollowed-out half-loaf of bread filled with curry; you use the loaf's innards to dunk in the gravy and slowly eat your way down. For the best bunnies, head to lowbrow **Gounden's** or **Hotel Britannia** (p. 381).

o **Chewing Biltong on a Road Trip:** *Biltong,* strips of game, beef, or ostrich cured with spices and dried, is sold at farm stalls and butcher shops throughout the country. This popular local tradition, dating from the Voortrekkers, is something of an acquired taste, but it's almost addictive once you've started.

SOUTH AFRICA IN DEPTH

South Africa, a.k.a. Mzansi, is one big country. Its north-eastern border, churned out by the waters of the Limpopo River, is some 2,000km (1,240 miles) from the Cape's craggy coastline, while the semi-arid West Coast, beaten by the icy waters of the Atlantic, is more than 1,600km (992 miles) from the lush East Coast. Surrounded by two oceans, it also borders some extraordinary countries to the north: Namibia, home to the ancient Namib desert; Botswana, southern Africa's premier wildlife destination; Zambia and Zimbabwe, both straddled by the world's most spectacular waterfall; and the subtropical beauty that is Mozambique. It's a region that is both vast and immensely varied, offering a correspondingly diverse array of experiences.

Historically, too, the contrasts are great: Some of the world's oldest hominid remains—some 4 million years old—make this one of the cradles of civilization, yet 2 decades ago the country was still living under the dark shadow of an oppressive policy that made it the pariah of the modern world. South Africa's peaceful transition to democracy, its combatants coauthoring one of the most progressive constitutions in the world, was one of the great miracles of the 20th century, but despite this feted achievement, the economic reality for far too many remains bleak. Most first-time visitors are, in turn, amazed at how sophisticated the infrastructure is on the southern tip of what is still sometimes referred to as the Dark Continent, and appalled by the contrast in living standards. This often unnerving combination of first and third worlds is also what makes it such a dynamic destination, full of unexpected contrasts, experiences and, yes, bargains. Add huge landscapes, iconic natural wonders, fascinating wildlife, superb wines, world-class restaurants, and an all-year temperate climate, and it is easy to see why South Africa amazed so many thousands during the 2010 World Cup.

But according to most newcomers, the greatest surprise was the warmth of the welcome they received; the inquisitiveness, joy and general desire to please and party with all nationalities. Locals attributed it to the traditional African philosophy of *"ubuntu,"* which says that no human being can exist in isolation; that one can only become human through another human, that we are defined by our interconnectedness. Regardless, the overwhelming success of World Cup showed South Africans what they were capable of. With the huge investment in gleaming new infrastructure (around R35 billion, including the creation of three world-class international airports), the emerging tourism ingénue has arrived as the most sophisticated destination in Africa, ready to welcome an ever-increasing number of visitors to its shores. As South Africa's national broadcaster tagged the 2010 World Cup: "Feel it; it is here."

2 SOUTH AFRICA TODAY

by Richard Calland

Political Analyst for Idasa, SA's leading Democracy Institute, and Associate Professor in Constitutional Law at UCT.

Author of *Anatomy of South Africa: Who Holds the Power?* and *The Vuvuzela Revolution: Anatomy of South Africa's World Cup*

In South African politics there are always two perfectly respectable and plausible answers to any decent question. So, for example: Is South Africa in good shape democratically and economically? Well, it really does depend where you look. In 2010, the country shimmered in the bright light of the global attention of the World Cup. Defying the Afro-pessimists and the naysayer preoccupations with high crime rates, South Africa delivered a very well run tournament. Perceptions not just of South Africa but of the continent shifted. Instead of famine, civil war, and corrupt leaders clinging to power, the world was provided with a completely different view—one of competence, first-world infrastructure, economic opportunity and growth, and social unity and a sense of purpose.

Indeed, as you board the smart new Gautrain at OR Tambo airport in Johannesburg, you are seductively exposed to South Africa's first-world capacity. But look carefully from the window as you speed toward Sandton's throbbing commercial heart and you will see the other side of South Africa: 63% of people do not have access to proper sanitation. Unemployment continues stubbornly at around 25%—the official figure—and 45% (the unofficial figure when taking informal employment out of the equation). "South Africa's is a precarious society," says Geoff Budlender, one of the country's leading human rights lawyers, commenting on the gap between the vision of social justice contained in one of the most modern and internationally renowned constitutions, and the reality of chronic poverty endured by the majority of South Africans.

Until recently, the poor do not seem to have placed blame for the slow rate of socioeconomic change on the ruling party, the African National Congress (ANC), which has won every democratic election since 1994, when Nelson Mandela was elected as South Africa's first black president. Although the ANC's total vote dropped by 4%, its election victory in 2009—South Africa's fourth election, and again, entirely free from violence—was still decisive, with 65.9% of the popular vote. But in the recent May 2011 local government elections, many traditional black working-class voters withheld their votes. As a result, the main opposition party—the Democratic Alliance (DA)—made further inroads, building on its early success in 2006 and 2009 when it became the largest party in the City of Cape Town council and the Western Cape Provincial government, respectively. Smaller parties—such as Mangosuthu Buthelezi's Inkatha Freedom Party (IFP) and the Congress of the People (COPE), which broke away from the ANC after Thabo Mbeki was unceremoniously removed from office by his own party in late 2008—have been further squeezed. South Africa is fast moving toward being a two-party electoral competition.

Having passed the 20% "glass ceiling" that had hitherto seemed beyond them, the DA will be looking ahead to a possible watershed election in 2019 when—should it do justice to its campaign promise of "delivery for all"—it may be strong enough to challenge the ANC for national power. Whether this is possible with a white leader is an uncertain question. The DA's dynamic new leader, Helen Zille, is a former journalist who speaks isiXhosa (one of the nine African indigenous languages recognized in South Africa), along with English and Afrikaans. While the ANC's young maverick, Julius Malema, stirs up racial division by describing Zille as "the madam" doing "a monkey dance" who must be crushed, Zille seeks to present herself and her party as one of probity and accountable government—in contrast to President Zuma and his corruption-blighted party. Jacob Zuma is a political leader who initially developed an international profile for all the wrong reasons: a rape charge he was acquitted of and a corruption charge that was dropped shortly before the April 2009 election that brought him to power. Famous for his populist tendencies and his ability to whip up a crowd with his traditional Zulu dancing and singing of his trademark song "Mashimi Wam" ("Bring Me My Machine Gun"), Zuma has to reconcile the urgent needs of the black, working-class poor who voted him into office with the anxieties of a corporate sector that is already under pressure from the global economic meltdown. Lucky, then, that Zuma's closest friends describe him as a "reconciler by instinct." However, in office, Zuma has proved to be indecisive, declining to make the tough policy choices on issues such as energy policy and labor market reform, as he seeks to hold together the political coalition that defeated Mbeki at the watershed ANC national conference in Polokwane in 2007.

On international affairs, Zuma has won credit for the invitation that brought South Africa into the influential BRICS group of large emerging economies—Brazil, Russia, India, and China. And, in fairness to the ruling party, the landscape of South Africa is unrecognizable from 1994 in many ways: the socioeconomic data show that millions of South Africa now have access to electricity and to water. But patience is now running out, and the increasing number of citizen protests against a lack of so-called "service delivery" is testimony to this. In April 2011, a protester, Andries Tatane, was shot dead by the police. It was a potentially tipping-point moment. Civil society organizations, such as the Council for the Advancement of the South African Constitution (CASAC), reacted with horror, claiming that the government was becoming increasingly repressive and losing sight of its constitutional responsibilities. As CASAC's chairman, Dr. Sipho Pityana, a former ANC activist and senior government official, put it with a potent reference to Nelson Mandela's epic autobiography *A Long Walk to Freedom*: "The walk to freedom may be long, but the return journey can be devastatingly short."

The robust debate about the shape we're in, or the age we're at, continues. It's always been a roller-coaster ride, and in that sense not much has changed. As South Africans like to say, "Africa is not for *sissies* [fainthearted]."

SOUTH AFRICA HISTORY 101

The history of South Africa, like any nation's, depends heavily on who is telling the tale. Under the apartheid regime, children were taught that in the 19th century, when the first pioneering Voortrekkers (predominantly Afrikaans-speaking farmers) made their way north from the Cape Peninsula, and black tribes were making their way south from central Africa, southern Africa was a vast, undiscovered wilderness. Blacks and whites thus conveniently met on land that belonged to no one, and if the natives would not move aside for the trinkets and oxen on offer, everyone simply

South Africa

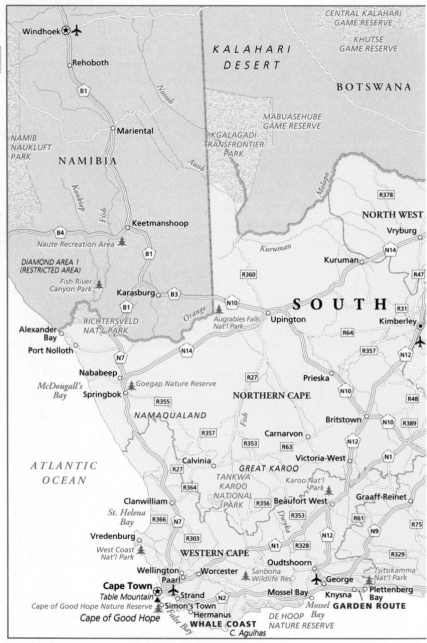

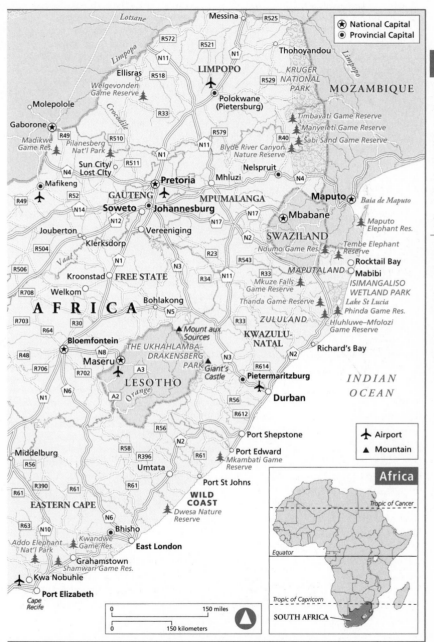

TRUTH + GUILT + APOLOGY = reconciliation?

Following South Africa's first democratic elections in 1994, the **Truth and Reconciliation Commission (TRC)** was formed to investigate human rights abuses under apartheid rule. The many victims of apartheid were invited to voice their anger and pain before the commission, headed by Archbishop Desmond Tutu, and to confront directly the perpetrators of these abuses in a public forum. In return for full disclosure, aggressors, regardless of their political persuasion, could ask for forgiveness and amnesty from prosecution. Although many white South Africans went into denial, many more for the first time faced the realities of what apartheid meant. Wrenching images of keening relatives listening to killers, some coldly, others in tears, describing exactly how they had tortured and killed those once officially described as "missing persons" or "accidental deaths" were broadcast nationwide. Those whom the commission thought had not made a full disclosure were denied amnesty, as were those who could not prove that they were acting on behalf of a political cause. While some found solace in the process, many more yearned for a more equitable punishment than mere admission of wrongdoing.

Twenty-seven months of painful confessions and $25 million later, the commission concluded its investigation, handing over the report to Nelson Mandela on October 29, 1998. But the 22,000 victims of gross human rights violations had to wait until April 2003 to hear that each would receive a one time payment of R30,000, a decision that was greeted with dismay by the victims. In contrast, big businesses (and most whites) were relieved to hear that the government had rejected the TRC's proposed tax surcharge on corporations, as well as the threatened legal action driven by New York lawyer Ed Fagan and others against companies that had benefited from apartheid, opting for

rolled up his sleeves and had an honest fight—which the whites, who believed they enjoyed the special protection of the Lord, almost always won. Of course, for those who pursued the truth rather than a nationalistic version of it, the past was infinitely more complex—not least because so little of it was recorded.

FROM APES TO ARTISTS Some of the world's oldest hominid remains have been found in South Africa, mostly in the valley dubbed the **Cradle of Humankind,** easily accessed from Johannesburg in Gauteng (see chapter 8)—ironic, really, if you think that before the 1990s, evolution was a banned topic in South African schools. These suggest that humanity's earliest relatives were born here more than 4 million years ago; if your ancestral origins are of interest, make sure you also visit the **Origins Centre** in Johannesburg, where you can apply for a DNA test to trace your origins. Much of the Centre is focused on the fascinating spiritual life of the San hunter-gatherers (or Bushmen, as they were dubbed by Europeans), the closest living relatives of Stone Age man. A few small family units of San still survive in the Kalahari Desert, but the most arresting evidence of their long sojourn in southern Africa are the many **rock paintings** they used to record events dating as far back as 30,000 years and as recently as the 19th century. The best places to see these paintings are in caves and rock faces of the Cederberg, in the Western Cape, and the Drakensberg, in Kwazulu-Natal (see chapters 5 and 10).

"cooperative and voluntary partnerships." Mbeki emphasized that the TRC was not expected to bring about reconciliation, but was "an important contributor to the larger process of building a new South Africa."

While it is true that the commission affected a more accurate rendition of recent history, its focus on an individualized rather than a collective approach to human rights abuses under apartheid demanded little by way of white acknowledgement of collective guilt for the suffering their fellow citizens endured. It is against this backdrop that the **Home for All** campaign launched in 2000. Initiated, ironically, primarily by whites involved in the liberation struggle, the campaign was supposed to indicate the willingness of white South Africans to accept that they had personally benefited from apartheid, with signatories pledging to use their skills and resources to contribute to "empowering disadvantaged people, and promoting a nonracial society whose resources are used to the benefit of all its people."

But apologies come hard in South Africa: According to a *Reconciliation Barometer,* published by the Institute for Justice and Reconciliation soon after (www.ijr.org.za), only 22% of whites believed they had benefited from apartheid, and only 29% believed that they should apologize. The debate continues today in discussions around the pros and cons of the government's enforced affirmative action policies (which appear to have done little but transfer a portion of wealth into the hands of a relatively small group, while entrenching racial friction) still dominate the pages of local newspapers. Despite this, it appears that forgiveness has taken place, albeit in individual hearts, and that the South African TRC went a long way toward cauterizing the cycle of retributive anger. You can read some of these transformative stories on the UK site **www.theforgivenessproject.com**.

From these paintings, we can deduce that Bantu-speaking Iron Age settlers were living in South Africa long before the arrival of the white colonizers. Dark skinned and technologically more sophisticated than the San, they started crossing the Limpopo about 2,000 years ago, and over the centuries, four main groups of migrants settled in South Africa: the **Nguni**-speaking group (including the Zulu and Xhosa), followed by the **Tsonga, Sotho-Tswana,** and **Venda** speakers. Iron Age trading centers were developed around copper and iron mines, such as those in and around Phalaborwa: The remains of one such center can be seen at the **Masorini complex** in **Kruger National Park.**

By the 13th century, most of South Africa's eastern flank was occupied by these African people, while the San remained concentrated in the west. In Botswana, a small number of the latter were introduced to the concept of sheep- and cattle-keeping. These agrarian groups migrated south and called themselves the **KhoiKhoi (men of men),** to differentiate themselves from their San relatives. It was with these indigenous people that the first seafarers came into contact. The KhoiKhoi saw themselves as a superior bunch, and it must have been infuriating to be called Hottentots by the Dutch (a term sometimes used to denigrate the Cape Coloured group, and still considered degrading today).

THE COLONIZATION OF THE CAPE   When spice was as precious as gold, the bravest men in Europe were the Portuguese crew who set off with **Bartholomieu**

Dias in 1487 to drop off the edge of the world and find an alternative trade route to the Indies. Dias rounded the Cape, which he named **Tormentoso (Stormy Cape),** after his fleet of three tiny ships battled storms for 3 days before he tracked back to what is today known as Mossel Bay. Suffering from acute scurvy, his men forced him to turn back soon after this.

Ten years passed before another group was foolhardy enough to follow in their footsteps. **Vasco da Gama** sailed past what had been renamed the Cape of Good Hope, rounding the lush coast of what is now called the **Garden Route,** as well as the East Coast, which he named **Natal,** and sailed all the way to India.

The Portuguese opened the sea route to the East, but it was the Dutch who took advantage of the strategic port at the tip of Africa. In 1652 (30 years after the first English settled in the United States), **Jan van Riebeeck,** who had been caught cooking the books of the Dutch East India Company in Malaysia, was sent to open a refreshment station as penance. The idea was not to colonize the Cape, but simply to create a halfway house for trading ships. Van Riebeeck was given strict instructions to trade with the natives and in no way enslave them. Inevitably, relations soured— the climate and beauty of the Cape led members of the crew and soldiers to settle permanently on the land, with little recompense for the KhoiKhoi. To prevent the KhoiKhoi from seeking revenge, van Riebeeck attempted to create a boundary along the Liesbeeck River by planting a bitter-almond hedge—the remains of this hedge still grow today in **Kirstenbosch,** the national botanical gardens. This, together with the advantage of firepower and the introduction of hard liquor, reduced the KhoiKhoi to no more than a nuisance. Those who didn't toe the line were imprisoned on **Robben Island,** and by the beginning of the 18th century, the remaining KhoiKhoi were reduced to virtual slavery by disease and drink. Over the years, their genes slowly mingled with those of slaves and burghers to create a new underclass, later known as the Cape Coloureds.

In 1666, the foundation stones were laid for the **Castle of Good Hope,** the oldest surviving building in South Africa, and still more elements were added to the melting pot of Cape culture. Van Riebeeck persuaded the company to allow the

DATELINE

Circa 8000 B.C. Southern Africa is believed by many paleontologists to be the birthplace of humanity, due to hominid remains dating back more than 4 million years. Millions of years later, the pastoral KhoiKhoi (Hottentots), joined even later by the Bantu-speaking people (blacks), arrive to displace the hunter-gatherer San (Bushmen).

A.D. 1488 Bartolomeu Dias is the first white settler to round the Cape, landing at Mossel Bay.

1497 Vasco da Gama rounds the southern African coast, discovering an alternate sea route to India.

1652 Jan van Riebeeck is sent to set up a supply station for the Dutch East India Company. Cape Town is born.

1659 The first serious armed conflict against the KhoiKhoi occurs; the first wine is pressed.

1667–1700 First Malay slaves arrive, followed by the French Huguenots.

1779 The first frontier war between the Xhosa and settlers in the Eastern Cape is fought. Eight more were

import of **slaves** from the Dutch East Indies; this was followed by the arrival of the **French Huguenots** in 1668. Fleeing religious persecution, these Protestants increased the size of the colony by 15% and brought with them the ability to cultivate **wine.** The glorious results of their input are still thriving in the valley of **Franschhoek (French corner),** augmenting the efforts of Simon van der Stel, second governor to the Cape, who planted the first vines in the shadow of what is still one of the most beautiful Cape Dutch homes and wine estates, **Groot Constantia.** Van der Stel also established **Stellenbosch,** lining the village streets with oak trees and Cape Dutch buildings, making this the most historic of the Winelands towns (see chapter 5).

The British entered the picture in 1795, taking control of the Cape when the Dutch East India Company was liquidated. In 1803, they handed it back to the Dutch for 3 years, after which they were to rule the Cape for 155 years.

One of their first tasks was to silence the "savages" on the Eastern Frontier—these were the **Xhosa,** part of the Nguni-speaking people who migrated south from central Africa. Essential to the plan was the creation of a buffer zone of English settlers. Between 1820 and 1824, the British offloaded thousands of penniless artisans and out-of-work soldiers in **Port Elizabeth,** in what is now the Eastern Cape; issued them basic implements, tents, and seeds; and sent them off to farm the land (much of it totally unsuitable for agriculture) and deal with the Xhosa. English-settler towns, such as **Grahamstown,** which has some fine examples of Victorian colonial architecture, were established, but at great cost. Four frontier wars decimated numbers on both sides, but it was the extraordinary **cattle-killing incident** that crippled the Xhosa. In 1856, a young girl, Nongqawuse, prophesied that if the Xhosa killed all their cattle and destroyed their crops, their dead ancestors would rise and help vanquish the settlers. Needless to say, this did not occur, and while four more wars were to follow, the Xhosa's might was effectively broken by this mass sacrifice. Today the **Eastern Cape** is still the stronghold of the Xhosa, many of whom still live a traditional lifestyle along the **Wild Coast,** and the province is the birthplace of their most famous son, **Nelson Mandela.** Massive tracts of failed farmland in the Eastern Cape have, since the advent of tourism, been rehabilitated

to follow in what is now known as the Hundred Years' War.

1795 The British occupy the Cape for 7 years and then hand it back to the Dutch.

1806 Britain reoccupies the Cape, this time for 155 years.

1815 Shaka becomes the Zulu king.

1820 The British settlers arrive in the Eastern Cape. In KwaZulu-Natal, Shaka starts his great expansionary war, decimating numbers of opposing tribes and leaving large areas depopulated in his wake.

1824 Port Natal is established by British traders.

1828 Shaka is murdered by his half brother, Dingaan, who succeeds him as king.

1834 Slavery is abolished in the Cape, sparking off the Great Trek.

1835–45 More than 16,000 bitter Dutch settlers head for the uncharted hinterland in ox wagons to escape British domination.

1838 A party of Voortrekkers manages to vanquish Zulu forces at the Battle of Blood River.

continues

and restocked with wildlife, forming the **Eastern Cape game reserves,** popular because they are near the **Garden Route** and malaria free.

THE RISE OF THE ZULU & AFRIKANER CONFLICTS

At the turn of the 19th century, the **Zulus,** the Nguni group that settled on the East Coast in what is now called **KwaZulu-Natal,** were growing increasingly combative, as their survival depended on absorbing neighbors to gain control of pasturage. A young warrior named **Shaka,** who took total despotic control of the Zulus in 1818, raised this to an art form. In addition to arming his new regiments with the short stabbing spear, Shaka was a great military tactician and devised a strategy known as the **"horns of the bull,"** whereby highly disciplined formations of warriors outflanked and eventually engulfed the enemy. Shaka used this tactic to great effect on tribes in the region, and by the middle of the decade, the Zulus had formed a centralized military state with a 40,000-man army. In a movement called **Mfecane,** or "Forced Migrations," huge areas of the country were cleared. The Zulus either killed or absorbed people; many fled, creating new kingdoms such as **Swaziland** and **Lesotho.** In 1828, Shaka's two brothers killed him, and one, Dingaan, succeeded him as king.

In the Cape, British interference in labor relations and oppression of the "kitchen Dutch" language infuriated many of the Dutch settlers, by now referred to as *Afrikaners* (of Africa), and, later, *Boers* (farmers). The abolition of slavery in 1834 was the last straw. Afrikaners objected to "not so much their freedom," as one wrote, "as their being placed on an equal footing with Christians, contrary to the laws of God and the natural distinction of race."

Some 15,000 people (10% of the Afrikaners at the Cape) set off on what is known as the Great Trek and became known as the *Voortrekkers,* or "first movers." They found large tracts of unoccupied land that, unbeknownst to them, had been cleared by the recent Mfecane. It wasn't long before they clashed with the mighty Zulu nation, whom they defeated in 1838 at the **Battle of Blood River.** A century later, this miraculous victory was to be the greatest inspiration for Afrikaner nationalism, and a monument was built to glorify the battle. Today the **Voortrekker Monument** is a place of pilgrimage for Afrikaner nationalists and can be seen from most places in Pretoria.

1843	Natal becomes a British colony.
1852	Several parties of Boers move farther northeast and found the Zuid Afrikaansche Republiek (ZAR).
1854	The Boer Independent Republic of the Orange Free State is founded by another party of Boers.
1858	The British defeat the Xhosa after the Great Cattle Killing, in which the Xhosa destroy their crops and herds in the mistaken belief that with this sacrifice their ancestors will destroy the enemy.
1860	The first indentured Indian workers arrive in Natal.
1867	Diamonds are found near Kimberley in the Orange Free State.
1877	The British annex the ZAR.
1879	Anglo-Zulu War breaks out, orchestrated by the British.
1880–81	First Anglo-Boer War is fought. Boers defeat British.
1883	Paul Kruger becomes the first president of the ZAR.
1886	Gold is discovered on the Witwatersrand, the range of

Impressions

The more of the world we inhabit, the better it is for the human race. Just fancy, those parts that are at present inhabited by the most despicable specimens of human beings, what an alteration there *would be if they were brought under Anglo-Saxon influence.*
　　—C. J. Rhodes, British imperialist and South African mining magnate of the 1800s

The Voortrekkers' victory was, however, short lived. The British, not satisfied with the Cape's coast, annexed Natal in 1845. Once again, the Voortrekkers headed over the mountains with their ox-wagons, looking for freedom from the British. They founded two republics: the **Orange Free State** (with similar boundaries to what is now the Free State) and the **South African Republic** or **Transvaal** (now Gauteng, the North-West, Mpumalanga, and the Northern Province). This time the British left them alone, focusing their attention on places of more interest than a remote outpost with only 250,000 settlers. Needless to say, the 1867 discovery of **diamonds** in the Orange Free State and, 19 years later, **gold** in the Transvaal, was to change this attitude dramatically.

GETTING RICH & STAYING POOR　In both the diamond mines and the gold fields, a step-by-step amalgamation of individual claims was finally necessitated by the expense of the mining process. In Kimberley, **Cecil John Rhodes**—an ambitious young man who was to become obsessed with the cause of British imperial expansion—masterminded the creation of **De Beers Consolidated,** the mining house that, to this day, controls the diamond-mining industry in southern Africa. (The discovery of diamonds was also the start of the labor-discrimination practices that were to set the precedent for the gold mines and the ensuing apartheid years.) The mining of gold did not result in the same monopoly, and the **Chamber of Mines,** established in 1887, went some way to regulate the competition.

hills between the Vaal River and Johannesburg.	1914–18 South Africa declares war on Germany.
1899–1902 The Second Anglo-Boer War is fought. British defeat Boers.	1923 Natives (Urban Areas) Act imposes segregation in towns.
1910 The Union of South Africa is proclaimed. Louis Botha becomes the first premier. Blacks are excluded from the process.	1939–45 South Africa joins the Allies in fighting World War II.
1912 The South African Native National Congress is formed. After 1923, this would be known as the African National Congress (ANC).	1948 D. F. Malan's National Party wins the election, and the era of apartheid is born. Races are classified, the passbook or bankbook system is created, and interracial sex is made illegal.
1913 The Native Land Act is passed, limiting land ownership for blacks.	1955 ANC adopts Freedom Charter.

continues

Paul Kruger, president of the South African Republic, became a spoke in the wheel, however. A survivor of the Great Trek and a Calvinist preacher (his home in Pretoria, a museum today, is directly opposite his church), Kruger did not intend to make things easy for the mostly British entrepreneurs who controlled the gold mines. He created no real infrastructure to aid them, and *uitlanders* (foreigners) were not allowed to vote. Britain, in turn, wanted to amalgamate the South African colonies to consolidate their power in southern Africa. British forces had already attempted to annex the Transvaal in 1877, just after the discovery of diamonds, but they had underestimated Paul Kruger; in 1881, after losing the first Anglo-Boer war, they restored the Boer republics' independence. In 1899, when the British demanded full rights for the *uitlanders,* Kruger invaded the coastal colonies.

At first, the second **Anglo-Boer War** went well for the Boers, who used hitherto-unheard-of guerrilla warfare tactics, but the British commander **Lord Kitchener** soon found their Achilles' heel. Close to 28,000 Boer women and children died in Kitchener's concentration camps—the first of their kind—and his scorched-earth policy, whereby the Boer farms were systematically razed to the ground, broke the Boer spirit. Ultimately, Britain would pit nearly half a million men against 88,000 Boers. In 1902, the Boer republics became part of the empire—the Afrikaner nationalism that was to sweep the country in the next century was fueled by the resentments of a nation deeply wounded and struggling to escape the yoke of British imperialism.

OPPRESSION & RESISTANCE   The years following this defeat were hard on those at the bottom of the ladder. Afrikaners, many of whom had lost their farms and families, streamed to the cities, where they competed with blacks for unskilled jobs

1956 "Coloureds" lose the right to vote.	**1963** Nelson Mandela and others are sentenced to life imprisonment in the Rivonia sabotage trials.
1958 H. F. Verwoerd, the architect of apartheid, succeeds D. F. Malan and creates the homelands—territories set aside for black tribes.	**1970s** Worldwide economic and cultural boycotts are initiated in response to South Africa's human rights abuses.
1959 Robert Sobukwe forms the Pan African National Congress (PAC).	**1976** Police open fire on unarmed black students demonstrating against the use of Afrikaans as a teaching medium; the Soweto riots follow.
1960 Police open fire on demonstrators at Sharpeville, killing 69 people. ANC and PAC banned. ANC ends its policy of peaceful negotiation.	**1977** Black-consciousness leader Steve Biko dies in police custody.
1961 South Africa leaves the Commonwealth and becomes a republic. Albert Luthuli is awarded the Nobel Peace Prize.	**1980–84** President P. W. Botha attempts cosmetic reforms. Unrest

on equal terms and were derogatively referred to as the "poor whites." It is worth noting here that black South Africans had also suffered immense losses during the Anglo-Boer War (including the loss of some 14,000 in the concentration camps), but in later years, when Afrikaner fortunes turned, this was neither recognized nor compensated. With the creation of the Union of South Africa in 1910, the country joined the British Commonwealth of Nations and participated in World War I and World War II. Back home, loyalties were divided, and many Afrikaners were bitter about forging allegiances with a country they had so recently been at war with. In 1934, a new "purified" National Party (NP) was established, offering a voice for the "poor white" Afrikaners. Under the leadership of Dr. D. F. Malan, another preacher who swore he would liberate the Afrikaners from their economic oppression, the NP won the 1948 election by a narrow margin—46 years of white minority rule were to follow before internal and international pressure would finally buckle the NP's resolve.

One of the first laws that created the segregationist policy named **apartheid** (literally, "separateness") was the **Population Registration Act,** in which everyone was slotted into an appropriate race group. This caused great division among those of mixed descent, now to become a new "race" (see "The 'Coloured' Vote" below). One of the most infamous classification tests was the pencil test, whereby a pencil was stuck into the hair of a person of uncertain racial heritage. If the pencil dropped, the person was "white"; if not, he or she was classified "coloured." In this way, entire communities and families were torn apart. This new group, dubbed the "coloureds," enjoyed slightly more privileges than their black counterparts—a

2

SOUTH AFRICA IN DEPTH

Dateline

> ## Impressions
>
> *I have cherished the ideal of a democratic and free society, in which all people live together in harmony and with equal opportunities. It is an ideal which I hope to live for and achieve. But if needs be, it is an ideal for which I am prepared to die.*
>
> —Nelson Mandela at the Rivonia Trial, 1963

escalates. Bishop Desmond Tutu, who urges worldwide sanctions, is awarded the Nobel Peace Prize.

1985 A state of emergency is declared, gagging the press and giving security forces absolute power.

1989 F. W. de Klerk succeeds P. W. Botha.

1990 De Klerk ends the state of emergency, lifts the ban on the ANC, and frees Mandela.

1993 De Klerk and Mandela win the Nobel Peace Prize.

1994 The first democratic elections are held, and on May 10, Mandela is sworn in as the first black president of South Africa. De Klerk and Thabo Mbeki become joint deputy presidents.

1995 The Truth and Reconciliation Commission is created under Archbishop Desmond Tutu.

1997 South Africa's new constitution, one of the world's most progressive, comes into effect on February 3.

1999 The second democratic elections are held. The ANC gets 66% of the vote; Thabo Mbeki becomes president.

continues

better standard of housing, schooling, and job opportunities—an overture to their white ancestors. Interracial sexual relations, previously illicit, were now illegal, and the Group Areas Act ensured that families would never mingle on the streets. The act required the destruction and relocation of total suburbs too, almost none of which were white.

Perhaps the most iniquitous new law was the **Bantu Education Act** that ensured that black South Africans would have a second-rate education, given that they were to be providers of semiskilled labor, and never to challenge the better-educated white South Africans for jobs. During this time, the majority of English speakers condemned the policies of what came to be known as the Afrikaner NP (as did certain Afrikaners); but because they continued to dominate business in South Africa, the maintenance of a cheap labor pool was in their interests, and life was generally too comfortable for most to actually do anything other than engage in robust debate over dinner tables.

By the mid–20th century, blacks outnumbered whites in the urban areas but resided "unseen" in **townships** outside the cities. Their movements were restricted by **pass laws;** they were barred from trade union activities, deprived of any political rights, and prohibited from procuring land outside their reserves or homelands. **Homelands** were small tracts of land, comprising a shameful 13% of the country, where the so-called ethnically distinct black South African "tribes" (at that time, 42% of the population) were forced to live. This effectively divided the black majority into tribal minorities.

The **African Nationalist Congress Party (ANC)** was formed by representatives of the major African organizations in 1912, but it was only in 1934 that it was to find the inspired leadership of **Anton Lembede, Oliver Tambo, Walter Sisulu,** and **Nelson Mandela,** who formed the **ANC Youth League** in that year. The ANC's hitherto passive-resistance tactics were met with forceful suppression in 1960 when police fired on unarmed demonstrators in **Sharpeville,** killing 67 and wounding 200. It was a major turning point for South Africa, sparking violent opposition within and ostracism in world affairs.

2000 UNESCO awards five sites in South Africa World Heritage status. The Kgalagadi, Africa's first Transfrontier Park, is created. UNAIDS reveals that South Africa has the largest AIDS population in the world.

2004 The ANC, with Thabo Mbeki at the helm, wins the country's third democratic election, with a landslide 70% victory.

2005 President Mbeki fires his deputy president, Zuma, when he is implicated in the corruption trial of his financial advisor. Zuma cries foul play and sweeps up populist support.

2007 Tony Leon steps down as leader of the opposition (DA), and Helen Zille takes over. At the ANCs national conference there is a strong shift in support for Jacob Zuma.

2008 The Zuma-led ANC party forces Mbeki to resign as national president in September.

2009 Hundreds of Zuma supporters revel in the streets after prosecutors said they would not

In 1963, police captured the underground leaders of the ANC—including the Black Pimpernel, Nelson Mandela, who was by now commander in chief of their armed wing, **UmkhontoWe Sizwe (Spear of the Nation).** In what came to be known as the **Rivonia Trial,** Mandela and nine other leaders received life sentences for treason and were incarcerated on **Robben Island.** The imprisonment of key figures effectively silenced the opposition within the country for some time and allowed the NP to further entrench its segregationist policies. But it wasn't all clear sailing: Hendrik Verwoerd, the cabinet minister for Bantu Affairs under Malan and the man named the "architect of apartheid," was stabbed to death one morning in the House of Assembly—strangely, not for political reasons; the murderer insisted that a tapeworm had ordered him to do it. In 1966, B. J. Vorster became the new NP leader. He was to push for the independence of Verwoerd's black homelands, which would effectively deprive black people of their South African citizenship, and enforce the use of Afrikaans as a language medium in all schools. Ironically, the latter triggered the backlash that would end Afrikaner dominance.

SOUTH AFRICA GOES INTO LABOR   On June 16, 1976, thousands of black schoolchildren in **Soweto** took to the streets to demonstrate against this new law, which, for the many non-Afrikaans speakers, would render schooling incomprehensible. The police opened fire, killing, among others, 12-year-old **Hector Pieterson** (you can see the photograph that shocked the world, taken minutes after, in the **Hector Pieterson Museum** in Soweto), and chaos ensued, with unrest spreading throughout the country. The youth, disillusioned by their parents' implicit compliance with apartheid laws, burned schools, libraries, and *shebeens*, the informal liquor outlets that provided an opiate to the dispossessed. Many arrests followed, including that of black-consciousness leader **Steve Biko** in the Eastern Cape, who became the 46th political prisoner to die during police interrogation. Young activists fled the country and joined ANC military training camps. The ANC, led by Oliver Tambo, called for international sanctions—the world responded with economic, cultural, and sports boycotts, and awarded the Nobel Peace Prize to **Archbishop Desmond Tutu,** one of the strongest campaigners for sanctions. The new NP premier, **P. W.**

pursue corruption charges against him. A month later, the ANC wins its fourth general election by 66% and Zuma is inaugurated as South Africa's third black president (Motlanthe having stood in for Mbeki).

2010   South Africa successfully hosts hundreds of thousands of visitors during the Soccer World Cup, the first country in Africa to do so.

2011   For the first time the Zille-led DA—promising "delivery for all"—starts to make inroads on the ANC stronghold, with about one in four votes cast in the DA's favor in local and provincial elections.

We have triumphed. We enter into a covenant that we shall build the society in which all South Africans will be able to walk tall, without any fear in their hearts, assured of their inalienable right to human dignity—a rainbow nation at peace with itself and the world.
—Nelson Mandela, inaugural address, 1994

Botha, or, as he came to be known, *die Groot Krokodil* (the Big Crocodile), simply wagged his finger and declared South Africa capable of going it alone despite increasing pressure—in the words of Allen Boesak, addressing the launch of the United Democratic Front, the students of Soweto wanted *all* their rights, they wanted them *here,* and they wanted them *now.* The crocodile's bite proved as bad as his bark, and his response was to pour troops into townships. In 1986, he declared a **state of emergency,** giving his security forces power to persecute the opposition, and silencing the internal press.

The overwhelming majority of white South Africans enjoyed an excellent standard of living, a state of supreme comfort that made it difficult to challenge the status quo. Many believed the state propaganda that blacks were innately inferior, or remained blissfully ignorant of the extent of the human rights violations; still others found their compassion silenced by fear. Ignorant or numbed, most white South Africans waited for what seemed to be the inevitable civil war, until 1989, when a ministerial rebellion forced the intransigent Botha to resign, and new leader **F. W. de Klerk** stepped in. By now, the economy was in serious trouble—the cost of maintaining apartheid had bled the coffers dry, the Chase Manhattan Bank had refused to roll over its loan, and sanctions and trade-union action had brought the country's economy to a virtual standstill. Mindful of these overwhelming odds, de Klerk unbanned the ANC, the PAC, the Communist Party, and 33 other organizations in February 1990. Nelson Mandela—imprisoned for 27 years—was released soon thereafter.

BIRTH OF THE "NEW SOUTH AFRICA" The fragile negotiations among the various political parties were to last a nerve-racking 4 years. During this time, right-wingers threatened civil war, while many in the townships lived it. **Zulu nationalists,** of the **Inkatha** party, waged a low-level war against ANC supporters that claimed the lives of thousands. Eyewitness accounts were given of security force involvement in this black-on-black violence, with training and supplies provided to Inkatha forces by the South African Defence Force. In 1993, **Chris Hani,** the popular ANC youth leader, was assassinated. South Africa held its breath as Mandela pleaded on nationwide television for peace—by this time, there was no doubt about who was leading the country.

On April 27, 1994, **Nelson Mandela** cast his first vote at the age of 76, and on May 10, he was inaugurated as South Africa's first democratically elected president. Despite 18 opposition parties, the ANC took 63% of the vote and was dominant in all but two provinces—the Western Cape voted NP, and KwaZulu-Natal went to Buthelezi's Zulu-based Inkatha (IFP) Party. Jubilation reigned, but the hangover was bad. The economy was in dire straits, with double-digit inflation, gross foreign exchange down to less than 3 weeks of imports, and a budget deficit of 6.8% of GDP. Of an estimated 38 million people, at least 6 million were unemployed and 9 million destitute.

Ten million had no access to running water, and 20 million no electricity. The ANC had to launch a program of "nation-building," attempting to unify what the NP had spent a fortune dividing. Wealth had to be redistributed without hampering the ailing economy, and a government debt of almost R350 billion ($52 billion) repaid.

Still, after 300 years of white domination, South Africa entered the new millennium with what is widely regarded as the world's most progressive constitution, and its murky history was finally held up for close inspection by the Truth and Reconciliation Commission, the first of its kind in the world (see "Truth + Guilt + Apology = Reconciliation?," above). South African sports heroes, barred from competing internationally for 2 decades, added to the nation's growing pride, winning the Rugby World Cup in 1995 (*Invictus,* a movie about the events surrounding this, directed by Clint Eastwood, was released in 2010) and its first gold Olympic medals in 1996. Augmenting these ideological and sporting achievements were those that have happened on a grassroots level: 1999, when the ANC won the second democratic elections with a landslide victory of 66% of the vote, saw a change in ANC leadership style, with new president **Thabo Mbeki** centralizing power and promising to focus on delivery rather than reconciliation. The fiscal discipline the ANC pursued resulted in a robust economic outlook, and by late 2000, 6 years after the first democratic election, more than one million houses had been completed, 412 new telephone lines installed, 127 clinics built, and 917,220 hectares (2.3 million acres) of land handed over to new black owners. Some 37,396 households had benefited from land redistribution, and water supply had increased from 62,249 recipients in 1995 to a whopping 6,495,205. Black-owned business grew, and an estimated four million blacks comprised half of the top earners in the country. But with unemployment estimated at between 30% and 40%, the concomitant rise in crime was hardly surprising. The specter of AIDS was also stalking South Africa, and by 2000, it would find itself with the highest HIV-positive population in the world. Equally distressing was the continued divide between black and white incomes, reinforcing South Africa's strange mix of first- and third-world elements, and prompting Mbeki's controversial "two nations" speech in which he stated that "the failure to achieve real nation-building was entrenching the existence of two separate nations, one white and affluent, and the other black and poor."

But the man who kick-started the concept of an African Renaissance became hamstrung by corruption (much of it shrouded in the secrecy surrounding the arms deal he oversaw in the 1990s) and political infighting. Mbeki's Oxford-don demeanor and his inner circle—members of a New Establishment of black intellectuals, industrialists, and professionals, many of them millionaires who benefited from the government's Black Economic Empowerment (BEE) policies—never sat well with the vast majority of South Africans. Into the gap marched the irrepressibly populist former deputy president, Jacob Zuma, whom Mbeki sacked in 2005 after Zuma's main business confidante and associate was convicted of corruption and sentenced to 15 years in jail. Encouraged by the ANC's two powerful alliance partners—the trade union federation, COSATU, and the South African Communist Party, which now represents the traditional social democrat wing—Zuma doggedly pursued the ultimate prize, despite facing his own serious corruption investigation and being dragged through a rape trial in 2006.

Mbeki's favorite rhetorical question, "Will the center hold?," written by Yeats, one of Mbeki's favorite poets, was finally answered in 2008, when the ANC, having chosen Jacob Zuma as their president, effectively fired Mbeki as president of the country, handing the baton to Zuma after the 2009 elections, which the ANC won by a nearly 70% majority. Despite being a more accessible president than Mbeki, apparently a pacifier trying to balance the needs of such vastly differing constituents as business and labor unions, Zuma has categorically failed to deliver "a better life for all", with unemployment (hovering at 24%), education and corruption his greatest challenges. In the mean time ANC Youth League Julius Malema continually grabs headlines with his populist rhetoric and what many whites regard as "hate speech." Will the center hold? The next major election will be in 2014.

THE RAINBOW NATION

South African stereotypes are no simple black-and-white matter. Historically, the nation was made up of a number of widely different cultural groups that under normal circumstances might have amalgamated into a singular hybrid called "the South African." But the deeply divisive policy of apartheid only further entrenched initial differences, and while "affirmative action" policies, still in place 16 years after the dismantling of apartheid, were intended to redress the balance, they have ironically further highlighted the importance of race.

At a popular level, Mandela appeared as the architect of the post-1994 "nation-building," utilizing Desmond Tutu's "rainbow nation" to capture the hearts and minds of black and white South Africans alike. But despite the ANC government's stated objective to end racial discrimination and develop a unique South African identity, this "rainbow nation" remains difficult to define, let alone unify. Broadly speaking, approximately 76% of the population (thought to be approaching 50 million) is black, 12.8% is white, 2.6% is Asian, and 8.5% is "coloured" (the apartheid term for those of mixed descent; see "The 'Coloured' Vote" below). Beyond these are smaller but no less significant groups, descendants of Lebanese, Italian, Portuguese, Hungarian, and Greek settlers, as well as the estimated 130,000-strong Jewish community. The latter has played an enormous role in the economic and political growth of South Africa, as seen at the Jewish Museum in Cape Town.

In an attempt to recognize the cultural diversity of South Africa, the government gave official recognition to 11 languages: Zulu, Xhosa, Afrikaans, English, Sotho, Venda, Tswana, Tsona, Pedi, Shangaan, and Ndebele. Television news and sports are broadcast in the four main language groups, English, Nguni (Zulu and Xhosa), Afrikaans, and Sotho. But while languages provide some clue to the demographics of the population, particularly where a specific language user is likely to live (another apartheid legacy), they give no real idea of the complexity of attitudes within groups. For instance, urban-born Xhosa males still paint their faces white to signal the circumcision rites that mark their transition to manhood, but unlike their rural counterparts, they may choose to be circumcised by a Western doctor. A group of Sotho women may invest their *stokvel* (an informal savings scheme) in unit trusts, while their mothers will not open a bank account. And an "ethnic" white Afrikaner living in rural Northern Cape is likely to have little in common with an Afrikaans-speaking "coloured" living in cosmopolitan Cape Town.

While life is better than it was under apartheid, and incidences of racial prejudice are now condemned in banner headlines, poverty and crime are the new oppressors. Even among the new black elite—the so-called "black diamonds," typified by conspicuous consumption (best observed striding through the glitzy shopping malls and clubs of Jozi)—there are those who feel that the New South Africa is taking too long to deliver on its promises. "There is no black in the rainbow," an embittered Winnie

Afrikaans-speaking people of mixed descent—grouped together as a new race called the "coloureds" during the Population Registration Act, from 1950 to 1991—were perhaps the most affected by the policies of apartheid. They were brought up to respect their white blood and deny their black roots entirely, and the apartheid state's over-ture to the "coloureds'" white forefa-thers was to treat them as second in line to whites, providing them with a better education, greater rights, and more government support than black people (but substantially less than "pure" whites). These policies were even evident on Robben Island, where Indian and "coloured" inmates were given better food and clothing than the black prisoners, despite the fact that they were mostly close political comrades. The destruction of the "coloured" sense of self-worth was made evident when the New National-ist Party (NNP) won the 1994 election race in the Western Cape (where the majority of "coloureds" reside). Voting back into power the same racist party that had created their oppressive new identity was seemingly a result of the false sense of hierarchy that apartheid created. Fear of *die Swart Gevaar* (an NP propaganda slogan meaning "the Black Danger") has been slow to dissi-pate, and in recent years been fanned by the increasingly Africanist policies of the ANC, in which "affirmative" posi-tions are seen as being held for blacks only. In February 2011, government spokesperson Jimmy Manyi said there was an "overconcentration of coloureds in the Western Cape" and that they needed to "spread" and "meet the sup-ply" elsewhere in the country, a horrid reminder of apartheid's group areas policies. Ideally, South Africans would heed the calls of those within the coloured ranks to do away with the label entirely, but as long as the major-ity believe that the "coloureds" are in a class of their own, this remains a pipe dream.

Madikizela-Mandela once said. "Maybe there is no rainbow nation at all." Hardly surprising, really. Despite the peaceful transition, years of fragmentation have ren-dered much of the nation cautious, suspicious, and critical. Many are still molded by the social-engineering experiment that separated them geographically and psycho-logically. But when our school-age youth stand up to sing their national anthem—proudly singing the verses in three languages—those old enough to remember the dark days of apartheid feel a thrill at new beginnings. A truly shared South African identity will take time to emerge—enough, at least, for the colors to mingle.

THE LAY OF THE LAND
South Africa

Geographically, much of South Africa is situated on an interior plateau (the highveld), circled by a coastal belt which widens in the eastern hinterland to become bush savannah, or lowveld, where South Africa's most famous reserve, Kruger National Park, is situated. For the first-time visitor, there are usually three crucial stops: a trip to **Big-Game Country,** most of which is located in and around Kruger National Park, which spans **Mpumalanga** and the **Limpopo Province;** a visit to **Cape Town** and its Winelands; and, time permitting, a self-drive tour of the **Garden Route** in the Western Cape. **Kwazulu-Natal** is another area worth considering, not least for the fabulous crafts, lush game reserves, and magnificent Drakensberg mountains.

THE WESTERN & EASTERN CAPE   The Western Cape is the most popular province in South Africa, primarily due to the legendary beauty of its capital city, **Cape Town,** the neighboring **Winelands,** and the scenic coastal belt called the **Garden Route,** which winds through South Africa's well-traveled Lakes District. It also offers some of the best beach-based whale-watching in the world on the **Overberg Coast;** the world's most spectacular spring flowers display on the West Coast, north of Cape Town; and, in the **Karoo,** the quaint *dorpies* (small towns) that typified rural Afrikaans culture. The mountains and hills that trail the coastline are a botanist's and hiker's dream, with the Cape Floral Kingdom—an awesome array of more than 8,000 species—a treat year-round. The Eastern Cape is where you'll find the Big 5 reserves (those parks where you can spot the Big 5 animals: lion, leopard, rhino, elephant, and buffalo) closest to Cape Town (also malaria free), as well as two of the country's top trails: the **Otter Trail,** in the Tsitsikamma National Park, the exit point of the Garden Route; and the **Wild Coast,** bordering KwaZulu-Natal.

Established as a port in 1652, Cape Town was the first gateway to southern Africa from Europe and still retains more of a colonial feel than any other major city. It is cut off from the rest of the country by mountain ranges and has its own distinctive climate—cool, wet winters and hot, windy summers—ideal for the wine and deciduous fruits that further cocoon the Cape's inhabitants from the harsh realties of the hinterland. This geographic insularity and the wounds inflicted by apartheid have bred their own set of unique problems, however. Gang warfare and drug trafficking in the Cape Flats—a region created by the notoriously draconian Group Areas Act, which relocated people of color to housing projects on the outskirts of town—as well as the increased rancor of the swelling homeless (further exacerbated by the stream of economic refugees from the Eastern Cape and beyond) are serious problems. In a city this size, such problems are hardly unusual, but what is surprising is how cut off from them you'll feel as a visitor.

MPUMALANGA & THE LIMPOPO PROVINCE   To the east of Gauteng and the Free State lies the **Escarpment**—the end of the Drakensberg mountain range that rises in the Eastern Cape, running up the western border of KwaZulu-Natal before dividing Mpumalanga and the Limpopo Province into the high- and lowveld. Traveling through the Escarpment to reach the lowveld's **Big-Game Country,** you will find some of the country's most gorgeous views, the continent's second-largest canyon, and the country's first gold-rush towns, one of which has been declared a living monument. Traveling east on scenic mountain passes, you will drop thousands of feet to the lowveld plains. For those who want to see Africa's wild animals on a budget, **Kruger National Park** offers the best deal on the continent—a high density of game combined with spotlessly clean, albeit spartan, accommodations. For well-heeled visitors (or those who want that once-in-a-lifetime treat), Kruger is also home to several high-end **private concessions** that combine ultraluxurious lodgings with great game-viewing (though you cannot go off-road). Along Kruger's western flank, with no fences between, lie the **private game lodges** in the **Sabi Sand, Manyeleti,** and **Timbavati reserves,** which offer a variety of experiences—from over-the-top-decadent luxury chalets with private plunge pools to rough huts with no electricity. Closer to Johannesburg, the malaria-free **Welgevonden** reserve (p. 355) offers a Big 5 alternative for those with limited time, while **Madikwe** (p. 357) likes to market itself as a Big 7 reserve—cheetah and the rare wild dog being the additional pull.

> ### Endemic: Occurring Nowhere Else
>
> Did you know that 15% of South Africa's mammals, 30% of its reptiles, 6% of its birds, and 80% of its plants are found nowhere else in the world?

KWAZULU-NATAL Hot and humid in summer, warm and balmy in winter, the KwaZulu-Natal coast makes for an excellent beach vacation. Temperatures never drop below 61°F (16°C), and the Indian Ocean is kept warm by the Mozambique Current, which washes past its subtropical shores. Unfortunately, this is no well-kept secret, and development along much of the south and north coasts (Durban being the center) has resulted in another paradise lost and an endless string of ugly, generic vacation and timeshare beach resorts. There are exceptions, the best of which lie north, such as the **iSimangaliso Wetland Park,** Africa's biggest estuary and home to large populations of Nile crocodile and hippo, and within easy striking distance of **Hluhluwe-Umfolozi,** the province's largest Big 5 reserve.

After Cape Town, **Durban** is the most enjoyable city in the country to visit; it's not in the same league in terms of natural beauty, although a thorough pre–World Cup revamp of its handsome Golden Mile beachfront promenade has people flocking to enjoy its warm Indian Ocean waters. It's sultry, with that run-down charm associated with the tropics, and home to a fascinating blend of cultures—besides the Zulu, the largest indigenous group in South Africa, the biggest population of Indians outside of India resides here. Perhaps this is why Durban is a design hothouse, producing the most talented interior and fashion designers in South Africa, and it's a great place to shop for crafts. It is also well situated, should you be interested in combining a visit to a Big 5 game reserve with diving or snorkeling, taking one of the historic battlefields tours, tooling along the Midlands Meander, or hiking through the vast and majestic Drakensberg range (top choice for local hikers). With Durban's shiny new King Shaka International Airport open for business, this relatively undiscovered region is set to offer the Cape some stiff competition.

Botswana

Straddling the Tropic of Capricorn in southern Africa, Botswana is truly one of the last pristine wilderness areas on the continent. Roughly the size of France, it is bordered by Namibia to the west and north, Zimbabwe to the east, and South Africa to the south.

A sparsely populated country of just over one million inhabitants, Botswana offers a varied wilderness experience, from forest to salt pan, bushveld to rolling savanna, ancient lake beds to palm-fringed islands. The waterless Kalahari covers two-thirds of its surface, so it is nothing short of incredible that it is also home to one of the world's largest inland delta systems: the **Okavango Delta,** highlight of Botswana. This 15,000-sq.-km (5,850-sq.-mile) inland flood plain fans into the northwestern corner of the country, creating a paradise of palms, papyrus, and crystal-clear channels and backwaters. The life-giving waters provide an oasis for birds and animals, and consequently unparalleled opportunities for humans to view them.

In addition to the delta, Botswana has **Chobe National Park** to the northeast, a 12,000-sq.-km (4,680-sq.-mile) park that is famed for its huge elephant herds, and between it and the Delta, three bordering concessions: the 23,000-hectare (56,810-acre) **Kwando** reserve in the north; the 125,000-hectare (308,750-acre) **Linyanti**

The **Cape Floral Kingdom** (69,930 sq. km/27,000 sq. miles) covers only .04% of the world's land surface, yet it contains 24,000 plant species; the most diverse of the world's six floral kingdoms—comparable only to the Boreal Kingdom, which comprises all of northern America, Europe, and Asia (51.8 million sq. km/20 million sq. miles). This high concentration makes it as important a conservation area as the Amazon basin. Although it is by no means as threatened, the battle to control alien invasive species introduced during the past century is ongoing.

The delicate inhabitants of the Cape Floral Kingdom are referred to as *fynbos* (literally, "fine bush," pronounced *feign*-boss)—an evergreen vegetation characterized by the ability to thrive on nutrient-poor soil and to survive the Cape's windy, baking summers and wet winters. They're thought to be the oldest floral kingdom, and they're certainly the most diverse. Three-quarters of fynbos species are found nowhere else—many are so specialized they grow only in one valley, while popular indigenous species that have found their way into gardens across the world include the gardenia, red-hot poker, arum lily, strelitzia (bird of paradise), agapanthus, gladioli, and freesia. The most well-known *fynbos* group is the sculptural protea (of which the King protea is S.A.'s national flower), tiny ericas (with fine, bell-shaped flowers), and restios (reeds). Appearing as a homogenous gray-green heathland from afar, the Cape Floral Kingdom has a delicacy and variety of textures best appreciated at close range. Beyond the Kirstenbosch Botanical Gardens in Cape Town, you'll find the best views at Table Mountain and the De Hoop Nature Reserve and Grootbos Private Reserve. For more information, see the Cape Town and Western Cape chapters.

reserve in the east, and to the west of Linyanti, the beautiful 135,000-hectare (333,450-acre) **Selinda** reserve. South are the spectacular wide-open spaces of **Makgadikgadi** and **Nxai Pans** in the Kalahari. Time and money allowing, visits to the Delta, greater Chobe and Kalahari areas are essential to your southern Africa itinerary.

Victoria Falls

Victoria Falls is easy to reach and safe to visit, with two airports within easy striking distance. Chapter 11 deals with the best way to experience what has justifiably been described as one of the wonders of the world, from both the Zimbabwean and Zambian sides of the falls. Note that the falls are also accessible as a day trip from Chobe National Park, Botswana.

RECOMMENDED BOOKS

As the first South African novel, *The Story of an African Farm* (1883)—a beautifully rendered account of daily life in the harsh Karoo—was written at the close of the 19th century by Olive Schreiner. The literature produced in this southern tip captured the imagination of its colonizers with its evocation of a bleak landscape and tough survival. This reached its apotheosis with the advent of the "Jim-comes-to-Jo'burg novel," a phrase coined by Nadine Gordimer to describe the plot in which a naive rural African moves into the corrupt and evil urban landscape—the most famous example being Alan Paton's *Cry the Beloved Country* (1948). Lesser known and more devastating is the work of Sol Plaatje, founding ANC member, who wrote *Native Life in South Africa* (1916), about the devastation of the Land Act in 1916. Even our best-known imports deal with the painful issues surrounding race, usually with love across the color bar. These authors include Nadine Gordimer, awarded both the Booker and Nobel Prize—read *The Conservationist* (1974), *The House Gun* (1998), or *The Burger's Daughter* (1979)—the prolific Doris Lessing, winner of the Nobel Prize for Literature, and J. M. Coetzee, first author to win the Booker prize twice. Coetzee's novels in particular explore the painful constraints of humanity when saturated in the racist fears of the "Dark Continent." He won the first Booker prize for *The Life & Times of Michael K,* in 1983, and the second, in 1999, for the book *Disgrace,* since made into a (not very successful) film. Both are brilliant reads, but my personal favorite remains *Age of Iron* (1990), in which a white woman who is dying of cancer befriends the black tramp living in her garden. Ironically it is this theme that won awards for the latest offering from the superbly talented Afrikaans writer Marlene van Niekerk: *Agaat* (2007; beautifully translated into English) features the relationship between a mute 67-year-old woman dying of ALS motor neuron disease and her "colored" nurse, Agaat. It is political in some sense, but mostly it is a psychological analysis of a relationship that reverberates on many levels—an absolute must for any serious lover of literature. Zakes Mda is another recommended novelist in this genre; either his first book *Ways of Dying* (1995), which follows the adventures of a self-confessed "professional mourner," or his third book, *The Heart of Redness* (2002), a fictional narrative inspired by the real-life story of Nongqawuse, the Xhosa prophet responsible for the tragic Cattle Killing of 1856 (see history above).

For a political overview of the country, packaged as rollicking read, you can't go wrong with Richard Calland and Allistair Sparkes, both eloquent, intelligent, and incisive political analysts, and a joy to read. Of course political autobiography often provides the most direct insights into the complex past of South Africa, and there is no shortage here. Mandela's *Long Walk to Freedom* (1995) is an obvious choice, as is—if you can stand the harrowing truth—*Country of My Skull* (1998), Afrikaans poet Anjie Krog's account of her work as a journalist reporting on the Truth Reconciliation Commission. Head of the Commission, Archbishop Desmond Tutu, authorized a good biography (*Rabble Rouser for Peace,* by John Allan, 2006), but look for the book by his successor, Njongonkulu Ndungane: *A World with a Human Face: A Voice from Africa* (2003) provides an excellent analysis of the challenges facing the country, and how the West exacerbates many of the problems. The gripping autobiography *My Traitor's Heart* (1989), written by the talented Rian Malan, gave eloquent voice to white South Africa's primal fears in the 1980s and is essential reading for anyone who finds it hard to understand how white people could live with themselves under apartheid. For a less intense read, but with plenty of insight, pick up a copy of *Playing the Enemy* (2008), in which John Carlin explores how Nelson Mandela used rugby to set South Africa on the path to reconciliation.

Other reads worth looking into are Fred Khumalo's autobiographical novels, *Touch My Blood* (2006) and *Bitches Brew* (2005), and Kopano Matlwa's *Coconut* (2007), a look at race and class in South Africa—the latter two are both winners of the EU Literary Awards. Equally so, *Dog Eat Dog* (2005), by hip newcomer Niq Mhlongo, dubbed the "voice of the *kwaito* generation," and—for comic relief—*Some of My Best Friends Are White* (2004), by the ever-satirical Ndumiso Ngcobo. *The Native Commissioner* (2006), by Shaun Johnson, and *The Good Doctor* (2003), by Damon Galgut, are both recipients of the Commonwealth Writer's Prize. If you like poetry, Gcina Mhlope is one of the country's most beloved poets; purchase *Love Child* (2002) and see why. If you'd like to dip into a compendium of South Africa's best writers, *Lovely Beyond Any Singing* (2008) is a good choice, with snippets and excerpts from some 30 authors.

However, if all you want to do is escape with a good crime thriller that happens to be set in South Africa, pick up anything written by Deon Meyer: *Dead at Daybreak* (2000) and *Heart of the Hunter* (2003) are both good, but most Meyer fans rate *Thirteen* (2010) and its precursor *Devil's Peak* (2008) as his best. Another popular local thriller writer is Margie Orford, whose heroine, Clara Heart tracks serial killers and the like in Cape Town. But if you like your thrillers gritty, with complex, flawed and compromised characters, opt for the superbly researched and excellent writing of Roger Smith: either *Mixed Blood* (2009), his debut in which four men are drawn into a web of murder and vengeance, or *Wake Up Dead* (2010) in which the dark underbelly of the Cape Flats and Pollsmoor prison infiltrates the conspicuously wealthy Atlantic seaboard. Not for the faint-hearted. Alternatively, discover your favorite crime writer in *Bad Company* (2009), a compendium of short stories by South Africa's top thriller writers (South Africa's *real* gold mine, according to master of suspense, Lee Child, who wrote the foreword). Or opt for light humor with Alexander McCall Smith's *The No. 1 Ladies' Detective Agency* (1998), a series set in Botswana. The sassy *Moxyland* (2008) by Lauren Beukes is worth highlighting; set in a futuristic Cape Town, and tackling issues such as globalization and consumerism, it transcends South Africa's past, and the lack of baggage is refreshing; her latest *Zoo City* (2010) won the Arthur C Clarke Award for sci-fi writing. Memoirs of a haunting African childhood have become a publishing trend and produced some fine reads, among them the superbly balanced and brilliantly told *Don't Let's Go to the Dogs Tonight,* by Alexandra Fuller (2001). Others worth a look in are *Ja No Man* (2007), by Richard Poplak; *Stealing Water* (2008), by Tim Ecott; and *A Fork in the Road* (2009), by Andre Brink, the latter one of South Africa's most respected writers, with a host of fictional titles worth browsing through if you are serious about your literature.

FILM OVERVIEW

By Dr. Keith Bain

Film Theorist

Sadly, there aren't yet many good South African–produced movies likely to give you a truly coherent picture of life in the country today. That's partly because there's such huge cultural and social diversity here that it's absolutely impossible to pack everything into a single story or within a 90-minute frame. Decent local cinema that has garnered critical acclaim usually fails dismally at the box office: South Africans tend to go to movies to be entertained and escape; with so much political intrigue and real-life soap opera in our daily news, you can't really blame us. After big budget Hollywood blockbusters, South Africans consume principally stupid films about stupid South Africans making fools of themselves. Our ability to laugh at ourselves is second to none. The best known example of this type of slapstick comedy event is *The Gods Must Be Crazy,* which astonished audiences when it was first released in 1980. Deceptively, that film was about a bushman traveling to the ends of the earth to dispose of a Coca-Cola bottle dropped into the desert from a passing plane, but in more metaphoric terms, it deals with the clash of cultures that's still, even 30 years later, apparent within South African society. If you can sit through something slightly silly and potentially embarrassing, it remains a classic of South African cinema, and is not without its charms.

Since then the only South African to consistently make money-spinning films has been Leon Schuster, a pranks and pratfalls comedy man who makes fun of the contradictions and paradoxes that are so obviously a part of life in a country that still has deep underlying racial resentment and wide social imbalance. Schuster—in films like *Mr. Bones* (2001, with a sequel in 2008), *Oh Shucks It's Shuster* (1989) and *Oh Shucks I'm Gatvol* (2004), and *There's a Zulu on my Stoep* (2009)—capitalizes on his knack for hitting on a collective funny bone that is inherently connected to the confusing, catastrophic, and potentially wonderful cultural stew. Watch these at your own risk.

Cheap slapstick films aside, early post-apartheid cinema tended to focus heavily on "issue" narratives. *Forgiveness* (2004), exploring the possibilities for redemption, was ultimately a bad reminder of the worst of apartheid-era South Africa—see it if you want to learn about some of the furious tensions that exist in our society. Picking up a number of international film festival awards, *Promised Land* (2003) deals with "white identity syndromes" evident in post-apartheid South Africa, but bewildered audiences with its cartoon stereotypes and art-house posturing; however, the film will give you a vague idea of how some people in this country have grown up with socialized hatred. Two small, but very memorable, late-1990s dramas that do justice to their subject matter are *Paljas* (1998), directed by South Africa's most prolific female filmmaker, Katinka Heyns (and quite possibly the best art-house film to have come out of South Africa), and *A Reasonable Man* (1999), directed by Gavin Hood, who went on to make South Africa's first-ever Oscar winner, *Tsotsi*, in 2005. *Paljas* is a small, riveting movie about a tiny, forgotten Afrikaans village and the intricacies of family and community life there. As a drama, it's searing, tender, and deeply moving, with some of the finest-ever screen performances by South Africans. *A Reasonable Man* explores the notion of justice in an unjust world (Hood, in fact, studied law and the legal system has always played some part in his movies).

In the last few years, three South African films have achieved international recognition: The much-lauded township opera, *U-Carmen e-Khayelitsha* (2005); the Oscar-nominated AIDS movie, *Yesterday* (2004); and the aforementioned *Tsotsi*, which won the Best Foreign Language Film Academy Award, albeit for a version of the film that featured not only a different soundtrack, but an alternate ending to the one shown in South Africa. Be that as it may, *Tsotsi* blew South African audiences away with its gripping story (and superbly sensitive acting) that humanizes both sides of the class fence. Another film worth seeing (this time by Darrell Roodt, director of *Yesterday*), is *Faith's Corner* (2005), starring Lelethi Khumalo, the singular talent who headlines *Yesterday*. It's a very simple tale of a homeless woman's struggle to beg for enough money to feed her hungry children; a heartbreakingly honest reflection of life for many South Africans struggling on the streets. More films worth looking at are *White Wedding* (2010), a romantic comedy about a road trip that somehow captures something of the spirit of this wonderfully diverse nation; *Jerusalama* (2008), a gritty crime thriller that looks at one of Jo'burg's more audacious crime heists—the hijacking of entire buildings by entrepreneurial slumlords; the well-made biopic of Nelson Mandela's prison warden *Goodbye Bafana* (2007), directed by Oscar-winning director Bille August; the gripping, stirring, Hillary Swank–starring *Red Dust* (2006), which uncovers some of the horrors of the past through episodes revealed at the Truth and Reconciliation Commission (TRC), and *Stander* (2004), which showcases the country as it looked and felt in the '70s—it's also a very good portrayal of the only South African bank robber to have attained cult status.

But perhaps the most accessible choices are the Clint Eastwood–directed film *Invictus* (2009), starring Matt Damon as a South African sporting hero and Morgan Freeman as Mandela, in a recounting of the country's memorable victory in the 1995 Rugby World Cup, one year after the first elections; and *District 9* (2009), a sci-fi film about aliens stranded in slums outside Johannesburg. The latter is a sensational film regardless of whether you see the interesting parody with the country's past and ongoing struggle with social geography and race politics.

While we clearly have exciting enough material upon which to base them, we seem to lack the industry capacity to locally produce films. What we do have, though, is a massively talented film industry—for years South African crews have been honing their skills on the plethora of international commercials and films that are shot here. Hopefully, now that the long awaited Cape Town Film Studios are up and running (and where the latest version of *Judge Dredd* was filmed), there will be a more concerted push toward establishing a thriving, consistent industry in S.A., and we can look forward to more brilliantly written, entertaining, and insightful films such as *Gums and Noses* (2004), perhaps the most underrated South African film of the last decade. A slick little comedy set in the world of contemporary advertising, it's one of the few intelligent, locally made films that sidesteps politics and discovers a South Africa that is both unique and globally accessible. Or we could continue to deliver small, interesting niche and art house films—such as 2011's *Skoonheid (Beauty),* which premiered among the *Un Certain Regard* selections at Cannes—that hone in on aspects of the South African psyche that makes this such an intriguing and oftentimes bewildering destination.

CUISINE IN SOUTHERN AFRICA

Southern Africa does not have a developed cuisine to call its own, and despite attempts by local and international chefs to inject menus with a South African or "Cape-inspired" cuisine style, you are far more likely to find restaurants showcasing the cuisines of Italy, Japan, Greece, China, India, and Thailand, or even more likely, some cross-continental hybrid. A *New York Times* journalist once said that our dining culture is almost defined by its fusion approach—a fair comment given the plethora of international chefs showcasing their talents in particularly the Cape, where beautiful surrounds augment the abundance of fresh produce available. That said, there are a few meals worth sampling.

The only truly local cuisine we can lay claim to is **Cape Malay,** an amalgam of imported influences brought by Dutch settlers, slaves from various parts of the East (including Indonesia and India), and the indigenous Khoi-San people, and characterized by mild aromatic curries, pickled fish, samoosas (pastry wrapped around meat or vegetable filling and deep-fried), and some lovely sweet treats. The most popular dish is probably *bobotie,* a baked meatloaf, mildly curried and served with chutney; and *bredie,* a tomato-based stew, usually with lamb, often served with pumpkin sweetened with brown sugar. Another Cape delicacy not to be missed is *waterblommetjie bredie,* or water lily stew, also usually cooked with lamb. *Snoek,* a firm white fish, is often served with *konfyt* (fruits preserved in sugar syrup, from the French *confit,* a legacy of

---

Is your fish "orange" or "red"?

The coastline supplies seafood in abundance: fish, abalone, mussels, oysters, crabs, squid, langoustines, and the Cape's famous rock lobster (crayfish), though here—as elsewhere—has seen an increasing concern about the plunder of stocks. To find out if the fish your restaurant is selling is endangered, simply SMS the name to the **SASSI hot line** (© **079/499-8795**) and an automatic reply message will tell you whether it's "orange" (vulnerable) or "red"; if the latter it's illegal and definitely shouldn't be on the menu.

---

the French Huguenots). Choice desserts you shouldn't miss are *melktert,* a cinnamon-flavored custard tart and *malva pudding,* a hot, sticky sweet Dutch pudding, served with custard or cream; *koeksisters,* plaited doughnuts deep-fried and dipped in syrup, or dusted with coconut and sugar, are a great favorite with local kids.

Interesting as it is, Cape Malay is hardly a staple in South African homes. What you will find is a preponderance of meat, best cooked over the **braai** (barbecue)—whether you are overlooking leafy middle-class suburbia or the sprawling shacklands, spiraling smoke signals the presence of the ubiquitous **braaivleis** (barbecues) or **tshisanyamas** ("burn the meat"), where men clutching cans of beer tend to every conceivable meat cut: from **Karoo lamb** (favored because the sweet and aromatic herbs and grasses of this arid region flavor the animals as they graze) and **boerewors** (a coriander-spiced beef-and-pork sausage, arguably South Africa's staple meat) to chicken feet and pork ribs. The most famous place to witness the butcher-style gatherings so popular in the townships is Mzoli's Place (p. 98), a vibrant informal restaurant attracting both locals and international tourists; more accessible, though, and with some emphasis on food quality (as opposed to popularity), is amaZink in the Stellenbosch township of Khayamandi (p. 158). With luck you will also sample **pap,** a ground-maize polenta-like stiff porridge, or the rougher wholegrain **samp.** Both are served with a tomato-and-onion sauce, usually with chili for bite. *Samp* goes very well with beans.

Aside from **ostrich**—a delicious lean red meat that tastes surprisingly like beef—game cuts such as springbok, kudu, eland, impala, and warthog are common on many menus (increasingly so as an emphasis on local, indigenous produce inspires many top chefs), but be warned that they are usually less tender than lamb or beef, so look for dishes that require slow, lengthy cooking. Unless you're a healthy eater, look out too for **vetkoek** (literally, "fat cake")—a deep-fried crispy bread-dough, stuffed with curried mince; in Durban, they serve a **"bunny-chow"**—a half-loaf of white bread, the soft innards pulled out for the crust to become a receptacle for various curries. Durban is, in fact, famed for its hot **Indian-style curries,** whose burn potential is usually indicated by names such as Honeymooners' Delight (hot) and Mother-in-Law Exterminator (damn hot!). Consume at own risk.

WHEN TO GO

Roughly speaking, the summer months are December to March, autumn is April to May, winter is June to August, and spring is September to November. Because southern Africa is such a large area, and each region's offerings change with the seasons, when you go may determine where you go.

THE COAST South Africa's southwestern coast (a large province known as Western Cape, with Cape Town its capital) tends to attract the majority of international visitors during the summer months, while local landlubbers tend to head for subtropical Kwazulu-Natal (nearest to densely populated Johannesburg and Gauteng). Certainly the Western Cape is big enough to absorb increased numbers without causing the discomfort most people associate with busy seasons, though parts of Cape Town become too crowded for locals' tastes. Be aware, however, that accommodation prices do increase in summer, some by as much as 70% in peak season; if you want better value and fewer crowds, avoid the coast during the busiest school holidays, which—like elsewhere—peak from around 20 December to the first week of January. Note that gale-force winds often occur in Cape Town during the summer months, but tend to die down in February. In fact, the hot months of February and March are considered by most Northern Hemisphere dwellers, desperate to escape what has felt like a very long winter, to be the best times to visit. April, too, is a great month, when the light takes on a softer hue, sunsets are often spectacular, and balmy temperatures are preferable for those who dislike baking heat. Note, though, that you'll need to book early if your visit coincides with Easter weekend, when you will compete with locals on their 10-day school vacation.

Depending on your interests, winter (June–Aug) brings substantial benefits, too: aside from inland game viewing (see below) July to November are the months when the southern right whales migrate to the Cape's southern coast, providing the best land-based whale-watching in the world (and plenty of opportunities to see them by boat). With the Cape a winter rainfall area, local tourism authorities have aptly dubbed the May-to-August period its "Green Season," and indeed the Cape's valleys and mountains are an ideal verdant backdrop to dramatic displays of *fynbos* (shrublike plant) in flower. While it can at times rain continuously, the pattern is usually broken every few days with balmy, sun-drenched days. Note that South African buildings are not geared for the cold, with insulation often low on the priority list; with fluctuating temperatures, you're best off layering. Inland the cold winter nights have real icy bite, but the wet, relatively temperate winters are a wonderful time for Capetonians, who get to air their winter coats for only these few months and reclaim the city, now virtually empty of visitors, as their own.

If you're looking for Southern Hemisphere winter sun, plan your safari during this time, or take a road trip from Cape Town into the semi-arid Klein Karoo, preferably along Route 62, where year-round sunshine ensures that any time of year is a great time, then head to the balmy, lush Garden Route—you can cover this journey with a few hours driving every day in 4 to 6 days; longer if you wish. Winter is also the ideal time to visit the east coast of Kwazulu-Natal, which can be oppressively humid in summer, but merely warm in winter.

October to November is when the Cape floral kingdom again wows her human inhabitants with a new batch of flowering species, while the beaches, still relatively empty, sparkle in the temperate sun, and guesthouses and hotels, hungry after the winter wait, offer some of the best deals of the season.

INLAND May to August are considered the best months for sighting big game in and around Kruger National Park. The foliage is less dense, malaria risk is lower, yet many of the private game reserve lodges drop their prices substantially as foreigners prefer to cavort in the sunny Northern Hemisphere during these months.

June to October, however, is very definitely peak season (prices too) in the Delta, Botswana; thanks to the rains, which flood the delta, luring high densities of game from the desert. Given the low-volume approach to tourism, lodges here are often booked months in advance, despite charging top dollar. The Delta is often combined with a visit to Victoria Falls, but the Falls are widely considered most impressive in full flood, between March and May, when some 500 million cubic liters of water cascade into the Batoka gorge every minute. The spray can obscure views, however, and prohibit riding the Batoka's Grade 5 rapids—renowned in rafting circles as one of the most exhilarating rides in the world—as they are out of bounds when the falls are in flood.

Rainfall

Please note that South Africa is a drought-prone region with two-thirds of the country receiving less than 500mm (20 in.) of rain a year. How to become more **water-wise** is drummed into school children every year, and it is a breach of social etiquette in an area suffering from a lack of water (look out for signs) to take extensive showers or leave the tap running while brushing your teeth.

In the interior, rain usually falls in the summer, and spectacular thunderstorms and the smell of damp earth bring great relief from the searing heat. The Garden Route enjoys rain year-round, usually at night. In Cape Town and surrounds, the rain falls mostly in the winter, when the gray skies are a perfect foil for the burnt-orange strelitzias, pink proteas, and fields of white arum lilies—and an equally good accompaniment to crackling fires and fine South African red wines.

Holidays

If you are traveling during the South African school holidays, make sure you book your accommodations well in advance. (Check exact school holiday dates with South African Tourism, as provinces differ, but they usually run 4 weeks in Dec and Jan, 10 days in Apr, 3 weeks in June and July, and 1 week in Sept.) Flights are more difficult to find, particularly over the Christmas holidays. Easter holidays (usually late Mar to mid-Apr) can also be busy, while the Kruger is almost always packed during the winter vacation (mid-June to mid-July). For public holidays in South Africa, see p. 451.

Zimbabwe/Zambia

Zimbabwe and Zambia's climates are similar to that in South Africa's northern provinces, with a rainy season in summer, mostly between December and mid-March. Summers are warm to hot (late Oct–Dec can be uncomfortable), and winters are mild. Malaria is still a danger in many areas. There are tsetse flies in parts of the Zambezi Valley and in the southeast. And certain rivers, lakes, and dams are infected with bilharzia. Victoria Falls are often at their fullest around mid-April, at the end of the rainy season (Nov–Apr), though this is also when the mist created by the falling water may obscure the view and malaria-carrying mosquitoes are at their most prolific. Temperatures range from 90°F (32°C) in October and November to 60°F (16°C) in June and July. Many think the best time to see the falls is from August to December, when the view is clearer (though the flow of the water is at its lowest). June through December is high season for many of the upmarket lodges, which raise their prices during these months. You are unlikely to be affected by public holidays.

Botswana

Botswana has a pleasant, temperate climate with low humidity, with a maximum mean temperature of 91°F (33°C) in January and a minimum mean temperature of

38°F (4°C) in June. There are effectively two seasons: summer (Sept–Apr), with frequent rains and thunderstorms, and winter (May–Aug), with cold and dry days and nights. Rainfalls make the summer months a great time to visit the delta if you're interested in birds and plants, but it can get very hot. From April to September, the days are mild to warm, but temperatures drop sharply at night and early in the morning, particularly around June and July. Most consider these 2 months the best time to visit the delta, when the rain that falls on the Angolan bushveld plains seeps down to create what is referred to as the "flood." At this time, water lilies bloom, countless aquatic creatures frolic in the water, and a huge diversity of game from the surrounding dry areas moves into the delta. You are unlikely to be affected by public holidays.

South Africa Calendar of Events

A comprehensive list of events throughout South Africa can be found at www.sa-venues.com/events—even the smallest of festivals, as well as the dates—useful to know even if you don't want to participate in festival gatherings, as parking and accommodation in the area can become more problematic. For a more broad-based yet specialist look at the South African calendar, take a look at the official website **www.southafrica.net**; choose the country "South Africa," then and click on any of the themed options (green season, beach, floral, adventure activities, and so on). For an exhaustive list of events beyond those listed here, check **http://events.frommers.com**, where you'll find a searchable, up-to-the-minute roster of what's happening in cities all over the world.

JANUARY

Cape Minstrels Carnival, Cape Town. Festive teams from the Cape's "coloured" community, with all ages dressed in matching glittering satin outfits and boaters, compete by parading and jiving through the city's streets, singing to banjo beats. Several days in the first weeks of January; dates and routes vary.

Kirstenbosch Summer Sunset Concerts, Kirstenbosch Gardens, Cape Town. One of the must-do activities: pack an early evening picnic on Sunday and sprawl on the lawns listening to some local act, with the towering back of Table Mountain as stunning backdrop. Get there by 4:30pm to grab a choice spot on the lawn before the concert starts at 5:30pm. (Season starts end of Nov; program runs to end Mar/first week Apr.)

Shakespeare Open Air Festival, Maynardville, Wynberg, Cape Town. Another place to pack a picnic to enjoy in the park (or dine at one of Wynberg's Chelsea restaurants), then take your seat for the annual Shakespeare play performed in the Maynardville Gardens. Mid-January.

J&B Metropolitan Horse Race, Kenilworth Race Course, Cape Town. The Western Cape's premier horse-racing event is Cape Town's excuse to party, and it attracts many of the country's socialites. Over 18s only. Last Saturday in January or first in February.

Duzi Canoe Race, Pietermaritzburg, KwaZulu-Natal. The country's most prestigious canoeing event covers the 115km (71 miles) between Pietermaritzburg and Durban. Late January.

South Africa Open, new venue every year. South Africa's golfing greats battle it out on one of the country's premier courses. Mid- or late January.

FEBRUARY

Infecting the City, Cape Town. Curated by agent provocateur Brett Bailey, one of the most innovative minds to come out of Cape Town's theatre scene, the city's most public arts festival takes place over a 1-week period, when a series of commissioned collaborative performances are staged in and around the inner city, many of them out on the streets; for schedule visit www.infectingthecity.com

Design Indaba Cape Town, Cape Town. Africa's premier design event is considered one of the best in the world, host to an impressive list of international designers (in the broadest sense, with speakers ranging from celebrated chef Ferran Adria to Mark Dytham and Bruce Nussbaum) who address the main conference (usually sold out), while South Africa's most talented designers hawk their wares at the Expo. It's a must for anyone looking for retail inspiration, or simply wanting to go home with a rare one-of-a-kind design piece.

Sangoma Khekheke's Annual Snake Dance, Zululand, KwaZulu-Natal. Some 6,000 to 8,000 Zulus gather to slaughter cattle and dance under the auspices of Sangoma Khekheke. Late February.

Dance Umbrella, various venues, Johannesburg. A platform for the best contemporary choreography and dance in South Africa. Mid-February to mid-March.

MARCH

Cape Argus Cycle Tour, Cape Town. The largest of its kind in the world, this race attracts some 35,000 cyclists (Lance Armstrong and Matt Damon have completed it) and covers 105km (65 miles) of Cape Town's most scenic routes. Second Sunday of March.

Cape Town International Jazz Festival, Cape Town. Considered one of the best in the world, this showcases the cream of local jazz talent, a line up that includes some international greats all of whom perform for enthusiastic audiences for 2 days; go to **www.capetownjazzfest.com**. Late March.

Klein Karoo National Arts Festival, Oudtshoorn, Western Cape. Showcases the country's most innovative dramas; many award-winning productions (often in Afrikaans) premier here. Predominantly drama, but also excellent dance and music acts. End of March or early April.

APRIL

Two Oceans Marathon, Cape Town. This 56km (35-mile) scenic route (similar to Argus cycling tour) attracts some 12,000 athletes; there's also a half-marathon, and two trail events. Easter Friday and Saturday.

Out in Africa Gay & Lesbian Film Festival. A gay and lesbian film festival held three times a year in Jo'burg and Cape Town, this covers the latest and best movies and documentaries available on the international circuit. www.oia.co.za; 6 days in April, August and October respectively.

AfrikaBurn, Tankwa Karoo. At the end of a rutted, tire-eating dirt road, this is Africa's version of the Nevada desert's Burning Man festival, set in a pristine empty landscape under a blazing sun and star-studded sky. It lasts almost a week and brings together artists, musicians, hippies, and hipsters in a joyous free-for-all celebration of lifestyle alternatives, based primarily on the economy of gifting—you can neither buy nor sell anything here, so bring all possible supplies and dream up a concept (costumes, artworks, theater, flying machine, whatever) that will surprise, entertain, bewilder, or charm your fellow revelers. www.afrikaburn.com.

MAY

Cape Times Waterfront Wine Festival, V&A Waterfront, Cape Town. Some 400 wines from 95 estates and wineries are represented, as well as a great selection of South Africa's finest cheeses—the easiest way to sample some of the culinary wonders of the Cape. Early May.

The Good Food & Wine Festival, Cape Town International Convention Centre. Various programs including celebrity chef appearances. **www.gourmetsa.com**. Mid-May. Note that the festival moves to Durban in July and Gauteng in September.

Franschhoek Literary Festival, Franschhoek. Thanks in part to the gorgeous surroundings—Franschhoek is one of the Cape's most beautiful Winelands villages—this relative newcomer is attracting some big names in local literature who see this as a great opportunity for debate and carousing.

Prince Albert Olive Festival, Prince Albert. This 2-day festival in the pretty rural hamlet of Prince Albert is a real treat—a gathering offering unpretentious entertainment (care to join in the annual olive-pit-spitting championship?), and great food. May.

JUNE

Standard Bank National Arts Festival, Grahamstown, Eastern Cape. The largest arts festival in the Southern Hemisphere features performances from cutting-edge to classical. Pack warm woolies. Late June to early July.

Comrades Marathon, Pietermaritzburg, KwaZulu-Natal. More than 13,000 runners participate in this 89km (55-mile) race. Mid-June.

JULY

Knysna Oyster Festival, Knysna, Garden Route, Western Cape. The festival encompasses the Forest Marathon, a mountain-bike cycling tour, a regatta, a golf championship, and flea markets. Very popular, and gets better every year. First Friday to second Saturday of July.

Pro Surfing Classic, Durban beachfront. This world-class watersports- and beach-related tournament includes what is still sometimes referred to as the Gunston 500, one of the world's premier surfing events. Mid- or late July.

The Sardine Run, Eastern Cape and Kwa-Zulu-Natal. Every year the east coast of South Africa is host to the greatest dive show in the world, when some three billion sardines, followed by hundreds of predators, move from the cold Atlantic to the subtropical waters of the Indian Ocean—a migration to rival that of the Serengeti.

AUGUST

Namaqualand Wild Flower Season, Western and Northern Cape. From mid-August on (sometimes Sept, depending on rain; watch press for details), the semi-arid West Coast is transformed into a floral paradise, with more than 2,600 species in bloom. August to October.

Jomba! Contemporary Dance Experience, Durban, KwaZulu-Natal. UKZN's Centre for Creative Arts presents a contemporary dance festival featuring the best of Kwa-Zulu-Natal's considerable dance and choreography talent. Late August to early September.

SEPTEMBER

Whale Festival, Hermanus, Western Cape. The Whale Festival includes drama performances, an arts ramble, a crafts market, and whale-route lectures and tours. Late September to early October.

S.A. Fashion Week, Sandton Convention Centre, Johannesburg. A great showcase of the abundance of new Afro-centric design talent, at the innovative Arts on Main in the city center.

Arts Alive International Festival, Johannesburg. This urban arts festival features local talent and international stars. Includes the Jazz on the Lake Concert held at Zoo Lake. www.artsalive.co.za.

King Shaka Day Celebrations and the **Zulu Kings Reed Dance,** Zululand, KwaZulu-Natal. King Shaka Day sees all the Zulu heads, from Chief Buthelezi (leader of the IFP party) to Prince Gideon, dressed in full traditional gear, addressing their minions in a moving day celebrating Zulu traditions. Later in the month, some 15,000 Zulu women participate in the colorful reed dance, in which the king would traditionally choose a new wife. Prince Gideon, mindful of the AIDS crisis, uses the opportunity to address some of the issues affecting the nation today by abstaining from the tradition. Both events are highly recommended. Last week in September.

Pan African Space Station, Cape Town. A month-long "cultural intervention," with performances from any imaginable genre, from across the African continent, and gathered in a number of the Mother City's more underused venues. It's among the worst-publicized festivals in the country, and probably the most exciting, even if organizers are frequently guilty of late starts. Abundant interactive online activity, including interviews and cyberspace broadcasts, holds the festival together for 30 days, commencing early September. www.panafricanspacestation.org.za.

OCTOBER

Shembe Celebrations, Zululand, KwaZulu-Natal. The prophet Shembe, the fourth successor of the first prophet, presides over a congregation of some 30,000 who gather to hear his words; Sunday, when Shembe leads the crowds into prayer-dancing, is the highlight. Last 3 weeks of October.

NOVEMBER

Oude Libertas Amphitheatre Season opens, Stellenbosch, Winelands. This lovely intimate '70s open-air stage hosts a program of sophisticated music (international chamber choir recitals, respected local singer-songwriters, a cappella groups, jazz, opera), as well as some dance and drama. Season ends March.

Turtle-tracking in Maputaland, Zululand, KwaZulu-Natal. Every year from November to January, the rare loggerhead and leatherback turtles return to the very beaches on which they were born, to nest and lay their eggs in the soft sands. The best place to witness this ancient ritual is at Rocktail Bay and Mabibi, both blessed with coral reefs and fabulous lodgings.

DECEMBER

Mother City Queer Project, Cape Town. This masked costume ball features loads of dance zones and costumed teams celebrating Cape Town's vibrant and creative gay culture. The biggest gay party on the African continent. Mid-December.

Million Dollar Golf Challenge, Sun City, North-West Province. This high-stakes tournament attracts some of the world's best golfers. Call Sun City at ✆ **014/557-1544** for exact dates.

Rezonance New Year's Eve Festival, within 100km (62 miles) of Cape Town. A nonstop multiday camp-out party, where Cape Town's hippest hippies, and most of the finest young things pay homage to the beat from dusk to dawn, partying like there's no tomorrow in a beautiful outdoor environment. It is the biggest New Year's party on the continent with food stalls, bars, and at least three distinct dance areas, the main one dedicated to full-on psychedelic trance music, but others covering everything from dubstep to world music—major South African bands perform too; www.rezonancefestival.com. Other unapologetically hedonistic outdoor festival-parties are held throughout the summer; also check out www.originfestival. com, www.aliensafari.net, and www.into thevortex.co.za.

RESPONSIBLE TOURISM

Tourism is big business here. According to the World Tourism Organization, the world's largest and fastest-growing industry generated $944 billion in revenue in 2008, with 922 million international arrivals recorded—despite the slowdown in 2009 (a worldwide decline of 4%, to 880 million international travelers), experts expect a slow but steady recovery. By 2020, the forecast is 1.6 billion. That's a lot of people tramping around our increasingly fragile planet! Faced with the long-term costs associated with this kind of rapacious growth, "responsible tourism" has become the 21st-century tourism buzz phrase, and recent years have seen a rash of new awards recognizing properties and operators making an effort to do the right thing. Even mainstream tourism has taken elements of this on board—though one cannot help suspecting that discreetly placed signs asking you to reuse your towels are geared more toward conserving laundry costs than the environment, or wondering just how big that percentage of profits donated to local schools really is.

Ironically, the seeds of global eco-tourism were laid in Africa's "nature" tourism. During the 20th century, vast areas, such as the Kruger, were unilaterally set aside for conservation, and local inhabitants were often forcibly removed to make way for reservation areas. This left tourism regions ring-fenced by poor communities, unable to graze herds, hunt, or forage for building materials and food. As human developments grew, problems were exacerbated. Such forward-thinking pioneers such as Dave Varty in Londolozi, a private reserve abutting Kruger (and founding father of what would become &Beyond tour company), as well as the founders of Wilderness

Safaris (regularly cited as Southern Africa's leading safari operator), realized that a different approach was called for, and pioneering partnerships between the government, private business, and locals were forged. With a proportion of "safari tourism" revenue now plowed into both wildlife protection *and* local community development, responsible tourism was in a sense born. As revenue grew out of ground-breaking rehabilitation projects such as Phinda in KwaZulu-Natal, where degraded farmland was slowly returned to its original pristine state, others followed suit, particularly in the Eastern Cape, while Madikwe, near Botswana, was restocked with game in the largest translocation operation in the world.

In 1996, South Africa became the first in the world to adopt responsible tourism as an official policy, and the 2002 Cape Town Declaration, basis for the international World Responsible Tourism awards, was formulated in accordance with this policy, as were the Imvelo Awards, Africa's Responsible Tourism awards (for past winners, visit **www.imveloawards.co.za**). South Africa is also the only country in the world to have a "fair trade" label for its tourism products. To find accredited operators (and it is a stiff audit, so these companies have earned our support) as well as various links providing tips on how to become an even more responsible traveler, visit **www.fair tourismsa.org.za**. Stringent criteria include fair wages, working conditions, distribution of benefits, and so on, and the site gives you a great selection across all price points and regions.

SPECIAL-INTEREST TRIPS & ESCORTED GENERAL-INTEREST TOURS

Safari Specifics

Wildlife viewing and interaction is the reason most set their sights on southern Africa, and there are numerous ways to experience the bush. Here are a few pointers to help make the most of it. Self-promotion alert: Should you require a custom-made itinerary at the best lodges for your budget, contact the authors of this guide at www. bestkeptshhh.com.

What kind of safari options are available?   Broadly speaking, you can opt for a **self-drive safari** within a national park like Kruger, Addo (Eastern Cape) or Hluhluwe (Kwazulu Natal), which will cost you less (but involves a fair amount of driving, less close encounters with Big 5, and the accommodation options are not stellar), or drive or fly straight to a luxurious lodge in a **private game reserve.** Specialist safaris include tracking game on **foot, horseback, bike, canoe,** or even the back of an **elephant.**

What reserve should I choose?   In South Africa, most of the best destinations are concentrated in and around **Kruger** (see p. 318), with the **Sabi Sands** private reserve the most reliable for close-up encounters in Africa. The best reason to visit a private reserve is that you are guaranteed to see more animals, and you will learn more about them as well as the intricacies of the ecosystem that supports them. If you're worried about malaria, the best malaria-free reserve is **Madikwe,** conveniently close to Johannesburg—a 3-hour self- or chauffeur drive. A good alternative is the malaria-free **Eastern Cape** where **Kwandwe** is the undisputed leader. Port Elizabeth is the gateway airport but visiting one here is the ideal start or end point of a road trip along the R62 and Garden Route to or from Cape Town, a wonderfully scenic drive that could take a few days or a week. The best lodges and reserves here are comparable with those in the top reserves in the country, but vegetation is not as lush. There are now a handful of reserves in the **Western Cape** claiming Big 5 destinations, and while Sanbona (about 3 hr. from Cape Town) and Gondwana, (near the western end of the Garden Route) are the best, offering great accommodation and wide open spaces, none afford the authentic bush experience you'll get in and around Kruger, the Eastern Cape, or in KwaZulu-Natal. Note that those desperate to see the Big 5 near Cape Town itself should still not opt for a day trip **Aquila.**

To reach **KwaZulu-Natal's** reserves, (the best here being **Phinda**), fly from Johannesburg or Cape Town to Durban or Richard's Bay airport. **KwaZulu-Natal's** semitropical climate creates a more junglelike environment—it's beautiful, but spotting animals can be more difficult in dense foliation—but visitors can combine a safari with diving and snorkeling excursions.

Most of **Botswana's reserves and camps** are accessible by charter flight from Maun or Kasane. You can also choose to fly to Livingstone airport in Zambia, close to Victoria Falls, and transfer by road to Botswana (90 min. to Kasane). Although the reserves surrounding Kruger are typical of the African bush and savanna, the **Okavango Delta** in flood offers a lush landscape that attracts an incredible variety of bird life and game; a mystical beauty makes it a must on any safari itinerary. Then there are the desert reserves such as **Tswalu, Kgaligadi Transfrontier Park,** and **Makgadigadi Pans.** With huge horizons and stark landscapes, these support species that have adapted to harsh conditions but visit these reserves more for the awe-inspiring landscapes as the animals.

What should I do if I'm on a budget?   One option is to rent a car and drive yourself around the reserves, concentrating on the national parks (such as Kruger); see our recommended itinerary for this. The roads in these reserves are in good condition, and offer the cheapest room in a Big 5 reserve (around R800 to R960 per night), each with a fridge, tea-making facilities, and a barbecue area. The more expensive units (R980–R1505) will have the added advantage of better views or slightly more privacy. An alternative is to book into a lodge on the outskirts of Kruger (like unpretentious and welcoming **Rissington Inn**/R1,000–R1,780 double) and do day trips into the park. But first prize is definitely to book into a lodge or camp within a private reserve, where meals (as well as virtually all drinks) and guided game activities are laid on, and accommodations make the most of the bush. In 2011 the best-value camps or lodge in private reserves close to Kruger included **Naledi** (R3,110–R3,500 double), **Gomo Gomo** (R3,420–R3,800 double), **Nottens** (R4,200–R6,700 double), **Honeyguide** (R5,000–R7,600 double), **Rhino Post Safari Lodge & Plains Camp** (R5,460–R6,100 double) and **Umlani** (R6,050 double)—rates include game activities, most drinks and all meals. For those prepared to rough it (shared bucket showers and bush toilets), **Mosetlha Bush Camp** in Madikwe offers one of the most authentic safari experiences for just R3,200 for two persons (meals and game activities included); offering quite a bit more luxury **Thakadu Tented Camp** (R6,200–R6900) and **Impodimo** (R5,500-R7,100) are next up as affordable Madikwe recommendations that still tick all the right boxes.

The best-value Big 5 private reserve options in KwaZulu-Natal are the five East African-style luxury tents at **Mkhuze Falls Private Game Reserve** (R4,900–R6,500 double), or the river suites at nearby **Amakhosi Lodge** (R4,400–R7,200 double), with rate always depending on season.

The only budget option in the delta is still **Oddballs**, where the tented accommodation has been upgraded but rates still kept in check ($580–$680 double). For more luxury but still a thoroughly authentic safari experience take a look at **African Bush Camps**; these are also marketed by **Ker & Downey** (www.kerdowney.com), who offer the best value walking and canoe safaris in the Delta.

Bird-Watching Trips

With so many habitats, southern Africa is one of the most rewarding bird-watching destinations in the world. Birders looking for escorted tours of the bush throughout the country, with the focus primarily but not exclusively on bird-watching, should contact **Lawson's** (© 27/13/741-2458; www.lawsons.co.za), the pioneer of birding tours in SA, with experience since 1983. For a full listing of operators in S.A. offering tours specifically for birders (as well as online guides, local events, and more) take a look at the excellent www.birdlife.org.za.

Cultural & Historical Tours

Cape Town is stocked full of cultural excursions—many of them geared around trips to the townships—but few are as innovative as any of the tours put together by **Coffeebeans Routes** (www.coffeebeansroutes.com). Their outings are likely to be a big eye-openers, with a refreshing approach to getting beneath the skin of a local culture. There's a Jazz Safari, Fashion Route and even a Township Futures tour, in which you meet some of the people orchestrating the future development of the districts where the majority of Cape Town's urban populations live. For more tours of this nature, refer to chapter 4.

Visitors to Johannesburg should not miss the award-winning **Apartheid Museum** (p. 293), and if possible combine your visit with a tour of Soweto, where many of South Africa's pivotal moments were played out. You will need around 3 hours at the Apartheid Museum, then lunch in Soweto followed by a tour of South Africa's largest "township." Wilro Tours offer both scheduled and "Go As You Please" tours to cover this option; choose between 5, 7, 9, and 12 hours as an individual or small group (www.wilrotours.co.za). Please note that you can also embark on cycling tours of Soweto—perfectly safe, these are rated as the most authentic way to really meet the people (www.sowetobicycletours.com).

If you're interested in more ancient history, consider booking with **Palaeo-Tours** (© 011/726-8788; www.palaeotours.com) offering specialist trips to some of the world's richest prehuman fossil sites in what has become known as the Cradle of Humankind, declared a World Heritage Site in 1999 (for more, see p. 282). The area is some 50 minutes from Johannesburg city; tours, comprising two site visits, usually last 5 hours. All Palaeo-Tours are by arrangement only, so book before you leave home.

Adventure Activities

From dropping like a stone into the Batoka ravine, to walking with lions, riding elephants and surfing the Zambezi as it churns the waters like a washing machine, Victoria Falls is a mecca for adrenaline junkies and outdoors enthusiasts. For a complete list of what to do in the Victoria Falls area, check out **Wild Horizons** (www.wildhorizons.co.za) and **Safari Par Excellence** (www.safpar.net; p. 404). South Africa (particularly Cape Town environs and the Garden Route) offer a great array of world-class adventure activities, from shark-cage diving to canopy tours; kloofing down river ravines to jumping off bridges (you'll find the highest commercial bungee jump in the world on the Garden Route). Check the selection out on www.adventure escapades.co.za and www.dirtyboots.co.za; the latter being particularly user friendly as it lists activities according to town and region.

Food & Wine Trips

The delightfully named **Samp and Soufflé** (www.sampsouffle.com; © **082/687-0442**) specializes in custom-designed luxury "food adventures," in which you can either just eat or learn to cook in self-driven or chauffeured gourmet tours that lead from one destination restaurant to the next. Excursions can include visits to authentic produce markets and working wine estates. For a short culinary tour, consider booking one of **andulela's** Cape Malay or African Cooking safaris (www.andulela. com), in which you visit a home in the local community and prepare a meal with your hostess.

There are countless wine tours on offer, but serious wine lovers need to book a tour with **Stephen Flesch** (© **021/705-4317** or 083/229-3581; www.gourmetwine tours.co.za). Former chairman of the Wine Tasters Guild of S.A. and an ardent wine lover, Stephen's knowledge of South African wines spans 4 decades. He will take into account your particular interests or wine preferences, and tailor an itinerary that covers both historical estates and rustic farms off the beaten track, in any of the wine regions surrounding the city. The day trip includes a stop at a great restaurant (he is, after all, secretary of Cape Town's Slow Food Convivium); you can request where this is or provide him with a budget and leave it to him. Rates for a full day are R1,600 for the first person and R800 for each additional person. Half-day is R1,100 for the first person and R500 for each additional person. (Rates exclude lunch.)

Gourmands should also check out these two sources: *Eat Out* (www.eatout.co.za) is an annual overview of restaurants throughout the country, with an annual top 10 that is highly rated (and coveted), is very thorough, and you can find a review on the restaurant closest to you with the click of a button. Far more discriminating and critical, *Rossouw's Restaurants* (www.rossouwsrestaurants.com) is an annual guide that is essentially a collaboration of diners review notes, so you're not being influenced by a few food critics' palates (though Rossouw does the final edit, and is opinionated).

SUGGESTED SOUTHERN AFRICAN ITINERARIES

3

Most people fly to southern Africa to reconnect with the raw power of Mother Nature; others just to party or relax in the "World's Best Destination" as voted by the millions of Tripadvisor users in 2011. However long your stay, these itineraries are designed to make the most of your precious time.

THE REAL RELAXER: CAPE TOWN IN 1 WEEK

You've chosen to stay put in one region. Sensible, really: You're in one of the most beautiful cities in the world, surrounded by vineyard-carpeted valleys and a whale nursery off the coast—why rush off? This tour starts off in Cape Town then takes you out of the city—but not too far. It's jampacked and could easily be extended to 10 days.

Day 1: Cape Town & Waterfront

Having arrived at your city or Atlantic seaboard lodgings (where you have booked for 3 or 4 nights; see recommendations in chapter 4), spend the first day sleeping late, then take a stroll around the city center or **Victoria & Alfred Waterfront** (sticking to the working harbor and dockside bits—don't get trapped inside the mall). Lunch at a table with a view of the iconic **Table Mountain** (even good during the summer evenings when it's magically lit up): We recommend either **Den Anker** (for delicious Belgian-inspired cuisine) or the flashier **Baia** (for expensive but good seafood); for the best sushi it has to in the mall, at Willoughby's. Alternatively, if you want to watch Capetonians at play, head for **Cape Quarter,** either to the original piazza where you can grab an outside table at one of the restaurants there, or in the new section. This is also the city's best shopping precinct (and incidentally where you'll find most of the city's gay-friendly bars and clubs). Get to bed early for a full day that follows.

The Real Relaxer: Cape Town & Environs in 1 Week

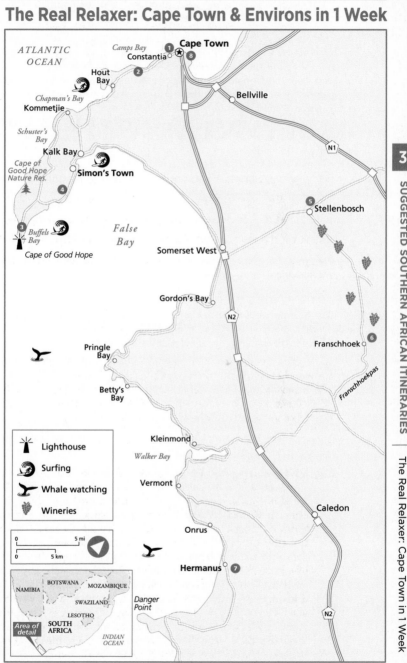

ATLANTIC OCEAN

Camps Bay

Cape Town

Constantia

Hout Bay

Chapman's Bay

Kommetjie

Schuster's Bay

Bellville

Kalk Bay

Cape of Good Hope Nature Res.

Simon's Town

Buffels Bay

False Bay

Cape of Good Hope

Stellenbosch

Somerset West

Gordon's Bay

Pringle Bay

Franschhoek

Franschhoekpas

Betty's Bay

Kleinmond

Walker Bay

Vermont

Caledon

Lighthouse

Surfing

Whale watching

Wineries

Onrus

0   5 mi
0   5 km

Hermanus

NAMIBIA   BOTSWANA   MOZAMBIQUE

SWAZILAND

LESOTHO

Area of detail   SOUTH AFRICA

INDIAN OCEAN

Danger Point

N1

N2

Day 2: Table Mountain's Eastern Slopes or Cape Town's Famous Beach Scene

Spend the morning on the eastern slopes of Table Mountain exploring **Kirstenbosch Botanical Gardens.** From Kirstenbosch, make your way farther south to sample the award-winning wines of the **Constantia wine route,** lunching at the manor house at **Constantia Uitsig,** for pastoral vineyard views and old-style elegance, or the modern South African combinations at **Catharina's** on the Steenberg estate. Alternatively, if you're a beach lover, skip the gardens and take a book, sunscreen, and sunglasses to **Clifton Beach,** where it's a short drive to a fabulous lunch at **Rumbullion** (reserve well ahead—it's the daytime version of The Roundhouse, and superpopular), set in a forest overlooking palm-fringed Camps Bay. Or worship the sun on Camps Bay and saunter over the road to one of the many restaurants and bars that line the beachfront for lunch or sundowners. If neither beach nor gardens appeal, stroll the **city streets,** taking a guided city tour or just wandering at will. Weather permitting, ascend **Table Mountain** in the late afternoon to watch as the sun sinks into the western horizon and the city lights start to sparkle. Come nightfall, foodies should choose between **The Test Kitchen** in nearby Woodstock and **Aubergine** in the central city. If you've still got energy after your meal, hit one of the bars or clubs on **Long Street,** one of the inner city's key nightlife nodes

Days 3 & 4: Cape Peninsula

Set off on the **peninsula drive** (see p. 124) to cruise the awesome **Chapman's Peak Drive** and explore the **Cape Point Nature Reserve.** (If you've not yet done Kirstenbosch Gardens, you could stop there en route.) It's also an opportunity to wander through the boho fishing town of **Kalk Bay,** where you'll get your fill of galleries and antique shops. Have lunch at **Harbor House** for the close-up views of crashing waves and seals catching fish, and then catch a boat in **Simonstown** to look for whales. Foodies might want to hold out for three-star Noordhoek options recommended in the chapter. With so much on offer in this southern part of the peninsula, rather than head back to the city, consider overnighting on the False Bay Coast, giving you more time to explore the laid-back coastal villages that surround Cape Point.

Days 5 & 6: Winelands: Franschhoek & Stellenbosch

On your 5th day, set off for **Stellenbosch,** where the majority of South Africa's award-winning wines are grown. Arrange in advance for a personal wine guide (see p. 150 for recommendations) to take you to a selection of wine estates. Lunch at either **Babel** (after touring the impressive gardens on the **Babylonstoren** estate), or **Rust en Vrede**, then spend the late afternoon exploring Stellenbosch's bustling town on foot. The town is alive with students, except in mid-summer, and it's packed with great restaurants. For the best take on New South African cuisine, book your place at **Cognito** for dinner. Then see if you can catch a local band later in the evening, before retiring to **Middedorp Manor.** Alternatively, get to **Franschhoek** by midafternoon to spend the night at the gorgeously located **Le Petite Ferme,** where you'll spend the night lording over the valley below. Next day, continue your oeno-expedition.

Day 7: Whale-Watching in Hermanus

You could easily spend another night in Stellenbosch (or Franschhoek). But if it's whale-watching season (June–Nov), keep following the magnificent **Coastal Road** turning off at Gordon's Bay to reach **Hermanus,** whale-watching capital of the world, approximately 112km (69 miles) from Cape Town. Spend the night here (the views from the pool terrace at **Birkenhead House** or **Mosselberg** are reason to linger), and check out some of the world's biggest fish at Shark Alley (p. 174) before returning to Cape Town. Or check out Hermanus's very own wine route, **Hemel-en-Aarde,** where some of the country's best vintages are being bottled—with great restaurants to match.

Day 8: Cape Town

Extend your stay by 1 day, returning to the city and—if you haven't yet dined here—celebrate with a meal at the **Roundhouse;** the food, service, and formidable list of South African wines and top-class spirits will put you in the mood for a party. Make sure you preorder a taxi, and if it's the right night of the week, hit the bar or club of your choice. Or head for bed, and dream of your return.

THE QUICK FIX: THREE COUNTRIES IN 1 WEEK

Botswana is generally considered the last untouched wilderness in Africa, Victoria Falls is a world wonder, and Cape Town is one of the most beautiful cities on Earth. A week covering these sights will leave you breathless.

Days 1, 2, 3 & 4: Okavango Delta & Selinda/Linyanti

From Johannesburg you will fly directly to Maun, gateway to the Delta. Your priority should be to spend at least 2 nights in the **Okavango Delta,** preferably between June and October, when the abundance of game attracts a huge number of predators, followed by 2 nights in one of the more remote camps in the nearby **Linyanti** and **Selinda reserves.** You'll find the best selection of camps in this region operated by just four companies: Wilderness Safaris; &Beyond; Ker & Downey (which also markets excellent-value African Bush Camps); and Orient-Express; see chapter 2 for more.

Days 5: Victoria Falls

Transfer to Kasane by air from your Linyanti or Selinda camp; then transfer by road to your lodgings on the Zambezi River, near Vic Falls (about a 90 minute journey from Kasane). For colonial pampering, book the **River Club;** for a real adventure, book an open-to-the-elements suite at **Tongabezi** or **Sindabezi** (the latter an island in the middle of the Zambezi) or if you're hankering for a hotel, **Royal Livingstone,** within sight and sound of the falls. Your Botswana lodging will arrange the transfer to Kasane; ask your Zambian lodging to arrange the road transfer from Kasane. *Note:* If you like to get your pulse racing, extend your stay here by another day and spend it either river rafting the Zambezi (the most exhilarating commercially run rapids in the world), or jumping off Victoria Falls bridge attached to a variety of harnesses.

The Quick Fix: Botswana, Victoria Falls & Cape Town in 1 Week

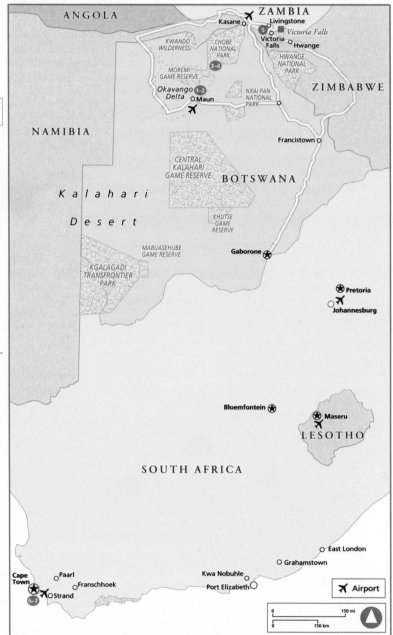

Days 6 & 7: Cape Town & the Winelands

Fly via Johannesburg to get to **Cape Town** the next day. There are wonderful places to stay all over town, but given that your time is limited, opt for lodging in the City Bowl (a natural amphitheater created by Table Mountain and the encircling arm of Signal Hill) or the Atlantic Seaboard, if it's summer; see chapter 4 for the top choices. If the weather is bad, book a personalized wine tour and spend the day sampling the superb red wines produced in the Stellenbosch region's tasting rooms, many of them heated with crackling fires. If the sun's out, spend the day driving the Cape Peninsula route (see chapter 5) and end your last day on **Clifton** or **Camps Bay beach,** or with a bottle of champagne on **Table Mountain** as the sun sets over the Southern Hemisphere and you toast your next trip here.

THE SPLURGE SAFARI: IN 10 DAYS

For the southern African safari experience of a lifetime, you really need to experience Botswana's Okavango Delta and/or Linyanti and Selinda reserves, a desert reserve, and the abundant wildlife of South Africa's Kruger Park region.

Days 1 to 3: Kruger National Park

From Johannesburg, it's an easy flight to world-renowned **Kruger National Park,** along South Africa's eastern border. Here, a choice of ultraluxurious game lodges offer smart design, impeccable comfort, and excellent game viewing. Spend 3 nights at **Singita's Lebombo Camp** for the ultimate style safari (or, if you prefer Afro-colonial chic, take a look at **Singita Ebony,** or **Royal Malewane**). If you're superkeen on seeing leopard, you should book a lodge or camp in **Sabi Sands;** see chapter 9 for the full spectrum of recommendations. Fly back to Johannesburg.

Days 4 to 9: Botswana

Fly directly from Johannesburg to Maun in Botswana, and spend 2 nights at one of our recommended **Okavango Delta** camps (start by looking at **Eagle Island Camp**) and 2 nights at one of our camp recommendations in **Linyanti or Selinda** (Wilderness Safari's **Selinda Camp** will completely wow you). Spend your first day relaxing and recovering from your long journey, watching the wildlife from the privacy of your deck. You'll wake the next day refreshed and ready for a day's intensive game-viewing. Alternatively, book the **Kanana mokoro (canoe) trail,** and camp out on an island with your own dedicated staff. Having spent 4 nights on the waters of the Delta and Selinda/Linyanti, fly south to spend 2 nights at **Jack's Camp** in Botswana's Kalahari wilderness, where the desolate desert is nature at its most surreal; take a quad-bike safari to view some **Bushman rock art,** or to **Kubu Island.**

Day 10: Zambia/Victoria Falls

From Jack's Camp, you can charter a flight directly to Livingstone, in Zambia, or fly to Kasane and transfer by road to your lodge on the Zambezi River. Opt to spend the night at the colonial-style **River Club** or open-to-the-elements **Tongabezi** or the charming **Toko Leya,** a laid-back tented camp about

The Splurge Safari in 10 Days

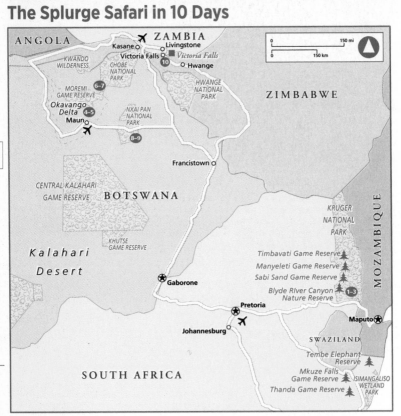

10 minutes from the falls. Or, if you'd prefer to be walking distance from the Falls, and feel like the anonymity of a large hotel, the Royal Livingstone, within sight and sound of the spectacular **Victoria Falls.**

THE BUDGET SAFARI: IN 10 TO 14 DAYS

Given the standards of the game-viewing and the public rest camps, this self-driving tour is definitely the best-value safari to be had on the continent: It will take longer, but you are likely to see everything you dreamed of, at a fraction of the price of the itinerary above. If you'd prefer not to self-drive or self-cater, and want the benefits of a camp in private reserve (being allowed to get close to animals by getting off-road, and the presence of a qualified ranger/tracker being prime), spend 4 nights in Kruger and 2 to 3 nights in a private reserve camp that doesn't charge the earth, then head south to Cape Town or Kwazulu-Natal. You can see our detailed recommendations on Frommers.com (search for "Safari Specifics: FAQ")—or go direct to Naledi Game Lodge, in 2011 our best-value camp choice in Southern Africa. Note that you can shave off the first 2 days by flying direct from Jo'burg to Nelspruit, the nearest airport

to southern Kruger, or even drive directly to Kruger from Johannesburg (about a 5- to 6-hr. drive via Nelspruit; see chapter 9 for details).

Days 1 & 2: Traversing the Escarpment to the Lowveld

Getting to the Kruger area by air from Johannesburg is pretty straightforward (and dealt with in detail in chapter 9), but flights are relatively expensive, particularly if there's more than one of you, and if you are self-driving within Kruger you will need to hire a car there anyway. A relaxed 5- to 6-hour drive will bring you directly from Jo'burg airport to the southern gates of Kruger, but time allowing, we recommend you take a more scenic route. You can either travel the Mpumalanga Escarpment, with its myriad viewpoints over the lowveld and Blyde River Canyon (this "Panorama Route" involves quite a bit of driving, so we recommend you overnight for 2 nights in Hazyview at **Rissington Inn**). However, we highly recommend you take the road less traveled: head north on a loop that takes you through the scenic Magoebaskloof Pass and Tzaneen, overnighting at **Kings**

Walden: With large suites surrounded by beautiful gardens and awesome views, this is one of the best-value guesthouses in the country.

Days 3 to 5: Southern Kruger

Southern Kruger is the most densely touristed part of the vast park, as it is also the best section for game-viewing. Several rest camps are scattered in the south, of which Lower Sabie is a firm favorite, not only for its relaxed atmosphere, lovely riverine location, and good selection of budget-friendly accommodation options, but also as the epicenter of three of the finest game-viewing roads anywhere in the park. Three days here will give you an excellent chance to see all the Big 5: Elephant, buffalo, and, to a lesser extent, lion are almost guaranteed and might be seen driving in any direction; rhino are most common along the road to Crocodile Bridge; and leopards hang in the riparian undergrowth that follows the Sabi River toward Skukuza. If Lower Sabie is full, other good camps in the south include sprawling Skukuza and the relatively intimate Berg-en-Dal. You could also choose to base yourself at Rissington Inn and do day trips into the park.

Days 6 to 7: South-Central Kruger

It's worth dedicating 2 nights to the central plains around Satara, an area known for its dense lion population, high concentration of cheetahs, and seasonal herds of zebra and wildebeest. Satara is the most central base here, but it's also the second-largest rest camp in the park, with an undistinguished setting and rather impersonal atmosphere; there's a strong case for booking one of the tented units at Tamboti Camp (near Orpen Gate) instead. The best game-viewing in this area is usually along the main road connecting Satara to Tamboti, and the loop road running between Satara and the Nwanetsi picnic site.

Days 8 to 9: North-Central Kruger

Wildlife is less varied north of the Olifants River, but it's an excellent area for large elephant and buffalo herds, and it feels decidedly untrammeled by tourism, comparison to the south. Olifants Camp, on a cliff overlooking the river, has the most spectacular setting in the park (which is why it's also the most expensive camp), usually complete with browsing elephants and giraffe along the bank. Alternatively, the tiny primitive camp of Balule is ideal for those seeking a real bush experience (and the huts are the cheapest of anywhere in the park), while the more northerly Letaba Rest Camp overlooks the eponymous river and is known for its wonderful birdlife. The area around Letaba also hosts localized antelope such as roan, sable, and tsessebe.

Days 10 to 14: Northern Kruger or Private Game Reserve (Optional)

Those who reckon 7 nights of Kruger is enough of a good thing should head to the nearest airport (Hoedspruit or, for a cheaper flight, farther south, Nelspruit) and fly to the reserves of subtropical KwaZulu-Natal; see below (or, if you've had enough of safari, to Cape Town; here you can Walk with Baboons near Cape Point (highly recommended), swim with penguins, go diving with sharks or enjoy the best land-based whale-watching in the world. However, to say you've experienced the full Kruger, you should continue northward for 4 nights, divided evenly between the rest camps of Shingwedzi and Punda Maria. The former is a riverside camp surrounded by a small network of great game-viewing roads; it feels strikingly remote even by comparison to Olifants or Letaba. More remote still is the hillside camp of Punda Maria, which is the best base for day trips to the lush Pafuri area, where a host of unusual birds can be seen in the vicinity of the confluence of the Levuvhu and Limpopo rivers (the three-way border with Zimbabwe and Mozambique). The Thulamela Heritage Site protects the remains of a large stone city built in the 16th century after Great Zimbabwe was abandoned. On Day 14, we recommend an early start to get back to Gauteng in good time (or fly from Phalaborwa).

Alternatively, Days 10 to 14: KwaZulu-Natal

Days 10 to 12   Fly into King Shaka International Airport, rent a car, and take an easy drive north up the scenic N2 through rolling green fields of sugar cane and indigenous forests on a well-designed, well-marked toll road. Take the turn-off for Cape Vidal in the heart of the iSimangaliso Wetland Park, a UNESCO World Heritage site, where you have prebooked a rustic KZN Wildlife chalet a stone's throw from the beach, under the welcome shade of the casuarinas. Snorkel, dive, fish, or walk on the deserted beach and around Lake Bhangazi. Diverse wildlife in the highest vegetated dune and sand forests in the world include elephant, hippo, buffalo, and an array of birdlife.

Days 13 to 14   A short 90 minutes' drive west from Cape Vidal and the eastern shores lies the **Hluluwe–Umfolozi Game Reserve,** one of the oldest wildlife sanctuaries in Africa and site of the Zulu kings' ancient hunting grounds. Make reservations for **Hilltop Camp** there, or consider the purely self-catering **Mpila Camp** in the Umfolozi section—a series of comfortable canvas tents, where you really are in the bush proper. If you are feeling adventurous and need to stretch your legs, book a Wilderness Trail, the best foot safari in southern Africa.

If, on the other hand, you've had enough of being on safari, drive or fly back to Johannesburg and catch a flight to Cape Town, booking into **Spicy Villa, Maremoto, Villa Zest,** or **The Backpack**—all good value options—and spend your last few days exploring the scenic wonder in and around Table Mountain National Park and the waters of the Atlantic coast.

ROAD TRIP: WESTERN CAPE IN 10 DAYS

There's nothing like a good road trip, with the freedom to stop exactly where and when you like. This drive will take you through incredible scenery from the slopes of Table Mountain to the thorny wilderness of the Eastern Cape. You could do the trip in less time, but the secret is to get off the beaten track and take it slow. See map p. 58.

Days 1 & 2: Route 62

Choose your vehicle with care: It will become your friend and chariot. Go for fuel efficiency and comfort (A/C in summer is a must). Travel north from Cape Town on the N1; branch off at Worcester and head for Robertson on the R60, then turn onto the R62 to Montagu soon afterward. Stretch your legs at the fabulous Kogmanskloof Pass, with its incredible fold mountains. If you're a wine lover, don't miss one of the multitude of estates on the Robertson–Montagu stretch. **Aasvoelkrans,** in Montagu, is worth a stopover; otherwise, press on

Western Cape Road Trip

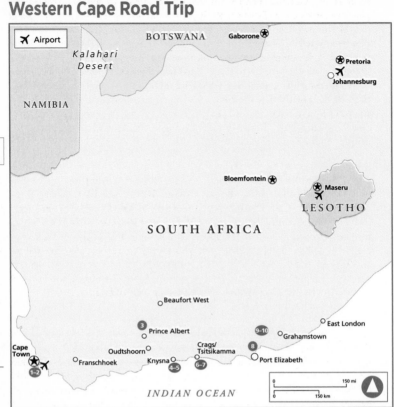

and perhaps spend the night at **Sanbona** for your first safari experience in the arid Karoo (you'll need time to see the entire reserve, but it's a unique wilderness, worth experiencing). Otherwise, press on past Barrydale (stopping there for lunch at **Clarke of the Karoo,** if you have time), and make your way to **Boesmanskop,** near Calitzdorp, which is a wonderfully remote stop, and one which you won't soon forget. The Karoo landscape is huge, starkly beautiful, and often empty: There are fewer towns along this stretch, so watch your gas gauge.

Day 3: Prince Albert

From Boesmanskop, it's a short journey to the start of the **Swartberg Pass,** which affords spectacular scenery at every knuckle-clenching turn and finally spits you out in the Karoo's most interesting village, **Prince Albert,** where there's heaps to do, plenty of dining experiences to enjoy, and the chance to spend the night in such idiosyncratic places as **Dennehof** or one of the **African Relish** cottages.

Day 4 & 5: Wilderness/Knysna

Take the spectacular Meiringspoort Pass to Oudsthoorn, possibly viewing the Cango Caves or one of the wildlife encounters here, then wend your way further south via the Outeniqua and Kaaimansriver Pass to **Wilderness.** If you like the peaceful atmosphere of this small village, surrounded by water, spend a night at one of the excellent-value guest houses (such as **Moontide**) and enjoy the deserted beaches (beware the currents) and the lakes of the Garden Route National Park. Alternatively, press on to nearby **Knysna,** which has plenty of accommodations; top choice here is **Phantom Forest.** While in Knysna, try to fit in a **forest walk** to admire centuries-old yellowwood trees (or choose a horse-riding trail), a boat trip to the Heads, and a visit to **Noetzie** beach. Golfers may want to play a round or two at Pezula or Simola (Fancourt courses in George are an even greater draw). Restaurant choices for all pockets and tastes abound, see chapter 6 for recommendations.

Days 6 & 7: Tsitsikamma

The drive from Knysna farther east is lovely: This is forest territory. Leave time to either paddle or cruise up the **Keurbooms River** (near **Plettenberg Bay**); visit **Monkeyland** (or **Tenikwa,** for cat lovers), in **The Crags;** or spend some time on **Nature Valley Beach** (a wonderful diversion from the N2). End up in the glorious coastal forest of **Tsitsikamma National Park.** Give yourself a full extra day to hike, swim, and relax in this natural paradise. Accommodations aren't swish, but it's the scenery that counts; if you'd prefer creature comforts and fine dining, trade this time for a stay at **Tsala Treetops,** just west of Plettenberg Bay, or **Hog Hollow,** in The Crags, east of Plett.

Days 8, 9 & 10: Port Elizabeth & Eastern Cape Reserves

Get acquainted with the struggle against apartheid at the **Red Location Museum,** or visit the beaches (if you need to stretch your legs, walk the **Donkin Heritage Trail** and take in some history). You could spend the night at one of the fine accommodation options (**Shamwari Townhouse** is top-notch) or push on to an Eastern Cape game reserve, most about 2 hours from the city.

You're spoiled for choice, but, budgetary concerns aside, our personal favorite in the P. E./Grahamstown region would be **Kwandwe;** while Shamwari's **Bayete** camp or **Gorah** in Addo are also fine options. Aim to spend 3 nights at your reserve of choice—2 nights at the very least. Those on a strict budget could book in at **Addo Elephant National Park** and search in their own vehicle for elephant and other beasts. It's a wonderful experience, though you are unlikely to see as much as you would with trained guides. (The other option is to stay at **Elephant House** and enjoy their safari tours into Addo—more expensive than the National Park camp options, but very relaxing and at nowhere near the prices you'll pay for the top reserves.) There are a fair number of midrange game lodge options, too, such as the lovely **RiverBend Lodge.** Another excellent option, farther into the Karoo, is the magical **Samara** (near Graaff-Reinet) where you can track cheetah on foot. (If you can extend your trip by 2 nights, spend them at one of the Graaff-Reinet lodgings, taking time to explore the breathtaking **Valley of Desolation** and to see the **Owl House** in Nieu Bethesda before heading back to P.E. and flying home via Jo'burg or Cape Town.) If you can extend your trip a week, head for the aptly named **Wild Coast,** and experience a way of life rich in the simple luxuries of good food, empty beaches, pristine rivers, and friendly communities living life as they have for centuries.

THE MOTHER CITY: CAPE TOWN & THE PENINSULA

4

stablished as the first garden in Africa for ships restocking en route to India, Cape Town is southern Africa's oldest city, and rightfully heralded as one of the most beautiful on Earth. The massive sandstone bulk of Table Mountain, often draped in a flowing "tablecloth" of clouds, forms an imposing backdrop, while minutes away, pristine sandy beaches line the cliff-hugging Atlantic coast. Mountainous slopes sustaining the world's most varied botanic kingdom (some 9,000 species strong) overlook fertile valleys carpeted with vines, while the relatively compact city center is a multifaceted hodgepodge of Cape Dutch gables, neo-Gothic churches, Muslim minarets, Georgian and Victorian terraces, Art Deco icons, and brutalist '70s monstrosities. With an equally varied population, it is by far the most cosmopolitan city in South Africa, with an uncanny ability to make everyone feel at home.

THINGS TO DO Cape Town's endowment of natural beauty means its mountains, beaches, and vast *fynbos*-covered coastal contours get first priority. Ascend **Table Mountain** by cable car or on foot. Get your toes into the sand on one of the sexy beach coves of **Clifton,** and explore **Kirstenbosch,** the oldest and biggest botanical garden in the country, where beautifully groomed lawns planted with thousands of fynbos species blend seamlessly into the natural foliage of the mountain. Explore **Cape Point**, stopping at **Constantia wine estates** and the quaint coastal villages like **Kalk Bay** and **Simonstown** en route. Back in the city, don't forget to check out the Victorian architecture on **Long Street** (at night the most happening bar and club strip), the colorful Georgian homes in cobblestone **Bo-Kaap,** and the stately **Parliament** and **St George's Cathedral** that border the original **Company's Garden.** But no visit to Cape Town is complete without one of our recommended cultural excursions into the **townships.** These informal settlements form a seamless ribbon of cardboard-and-corrugated-iron housing that many visitors only glimpse on their way from or to the airport. You'll discover a very different way of life here, but a shared love of music, food, and humor.

ACTIVE PURSUITS Looking good is a priority in a city this sexy; biking, running, and hiking are natural preoccupations centered on the abundant trails and routes on Table Mountain and all around the peninsula. Jumping off Signal Hill attached to an experienced paraglider is possibly the most exhilarating way to see the city. Many opt to simply lounge on the beaches, but while you may not want to spend time lingering in the chilly Atlantic waters, it's worth getting wet for the chance to dive with great white sharks (in a cage, of course).

RESTAURANTS & DINING Cape Town is South Africa's culinary capital, with a dynamic lineup of venues in every possible category. Most of the best haute cuisine venues are located in the **Winelands** (see chapter 5 and the Constantia section of this chapter), but in town you should look at **The Roundhouse** (which serves up great views along with meals in a heritage-listed former hunting lodge), perennial favorite **Aubergine, Nobu,** and **The Test Kitchen,** the latter secreted away in an old warehouse building in Woodstock (incidentally where you can pick up the most delicious fare every Saturday from the city's famous **Neighbourgoods Market**). Quirky neighborhood bistros like **Bombay Bicycle Club** are all the rage these days, ideal if you want to mix in a bit of people-watching while you eat. For seaside dining you won't do better than **Harbour House,** in Kalk Bay.

NIGHTLIFE & ENTERTAINMENT A genuine cultural melting pot, the city has a dynamic music, theater, and party scene. The summer social calendar is filled with outdoor concerts (don't miss a Sunday evening on the lawns at Kirstenbosch), music festivals (jazz a real highlight), and DJ-fueled dance celebrations starring the partying tribes of Cape Town at their unhinged, magnificent best (hedonist's note: the **Balkanology** and **trance parties** are unmissable). The city's clubs are a mixed bag: **Assembly** hosts regular electronic parties, **Fiction** has the best reputation for quality urban beats, and **Trinity** is the only real superclub in town. The best bar in the Camps Bay strip is still the überpopular **Caprice;** in Long Street we like **Julep,** but our favorite place to knock back a drink is probably hip **Asoka.** Alternatively (in every sense), head for Cape Town's **"Queer Quarter"** and get down with the boys (and girls) at **Crew** or **Bronx.**

ORIENTATION

Arriving

BY PLANE Revamped and expanded **Cape Town International Airport** (✆ **021/937-1200,** or 086/727-7888 for flight information) is 17km (11 miles) from the center of town; it should take 20 to 30 minutes to get into the city and environs (set aside at least twice that amount of time if traveling toward the airport during evening rush hour, 4–6pm). See "Airport Transfers" for recommendations. Alternatively, the **MyCiti Bus** is an efficient service running between the airport and the Civic Centre terminal in the city center (R50 one-way); it's the most carbon-neutral way of getting to town, and you can pick up a taxi or prearranged transfer from the bus terminal, or jump on another MyCiti bus for destinations within the city or the Waterfront. Car-rental desks are inside the arrival terminals, and a *bureau de change* stays open for international flights; the rates aren't always the best, so use an ATM instead. *Tip:* If you've arrived early or are waiting for a connection, you can relax in a **Premier Lounge** (www.comfortguaranteed.co.za), which offers relaxing facilities, light meals, drinks, business facilities, and showers; entry costs R210 (international terminal; ✆ **021/936-2127**) or R110 (domestic; ✆ **021/936-3014**).

In the rare instances that a hotel offers a complimentary airport transfer, we have mentioned this. All lodgings will arrange this transfer, but you will definitely save money by dealing directly with **Centurion** (📞 021/934-8281; centuriontours@telkomsa.net), a reliable company offering an efficient door-to-door service in clean minibuses. Ideally, book your ride 2 days in advance. From the airport to the city center, it costs R180 for the first person and R30 per person thereafter. Mail or call them, and they'll be waiting at the airport arrivals area with your name on a sign board; note that there's an early morning (before 7am) and late-night (after 10pm) surcharge of R40. Eco-friendlier than its competitors, **The Green Cab** (📞 086/184-3473) charges R300 for the first person and R30 per additional passenger into the city. **Rikkis** (📞 086/174-5547) offers an efficient airport taxi service costing a flat R250 (city center) or R300 (Atlantic seaboard) for one to four passengers. You'll also find taxis directly outside the terminals (usually much more expensive), or use the **MyCity** bus service (see "Arriving by Plane").

BY CAR If you're driving directly from Johannesburg, you will arrive on the N1; from Port Elizabeth, via the Garden Route, you'll approach on the N2. The N2 splits into the M3 (the highway, known as De Waal Dr., that connects the southern suburbs to the City Bowl suburbs on the slopes of Table Mountain) and Eastern Boulevard, which joins the N1 as it enters the perimeter of town. The entrance to the Waterfront is clearly signposted off here, and there are signs pointing the way to the Table Mountain cableway as well as Camps Bay.

BY BUS The main intercity buses, **Greyhound, Intercape Mainliner,** and **Translux,** all terminate at the junction of Strand and Adderley streets. Note that the **Baz Bus**—a minibus service aimed at backpackers—offers a more flexible hop-on, hop-off option throughout the country. (See chapter 13 for regional numbers.)

BY TRAIN The luxurious **Blue Train** (📞 021/449-2672; www.bluetrain.co.za) and **Rovos Rail** (📞 021/421-4020; www.rovos.co.za) roll into Cape Town station (📞 021/449-2991) from Pretoria. A more affordable alternative is a Premier Classe coupe from Johannesburg on **Shozoloza Meyl** (📞 086/000-8888; www.shosholoza-meyl.co.za), South Africa's main-line passenger services (see chapter 13 for more).

Visitor Information

You'll find a Cape Town tourism desk at the airport (📞 021/934-1949; Mon–Fri 6am–9pm, Sat–Sun 8am–8pm), but the best place to gather information is at **Cape Town Tourism,** in the city center at the corner of Burg and Castle streets (📞 021/487-6800; www.capetown.travel; Mon–Fri 8am–5 or 6pm, Sat 8:30am–2pm, Sun 9am–1pm). Staff is knowledgeable and helpful and there are hundreds of brochures; look out for the *Footsteps to Freedom Cape Town City Guide,* which has a good map covering the top sites. The hop-on, hop-off CitySightseeing bus (see "Getting Around," below), and city walking tours depart regularly from here.

A satellite tourism office at the **Waterfront Rocket Shed** (📞 021/408-7600) has similar services and longer hours (9am–9pm), and there are many more information offices scattered throughout the region.

The **Netcare Travel Clinic,** 1107 Picbell Parkade, 58 Strand St. city center (*©* **021/419-3172;** www.travelclinic.co.za) offers expert advice and medical services (inoculations, malaria tablets), should you be traveling farther afield. **MTI Medi-Travel International** (*©* **021/419-1888;** www.meditravel.co.za) has similar services; you may find its Waterfront Clock Tower location more convenient.

City Layout

Cape Town lies on a narrow peninsula that curls southward into the Atlantic Ocean. Its western and eastern shores are divided by a spinal ridge of mountains, of which Table Mountain is the most dramatic landmark. On the western shore, the relatively small **city center,** together with the residential suburbs that cradle it, is known as the **City Bowl**—the "bowl" created by the table-topped massif as backdrop, flanked by jagged Devil's Peak to the east and the embracing arm of Signal Hill to the west. Upmarket family homes, small businesses, and apartments—as well as a plethora of excellent guesthouses—range along these slopes and make up the neighborhoods of Tamboerskloof, Higgovale, Oranjezicht, and Gardens. From here, views north look over the city center and harbor, where the **Victoria & Alfred Waterfront** is situated at the icy waters of Table Bay. On the slopes of Signal Hill, close to the center, is the **Bo-Kaap** (literally, "Upper Cape"), where most of the population are descendants of Cape Town's original Muslim slaves.

Within easy striking distance of the city center and the slightly isolated **Waterfront,** are the dense, built-up suburbs of tiny **De Waterkant** (a must-see destination for shoppers), and **Green Point,** where the visually spectacular Cape Town Stadium (built specifically for the 2010 FIFA World Cup) stands amid a brand new urban public park. Adjacent Green Point is the high-density coastal suburb of **Sea Point,** which has an ever-bustling, rather rough-and-ready Main Road, lined with shops, bars and eateries, and a generous promenade where Capetonians like to walk and jog during the summer. The promenade runs north-east to **Mouille Point,** which in turn runs into the V&A Waterfront. Moving farther south from Sea Point, the western slopes of the Cape Peninsula mountain range slide almost directly into the sea, and it is here, along the dramatic coastline referred to as the **Atlantic seaboard,** that you can watch the sun sinking from Africa's most expensive real estate. Of these, the beaches of **Camps Bay** ★ and **Clifton** ★★★ are the most conveniently located—easily reached from the City Bowl via Kloof Nek, they are a mere 10- to 15-minute drive from the city center (although in summer, traffic can seriously irk). **Bakoven** ★ is the choice for those who don't want sand or looking to escape the crowds—two relatively tiny patches (one called Big Beach, the other Little Beach) hidden between massive boulders. Farther along the coast, totally isolated and free of any kind of commerce is **Llandudno** ★★★, a privileged village mounted on a steep slope culminating in a gorgeous beach bounded by boulders— needless to say, on a perfect day it gets packed.

Traveling along the Atlantic seaboard is the most scenic route to Cape Point, but the quickest route is to travel south along the eastern flank of the mountain, via the M3, past the **southern suburbs** (and the turn off to Kirstenbosch Gardens) and **Constantia** (the closest wine route to the city, some 30 min. away), then snake along the False Bay seaboard to the Point. These eastern slopes, which overlook False Bay (so called by early sailors who mistook it for Table Bay), are the first to see the sun rise. Northwest of the southern tip are the city's sleepiest seaside villages, Kommetjie and **Scarborough,** ideal if you want to be right near the unspoiled wilderness of

Cape Point and have utterly pristine beaches at your fingertips. Heading further north through Noordhoek and Chapman's Peak, you complete the "peninsula loop" to arrive back in the city via **Hout Bay** and the Atlantic seaboard suburbs.

East of the peninsula are the **Cape Flats,** where the majority of so-called "Cape coloureds" live (see "The 'Coloured' Vote" in chapter 2), as well as the **"townships"** where the majority of the black population resides—proof that, sadly, despite nearly 2 decades of democracy, an unenforced geographic apartheid still keeps the Cape's communities effectively separate.

With their kitsch postmodern palaces and endless "first-home" developments, these suburbs don't really warrant much attention. However, if you're heading north to see the West Coast (chapters 5 and 6), consider stopping at **Blouberg Beach** for the classic postcard view of Table Mountain across the bay.

🖊 Consider investing in a detailed street atlas, such as *Mapstudio Street Guide,* sold at most bookstores; but if you get lost, don't despair: With Table Mountain (and relatively excellent street signage) as a visual guide, it's difficult to stay lost for long.

4 The Neighborhoods in Brief

CITY CENTER (CBD) ★★ & WOODSTOCK

Cape Town's **CBD** is compact and designed to a grid system of roads, with most of its financial high rises clustered near the harbor-end of the city close to the **Foreshore** (where the Cape Town Convention Centre is located); closer to the mountain end of the city are more Victorian-era constructions, government buildings, the country's Parliament, and the Company's Gardens. East of Parliament, long-neglected quadrants of the city are being revitalized as warehouses are converted into clubs and innovative designers move in. **Woodstock,** with its totally unglamorous, semi-industrial feel is really an extension of the emerging East City precinct—distinct from the city center in terms of geography and socioeconomy; it's always been relatively poor. But it may well be setting the tone for the future as it sees an injection of capital and creative energy that is transforming it into the next residential hub, already boasting the city's most fabulous Saturday market, many top galleries, enticing new shopping venues, a boxing gym, its first serious hotel, and many fine little eateries.

CITY BOWL ★

Near the Waterfront, beaches, and Winelands, and in easy reach of most of the city's best restaurants, with great views, the residential suburbs that flank the **city center** are the most convenient place to stay. Opt for one of the many elegant guesthouses on the mountain slopes of the upmarket suburbs of Oranjezicht, Higgovale, and Tamboerskloof, with excellent views of the city and harbor.

BO-KAAP ★

Stretching from the edge of the inner city and up the slopes of Signal Hill, this lively suburb of historic houses painted in a rainbow of pastels and bold colors is historically one of the most interesting parts of Cape Town. With its concentration of historic mosques, rough cobbled streets, and a distinctive sense of community and vibrant "Cape Malay" culture, this is a great place to experience Cape Town's much-vaunted "diversity," although it's slowly changing under the influence of foreign investment.

DE WATERKANT ★★, GREEN POINT ★, MOUILLE POINT & SEA POINT

Wedged into a strip of land between Signal Hill and the Atlantic Ocean, this area—with a mix of residential and commercial property—has been the most dynamically evolving part of Cape Town. **De Waterkant** is a tiny enclave that has evolved into a chi-chi shopping area, with cobbled streets and two swanky side-by-side shopping centers (Cape Quarter) with many restaurants. It's world renowned for its popularity with gay travelers, who spend a lot of their vacation time swinging through the densely concentrated bars and clubs located here and in neighboring **Green Point.** Closer to the water, the beachfront that stretches along the coast of Mouille Point and Sea Point has been largely ruined by the construction of dense high-rise apartments, but its **seaside promenade** is where Capetonians from all walks of life come to walk, jog, or hold hands, particularly at sunset. The playpen has been extended with the new **Green Point Park** with its up-close views of the new **Cape Town Stadium.** You'll find a wide selection of restaurants on Main Road, from the start of Green Point to the very end of Sea Point, but be mindful after dark.

THE WATERFRONT ★★

The Victoria & Alfred (V&A) Waterfront, one of the most successful in the world, is one of Cape Town's top attractions. Hotels have glorious sea and mountain views, and shopping, dining, and entertainment options are right at your doorstep. You'll pay for the privilege of staying here, though (the cheap options aren't worth it). And it's a little out of touch with the rest of the city; most of the locals you'll meet here are the ones working the shops.

ATLANTIC SEABOARD ★★★

If you're looking for a beach vacation, stay on the Atlantic seaboard, where Table Mountain drops steeply into the ocean, creating a magnificent backdrop to the seaside "villages" of Bantry Bay, Clifton, Camps Bay, Bakoven, and Llandudno. The beaches are the most beautiful (Camps Bay, lined with restaurants and cocktail bars, is the most accessible), and the sunsets are awe inspiring.

SOUTHERN SUBURBS

Worth highlighting are Observatory and Constantia. **Observatory** (less than 10 min. from town), with its quaint Victorian buildings and narrow streets, has an interesting bohemian feel; its proximity to both the University of Cape Town and the huge Groote Schuur hospital makes for a particularly eclectic mix of people. Farther south (about 20 min. from town), the oak-lined streets and old, established mansions of **Constantia ★★★** are arguably the city's most exclusive addresses, with the lush surrounds of the Cape's oldest wine-producing

area attracting the rich and famous who prefer privacy to the glare of the sun-soaked hoi polloi in Camps Bay.

FALSE BAY ★★

Distance from city attractions is a drawback: Nevertheless, Victorian-era **Simons Town,** overdeveloped Fish Hoek, **Kalk Bay ★★★,** St. James, and Muizenberg are definitely worth a day or two of your attention, particularly if this is not your first visit to Cape Town. Kalk Bay, in particular, has a plethora of quaint restaurants and shops—even a dinner theater.

SOUTHERN PENINSULA & CAPE POINT ★★★

Surrounded by mountains, the fast-developing town of **Hout Bay** has its own harbor and marks the start of the breathtaking **Chapman's Peak Drive ★★★,** which snakes past the burgeoning town of **Noordhoek,** and the sweet villages of **Kommetjie** and **Scarborough ★★,** before reaching **Cape Point Nature Reserve ★★★.** Close to the shore, the best of these seaside enclaves have superbly white sandy beaches backed by magnificent cliffs, and they retain a dreamy, villagelike feel. Some, such as Noordhoek, though, have spawned huge housing developments. If you need to be near the action rather than surrounded by nature, you'll probably find these places a little too far from the city.

CAPE FLATS

This is where the majority of "coloureds" (the apartheid name for people of mixed descent) live, many forcibly relocated from District Six (a now-razed suburb adjacent to the city) by apartheid policies. The residents of the Cape Flats suffer from a high unemployment rate and lack of cohesive identity and hope, and the area has become a fertile breeding ground for drug-fueled gang wars. Even farther east are the "black suburbs" (historically referred to as "townships") of Gugulethu, Langa, and Nyanga, and the vast shantytowns and new residences of Khayalitsha (visible from the N2 as you drive in from the airport). To get a balanced view of Cape Town, a cultural tour here is highly recommended; see "Getting Around," below).

GETTING AROUND

The city center is small enough to explore on foot; even more so with the new pedestrian walkways and cycling routes that link the center with Green Point, Sea Point, and the entire Atlantic seaboard. The city's upgrade includes a long-awaited plan (now in its infancy) to establish an integrated public transport system with **MyCiti buses,** but aside from this and the **CitySightseeing** bus (see below), you'll need to rent a car. Beyond the city, with some frustrating exceptions, roads are relatively uncongested, parking is easy to find, and signs are straightforward.

By Public & Private Transportation

BY TRAIN Despite the dramatic improvement of Cape Town's train station, you still need to queue for tickets, and trains are not always reliable, clean, or safe; choose cars with other occupants, and watch your bags.

BY BUS After a series of stops and starts, Cape Town's new **MyCiti** integrated public transport system finally got underway in early 2011; for the latest updates, maps, and routes visit **www.capetown.gov.za/en/MyCiti**, or call ✆ **0800/656-463;** or contact the Cape Town tourism offices.

The public buses won't get you to all of the major tourist attractions, though; the most expedient way to take it all in is with a red **CitySightseeing** bus (see "Organized Cruises & Tours," below).

BY CAR If you can possibly avoid driving into the city center, do so, as the narrow streets can become quite congested. As cities go however, it's relatively easy to find parking; the need to pay the mobile meter-carrying attendants upfront (R4.50 per ½ hr.); if you overstay, you simply pay the difference when you return. Apart from the city center and Sea Point's Main Road, there is no charge for street parking, but business- or self-appointed "parking attendants" will offer to watch your car; although you are under no obligation to reward them, it is customary to tip those who are hired by local businesses (they will usually wear a bib or hand over a card) on your return; R2 to R7 is fine, but ignore aggressive and threatening tactics used by a rare few—you are under no obligation to pay.

You'll find numerous car-rental companies in Cape Town. For a cheaper deal, try **Penny K's** (✆ 072/736-6957; www.pennyks.co.za; from R175 per day) or **Value** (✆ 021/386-7699; www.valuerentalcar.com; from R159 per day). Both include some insurance and unlimited mileage. For a one-way rental to another province, you'll have to use a company with nationwide offices—**Avis** (✆ 021/424-1177) is the most consistently priced, and great because you can book online without inserting your credit card details (www.avis.co.za); also check out the deals on offer at **Tempest** (www.tempest.co.za), which often comes in cheapest for the same deal. To tool along the coast with the wind in your hair, rent a classic convertible, with or without chauffeur, from **Motor Classic** (✆ 021/461-7368 or 072/277-5022; www.motor classic.co.za; from R1,290 per day self-drive) or **Cape Cobra Hire** (✆ 083/321-9193; www.capecobrahire.co.za).

BY TAXI **Metered taxis** generally don't cruise the streets looking for fares (those that do should be avoided); you'll have to phone. Most charge around R12 per kilometer: **Excite** (✆ 021/418-4444) and **Unicab** (✆ 021/486-1610) have been around for years. Or make a difference and contact **The Green Cab** (✆ 086/184-3473 or 082/491-5972; www.thegreencab.co.za), the only company to offer an eco-friendly fleet (small seven- and four-seaters that run on liquefied petroleum gas and biodiesel) operating door-to-door. Drivers are mostly women (it's also entirely woman owned); note that fares are run on a share-ride system that keeps prices down. Also much cheaper than a metered taxi are **Rikkis** (© **086/174-5547;** www.rikkis.co.za), London-style cabs that keep continuously picking up and dropping off passengers on set routes. You pay according to city zones, priced from R22 to R35 (after 7pm, a R5 surcharge applies). These are operational 24/7 and will drop you off anywhere in the center, City Bowl suburbs, the Waterfront, or Camps Bay, and they now also service Hout Bay (R60) as well as Constantia and Claremont in the Southern Suburbs (R65–R75). You can also contact Rikkis from dedicated telephones they have set up in locations around the city; if you'd rather not share your fare, you pay extra for sole use. Trips farther afield—even to Cape Point—are charged at a flat rate or by the hour.

BY MOTORCYCLE If you just want to get from the beach to the city, zip around on a scooter from **La Dolce Vita Biking,** 57 Regent St., Sea Point (© **083/528-0897;** www.ldvbiking.co.za; R265 per day, including unlimited mileage, a helmet, and insurance; R1,500 deposit)—they also rent motorbikes. If you require more muscle, you can hire a real machine from **Motorcycle Tours** (© **021/794-7887;** www.sa-motorcycle-tours.com; prices vary). You can also go top-end by contacting **Cape Bike Travel** (© **084/606-4449;** www.capebiketravel.com) a Harley-Davidson goes for R1,200 to R1,500 per day; off-road BMWs start at R750 per day. They also organize "chauffeured" Harley rides where you ride on a pillion with a local. The regular Sunday morning breakfast run to Stellenbosch and Franschhoek is worth joining; ask owner Jörg Vogel about these routes and other rallies. Alternatively, get off the road and explore the mountain on a bike from **Downhill Adventures** (© **021/422-0388;** R140 per day).

Organized Cruises & Tours

These tours concentrate on the city and immediate surroundings; for tours farther afield, see chapter 3.

ON FOOT CITY TOURS The excellent 3-hour guided walk **Footsteps to Freedom** ★★★ (© **083/452-1112** or 021/671-6878; www.footstepstofreedom.co.za) departs Monday to Saturday at 10:30pm from Cape Town Tourism (at Castle and Burg sts.) and covers the most fascinating parts of the city center. It's a good way to get oriented and come to grips with Cape Town's history; your guide will take you to some secret spots—like the balcony where Nelson Mandela first addressed the public as a free man on February 11, 1990. The scheduled tour costs R150; **personalized tours** are also available (© **083/452-1112;** info@footstepstofreedom.co.za;

📷 **Sidecar Tours ★★★**

Tim Clarke's **Cape Sidecar Adventures** ★★★, 2 Glengariff Rd., Three Anchor Bay (© **021/434-9855;** www.sidecars.co.za), offers another unusual way to see the city—you can either motor yourself and a partner (or two!) around the city and beyond, or opt to travel in the road-level sidecar with a chauffer/guide. The sidecars were modeled on original 1938 German BMW sidecars and manufactured for the Chinese Red Army from as early as the mid-1950s. A self-drive day rental costs R884, including gear; a full-day chauffeured excursion with two passengers costs R2,400. Tim can fashion bespoke itineraries, such as Constantia wine tours by sidecar.

ask specifically for Garth Angus, whose expertise is unparalleled). If you're looking for something a little different, the street performance–style **Sex and Slaves in the City** tour put on by **Cape Town Walks** (✆ 021/785-2264; www.walkinafrica.com; R150) features two young acting graduates singing, reciting, and joking their way through a condensed city history as you visit several salient corners (including Bo-Kaap and the Castle).

BY BOAT   One of the best vantages of Cape Town is from the sea, particularly at sunset when the water is aglow and the lights of the city effervesce in the background. We highly recommend the 90-minute **sunset cruise** ★★★ from the harbor to Clifton (R220), offered by the **Waterfront Boat Company** (✆ 021/418-5806; www.waterfrontboats.co.za). They also have two gaff-rigged schooners—the *Spirit of Victoria* and *Esperance*—that cruise the Table Bay and Blouberg area, and luxury motorboats that cruise to Clifton Bay. The company also has a whale-watching permit. *Tigresse* (✆ 021/421-0909; www.tigresse.co.za), a huge luxury catamaran, is another great way to get to Clifton (R120 adults, R200 sunset cruise with bubbly). Alternatively, get your pulse racing and strap up with **Atlantic Adventures** (✆ 021/425-3785; www.atlanticadventures.co.za), which reaches speeds of up to 130kmph (81 mph) across Table Bay or around Robben Island in an 11-passenger rubber duck (R400 per person per hour). In Hout Bay harbor, **Drumbeat Charters** (✆ 021/791-4441; www.drumbeatcharters.co.za) offers 40-minute trips to see the Cape fur seals on Duiker Island (R65 adults, R25 children under 14; daily in season).

BY BUS   The 2-day ticket for the hop-on, hop-off **City Sightseeing bus** (✆ 021/511-6000; www.citysightseeing.co.za; R220 for 2 days; R110 for 1 day; prices cheaper if purchased online) is an efficient way to get around and see many of the highlights at more or less your own pace. In 2 days, you can cover both available routes—one takes in some top peninsula sights (including Kirstenbosch) and the other covers top city sites, even trundling through glamorous Camps Bay. There are a variety of extra-value tickets available, including one that includes a helicopter flip, and another that gives you an hour-long sunset cruise. The 1-day Go Cape Town card (R375) gets you a space on the Table Mountain cable car and admission to the aquarium.

African Eagle (✆ 021/464-4266; www.daytours.co.za), **Hylton Ross** (✆ 021/511-1784; www.hyltonross.co.za), and **Springbok Atlas** (✆ 021/460-4700; www.springbokatlas.com) are long-standing operators offering a variety of half-day, full-day, and multiday tours. You might want to check on the size of any tour group, and bear in mind that seeing the Cape through a bus window is not ideal.

BY AIR   Based at the V&A Waterfront, **The Hopper,** Quay 5 (✆ 021/419-8951; www.thehopper.co.za), promises to take single bookings (from R600 per person for short scenic hops) any day of the week. Also here, on East Pier Rd., is **The Huey Helicopter Co.** (✆ 021/419-4839; www.thehueyhelicopterco.com), offering half-hour low-flying "simulated combat" tours (R1,800 per person; seven-passenger minimum) in a retired Vietnam combat chopper, plus exhilarating scenic flights (R32,400 for a 60-min. full peninsular tour); they incorporate **Sport Helicopters** (✆ 021/419-5907/8; www.sport-helicopters.co.za), which has aerial tours of the city or peninsula, from R2,700 per lift-off. **Aquila** (✆ 021/712-1913; www.aquilamicrolight.com) takes to the sky in microlights.

TOWNSHIP TOURS   For a more holistic view of the still essentially segregated Cape Town community, and an insight into the Cape Muslim culture of the Bo-Kaap, a so-called "township" tour is essential. A most refreshing way is the unhurried,

2-hour guided **cycling tour** (R250) tour with Siwe Mbinda's **Vamos** ★★★ (📞 072/499-7866; www.vamos.co.za); its starts at Guga S'Thebe cultural center in Langa and gives a great overview of life here, and (during afternoons and on weekends) usually includes a virtuoso performance by Siwe's own children's dance troupe, Happy Feet. Vamos also offers a number of other ways of experiencing the townships, including a **walking tour** (R200), a **Sunday gospel tour** in which you attend a church service and finish up at Mzoli's for a vibrant barbecue lunch (R430). Vamos also runs a **full-day combination tour** (R520) in conjunction with Garth Angus's Footsteps to Freedom tour (see "On Foot City Tours," above), which gives you half a day exploring the city center, lunch at Mzoli's, and then a 2-hour township tour; this is a brilliant way to learn more about the city than most locals ever will. Another good option is the "Cape Care Route—A Trail of Two Cities," run by **Cape Capers** ★★★ (📞 021/448-3117; www. tourcapers.co.za; R690 adult, R520 children under 12, full day). It introduces visitors to some of the interesting entrepreneurs, including a visit to Philani Nutrition Centre in Khayelitsha, where women can bring their children to an on-site day care that operates while they're weaving, silk-screening, and painting; and Abalimi Bezekhaya, who inspires township greening efforts. Another outfit offering cultural tours of the townships is **Camissa Travel & Marketing** ★★ (📞 021/510-2646 or 078/657-7788; www. gocamissa.co.za), whose tours, like those of Cape Capers, help you forgo the sense of being a voyeur. They also run a **township eco tour** (R400; weekdays only) in which you spend time assisting in a community garden and working at a soup kitchen where needy people are given a meal. **Uthando** (📞 021/683-8523; www.uthandosa.org) offers a chance to learn and feel inspired rather than emerging guilt-ridden from a tour of the townships. For more possibilities, see "Cultural Sights: Cape Muslim to Khayalitsha," on p. 118, and "Specialist Tours," below.

SPECIALIST TOURS   For reality-shifting cultural tours that range from interactive jazz, reggae, or hip-hop evenings (where you meet legendary musicians and even dine and possibly jam with them), to community soccer expeditions and art tours, get in touch with **Coffeebeans Routes** ★★★ (📞 021/424-3572; www.coffeebeans routes.com). Within their innovative portfolio is a **spirituality route** (R595 per person), where you meet two very different spiritual leaders, perhaps a *sangoma* (traditional healer) and a Muslim imam, in the course of a 4-hour Friday afternoon tour; and we love their **storytelling route,** where you meet and listen to a couple of engaging local residents in their own homes (R595 per person including dinner; Tues and Thurs 7–11pm). Their popular **Jazz route** (R795) is a must-do for anyone interested in music; or if fashion and local design interest you, join their fashion route (R595), which goes behind the scenes of the local scene, meeting designers and fashion entrepreneurs in their studios to get a sense of how things tick creatively in a city hoping to be World Design Capital in 2014. For more intriguing tour options, visit their website, or pop into their office at 70 Wale St. in the city center; tours can be booked online at **www.webtickets.co.za**. Community-geared Cape Malay and African **"cooking safaris"** (R570–R595) are offered by **andulela experience** ★★★ (📞 021/790-2592; www.andulela.com; see p. 118). This excellent outfit, which works closely with Coffeebeans, also conducts music, art and poetry, and township tours, always with a commitment to local communities—and they've introduced an **"Opera Safari"** (R790), which includes a private performance by a local virtuoso as well as a light meal with them in their own home. **Cape Fusion Tours** (📞 021/461-2437; www.capefusion.co.za) runs culinary tours and cooking classes with some of the Cape's top chefs. **Daytrippers** (☎ 021/511-4766; www.daytrippers.co.za) specializes in hiking and biking trips. For specialist **wine tours,** see chapter 5.

[Fast FACTS] CAPE TOWN

Airport See "Arriving," earlier in this chapter.

American Express Main local offices are in the city center at Thibault Square (☎ 021/425-7991; Mon–Fri 8:30am–4:30pm) and at the Waterfront, Shop 11A, in Alfred Mall (☎ 021/419-3917; Mon–Fri 9am–7pm, Sat–Sun 10am–5pm).

Area Code The area code for Cape Town is 021.

Babysitting Contact **Supersitters** (☎ 021/552-1220; www.supersitters.net; around R50 per hour 7pm–midnight; R63 per hour all other times).

Bookstores Cape Town's best independent is **The Book Lounge** (see p. 131). The biggest commercial outlets are **Exclusive Books** (☎ 021/419-0905) and **Wordworth Books** (☎ 021/425-6880), both in Victoria Wharf at the Victoria & Alfred Waterfront.

Climate See "When to Go," in chapter 13.

Doctors & Dentists Call ☎ 021/671-3634, or 021/671-2924 for a 24-hour referral service. For travel clinics see "Visitor Information," above.

Driving Rules See "Getting Around," above.

Embassies & Consulates **U.S.:** 2 Reddam Ave., Westlake (☎ 021/702-7300); **U.K.:** 15th Floor, Deneys Reitz House, 8

Riebeek St. (☎ 021/405-2400).

Emergencies For an ambulance or general emergencies, call ☎ 10177; for police, call ☎ 10111; in case of fire, call ☎ 021/535-1100; for a sea rescue, call ☎ 021/449-3500; for Mountain Rescue Services, call ☎ 021/873-1121.

Hospitals **Groote Schuur** (☎ 021/404-9111), in Observatory, is the Cape's largest hospital. However, for immediate attention in more salubrious surroundings, you're best off heading for a private clinic (medical insurance is recommended). The **Netcare Christiaan Barnard Memorial Hospital** (☎ 021/480-6111) is in the center of town, at 181 Longmarket St., while the **Cape Town Mediclinic** (☎ 021/464-5500) is at 21 Hof St., in Oranjezicht. **Netcare Hospital** is South Africa's biggest private hospital group; to find the nearest Netcare hospital or hospital pharmacy contact its call center at ☎ 0860/638-2273.

Hot Lines **Automobile Association** (☎ 082/161-11, for vehicle breakdown); **Rape Crisis** (☎ 021/447-9762, for 24-hr. advice and counseling).

Internet Access There are numerous Internet cafes all over the city (especially on Long and Kloof sts., and

along Main Rd. in Sea Point). Just about every hotel and guesthouse in town offers free (or prepaid) Wi-Fi. Many of Cape Town's cafes and restaurants offer a limited amount of free browsing (if you have a laptop), via either **RedButton** (www.redbutton.co.za) or **SkyRove** (www.skyrove.com)—you can purchase time with your credit card.

Maps See "City Layout," earlier in this chapter.

Newspapers & Magazines The morning paper, *Cape Times,* and the more sensationalist afternoon and evening paper, *Argus,* are sold at most street corners. The *Mail&Guardian* offers a serious weekly overview of events. You'll find international titles at the Waterfront's bookstores (see above).

Pharmacy **Lite-Kem** (☎ 021/461-8040), 24 Darling St., opposite the city post office, is open Monday through Saturday from 7:30am to 11pm and Sunday from 9am to 11pm. **Sunset Pharmacy** (☎ 021/434-3333), in Sea Point Medical Centre, Kloof Road, is open daily from 8:30am to 9pm.

Post Office The best-located city branch, if you want to park easily and get served relatively quickly, is the Vlaeberg branch on

Loop Street (corner of Pepper; ☎ **021/424-7477**), near the center of town. Better still is the branch in the Promenade center in **Camps Bay** (the center offers 30 min. free parking and the post office gets few customers). Hours are Monday through Friday from 8am to 5pm (Wed from 8:30am) and Saturday from 8am to 1pm.

Restrooms The city's large population of homeless people means that the hygiene of public restrooms can be of varying quality. You're best off going to a shopping center or coffee shop, or visiting a gas station.

Safety The formation of the Central City Improvement District (CCID), the ongoing installation of closed-circuit cameras, a dedicated city police force, and 24-hour care centers for Cape Town's street children has resulted in a marked reduction in crime in the city center. This is no reason to let down your guard, however. Muggings can be avoided by taking the same precautions you would in any large city—lose the jewelry and stash the wallet. Be aware of street children, many of whom beg at large intersections and along Long Street at night. Visitors are requested to give them food coupons (inquire at the CCID Kiosks in St George's Mall and Company Gardens) or make a donation to one of the child-care centers rather than giving them cash, which keeps them on the streets. Be particularly vigilant on the beach—taking a dip while leaving your belongings unattended is asking for trouble. Note that it is inadvisable to pull over and stop on the N2 (the airport highway), and always travel with a cellphone in case your car breaks down. Driving into the townships at night (unless on a guided tour) is definitely not advisable.

Taxis See "Getting Around," earlier in this chapter.

Weather Call ☎ **082/231-1640;** better still, visit www.windguru.cz.

WHERE TO STAY

Cape Town's popularity has produced an ever-expanding list of accommodation options, and many seasoned globetrotters contend it offers the best selection of guesthouses in the world. Following the opening of many new large hotels in 2010, supply has, for the first time, seriously outstripped demand, and rates have in most cases finally dipped—good news for visitors in these tough economic times.

The City Bowl, V&A Waterfront, and Camps Bay remain the most popular areas to stay offering great views and/or good access to restaurants, attractions, and beaches. If you're traveling between May and September, you'll inevitably get a fantastic low-season rate (also called "green-," "shoulder-," or "secret-" season).

Note: The airport is no more than a 20- to 30-minute drive from most hotels, so it's not necessary to move to an airport hotel for early morning or late-night flights.

City Center, Bo-Kaap & Woodstock

As the **city center (CBD)** tries to reinvent itself as a residential hub, an increasing number of smart places to stay are offered—described here are the best city-center options, but given Cape Town's topography, our money is on the options in the residential City Bowl neighborhoods, reviewed later.

Best For: Cape Town's CBD is great for daytime exploration on foot, and you'll have the city on your doorstep. Some of the taller hotels afford extraordinary views of the cityscape—with either Table Mountain in the background or Table Bay stretching away beyond the harbor.

Cape Town Hotels

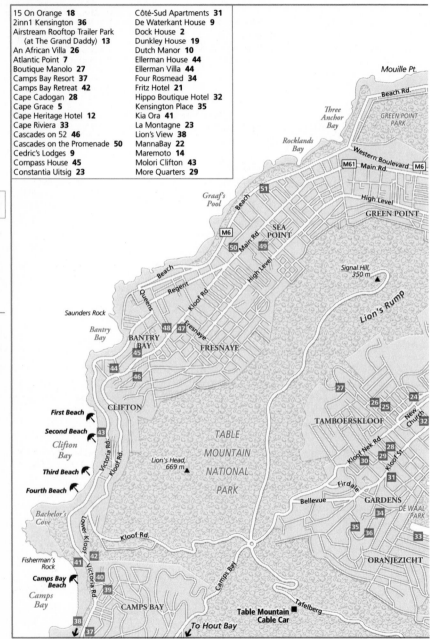

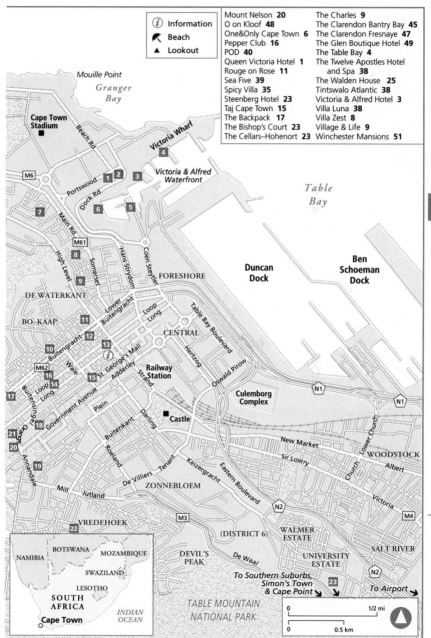

Mount Nelson **20**
O on Kloof **48**
One&Only Cape Town **6**
Pepper Club **16**
POD **40**
Queen Victoria Hotel **1**
Rouge on Rose **11**
Sea Five **39**
Spicy Villa **35**
Steenberg Hotel **23**
Taj Cape Town **15**
The Backpack **17**
The Bishop's Court **23**
The Cellars–Hohenort **23**

The Charles **9**
The Clarendon Bantry Bay **45**
The Clarendon Fresnaye **47**
The Glen Boutique Hotel **49**
The Table Bay **4**
The Twelve Apostles Hotel and Spa **38**
The Walden House **25**
Tintswalo Atlantic **38**
Victoria & Alfred Hotel **3**
Villa Luna **38**
Villa Zest **8**
Village & Life **9**
Winchester Mansions **51**

(i) Information
Beach
▲ Lookout

YOUR OWN CAPE TOWN HOME: MORE SPACE, MORE PRIVACY, MORE freedom

Renting an apartment or home can be a great-value option, particularly for families, or couples looking for absolute privacy. Even the luxurious villas (and there are plenty of those) compare well with five-star hotels if you're traveling as a small group or extended family, plus you have added space and exclusivity. If you prefer a contemporary edge, take a look at the various cottages and apartments offered by **inAWEstays** ★★ 🏷 (**www. inawestays.co.za**), which has a variety of well-priced efficiency options in different residential neighborhoods across the city, including miniature Studio Uno in wind-free Fresnaye (R850 double) and two-bedroom Garden Cottage (R990 for four people) done out in smoldering charcoal and featuring local designer furniture. Another well-priced option is **Côté-Sud Apartments** (www. cotesud.co.za; 🕭 **072/608-1889**; R900–R1,600 for four, according to season)— four neat two-bedroom apartments (book an upstairs apartment for views) with separate entrances and a communal plunge pool conveniently located on busy Kloof Street (plenty of dining options within walking distance, plus a 1 minimart)—the drawback is a fair amount of traffic noise. Or take a look at **More Quarters** ★★★ on a little side street off bustling Kloof Street (www. morequarters.co.za; 🕭 **021/480-8080**). A cluster of historic semidetached cottages that have been converted into efficiency apartments, each one is individually styled and provided with all the conveniences of a small but spacious modern home. There's a dedicated check-in, with an upstairs breakfast room (included in the good-value rate; R2,670–R3,000 for two people sharing in high season; low-season rates are much lower). There's also their four-bedroom Redcliffe House (with a pool) that you can take over (from R5,340 per night in high season). If you're prepared to splurge, we'd like to give you a sample of some of our favorite villas: Start by taking a look at **Lion's View** ★★★ (www.lionsview.co.za; 🕭 **021/438-0046** or 083/719-5735), an architect-designed modern dream pad in Camps Bay that's featured in a string of glossies. The two-bedroom Penthouse Apartment is good

Drawbacks: Unless you're high up, you're unlikely to have a view; in some areas, all-night noise can be a real problem. If you have rented a car, parking can be an issue.

Recommended Neighborhood Restaurants: There's an endless supply of reliable restaurants within easy reach of any of these suggestions. The best are reviewed later in this chapter. However, if there's one place that we think defines Cape Town's emerging inner-city sensibility, it's the former **L'aperitivo** ★★★, 170 Loop St. (🕭 **021/426-1001**), a wine and cocktail bar that spills out onto the sidewalk, and serving fresh bistro-style food that you can choose from the chalkboards. Ownership is changing hands as we go to print, but we imagine it will retain its Cape vibe (and hopefully its mean gin and tonics).

VERY EXPENSIVE

Taj Cape Town ★★   It's one of the inner-city's most prestigious corners of real estate, directly across the road from the Company's Gardens, Parliament, and St. George's Cathedral, and the best of the large posh hotels that opened just before the 2010 World Cup. A modern tower cleverly grafted onto the elegant stone masonry of the original Reserve Bank, it combines old-world elegance in the double-volume

for families (up to four people; R3,900–R5,900 in summer, 2-week minimum in peak), while the five-bedroom Main House down below is ideal setting for memorable celebratory gatherings (R7,900–R12,000 per night in summer). Other villas we love are **Villa Luna** ★★★ (www.villaluna.co.za; R5,000–R12,500 per night in summer); **Kia Ora** ★★★ (www.kiaora.co.za; R7,500–R20,000 per night in summer), and the show-stopping **Molori Clifton** ★★★ (**www.molori.com**)—the sexiest, most luxurious beach villa on the continent, at celeb prices. Molori rents for between R48,000 and R115,000 per night (for up to 12 people); or R140,000 in peak season, and comes with a long list of add-ons, including a chauffeured Bentley at your disposal, a spa, gym, bikes, and direct access (via one of Clifton's winding pathways) to the beach—next door is Molori's Beach House Villa (also an apartment) which has just three bedrooms and costs R65,000 per night. There are plenty of villa agents, but we recommend the following two: **Icon Villas** (www.iconvillas.travel; ✆ **086/184-5527**) offers a broad spectrum of well-dressed apartments and luxury villas, all hand-picked by the proprietor, Therese Botha, as well as a full concierge service if needed. Although dotted all over the Western Cape, many of the stunning villas and cottages rented out through **Perfect Hideaways** (www.perfecthideaways.co.za) are in fact right in the city, and often at the edge of the beach, and they live up to the name. If it's peak season and you're struggling to find a spot, other rental agents worth checking out are **www.campsbayapartments.com**, **www.cliftononsea.co.za**, and **www.platinumplaces.co.za** and **www.capeportfolios.com**. If push comes to shove, you may be forced to contact overextended **Village & Life** (www.villageandlife.com; ✆ **021/438-3972**), which runs a bloated assortment of efficiency spots. If looking at all this seems a lot like work (and finding the right place does take time), feel free to contact us at **www.bestkept.co.za**. We're constantly scouring the city (and beyond) for new, old, and novel places to stay, and we'll find the perfect match for your needs and budget.

lobby with plush bedrooms—lots of high-sheen dark wood and furniture, freestanding lamps, modern artworks, and marble bathrooms, with large picture windows. The "mountain view" luxury rooms (specify) are the ones to book; they improve the higher up in the tower block you go. Numerous attractions are within walking distance, as are restaurants and bars (chi-chi nightclub The Reserve is next door). Service is a bit patchy: charming doorman vs. awkward, cheerless restaurant service.

Wale St., Cape Town. www.tajcapetown.co.za. ✆ **021/819-2000.** Fax 021/819-2001. 176 units. High season R5,200–R6,600 double, R7,200–R7,900 Taj Club double, R10,000–R37,500 suite; low season R3,500–R5,600 double, R7,500–R25,000 suite. Rates include breakfast. AE, DC, MC, V. **Amenities:** 2 restaurants (including **Bombay Brasserie,** see p. 98); bar; lounges; airport transfers (R480); concierge; club level rooms; heated indoor lap pool; room service; spa. *In room:* A/C, TV, movies-on-demand, hair dryer, minibar, MP3 docking station, Wi–Fi (30 min. free, R60 per hour).

EXPENSIVE

15 On Orange ★★ ☺ Step inside the vast, high-ceilinged atrium lobby of this glitzy design-centric hotel and it's difficult to say if it's a gallery, an airport, or perhaps a superspacious nightclub. From the supermodel-baiting Murano Bar to the purple felt on the white pool table in the Judge's Lounge and the gold-upholstered armchair in the elevator, everything is designed for effect. Things are marginally more restrained in your living quarters, although still appealing to look at and very comfortable—definitely book a room with a Table Mountain view, but there are also rooms with a twist—glass boxes fitted with hanging Perspex pods for you to lounge in while watching the scene in the hotel atrium below. Rates fluctuate with demand (below are indicative), when it's low you could be bagging a bargain. Patchy service is the only downside—perhaps there are just too many design curiosities distracting an inexperienced staff.

Corner of Grey's Pass and Orange St., Cape Town. www.africanpridehotels.com/15onorange. ℂ **021/ 469-8000.** Fax 021/469-8001. 129 units. Peak season R2,648–R3,950 double; rest of year R1,883– R3,050 double. AE, DC, MC, V. **Amenities:** Restaurant; cafe; bar; lounge; pool; room service; spa. *In room:* A/C, TV/DVD, hair dryer, minibar, free Wi-Fi.

Cape Heritage Hotel ★★

On buzzing Bree Street, this imaginative revamp of one of Cape Town's original Georgian townhouses (dating back to the 1770s) stands betwixt some of the city's hippest shops, bars and eateries. It's an ideal base if you want to be close to the action in a genuinely gracious heritage property (with creaking floorboards and walls that aren't always at regular angles). Interiors are individually crafted and hung with local art (most of which is for sale) and evidence of the depth of South African creativity. Every room is uniquely proportioned, and every space has a particular personality, combining contemporary flair with original architectural elements (high ceilings, exposed wood beams, and sash windows overlooking the street). In the standard category, book room 111—or upgrade to the more spacious (and better-dressed) luxury category. A rooftop Jacuzzi with mountain and city views compensates for the lack of pool or real outdoor space.

90 Bree St., Cape Town. www.capeheritage.co.za. ℂ **021/424-4646.** Fax 086/616-7281. 17 units. High season R2,390 double, R2,960 luxury double, R3,310 junior suite, R3,870 suite; low season R1,950– R2,450 double, R2,710–R3,170 suite. AE, DC, MC, V. Rates include breakfast. **Amenities:** Breakfast room; bar; 2 lounges; airport transfers (R450 for 2 people); babysitting; library. *In room:* A/C, TV/DVD, movie library (R25/title), hair dryer, heated towel rack, minibar, underfloor heating in bathroom, free Wi-Fi.

Pepper Club ★★

Another slick contemporary option with a sense of fun and astonishing views: Book a room as high up in the North Tower as possible and claim your preference—either a full-on view of Table Mountain, or have the city spreading out beneath your feet, culminating in the harbor and Table Bay (insist on a room with a balcony—a few don't have). Aside from the bar (frequented by locals) there's an in-house cinema (over 1,000 titles to choose from; popcorn and drinks available), an elegant spa, and—besides the pool up on the eighth floor—a dedicated beach club and restaurant over on the Camps Bay strip (free shuttles to get you there). Bustling Long Street is very close by—perfect for party hounds. The entry-level studios are large and well equipped, but if you can, bag a suite on the 18th floor (though note that the elevators can be slow and the A/C noisy).

Corner of Loop and Pepper sts., Cape Town. www.pepperclub.co.za. ℂ **021/812-8888.** 210 units. High season R3,050–R3,325 studio, R3,805–R5,640 1-bedroom suite, R6,100–R8,810 2-bedroom suite, R16,000–R64-895 3-bedroom suite; low season R1,960–R2,090 studio, R2,450–R3,580 1-bedroom suite, R3,920–R5,190 2-bedroom suite, R6,180–R30,980 3-bedroom suite. Rates include breakfast. AE, DC, MC, V. **Amenities:** 2 restaurants (1 offsite with beach facilities); bar; lounge; airport transfers (R400 one-way); cinema; pool; spa. *In room:* A/C, TV/DVD, movie library, kitchen, free Wi-Fi.

MODERATE

Airstream Rooftop Trailer Park/The Grand Daddy ★

The Grand Daddy—a revamp of one of the city's oldest hotels—offers rooms that are bright and contemporary, but hardly a match for the innovation up on the roof—the world's first rooftop trailer park hotel. A collection of reconditioned vintage trailers artfully rejigged as psychedelic hotel quarters. We wouldn't recommend these for extended stays (interiors are great fun but spatial constraints can be a bit overwhelming, and in summer you'll need the A/C on 24/7), but for a night of rollicking rock-star-style madness, they're worth checking out: The Ballad of John and Yoko is the one to go for (it's almost all bed, with musical instruments to keep you occupied). If this sounds like fun, check out the swankier version in nearby Elgin valley (p. 170).

38 Long St., Cape Town. www.granddaddy.co.za. ℗ **021/424-7247.** Fax 021/424-7248. 7 units. High season R1,925–R2,200 double, R2,200–R2,475 suite; low season R1,455–R1,760 double, R1,730–R2,035 suite. AE, DC, MC, V. **Amenities:** Restaurant; 2 bars; airport transfers (R300); room service. *In room:* A/C, TV, hair dryer, minibar, Wi-Fi (50 MB free).

Dutch Manor ★★ Described as an "antique hotel," this feels a bit like a house museum, with just six compact rooms stuffed full of vintage furniture and artifacts from a cross-section of earlier eras. The thick-walled house was built in 1812, and you'll get a strong sense of that history just by looking at the mustard-color facade (sadly blighted by iron burglar bars), which faces the city from an elevated position at the edge of Bo-Kaap. Interiors are seriously old-fashioned—the heavy floral drapes, ancient rugs, prodigious use of lace and antiques are in keeping with the historic theme, but if you're used to a more contemporary style, might feel a bit claustrophobic. Choose room 5 for the most romantic ambience (although the tiny antique bed may spoil any plans for true romance). It'll all feel a bit like overnighting in a time-trapped home rather than a hotel—you're even allowed to use the kitchen to make tea or coffee.

158 Buitengracht St., Bo-Kaap. www.dutchmanor.co.za. ℗ **021/422-4767** or 072/847-5239. 6 units. High season R1,500 standard double, R1,700 luxury double, R2,500 suite; low season R950 standard double, R1,200 luxury double, R2,000 suite. Rates include breakfast. AE, DC, MC, V. **Amenities:** Dining room; lounge. *In room:* A/C, TV, hair dryer, heated towel rack, free Wi-Fi.

Rouge on Rose ★★ 🍴 ♨ On Bo-Kaap's burgeoning Rose Street strip, this little boutique guest house offers suite-size digs at rates that'll knock your socks off. Bedrooms are a blend of modern chic (all clean lines, fabulous white linens, extralong king-size beds, and excellent bathrooms) and Bohemian styling (antiques collected over 3 decades, chunky armchairs, hand-carved armoires, random *objets*, and rainfall showers folded into curved walls); there's a mix of deluxe rooms and efficiency suites (with space for kids on a sleeper couch). Room 302 is especially fabulous. De Waterkant and the city center are within easy reach, and there are several interesting shops nearby, not to forget Bo-Kaap's ancient cobbled roads and mosques (we love the melodious call to prayer, but be prepared, as there's no escaping it).

25 Rose St., Bo-Kaap. www.rougeonrose.co.za. ℗ **021/426-0298.** Fax 021/422-2355. 9 units. R1,000–R1,400 double; extra person R350. Rates include breakfast. MC, V. **Amenities:** Dining room; airport transfers (R350). *In room* A/C, TV/DVD, hair dryer, kitchenette (some), minifridge, free Wi-Fi.

INEXPENSIVE

The Backpack ★ ♨ The UK's *Guardian* rated it one of the world's 10 coolest hostels, and we agree. It's reasonably central (a short stroll from the restaurant/nightlife options on Kloof and Long streets—walking is inadvisable late at night, though), and comprises four interconnected Victorian-era houses, which makes for interesting indoor/outdoor spaces. Aside from that it's clean, comfortable, and efficiently managed; there are also plentiful useful amenities on-site, including a pool with full-on mountain views. Aside from dorms, there's a focus on private rooms, including en suites, and even the shared bathrooms are immaculate. Rooms are thoughtfully decorated, too, with handpicked pieces you don't often see in a backpacker. All of which makes it extremely popular, not just with single budget travelers but with couples and families seeking excellent value, so book early.

74 New Church St., Cape Town. www.backpackers.co.za. © **021/423-4530.** Fax 086/271-4165. 34 units. R650–R750 double, R900 3-bed loft, R1,200 4-bed family room, R500–R600 single, R160–R320 dorm bed. MC, V. **Amenities:** Cafe; bar; lounge; airport transfers (R200 plus R70 per each additional person); kitchen; pool. *In room:* Fan, no phone.

Maremoto ★ 🛥 One of the best-value spots in the city, and an excellent option for anyone who's here to live it up, this small inn (a handful of elegant rooms above a relaxed bar-cum-restaurant) is in the center of the hardest-partying section of Long Street: Stumble down the stairs and you're right in the zone, back upstairs—aside from the noise—you'd hardly guess. Much of the original architecture (it's a three-story early-20th-century building with a nine-column colonnade along the curved facade) has been left intact and bedrooms are spacious and individually decorated with antiques from the family's private stash (Art Deco mirrors, hand-carved side tables, reupholstered armchairs). Wooden floors have been whitewashed, walls coated in soft gray, and comfy beds wrapped with Egyptian cotton. Room 6 affords views of Table Mountain straight from the bed. Really agreeable, considering the price.

230 Long St., Cape Town. www.maremoto.co.za. © **021/422-5877.** 6 units. R750–R850 double. AE, DC, MC, V. **Amenities:** Restaurant; bar. *In room:* A/C and fan, TV, hair dryer, Wi-Fi (by credit card).

City Bowl: On the Slopes of Table Mountain

Best For: For access to sights, top restaurants, and beaches, you can't beat the City Bowl, the residential neighborhoods that tumble down the slopes of the mountain. Most enjoy fabulous views of the city center and the best vistas of the mountain.

Drawbacks: You will need to drive to the beach, and you probably won't be able to walk into the city at night either (by day you should be fine, although it can be a stiff walk back up).

Recommended Restaurants Within Walking Distance: There are dozens of places along Kloof Street (and on some of the side streets off it), accessible from most of the City Bowl neighborhoods, although it's a short cab hop into the city or various dining precincts from any of the places listed here—walking at night is not recommended.

VERY EXPENSIVE

Mount Nelson ★★★ ☺ The Nellie opened her doors in 1899 to accommodate passengers of the Union and Castle lines, and remains the undisputed grande dame of colonial hotels. It enjoys a great location on the edge of the city—a 10-minute stroll through the Company's Gardens to the center, or exit straight onto bustling Kloof Street—yet feels as though it's out in the country. Gorgeous gardens (3½ hectares/ 9 acres of them), rambling old buildings (divided into various charmingly old-fashioned wings), antiques and collectibles, and an astonishingly mixed clientele—from international celebs to cruise liner passengers—is why this is our favorite city hotel. Locals visit all the time, popping in for high tea, cocktails, spa treatments, weddings, and more recently dinner—see the review for slinky new fine-dining restaurant Planet. Staff is genuinely warm, and the kids' facilities are great.

76 Orange St., Gardens. www.mountnelson.co.za. © **021/483-1000.** Fax 021/483-1001. 209 units. High season R5,300 superior double, R6,900 deluxe double, R8,500–R13,300 suite; low season R4,000

superior double, R5,300 deluxe double, R6,600–R10,500 suite. Children 3–12 pay R245 if sharing with 2 adults; children over 12 pay R690. Rates include breakfast. AE, DC, MC, V. **Amenities:** 2 restaurants (including **Planet,** p. 98); bar; airport transfers (from R500 one-way); babysitting; 2 pools; room service; spa; 2 flood-lit tennis courts. *In room:* A/C, TV/DVD, hair dryer, heated towel rack, minibar, free Wi-Fi.

EXPENSIVE

Boutique Manolo ★★★ ♣   Magnificently located—high above the city, along Cape Town's very own "Mulholland Drive"—this modern, peppermint-colored cliff-side mansion ranks among the most fabulously designed places to bed down. Accommodations spill over various levels: Each room has an outdoor area with seating arrangements, and besides the luscious red pool, there's a secret garden, too. The chic white interiors are immaculate and outfitted with books, fine linens, useful gadgets, and heating, but the jaw-dropping vistas of Table Mountain and the city—glittering and pulsating beneath your feet at night—are what make this a top choice. Anyone seeking sublime romance should book the top-of-the-world, two-story Penthouse suite, which has a fireplace and god-gifted terrace.

33 Leeukloof Dr., Tamboerskloof. www.boutique-manolo.co.za. 🕾 **021/426-2330.** Fax 021/426-0022. 5 units. High season R2,350–R2,950 double, R4,500 suite; low season R2,000–R2,500 double, R4,000 suite. Rates include breakfast; suite rates include minibar and laundry. AE, MC, V. **Amenities:** Dining area; lounge; library; pool; wine cellar. *In room:* A/C, TV/DVD/CD, movie library, music library, hair dryer, minibar, MP3 docking station, underfloor heating, free Wi-Fi.

Four Rosmead ★★★ ♣   This small, well-bred boutique guest house (in a 1903 monument-status house) scores top marks for excellent service and thoughtful touches like kitted beach bags. Decor manages to be both soothingly tasteful and full of character—the entire house functions as an art gallery, so it's fascinating, too. Rooms are spacious and airy—the luxury (shower only) category is just fine, but if you decide to splash out on a deluxe room (with balcony), book Oranjezicht or Leeuwen-zicht for the city views. The "cottage" in the Provençal-inspired garden is a honeymooner's choice—big, without views, and with an al fresco shower. There is also a thorough, personally tested restaurant guide, suggesting walking-distance eateries and places as far afield as Constantia; they'll even plate take-out meals for you.

4 Rosmead Ave., Oranjezicht. www.fourrosmead.com. 🕾 **021/480-3810.** Fax 021/423-0044. 8 units, 5 with shower only. High season R2,050–R2,400 luxury double, R2,400–R2,800 deluxe double, R2,750–R3,100 suite; low season R1,525 luxury double, R1,750 deluxe double, R1,975 suite. Rates include breakfast. MC, V. No children under 12. **Amenities:** Dining room; lounge; airport transfers (R430–R630 one-way, depending on time and guest numbers); library; heated pool; room service. *In room:* A/C, TV/DVD, movie library, fireplace (some), hair dryer, MP3 docking station, minibar, free Wi-Fi.

Kensington Place ★★★   This sophisticated award-winning boutique hotel has beautiful views of the city, harbor, and mountain (although the views are better at Boutique Manolo). Each bedroom is the size of a minisuite, with expensive finishes, fabrics, and furnishings; ready for the next magazine shoot. Thoughtful touches include personal laptops, an "emergency box" stocked with condoms and headache pills, ready-to-go beach kits, and a gym-in-a-bag. The best rooms on the second floor have balconies overlooking the city—ask for nos. 1, 2, or 3. Near the pool, room no. 7 is larger than most; no. 8 has a private entrance, and privileged views through massive picture windows. The small, timber-decked pool is fringed by a comfortable casbah-style lounge with billowing curtains—a calm oasis that belies the proximity of bustling Kloof Street, with its choice of restaurants.

38 Kensington Crescent, at Leeuwenhof and Kensington, Higgovale. www.kensingtonplace.co.za. 🕾 **021/424-4744.** Fax 021/424-1810. 8 units. High season R3,100–R3,290 standard double, R3,410–R3,600

superior double; low season R2,086 standard double, R2,568 superior double. Rates include breakfast. AE, DC, MC, V. Credit card payments attract 5% surcharge. No children under 10. **Amenities:** Dining area; bar; lounge; airport transfers (R3500); gym access (in the city); pool; room service. *In room:* A/C, TV/DVD, gym-in-a-bag, hair dryer, laptop, MP3 docking station, minibar, free Wi-Fi.

MODERATE

Besides our favorites, fully reviewed below, Cape Town has a few more guesthouses worth considering in this price category. All are in gorgeous historic homes high up on the slopes of Oranjezicht, with great views of the city and harbor lights, but one that we fancy for its marriage of location, style, and great value is **Cape Riviera ★**, 31 Belvedere Ave. (www.caperiviera.co.za; ℂ **021/461-8535;** R825–R1,800 double). It's also on one of Cape Town's most beautiful streets, amid grand turn-of-the-20th-century homes overlooking the Molteno reservoir. Rooms, featuring dark wood and a pale palette, are mostly elegant and all equipped with all the comforts (A/C, Wi-Fi, satisfying linens). Pricier rooms have more space and better views, but do insist on one in the original house; the new construction at the back is a little off-putting.

An African Villa ★★ ● Make yourself at home: Your four hands-on hosts have skillfully reworked the spaces in several adjoining 19th-century double-story Victorian houses into a boutique guesthouse that is both chic and cozy. Using a clever mix of ethnic and modern furniture, they've created a stylish, good-value, and above all warm, welcoming environment—one of Cape Town's loveliest. The upbeat public interiors (including a big, homey kitchen) all lead to an outdoor area with plunge pool and timber loungers. For privacy and views, the rooms on the second floor are marginally preferable to those on the ground—those facing Table Mountain (like no. A2) have great ambience; but the platinum units, with doors that lead to the Victorian balcony overlooking the street, are the ones with space.

19 Carstens St., Tamboerskloof. www.capetowncity.co.za. ℂ **021/423-2162.** Fax 021/423-2274. 13 units. R1,100–R1,600 double. Winter discounts available. Rates include breakfast. AE, DC, MC, V. **Amenities:** Breakfast areas; honor bar; small library; pool; Wi-Fi. *In room:* A/C, TV, hair dryer, free Wi-Fi.

Cape Cadogan ★★ ● One of the original farmhouses built on the slopes of Table Mountain, this elegant double-storied Georgian (Victorianized in 1912) is just steps away from bustling Kloof Street, yet it's a thoroughly peaceful and very stylish. It's decorated with lovely touches that are offset by cool white-and-gold minimalism—a well-placed plush Victorian chair or large gilt-framed mirror—and even the smaller standard rooms ooze a kind of quiet grandeur. Rooms to book are nos. 2 and 8, both huge, beautifully furnished, and airy, with vast travertine bathrooms and double-volume showers—no. 8 has an especially interesting view from a little balcony. Adjacent, the double-story Owner's Villa is a cushy home for two, with added privacy, a large personal outdoor area, and a plunge pool.

5 Upper Union St., Gardens. www.capecadogan.co.za. ℂ **021/480-8080.** Reservations ℂ **011/484-9911.** Fax 011/484-9916. 12 units. High season R2,120–R2,340 standard double, R2,670–R2,900 luxury double, R4,060 villa double; low season R1,440 standard double, R1,920 luxury double, R2,900 villa double. Rates include breakfast. AE, DC, MC, V. **Amenities:** Dining room; bar; lounge; airport transfers (R370 one-way); small pool. *In room:* A/C, TV/DVD, hair dryer, minibar, free Wi-Fi.

MannaBay ★★★ An architectural oddity in powdery blue, this fashionable new guesthouse is even more theatrical on the inside; perfect if you find most contemporary digs rather bland. Decor is bold and slightly over the top, with interesting wallpaper, big glittery chandeliers, rich fabrics, and deep, vibrant colors creating a sensual space that's a pleasure to inhabit. Each bedroom is themed, from the cerise-tinged

Versailles Suite, to war chests and tongue-in-cheek Portuguese *padrões* in the Explorer Room, or the psychedelic wallpaper and restrained monochromatic black-and-white decor. Ask for a room with city views; outside, loungers at one end of the pool provide a great perspective on Table Mountain. Staff is charming and treats you like royalty.

1 Denholm Rd., Oranjezicht. www.mannabay.com. © **021/461-1094.** Fax 021/469-2628. 7 units. High season R1,425–R2,110 double, R3,250 luxury double, R3,990 suite; low season R1,000–R1,475 double, R2,275 luxury double, R2,795 suite. Rates include breakfast, high tea, and all drinks (within reason). No children under 6. AE, DC, MC, V. **Amenities:** Breakfast room; 2 lounges; free bar service and 24-hr. butler service; library; heated outdoor pool. *In room:* A/C, TV, hair dryer, MP3 docking station, free Wi-Fi.

2inn1 Kensington ★★ Across the road from the pretty estate of the Western Cape Premier, this is one of the slickest luxury guesthouses in town: two side-by-side reno-vated houses with cleverly refurbished spaces and personalized service at the hands of the European owners (though not as warm as say African Villa). In-room amenities are exhaustive (even a local cellphone) and the look is a blend of contemporary Euro-Afro chic (leather sofas, zebra skins on the white wooden floors, horns and snakeskin light fittings), which somehow complements the original Victorian architecture. Standard rooms lack views, so we definitely recommend the larger luxury units; suites accom-modate four people. Poolside sunbeds afford good views of Table Mountain.

21 Kensington Crescent, Oranjezicht. www.2inn1.com. © **021/423-1707.** Fax: 021/423-1445. 10 units. High season R1,700 double, R2,100 luxury double, R2,800 suite; low season R1,350 double, R1,550 luxury dou-ble, R2,100 suite. Rates include breakfast and minibar soft drinks. AE, MC, V. No children under 12. **Ameni-ties:** Breakfast room; lounge; bar; airport transfers (R300); Jacuzzi; saltwater pool. *In room:* TV/DVD, movie library, CD player, music library, fridge, MP3 docking station, underfloor heating, free Wi-Fi.

The Walden House ★ This quiet, turn-of-the-20th-century guesthouse offers stylish rooms in one of the city's oldest residential areas. White is predominant—from the floorboards to the linen—with many wicker touches and handsomely tiled bath-rooms. Standard double rooms are compact, no-nonsense, and comfortable, with a choice of twin or queen-size beds. The spacious garden suite is a personal favorite, but the most popular room is the upstairs honeymoon suite, with a door opening onto the first-floor veranda with a great view of Table Mountain. Kloof Street, with its large selection of restaurants, bars, and cafes, is within easy walking distance.

5 Burnside Rd., Tamboerskloof. www.walden-house.com. © **021/424-4256.** Fax 086/689-4802. 7 units. High season R1,480 standard double, R1,780–R1,990 suite; low season R1,100 double, R1,320–R1,700 suite. Rates include breakfast. AE, DC, MC, V. No children under 12. **Amenities:** Breakfast room; lounge; airport transfers (R220); pool. *In room:* A/C, TV, hair dryer, heated towel rack, minibar, free Wi-Fi.

INEXPENSIVE

The Fritz Hotel ★ 🍴 It's within easy reach of the Kloof Street restaurant strip, right on the edge of the city center, and furnished with an eclectic selection of Art Deco and 1950s antiques (collected by Swiss owner Arthur Bisig). It's more like a large colonial-style guesthouse (Edwardian, with Victorian bits) than a hotel, and it's a bar-gain, with neatly maintained, individually styled bedrooms, all with knock-off designer beds. Ask for a room that opens onto the first-floor wraparound veranda; they have high ceilings and wood floors—rooms 6 and 14 are the biggest. Room no. 11 is small but has a great view of Table Mountain from the bed. Breakfasts and drinks are served in the relaxed, breezy courtyard.

1 Faure St., Gardens. www.fritzhotel.co.za. © **021/480-9000.** Fax 021/480-9090. 13 units. High season R800–R1,000 double; low season R500–R650 double. Rates include breakfast. AE, DC, MC, V. *In room:* Fan, TV, hair dryer, minibar, free Wi-Fi.

Waterfront

Best For: You're in the heart of one of Cape Town's top attractions, a working harbor, with a huge variety of shops, restaurants, and activities at your fingertips

Drawbacks: It's very much a tourist enclave, and can feel a bit disconnected from the city (and is definitely cut off from the beaches).

VERY EXPENSIVE

Cape Grace ★★★ ☺   Aside from the more exclusive (and tiny) Dock House, this is the best of the Waterfront hotels. The difference between this hotel and the Mount Nelson (our other favorite) is primarily one of location; the Grace is on a busy marina, surrounded by waterside apartments, the nearby V&A mall, and plenty of boating activity (the Nellie is surrounded by lush, tranquil gardens at the edge of the city center). Since its last refurbishment, the Grace resembles a chic museum (with polished artifacts and antiques, glass display boxes, and experimental chandeliers), albeit one for lounging in. Bedrooms are all dressed up in locally printed textiles and detailed finery; they're smaller than at the more modern and brash One&Only, across the marina, but truly luxurious, with French doors opening onto mountain or harbor views. Children are welcomed with gift baskets, story time, and milk before bedtime, and the hotel rents gear like car seats and strollers. Service is unparalleled—consistent and personal.

West Quay, V&A Waterfront. www.capegrace.com. ℂ **021/410-7100.** Fax 021/419-7622. 120 units. Rates fluctuate according to demand: R4,510–R7,975 double, R10,275–R19,320 suite; child age 3–11 pays R110 if sharing with 2 adults; extra person over 12 pays R725. Rates include breakfast and chauffeured city-wide transfers as far as Kirstenbosch Gardens. AE, DC, MC, V. **Amenities:** Restaurant; bar; lounges; airport transfers (R650 one-way); babysitting; concierge; library; pool; room service; spa. *In room:* A/C, TV, minibar, free Wi-Fi.

Dock House ★★★   Originally the Harbor Master's residence, this heritage building has been transformed into one of the most intimate hotels in Cape Town: Just six individually designed neobaroque bedrooms (modern art, pretty chandeliers, silk drapes, gigantic framed mirrors, original plasterwork and fireplaces, and epic bathrooms) and so discreetly situated, hardly anyone knows of its existence. Yet, overlooking the V&A and enjoying access to so many useful amenities (own pool, spa and a nightly sunset cruise), you'll feel yourself at the epicenter of Cape Town. Service is highly personal—there's no reception or lobby, and relaxed, gracious staff members (dressed in white caftans) treat you like guests in a private home. *Note:* Avoid the ground-floor bedrooms, as they can be noisy early in the morning.

Portswood Close, Portswood Ridge, V&A Waterfront. www.dockhouse.co.za. ℂ **021/421-9334.** Fax 021/419-7881. 6 units. High season R5,770–7,220 double, R8,660 suite; low season R4,330–R5,415 double, R6,495 suite. Rates include breakfast and tea and coffee service. AE, DC, MC, V. **Amenities:** Breakfast room; bar; airport transfers (R395); pool; room service; spa. *In room:* A/C, TV, hair dryer, free minibar, free Wi-Fi.

EXPENSIVE

Queen Victoria Hotel ★★   This is the latest Waterfront lodging to open its doors mid-2011: a slick, chic little boutique hotel crafted from a Georgian shell, tucked behind sister hotel, Dock House. Bedrooms are down out in shades of gray, silver, and taupe, each with a large image of a younger Victoria gazing down over the bed, and all manner of modern luxuries and swish finishes to keep you amused. The best rooms have views of Table Mountain, with the city filling out the foreground—the pricier the room the better the view. The dashing, eager-to-please staff creates an upbeat vibe that starts at breakfast (excellent) and continues until you're propped up at the bar late at night. The restaurant, **Dash,** is absolutely superb.

Portswood Close, Portswood Ridge, V&A Waterfront. www.queenvictoriahotel.co.za. © **021/418-1466.** Fax 021/418-1475. 36 units. High season R4,195 classic double, R5,245 deluxe double, R6,295 premium double, R7,615 suite, R21,000 presidential suite; low season R3,145–R4,725 double, R5,710–R15,750 suite. AE, DC, MC, V. **Amenities:** Restaurant; bar; lounge; airport transfers (R395); babysitting; pool and spa access (at Dock House); room service. *In room:* A/C, TV, hair dryer, minibar, free Wi-Fi.

Victoria & Alfred Hotel ★★ ✿   Situated alongside a working dock in what was once a warehouse (now called Alfred Mall), this was the Waterfront's first hotel, and it remains the most centrally located choice, and also the Waterfront's best value, with gorgeous harborside views. Guests have access to a superb spa and lawn-fringed pool at nearby Dock House (see above), and also the intimate, excellent restaurant, Dash, at the Queen Victoria Hotel. Bedrooms are spacious; each features a king-size bed and a warm, rich palette. You pay a small premium for rooms with Table Mountain views, but it's worthwhile to wake up to that classic vista.

Pierhead, V&A Waterfront. www.vahotel.co.za. © **021/419-6677.** Fax 021/419-8955. 94 units. High season R3,620 piazza-facing double, R4,145 superior loft double; R4,880 mountain-facing double, R4,330–R5,770 junior suite; low season R2,715–R3,660 double, R3,660–R4,330 junior suite. Rates include breakfast. Child sharing parent's room pays R805, or R1,095 for extra bed. AE, DC, MC, V. **Amenities:** Restaurant; bar; airport transfers (R395); babysitting; gym, pool, and spa access (at Dock House); room service. *In room:* A/C, TV, hair dryer, minibar, free Wi-Fi.

De Waterkant, Green Point, Mouille Point & Sea Point

Best For: A sense of community—there's always something going on here, and not just for tourists. The promenade is one of the best places in the city to stretch your legs and observe Capetonians walking, jogging, holding hands. Plus, many options here represent good value, particularly when compared with accommodations in the adjacent (walking distance if you don't mind a brisk one) Waterfront.

Drawbacks: Beach access a little more time-consuming than from the City Bowl. The De Waterkant end of Green Point can be especially noisy at night, while Sea Point still has a few rough patches.

Recommended Neighborhood Restaurants: In Green Point, Mediterranean **Manos,** 39 Main Rd. (© 021/434-1090), is a reliable choice with better value than most. A few local gems are worth investigating along Sea Point's main drag (once renowned for having the highest concentration of restaurants in the world). Hearty meals are served at **La Boheme,** 341 Main Rd. (© **021/434-8797**), a tapas and wine bar that sits side-by-side with sister bistro **La Bruixa.** We find it hard to distinguish between the two, but if you stroll by on a warm summer evening, you'll see the sidewalk tables packed with locals tucking into fairly priced dishes (two courses for around R100)—it's hardly mind-blowing cuisine, but it does the trick. **La Mouette,** 78 Regent Rd. (© **021/433-0856**), occupies a gorgeous Tudor-style house that—in the late 1970s—belonged to the mayor of Cape Town. Now, Henry Vigar (who cut his teeth in several Michelin-starred London kitchens) prepares predominantly French and Mediterranean dishes with a modern twist and local ingredients; mostly it's good (the line fish works well) and things can get quite lively. On a warm day you can sit in the terrace style garden around the central fountain; later at night the upstairs bar is the setting for a grown-up party.

EXPENSIVE

O on Kloof ★★   One of *Tatler's* Top 101 Hotels in the World, this posh urban sanctuary is a great addition to Cape Town's boutique hotel scene. Ideal if you like your lines straight and your aesthetic modern, Olaf Dambrowski's meticulously design-conscious pad is situated on busy Kloof Road, at the junction of Sea Point and Bantry Bay; and although it's wedged into a high-density residential neighborhood, it makes excellent use of space. The best rooms—massively proportioned and super-luxurious—have views over the cityscape, and Lion's Head rears up right behind; from here, it's a gorgeous sunset walk along the promenade that stretches all the way past Clifton to Camps Bay. Reserve suite no. 1 or 5, with large private rooftop terrace on which there's a Jacuzzi, pair of chaise longues, and view of the sea.

92 Kloof Rd., Sea Point/Bantry Bay. www.oonkloof.co.za. © **021/439-2081.** Fax 086/297-1721. 8 units. High season R2,130 standard double, R2,700 luxury double, R3,950 suite; low season R1,472 standard double, R1,888 luxury double, R2,720 suite. Rates include breakfast. AE, MC, V. **Amenities:** Restaurant; bar; airport transfers (R350 for 2, R500 for 4); library; heated indoor pool; room service; spa. *In room:* A/C, TV/DVD, movie library, music library, hair dryer, MP3 docking station, minibar, free Wi-Fi.

MODERATE

Cascades on the Promenade ★★ 🖋   A superslick overhaul of a century-old building, this is in densely developed Sea Point yet spitting distance from the Promenade, and a top choice for anyone who likes state-of-the-art bathrooms (enormous showers; no bathroom) and technologically enhanced bedrooms (all with Apple Macs), decked out in plush linens, black rugs on hardwood floors, and big, excellent beds. In its favor, it's small and has an intimate atmosphere—staff will remember you by name, and you'll be bumping into neighborhood locals in the bar and bistro that spills onto the citrus-hued veranda. Fractionally pricier deluxe rooms (upstairs) have balconies (no. 7 has a bit of a sea view; no. 6 is more spacious). Cascades has a complimentary shuttle that takes guests to a select few restaurants.

11 Arthurs Rd., Sea Point. www.cascadescollection.com. © **021/434-5209.** Fax 021/439-4206. 7 units. R1,550 double, R1,750 deluxe double. AE, DC, MC, V. **Amenities:** Restaurant; bar; airport transfers (R350); babysitting; room service. *In room:* A/C, TV, video-on-demand, CD-player, computer/free Internet, hair dryer, heated towel rack, minibar, MP3 docking station.

The Clarendon Fresnaye ★★ 🖋☺   Comprising two houses linked by a lawned garden and pair of swimming pools, this big-boned, gracious home was built a century ago for the Earl of Clarendon, and offers more space; a better bet than Cascades or Zest for older travelers or families. Although there's a nod to contemporary style, the overall look is one of timeless elegance—parquet flooring in the breakfast room, broad passageways, high ceilings, flamboyant chandeliers, and plush carpets. Huge mirrors amplify the neat, comfortable, unfussy spaces, and modern artworks offset classical elements. Although they don't advertise the fact, several rooms have partial sea views. Superior rooms are considerably bigger than entry-level units; the two-bedroom family "room" is a great value, with a private entrance and beautiful bathroom.

67 Kloof Rd., Fresnaye. www.clarendon.co.za. © **021/434-6854.** 14 units. High season R1,750–R2,200 double, R2,200–R2,750 superior double, R3,250–R3,500 family room; low season R1,100 double, R1,350 superior double, R1,500 family room. Rates include breakfast. AE, DC, MC, V. **Amenities:** Dining room; airport transfers (R280); babysitting; 2 pools. *In room:* A/C, TV, hair dryer, minibar, free Wi-Fi.

Villa Zest ★★   Small, swanky, and highly personal, this large, four-level guest house features sleek, minimalist interiors, and a Zen garden with a chic pool area. It will appeal to younger travelers looking for a space that's upbeat, fashion-conscious, and surgically clean. It's also near favorite hotspots and walking distance from De

Waterkant and (by day) the Waterfront. Bedrooms, each named for a 1970s cult movie, are extremely comfortable, with great beds and quality linens, and spunky retro-inspired wallpaper against an all-white palette. They're not terribly spacious, so make sure you secure Studio 54 if you need room enough to disco. San Diego–born owner Kevin Gerlach is very hands-on and committed to sustainability, evident in organic toiletries and eco-friendly cleaning products.

2 Braemar Rd., Green Point. www.villazest.co.za. © **021/433-1246.** Fax 021/433-1247. 7 units. High season R1,290–1,690 deluxe double, R1,790–2,090 superior deluxe double, R2,190–R2,590 superior double; low season R1,090 deluxe double, R1,590 superior deluxe double, R1,990 superior double. Rates include breakfast. AE, DC, MC, V. **Amenities:** Dining area/lounge; heated pool. *In room:* A/C, TV/DVD, hair dryer, MP3 docking station/radio, free Wi-Fi.

Winchester Mansions ★★ ☺ Built in the 1920s in the Cape Dutch style, this gracious, low-slung hotel faces the sea, though it's separated from the ocean by a busy road and broad swath of park (with play areas). Still family owned, the hotel is distinguished by its friendly service. Rooms vary by size, style, and configuration. Those in the converted loft feature classy modern interiors, earthy tones, and dark wood. The best "classic" rooms marry modern design with old-fashioned charm (a few antiques, floral artworks)—ask for no. 306. The sea-facing "junior suites" are best value: From loft-style Robben Island suite guests can watch as health-conscious Capetonians jog along the promenade. Harvey's, the bar spilling out onto the terrace, is popular with locals, and on Sundays a jazz brunch draws a crowd to the beautiful colonnaded central courtyard, built around a fountain and encircled with trees.

221 Beach Rd., Sea Point. www.winchester.co.za. © **021/434-2351.** Fax 021/434-0215. 76 units. High season R2,025–R2,775 double, R2,460–R3,050 junior suite, R3,760–R5,850 suite; low season R1,550–R2,025 double, R1,850–R2,250 junior suite, R2,825–R3,550 suite. Extra person R195; children under 6 stay free if sharing with 2 adults. Rates include breakfast. AE, DC, MC, V. **Amenities:** Restaurant; bar; airport transfers (R300 for 2; R100 each extra person); pool; room service; spa. *In room:* A/C, TV/DVD, CD player (in suites), hair dryer, minibar, Wi-Fi (R60 per hour; R250 per day).

INEXPENSIVE

Atlantic Point ✎ Budget travelers looking to be near the action in Green Point and wanting something a little more thoughtful than a standard hostel would offer should consider this neat option, occupying a converted 1930s home. It's design-conscious—pop art canvases, funky murals, artworks referencing Cape Town, and school lockers painted in bright primaries—offset by touches like luxurious duvets. The upstairs lounge features faux grass-covered floor, comfy sofa, ottomans, huge plasma screen, and DVD player; there's a fireplace, games for downtime, and private booths for eating in. Music is piped into the communal bathrooms, which are scrupulously clean. Staff is on the ball and will help you arrange itineraries or bookings.

2 Cavalcade Rd., Green Point. www.atlanticpoint.co.za. © **021/433-1663.** 7 units. High season R495–R680 double with shared bathroom, R660–R840 en suite double, R140–R200 dorm bed; low season R475 double, R630 en suite double, R135–R165 dorm bed. Rates includes breakfast. MC, V. **Amenities:** Dining area; lounge; bar; pool table; table tennis. *In room:* Fan, TV/DVD (in private rooms), hair dryer (on request), no phone, free Wi-Fi.

Atlantic Seaboard

Best For: Most visitors want to wake up to a seascape and stroll down to the beach, and this stretch—particularly residential **Camps Bay**—offers just that. It's lined with bars, coffee shops, and restaurants (few of them recommended for much more than posing, people-watching, and toasting the sunset, but popular nonetheless). It's also a mere 10-minute drive from the center of town. Neighboring **Clifton,** which is less accessible (and more secluded), is even more beautiful, but you'll probably need to rent your own seaside bungalow to stay here, or look at what's available on **Glen Beach,** squeezed between the two (see "Your Own Cape Town Home: More Space, More Privacy, More Freedom," earlier in this chapter).

Drawbacks: In summer locals lament the hordes of tourists that descend on this tiny enclave. You'll need to book early and shell out. There is also, relative to the City Bowl options, a dearth of good taste on the Atlantic seaboard; the rare exceptions are reviewed below. Note that **Bantry Bay** has dizzying sea views but lacks a beach.

Recommended Neighborhood Restaurants: Camps Bay is known for it's indifferent food and rip-off prices. That said **The Hussar Grill** (© 021/438-0151) on Camps Bay Drive is good for steak (at bargain prices)—it's in a crappy location (above a minimart), so doesn't charge outrageous prices. Locals also trust **Primi Piatti** (© 021/438-2923), a casual eatery (part of a nationwide chain) offering quick-fix Italian dining and fast-as-lightening service, and **Col'cacchio** for its wide variety of thin-crust pizzas. Prices are low and portions filling. In Bantry Bay's Ambassador Hotel, **Salt** (© 021/439-7258) affords sensational views of the pounding surf through floor to ceiling foldaway glass walls (it's a well-documented sunset crowd-puller) but food is not as consistently pleasing as the views.

VERY EXPENSIVE

Ellerman House ★★★   On an elevated site overlooking the Atlantic Ocean and the cliffside suburb of Bantry Bay, this classy Edwardian mansion is in a league of its own, and our favorite seaside mansion by far. It's arguably the most exclusive address in Cape Town: Views evoke comparisons with the Riviera, and the sheer grace and style of the place make you feel like royalty. Everything—from walls hung with the country's most important private art collection to the perfect flavor of the seared tuna and the "treat" room—is pitch perfect. That said, the hushed atmosphere and privacy (only resident guests allowed, unless by prior arrangement) is ideal if you want a tranquil, romantic retreat; not if like the bustle of a hotel. (Note that until mid-2012 the construction of a second villa alongside Ellerman House might mean construction noise.)

180 Kloof Rd., Bantry Bay. www.ellerman.co.za. © **021/430-3200.** Fax 021/430-3215. 11 units. High season R5,300–R9,900 double, R14,500 suite; low season R4,500–R8,400 double with balcony, R12,300 suite. Rates include airport transfers, breakfast, laundry, drinks, pantry snacks, and Waterfront shuttles (3 daily). AE, DC, MC, V. No children under 12. **Amenities:** Restaurant; bar; art gallery; concierge; gym; library; pool; room service; spa; wine cellar. *In room:* A/C, TV, hair dryer, minibar, free Wi-Fi.

The Twelve Apostles Hotel and Spa ★★ ☺   Following a thorough makeover and room refit, this is an isolated choice (about 3km/2 miles beyond the edge of Camps Bay/Bakoven, overlooking the road and ocean but surrounded by reserve), and showcases a no-expenses-spared aesthetic, with plenty of over-the-top luxury on display. To escape the flamboyant decor, there are a couple of small coves and beaches within walking distance, and trails through the surrounding fynbos mountain reserve are mapped out. Thrown in, too, are neat extras—a mini-cinema with children's matinees, and gazebos in the bush for outdoor massage. Entry levels rooms are very boxy (with teeny bathrooms), and don't deserve the high price tag.

Victoria Rd., Camps Bay (midway btw. Camps Bay and Llandudno). www.12apostleshotel.co.za. © **021/437-9000.** 70 units. High season R5,125–R5,595 classic double, R5,665–R6,175 mountain-facing double, R6,370–R6,945 luxury double, R8,260–R9,280 superior sea-facing double, R10,695–R38,530 suite; low season R4,165–R6,520 double, R8,330–R38,530 suite. Children under 12 stay free if sharing with adults; children 12–16 pay R450. Rates include breakfast. AE, DC, MC, V. **Amenities:** 2 restaurants; bar; cinema; concierge; helipad; pool; room service; spa. *In room:* A/C, TV/DVD, CD player, hair dryer, minibar, free Wi-Fi.

EXPENSIVE

Camps Bay Retreat ★★ 🏠 A choice of three quite different lodges, each with markedly different ambience and united by the tucked away, jungly location—and yet you're walking distance to the Camps Bay beach and its bars; it's also a short walk through the forest to reach The Roundhouse (Camps Bay's best restaurant). Built as a ultra-luxurious family home 1929, Earls Dyke Manor retains its sophisticated manor house feeling—wood-paneled walls, comfy fire-warmed lounges, cabinets packed with polished silverware antiques and vintage furniture, hunting trophies, animal skins, Art Nouveau statues, and so on. To reach the more modern units, you cross a big swing bridge suspended above a ravine; the Deck House is fashioned to simulate a sophisticated treehouse, with a number of wooden decks and terraces and views into the surrounding trees; the Villa is even more contemporary and pared down. The sprawling grounds provide a very relaxing atmosphere, and the spa includes two Victorian-era "nature baths" surrounded by lush vegetation.

7 Chilworth Rd., Camps Bay. www.campsbayretreat.com. © 021/437-8300, or 021/437-9703 reservations. 15 units. High season R3,020–R4,380 premier double, R3,380–R4,900 luxury double, R4,000–R5,850 superior double, R4,600–R10,050 suite; low season R2,300–R3,050 double, R3,500–R5,250 suite. AE, DC, MC, V. **Amenities:** Restaurant; lounges; bar; airport transfers (R395); bikes; library; 3 pools (1 solar-heated); room service; spa; floodlit tennis court. *In room:* A/C and fan, TV/DVD, movie library, hair dryer, minibar, free Wi-Fi.

The Clarendon Bantry Bay ★★★ 🪙 🏠 An exclusive, hidden guesthouse (no signage), lording it above a magical Atlantic Ocean vista, this is tantalizingly under the radar, and agreeably priced—you can bag a broad-balcony suite here for less than the cheapest rooms at nearby Ellerman House (see above). Foldaway glass walls and large windows bring much of the scenic drama—shimmering light reflected off the water below—inside. Rooms are arranged over three floors; no two are alike, but all feature understated opulence with luxurious finishes, plush fabrics, and smart furniture. Most of bedrooms have private balconies, some with direct pool access. Gracious butlerlike staff is effortlessly warm and attentive. Installed in the expansive top-floor penthouse suite you will feel like royalty—the view from the massive marble terrace is breathtaking, with such a luxurious, uncluttered layout that you'll be loath to step outside (quite possible; staff can arrange meals). It lacks an expansive garden, so don't come here if you want a lawn.

158 Kloof Rd., Bantry Bay. www.clarendon.co.za. © **021/439-3224.** Fax 021/434-0327. 10 units. High season R2,950–R3,500 standard double, R3,950–R4,250 superior double, R4,750–R4,950 superior suite, R7,500 penthouse; low season R1,750 standard double, R1,950 superior double, R2,200 superior suite, R3,500 penthouse. Rates include breakfast and afternoon tea. AE, DC, MC, V. Children under 4 by arrangement only. **Amenities:** Dining room; lounge; airport transfers (R280); bar service; babysitting; pool; room service. *In room:* A/C, TV/DVD, movie library, hair dryer, minibar, underfloor heating, free Wi-Fi.

Compass House ★★ It's a real privilege waking up to this view—the Atlantic views spread out before you, just beyond your toes, at the end of your bed. The entire house is poised to take advantage of the showstopper scene, so it's easy to find excuses just to spend the day lounging around the pool—you can even order a poolside massage. The owner is a fan of the sleek, unfussy look—entry level "cabin" rooms don't even have distracting TVs. Room no. 8 is the one to go for; it has a private entrance, full kitchen, and unfettered views. Staff follows a policy of noninterference, leaving you as much to your own devices as possible; if you see this as independence rather than neglect it's just perfect.

154 Kloof St., Bantry Bay. www.compasshouse.co.za. *C* **021/430-3330.** Fax 086/620-6488. 8 units. High season R2,700–R3,100 double, R3,900–R4,500 deluxe, R6,000-R6,500 suite; low season R2,000 double, R2,900 deluxe, R5,000 suite. Rates include breakfast. AE, DC, MC, V. **Amenities:** Dining area; honor bar; lounge; pool. *In room:* A/C, TV (not standard rooms), hair dryer, heated towel rack, free Wi-Fi.

Les Cascades ★★★ 🌶 High on Bantry Bay's mercifully wind-free cliffs, this beautifully appointed boutique villa, one of our perennial tip-top recommendations, offers excellent value, considering the privileged position, attentive service, sumptuous decor and want-for-nothing in-room amenities (Apple Mac, Nespresso machine, Bose sound system, and so on). Spacious rooms and ultraplush suites have a distinctive Eastern influence but beautiful arrangements of brass sculptures, giant cowbells, tantric wood paintings, and sophisticated designer furniture are a small distraction from dazzling blue skies and extraordinary ocean views. Hosts Luc and Els are always on hand to assist, and their eye for the finer things in life means that everything from the choice of wine in your minibar to the selection of cold meats at breakfast is of the finest quality. All but standard and deluxe rooms have private balconies; the two-bedroom suite has a private pool.

48 de Wet Rd., Bantry Bay. www.cascadescollection.co.za. *C* **021/434-5209.** Fax 021/439-4206. 6 units. High season R2,150–R3,250 double, R3,750–R5,200 2-bedroom suite (2–5 people), R3,750 penthouse suite; other seasons R1,800–R2,550 double, R2,900–R4,150 2-bedroom suite (2–5 people), R2,900–R3,250 penthouse suite. Rates include breakfast. AE, DC, MC, V. **Amenities:** Dining room; bar service; airport transfers (R450); pool; room service. *In room:* A/C, TV/DVD, CD player, computer, hair dryer, MP3 docking station, minibar, free Wi-Fi.

POD ★★ Squeezed into a tight piece of real estate, this small, a la mode hotel is a great addition to the Camps Bay line up, ideal for the design-savvy *Wallpaper** reader who wants to be walking distance to the beach. Replacing the standard hotel look is a wood-framed space-within-a-space bed design; organic shapes and natural materials are a striking counterpoint to the slick minimalism. You need to cough up for a sea view; mountain (no balcony) and classic rooms face the mountains rather than the ocean. Then again, simply head for the pool—it overlooks Camps Bay beach and is served by a fantastic indoor-outdoor bar spilling from POD's sophisticated lounge. Staff will give you whatever you need for the beach, and even take care of you while you're down there. Initial problems with service should have been smoothed out by now.

3 Argyle Rd., Camps Bay. www.pod.co.za. *C* **021/438-8550** or 082/600-9438. Fax 021/438-8552. 15 units. High season R2,700 mountain double, R3,700 classic double, R4,100 luxury double, R5,500 luxury double with plunge pool, R7,100 suite; low season R1,800 mountain, R2,200 classic, R2,500 luxury, R3,300 luxury with pool, R4,300 suite. AE, DC, MC, V. Children under 14 by special arrangement. **Amenities:** Dining area; bar; lounge; beach service; pool. *In room:* A/C, TV/DVD, movie library, hair dryer, MP3 docking station, free Wi-Fi.

Sea Five ★★★ Like POD, Sea Five is within easy reach of the beach, yet removed from Camps Bay's busy sunset strip, but this is a more intimate clapboard-style guesthouse—a classic barefoot-chic beach house. Fabrics are as natural as the wheat, mushroom and off-white palette, and there's plenty of glass to allow in the light and views. All rooms have some kind of private terrace, or—as with the entry-level garden room—open to a large open courtyard with herb garden and lemon tree. Some rooms have Table Mountain vistas but in addition to the cozy lounge and bar is the poolside lounging space with ocean views. Especially lovely is the two-bedroom penthouse, with 360-degree views, not to mention a private dining area, four sun-soaked terraces, a spa bath, and DVD-player and minibar.

5 Central Dr., Camps Bay. www.seafive.co.za. ⓒ **021/438-0743.** 6 units. High season R3,900 garden double, R4,750 mountain view double, R5,200 sea view suite, R7,800–R9,000 penthouse (2–4 people); low season R2,500, garden double, R3,000 mountain view double, R3,250 sea view suite, R4,650–R6,500 penthouse suite (2–4 people). Children under 12 sharing with adults pay R600. Rates include breakfast and local drinks. AE, DC, MC, V. No children under 8. **Amenities:** Dining room; bar; lounge; airport transfers (R350); babysitting; pool. In room: A/C, TV, hair dryer, underfloor heating in bathroom.

MODERATE/INEXPENSIVE

Although it's generally pricey on the seaboard, there are a few decent exceptions. If you're on a more restrictive budget, take a look at the various options on offer at **Camps Bay Resort** (www.campsbayresort.com; ⓒ **021/438-5560**): The so-called **Traveller's Places** are aimed at backpackers looking for a smart alternative to shared dorms—instead you get a neat and comfortable en suite pad to yourself (R590–R790 double); they have pool access and they're close to the beach (two even have sea views), but they're small, so best suited to those who intend being out and about. Also great value is the selection of **studio apartments** on offer (R830–R1,900 double). These all come with a kitchen, and some with A/C and other luxuries, including proximity to a pool. Families could opt for a **one- or two-bedroom apartment** (R2,500–R3,800 in summer). There's a wide range of options and prices vary according to demand and seasonal fluctuations—best is to call or e-mail for a quotation.

Southern Suburbs

If you prefer your landscapes more rural, with mountains and vineyard vistas, you'll find blissful peace in **Constantia,** the wine-producing area closest to the city, some 20 to 30 minutes away (halfway between the city and Cape Point). A little closer to town are leafy **Bishops Court** (Cape Town's embassy district) and **Newlands. The Vineyard Hotel & Spa** ★, Colinton Road, Newlands (www.vineyard.co.za; ⓒ **021/657-4500**) offers a good-value alternative (from R2,175 double in summer) to the pricey hotels at the Waterfront, and offers a sylvan 15-hectare (6-acre) garden amid dense residential environs, a great fine-dining restaurant, **Myoga,** and superb **Agsana Spa;** it's also close to Cavendish, a popular local shopping mall. It's also worth browsing **www.thelastword.co.za**, a collection of luxury guesthouses offering chauffeurs and managers who administer advice and arrange tours; check out are the lavish rooms at **The Bishop's Court** ★, 18 Hillwood Ave., Bishopscourt (www.the bishopscourt.com; ⓒ **021/794-6561;** from R3,900 double in summer)—particularly lovely is room no. 3, with its commanding vista.

Best For: If you want to feel like you're out in the country, while being relatively close to both the city and the Peninsula sights (both around 20–30 min. away, depending on traffic).

Drawbacks: If you prefer the buzz of urban life, this area won't work for you; the beach, too, will require some driving, as will sights, restaurants, and attractions.

Recommended Neighborhood Restaurants: All the hotels reviewed here have commendable restaurants of their own, but you'll need to drive to get to any other Southern Suburbs eateries.

The Cellars-Hohenort ★★★ This gracious historic hotel affords expansive views of the densely forested eastern slopes of Table Mountain. It's a genteel hotel, much smaller and more intimate than the Mount Nelson—an oasis of sorts, it's perfect if you're interested in a country or mountain retreat. Nearby are excellent trails up the back of Table Mountain, and Kirstenbosch Gardens is very close. Antique furnishings and original artworks adorn the original Hohenort manor house, where the best rooms are. Considerable pluses are the beautifully manicured 3.5-hectare (9-acre) garden and, opening onto it, a fabulously appointed bar-lounge, serving Cape Town's best martinis—*sans* sunset, alas.

93 Brommersvlei Rd., Constantia. www.collectionmcgrath.com. (C) **021/794-2137.** Fax 021/794-2149. 53 units. High season R4,200–R4,400 double, R5,350–R6,600 luxury double, R7,350–R11,000 suite, R15,750–R19,250 villa; low season R2,600 double, R3,500–R3,950 luxury double, R4,650–R6,950 suite, R11,550–R14,950 villa. Rates include breakfast. AE, DC, MC, V. No children under 12. **Amenities:** 2 restaurants; 2 bars; croquet lawn; full-scale golf green (designed by Gary Player); 2 pools (1 heated); room service; spa; tennis court. *In room:* A/C, TV/DVD, hair dryer, free Wi-Fi.

Constantia Uitsig ★★   A wine estate on the lower slopes of Table Mountain, this aptly named hotel (*uitsig* means "view") has superb vistas of the surrounding vineyards and jagged mountains. A real sense of rural peace prevails here, underscored by the rhythms of genuine everyday farm life. Still, it's the award-winning restaurants that draw the well-heeled crowds. After feasting, you can simply roll back to one of the well-appointed cottages spread around the tranquil gardens (each suite has a fireplace and kitchenette). Much of the architecture is Cape Dutch, echoing that of the 17th-century manor house, and the decor tries to reflect this influence. It's nowhere near as elegant as the guest rooms at Cellars-Hohenort, but it's generally more relaxed, with less of a hotel atmosphere. And there's a spa and plenty of wide-open space to roam.

Spaansgemacht River Rd., Constantia. www.constantia-uitsig.com. (C) **021/794-6500.** Fax 021/794-7605. 16 units. High season R3,600 garden twin, R4,500 Victorian double, R5,200–R7,600 suite; low season R1,750–R2,050 double, R2,500–R3,500 suite. Children under 12 pay R700 if sharing. Rates include breakfast. AE, DC, MC, V. **Amenities:** 3 restaurants (including **La Colombe** and **Constantia Uitsig,** p. 107); lounge; babysitting; airport transfers (R375–R440); pool; room service; spa; wine cellar. *In room:* A/C, TV, hair dryer, minibar, Wi-Fi (R30 per day).

Steenberg Hotel ★★★   At the foot of the Steenberg Mountains, on Constantia's oldest farm—now planted with vines and producing notable wines—this is another spot with countryside charisma, attached to one of the city's best golf courses. Accommodations are arranged around a garden of manicured hedges and mature trees: There's a choice of styles here, but we love the antique-filled 17th-century Manor House, filled with gorgeous old wood smell and original furniture, old photos, porcelain plates, rugs on hardwood floors, and a grandfather clock. There are just five rooms in this National Monument; of these, rooms 1 and 12 get the best light and have direct outdoor access. The three Heritage Suites, which work as private villas, have kitchens, butler service, working fireplaces, and access a private pool terrace—decor is original and bold, with a contemporary take on historical themes.

10802 Steenberg Estate, Tokai Rd., Constantia. www.steenberghotel.com. (C) **021/713-2222.** Fax 021/713-2251. 24 units. High season R3,435–R5,850 double, R5,575–R6,850 family rooms and suites; low season R2,255–R4,125 double, R4,125–R5,195 family rooms and suites; Heritage Suites R9,720–R14,580 year-round. AE, DC, MC, V. **Amenities:** 2 restaurants (**Catharina's** and **Bistro Sixteen82;** p. 107); bar; lounge; 18-hole championship golf course; pool; spa; wine cellar. *In room:* A/C, TV, hair dryer, heated towel rack, minibar, free Wi-Fi.

The Peninsula's Coastal Villages

Even Capetonians look at this part of Cape Town as a totally different city experience and talk about moving here in the same dreamy tones as they would of moving "to the country." Kalk Bay is considered the peninsula's quaintest village, offering a plethora of dining options and dinky antiques shops, art galleries, quirky clothing boutiques, cobbled streets, a fisherman's harbor, and a theater; Simonstown has a distinctive naval atmosphere and distinctive Victorian architecture—these are the two best suburbs in which to base yourself if you want to enjoy coastal village life. We have also included a few options for those who want isolation, one in the sleepy hamlet of Kommetjie, one in Scarborough (so small it doesn't have streetlights) and one tucked away just outside Hout Bay.

Best For: A decidedly laid-back atmosphere, probably more suited to someone who's been to Cape Town before. Staying on this side of the mountain, you are well positioned to visit major attractions like the penguins at Boulders and dramatic sea cliffs at Cape Point (some 10–20 min. away); the city center is a mere 40 to 60 minutes away.

Drawbacks: The main route through St James (linking Muizenberg to Kalk Bay), has been a construction site—with annoying roadwork—for well over 2 years, and no end in sight.

The Last Word Long Beach ★★ With the roaring False Bay waters just moments from the foot of your bed, you'll feel as though you're right on top of Long Beach, an aptly named stretch of sand that runs all the way to the foot of Chapman's Peak. Converted from a spacious beach house in sleepy Kommetjie, it offers old-style comfort, with simple watercolors evoking a vacation atmosphere. For views, bedrooms aren't all equally well situated; those downstairs open directly onto a pool garden with gate access to the beach (only the premiere suite has a view from the bed). Two upstairs rooms take better advantage of the vista. Plenty of excuses here to do absolutely nothing, but Kommetjie is a great spot to join tribes of surfers (there's a shop for equipment rental nearby), set off along the beach on horseback, walk to the nearby lighthouse, or—in the other direction—to the shipwreck on Noordhoek beach.

1 Kirsten Rd., Kommetjie. www.thelongbeach.com. © **021/783-4183.** Fax 021/783-4735. 6 units. R3,000–R4,750 double, R3,900–R6,600 elegant suite. Children under 12 sharing with adults in a suite pay R600. AE, DC, MC, V. No children under 8. **Amenities:** Dining room; lounge; bar; airport transfers (R410 double one-way), pool; room service. In room: A/C, TV/DVD, hair dryer, heated towel rack, minibar free Wi-Fi.

Rodwell House ★★★ Built—like so many of the mansions on this seaboard— by a Randlord millionaire (gold-mining entrepreneur) in the 1930s, this gracious guesthouse offers luxury on a grand scale, yet you're invited to kick off your shoes and let your hair down. Start your day with a refreshing dip in the famous St James tidal pool right across the road, and spend time hanging with local surfers or simply watching them from the balcony of this classically proportioned manor house. Your view across the terraced gardens stretches far across False Bay, and at your back are the looming Kalk Bay mountains. Stylish suites all have either sea or mountain views. The house also holds a dynamic collection of artworks and an exciting wine cellar. Kalk Bay is a hop away, and you're 10 minutes by car from Simons Town; 20 minutes from Cape Point; 15 minutes from Constantia.

Rodwell Rd., St James, 7945. www.rodwellhouse.co.za. © **021/787-9880.** Fax 021/787-9898. 8 units. High season R2,620–R3,150 double, R3,150–R5,300 suite, R6,375–R8,500 apartment; low season R1,850–R1,980 double, R2,450–R3,150 suite, R5,950–R6,375 apartment. Children under 12 pay R500 if sharing with 2 adults in a suite. Rates include breakfast. MC, V. No children under 7. **Amenities:** Restaurant; 2 lounges; airport transfers (R470–R500 one-way); art gallery; *pétanque* court; gym; library; massage; pool; wine cellar. In room: A/C, TV/DVD, hair dryer, minibar, free Wi-Fi.

To experience real *ubuntu* and the warm spirit of African hospitality, you can spend a night in one of the city's "townships," or black suburbs. The experience will be enlightening on many levels, so keep an open mind: In Khayelitsha, there's **Kopanong** (www.kopanong-township.co.za; ✆ 021/361-2084) and **Malebo's B&B** (www.malebos-bed-and-breakfast.com; ✆ 021/361-2391), an unlikely seeming brick-face house; in Guguletu, try **Liziwe's Guest House** (www.liziwes-bed-and-breakfast.com; ✆ 021/633-7406), which even has a bit of a lawn garden; and **Ma'Neos** is in Langa (www.maneos.co.za; ✆ 073/146-0370). Expect to pay around R600 to R1,000 for a double, and prepare for a display of unbridled hospitality. Even if bedrooms are small and lack the amenities of a big hotel, the welcome and personal insight you'll get more than compensates. Ask in advance if your hosts will be willing to take you to their neighborhood restaurant, and get them to recommend the best time to come to catch local musicians in action. A night at one of these establishments will be a major talking point of your stay in the Cape.

Tintswalo Atlantic ★★★ There's nowhere like it anywhere in Africa—a luxury safari-style lodge tucked among a grove of milkwood trees, and backed by the looming craggy cliffs of famous Chapman's Peak Drive. A chauffeured Mercedes whisks you down a steep, winding driveway culminating in the beautifully designed, ecologically sensitive hideaway, completely invisible from above. Suite-size water's edge cottages with balconies on stilts let you feel as if you're hovering over the water: Soothed by a symphony of crashing waves, you can watch southern right whales just off shore; and at night, Hout Bay twinkles across the bay, while fishing vessels trawl the waters like fireflies. Each island-themed cottage features wood floors, elaborate chandeliers, Persian rugs, ceramic fireplace, and rustic touches. One drawback (besides the price tag) is that you can't jump into the ocean here. It's also rather isolated from attractions (though for some, there'll be no desire to leave at all).

Chapman's Peak Dr., Hout Bay. www.tintswalo.com. ✆ **011/300-8888** or 087/754-9300. Fax 086/543-1510. 10 units. R7,800 double, R25,000 presidential suite. Rates include breakfast, high tea, and house beverages. AE, DC, MC, V. No children under 17, except in presidential suite **Amenities:** Restaurant; bar; lounges; Jacuzzi; library; free Wi-Fi (in main lodge); wine cellar. *In room:* A/C, TV/DVD, movie library, hair dryer, heated towel rack, minibar, underfloor heating in bathroom, free Wi-Fi.

Zensa Lodge ★★ If you're after a restful, shoeless, Zen sort of seaside holiday, this sexy retreat in a dreamy village is heaven sent. Scarborough's original homestead has been transformed into a delightful guesthouse: Small, yet beautifully detailed, the informal, uncluttered lodge consists of two interconnecting houses with an assortment of pretty, all-white bedrooms, each with unique artworks and other collectibles. A third bungalow serves as a lounge, bar and dining area. You won't find lavish luxury or an endless lineup of services. Part of Scarborough's great charm is that it's a genuine backwater, and walking distance from one of the world's most pristine beaches.

534 Egret St., Scarborough. www.zensalodge.com. ✆ **021/780-1166** or 082/352-0740. 9 units. R1,400–R1,700 double, R2,350 loft, R2,700 family apt (additional R100–R150 per child). Rates include breakfast. MC, V. 2 night minimum. **Amenities:** Dining area; honor bar; airport transfers (R500–R700); bikes (R150 per half day, R300 per day); lounges; Jacuzzi; massage; 2 pools; free Wi-Fi. *In room:* CD, hair dryer.

WHERE TO EAT

For centuries, Cape Town has set the table for a varied and increasingly discerning public. Visitors have raved about its world-class fare, augmented by historical venues and great views. For harbor settings and Table Mountain views, there's the touristy Waterfront. For uninterrupted ocean views and great sunsets, the Atlantic seaboard is tops—but with most restaurants here resting on their location laurels, not ideal if you care about what's on your plate. For plenty of casual dining options we'd head back over the Nek to Kloof Street, the road that runs down the slope of Table Mountain into Long Street. Whatever you do, enjoy at least one lunch in the Winelands (see chapter 5), where you can drink in views of the vineyards and mountains along with a selection of fine Cape wines. If you're setting off for Cape Point, a journey that will take you most of the day, time lunch at one of the recommended restaurants in the Constantia area, among the vineyards, or one overlooking the False Bay coast, in Kalk Bay.

Be sure to sample at least one dish inspired by the unique hybrid of Cape cultures—the traditional fare is referred to as Cape Malay cuisine, but there's more to Cape cuisine than *bobotie* and *denningvleis*. Cape Town's scenic setting and regular influx of cosmopolitan visitors has attracted some of the world's top chefs, many of whom are creating (and inspiring) an exciting modern Cape cuisine, combining local ingredients with elements of the Portuguese, Dutch, French, German, English, Indian, and Malaysian influences that have made up the city's multicultural past.

> ### Eating In
>
> If you're dining in, contact **Mr. Delivery** (℅ 021/423-4177 in City Bowl; ℅ 021/439-9916 in Sea Point; ℅ 021/761-0040 in Constantia) and ask them to drop off a menu (or browse at www.mrdelivery.com). They deliver meals from almost 40 restaurants and take-out joints, as well as groceries, directly to your door.

The City Center & the City Bowl

There is simply not enough space to cover the many superb restaurants concentrated in this area, so in some cases, a simple mention will have to suffice.

VERY EXPENSIVE

Aubergine ★★★ INTERNATIONAL/MODERN CAPE A timeless venue, with seating beneath the stars or inside the beautifully converted 1830s home of the Cape's first Chief Justice, Aubergine is widely revered as the inner city's best fine dining option. Harald Bresselschmidt is a genius, conjuring up new magical combinations month after month, making it hard to decide what to order. By the time one of his polished waitstaff has recited the options on the degustation menu, you're likely to be even more flummoxed—everything sounds wonderful. Yet, it's his simplest creations (such as the signature Aubergine soufflé, filled with goat's milk cheese) that remain among our favorites. It's a superlative experience and the chance to sample Cape Town's most complex cuisine (perhaps a little rich for some palates), using the freshest local produce to sublime effect. There's a more affordable *cinq à sept* menu catering to the after-work crowd, and in winter there's a reduced bistro menu.

39 Barnet St. ℅ **021/465-4909.** www.aubergine.co.za. Reservations essential. Lunch menu R184 (2 courses) or R235 (3 courses). Dinner main courses R120-R195. Dinner degustation menu R345 (3 courses) or R485 with wine; R420 (4 courses) or R600 with wine; R525 (5 courses) or R745 with wine. AE, DC, MC, V. Wed-Fri noon-2pm; Mon-Sat 5pm-10pm.

Cape Town Restaurants

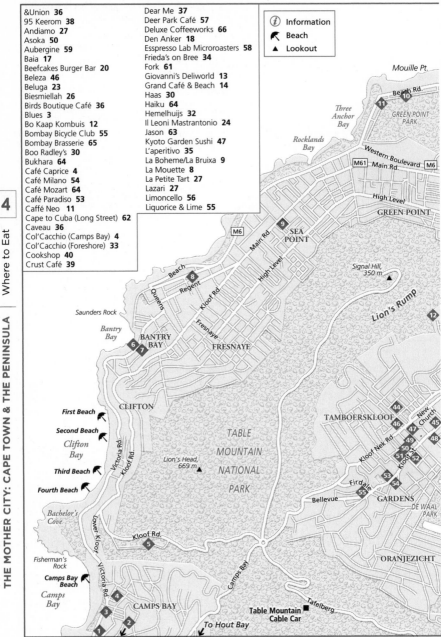

Information
Beach
Lookout

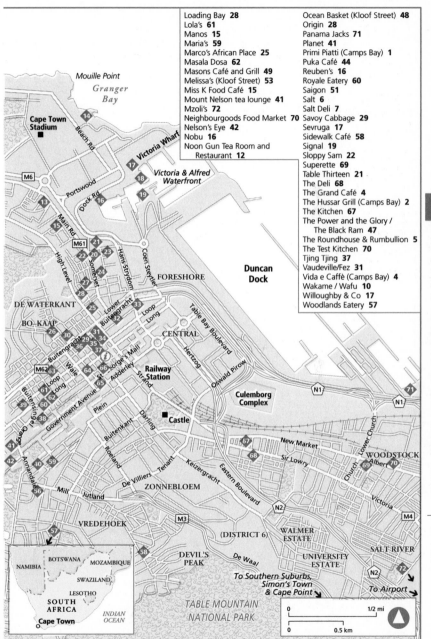

Loading Bay **28**
Lola's **61**
Manos **15**
Maria's **59**
Marco's African Place **25**
Masala Dosa **62**
Masons Café and Grill **49**
Melissa's (Kloof Street) **53**
Miss K Food Café **15**
Mount Nelson tea lounge **41**
Mzoli's **72**
Neighbourgoods Food Market **70**
Nelson's Eye **42**
Nobu **16**
Noon Gun Tea Room and
   Restaurant **12**

Ocean Basket (Kloof Street) **48**
Origin **28**
Panama Jacks **71**
Planet **41**
Primi Piatti (Camps Bay) **1**
Puka Café **44**
Reuben's **16**
Royale Eatery **60**
Saigon **51**
Salt **6**
Salt Deli **7**
Savoy Cabbage **29**
Sevruga **17**
Sidewalk Café **58**
Signal **19**
Sloppy Sam **22**
Superette **69**
Table Thirteen **21**
The Deli **68**
The Grand Café **4**
The Hussar Grill (Camps Bay) **2**
The Kitchen **67**
The Power and the Glory /
   The Black Ram **47**
The Roundhouse & Rumbullion **5**
The Test Kitchen **70**
Tjing Tjing **37**
Vaudeville/Fez **31**
Vida e Caffè (Camps Bay) **4**
Wakame / Wafu **10**
Willoughby & Co **17**
Woodlands Eatery **57**

4

THE MOTHER CITY: CAPE TOWN & THE PENINSULA | Where to Eat

cafe culture MOTHER CITY-STYLE

Kloof Street & Environs: At the very top end of Kloof Street (next to Bombay Bicycle Club, reviewed), **Liquorice & Lime** (📞 021/423-6921), with its Art Deco accents and great big picture window framing Table Mountain views, turns out well-prepared breakfasts and great lunch plates. The owner, ex-chef at the Mount Nelson, takes pride in his own handmade burger patties, served flame-grilled. A little further down, on the opposite side of the street, **Café Milano** ★ serves imported coffee and brilliant, well-priced pastries, as well as a light luncheon menu that has the ladies-who-lunch flocking to claim their space in the well-bred interior. **Melissa's,** one of the first classy delis to open in the city (📞 021/424-5540), set a bit of a trend, tuning locals in to the possibility of heaping a home-cooked style lunch from a small but excellent buffet. Sadly, Melissa's prices have driven off the locals, but what's on your plate (charged according to weight) is still freshly made and wholesome. With so many Capetonians engaged in creative industries, where the office travels along in the laptop, you're likely to see many locals perched over their Macs as they sip cappuccinos or tuck into a croissant. One of the popular spot for a daytime confab is **The Power and the Glory** ★, on the corner at the busy intersection of Kloofnek and Burnside roads (📞 021/422-2108); it's a glorified boho deli-style cafe-cum-bar that's part Parisian cafe, and part retro junk shop. It's been an instant draw for the trendy tribe, and like many of Cape Town's new school old-school cafe venues, operates on the shimmied-up Starbucks formula, with a counter where you order coffee, a few baked offerings, and very simple all-day breakfasts (no serious cooking), and—after noon—meaty salads, sandwiches, and hot dogs with free-range pork sourced from Happy Hog. Across the road, at **Beleza** (📞 021/426-0795) you can get a seriously cheap breakfast, although service can be a bit hit-and-miss. They're open all day, with some good-value Portuguese style dishes. Tucked away around the corner, glove-compartment-size **Puka Café** ★ at Brunswick and Tamboerskloof roads (📞 021/423-6715) is Tamboerskloof's best-kept secret, serving fabulous potato rösti heaped with generous toppings; there are wraps, salads, and stuffed rolls, too. Coffee is excellent, and there's a park across the road for parents with children in tow.

Bree Street: In an unlikely location (near the bustling intersection where Kloof St. becomes Long), **Crust Café,** 243 Bree St. (📞 021/422-2222), does wonderful sandwiches, breakfasts, and light meals for the local work crowd. It's owned by two Brits, Phil and Andrew—they moved here after falling in love with the city, and now welcome the world with gourmet sandwiches made with a variety of fresh-baked breads, and lean beef handmade burgers, soup of the day, salads, and great muffins. **Jason** ★★★ (📞 021/424-5644, visible from Bree street) started as a hole-in-the-wall side-venture for the erstwhile fine dining establishment, Jardine (now in the Winelands; see p. 160); it's now in the capable hands of Jason Lilley, aka Captain Bread, whose team still churns out the most popular and tasty sandwiches in Cape Town, not to mention unique pies (the macaroni cheese pie will knock your socks off)—they're also now serving wine and artisan beer. With its emphasis on organic produce and making everything naturally, **Birds Boutique Café** ★★, 127 Bree St. (📞 021/426-2534), is a refreshing counterpoint to the bustling city outside. The kitchen (preparing wholesome lunches, freshly prepared juices, teas, and Austrian-influenced tarts and cakes that will tempt even a savory tooth) is hidden behind a curtain, while customers sit on plastic crates at wooden trestle tables, entertained by recorded birdsong and a good-looking clientele. But perhaps the most exciting daytime venue to open in 2011 is **Dear Me** ★★★ (☏ 021/422-4920)—tucked into a Dutch Victorian house on Longmarket Street, a narrow side-road linking Long and Loop. Although it's not exactly a health restaurant (there's a bar, Tjing Tjing, upstairs; see p. 143), the ladies source the finest local ingredients and work strictly with seasonal produce. They refuse to serve bottled water, filtering their own, and carbonating it for diners who prefer bubbles in their aqua. There's always sustainable fish, organic pork, and grass-fed beef on the menu, and the baking team caters to all kinds of special diets, so gluten-free bread (and exquisite muffins), vegan dishes, and diabetic meals (and desserts!) are almost always available. Lunchtimes get very busy, so book ahead. Much further down toward the Foreshore, **Frieda's on Bree** ★ (☏ 021/421-2404) is a wonderfully retro-funky space that feels a bit like your grandmother's lounge—with plenty of quirky, offbeat styling detail thrown in for good measure. Great-tasting burgers, warm salads, and stir-fries are on the menu for lunch.

Near Company Gardens & Museums: A hub of wholesome tastes and healthy salads, fresh-squeezed juices, and wraps, soups, and imaginative recipes dished up from the small buffet table (and paid for by the plate or bowl), **Cookshop,** 117 Hatfield St. (☏ 021/461-7868), is another tucked away secret attracting a the luncheon crowd from nearby offices. With more space (and tables spilling out onto the sidewalk around the Dunkley Square parking lot, **Maria's** ★, Barnet St. (☏ 021/461-3333) is a fabulous spot serving Greek dishes such as slow-cooked lamb with ouzo and artichoke sauce, mint-flavored meatballs with tzatziki, and various other mezzes (appetizers), of course.

Long Street: In summer Long Street is where you'll find the city's most energetic nightlife. It's decadent atmosphere but best ignore the frequent offers of cannabis (known here as "dagga") from casual dealers. Many of the eateries are also best ignored; not so **Lola's** ★, 228 Long St. (☏ 021/423-0885), where you pick something from the chalkboard. On the other side of the street, look out for **Masala Dosa** ★, 167 Long St. (☏ 021/424-6772) for the tongue-in-cheek Bollywood kitsch decor and mild South Indian selection—order a couple of curry-filled *sev puris,* and a mixed *thali* (platter)—to share.

Bo-Kaap: If you're notching up supercool daytime dining experiences, don't miss a stop at **Haas** ★★★, 67 Rose St. (☏ 021/422-4413), in Bo-Kaap. It's one of the most beautiful homeware and decor shops in the city, a collective of highly sought-after designers pooling their talents and also branching into coffee (they roast their own; see "Cape Town's Caffeine Fix," on p. 117).

Woodstock: Originally a corner store built in 1902, **Superette** ★, 218 Albert St. (☏ 021/802-5525), offers cool, retro-inspired design and a buffet table packed with great breakfast and lunch choices. It's right next door to Whatiftheworld, one of the city's top galleries (p. 136) and attracts an interesting crowd.

The Kitchen ★★, 111 Sir Lowry Rd. (☏ 021/462-2201), is a deli-style emporium from the imagination of catering expert Karen Dudley. It's enough just to sit here watching the constant stream of locals stopping by for their daily fix of healthy plates—heaped with a choice of six superb salads (for only R45) and optional meat dish—or to watch the charming lasses working the salad counter. Almost directly across the road from here, **The Deli** ★★ (☏ 021/461-8056) is another good spot, with more variety and the sweetest hands-on owners.

Bombay Brasserie ★★★ CONTEMPORARY INDIAN   Just when you thought you knew everything about food from the subcontinent, along comes Harpeet Kaur's updated interpretation of one of the world's great cuisines. It's a small, opulent space tucked into a wood-paneled former banking room richly augmented by jewel-like chandeliers, plush armchairs, and rich velvety drapes. Ignore the menu: The maitre'd is intimately acquainted with each dish and gives a very personal rundown of what's on offer. Norwegian salmon flavored with Bishop's weed; apricot and potato cakes with yogurt and tamarind chutney; chili-flavored stir-fried potatoes; prawns cooked with spring onion; smoked eggplant mash; masala tea flavored crème brûlée—all heavenly. If you can't make up your mind the maitre'd has compiled a tasting menu and paired wines to match those Indian spices. A most distinguished dining experience.

Taj Cape Town, Wale St., City Center. ✆ **021/819-2000.** www.tajcapetown.co.za. Reservations essential. Main courses R65–R150; Maitre'd menu R395, with paired wines R575. AE, DC, MC, V. Mon–Sat 6–10:30pm.

Planet ★★★ CONTEMPORARY CAPE   Arrive early and kick off with cocktails from the champagne bar (on a balmy evening you can sit outside) and then slink across the Milky Way–patterned carpet into this grand space, with its high vaulted ceiling and opulent, opera set design. Chef Rudi Liebenberg is adept at composing unusual flavor combinations with local ingredients, not only intriguing on the page, but good to taste, like rooibos-cured ostrich, and springbok glazed with beets and honey. For vegetarians and vegans, there's a specialized menu, including dishes you won't ever find again, such as mushroom and fynbos broth, and chakalaka stuffed onion.

Mount Nelson Hotel, 76 Orange St. ✆ **021/483-1000.** www.planetbarandrestaurant.co.za. Reservations essential; book online. Main courses R95–R295, set menu R380. AE, DC, MC, V. Daily 6:30–10:30pm.

EXPENSIVE

95 Keerom ★★★ ITALIAN   An urbane, good-looking space, 95 Keerom offers affordable glam, and Capetonians love it, not only because it feels good to walk

---

🎁 Where Locals Dine

Although recommended, Africa Café and Gold cater primarily to well-heeled foreigners, and visitors come away nonplussed at how European the Cape Town scene is. If you'd like to sample South African cuisine along with other Africans (for considerably less money), head for the balcony of the **Pan African Market,** Long Street (✆ **021/426-4478**), for lunch with the traders. Out of town, in Gugulethu (you'll need to arrange reliable transport to get here), is **Mzoli's** (✆ **021/638-1355**), where you choose your meat from the butchery (vegetarians strongly cautioned), which is then barbecued while DJs pump out loud electronic beats. The place rocks

on weekends (although it closes at 8pm), drawing local celebs and politicos as well as a smattering of tourists; it's become a place where Capetonians of all persuasions (except one or two snooty restaurant critics we've met) can really hang out together. In the city, though, it's **Marco's African Place,** 15 Rose Ln. (✆ **021/423-5412**), at the edge of Bo-Kaap, which serves popular African dishes such as steamed ox tongue, tripe, and *umngqusho* (samp and beans). There's usually live musical entertainment (including marimba bands and jazz), and plenty on the menu if you want to play it safe or don't eat meat.

High tea at the **Mount Nelson** (℃ 021/483-1850; R165; daily 2:30–5:30pm) is a Cape Town institution. As you sink into the comfortable armchairs in the elegant chandeliered room, you'll sink your teeth into savory smoked salmon grissini and cucumber sandwiches, as well as sinful tarts, scones, cakes, and tea-themed confectionary such as forest berry tea–infused Turkish delights, green tea cake, and chamomile lemon loaf, served buffet style.

Whether you stay indoors and hum along with the tinkling piano or escape to the verdant shady gardens, it's a wonderful way to experience Mount Nelson's gracious ambience and watch those who frequent the place. The experience is enhanced by Nigiro loose-leaf teas supplied by **Origin,** one of the city's top coffee and tea venues (p. 104); each blend comes to you DIY style with boiling water and an egg timer.

through, but because the food is simple and straightforward, and the service slick and attentive (with personal table visits by restaurateur Giorgio Navara). It's also wonderfully pared down, free of the rich, sauce-heavy dishes favored by many top chefs. The menu is extensive, starting with a long list of carpaccio options; to follow, we love the tuna, seared slightly New York–style, with capers, olives, and tomatoes. If fish isn't fresh off his boat, Giorgio doesn't serve it. For meat eaters, the slow-cooked springbok and pork belly are both popular; a good vegetarian choice is the butternut ravioli, tossed in browned sage butter, and topped with Parmesan.

95 Keerom St., City Center. ℃ **021/422-0765.** www.95keerom.com. Reservations essential. Main courses R90–R180. Minimum 2 courses. AE, DC, MC, V. Thurs–Fri noon–2pm; Mon–Sat 7–10:30pm.

Gold ★ PAN-AFRICAN Drumming lessons, traditional dancers, Mali puppets, and stirring voices belting out kitschy African tunes—it's touristy but entertaining. Adapted from traditional African and Cape Malay recipes, the range of dishes gives a good feel for what the people of Africa eat (though prepared with a global palate in mind); the line-up changes from time to time, but may include West African–style chicken, prepared in a rich, creamy sauce of peanuts, garlic, chili, ginger, and thyme; masala-grilled sweet potatoes; spicy braised butternut from East Africa (with a tomato and coconut cream); and smoked fishcakes topped with apple and mint relish. Staples that you should try are putu pap (thick maize porridge that—like polenta—goes with most anything), and African spinach (imfino in Zulu, or morogo in Setswana), which is traditionally gathered in the bush, and here gets a modern spin with tomato and pumpkin seeds. End with pumpkin fritters, dusted with 24-carat gold.

Gold of Africa Museum, 96 Strand St., Cape Town. ℃ **021/421-4653.** www.goldrestaurant.co.za. Reservations highly recommended. Dinner R250 adults, R125 children under 12. AE, DC, MC, V. Mon–Sat 10am–11pm; Sun 6:30–11pm.

Hemelhuijs ★★ LIGHT FARE One of our favorite luncheon spots in the city, this is on a new pedestrian thoroughfare walking distance from De Waterkant's shopping district. The white-and-charcoal glass-fronted room has quickly become a fashionable all-day lunching spot, with quirky decor (a reindeer trophy's horns are hung with broken white crockery; a mural made of burned toast) and slick service from the camp waitstaff. The wholesome food is even more interesting than the decor: Duck and beet salad; scrambled eggs with salmon trout and fresh marmalade toast; asparagus salad with salmon, dates, Parmesan, and watercress; calamari dusted in coconut and spices with a pine kernels and rocket side salad. It's not the most interesting choice but the homemade burger with mushroom sauce is out of this world.

71 Waterkant St. *C* **021/418-2042.** Main courses R55–R130. MC, V. Mon–Fri 9am–4pm; Sat 9am–3pm; Wed 7–10pm.

Kyoto Garden Sushi ★★ 👔 JAPANESE   With eccentricities aplenty (including the Californian owner, Scott), this is among the finest sushi restaurants in Cape Town. Tucked away at the intersection at the bottom of Kloofnek Road, it features interiors styled with near-surgical precision to create a Zen-like beechwood temple. Obsessed with detail, Scott imports real wasabi root (ask for some—it's far better than the ready-made paste) and has a very serious Japanese chef controlling the kitchen. Expect ultrafresh sushi and sashimi (made with local fish, like kabeljou, but also octopus and eel), as well as delicious cooked noodle broths and delicate vegetable and seafood sautés. Desserts are also intriguing—how about green tea crepes? There's an exacting bar service: shots of *shochu*, a hand-picked wine list, and brilliant cocktails.

11 Lower Kloofnek Rd. *C* **021/422-2001.** Main courses R90–R160. AE, MC, V. Mon–Sat 5:30–11pm

Nelson's Eye ★ 👔 STEAKHOUSE   Ask local steak lovers where they get their fix, and they'll point you to this publike facade, walking distance from the Mount Nelson. It's very old-fashioned, and the prize for the steeper-than-expected prices is a large meat cut that reminds you that South Africans are first and foremost carnivores. Service can be slow and slack, but do as the others have done for years as they wait their turn at this always-packed venue—order more wine. It's worth it.

9 Hoff St., Gardens. *C* **021/423-2601.** www.nelsons-eye.co.za. R89–R240. AE, DC, MC, V. Tues–Fri 12:30–3pm; Mon–Sun 6–10:30pm.

Savoy Cabbage ★★★ INTERNATIONAL   Having outlived many overhyped upstarts, this stylish restaurant still celebrates what it terms "sophisticated peasant food." Successfully bridging the gap between homestyle comfort food and elaborate fine dining, there's always something innovative to try. Chef Peter Pankhurst changes the menu daily to make the best of what's available, but if you haven't yet tried Karoo lamb, try his extraordinary three-way variation—roasted rack, braised shoulder, and grilled Merguez sausage (made on-site), all served with a braised fennel and red wine sauce. If you want to venture beyond the usual suspects, there's loin of warthog (fennel dusted and brined); gemsbok (or perhaps wildebeest) crusted with spice; or a delicious pork chop with smoked filet served with sautéed apple and cider jus. The classic soundtrack-free venue remains fairly unchanged since we first dined here in 1998—a narrow double-volume L-shape with old brick walls exposed and juxtaposed with glass-and-steel fittings.

101 Hout St., Heritage Sq. *C* **021/424-2626.** www.savoycabbage.co.za. Reservations essential. Main courses R110–R165. AE, DC, MC, V. Mon–Fri noon–2:30pm; Mon–Sat 7–10:30pm.

MODERATE/INEXPENSIVE

Wonderful tapas plates are in abundance at **Fork** ★★, 84 Long St. (*C* **021/424-6334**), located in a pretty, exposed-brick space. Kick off with puff pastry stuffed with oven-roasted peppers, asparagus, and caprino; slices of tuna on cannellini beans; or slightly overdone but extremely tender lamb cutlets.

Up in the City Bowl, the multifarious options along Kloof Street can be very hit or miss, but there some good choices for well-priced, relaxed dining: **Bombay Bicycle**

Run by two generations of the Osman family in the historic former slave quarter of Bo-Kaap, **Biesmiellah,** 2 Upper Wale St. (📞 **021/423-0850;** www.biesmiellah.co.za), has been serving the local Cape Muslim community for over 2 decades—although these days it caters overwhelmingly to tourists. Start with a selection of *samoosas* or *daltjies* (chili bites), and then try *denningvleis*—this sweet-sour mild lamb stew flavored with tamarind—with *roti* (flatbread). Or try the *penang* curry, with beef, bay leaves, and spices, served on rice that's boiled, then fried in olive oil, then flavored with nuts, raisins, and almonds. As a Muslim establishment, it prohibits alcohol on the premises. Order a refreshing *falooda* (sweet beverage typically made with vanilla ice cream, rose syrup, basil seeds, and tapioca pearls) instead. **Bo Kaap Kombuis** (Kitchen), 7 August St. (📞 **021/422-5446;** www.bokaapkombuis.co.za) serves a less adventurous menu, which is a bit hit and miss, but affords showstopper views of Table Mountain through floor-to-ceiling glass walls. It's also family run and you'll find neighbors dining here or locals celebrating weddings; prices are lower than the more tourist-geared places (like the **Noon Gun Tea Room,** farther up the slopes of Signal Hill). It's worth arriving in time to see the city bathed in a sunset glow, and then glittering when the lights come on—or come for lunch, making sure you reserve a table with a clear view.

Club and **Café Paradiso** are two extremely popular spots (with the same owners) for which you'll need to reserve (reviewed below). Check out **Mason's Café and Grill** ★, 64 Kloof St. (📞 **021/422-5325**), for its hearty bistro fare and friendly welcome; it a good choice for daytime dining when you can grab a table with a view of Table Mountain. Nearby, **Saigon** ★★, on the corner of Kloof and Camp streets (📞 **021/424-7670**), is an elevated venue with great views, specializes in Vietnamese cuisine (don't miss the crystal prawn spring rolls or the karma-free curry with pumpkin and sweet potato). Many locals rate this their ultimate city eatery. Farther down is the good value **Ocean Basket,** 75 Kloof St. (📞 **021/422-0322**), with a patio-style back garden and decent waitstaff. The fish is superfresh (hardly surprising, considering the volumes they move), perfectly cooked, served in the pan, and seriously cheap. If you like the idea of pizza but could do without the cheese, head over to **Limoncello** ★, 8 Breda St. (📞 **021/461-5100**), a tiny restaurant in Gardens frequented by locals who love the ultrathin, crispy pizza base (tomato free), topped with smoked salmon (or eggplant), lemon juice, and fresh rocket (arugula). Equally good is the tender baby squid, flash-fried with chili and garlic, and its risotto of the day.

The Bombay Bicycle Club ★★ 📷 BISTRO   If you're in the mood for a bit of a party, hit the Bombay and fill your stomach at the same time. With its motley bohemian styling—a cross between an antiques store an insane asylum, really—and heady buzz, this is currently the city's most popular place to see and be seen, frequented by a cool crowd that's as eclectic as the vintage soundtrack. It's reliable comfort food—nothing too complicated—and your waiter (inevitably offbeat) will work hard to win you over and have you ordering shots (two-for-one specials start kicking in by the time you've ordered dessert). There's good reason why this place is *always* packed to the gills (some may find it too crowded) and why, after 10pm, things get out of hand; book for the second seating (8pm) and do so at least a week ahead.

158 Kloof St., Tamboerskloof. ✆ **021/423-6805.** www.thebombay.co.za. Reservations essential. Main courses R70–R145. AE, MC, V. Mon-Sat 6pm–midnight.

Café Paradiso ★★ ☺ BISTRO/MEDITERRANEAN   An unpretentious, laid-back bistro with appealing atmosphere and robust staff, and an outdoor terrace under the trees with Table Mountain views. Hearty, comforting dishes are served with a bit of flair. Everything, including the butter, is prepared on-site. Old kitchens have been transformed into a bustling bakery, where farm-style cakes, *melktert* (milk tart, often sprinkled with cinnamon), puddings, and breads are produced, along with homemade tagliatelle. Children are looked after: storytelling beneath the trees (or next to the fire), muffin- and pizza-making in the farm-style bakery, and grandmotherly supervision while you enjoy a relaxed grown-up meal. We love the tiny outdoor courtyard at the back, with just two tables.

110 Kloof St., Tamboerskloof. ✆ **021/423-8653.** www.cafeparadiso.co.za. Main courses R60–R135. AE, MC, V. Daily 8am–10pm.

Royale Eatery ★ 🍴 GOURMET BURGERS   It's hip and trendy, with the biggest selection of burgers in town, and if you're lucky, you'll be served by a demure Gwyneth Paltrow look-alike. Interesting choices include the lamb with mint (referred to as the "baaa baaa" burger); the fish-of-the-day burger with mango, Peppadew, and coriander salsa; the "big bird" (ostrich with beet relish); or the "fat bastard" (double everything). Even vegetarians will be happy: Try the "googamooly"—made from soy, lentils, sunflower seeds, and chickpeas, topped with guacamole, feta, and hummus. Upstairs, Royale Kitchen is a little more grown-up (no under-23s), but still with the same feisty, artful, retro-diner atmosphere. Royale milkshakes are second to none (ask for avocado, if available)—and not to be taken lightly. Pizzas are terrible.

273 Long St., Cape Town. ✆ **021/422-4536.** www.royaleeatery.com. Main courses R53–R84. AE, DC, MC, V. Mon-Sat noon–11:30pm.

The Woodlands Eatery ★★ 🍴 BISTRO   Owner Larry Steenkamp (a cook, not a chef, he claims) has opened a low-key, cozy spot for a good-value meal catering to the neighborhood rather than to tourists. There's something for everyone (including beleaguered vegetarians and celiacs—the best gluten-free pizzas in town are served here, and the chickpea, butternut, and lentil burger can be served on a gluten- and lactose-free bun). There's a pleasant courtyard; inside the atmosphere is boho and homegrown—clusters of mismatched frames, lampshades, and chairs; a rustic antiques shop look currently very popular in the city. Each night's menu is slightly modified from the previous day, but there's always a secret slow-cooked tomato and carrot sauce for thin-crust pizzas (great toppings, too), a few pasta options, and perhaps veal or Cajun-grilled line fish. Larry is a bit of a character, occasionally moonwalking between the tables checking that you're having a good time.

2 Deer Park Dr., Vredehoek. ✆ **021/801-5799.** Reservations highly recommended. Main courses R40–R95. MC, V. Tues-Thurs 5pm–late; Fri-Sun noon–late.

The East City & Woodstock

The Test Kitchen ★★★ INNOVATIVE   In many ways, celeb chef Luke Dale Roberts' private venture in Woodstock's Old Biscuit Mill is much better than world-class La Colombe, which he previously headed up. It's a more inviting, more intimate, more personal space. Luke scours the local markets, butcheries, and fisheries for the freshest ingredients—Salt River Market is smack on his doorstep—and then he does what he loves doing best: inventing, creating, experimenting. This is a real *test* kitchen where new ideas are tried out and imagined tastes are made real. Bring no expectations, but prepare to be impressed. The vast open kitchen takes up half the semiwarehouse space at least, with counter seating where you can perch at the lip of the kitchen theater and observe goings-on. Dishes are cleverly paired with fairly unexpected vintages—from a stock of wines perched up on library-like shelves accessed via a red ladder.

The Old Biscuit Mill, 375 Albert St., Woodstock. ☎ **021/447-2337.** www.thetestkitchen.co.za. Lunch mains R85–R130; dinner: 3 courses R345, 5 courses R440, 8 courses R550 or R750 with wine. MC, V. Tues–Sat 12:30–2:30pm and 7–10pm.

The Waterfront & Docklands

There's quality at the Waterfront, sure, but nothing so fine that we make a regular pilgrimage, with the exception of Willoughby & Co. (reviewed below), where we join the queue for the best sushi in town. Of the hotel restaurant chefs we like Malika van Reenen (probably the best female chef working in Cape Town today) who heads up the kitchen at the Cape Grace's **Signal ★★** (☎ **021/410-7100**). She takes her inspiration from the kitchens, cookbooks, and word-of-mouth recipes handed down through the generations, and then gives them a unique and personal spin. While dinner choices are pricey, you can get a two-course lunch (with such laid-back options as fish and chips, and barbecued beef burger) for R145.

If eating in a mall (or hotel) in the most beautiful city in the world depresses you, head upstairs to the terrace at **Baia ★★** (☎ **021/421-0935**), for linen tablecloths and picture-perfect harbor and mountain views; the seafood's excellent, too, but prices mean that it caters predominantly to a foreign market. Down below, with some open-air tables just a few meters from the harbor, **Sevruga** (☎ **021/421-5134**) is sister establishment to Greenpoint's very popular **Beluga.**

Den Anker ★★ 📷 BELGIAN If you'd rather be seated on the water's edge than inside the a Waterfront mall or hotel, then this is our top Waterfront pick, with a great view of Table Mountain and bathing seals for company. It offers a casual atmosphere and unpretentious menu; top choice is to wolf down a pot of the freshest West Coast mussels, accompanied by Belgian beer, and there's plenty more seafood to choose from. Rabbit, simmered in Belgian beer and served with applesauce and potato croquettes, is another specialty.

Pierhead, V&A Waterfront. ☎ **021/419-0249.** www.denanker.co.za. Main courses R75–R250. AE, DC, MC, V. Daily 11am–4pm and 6–10:30pm.

Nobu ★★★ JAPANESE Yes, it's *that* Nobu—as good as any of the others, and a bit of a bargain by comparison. Sit at the counter if you can and observe as sushi master Hideki Maeda and his team prepare one of their *omakase* ("from the heart") multicourse taste experiences, best if enjoyed with paired *sakes*. Service, like the food, is exceptional, and the overall experience memorable, taking Japanese food far beyond the sushi and sashimi most Westerners have grown accustomed to.

One & Only, V&A Waterfront. ☎ **021/431-5222.** www.noburestaurants.com. Main courses R70–R385. AE, DC, MC, V. Daily 6–11pm

Willoughby & Co. ★★★ SUSHI/SEAFOOD Even those who abhor dining in shopping centers queue (no bookings) to dine on the freshest, best prepared sushi in the city; like a well-oiled machine the various kitchens spit out Japanese and more traditional seafood dishes at an amazing rate, so you don't queue for long. Avoid the tables out in the mall, and sit instead on high stools at the counters or long shared

grazing WHILE BROWSING IN DE WATERKANT

This tiny enclave within Green Point has always enjoyed a reputation as a Cape Town nightlife hot spot and center of the gay scene, but in the past few years, De Waterkant has also developed into the city's most exciting shopping precinct (see "Shopping," later in this chapter). But one needs sustenance to plunder, and the restaurants and eateries in and around the two Cape Quarter piazza-style shopping centers don't disappoint—to be honest, though, it's the places on the fringes that really steal the show. With the upbeat slogan "TODAY IS A GOOD DAY," **Loading Bay ★★★**, on 30 Hudson St., is one of our favorite places to load up while indulging the visual senses; they serve excellent coffee, great breakfasts, and wonderful sandwiches (try the man'oushe, served on Lebanese flatbread). Next door is **Origin ★★**, a good stop for serious coffeehounds, with a buzz as heady as the blends served by a knowledgeable crew (they also run barista and coffee appreciation courses here). Tea lovers should head directly for the glass-enclosed room at the back—the fishbowl-like venue is said to heighten the experience. For more dining choices, head to the central cobbled piazza-style courtyard of the first Cape Quarter development, where a couple of places have tables spilling out around the central fountain: Popular with locals is **Andiamo** (✆ 021/421-3687), which has a small but good Italian menu and a testosterone-strong staff pumping up the action. Food is good, but when it's packed, tables are a little too close together and the vibe is frenetic. Inside the actual deli-shop, you'll find the greatest selection of edible items this side of the equator. It's a good place to stock up for a picnic or gifts for foodie friends. If it's a delicious light meal you're after, pick a table at tiny **La Petite Tart ★**, on the "outside" of the original Quarter, on Dixon Street (✆ 021/425-9077). It has the most wonderful tart selection (sweet and savory) or try the traditional croquemonsieur, or interesting quiches, all baked that morning. Attached to a gorgeous furniture and homeware store, **Table Thirteen ★**, 78 Victoria Junction, Ebenezer Rd. (✆ 021/418-0738), is another great, slightly secreted-away eatery with freshly baked cakes, salads, and a handful of hearty homestyle dishes served mostly to people from offices in the surrounding buildings.

tables—ideal if you like to watch the sushi chefs stacking plates with fat slices of fresh, raw fish. The menu is a bewildering array of choices but one of the most popular rolls remains the Rainbow Nation, while the 4x4 is the deluxe sushi choice. Tempura is perfect, like everything else that comes out of the bustling kitchen.

Victoria Wharf, V&A Waterfront. ✆ **021/418-6116.** Main courses R79–R229. AE, DC, MC, V. Daily 11:30am–10:30pm.

De Waterkant, Green Point, Mouille Point & Sea Point

Even before Green Point's pre-2010 transformation, these bustling, adjoining neighborhoods experienced an explosion in growth. New restaurants and retail outlets opened monthly along their respective main roads, while the modern apartment blocks that rise above them were being renovated faster than the restaurants could handle. Green Point has a number of fashionable and good-value restaurants; our favorites are described below, but do look at our recommended neighborhood eateries on p. 83.

Il Leoni Mastrantonio ★★★ 🏠ITALIAN   Tucked away on a Green Point backstreet, this is hailed by its loyal local followers as the best Italian joint in the city. It's part of a small family-owned chain with handed down recipes: Ebullient young Daniel Toledo mans the kitchen and makes regular turns at the tables to check on customers, most of whom are digging in to spot-on al dente pastas topped with delicious sauces. Classic veal, fish, and steak dishes also feature. The space—in a double-story building dating back 3 centuries (once a water's edge hotel for sailors)—is totally unassuming.

22 Coburn St., Green Point. ✆ **021/421-0071.** www.mastrantonio.com/illeone. Main courses R55–R170. AE, DC, MC, V. Tues–Sun noon–3pm and 6:30–10:30pm.

Sloppy Sam ★★★ EAST MEDITERRANEAN   Despite its neon sign, it's still easy to miss this gem among the faceless traps in this bustling part of Green Point. Iran-born Hooman Saffarian cooks up a storm, taking inspiration from his roots, but paying attention to Greek and other cuisine influences, too. The two-level space is stocked like a motley deli, piled with jars and cans and sacks suggesting the provenance of much of his produce. Expect delicious homestyle cooking from a man who simply loves working with food—his lamb shank is said to have converted more than a handful of vegetarians.

51A Somerset Rd., Green Point. ✆ **021/419-2921.** www.sloppysam.co.za. Main courses R69–R97. MC, V. Mon–Sat 6:30–10pm.

Wakame ★★ SUSHI/ASIAN FUSION   A stylish, clean-lined place with a great sea vista and airy modern interior where Japanese chefs skillfully slice, dice, wrap, and roll. Ceiling-length glass doors fold back entirely to reveal a postcard-perfect view of the ships sailing in and out of the nearby harbor. Start upstairs at one of Cape Town's sexiest cocktail venues, **Wafu** (open all afternoon), and watch as a cosmopolitan crowd schmoozes on the lounge-style wooden deck (see "Cape Town After Dark," below). Then, when a hunger sets in, go for hot offerings rather than sushi; the menu's superstar is seared tea-smoked tuna served on wasabi mash. All in all, potentially a great night (or afternoon) out, if only the staff wouldn't confuse the restaurant's popularity status with theirs.

Corner of Beach Rd. and Surrey Place, Mouille Point. ✆ **021/433-2377.** www.wakame.co.za. Dinner reservations recommended. Main courses R75–R135. AE, DC, MC, V. Mon–Thurs noon–3pm and 6–10:30pm; Fri–Sat noon–3:30pm and 6–11pm; Sun noon–3:30pm and 6–10pm.

Atlantic Seaboard

When the summer sun starts its slow descent into the ocean, most Capetonians feel compelled to head over to the Atlantic seaboard to soak up the last of its pink rays and watch the kaleidoscope unfold. Toasting nature's miracle with fast-flowing refreshments usually happens on Victoria Road—the street that hugs Camps Bay's palm-fringed beachfront—where you'll find tightly packed refreshment stations mostly posing as restaurants, but all boasting good-to-glorious views of the ocean. Bucking this trend to some degree is **Grand Café** (reviewed below), which—in terms of atmosphere at least—is memorable. But if your first priority is the quality of your meal, make every effort to get to **The Roundhouse** (high above the sea; reviewed below), which offers magnificent views by day and extraordinary romance in a (pricy) fine dining setting once the sun descends over the Atlantic.

> ⚠ **Sunset Strip Mayhem**
>
> In summer, the atmosphere along Camps Bay's sunset strip gets frenzied, and any genuine desire to service individuals' needs or produce noteworthy food takes a backseat to turning tables as fast as possible (Blues and Grand Café being notable exceptions); if you're looking for a more laid-back seaside alternative, where views are not tainted by brash punters or low-level aggressive staff, escape to one of the sleepy village-size towns in the southern part of the peninsula.

The Grand Café ★ ▣ BISTRO/ SEAFOOD   This is the most romantic of the water-facing options along Camps Bay's rowdy bling-bling sunset strip. It's also currently the only semismart dining option with any sort of individual personality (the rest have all gone for a polished plastic). This has more to do with the venue's theatrical Parisian cafe good looks—bohemian chic accented by casual collectibles, antiques, casual *tromp l'oeil* effects, and fab pieces of vintage furniture—than with the menu offerings. Most of what's offered is simple bistro fare at inflated location-related prices: grilled line fish of the day, very good steak, and crayfish linguine. Watch the sun sink from the gallery-style upstairs terrace table (it's worth reserving an upstairs table) and see how the fairy lights and flickering candles transform this place into a dreamy cocoon. *Note:* Sister outfit Grand Beach Café, on Granger Bay Road, near the Waterfront, is another seaside option worth checking out; we review it under bars below for its superb location, but it's also good for pizzas and light meals, though very overpriced.

35 Victoria Rd., Camps Bay. ✆ **021/438-2332.** www.thegrand.co.za. Dinner reservations essential. Main courses R60–R220, seafood platter for 2 R740. AE, MC, V. Tues–Sun 12:30–11pm.

The Roundhouse & Rumbullion ★★★ ▣ CONTEMPORARY FRENCH FUSION   This is the most romantic dining experience in Cape Town: an 18th-century hunting lodge with extraordinary views and an enchanting location, hidden away in a little-known woodland part of Camps Bay. It offers two very distinctive dining experiences. Rumbullion's affordable al fresco bistro-style **lunch** is all about the views, and designed to fit the languid mood beneath the trees overlooking Camps Bay. The Roundhouse is fine-dining **dinner** in a beautiful heritage building (but in line with international prices). Chef P. J. Vadas (who worked under Gordon Ramsay in New York) captains the kitchen, where they aim to keep things local, seasonal, and organic—guinea fowl with celeriac, blueberry, and baby onions; smoked trout risotto; roasted eland filet; slow-braised pork belly; and a delicious cut of a local variety of fallow deer, known as *takbok,* are just some of the items that may be available.

The Glen on Kloof Rd., Camps Bay. ✆ **021/438-4347.** www.theroundhouserestaurant.com. Reservations essential. **Roundhouse:** 4 courses R420, R640–R800 with wine. **Rumbullion:** Main courses R85–R120. AE, MC, V. **Roundhouse:** Tues–Sat 6–9pm, also open Sun in summer. **Rumbullion:** Oct–Apr/May Wed–Sun noon–2:30pm; Fri–Sun 8am–11am.

Southern Suburbs & the Constantia Wine Route

The Constantia wine estate, **Uitsig,** is fortunate enough to house two fabulous dining options: The first, **Constantia Uitsig,** is reviewed in full below because the setting is just the best, but foodie accolades tend to accumulate around ultrapricey sister establishment **La Colombe ★★** (✆ **021/794-2390**), where the seven-course tasting menu will run you around R850 (in winter this drops to a bargain price of R390 for five courses with wine; a la carte main courses cost R135–R275). With new chef Scot Kirton in charge, the critics are still debating La Colombe's future, but local diners have been raving about **Catharina's** (reviewed below) at the Steenberg. Steenberg Estate's second option is the fresh, hip-looking **Bistro Sixteen82 ★★** (✆ **021/713-2211;** www.steenberg-vineyards.co.za), a stylish cellar door-cum-tasting room that's developed into a daytime favorite (with drinks and tapas available until early evening, when the after-work crowd piles in); there's a children's menu, too.

The biggest tourism drawing card in this area—with a gracious manor house museum and lovely grounds—is **Groot Constantia.** The relaxed **Jonkershuis Restaurant ★** (✆ **021/794-6255**), also in a historic building, is another wonderful venue, serving well-priced comfort food. On a fine day, grab a table under the oaks; when it's wet, one beside the fire will do; it's popular, so bookings are essential.

Another Constantia option worth considering, with a lovely garden setting but a great deal more formal, is **The Greenhouse ★★** (✆ **021/794-2137**), at the Cellars-Hohenort hotel, where chef Peter Tempelhoff offers a seasonal menu, using herbs from the hotel garden to create what he calls "progressive South African" cuisine. On the same property is **The Cape Malay Experience,** with a more traditional menu as the name suggests.

Catharina's ★★★ MODERN SOUTH AFRICAN An old Cape Dutch farm house has been given a fitting makeover—the designer was charged with bringing the outside in, so you can virtually touch the vineyards. Beyond them, the mountains sweep down to False Bay—an awesome scene on a warm summer's day when you can sit on the terrace. Continuing to make waves in Cape Town's culinary ocean chef Garth Almazan's contemporary take on South African cuisine offers clever (but uncomplicated) combinations. Lunch is a lighter menu, while dinner sees him flexing his muscles with warthog loin served with butternut gnocchi, sautéed baby spinach, Gorgonzola cream, shemeji mushrooms, and secret Catharina jus; or springbok with sultanas, pine nuts, seared asparagus, spinach tortellini, and red wine jus; or a delicious wild mushroom and winter squash risotto, and so on.

Steenberg Hotel, Tokai Rd., Constantia. ✆ **021/713-2222.** www.steenberghotel.com. Main courses R85–R165. AE, DC, MC, V. Daily noon–3pm and 7–10pm; closed Sun dinner and Mon in winter.

Constantia Uitsig ★★ 🖻 ITALIAN La Colombe (on the same estate) is the more famous of the two but frankly, we'd book here any day for the setting alone—the mountain and vineyard vistas are mesmerizing, while the ambience in the original Cape Dutch manor house is gracious and comforting. It's not an award-winning menu but you get good, comforting food from Chef Clayton Bell's kitchen. His paper-thin fish carpaccio comes with a ginger-seaweed dressing; the risotto with crayfish is a firm favorite as is the linguine with salmon and asparagus. Steaks are legendary; fish dishes not consistent. Whatever you do, finish up with the most sinfully rich dessert ever: Marquise au Chocolat.

Spaanschemat River Rd., Constantia. ✆ **021/794-4480.** www.uitsig.co.za. Reservations essential. Main courses R110–R220. AE, DC, MC, V. Daily 12:30–2pm and 7:30–9pm. Closed 1 month in winter.

Myoga ★★★ INNOVATIVE/FUSION If you like experimental fusion cuisine, Myoga is hard to beat (but not ideal if you prefer things unfussy). Oriental influences (Myoga is Japanese for "Ginger Blossom") mean slow-roasted pork comes with *kung pao* sauce and sweet kumara, and the seafood chowder is spiced like a Thai green curry. Although restaurateur Mike Bassett (whose much-loved city-side venture, Ginja, folded in 2010) loves Asian flavors, you'll probably find an interesting risotto,

😊 family-friendly RESTAURANTS

Since its reinvention at the hand of the same imaginative team behind Madame Zingara (the Cape Town–originated circus-themed dinner tent) and Bombay Bicycle Club, **Restaurant Paradiso ★★★**, 110 Kloof St. (✆ **021/423-8653**), has filled its tables with parents wanting a charming place to eat, while children have an absolute ball in the care of a dedicated team who do everything with them from story-telling beneath the trees (or around the fire in winter) to pizza and muffin prepa-ration in the kitchen. Service is charming but can be atrociously slow. Most city res-taurants have limited space, but **Deer Park Café ★** (✆ **021/462-6311**) opens onto a shady large children's park in Vredehoek, completely fenced, so you can sip a quiet cappuccino or enjoy a light meal and relax while they play. At 75 Kloof St., **Ocean Basket** (✆ **021/422-0322**) has a lovely terraced back garden and kiddy portions of perfectly cooked fish in minipans. If the kids are clamoring for pizzas, head down to the Foreshore or Camps Bay to grab a table at **Col'Cacchio** (✆ **021/438-2171**)—ask for a bit of dough to make and bake in the pizza oven. Moving south, **Jonkershuis,** on the Groot Constantia Estate (see above), doesn't have a play area, but it's a fine child-friendly venue, with a children's menu and an outdoor area in which to run around. Over in Hout Bay, at **Dunes Bar & Restaurant** (✆ **021/790-1876**) you can relax at a table with your feet in the sand and watch Junior play on the swings and climbing frame—just don't forget the sunblock. If you're heading toward Cape Point, consider stopping at the Noordhoek Farm Village for brunch at the totally unpretentious **Café Roux ★★★** (✆ **021/789-2538**). It's extremely child friendly, with a super-vised, fenced-off playground and special kiddies menu, as well as ultrahealthful items such as salads made with organic quinoa and adzuki beans.

spring lamb loin (served with mint chimichurri, black eggplant, and pomegranate jus), and lemon cheesecake on the eclectic menu. The sommelier is excellent (though wines are expensive), and the appreciative local clientele makes for a *lekker* (great) buzz.

Vineyard Hotel, Colinton Rd., Newlands. ✆ **021/657-4545.** Reservations highly recommended. Main courses R75–R110 lunch, R95–R150 dinner; 2-course lunch R120, 3-course lunch R145, 6-course dinner R195–R230, 8-course dinner R450. AE, DC, MC, V. Tues–Sat 11:30am–3pm and 7–10:30pm.

The Southern Peninsula

There's plenty of unpretentious and sociable places to eat while touring the southern peninsula; again too many to review in full so we've simply listed the best. Note that you may not always find the same kind of snappy service and cosmopolitan crowd that you might expect in the city, but a mellow vibe is part of what's best about this part of the world.

MUIZENBERG With it's upstairs art gallery, classy Africanova boutique craft store, and formal garden, **Casa Labia ★★**, 192 Main Rd. (✆ **021/788-6062**), is a great lunch stop. Interiors are as lavish as they might have been when this was the residence of the Count and Countess Natale Labia (whose descendants restored the building). It's filled with period detail and beautiful antiques; the menu, designed by Cape Town food maven Judy Badenhorst, is a clever integration of Italian inspiration and local produce.

KALK BAY You'll find the most atmospheric False Bay restaurants in the charming and increasingly trendy fishing village of Kalk Bay. In the small fishing harbor, where fishermen still hawk their hand-caught fish directly to the public and surrounding restaurants, three options are right on the water. For its unpretentious crisp clean look and on-the-harbor's-edge views of the crashing waves below, the best choice by far is breezy **Harbour House ★★** (✆ **021/788-4133**)—book a table by the window, order the line fish and be prepared to be mesmerized by the rhythmic sound of the sea. Line fish are listed in chalk on the board and scratched off as they disappear down the hungry maws of patrons. Downstairs, **Live Bait** (✆ **021/788-5755**) is a more casual affair, with mosaic tables, mismatched chairs, and a similarly dramatic full frontal assault of waves. Just as well the views and surroundings are convivial, for you will surely be kept waiting for your meal.

If you have a yen for something other than seafood, scruffy **Olympia Cafe & Deli ★**, Main Road, diagonally opposite the turnoff to the harbor (✆ **021/788-6396**), is a cult status deli-restaurant serving light meals to the hippies and trendy bohemians who frequent this side of the mountain to haunt this scruffy old favorite. The crowd may be gorgeous, but you'll need to fight them off for a table, and then deal with obnoxious staff—house rules strictly forbid "smoking, split bills, self-discipline, bullshit. . . ever" so you're advised to keep it real. Occupying a 98-year-old building, and tucked into the back of Kalk Bay Books, **The Annex ★★**, Majestic Village, 124 Main Rd. (✆ **021/788-2453**), may not have the notoriety, but it's a far more warm, welcoming space with fires in winter, comfy antiques, tidily exposed brick walls, and books to browse. The menu changes daily, but has never let us down: fresh fish simply prepared, or salads bursting with ingredients (wild mushrooms, artichokes, fine beans, and greens tossed in a delicate dressing). A rather sexy-looking spot near the train lines is **Cape to Cuba,** Main Road (✆ **021/788-1566**)—eclectically decorated with mismatched chairs, numerous chandeliers, and Catholic kitsch on rich, saturated-color walls, it's comfortable, and the mojitos are drop-dead delicious; pity the food isn't up to snuff.

SIMONS TOWN We love **The Meeting Place** (✆ **021/786-5678**), located on the main road, a casual cafe-deli-bistro with fresh, delicious produce and light meals. Upstairs is where you'll head at night, where the menu gets more serious; we've never had a bad meal at either venue (female shoppers should pop into Mauve, a great little clothing boutique just around the corner). On the way out of Simons Town, heading for Cape Point, you'll see the **Black Marlin,** Main Road (✆ **021/786-1621**), a

---

Fish & Chips with Real Cape Locals

Diagonally across from Harbour House is rough and ready **Kalky's ★** (✆ **021/788-1726**), the most unpretentious restaurant in Cape Town, attracting a diverse cross-section—from flat-capped and tattooed roughnecks to Constantia types twirling their wineglasses and tittering at the large ladies who dispense plates and keep up a great running commentary with regular patrons. There's a substantial seafood menu, but everyone is here for the succulent fish (hake) and chips—superbly battered, 100% fresh—for a paltry R35 per portion. Order at the till and wait for your number to be screamed out; help yourself to cutlery and crockery. There's no corkage, so pick up some chilled vino or beer beforehand.

venue that enjoys one of the best sea views in the Cape, making it a popular tourist spot (arrive early to avoid the tour buses).

NOORDHOEK   On the southern side of Chapman's Peak Drive, **The Food-barn ★★★** (☏ 021/789-1390), in the Noordhoek Farm Village, is a darn fine restaurant; the best on the southern peninsula. It is co-owned by Franck Dangereux, the celebrated French chef who, after putting La Colombe on the map (it was restaurant of year six times under his watch; see p. 107), opted for a more laid-back lifestyle (and cuisine style) and relocated here in 2007. The food is simple and well presented, ingredients are predominantly organic, and the ambience, after a shabby chic make-over by Franck's wife, is comfortable and family friendly. Franck also has one of the best deli-cum-bakeries in the country here, with a dining area if you can't bear to leave the wonderful aromas behind. A few steps away is **Café Roux ★★★☺** (☏ 021/789-2538), perfect for a long, languid lunch beneath the trees, and another great venue for parents: Aside from the great menu, there's an enclosed play area within sight.

HOUT BAY   The family-run restaurant at the **Chapman's Peak Beach Hotel ★★★**, Chapman's Peak Drive, at the base of the Peak on the Hout Bay side (☏ 021/790-1036), is famous for its fresh calamari and fish—served still sizzling in the pan with fat fries—and wide veranda with views of the small fishing harbor. It's a jolly, unpretentious place that long predates Cape Town's burgeoning restaurant scene, yet it still pulls in the punters from all over the city, all of whom leave as satisfied as they did 30 years ago. Hout Bay is also where you'll find one of the best-loved Asian restaurants in the Cape: **Kitima ★★★** (☏ 021/790-8004), good not only for the spectacularly renovated Kronendal Manor, the heritage building in which it's located but also for the delectable food (mostly Thai, but with other parts Eastern cuisines represented, too), lively buzz, and formidable cocktails.

EXPLORING CAPE TOWN

From ascending its famous flat-topped mountain to indulging in the sybaritic pleasures grown on its fertile slopes, Cape Town has much to offer sightseers. You could cover the top attractions in 3 days, but to really get a sense of how much the city and surrounds have to offer, you'll need to stay at least a week.

Table Mountain National Park

Nowhere else in the world does a wilderness with such startling biodiversity survive within a dense metropolis; a city housing some 3.5 million people effectively surrounds a national park, clinging to a mountainous spine that stretches southward from Table Mountain's Signal Hill massif to the jagged edges of Cape Point at the tip of the peninsula. Hardly surprising, then, that the city's best attractions are encompassed by Table Mountain National Park: world-famous **Table Mountain,** also known as Hoerikwaggo (Mountain of the Sea); **Kirstenbosch Botanical Gardens,** showcase for the region's ancient and incredibly varied floral kingdom; **Boulders,** home to a colony of rare African penguins and the dramatic **Cape Point,** most southwesterly tip of Africa. Ascending Table Mountain warrants half a day, as does a visit to Kirstenbosch—though you could include it as part of a (rather rushed) daylong peninsula driving tour, which encompasses Boulders and Cape Point.

Table Mountain ★★★   This huge, time-sculpted slab of shale, sandstone, and granite that rose from the ocean some 250 million years ago is Cape Town's most instantly recognizable feature. A candidate for selection as one of the New 7 Wonders

Legend has it that the "tablecloth," the white cloud that tumbles over Table Mountain, is the work of retired pirate Van Hunks, who liked nothing more than to climb Devil's Peak and smoke his pipe while overlooking Cape Town. One day the devil, not happy that someone was puffing on his turf, challenged him to a smoking contest. Needless to say, the competition continues to rage unabated, particularly in the summer months. The downside of this magnificent spectacle is that hurricane-force winds will simultaneously whip around Devil's Peak and rip into the city at speeds of up to 150kmph (93 mph). The "Cape Doctor," as the southeaster is often called, is said to clear the city of pollution; but most just wish Van Hunks would give it up and stop infuriating the devil. For sanity's sake, head for Clifton, Bantry Bay, or Newlands, the most protected suburbs. See chapter 5 for escapes further afield.

of Nature (www.n7w.com; to be announced Nov 11, 2011), the flat-topped mountain dominates the landscape, climate, and development of the city at its feet, and provides Cape Town with a 6,000-hectare (14,820-acre) wilderness at its center.

The best view of the mountain is from Table Bay (another good reason to take a sunset cruise; see p. 68), from where you can get some idea of the relative size of the mountain—while the city shrinks to nothing, the "Mountain of the Sea" is visible some 150km (93 miles) from shore. Other views of the mountain are no less beautiful, particularly of the wooded eastern flanks of **Constantiaberg,** which greet the sun every morning, and the bare buttresses of the **Twelve Apostles,** kissed by its last rays. The mountain is thought to be the most climbed peak in the world, with some 350 paths to the summit and more plant varieties (some 1,470 species) than the entire British Isles.

You can ascend the mountain on foot or via cable car and, once there, spend a few hours or an entire day exploring. The narrow table is 3km (1¾ miles) long and 1,086m (3,562 ft.) high. **Maclear's Beacon** is its highest point, and really suitable only for serious hikers. From Maclear's, it's another hour's trek to the upper cable station and restaurant, which are on the mountain's western edge, from where you can view the Twelve Apostles towering over Camps Bay; the eastern edge overlooks the southern suburbs.) The back table, with its forests, *fynbos* (shrublike vegetation), and the reservoirs that supply Cape Town with its water, is a wonderful place to hike, but much of it is off limits.

By aerial cable car: Cars depart every 15 minutes from Tafelberg Road (☎ **021/ 424-8181;** www.tablemountain.net) daily from 8:30am until between 5 and 8:30pm, depending on the season—and weather permitting. A round-trip ticket costs R180 for adults, R90 for children (children under 4 free). The floor rotates 360 degrees, giving everyone a chance to gape at the breathtaking views during the 4-minute journey up. Afternoons are usually less crowded but even during the busiest months (Nov–Apr) you shouldn't have to wait longer than 15 minutes to board.

On foot: The most commonly used route to the top is via **Platteklip Gorge**—the gap is visible from the front, or north face, of the mountain. The route starts just east of the lower cable station (see below) and will take 2 to 3 strenuous hours. Be sure to bring water. A more scenic route starts at the Kirstenbosch Botanical Gardens and climbs up the back via **Skeleton Gorge.** It's steep, requiring reasonable fitness, in

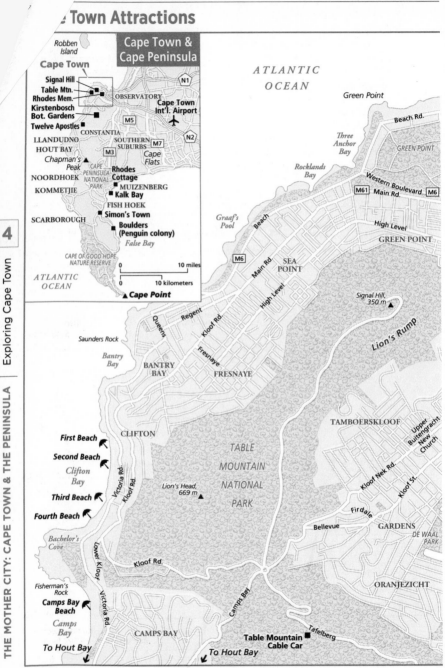

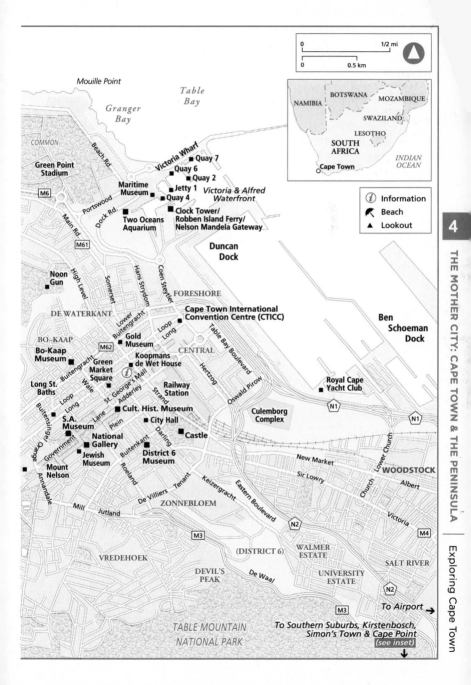

Mouille Point

Table Bay

Granger Bay

COMMON

Green Point Stadium

Beach Rd.

M6

Portswood

Dock Rd.

Main Rd.

M61

Maritime Museum

Victoria Wharf

Quay 7

Quay 6

Quay 2

Jetty 1

Quay 4

Victoria & Alfred Waterfront

Two Oceans Aquarium

Clock Tower/ Robben Island Ferry/ Nelson Mandela Gateway

Duncan Dock

Noon Gun

High Level

Somerset

Hans Strydom

Coen Steytler

Lower Buitengracht

FORESHORE

DE WATERKANT

BO-KAAP

Bo-Kaap Museum

M62

Gold Museum

Cape Town International Convention Centre (CTICC)

Loop

Long

Table Bay Boulevard

CENTRAL

Ben Schoeman Dock

Buitengracht

Green Market Square

Koopmans de Wet House

Hertzog

Oswald Pirow

N1

N1

Long St. Baths

Waal

St. George's Mall

Adderley

Strand

Railway Station

Royal Cape Yacht Club

Loop

Long

Lane

Plein

Cult. Hist. Museum

City Hall

Culemborg Complex

S.A. Museum

National Gallery

Buitenkant

Darling

Castle

Jewish Museum

District 6 Museum

New Market

Church

Lower Church

WOODSTOCK

Mount Nelson

Government

Roeland

Sir Lowry

Albert

Orange

Buitensingel

Annandale

De Villiers

Tenant

Keizergracht

Eastern Boulevard

Victoria

M4

Mill

Jutland

ZONNEBLOEM

N2

SALT RIVER

M3

(DISTRICT 6)

WALMER ESTATE

VREDEHOEK

DEVIL'S PEAK

De Waal

UNIVERSITY ESTATE

N2

M3

To Airport →

TABLE MOUNTAIN NATIONAL PARK

To Southern Suburbs, Kirstenbosch, Simon's Town & Cape Point (see inset) ↓

0   1/2 mi

0   0.5 km

NAMIBIA   BOTSWANA   MOZAMBIQUE

SWAZILAND

LESOTHO

SOUTH AFRICA

INDIAN OCEAN

Cape Town

ⓘ Information

↖ Beach

▲ Lookout

e it should take approximately 3 hours to the summit; your efforts will be
d with fine views of False Bay and the Constantia Valley. From here it's
er hour to the upper cable station. Be aware that the mountain's mercurial
ther can surprise even seasoned Capetonians—more people have died on Table
Mountain than on Mount Everest. Don't climb alone, stick to the paths, and take
water and warm clothes. The **Mountain Rescue** number is © **10177** or 021/948-
9900. For guided hikes, you can contact **Table Mountain Walks** (© **021/715-
6136**); better still, call **Riaan Vorster ★★★** (© **021/438-6073** or 083/683-1876;
cauaburi@yahoo.com), who will take you up the mountain—on any of more than 20
routes—armed with an extensive knowledge of its geology, flora, fauna, and history.
He also specializes in off-the-beaten-track routes, so it's possible to experience the
mountain as a true wilderness. Rates start at R300 per person for a half-day, and
R400 for a full-day hike. The 75km (46½ mile) **Hoerikwaggo Trail** (www.sanparks.
org) is a 4-night, 5-day hiking route from Cape Point to Cape Point. Hikers can book
3-, 2-, and 1-night hikes covering those sections of the trail that are already complete. The trail is unsignposted but has designated tented camps along the way;
there is no charge for hiking, but you're required to pay all park entrance and conservation fees as well as accommodation (R400 double with shared ablutions; no
bedding or towels provided, which must be booked in advance (© **021/422-2816;**
hoerikwaggobookings@sanparks.org). For assistance with hiring an accredited guide
for the trail (recommended), call © **021/465-8752** or 021/462-7861; you'll pay for
your guide's accommodation, too.

Boulders ★★ ☺   A few minutes from the center of Simons Town, on the way to
Cape Point, is the turnoff to pretty Boulders (signposted PENGUIN VIEWING), named
after a cluster of large granite boulders that form a number of small sheltered bays
that provide sanctuary for a breeding colony of African penguins (colloquially known
as jackass penguins because of their braying). You can swim at either Seaforth Beach
or Boulders Beach, which the penguins visit, but the best place to view them is from
the raised boardwalk overlooking Foxy Beach (accessed via the cashier kiosk); they
are a treat to watch, almost human in their interactions. A monogamous species, the
penguins mate in January and nest from February to August.

Boulders Beach (off M4), Simons Town. © **021/786-2329.** R40 adults, R15 children. Dec–Jan daily
7am–7:30pm; Feb–Mar daily 8am–6:30pm; Apr–Sept daily 8am–5pm; Oct–Nov daily 8am–6:30pm.

Cape of Good Hope Nature Reserve ★★★ ☺   Best known for **Cape Point,**
the farthest tip of the peninsula, this slither of protected reserve horns its way into
the ocean. Various scenic drives and picnic sites put you in the midst of a fabulous
terrain that's home to baboons, zebras, elands, red hartebeests, ostriches, and the
pretty bontebok. Often windswept, the reserve can be pretty bleak, but the coastal
views are arresting, and the beaches almost always deserted. The walks from
Gifkommetjie and **Platboom Beach,** on the western coast (good for windsurfing),
are recommended, or follow the turnoff to Bordjiesdrif or **Buffelsbaai** on the east
coast, where you can swim in protected tidal pools or even *braai* (barbecue); at the
latter you can see the remains of one of the more than twenty ships that have wrecked
on this coast.

Most head straight for Cape Point, taking the **Flying Dutchman funicular** (R45
round-trip; 9am–6pm summer, 9am–5pm winter) to the viewing platforms surrounding the old lighthouse (built too high, it was often obscured by mists) and walking to
the "new" lighthouse—the most powerful in the country, built after yet another liner
wrecked here in 1911. From these cliffs, towering more than 180m (600 ft.) above the

> ### ⚠ Don't Feed the Monkeys
>
> Be aware that the peninsula's baboons have become habituated to humans, and can be dangerous. Don't approach them, keep your car windows closed, your doors locked, and never feed them. Newspapers are regularly plastered with pictures of these crafty fellows opening car doors and helping themselves to the contents while the passengers rush to fend them off.

lashing ocean, the view is truly "bird's-eye"—hundreds of seagulls wheel below. *Note:* Despite the T-shirt slogans and the name of the Two Oceans Restaurant, this is not the meeting place of two oceans; that would be Cape Agulhus, southeast of here.

Entrance off M4 and M65. ℂ **021/780-9204.** www.capepoint.co.za. R80 adults, R20 children age 2–12. Oct–Mar daily 6am–6pm; Apr–Sept daily 7am–5pm.

Kirstenbosch National Botanical Gardens ★★★ ☺ Situated on the eastern slopes of Table Mountain, Kirstenbosch is the third-most-visited attraction in Cape Town and is without a doubt one of the most beautiful gardens in the world. Its shaded lawns and gurgling streams are the perfect antidote to the searing summer heat, and they're equally glorious in winter, when the rain coaxes out protea and aloe blooms. With the cultivated sections seamlessly blending into the adjoining Table Mountain nature reserve, some 8,000 of South Africa's 22,000 plant species (including a giant baobab tree) grow here. There are a number of themed walks and areas; as an introduction to the indigenous flora, the *fynbos* walk is recommended. Of historic interest are the remains of the wild almond hedge that Jan Van Riebeeck planted in 1660 to demarcate the colony from the indigenous Khoi. Easiest is to hire an audio guide, or take the free guided garden walks that take place on Tuesday, Wednesday, and Saturday (or take a golf cart tour—see below). **Summer sunset concerts ★★★** are held every Sunday at 5:30pm from late November to mid-April and feature an eclectic mix of mediocre-to-brilliant bands, orchestras, and solo artists. It's usually worth attending simply to check out the crowd (seating is on the lawn—bring a blanket, food, and drinks, and arrive very early if you want a spot near the stage). At the main entrance there are two restaurants (ℂ **021/762-9585**): the self-service **Fynbos Deli** (9am–5pm) and adjacent **Silver Tree,** serving a la carte lunches and dinners. The venue and views are lovely, but the food is pricey and unremarkable. Locals and visitors in the know avoid these tourist traps and opt to enter through Gate 2, and eat breakfast or lunch at the small, thatched **Kirstenbosch Tea Room** (ℂ **021/797-4883**), with tables outside and a well-priced menu.

Rhodes Dr., Newlands, 13km (8 miles) from the city center. Take De Waal Dr. (M3) toward Muizenberg, at the 1st traffic light intersection turn right (southward) into Rhodes Dr. (M63), and follow the signs. ℂ **021/799-8783** or 021/799-8899. www.sanbi.org.za. R37 adults, R10 children 6–17. Sept–Mar daily 8am–7pm; Apr–Aug daily 8am–6pm. Free guided garden walks Mon–Sat at 10am. Audio guides R40. Shuttle car tours (R45) depart every hour 9am–3pm. Concert prices vary.

Rhodes Memorial Stop here for the view alone; there's a coffee shop attached if you feel like doing so while enjoying it with a (mediocre) meal and a drink. Designed by Herbert Baker and Francis Macey, the monument was erected in honor of Cecil John Rhodes, the man who made his fortune in the Kimberley diamond mines and became prime minister of the Cape in 1890. A true British imperialist, he "owned" Zimbabwe (previously known as Rhodesia), and it was his lifelong dream to see a

Cape-to-Cairo railway line built so that the "sun would never set on the British Empire." A bust of Rhodes is at the top of an imposing lion-flanked granite staircase flanked by lions and overlooking the Cape Flats and Table Bay. Wildebeests and zebras graze on the slopes below, oblivious to rubberneckers driving the M3 below.

Groote Schuur Estate (from the M3/De Waal Dr., follow the signposted turnoff just after the University of Cape Town). Free admission. Daily 9am–5pm.

Attractions in the City Center

Cape Town is South Africa's oldest and most pleasant city center, featuring a combination of Cape Dutch, Georgian, Victorian, and 20th-century architecture, all framed by the backdrop of Table Mountain. Hardly surprising, then, that Cape Town is, with the efforts of the Cape Town Partnership, slowly transforming itself from sole-business to multi-use residential enclave, with many of the city's period buildings being redeveloped into apartments and hotels, and new retail and restaurant outlets to service them.

The prettiest axis, **Adderley Street,** runs past the revamped railway station, cutting the city in half—there's some gorgeous architecture (lots of solid bank buildings) and most visitors enjoy stopping by the **flower market,** where the sellers can be extremely engaging. East of Adderley is the **Castle of Good Hope, Grand Parade,** and **City Hall.** West are the more charming shopping areas, the best of which, **Long Street, Bree Street** and, to a far lesser extent, **St. George's Mall** (a pedestrian street), run parallel to Adderley—the side streets are full of surprises, too. **Greenmarket Square,** a lively flea market surrounded by coffee shops, lies between these two streets and Longmarket and Shortmarket streets.

South of Adderley Street (where it takes a right turn at The Slave Lodge and melds with Wale St.) are the **Company's Gardens,** Cape Town's very own central park, and the green lung where most of the museums are situated. These Gardens started out as the vegetable patch to supply the Dutch East India Company, which first established Cape Town as a refreshment station for passing ships in the 17th century. From the gardens, you can also get a clear view of **Tuinhuis,** where world dignitaries are received by the president. Also adjacent to the Gardens and Tuinhuis is **Parliament,** scheduled for expansion in the next few years. To arrange a free **tour** through the halls of one of the world's most hard-won democratic parliaments, call ✆ **021/ 403-2266,** and ask Mrs. Nhlanhla Mrwerwe to book you in—and perhaps arrange gallery tickets, if available. You'll need to bring your passport along for security purposes—the entrance to Parliament is at the junction of Roeland and Plein streets.

The city is small, so the best way to get to know it is on foot; we recommend you take a 3-hour guided walking tour (see "On Foot City Tours" on p. 67), or enjoy your own pace: Start at the Castle, then head down Darling Street to Adderley Street. Either turn right to look at the Trafalgar flower market before continuing up Darling to browse the markets and shops at Greenmarket Square, Church Street, and Long Street, or turn left onto Adderley to complete a loop that takes in The Slave Lodge, the Company Gardens, the National Gallery, and/or the South African Museum before returning down Queen Victoria Street or Long Street to Greenmarket Square. Besides the recommended museums and galleries below, you might want to take a look at **Koopmans–De Wet House,** 35 Strand St. (✆ **021/481-3935;** R10 adults; Mon–Fri 10am–5pm), the country's oldest house museum, and a repository for some of the finest Cape furniture, ceramics, and silverware to survive the 18th and 19th centuries. Originally built in the 18th century, the facade of this urban mansion really

For an essential Cape Town experience, be sure to stop by **Deluxe Coffee-works ★★★**, 25 Church St. (**📞 072/903-0319**), absolutely our favorite spot to quaff a rich blend (co-owner Judd Francis claims he doesn't really know what he's doing—he just loves the sensation of mixing the beans by hand) among a band of loyal regulars: *Wallpaper** called it one of *the* reasons to visit South Africa. After browsing through rooms stocked with rare- and beautiful-looking homeware, **Haas ★★★**, 67 Rose St. (**📞 021/422-4413**), in Bo-Kaap, also serves brilliant coffee (with creatively designed take-home sachets) roasted in-house after being sourced from relationship farms around the globe. Besides their own excellent blends, they also serve superexpensive kopi luwak (the world's rarest coffee; R80 per cup), famous for its unusual provenance (the beans are harvested from the droppings of the Asian palm civet).

stands out among some of the city's towering modern structures. An even grander example of 18th-century townhouse architecture is **Rust en Vreugd ★**, 78 Buitenkant St. (**📞 021/481-3800;** free admission; Mon–Fri 10am–5pm), built in 1778 and sporting a remodeled period garden. Part of the **William Fehr Collection,** donated by the super-conservationist, Dr. Fehr (1892–1968), is housed here; his collected historical paintings, etchings, and lithographs provide insight into the early colonists before they changed the face of the Cape completely.

Castle of Good Hope ★★   Built between 1666 and 1679, the castle—really a pentagonal fortress typical of the Dutch defense system adopted in the early 17th century—is the oldest surviving building in South Africa and marks the original shoreline. Once the hub of civilian and administrative life, the long-serving castle is still the regional headquarters of the South African Defence Force, though the most invasive force it's ever dealt with are the tourists ambling through its ramparts (and, in a wonderful exorcism of the ghosts of the past, more than 5,000 camp brides and other gay revelers at "The Wedding," a costume ball that MCQP hosted here in 2002). The fort combined local materials with European imports—note the slate paving stones, taken from Robben Island in the 17th century, and the bell at the entrance, cast in Amsterdam in 1697. It still looks much as it has for centuries.

Unless you're fascinated with colonial military might, you can skip the **Military Museum,** but the **William Fehr Collection** offers an entertaining way to brush up on your colonial history. Witness the crazy scene, for example, in Thomas Baines's spectacular painting *The Greatest Hunt in Africa,* which depicts the mindless slaughter of 30,000 animals in honor of the visiting Prince Alfred.

Corner of Buitenkant and Strand sts., opposite the Grand Parade. **📞 021/481-7223.** www.iziko.org.za. R28 adults (R20 on Sun), R12 children 5-16 (R5 on Sun). Mon–Sun 9am–4pm.

Gold of Africa Barbier-Mueller Museum ★★   Created in Mali, Senegal, Ghana, and Cote d'Ivoire during the 19th and 20th centuries, the gold artifacts here—purchased from the Barbier-Mueller Museum in Geneva for R11 million—represent a refreshing change from the chiefly Eurocentric designs available commercially, and the intention is to foster an appreciation for and pride in African design. The museum is housed in the historic **Martin Melck House,** constructed

On the slopes of Signal Hill—the arm that stretches out of Table Mountain to overlook the city and harbor—is the suburb of **Bo-Kaap.** Home to a section of the Cape's Muslim community (often referred to as the Cape Malays, despite the fact that only 1% of their forefathers, skilled slaves imported by the Dutch, were born in Malaysia), this is one of the city's oldest and most interesting areas. Its character is somewhat under threat, though, from property speculators and foreign investors keen to own a piece of the city's quaintest suburb. Narrow cobbled streets lead past colorful 19th-century Dutch and Georgian terraces and tiny mosques; try to visit at sunrise and sunset when the air is filled with the song of the muezzins in their minarets, calling the community to prayer.

The protected historic core of the Bo-Kaap ranges from Dorp to Strand streets, and between Buitengracht and Pentz streets. The best way to visit is on foot, with a local guide and, preferably, one who will expose you to more intimate aspects of the community and its culture, such as with **andulela experience ★★★** (*©* **021/790-2592;** www. andulela.com), on their half-day **Cape Malay Cooking Safari.** It's a great way to take in the entire area, with a detailed, lively account of its history, culture, architecture, and, of course, cuisine. You'll finish in a Bo-Kaap family home, where you'll get a hands-on cooking

lesson, learning to roll *rotis* and also fold and stuff *samosas,* then enjoy the three-course fruits of your labor (with a few more complicated dishes prepared by your delightful hostess).

If you're visiting the neighborhood on your own, consider starting at the **Bo-Kaap Museum,** 71 Wale St. (*©* **021/481-3939;** Mon–Sat 10am–5pm; R10 adults, children under 19 free), set in a house dating from the 1760s, and set out to give a basic idea of how a relatively wealthy 19th-century Cape Muslim family lived. Curatorship is lackluster, though, and proper explanation lacking. One block south of the museum, at Dorp Street, is **Auwal,** South Africa's oldest mosque, dating from 1795 and said to be where Afrikaans was first taught.

The charm of the Bo-Kaap provides some measure of what was lost when **District Six** was razed; across town from the Bo-Kaap, and clearly visible from any raised point, this vacant land is located on the city's southern border. Before bulldozers moved in to flatten the suburb in 1966, an estimated 60,000 people from every walk of life—musicians, traders, teachers, craftsmen, *skollies* (petty criminals), hookers, and pimps—had been living in one of the most creative communities, producing potent poets, jazz musicians, and writers. When the bulldozers finally moved out, all that was left were a few

in 1781 as the parsonage for the pretty Lutheran church, located next door. There are weekly courses, such as a Byzantine jewelry-making workshop where you'll make a gem-studded chain out of brass or copper. Targeting tourists, the attached Gold restaurant turns out tasty pan-African flavors and presents drumming lessons as part of the predinner entertainment.

Martin Melck House, 96 Strand St. *©* **021/405-1540.** www.goldofafrica.com. R35 adults, R25 children. Guided tour R60 adults, R40 children. Mon–Sat 9:30am–5pm; night tours 6–8pm.

Slave Lodge   Built in 1679 to house the Dutch East India Company's slaves, this building is just meters away from the very spot where people were once inspected by

churches and mosques (in a weird attempt at morality, religious buildings were exempt from the demolition order). The community was relocated piecemeal to the Cape Flats—a name that accurately describes both the geography and the psychology of the area. Many argue sensibly that Cape Town's ongoing gangster problems, spawned in the fragmented, angered, and powerless Cape Flats communities, are a direct resulted of the brutal destruction of District Six.

Renamed Zonnebloem (Sunflower), the so-called white area of District Six remained largely vacant, as even hardened capitalists spurned development in protest, and only the state-funded Cape Technicon was ever built on the land (purchased, incidentally, for R1). Restitution is underway, and it's hoped that the land can be returned to the original families, but the process has been weighed down by bureaucracy and infighting. Until then, the scar on the cityscape is a constant reminder; a poignant place to revisit this sad history is the **District Six Museum** ★★, 25A Buitenkant St. (✆ **021/466-7200;** Mon 9am–2pm, Tues–Sat 9am–4pm), a richly curated exposition of the life of the community.

Most organized tours of District Six are part of a trip to **Gugulethu** and **Langa,** two of Cape Town's oldest "townships," as black suburbs are still referred to, and kick off from either the Bo-Kaap or District Six museums, then head for a short visit to the townships to visit a crafts center, an "informal" home, a *shebeen* (traditional drinking house), and a housing project. A number of operators offer these but for a more specialized, thoughtful and personal approach, check out the bicycle tours (and others) offered by **Vamos** ★★★ (www.vamos.co.za) or those offered by **Camissa** ★★ (www.gocamissa.co.za), as well as the aforementioned **andulela experience** ★★★ and the excellent **Coffeebeans Routes** ★★★ (www.coffeebeansroutes.com). The latter two cooperate to offer a wide variety of eye-opening experiences, such as the innovative **Township Futures** tour, where you visit township revival zones and major transformation projects in order to get at look at a vision for Cape Town, circa 2030, with the townships at the center of the city (rather than at the margins). The extremely successful, interactive **Jazz Safari** is a fantastic nighttime trip into the heart of the pioneering music scene, much of which happens in the Cape Flats suburbs. You'll meet legends such as Mac McKenzie, the "king of Goema" (a fusion of jazz, samba, and traditional drumming), and engage with musicians in casual living room conversations, listening to impromptu recitals.

potential buyers before being sold off to the highest bidders. The museum is slated to become a world-class memory bank that honors the slaves who have featured in the colony's history. This museum's curators have been slow to develop a consistent body of work such as you'll find at Johannesburg's Apartheid Museum (p. 293)—it's good in parts, but feels incomplete. Watch, however, for temporary exhibitions, some of which are excellent, and intended to draw attention to issues relevant to S.A.'s turbulent history.

Cnr. Adderley and Wale sts. ✆ **021/460-8242.** www.iziko.org.za. R20 adults, children under 19 free. Mon–Sat 10am–5pm.

South African Jewish Museum ★ Opened by Nelson Mandela in 2000, this museum—like the nearby District Six Museum—celebrates the history of a particular South African community. It is architecturally leagues ahead, a contemporary arena gallery grafted onto Cape Town's original Old Synagogue (South Africa's first, consecrated in 1863). It's creatively curated, and there are a few stirring moments—a film in which Mandela talks respectfully about the Jewish community is particularly poignant, as are sound bites by Jews discussing their views on apartheid. Downstairs, reached via a fantastic spiral staircase, is a digital repository of Jewish identity and family trees—useful if you'd like to trace your own roots or connections here. Although the earliest records of Jewish settlers date from 1669, most of South Africa's Jewish immigrant community arrived after 1880 from the Baltic region, especially Lithuania; their roots are memorialized through a miniature version of a *shtetl* (Lithuanian village), reproduced here in exacting detail. It won't appeal to everyone, but this is the city's most meticulously curated museum.

88 Hatfield St., Gardens. ℂ **021/465-1546.** www.sajewishmuseum.co.za. R15 adults, children under 16 free. Sun–Thurs 10am–5pm; Fri 10am–2pm. Closed on Jewish holidays.

South African Museum & Planetarium In addition to the vast, often macabre taxidermy project, there's a fairly extensive shark and whale section, which includes a four-story whale well, hung with two massive whale skeletons. Unless dinosaurs are your thing, the most significant exhibits are those documenting the abundance of tribal and indigenous culture that makes up the local social fabric. Though the ethnographic displays don't compare with the engaging work being done at the ultra-contemporary Origins Centre in Johannesburg, they offer some insight into the role and nature of San trance dancing and rock art. The Planetarium has a varied program of shows, including some for children.

25 Queen Victoria St. Museum: ℂ **021/481-3800.** R20 adults, children under 18 free. Planetarium: ℂ **021/481-3900.** www.iziko.org.za. R25 adults, R10 children. Daily 10am–5pm.

South African National Gallery ★★★ This small gallery, started with an initial donation by Victorian landlord Sir Thomas Butterworth Bayley, has room to exhibit only a fraction of its collection of more than 8,000 artworks. Despite a chronic lack of funding it is considered by many to be the country's premier art museum, with a huge collection of artworks reflecting South Africa's turbulent and painful history. There's been a marked shift toward guest curatorship, which means there's always something new and interesting on the go. Dispelling the gallery's image as a highbrow enclave, 2011 saw the first-ever major showing of the work of internationally acclaimed Cape Town–based artist Vladimir Tretchikoff, widely known for his overtly kitsch canvases. Recent years have also seen the gallery collecting works neglected by other national institutions, including rare examples of what used to be considered crafts, such as Ndebele beadwork and *knobkierries* (fighting sticks).

Government Ave., Company's Gardens. ℂ **021/481-3970.** R20 adults, children under 18 free. Daily 10am–5pm.

Attractions in & Around the Waterfront

Redevelopment of this historic core started in the early 1990s, and within a few years, the Victoria & Alfred Waterfront (www.waterfront.co.za) had been rated as the best of its kind, successfully integrating a top tourist attraction with southern Africa's principal passenger-and-freight harbor. Views of Table Mountain and the working harbor, as well as numerous restored national monuments and a wide array of

Many of the Waterfront activities have been designed with children in mind, making it Cape Town's foremost family destination after the beach and Kirstenbosch. The top attraction here is the **Two Oceans Aquarium.** Face painting, drawing, and puzzles are on offer in the aquarium's Alpha Activity center, and staff often arranges sleepovers and excursions to interesting and educational locations for ages 8 to 12. Call ☎ **021/418-3823** to find out what's on. Virtually opposite is the **Scratch Patch,** where kids literally scratch through mounds of semiprecious stones, selecting their own "jewels," after which they may want to play a round of crazy golf. Afterward, you may want to hop aboard the **Jolly Roger Pirate Boat** (☎ **021/421-0909**), the only authentic pirate ship in the country, which departs from the Waterfront and goes on an assortment of pirate-themed jaunts along the coast—a good opportunity for youngsters to play with other children.

Catch the kiddies' **Blue Train** in nearby Mouille Point (☎ **021/434-8537;** Mon–Fri 3–5pm, Sat–Sun 11–5pm); next door is an outdoor putt-putt (crazy golf) course. In town, the noon **Planetarium** show is held every Saturday and Sunday, where they attempt to answer such simple astronomy questions as "Why is the sky blue?" and "Is the sun round?" To get there, take a stroll through the **Company's Gardens** (enter either from Orange St., opposite the Mount Nelson, or from the top-end of Adderley St., next to St George's Cathedral), armed with a bag of nuts to feed the almost-tame (but not!) squirrels. Afterward, take **high tea at the Mount**

Nelson (p. 99), or head for **Deer Park Café,** which opens onto a large public play park shaded by stately trees. Or book a table at **Café Paradiso ★★** (p. 102) during one of its "happy hours," designed with parents in mind—children are read stories and spend time in the kitchen baking and preparing pizzas. End the day by ascending **Table Mountain** in the rotating cable car—a thrill for kids, with rewarding views for adults. Pack a picnic as well as sunblock, hats, and a jacket, in case the weather turns.

An absolute must is to chill out with a picnic next to a burbling stream or under a huge tree at **Kirstenbosch Gardens,** or—if you don't want the hassle of shopping at a deli—head for the shady oaks at **Groot Constantia,** where Jonkershuis restaurant supplies the goodies. If you're doing the peninsula tour you'll have to make time to stop for a dip at **Boulders,** where the temperature is slightly warmer, tidal pools are safe, and the penguins are genuinely entertaining. Visit the **Warrior Toy Museum** (☎ **021/786-1395**), on Georges Street, in Simons Town, on your way, then go for a tame game drive in Cape Point. **Imhoff Farm** (☎ **021/783-4545**), in Kommetjie, offers country-style refreshments, camel rides, horseback riding, crafts shops for kids, and a snake and nature park to entertain, but parents looking for a great meal while the kids play should push onto Noordhoek to dine at either Café Roux or The Foodbarn. When in Hout Bay catch a cruise to **Seal Island,** departing from Hout Bay Harbour. And when all else fails, there's always the beach.

entertainment options, attract an estimated 20 million visitors a year. The smells of diesel and fish mingle with the aromas wafting from pavement bistros, tugboats mingle with catamarans, and tourists mingle with, well, tourists. (If you're seeking tattooed sailors and ladies of dubious repute, you'd be better off taking a drive down to Duncan Dock, where the large working ships pull in.)

A rather sanitized place, the shopping precinct is concentrated in the Victoria Wharf Mall, which on its own contains over **500 stores** (open until 9pm daily) and a choice of more than **80 eateries,** as well as **mainstream-movie screens** (Nu Metro; ℭ **021/419-9700**) and a smaller **art-movie cinema complex** (Cinema Nouveau; ℭ **0861/300-444**). Try to avoid getting stuck within the V&A buildings too long—the waterside action between Quay 5 and Pierhead Jetty is far more appealing, and you get splendid mountain vistas, to boot.

If you do only two things on the Waterfront, you should book a **boat trip,** preferably at sunset, and visit the **Two Oceans Aquarium** (see below). Most cruises (see "Organized Cruises & Tours," earlier in this chapter) take off from Quay 5. From June to November, you can also book a **whale-watching** cruise (p. 129).

Robben Island Museum ✋   To limit access to the delicate ecosystem of this infamous island, only government-run tours are allowed to land on this World Heritage Site, for many years a source of controversy and mismanagement (including ongoing scandals of disappearing funds) yet still one of the most popular attractions in the city. Visitors are transported via a large catamaran that takes approximately 25 minutes; views of Table Mountain and Cape Town as you pull out of the harbor are fantastic—arrive first to ensure you have a top-deck, open-air seat. Unfortunately, the tour of the island itself is underwhelming; passengers are packed like sardines in a bus, and chances are, you'll be on the receiving end of an unexciting narrative that does little to evoke empathy for the people who suffered here. The 45-minute bus tour provides passing glimpses of the **lepers' church and graveyard;** PAC leader **Robert Sobukwe's house,** where he was imprisoned; the **warden's village,** a collection of houses and a school that seem stuck in some period movie; the **lighthouse; World War II fortifications;** and colonies of African penguins. At one point, you'll be stationed beside the **lime quarry,** once worked by political prisoners (take sunglasses—the brightness ruined many inmates' and wardens' eyes). Mercifully, you're let off the bus to admire the view of Cape Town across the water—by far the best part of the bus ride. The tour's real highlight, though, comes right at the end, when an ex–political prisoner takes you through the "maximum security" facility, where you can view the tiny cell in which Mandela slept for 18 of his 27 years of imprisonment ★★★. Unfortunately, this does not really make up for a 3½-hour tour that feels terribly cloying and formulaic. Many visitors leave feeling thoroughly ripped off; the best feedback almost certainly refers to a VIP tour experience.

Tickets and departure from the Nelson Mandela Gateway at the Clock Tower terminal on Quay 5. ℭ **021/413-4220.** Advance bookings: www.robben-island.org.za. R220 adults, R110 children under 18. Ferries depart daily at 9am, 11am, and 1pm. Tours may be increased to include sunset tours in summer, and decreased because of inclement weather—call ahead. Advance bookings ((ℭ 021/413-4233) are highly recommended and essential during the busy summer months; you can book online through the website, but be sure to do this well in advance, and note that ticket dates and times are not transferable.

Two Oceans Aquarium ★★★ ☺   This is by no means the biggest but it is one of the best in the world, and by far the most exciting attraction at the Waterfront itself. From the brightly hued fish found on coral reefs to exhilarating encounters with ragged tooth sharks, more than 3,000 live specimens are literally inches from your nose. Besides the Indian and Atlantic underwater tanks displaying the bizarre and beautiful, there are a number of well-simulated environments, including tidal pools, a river ecosystem, and the magnificent Kelp Forest tank. The walk through the aquarium (30–90 min., depending on how long you linger) ends with a pretty cool display on deep-sea predators. There are child-height window benches throughout and a "touch pool" where kids can touch kelp, shells, and anemones. On weekends, kids are entertained in the Alpha Activity center with face painting and puppet shows. The Penguin Encounter is a personal (two people per slot) interaction with the aquarium's rockhoppers; it happens only on Saturdays from 11am. Predators are fed at 3pm daily (the sharks on Sun), but if you have a diving license, you can jump into the tank and swim with the shark—no cage, no need to fear, as raggies are considered nonaggressive (although you might not think so, judging by the bite marks on some of the smaller fish).

Btw. New Basin and Dock Rd. ✆ **021/418-3823.** www.aquarium.co.za. R100 adults, R48 children 4-13, R75 children 14-17. Daily 9:30am-6pm. Penguin Encounter R350 adult, R300 children 8-17. Shark diving R595 including equipment.

Farther Afield: Southern Suburbs & Constantia

Groot Constantia is a good place to start your exploration of what is not only the city's oldest and closest Winelands, but the densest award-winning terroir and a manageable area comprising just eight wineries, the most famous being **Groot Constantia, Klein Constantia, Buitenverwachting, Uitsig,** and **Steenberg** (though wine lovers note: **Eagles Nest** is worth a visit for its superlative boutique wines). The big estates all feature Cape Dutch homesteads, oaks, and acres of vineyards, and they're only about 30 minutes from town, ideal if you don't have time to venture into the surrounding Winelands. If you're looking for an ideal luncheon venue, see "Where to Eat," earlier in this chapter.

Groot Constantia ★★★ Groot Constantia was established in 1685 by Simon van der Stel, then governor of the Cape, who reputedly named it after his daughter Constancia and planted the Cape's first vines. A century later, the Cloete family put Constantia on the international map with a dessert wine that became the favored tipple of the likes of Napoleon, Bismarck, King Louis Philippe of France, and Jane Austen. An outbreak of phylloxera in the 1860s bankrupted the family, however, and the land lay fallow until 1975, when substantial replanting began. Today Groot Constantia is more known for its reds, but is essentially a must-see stop for hundreds of tourists, most of them not wine lovers. However, unless you've been unfortunate enough to arrive along with a couple of buses, it is large and gracious enough to still provide a lovely experience: In addition to tasting the wines, you can visit a small museum showing the history of the manor, as well as the beautiful Cape Dutch house itself, furnished in beautiful late-18th-century Cape Dutch furniture. Behind the house are the old cellars, originally designed by French architect Louis Thibault; note the celebrated pediment sculpted by Anton Anreith in 1791. The cellars also contain an interesting **wine museum.** A cozy, pleasant restaurant within the thick walls of the original homestead complex (with courtyard tables), **Jonkershuis** (✆ **021/794-6255**), is well worth your money (but you should book if you can); nearby **Simons** (✆ **021/794-1143**)—surrounded by vineyards and lawns—is a more modern bistro, where the locals can be found quaffing from the extensive wine list and marveling at the pinkness of the seared tuna or lamb.

Groot Constantia Rd., Constantia (from the M3, take the Constantia turnoff; follow the GROOT CONSTANTIA signs). Estate: ✆ **021/795-5128.** www.grootconstantia.co.za. Cellar tour and wine tasting R35 adults, R5 scholars (tour only). Museum: ✆ **021/795-5140.** www.iziko.org.za. R20 adults, children under 19 free. Daily 10am-5pm.

A PENINSULA DRIVE ★★★

START:	**Take the M3 out of town; this follows the eastern flank of the mountain, providing access to the southern suburbs.**
FINISH:	**Kloof Nek roundabout in town.**
TIME:	**The full tour will take at least 1 full day.**

Not all the sites listed below are must-sees; personal interest should shape your itinerary. That said, get an early start, and make an effort to fit Kirstenbosch and Groot Constantia into the morning, leaving Cape Point for the afternoon and Chapman's Peak Drive for the evening. Because this is a circular route, it can also be done in reverse, but the idea is to be back on the Atlantic seaboard at sunset. Should Chapman's Peak be closed (it sometimes is due to rockfalls), return from Cape Point via Ou Kaapse Weg and Silvermine Nature Reserve, rejoining the M4, this time north. Then head through Constantia (past the Alphen Hotel) over Constantia Neck and descend into Hout Bay. Drive the Atlantic seaboard back to Cape Town, passing the coastal suburbs of Llundudno, Bakoven, and Camps Bay as the sun sets.

As you approach the Groote Schuur Hospital on your left, scene of the world's first heart transplant, look for the wildebeest and mountain zebras grazing on the slopes of the mountain. Art lovers should consider taking the Mowbray turnoff to the:

1 Irma Stern Museum

Stern, a follower of the German expressionist movement—and acknowledged as one of South Africa's best 20th-century artists—was also an avid collector of Iberian, African, and Oriental artifacts. The museum, on Cecil Road (© **021/685-5686;** Tues–Sat 10am–5pm; R10), also exhibits new talents.

Back on the M3, still traveling south, you will pass Mostert's Mill on your left, another reminder of the Cape's Dutch past, and look out for left-hand turn to:

2 Rhodes Memorial

You can see the imposing memorial high up on the slopes on your right (see "Table Mountain National Park," earlier in this chapter); both it and the restaurant behind the memorial have awesome views. Back on the M3, you will pass a series of imposing ivy-clad buildings, which comprise the **University of Cape Town,** built on land donated by Rhodes. If you're interested in colonial architecture, you can make an appointment to visit **Groote Schuur,** also donated by Rhodes, and designed by Herbert Baker, "the architect of the Empire," and up until the end of Mandela's term, the official government residence; call © **021/686-9100.**

From here, the suburbs become increasingly upmarket. Take the turnoff right to:

3 Kirstenbosch National Botanical Gardens

Consider visiting Kirstenbosch (you'll need at least an hour, preferably more) before heading back to the M3 and wending your way through the suburbs of Bishop's Court and Wynberg for Constantia. See "Table Mountain National Park," earlier in this chapter.

If you've decided against Kirstenbosch, or made it a quick trip, you may have time along the way to visit the:

Peninsula Driving Tour

Legend:
- ★ Start here
- Take a Break
- Lighthouse
- Beach
- Surfing
- ▲ Lookout
- ✈ Airport
- -- Driving Route
- --- Alternate Return Route
- .... Trail

1 Mowbray turnoff/
   Irma Stern Museum
   & Mostert's Mill
2 Rhodes Memorial
3 Kirstenbosch National
   Botanical Gardens
4 Groot Constantia Estate
5 Casa Labia
6 Kalk Bay
7 Simon's Town
8 Boulders Beach
9 Cape of Good Hope
   Nature Reserve
   (entrance)
10 Chapman's Peak Drive
11 Hout Bay
12 Victoria Road
13 Signal Hill

4 Groot Constantia Estate

You can visit the 17th-century manor house and wine museum, and possibly try a wine tasting (see above). Alternatively, set aside a full afternoon to travel the full Constantia Wine Route, visiting at least three estates (don't miss Klein Constantia).

Keep traveling south on the M3 until it runs into a T-junction, then turn left to the next T-junction, where you join the M4; turn right and look for Boyes Drive and the gorgeous elevated views of False Bay. This short detour of the coastal route is often less congested than the narrow road (currently plagued by eternal roadworks) that runs through the coastal suburbs of Muizenberg, St James, and Kalk Bay, though you'll miss much of the interesting turn-of-the-20th-century architecture that spawned the city's first Millionaire's Mile. If this latter interests you, try to time your visit to coincide with lunch at:

5 Casia Labia

Built in the Venetian style, **Casia Labia,** Main Road, Muizenberg (© **021/788-4106** or 021/481-3800), was the sumptuous home of the Count and Countess Labia, and is a fabulous example of the vacation homes built by Cape Town's glam society in the last century, when False Bay was the favored seaboard of wealthy gold barons. It was graciously transformed into a lovely restaurant and (upstairs) art gallery in 2010, and is now amongst the loveliest places anywhere along this stretch of coast to stop off for a bite to eat or to buy excellent arts and crafts.

Another popular stop along this tight coastal road cutting between Muizenberg and Kalk Bay, is the St James tidal pool beach (right near the St James train station; look for the sign), with its trademark bathing boxes painted in different colors. Continue on Main Road to the quaint fishing village of Kalk Bay, which has a number of good places to eat and shops to explore.

6 Kalk Bay

Whether you've taken Muizenberg's main road or Boyes Drive, stop in at quaint **Kalk Bay** to browse the proliferation of shops and galleries. If you're ready to break for lunch, see "Where to Eat," earlier in this chapter.

The drive then resumes south along the M4 to Fish Hoek (push straight through) and the naval village of:

7 Simon's Town

This vies with Kalk Bay as the most charming of the False Bay towns, lined with double-story Victorian buildings. If you feel like lingering, take a 40-minute cruise around the bay (© **021/786-2136**). For more details on what the town has to offer, visit the **Simon's Town Tourism Bureau,** also on Court Road (© **021/786-8440**).

If you're hot and bothered, don a bathing suit and join the penguins at nearby:

8 Boulders Beach

View the large breeding colony of jackass (African) penguins that settled here in the early 1980s—to the horror of residents, who now have to deal with the attendant coachloads of tourists.

From Simons Town, it's 15 minutes to the entrance of the:

9 Cape of Good Hope Nature Reserve

Once inside, take Circular Drive to spot game, or head for one of the usually deserted beaches. If you're pressed for time, head straight for Cape Point (see "Table Mountain National Park," earlier in this chapter). From the nature reserve, it's a relatively straightforward and spectacular drive back to town (if Chapman's Peak is open; if not, see above). Take the M65 left out of the reserve past the **Cape Point Ostrich Farm** (© 021/780-9294; daily 9:30am–5:30pm; tours are R45), and travel through the pretty coastal town of **Scarborough** (where there's a lovely place to stay overnight, by the way; see p. 92), the aptly named **Misty Cliffs,** and **Kommetjie** (also with some fabulous beachfront accommodations options) to **Noordhoek.**

Noordhoek has a famously beautiful beach, the aptly named Long Beach (make sure you don't walk it with valuables) as well as two excellent restaurants (See "Where to Eat," earlier in this chapter), but if you're pressed for time, follow the signs and head north to ascend the exhilarating:

10 Chapman's Peak Drive

Built between 1915 and 1922, this winding 10km (6¼-mile) drive must rate as one of the world's best, with cliffs plunging straight into the ocean, dwarfing the vehicles snaking along its side. Not surprisingly, hundreds of international car commercials have been shot here. Note that this opened as a toll road in 2003 (count on paying around R30), but closes to traffic during hazardous weather or rockfall situations; look for signs alerting you to any closure, or ask your host to find out before you set off.

From Chapman's Peak, you descend into:

11 Hout Bay

Here you could either stop for the most delicious calamari, on the veranda at the **Chapman's Peak Hotel,** or head for the harbor and book a cruise to view the seal colony and seabird sanctuary on **Duiker Island** (see "Organized Cruises & Tours," earlier in this chapter).

From Hout Bay, you can now take the coast-hugging:

12 Victoria Road (or M6)

Take this road to Camps Bay—with any luck, it will coincide with sunset, or you'll have a moon to guide you.

Follow the M6 through Camps Bay and turn right at the KLOOF NEK ROUNDHOUSE sign to snake up the mountain to the Kloof Nek roundabout and take the turnoff to:

13 Signal Hill

The views from the hill are breathtaking, particularly at night, when the twinkling city lies spread before you.

STAYING ACTIVE

For one-stop adrenaline activity shopping, contact **Downhill Adventures** (© 021/422-0388; www.downhilladventures.com), which offers everything from its own surf school to helicopter rides.

Fight Club Comes to Woodstock

Getting and staying physically fit is important to many Capetonians, and you'll see them walking, running, and cycling, while gyms tend to fill up during peak hours. But the place to be for a specialized workout is **The Armoury Boxing Club ★★★**, Buchanan Square in Woodstock. You can sign up for one-on-one boxing training (often under the tutorship of a professional), or join sweat-inducing classes (from kettle bells to TRX suspension training) that are the antithesis if the average gym experience. The set-up is attention grabbing, too, with vintage upholstery, exposed brick, black-and-white tiled floors, a library, cool boxing-related artwork, and chandeliers. It also offers an arena for amateur white-collar boxers from the gym to engage in real physical bouts in front of a paying crowd. There are around three or four **Fight Night ★★★** events each year, usually with opponents who fly down from Johannesburg. With bars, a DJ, an emcee, ring girls, and a tremendous crowd of in-the-know Capetonians, it makes for a riveting night out (always on a Fri), often a starting point for more after dark adventures on the town. Call ✆ **021/461-9141** or visit www.armouryboxing.com.

ABSEILING ★★★   Abseil Africa (✆ **021/424-4760;** www.abseilafrica.co.za) will throw you 100m (328 ft.) off Table Mountain—attached to a rope, of course (R595, excluding cable car fees; R750 hike and abseil combo). But their best trip is **Kamikaze Kanyon ★★★**, a day's *kloofing* (scrambling down a river gorge) in a nature reserve, ending with a 65m (213-ft.) waterfall abseil (R795).

BOATING   See "Organized Cruises & Tours," earlier in this chapter.

CANOEING/KAYAKING   Between his two stores, **PaddleYak** and **Real Cape Adventures** (✆ **021/790-5611** or 082/556-2520; www.seakayak.co.za), Johan Loots covers almost every sea-kayaking route on the western and southern coasts and caters to all levels of ability.

FISHING   **Big Blue Fishing Charters** (✆ **021/786-5667**) operates on a 8.5m (28-ft.) catamaran and offers inshore and offshore fishing—they have the highest catch rate in Simons Town. You can also charter a deep-sea fishing trip with **Cape Sea Safaris** (www.capeseasafaris.com).

GOLFING   The **Royal Cape** (✆ **021/761-6551**) has hosted the South African Open many times. **Milnerton Golf Club ★** (✆ **021/552-1047;** www.milnerton golf.co.za) is a true links course, with magnificent views of Table Mountain; best avoided when the wind is blowing. **Clovelly** (✆ **021/784-2100**), near Fish Hoek, is a tight course requiring some precision. In Constantia, the Peter Matkovich-designed **Steenberg ★★** (✆ **021/715-0227**) is considered the top course in the city, but some of the nearby Winelands options are even better (see chapter 5).

HIKING & CLIMBING   See "Table Mountain," earlier in this chapter. For hikes (or climbs) farther afield, contact Ross Suter at **High Adventure** (✆ **021/689-1234;** www.highadventure.co.za).

HORSEBACK RIDING   Take an early morning or sunset ride on spectacular Long Beach, Noordhoek, by contacting **Sleepy Hollow** (✆ **021/789-2341**).

KITE-SURFING ★★★   Cape Town is considered one of the world's best kite-surfing destinations. For lessons and rentals, contact the **Cabrinha Kiteboarding**

School (© 021/556-1729; www.cabrinha.co.za; R495 per 2-hr. lesson or R1,200 full-day), or visit their shop at Eden On The Bay Shopping Center, Big Bay (at Sir Baird and Otto Du Plessis, Bloubergstrand). Or head north to Langebaan Lagoon (see chapter 5).

MOUNTAIN BIKING   There are a number of trails on Table Mountain, Cape Point, but the Tokai Forest network and Constantiaberg trails are the best. Contact **Day Trippers** (© 021/511-4766) for guided rides (R495 half-day).

PARAGLIDING ★★★   An unparalleled way to see Cape Town is while soaring weightlessly on the thermals above the city. The most reliable starting point is Signal Hill, but bear in mind that if the wind doesn't cooperate, you can't fly, so it's best to call at the start of your holiday and provide a mobile number where you can be reached on short notice when conditions are right. This is an exhilarating trip; no prior experience is necessary for the carefree tandem session (R950; 10–25 min.). Contact Barry or Candice at **Birdmen** (© 082/658-6710; www.birdmen.co.za).

SANDBOARDING   South Africa's answer to snowboarding takes place on the tallest dunes all around the Cape. Contact **Downhill Adventures** (R695 full-day).

SHARK-CAGE DIVING ★★★   Most Gansbaai/Hermanus (see chapter 5) shark-cage diving companies will do Cape Town hotel pick-ups, though some commence as early as 3:45am. If you're in or near Simon's Town you can join **African Shark Eco Charters** (© 021/785-1947; www.ultimate-animals; R1,450–R1,750 per person), which claims to be eco-sensitive and is accredited by Fair Trade in Tourism; they allow only two people in a cage at a time and have high success with sightings of sharks breaching in False Bay. You may want to consider taking sea-sickness medication and definitely take warm clothing (water is icy and the onboard breeze fresh).

SKYDIVING ★★★   Free-fall for up to 30 seconds, attached to an experienced instructor. **Skydive Cape Town** (© 082/800-6290; www.skydivecapetown.za.net) offers tandem dives (R1,500) 20 minutes north of the city, some 3,600m (11,808 ft.) above Melkbosstrand. Or jump solo by undertaking a basic static line course; R900 includes the theoretical and practical training, as well as the first exhilarating jump.

SURFING ★★★   For the daily surf report, call © 082/234-6370. The beaches off Kalk Bay reef and Noordhoek are considered hot spots, but Muizenberg and Big Bay, at Blouberg (take R27, Marine Dr., off the N1), are good for beginners. **Gary's Surf School** (© 021/788-9839; www.garysurf.com) in Muizenberg is considered one of the best places to learn (R500 per 2-hr. lesson with full-day equipment use).

WHALE-WATCHING   For the city's best whale-watching, drive along the False Bay coast, or contact Evan at **Atlantic Adventures** (© 083/680-2768; R600 per person), which operates trips out of the Waterfront. The **Waterfront Boat Company** (© 021/418-5806; www.waterfrontboats.co.za; R500 for 3–4 hr.) also leaves from there. For sighting information, call the **Whale Hot Line** (© 083/910-1028).

SHOPPING

You'll find a large selection of shops and hundreds of street hawkers catering to the African arts-and-crafts market, but very little of it is produced in South Africa. Beadwork, however, is a local tradition; a variety is for sale at the tourism bureau, also the place to pick up an *Arts & Crafts Map*. But Cape Town shopping offers a great deal more than naive wooden carvings and beaded trinkets. Sophisticated Eurocentric products with superb local twists are finding their way into design-savvy shops all over the world; from minimalist handbags made with patterned Nguni hides to gorgeous lamps made with polished horn, you'll find them here, particularly in the De Waterkant area, for far less. For more listings, page through the annual *Time Out Cape Town for Visitors,* available in the city's bookstores. And remember you are entitled to a 14% VAT refund before you leave.

Serious shoppers who want the lowdown on the city's hottest consumer venues should contact Sandra Fairfax of **Blue Buyou** ★★★ (✆ **083/293-6555** or 021/762-5689; www.bluebuyou.co.za) for one of her highly personalized **shopping tours.** She'll pick you up and put together a shopping and browsing itinerary that takes into account your tastes and interests.

Great Shopping Areas

CITY CENTER

In the heart of the city center, historical **Greenmarket Square** (Mon–Sat 9am–4pm) has become little more than a tourist trap (most of the stalls are owned by the same wholesaler, and goods here have little to do with local crafters). However, the atmosphere is pleasant (staffed largely by charming albeit foreign Africans, and surrounded by some of the loveliest buildings in Cape Town), then stroll across to nearby **Church Street,** where the pedestrianized cobbled walkway that links to Long Street attracts casual traders dealing in antiques, hand-fashioned leather jewelry, and T-shirts emblazoned with logo-style township names. Check out **African Image,** on the corner of Church and Burg (see below); the **Collector,** 52 Church St. (✆ **021/423-1483**), trading in the expensive end of what they term "tribal" artifacts and antiques; and the **Cape Gallery,** 60 Church St. (✆ **021/423-5309**), selling fine artworks with an emphasis on plant, animal, and birdlife. Opposite, the **Association for Visual Arts,** 35 Church St. (✆ **021/424-7436**), is an important nonprofit art gallery, while **Imagenius** (see below), just beyond Café Mozart (see "Take a Break," below) is the heavyweight specialist in desirable modern African *objets,* and plenty else besides.

Where Church meets Long, turn right and head for the **Pan African Market,** probably the best place to pick up African crafts (albeit mostly "mass carved") in Cape Town (see "Best Buys," below). It's a total contrast to the swanky interior of **Tribal Trends,** 72–74 Long St. (✆ **021/423-8008**), which showcases an audacious (but pricey) selection of great African-inspired design.

A Harmonious Meal Idea

There are plenty of places to eat around Greenmarket Square, but the best little daytime eatery is quirky little **Café Mozart** ★, which spills onto pedestrian Church St. (✆ **021/424-3774**): Beautiful breakfasts (stacked pancakes with crème fraîche and honey; eggs with salmon and spinach on a fresh croissant), generous sandwiches (try their open babotie sandwich on whole wheat molasses bread), and a wonderful choice of comforting lunch dishes, including burgers, chicken and mushroom pie, and a rich, flavorful melanzane parmigiano. The atmosphere is marvelously laid back, and they serve excellent teas, coffees (from nearby Deluxe Coffeeworks; see "Cape Town's Caffeine Fix," p. 117), and fresh-baked cakes.

Although Exclusives is probably the best-stocked bookstore in the Waterfront, the best place to browse for quality reads (no rubbish stocked) is **The Book Lounge ★★★**, 71 Roeland St. (✆ **021/462-2425**), with seating for bookworms and a cafe on the downstairs level. It's also where you can catch regular literary events (held almost every Tues, Wed, and Thurs, but occasionally on other nights, too, usually commencing 5:30 or 6pm); these include book launches and discussions involving some of the biggest names in South African literature and publishing. Pick up a program of forthcoming events in-store.

From Church Street head down **Long Street** toward the mountain; in many ways the city's most interesting street—lined with Victorian buildings, Long Street houses, antiques shops, galleries, gun shops, porn outlets, hostels, cafes, bars, a church or two, and eventually a Turkish bathhouse (though **Bree Street**, running parallel, is starting to give it a good run for its money). Be on the lookout for **210Long**, a small, sustainable shopping "mall" at 210 Long St., where you'll find a small selection of good South African stores; **Gravy** sells T-shirts by local designer Craig Native (under the Electric Zulu label), which make perfect gifts for younger friends back home. On the other side of the road is **Still Life,** stocked with cool homeware items. Continue up Long and cross onto **Kloof Street:** it's definitely worth looking at the intriguing local homeware and design parody items displayed at all-white **O.live** (next to the Chinese eatery), where you'll fall under the spell of the dreamlike soundtrack; next door is **laLesso,** a boutique selling ladies' exotic garments made from Kenyan fabrics—the Swahili logos on the dresses are good wishes; the innovative label has already found its way to Tokyo, London, Paris, Barcelona, and New York.

DE WATERKANT

With lovely cobbled streets, two lively dining squares (both with good protection when the wind is up), and loads of excellent shops and cafes, this gentrified area has developed into one of the most exciting shopping precincts in town. There are two distinct "Cape Quarter" shopping centers to explore, plus plenty of shops at street level. You could start anywhere, but Jarvis and Waterkant streets are proven stomping grounds. Whatever you do, don't miss **Africa Nova** or **Fibre Designs** (details below). If you're interested in art, check out **VEO Gallery,** 8 Jarvis St. (✆ **021/421-3278**), and **Lisa King Gallery,** Shop B14, Cape Quarter (✆ **021/421-3738**). Already referred to as the South African Abercrombie & Finch, the new **Kingsley Heath,** 117 Waterkant St. (✆ **021/421-0881**) offers a stylish look for adventures in the African bush. The sophisticated clothing and fashion accessories, including leather jewelry and cowhide shoes are a welcome preshop safari stop.

WATERFRONT

Shopping here is a far less satisfying experience than in the bustling streets of town or the gentrified cobbled streets of De Waterkant; at the end of the day, Victoria Wharf is simply a glam mall with a famous and fabulous location. There are, however, a few gems, such as **Out of Africa** (adjacent to **Exclusive Books,** which we have to grudgingly admit is a good bookstore with a huge selection albeit a chain), for a fantastic, albeit pricey, range of items from all over the continent. And if you're

4

THE MOTHER CITY: CAPE TOWN & THE PENINSULA

Shopping

THE OLD biscuit MILL

Every Saturday morning, a selection of the city's hippest congregate at **The Old Biscuit Mill ★★★**, 375 Albert Rd., Woodstock, a warehouse space that's been cleverly transformed to make way for the weekly **Neighbourgoods Market ★★★** (✆ 021/462-6361; Sat), now a defining Cape Town event, packed tables groaning under organic produce and great on-site prepared meals. Most are here for the vibe and good times (it quickly turns into a bit of a party, with wine, mixed drinks, and artisanal beers flowing from very early), but the food moves quickly—either wolfed down a the long tables here or taken home, with upcoming artisans waiting patiently in the wings as they move up the impossibly long waiting list for a stand here. There's now also a separate section where locally produced clothing (a great kids section), jewelry, and other accessories are sold, and this is also not to be missed. Even when the market isn't on, it's worth a visit: Refurbished warehouses and factory spaces are now filled with boutiques and artisanal shops—there's a place selling only furniture made form recycled wood, and **Oded's Kitchen ★★**

(✆ 084/804-0748) is a marvelous emporium that showcases Oded Schwartz's Israeli pickling talent—he offers cooking classes, too. It's worth your while to check out some of the permanent shops opposite the market: **Imiso Ceramics ★★** (✆ 021/447-7668) is owned by three young black ceramicists whose work is among the most exciting in the country; their scarified vases, bowls, and plates are great to use or display. In fact you could do all your gift shopping here, or at nearby **Clementina**, although you'll also want to pop into **Quirky Me** (which shares space with **Abode**), especially if your taste stretches to slightly offbeat design and decor items. And tucked away in the back, one of the city's most serious coffee roasters, **Espresso Lab Microroasters ★★** (✆ 021/447-0845), will help fight off any shopping exhaustion. Done out like a laboratory—with white tiles and a sexy industrial vibe—even their package labeling mimics the symbols on a chemist's elemental chart. It's a place for serious coffee connoisseurs, although they do do a very good cappuccino. And, then, of course, there's **The Test Kitchen** (p. 102).

looking for a dress or shirt that will really make heads turn—we're talking proper African designer wear—head straight upstairs for **Sun Goddess** (✆ 021/421-7620). Outside the shopping center, in the old offices of the Port Captain (on the way to the Clock Tower), is the truly excellent selection of sculptures, jewelry, tableware, textiles, ceramics, and furniture at the **African Trading Post,** Pierhead, Dock Road (✆ 021/419-5364); spread over three stories, this is worth a visit even if you're not buying. **Woolworths** is a national chain that offers a wide selection of average to good clothing (including sandals, bathing costumes, linen tops, and so on), and the best quality national food retailer. Wine selection is pretty poor though.

WOODSTOCK & SOUTHERN SUBURBS

You probably won't need to go beyond the Old Biscuit Mill (see box below), but farther south, in Newlands, there's plenty of creative flair (as well as opportunities to join pottery workshops, watch ironmongers, and grab a bite) at the **Montebello Design Centre ★★★**, 31 Newlands Ave. (✆ 021/685-6445), where you could spend anywhere between an hour and an afternoon browsing the shops.

Best Buys

SOUVENIRS, GIFTS & MEMORABILIA FROM AFRICA

African Image   This store offers a well-chosen selection of authentic crafts and tribal art ranging from headrests and baskets to beadwork and cloth. 52 Burg St. ℰ **021/423-8385.**

Africa Nova ★★★   Arguably the best of its kind, this large selection of contemporary handmade African goods has been chosen by someone with a keen eye; it's where craft meets art. Find it on the cobbled square of the Cape Quarter (right next to Andiamo). 72 Waterkant St. ℰ **021/425-5123.**

Amulet ★★★   For unique, well-priced jewelry, Gerika and Elizabeth's studio is a must-see, particularly for romantically inclined men wanting to impress their female partners (or just drag him here anyway). 14 Kloof Nek Rd., Tamboerskloof. ℰ **021/426-1149.**

Church   A fun place to browse after visiting the Slave Lodge, Parliament, or Company's Gardens this tiny store (with monthly-changing theme) is packed with nonsense items and random frivolities, including good books on art and design. Conceived and owned by leading conceptual artist, Peet Pienaar (famous for undergoing adult circumcision on videotape in 2000, his innovative design company, The President, is responsible for all kinds of reflections on South African art and culture). 12 Spin St. ℰ **021/462-6092.**

Haas ★★★   Filled with unusual, edgy, and imagination-tickling artworks and homeware items. They also have a cafe serving all-day meals and excellent coffee. Rose St., Bo-Kaap. ℰ **021/422-4413.** www.haascollective.com.

Heartworks ★★   A well-picked crafts showcase, more often than not at brilliant prices; look for beautiful ceramics, bags, bead- and wirework, tiny plastic pigs, embroidered teddy bears, or native carvings. Old Biscuit Mill, ℰ **021/447-7183;** Cape Quarter (De Waterkant), ℰ **021/418-0772;** 98 Kloof St., ℰ **021/424-8419.** www.heartworks.co.za.

Imagenius ★★★   Three floors of a refurbished turn-of-the-20th-century building are jampacked with great gear, from Shirley Fintz's ceramic hunting trophies to interesting furniture pieces by Haldane Martin (www.haldanemartin.co.za) and Gerard Back. 117 Long St. ℰ **021/423-7870.** www.imagenius.co.za.

Pan African Market   Three stories of rooms overflow with goods from all over Africa, from tin picture frames to large, intricate carvings and beadwork. There's also a small cafe with traditional food on the first-floor balcony. 76 Long St. ℰ **021/426-4478.** www.panafrican.co.za.

SOPHISTICATED AFRICAN INTERIOR DESIGN

Colonial House Design   Another interior shop producing wonderful furniture and accessories with a unique African twist, this is a one-stop shop if you're looking to furnish an upmarket game lodge. Shop A17 Cape Quarter, De Waterkant. ℰ **021/421-1467.** www.colonialhouse.co.za.

Fibre Designs   Perhaps the best carpet shop on the continent, with the exciting designs, in wonderful color combinations. You'd be hard-pressed to find any of the items anywhere else in the world, with carpets designed in Africa and woven by master weavers in the East; they do bespoke carpets to your specifications, too. 16 Dixon St., De Waterkant. ℰ **021/418-1054.** www.fibredesigns.co.za.

THE GREAT gay ES-CAPE

Cape Town is promoted as "The Gay Capital of Africa" (South Africa's constitution was the first in the world to expressly protect the rights of homosexuals). Its queer tribes are increasingly rich and varied, with an excellent rapport between straights and gays, and plenty of boundary crossing to keep the scene interesting.

Most gay-friendly venues are situated in and around the City Bowl, particularly in Green Point's "De Waterkant Queer Quarter" and Sea Point's Main Road. Check the local press or *The Pink Map* (produced annually and available from tourism bureaus), or visit either www. cape-town.org or www.capetown.travel.

GAY EVENTS Africa's biggest gay circuit party is the annual **MCQP** (Mother City Queer Project) costume party, an extraordinary themed dress-up spectacular (celebrating 19 years in 2012), held at various venues and attended by thousands of queers and straights of all ages and persuasions—expect a red-carpet arrival, numerous DJ-controlled dance floors, and riotous entertainment. For details of this mid-December event, go to www.mcqp.co.za. **Cape Town Pride** is a 10-day festival in late February (www. capetownpride.org; ℂ **021/820-4554**); there are new cultural and entertainment events each year (Feb 24–Mar 4, 2012), but the highlight is the Pride Parade through the center of Cape Town. Now held three times a year, **Out in Africa** (www.oia.co.za; ℂ **021/461-4027**) is the continent's most important gay and lesbian film festival, with something to satisfy all celluloid tastes. Also worth planning around is the **Pink Loerie Mardi Gras,** held at the end of May, when some 5,000 camp revelers take to the streets of Knysna on the Garden Route—a welcome extension to a trip to Cape Town, with plenty of gay-friendly places to stay along the way.

RECOMMENDED GUESTHOUSES & TOURS A variety of options can be had in **De Waterkant Village,** in the heart of the "Queer Quarter," within easy walking distance of clubs and bars (which also means it's extremely noisy). The most tasteful men-only choice, though, is the **Glen Boutique Hotel** ★★ (www.glenhotel.co.za; ℂ **021/439-0086**), in Sea Point, which has good facilities and very, er, well-equipped rooms. The Glen is known for its regular all-male gatherings—especially around the pool—a great place to meet new friends. Standard rooms go for R1,200 to R1,450 double, in the summer months, and just R500, in winter; for more luxury, book one of the lavish suites (from R2,350, in summer). And if you feel the need to clear your head and get out of town, the men-only **Shisa Guest Farm** (www.shisafarm.com; p. 184), near the Winelands town of Tulbagh, is just 80 minutes away. Franschhoek is also known as a gay-friendly town; if you spend the night, check out **Ashbourne House** (www.ashbourne. co.za; ℂ **021/876-2146;** from R1,180 double). If you're heading farther afield and want to search for gay-friendly accommodations, visit www.pinksa. co.za, or pick up a free copy of the **Pink South Africa Guide.** There are plenty of competent tour operators in Cape Town, but if you want to make friends, book with **Friends of Dorothy Tours** (ℂ **021/ 465-1871;** www.friendsofdorothytours. co.za). They cover pretty much everything in Cape Town, as well as the multiday tours of the Garden Route and whale-watching excursions. **Cape Classic Tours** (✆ **021/686-0013** or 083/251-7274; www.classiccape.co.za) is a gay-owned operator specializing in Cape Town and the Garden Route (but also handling safaris), and will provide you with a gay guide wherever possible.

BEST BEACHES Clifton's **Third Beach** is where you'll find international male models parading in garments so tight you can tell what religion they are. **Sandy Bay** is Llandudno's famous nudist spot, with discreet cruising at the far end of the beach. *Beware:* The freezing ocean will bring you down to size.

A GAY NIGHT OUT Kicking off in the Queer Quarter, there's usually plenty to see at Andrew and Grant Eglin's **Beefcakes Burger Bar,** 40 Somerset Rd. (✆ **021/425-9019**), a camp eatery (specializing in saucily named meat sandwiches) with regular drag acts, mincing waiters, and a tattooed stud behind the bar. Alternatively head for buzzy **Café Manhattan,** 74 Waterkant St. (✆ **021/421-6666**), a friendly, chatty bar with a good-value restaurant, which gets busy after 9pm. The Cape Quarter's **Lazari** (✆ **021/419-9555**), a light-filled space (by day) done out in lots of shocking pink, is popular with boys (and men) who like to eat and be seen (and see others doing the same)—food's not half bad, either. Girls might want to head for **Beaulah Bar** (named for the local gay-speak term meaning "beautiful"; ✆ **021/421-6798**), a favorite lesbian hangout where boys needn't feel left out; it's at 28–30 Somerset Rd. Virtually next door is legendary **Bronx ★** (✆ **021/419-9216;** www.bronx.co.za),

which doesn't pick up until much later; the upstairs nightclub, **Navigaytion** (www.navigaytion.co.za), gets a dedicated dance crowd pulsating and sweating to house every Wednesday, Friday, and Saturday from 11pm until late. Bronx is on the corner of a side-street strip called Napier—head down here to discover **Crew ★★** (✆ **021/418-0118**), the most popular gay club in town, where the night kicks off rather early and bodies just get increasingly squashed together as the night wears on (barmen are hot and friendly, and there's likely to be someone dancing near-naked on the counter). Later in the evening they open the upstairs dance floor, **Madison.** Cape Town's leather men and uniform-fetishists hang out at **Bar Code,** 18 Cobern St., off Somerset (✆ **021/421-5305**), a men-only cruise bar with slings, dark rooms, a maze, and more—ask at the bar about the underwear parties and naked nights, when a strict (un)dress code applies. Nearby, but even steamier, the **Hothouse Steam & Leisure,** 18 Jarvis St. (✆ **021/418-3888**), is a European-style men-only leisure club, with sauna, steam room, and outdoor sun deck with spectacular views over the city and the harbor. Finally, in this predominantly male-oriented gay scene, it's good to know that there's an outlet for women who love women to have some fun: **Lush** is just such a party—gorgeous girls gather every 2 weeks in a funky, safe environment at various venues around the city; contact Myrna Andrews (myrna@lushcapetown.co.za) for details, or join the Facebook group "LUSH—Events for women who love women."

LIM ★ This tiny shop produces excellent homegrown, simple, modern furniture and accessories—be it an asymmetrical Mozambican vase, a paper-thin Shapiro bowl, or chunky tambotie stool. 86a Kloof St. ✆ **021/423-1200.** www.lim.co.za.

Merchants on Long ★★★ Behind the lovely Victorian facade, museum quality displays of high-end African designer brands celebrate what owner-designer Hanneli Rupert likes to call a "precolonial aesthetic." The stripped-down space—rich with architectural detailing, displays of antique taxidermy, and beautiful furniture—is worth coming to see. Everything here—from fashion to homeware and art—comes from this continent. 34 Long St. ✆ **021/422-2828.** www.merchantsonlong.com.

T&Co This smart, ethical lifestyle store has a little cafe attached, and plenty of beautiful pieces of furniture and designware items to take home. 78 Victoria Junction, Ebenezer Rd., Green Point. ✆ **087/808-7064.**

FINE ART & GALLERIES

Erdmann Contemporary & The Photographers Gallery ZA Heidi Erdmann has a knack for unearthing new talent—she also handles work by brilliant talents such as Varenka Paschke, whose beautiful canvases are well worth snapping up. Renowned South African photographers contribute regularly. 63 Shortmarket St. ✆ **021/422-2762.** www.erdmanncontemporary.co.za.

Everard Read Gallery For one of the best selections of South African art, this is your best bet—though you won't find a bargain here. 3 Portswood Rd., Waterfront. ✆ **021/418-4527.** www.everard-read-capetown.co.za.

iART Upstairs, you'll find heftier price tags attached to some of the country's exemplary, well-established artists' pieces; downstairs is the terrain of up-and-coming and less-mainstream canvases and sculptures. 71 Loop St. ✆ **021/424-5150.** www.iart.co.za.

Misael SA Art and Design It's not all fine art here, but this Italian/South African collaboration includes plenty of unique design, fashion, furniture, photography, and other art curated in a beautiful all-white space. 103B Bree St. ✆ **021/424-8540.** www.misael.co.za.

João Ferreira Gallery Also a good bet for contemporary works by such artists as William Kentridge—whose video work *History of the Main Complaint* has a room all to its own in the Tate Modern in London—which João both exhibits and sources. 70 Loop St. ✆ **021/423-5403.** www.jaoaferreiragallery.com.

Rose Korber Art One of the city's most distinguished art dealers, Rose Korber is a former art critic; some of the top names in the business have canvases in her collection, which are kept in her Camps Bay home. Call to arrange a visit. 48 Sedgemoor Rd. ✆ **021/438-9152.** www.rosekorberart.com.

Salon91 One of the coolest art galleries in town. Owner Monique du Preez has envisaged this intimate new space as an affordable showroom for emerging talent. Investors with lighter wallets and vision should browse here first. 91 Kloof St. ✆ **021/424-6930.** www.salon91art.co.za.

Whatiftheworld/Gallery Having started the reinvention of Woodstock as a gallery precinct, it was selected in 2007 by *Contemporary Magazine* (London) as one of the Top 50 Emerging Galleries from Around the World. It's become a destination point for curators and collectors trawling for innovative work and rising stars. 1 Argyle St. (at Albert Rd.), Woodstock. ✆ **021/448-1438.**

FOOD & WINE

Atlas Trading Co. 🎁 Re-create the mild, slightly sweet curry flavors of Cape Malay dishes back home by purchasing a bag of mixed spices from the Ahmed family, proprietors of Atlas, who've been trading here for over a century. 94 Wale St. ✆ **021/423-4361.**

by nature 🎁 Although it's without any outlet to call its own just yet, it's worth tracking down Peter Owen's organic and totally natural produce, including the purest honey. He makes an appearance at the weekly Neighbourgoods Market, but has stalls at other markets, too. ✆ **083/658-3998.** www.bynature.co.za.

Caroline's Fine Wine Cellar Caroline Rillema has an exceptional nose for finding those out-of-the-way gems most Capetonians, let alone visitors, simply don't have the time or know-how to track down. Arguably the best wine shop in Cape Town. V&A Waterfront. ✆ **021/425-5701.** Also at 62 Strand St. ✆ **021/419-8984.**

Foodbarn Deli ★★★ The mind boggles at the shelves bulging with locally produced goods, while the senses delight in the wonderful aromas coming out of the bakery (considered the best in the country and on the go from very early every morning using stone ground flour); you can dine in, too. Noordhoek Farm Village, Village Ln., Noordhoek. ✆ **021/789-1390.**

Joubert & Monty This is one of the best places to sample good biltong; try a bit of kudu and beef—ask for the latter to be slightly moist and sliced. Waterfront. ✆ **021/418-0640.**

Steven Rom This liquor merchant (with two other branches) has a large selection in stock but will also track down and order anything you request (even once you're home) and arrange shipping. Galleria Centre, 76 Regent Rd., Sea Point. ✆ **021/439-6043.** www.stevenrom.co.za.

CAPE TOWN AFTER DARK

021 Magazine (www.021club.co.za) has probably the most extensive local listings; alternatively pick up a copy of the monthly *Cape etc.* or the annual *Time Out Cape Town.* Alternatively, the weekly *Mail & Guardian* covers all major events, as does the *Argus,* a local daily—look in the "Tonight" section—or consult Friday's "Top of the Times" insert in the *Cape Times.* You can book tickets to theaters and movies and most major music/party events by calling **Computicket** (✆ **083/915-8000;** www.computicket.com) and supplying your credit card details; the alternative online ticketing agent is **Webtickets** (www.webtickets.co.za), which is more efficient (and now the sole agent for many Cape Town venues, events, tours and cultural experiences), but requires you to print out your own tickets.

The Performing Arts

Cape Town showcases the very best of the country's stage productions. Critics can be appallingly sycophantic, though, so take whatever you read in the press with a pinch of salt (reviews in the *Mail & Guardian* tend to be more reliable). In summer, take in one of the outdoor concerts (see below), and keep abreast of anything that forms part of the slightly under-the-radar **Pan African Space Station ★★★** (www.panafricanspacestation.org.za), the city's edgiest and most progressive music festival, with some brilliant performances from across the continent—not to be missed if you're here in September/October. Since opening in 2010, **The Fugard,** on the corner of Harrington and Caledon streets in the East City (© 021/461-4244; www. thefugard.com) has emerged as the city's top space for good, homegrown theatre. When productions are in Afrikaans, they're subtitled, too, so you'll be able to follow. Also take a look at what's on at either of the city's main theater venues: **ARTscape** (© 021/421-7839) in the city center puts on everything from top-end Broadway musicals to important new South African theater, while the **Baxter Theatre,** Main Road, Rondebosch (© 021/685-7880), is a vibrant hub for culture hounds. If you like your entertainment light, Camps Bay's **Theatre on the Bay** (© 021/438-3301) hosts a mix of frothy comedies, big musicals, and farces. Attracting a wider audience than it's Gay Quarter location might suggest, **Beefcakes Burger Bar,** 40 Somerset St. (© 021/425-9019) puts on assorted drag cabarets, bitchy bingo sessions, and rock-lesbian shows; the performance worth looking out for is sizzling-hot Odidi Mfenyane (who goes by Odidiva).

Outdoor Performances

Summer brings a wealth of fantastic outdoor concerts; tops for venue are the Sunday **Kirstenbosch Summer Concerts** (© 021/799-8783; www.sanbi.org): Bring a hamper of food and wine and relax (or party) to great music, from jazz bands to some of the biggest pop and rock outfits in the country (Goldfish and Freshly Ground are possibly the most popular), playing to an enormous picnicking audience with the sun setting behind the mountain in the background. Concerts start at around 5pm, but get there very early in order to secure your patch of lawn. Early each year, **Maynardville Open-Air Theatre** in Wynberg (www.maynardville.co.za) hosts a Shakespearean play against a lush forested backdrop. Performances vary from year to year but invariably put a contemporary (or local) spin on the Bard. Arrive early with a picnic basket and bottle of wine, and join Cape Town's culture-loving crowd on the lawns for a preshow picnic. Summer (Feb–Mar) is when the city's public spaces become venues for **Infecting the City** (www.infectingthecity.com), a weeklong festival of site-specific (buildings, monuments, fountains, street corners) performances aimed at getting the general public talking about relevant issues. Free concerts are held at the **V&A Waterfront Amphitheatre** (© 021/408-7600); acts range from winners of school talent contests to good jazz.

The Club, Bar & Music Scene

During the summer season, Cape Town becomes one big party venue, despite the fact that die-hard dance animals rue the end of a proper club scene. Get into the mood with sundowners at a trendy bar in **Camps Bay** (**Café Caprice** is always packed to the gills in season, while **Sapphire** gets in some excellent DJs, especially on Friday evening, for chilled electronic sets) or with a bottle of bubbly on a well-situated beach (strictly speaking, this is illegal, so be discreet) or the top of Table Mountain. You will want to pace yourself, however—getting to *any* indoor party before 11pm will see you counting barstools. Arguably the city's most exciting parties are the bacchanalian **Balkanology** ★★★ (and slightly tamer **Fiddle East**) events, where the lineup is always astonishing (usually with an international live band or DJ playing thumping Balkan tunes), and there's a cool crowd of crazies (a wonderful mix of Cape Town's tribes) to match.

Listings below were hip at press time, but as in most cities, sell-by dates are unpredictable. To play it safe, expect good nights out from Wednesday onward, and head for one of the following two areas: **Long Street,** particularly the mountain end (near the Turkish-style Long Street Baths), is the central city's hot party area. Here there's a multitude of quite grungy bars—most notable is **Jo'burg** (✆ **021/422-0142**), where the heady crowd is often entertained by live local music, but the better sections are more intimate bars hidden behind discreetly located doors—make the effort to look for them. Definitely, if you're looking to dance on this street, your best bet is **Fiction,** which is tiny, but takes electronic music extremely seriously. Across the road, single-malt devotees frequent the plush leather settees of **The Dubliner @ Kennedy's** (✆ **021/424-1212**). Far cozier is the cigar bar hidden in the back of **Cape to Cuba** (✆ **021/424-2330**), a prettily designed upstairs restaurant (above similarly themed **Che Bar**) that also has a lovely terrace for early evening cocktails. On this side of the road, all the better watering holes are in upstairs venues (do seek out **Neighbourhood Bar**) or hidden down side streets (ask for **Julep**); in fact, our rule is that those that spill out onto the sidewalk are a little dodgy. The other, slightly more spread out party strip, catering to (generally speaking) an older, more sophisticated audience, is in Cape Town's "Gay Quarter," centered on De Waterkant.

LIVE MUSIC

In Zonnebloem (near District Six), **Mercury Live & Lounge ★★**, 43 de Villiers St. (✆ **021/465-2106;** www.mercuryl.co.za), is hardly the most slick or sophisticated venue, but it's still the only place in the city where you'll find a regular lineup of original South African bands—there are often some very pleasant surprises. **Assembly** (see below), a massive converted warehouse still occasionally gets in live bands, but has become more of a focal spot for electronic dance music events, thanks to huge support from a younger crowd. **Zula Sound Bar** (✆ **021/424-2442**), on cosmopolitan Long Street, is a much smaller but no less vibey music venue with eclectic live music, featuring something for everyone depending on the day of the week (or hour of the night) you arrive. Also in Long Street is the intimate **Waiting Room,** where you feel like you're watching a show, often by emerging bands and solo artists, in someone's lounge. In a totally different league are the international concerts hosted at the new **Cape Town Stadium** and at the more lackluster indoor space at the **Grand West Casino.**

CLUBS

Assembly ★★   The club that kick-started the rejuvenation of Cape Town's East City district started out as a host venue for the country's top bands; they still get live music in, but the focus has shifted to electronic music events (including loads of ho-hum electro), the best of which include savvier DJ talent such as the Killer Robot crew, or producer-DJ, Artelligent. Harrington St., East City. ✆ **021/465-7286.** www.theassembly. co.za. Cover varies.

Crew ★★   With better-looking bare-chested bar staff than neighboring Bronx, this has become the establishment of choice along Cape Town's bleary-eyed gay strip. Things start up early downstairs, with a squeeze-your-way-through crowd of muscled studs and pretty waifs—then a second bar and dance floor, **Madison,** opens upstairs. 30 Napier St., Green Point. ✆ **021/418-0118.** Free admission.

Decodance ★   A hangout for the 30-plus crowd—who would have thought the '80s and '90s could be so cheerfully revived? 120B Main Rd., Sea Point. ✆ **084/330-1162.** www.decodance.co.za.

The Fez ★   The long queue of shimmying models and coiffured hunks who plan on picking them up, may put you off, but if you arrive early enough you'll beat the crowds. DJ sets are varied but will get your toes tapping, and the pseudo-Moroccan styling somehow works. (Avoid dinner at the attached Vaudeville restaurant—sadly downhill since it opened.) Mechau St. ✆ **021/419-7000.** www.fez.co.za.

Fiction ★★★   Space may be at a premium at this DJ-centric club, the best in Long Street, but the music lineup is the stuff of legend. Find a spot on the matchbox dance floor early, and prepare to sweat among an electric mob of musically educated party enthusiasts. The Killer Robot events are, well, killer, and drum 'n' bass special-ist Niskerone quite extraordinary. 227 Long St. ✆ **021/424-5709.** www.fictionbar.com.

Jade ★★   Let down your hair, lounge on antique-style sofas, pose, stare, boogie, and meet gorgeous people from all over the world. Like the crowd, music is eclectic, and runs the gamut from messy hip-hop to kitsch commercial tracks; regardless, the crowd always appears to be having a great time. Entrance is unmarked. 39 Main Rd. just around the corner from Manos Restaurant, Green Point. ✆ **021/439-4108.** www.jadelounge.co.za.

The Reserve ★★★   With an ultra-beautiful crowd, this is a grown up club cater-ing to sophisticated (and expensive) tastes. It's tucked into a 150-year-old former banking building, overhauled by designers who added plenty of floral fabric, leopard skin, and palm trees-meet-African jungle murals. The music extends to hideous com-mercial tracks, defiantly lapped up by bopping scenesters. Dress like you mean busi-ness. 111 St. Georges Mall. ✆ **021/424-0102.** www.the-reserve.co.za. Cover varies. Fri–Sat 11:30pm–3am.

St Yves ★★   With its gazebo seating on a large balcony overlooking Camps Bay's sunset strip, it's little wonder this is popular in summer when there's a wild assort-ment of musical genres and an upmarket air-kissing crowd that's ready to party. A great place to listen to major South African electronic act, Goldfish, on a Sunday night. The Promenade, Victoria Rd. ✆ **021/438-0826.** www.styves.co.za. Cover varies.

Trinity ★★★   After a year of club closures, Cape Town's biggest, boldest night time space launched to a heaving crowd with DJ darling James Sabiela, and the party atmosphere shows little sign of abating; expect plenty of big name local DJs (dishing out everything from trance to good old-fashioned techno). Weeknights see live Jazz, and a stand-up comedy evening. An old warehouse, with exposed brickwork and a bit of a monastic industrial feel, it offers multiple spaces to play. No under-23s are allowed into the club (hard to believe it's strictly enforced); dress code is smart casual (no shorts or sneakers). 15 Bennett St., off Prestwich St., Green Point. ✆ **021/418-0624.** www.trinitycapetown.co.za. Cover varies. Mon–Tues noon–2am, Wed–Sat noon–4am.

BARS

Asoka ★★★   This chocolate-colored house with intimate Balinese-style interiors offers comfy seating in a courtyard centered on an old tree and attracts a cool crowd to imbibe drinks and light meals. With soothing lighting and groovy music, it's highly recommended for a pre- or postdinner drink. The vibe, fed by Cape Town's happening young crowd (mid-20s and up), is invariably great. 68 Kloof St., Tamboerskloof. ✆ **021/422-0909.** www.asokabar.co.za.

Bascule ★★★   With the millionaire yachts parked right outside, and countless whiskeys to chose from, this itty-bitty hotel bar is classy and intimate and situated on the edge of the marina. Cape Grace, V&A Waterfront. ✆ **021/410-7100.**

Brewers & Union ★★★   This a slick-casual "beer and charcuterie" venue beneath the church near Heritage Square; place your order at the counter (the cured meat platters and tapas are perfect accompaniment to the high-end hangover-free artisanal German-style beers) and park yourself at one of the benches beneath the trees outside (or settle for a bar stool inside). In summer, owners Brad and Rui host acoustic sets by some great talents, and they're always thinking up ways to reward locals with fun, after-work events. 110 Bree St., City Center. ☎ **021/422-2770.**

French Toast ★   This popular new tapas wine bar offers over 100 bottles of wine by the bottle or glass, not only from S.A.—head upstairs and grab a table. V&A Waterfront. 199 Bree St. ☎ **021/421-3753.** Mon–Sat 5–11pm.

Black Ram ★★   Owner Adam says he opened Black Ram because he could no longer afford to host his friends at home, so he moved his furniture into the small room behind Power & Glory, and now charges for drinks! It attracts a very cool, trendy crowd. Kloofnek and Burnside rds. (unmarked). ☎ **021/422-2108.**

Boo Radley's ★★   Classic cocktails—made according to authentic, original recipes—are signature at this slick bistro with a long, sociable, polished bar counter; order a perfectly mixed sazerac, made to original specifications, with rye bourbon and aged brandy. 62 Hout St. ☎ **021/424-3040.** www.booradleys.co.za.

Cape to Cuba ★★   After dark, come to this restaurant and head straight for the clubby, library-style cigar bar in the back. Slam back a chocolate tequila or two, and follow through with a delicious daiquiri or mojito—or ask the engaging barmen to make more suggestions. 227 Long St. ☎ **021/424-2330.**

Café Caprice ★   One of Cape Town's favorite see-and-be-seen bars, opposite Camps Bay beach, is like something out of a Ryan Reynolds movie, forever wearing a naughty grin. When it's quiet, it's surprisingly good for light meals, but when it's heaving (during the summer, it can flood out into the street), it's all about the bar. There's vibe and views and fairly on-the-ball bar service; sometimes there's a decent DJ spinning tunes in the background. 37 Victoria Rd., Camps Bay. ☎ **021/438-8315.**

Caveau ★   A favorite place to kick-start the evening (or end the day) this wine bar is within strolling distance of Long Street. It's a wonderful, warm, informal venue that spills out onto the cobblestones, with excellent wines by the glass to accompany a range of tapas and more filling meals. It's a hugely popular after-hours watering hole. Adjacent is **HQ,** a stylish sirloin and chips restaurant. Heritage Sq., Bree St. ☎ **021/422-1367.**

Fatback Soul ★★   With its stringent door policy (definitely worth dressing the part) and gloriously retro-chic decor, this is where you come for a well-mixed cocktail along with a dose of quality eye-candy. It feels like a private party for a cool, in-the-know crowd. Music is of the Motown, funk, and soul variety—very smooth, very ballsy. 289 Long St. ☎ **021/422-4086.**

Grand Café & Beach ★★★   The setting—a faux pocket beach overlooking Table Bay—is sublime. Tables and boho-chic atmosphere spill out of a ramshackle warehouse, cleverly transformed into a dining boudoir with chandeliers, velvet fabrics, and pretty antiques. Food is ridiculously expensive (but not bad), while service is erratic (and sometimes awful); however, you don't have to eat and there are few finer places to enjoy a drink with your toes in the sand, trying to decide whether to stare at the sunset glistening off the water or check out the übersexy crowd. In summer reservations are absolutely essential. Granger Bay Rd., off Beach Rd., Granger Bay. ☎ **021/425-0551.** Reservations by SMS text: ☎ **072/586-2052** or e-mail beach@thegrand.co.za.

Julep ★★★ 🎒   A favorite, well-kept secret where you'll find a buzzing crowd clamoring for what many consider to be the best cocktails in town. If you can't find the discreet, unpublicized entrance, just ask—it's down a little lane that runs off Long Street, more or less opposite Lola's. Vredenburg Lane. ☎ **021/423-4276.**

THE love PARTIES

If you're a party animal, make a point of lining up at least one **outdoor trance party** ★★★ as part of your hip-swinging sojourn. It's probably the best place to catch Capetonians at their unabashed, sweaty, unpretentious best—they'll be dressed down, barefoot, and up to all kinds of mischief, but united in their heady pursuit of the most intoxicating beats and tunes, spun by world-class DJs. Parties—in some of beautiful locations just outside the city—can go for 1 night or up to 4 days; thousands of dedicated pups set up camp, or just keep stomping for hours on end. While there's music day and night, the scene is more sociable while the sun is out (and sometimes utterly crazy after midnight), and there's no better way to witness sunrise. Bars, food stalls, and hippies selling healing crystals are plentiful, but you're welcome to bring all your own supplies (a cooler box with plenty of ice is a good idea; don't bring anything made of glass, though)—just remember to take everything, except your ego, home with you. There's a strong mix of old, young, and in between—the youngsters tend to fizzle out and leave early, leaving the best part of the party to a more "mature" crowd (so you can even just turn up on the last day). By far the best parties are organized by **Alien Safari** ★★★ (www.alien safari.net) and **Vortex Trance Adventures** ★★★ (www.intothevortex.co.za), while a stand-out one-off event is the annual **Origin Festival** ★★★ at the end of January (www.originfestival.com). For New Year's Eve, **Rezonance** ★★★ (www.rezonancefestival.com) is arguably the biggest party on the African continent. And, if catching up with the sixties is in your DNA, make a date (late Apr) with **AfrikaBurn** ★★★ (www.afrika burn.com) in the Tankwa Karoo desert (3–4 hr. from Cape Town)—it's Africa's version of Nevada's Burning Man, where festival goers participate in a "gifting economy" and celebrate life and art in a weeklong free-for-all with absolutely nowhere to buy anything. It's a surefire way to befriend thousands of South Africans.

L'aperitivo ★   This is a most sociable spot (preferably sitting on the sidewalk) to enjoy an early evening drink. Ownership is changing as we go to print, but we hope the vibe (and the excellent gin and tonics) stay intact. 70 Loop St. ℭ **021/426-1001.** www.laperitivo.co.za.

The Martini ★★★ 🍸   Deep in the Southern Suburbs green belt is where you'll find this most elegantly designed lounge-bar, looking out at the gardens of the impeccable Cellars-Hohenort hotel, offering an exhaustive martini menu. 93 Brommersvlei Rd., Constantia. ℭ **021/794-2137.**

Planet Champagne Bar ★★   If you haven't been to the gracious Mount Nelson hotel for tea, then come for its sexy bar. The interior is chic, the gardens are wonderful, barmen charming, and the crowd a mix of tourists and locals. 76 Orange St. ℭ **021/483-1000.**

Sapphire ★★   Elevated views of Camps Bay's palm-fringed beach still pull in a crowd of cocktail-sipping and beer-swilling Capetonians who can't get enough of the setting sun. Cool tunes are de rigueur, too. The Promenade, Victoria Rd., Camps Bay. ℭ **021/438-1758.** www.blues.co.za.

Tjing Tjing ★★★ Under the excavated rafters of a 180-year-old house on a mid-city side street, this gorgeous watering hole features a red-lacquered bar and counter that looks like a Japanese shrine. While you sink cocktails with names like Nutty Slutty and Ginger Ninja, fend off a hunger by ordering one of their superb tapas boards—you'll be hard-pressed to tear yourself away. It's an addictive, comfortable space with hand-picked music, plush seating, and elegant Sino-inspired decor; there's also a lovely open-air rooftop for a look at the surrounding cityscape. Be warned that it gets packed to the gills on Friday nights, so you'll want to arrive early to stake your piece of the action. 165 Longmarket St. (above Dear Me). ✆ **021/422-4920.**

Wafu ★★ This indoor-outdoor bar (above Wakame restaurant) features great ocean views, stylish decor, and good tapas—Cape Town's beautiful people pile in just as soon as they leave the office (or the fashion shoot comes to an end). Service can be haughty however. Beach Rd., Mouille Point. ✆ **021/433-2377.**

EVENTS

Balkanology ★★★ Cape Town's best city parties are swinging festivals at their unhinged, rollicking best. Each one is held in a new venue with an accompanying outrageous theme, and often a major Balkan-style international act supported by several local wonders. Mind-altering stuff. www.balkanology.com.

Cape Town Jazz Festival ★★★ Local and international artists combine in S.A.'s premier jazz event, held toward the end of summer. Celebrating 12 years in 2012, the festival attracts thousands of music fans for a huge variety of preeminent jazz performances. www.capetownjazzfest.com.

J&B Met ★ It's a horse race, but no one really watches the ponies. As one of the biggest events of the Cape Town social calendar, the J&B Met attracts the cream of S.A.'s best-dressed celebrities (and a few clots, too). www.jbmet.co.za.

MCQP ★★★ More than just an excuse to party in various states of undress, Cape Town's Mother City Queer Project costume party has mushroomed into Africa's quintessential gay (but very straight-friendly) extravaganza, held each December. A new venue and theme are revealed every year. www.mcqp.co.za.

SIDE TRIPS FROM CAPE TOWN: WHALES, WILDFLOWERS & WINE

5

Virtually surrounded by wine-growing valleys, with the coastline spilling away north and east from its peninsula, the city offers an infinite variety of easily accessible escapes. Servicing farmers or sheltering communities of fishermen are all manner of towns and villages—including some of the prettiest hamlets in the country—that are today destinations in their own right, but an easy day trip should you be limited in time. Many arrive in Cape Town and whip straight from the airport (a mere 45 min. away) to a rural idyll in the Winelands, where you can marvel at the superlative views from various mountain passes, stay amid some of the best-preserved examples of Cape Dutch architecture, sample award-winning wines, and dine at the best restaurants on the continent. In fact, with the bright lights of the city a mere 60- to 100-minute drive away, no vacation to Cape Town would be complete without at least a day exploring one of the Winelands areas.

If you're a serious wine lover, particularly of reds, the wine produced by the terroir surrounding the university town of **Stellenbosch** is generally considered the best. Aside from offering in an almost limitless choice of wines, it is the cultural epicenter of the Winelands, its oak-lined streetscape offering the greatest sense of the Cape's Dutch colonial history. However, it is surrounded by new developments—gated communities and corporate headquarters—that mar the once rural ambience. If you're looking for something more pretty, **Franschhoek**—reached via either Stellenbosch or Paarl—is located in a gorgeous valley and has a well-developed, albeit very touristy, infrastructure. By contrast, the town of **Paarl** has only limited appeal. Farther away from the three big-name Winelands destinations are quaint Winelands villages worth consideration as a base or a day trip. The lack of pretense, scant traffic, and prime accommodations at a fair price make **Tulbagh** one of the sweetest little destinations in the country. Much the same can be said of quiet, rural gems like **Riebeek Kasteel, Darling,** and **Elgin,** with their majestic mountain backdrops and the chance to savor great wines on estates that don't attract the kind of hype flung at Stellenbosch and Franschhoek.

Besides the sybaritic pleasures of the Cape's many wine routes, there are the coastal treasures that lie just an hour or two's drive southeast or north of the Mother City. The vast southern right whale nursery that stretches along the Cape's southern coast is said to be the best land-based whale-watching on earth. Quaint rural villages are found along many of the roads and byways that radiate out from the ever-expanding holiday resort town of **Hermanus,** long known as the "Whale Capital," and hugely popular because of its relative proximity (90 min.) to Cape Town. It is also the gateway to some of the less known but superb winegrowing areas of **Hemel-en-Aarde** (literally Heaven and Earth) and **Elim,** both boasting unique terroirs that produce a small but superb selection of award-winning wines. And if you've had your fill of wine and whale song, there's the underrated thrill of seeking out seasonal wildflower carpets that emerge (after the first rains fall, usually in Aug) from the vast, rugged emptiness stretching north of Cape Town toward semi-arid Namaqualand. Along what is known as the **West Coast,** you'll find salty lagoons and laid-back beach restaurants. Farther north still attracts the true solitude-seekers, into the bewitching **Cederberg Mountains,** its craggy weathered walls adorned in ancient rock art. Here, life couldn't be more different from the heady party atmosphere with which the Mother City is synonymous. The area farther north of this is no easy Cape Town excursion, but if you love desert landscapes, make every effort to travel to the sunbaked lunar landscapes of the **Kalahari Desert** and **Richtersveld,** where you can spot rare and unusual desert-dwelling animals beneath a vast and limitless sky.

STAYING ACTIVE

BALLOONING Winelands Board a balloon in the early morning and glide over the Paarl Winelands—the 1-hour flight (R2,800 per person) takes off every morning from November to early May and includes a champagne breakfast at the Grande Roche. Contact **Wineland Ballooning** (✆ **021/863-3192**).

BOARDSAILING & KITE-SURFING Langebaan Lagoon, north of Cape Town on the West Coast, is considered one of the best sites in South Africa for those who get a rush from the combined power of water and air—particularly in the early afternoon, when the wind picks up (wind speeds average 20–30 knots). Book lessons and rent equipment from family-run **Windchasers ★★**, 79 Main Rd. (✆ **082/079-0500**; www.windchaserssa.com), in Langebaan; besides offering the best kiting service in town, they have a comfortable guesthouse with an excellent rate if you cook for yourself (R520 double)—or they'll throw in breakfast (R600 double).

FISHING Trout fishing is popular in the crystal-clear streams found in the Du Toits Kloof Mountains near Paarl and in Franschhoek, where salmon trout is a specialty on every menu. You can catch brown and rainbow trout at **La Ferme** (✆ **021/867-0120**; www.laferme.co.za; R100 per adult). They also have a couple of cottages for rent (R850–R1,500 per night).

GOLFING In Hermanus The Peter Matkovich–designed course at **Arabella Golf Club ★★★**, 20 minutes from town, is among the best in the Western Cape.

It's attached to a luxury hotel (**www.arabellawesterncapehotel.com**) with a spa. Call ℂ **028/284-0105** (18-hole greens fees R795 for day visitors or R625 for hotel guests; club rental R325; golf cart R275; caddie R135). There are huge discounts in winter.

In the Winelands   Nestled in the Franschhoek valley, Jack Nicklaus's **Pearl Valley Golf Estate ★★** (ℂ **021/867-8000;** www.pearlvalleygolfestates.com), which has hosted the South African Open three times since opening in 2003, is considered one of the top five courses in the country; the 13th hole is legendary, and views provide a great distraction throughout. Gary Player-designed **Erinvale ★**, Lourensford Rd. (ℂ **021/847-1144**), in Somerset West, has a big following, but **Stellenbosch** (ℂ **021/880-0103**), on Strand Road, is also worthwhile, with a particularly challenging tree-lined fairway.

HIKING   The Overberg   Nature lovers based in either Elgin or Hermanus should explore the *fynbos*-rich **Kogelberg Biosphere Reserve ★★** (ℂ **028/271-5138;** www.capenature.co.za). Protecting more than 1,600 plant species, it's considered the heart of the Cape floral kingdom because of the sheer density of plant life; most trail access points are near Kleinmond, on the R44 (see "The Coastal Route: Gordon's Bay to Hermanus," below), but the more challenging 16km (10-mile) **Perdeberg Trail ★★** starts near Iona, one of Elgin's must-see wine farms. If you want a knowledgeable **private guide** for tailor-made walks in this region, contact **Bill Robertson ★★** (ℂ **072/926-3612;** www.walkerbaytours.co.za); he charges R300 per person for an excellent 4-hour hike. For longer trails the top pick is the **Whale Trail ★★★** (ℂ **021/659-3500;** www.capenature.org.za) in the De Hoop Nature Reserve, a 5-day walk through its *fynbos* paradise, with the last 3 days hugging the coast—in season, whales are constantly within view and earshot. The first day is the hardest (15km/9.3 miles), but it gets much easier after that (day 3 is only 8km/ 5 miles)—luggage is portaged. Covering 60km (37 miles) in 4 days, the **Green Mountain Trail ★★★** (ℂ **028/284-9827;** www.greenmountaintrail.co.za; R1,110 per person per day, all inclusive) around the Groenland mountain (flanking the Elgin Valley) is another portaged trail that is well worth consideration. Nights are spent at warmly hosted guest farms, there's wine tasting en route, and you dine at country establishments you'd otherwise miss out on.

Stellenbosch   The trails (5.3km–18km/3.2–11 miles) in the mountainous **Jonkershoek Nature Reserve** are recommended.

Cederberg   With its strange twisted rock formations and tea-colored streams, the **Cederberg Wilderness Area ★★★** (ℂ **0861/227-362-8873;** www.capenature. co.za), some 3 to 4 hours north of Cape Town, is a hiking and climbing paradise but one that's relatively off the beaten track. If you can get a group (or extended family) together for an all-out wilderness adventure with a guide, contact **Peter Raimondo ★★★** (ℂ **082/498-5445;** www.purelywild.co.za), a superlative wilderness guide who will interpret the Cederberg for you as he leads you through it. If you've sufficient numbers, the experience is very reasonably priced (R18,000 for 5 days for up to eight people; includes everything, including your Cape Town pickup).

HORSEBACK RIDING   The Overberg   Using unbroken horses trained in accordance with their herd's natural hierarchy, the **African Horse Company ★★★** (ℂ **082/667-9232;** www.africanhorseco.com) offers both shorter rides (1–6 hr.) and longer overnight trails (2–10 days), covering beach and mountain terrain; all experience levels are catered for—stay at Farm 215 (p. 181). You can also contact **Klein**

Diving with Apex Predators ★ ★ ★

One of the world's greatest concentrations of **great white sharks** is found in South African waters—in particular, around Dyer and Geyser Islands, near Gansbaai, considered the global capital for shark-cage diving. Recent studies have shown that this impressive apex predator (large specimens can reach lengths of up to 6m/20 ft., although 4m/13 ft. is more usual) is a very particular hunter, and most of the (extremely rare) attacks on humans are thought to be mistakes. In Cape Town, shark spotters placed on mountain slopes keep a sharp lookout for sharks and warn bathers of their presence. But for many, one of the highlights of a trip to the Cape is the chance to eyeball the creatures on their home turf: Eight operators offer similar services for around the same price; for our favorite, see p. 129.

Paradys Equestrian Centre (✆ **028/284-9422** or 083/240-6448; www.klein paradys.net), which is based in Bot River, between Elgin and Hermanus.

MOUNTAIN BIKING The mountains above the Elgin Valley are ideal for biking; check out the **Green Mountain Eco Route** (www.greenmountain.co.za).

PARAGLIDING **Walker Bay Adventures** (✆ **082/739-0159;** www.walkerbay adventures.co.za) arranges half-hour tandem flights (R950) off the mountains around Hermanus.

SANDBOARDING Contact Cape Town's **Downhill Adventures** (✆ **021/422-0388;** www.downhilladventures.co.za) to surf the dunes near Hermanus.

SHARK-CAGE DIVING See p. 222.

SKYDIVING/PARACHUTING Drop from a height of 900m (3,000 ft.) with **Skydive Robertson** (✆ **083/462-5666;** www.skydive.co.za), based in Robertson, another wine-growing area 90 minutes outside of Cape Town. With 1-day training for the novice costing R1,200, including the first jump (or R1,740 with three jumps included), and additional jumps costing R320, this is one of the cheapest drops from a plane in South Africa. *Tip:* The best place to stay in Robertson is at **Die Laaitjie ★★** (www.dielaatjie.com; ✆ **023/626-4035**), a gorgeous renovated mid-Victorian farmhouse just 7km (4⅓ miles) outside town. You can either rent the entire main house (R4,000 for up to eight people; no children), or opt for one of the smaller, simpler, all-white cottages overlooking the dam (R550 double).

SURFING **Elands Bay ★★** (220km/137 miles north of Cape Town) is considered the best surf spot on the west coast. The big drawback is its huge growth in popularity, especially among kiteboarders who come for the howling offshore. The best place to stay is **Straw House ★★** (www.strawrevolution.co.za; ✆ **072/130-1755;** R1,100–R1,650 per day), an eco-friendly architect-designed beach house made from straw bales and sleeping six people in three bedrooms—just bring your own food and surfboards. Alternatively, the **Eland's Bay Hotel** (www.elandsbayhotel.co.za; ✆ **022/972-1640**) has clean, simple sea-facing en suite rooms for R560 double, as well as cheap backpackers rooms with shared bathrooms for R100 per person.

WHALE-WATCHING Some of the best land-based whale-watching in the world happens on the Overberg coast, particularly Hermanus, from June to October or November. For boat-based encounters, note that a limited number of whale-watching

5

SIDE TRIPS FROM CAPE TOWN

Staying Active

147

permits are issued for operators along the entire South African coast—so make sure your boat has a permit. Skippers are allowed to get no closer than 50m (164 ft.), but the curious whales will often swim right up to the boat. For recommended companies, see "The Overberg & Whale Coast," below.

WHITE-WATER RAFTING   The River Rafters (✆ 021/975-9727; www.riverrafters.co.za) organize all-inclusive weekend trips on the **Doring River** for R1,450 per person; base camp is 4 hours from Cape Town, in the Cederberg area. More accessible is their 2-day stint on the **Breede River** (R1,350 per person with dorm-style accommodation; room upgrades possible), based near Worcester, about an hour from Cape Town. They also run multiday trips on the Richtersveldt section of the **Orange River** (R2,500 for 4 days); the river runs through one of the largest mountain deserts in the world. Trips start 680km (422 miles) north of Cape Town.

THE WINELANDS

Stellenbosch

46km (29 miles) E of Cape Town

The historic town of Stellenbosch was founded in 1679 by Gov. Simon van der Stel, who, among his many other enduring investments, planted hundreds of oak trees here, resulting in the informal name for Stellenbosch of *Eikestad,* or "City of Oaks." The beautifully restored and oak-lined streetscapes of **Dorp, Church,** and **Drosdty** make Stellenbosch the most historic of the Winelands towns, with the largest number of Cape Dutch buildings in the region, but outside the historic center suburban sprawl surrounds otherwise exceptional wine estates, many of them now boasting restaurants with spectacular views—in fact, Stellenbosch has overtaken Franschhoek as culinary capital of the Cape.

Owning a Stellenbosch vineyard is the most prestigious asset for South Africa's wealthy elite, and the presence of their disposable income, mingled with the needs of the 25,000 students enrolled at what is the country's most prestigious Afrikaans university, gives Stellenbosch town center a special buzz, with a myriads cafes, bars, and interesting cultural and shopping hubs vying for their—and your—attention. There are several good performance spaces around town, too, including the **Oude Libertas** open-air amphitheater, and the university's **Endler,** for classical music concerts.

ESSENTIALS

VISITOR INFORMATION   Stellenbosch Tourism, 36 Market St. (✆ 021/883-3584; www.stellenboschtourism.co.za; summer Mon–Fri 8am–6pm, Sat 9am–5pm, Sun 10am–4pm; winter Mon–Fri 9am–5pm, Sat 9:30am–2pm, Sun 10am–2pm), is by far the most helpful in the Winelands. They'll provide expert advice on where to stay and what to do, and they distribute a *Discover Stellenbosch on Foot* leaflet, describing more than 60 historical sites with an accompanying image. Adjacent is the **Adventure Centre** (✆ 021/882-8112; www.adventureshop.co.za).

GUIDED TOURS   Guided **walking tours** (R100 per person; 90 min.) led by **Sandra Krige** (✆ 021/887-9150 or 083/218-1310; hkrige@iafrica.com) depart from Stellenbosch Tourism every weekday at 11am and 3pm (also by appointment for private early morning and twilight ghost story walks. The town center is small enough to explore on foot, but you can also rent a bicycle from **Piet se Fiets** (✆ 021/887-3042; R25 per hour, R100 per day). See "Exploring the Winelands," on p. 150, for wine tours and self-drive tips.

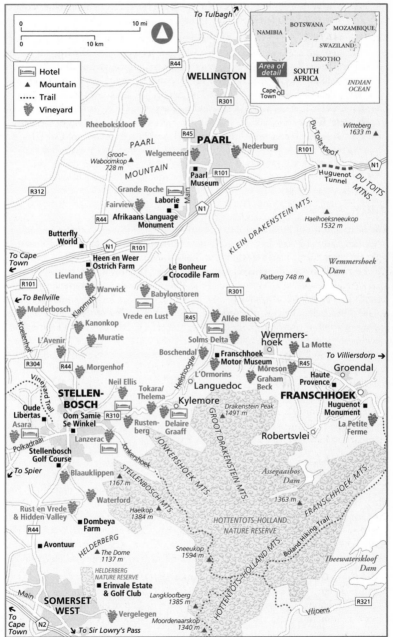

EXPLORING THE winelands:
MAKING THE MOST OF IT

South Africa has well over a dozen designated wine routes, but the best known are Stellenbosch (including Helderberg/Somerset West), Paarl, and Franschhoek. These three towns are all within easy driving distance of Cape Town (and each other: Franschhoek and Paarl are about 30 min. from the center of Stellenbosch), but there are literally hundreds of estates and farms to choose from en-route (and so many routes!). If you are serious about your wines, start by purchasing the latest copy of the award-winning *John Platter's South African Wines* (www.wineonaplatter.com) and study the five-star wines listed and their locations. Updated annually since 1980, the Platter guide is considered one of the best the world; certainly it's the definitive guide to wine in South Africa, listing not only all the producers, but providing ratings to all their wines (some 6,000 tasted annually) and where they are located; wines rated three stars are incidentally very drinkable, while the coveted five stars are awarded only to the very best. Most first-time visitors will want to combine a tour of pretty **Franschhoek** and **Stellenbosch,** the latter producing the highest concentration of great red wines. Both are within easy driving distance of one another, via the scenic

Helshoogte Pass. Then again, Hermanus's **Hemel-en-Aarde** is probably the smallest most rewarding wine route in the country, with some strong character wines to taste in gorgeous surroundings, while **Elgin Valley** offers the most rural experience, and boasts some of the country's top sauvignon blancs. Whichever region you choose, don't try to cover more than **four to six estates** in 1 day, arrange a dedicated driver, and don't forget to **book a luncheon table,** preferably with a vineyard view, in advance (as much as a month for the top restaurants).

Far better than trying to plan a self-drive wine tour is to **book a wine tour with an expert** who can tailor a tour to suit your specific interests, and find the most scenic way to get around. The tours offered by large companies tend to focus on large producers and give no sense of the wealth of environments and tastes to be had. For tailor-made trips to a carefully selected group of cellars based on your interests, including the lesser known and those that require appointments, schedule a tour with **Stephen Flesch ★★★**. Former chairman of the Wine Tasters Guild of S.A. and leader of the Cape Town Slow Food Convivium, Stephen is an ardent wine

EN ROUTE TO STELLENBOSCH VIA THE N2

EXIT 33   The lineup of gorgeous estates starts long before you hit town; just after you turn off the N2, taking exit 33 (Baden Powell Dr.) toward Stellenbosch, you will see the sign for **Vergenoegd ★★★**, which opened the doors of its old Cape Dutch homestead to the public at the end of 2003—great news for red-wine lovers. In fact, the combination of superbly smooth red wines and the gorgeous setting makes it a firm favorite, so don't miss it (ⓒ **021/843-3248;** Mon–Fri 9am–5pm, Sat 9:30am–1:30pm). Vergenoegd forms part of the Stellenbosch-designated Helderberg Wine Route, which includes all the wine estates situated in and around Somerset West, some of which (**Vergelegen** and **Waterkloof**) are best visited en route to the Overberg (p. 168). However, you can cut across to Somerset West from Vergenoegd using the R102. Otherwise, continue on the R310 for Stellenbosch. Consider stopping at

lover and personally knows many of the winemakers and proprietors, and his knowledge of South African wines spans 4 decades. He will take into account your particular interests, be it area, architecture, or cultivar, and create an itinerary that covers both flash estates and rustic farms; lunch too can be at one of the top award-winning restaurants or a lesser-known gem—influenced by your interests and budget. Rates are R1,700 per day for the first person (lunch extra), R850 extra for each additional person (a half-day starts at R1,100). Book well in advance ☎ **021/705-4317** or 083/229-3581; sflesch@iafrica.com; www.gourmet winetours.co.za.

Covering far fewer estates (usually two) per outing, Reiner Kloos's **Gourmet Travels ★★** (☎ **082/449-7666;** www. gourmettravels.co.za) offers personalized epicurean adventures where the focus is more on an extensive wine-paired lunch, or catering for those with a more active bent (cycling between estates) as well as those with families (lunch is then a gourmet picnic, or a crayfish or seafood barbecue). If you're watching your budget, **Bikes 'n' Wines** (www.bikesnwines.com) offers a great alternative to driving. Tours start in Stellenbosch or Cape Town (on Long

St., and you travel to Stellenbosch by train); tours are from 9 to 21km (5½–13 miles) with stops at two to four farms, and frequent tasting (R450–R690 per person); there'll be cellar tours, cheese and chocolate pairings, and possibly brandy tasting, too. Then it's back to town by train. A more conventional approach is with **Adventure Wine Tours** (☎ **021/859-1989** or 083/461-4567), running small-group tours in three different wine areas: Stellenbosch, Franschhoek, and Elgin. You travel in a converted game-viewing style vehicle with a qualified guide and visit a selection of estates with tastings and cellar tours included (R550 per person for a half-day tour). In Stellenbosch a great-value option is to use the hop-on, hop-off **Vinehopper bus** (☎ **021/882-8112;** www.vinehopper.co.za; R190 per person, excluding tasting fees). Choose between two routes (northern route is preferred if you like good reds), each visiting six Stellenbosch estates. In Franschhoek you can catch the **Vineyard Hopper** (☎ **083/301-6774;** www.larochelletours. com; R300 per person, excluding tastings and lunch), traveling between three wine estates: Grande Provence, La Petite Ferme, and Haut Espoir.

the touristy but well-designed **Spier** (☎ **021/809-1100;** www.spier.co.za; daily 9am–5pm), with plenty for families to do. You can for instance watch raptors in flight at their **Eagle Encounters ★★** center (☎ **021/858-1826;** daily 10am–5pm). Note that Spier's offerings were cut significantly with the loss of its **Cheetah Outreach** operator, a conservancy for captive-born cats (try www.cheetah.co.za to see where Cheetah Outreach is now operating). Spier is still a large property, and if it sounds like hard work, hold out for nearby **Stellenbosch Hills,** a low-key estate where five wines are paired with different varieties of biltong (jerky)—from kudu to springbok—and *droewors* (dried sausage), chosen by the winemaker (☎ **021/881-3828;** www.stellenbosch-hills.co.za; R40; Mon–Fri 8am–5pm, Sat 10am–3pm; reservations essential).

EXIT 43 If you don't mind skipping Vergenoegd and Spier, or are perhaps coming from Somerset West (or the Overberg region), there's a string of excellent wine estates to see along the R44 (which links Somerset West to Stellenbosch). Red-wine lovers should look for the sign to **Rust en Vrede** (Rest and Peace) ★★★ along the way—turn right onto Annandale Road to sample these reds (✆ **021/881-3881;** Mon–Fri 8am–5pm, Sat 8:30am–4pm in season); the estate also hosts the most decadently priced restaurant in the region, crowned Restaurant of the Year in 2010 (see "Where to Eat," below). Annandale Road also leads to **Hidden Valley Wines,** which boasts another top-10 eatery, **Overture** (reviewed below), perfect for a long lunch, this time served with an incredible view.

Back on the R44, take either the Stellenrust or Blaauwklippen roads to get to family-run **Waterford** ★★★—a good example of the Cape's love affair with Tuscany (✆ **021/880-0496;** www.waterfordestate.co.za)—where Von Gesau chocolates (handcrafted in Greyton) are matched to appropriate wines so you can discover just how perfectly the tannins of the two complement one another. Next door is **Dornier** (✆ **021/880-0557;** www.dornier.co.za), one of the most attractive modern-style wineries, and you'll be within view of another fine restaurant, **Bodega** (reviewed below).

WHAT TO SEE & DO IN TOWN

If you have time for only one historic stop in town, make it the **Village Museum** ★★, 18 Ryneveld St. (✆ **021/887-2902;** Mon–Sat 9am–5pm, Sun 10am–4pm; admission R30), which comprises the Schreuderhuis Cottage (1709), the Cape Dutch Blettermanhuis (1789), the Georgian Grosvenor House (1803), and the Victorian-era home of O. M. Bergh (1850). Each house has a guide in period dress, and the artful styling of the furniture, combined with the accessible explanations on the architecture and fashion of these eras, make these the best house museums in the country. Just around the corner from the museum is the neo-Gothic **Moeder Kerk,** or "Mother Church," still a vital part of Stellenbosch community life.

From here, head south along Drosdty Street, turn right onto Dorp Street, and then stroll down the oak-dappled street to visit **Oom Samie Se Winkel** (✆ **021/887-2612;** 9:30am–6pm Mon–Fri, 9am–5:30pm Sat–Sun, till 6pm in summer), a Victorian-style general dealer bursting at the seams with kitschy souvenirs; save your money for the stores housed in the **Black Horse Centre** a little further down the street. In fact, back nearer the center of town, you'll find plenty of superb little boutiques selling quality crafts, homeware, clothing, and art. Definitely worth checking out is the **Dorp Street Gallery** ★ (✆ **021/887-2256**), which is now actually on Church Street. While here, pop through the back door into the dreamy little bakery **De Oude Bank Bakkerij** (see "Where to Eat," below). Across the road, you'll find the entrance to the **SMAC (Stellenbosch Modern and Contemporary) Art Gallery** ★★★, De Wet Centre (✆ **021/887-3607**), where good exhibitions are curated in a several renovated room within a vast first-floor space—simply press the door buzzer to be admitted. Art lovers shouldn't miss the permanent 20th-century South African works displayed at the **Rupert Museum** ★★★, Stellentia Ave. (✆ **021/888-3344;** R20 adults; Mon–Fri 9:30am–1pm and 2–4pm, Sat 10am–1pm), often alongside important temporary exhibitions.

THE STELLENBOSCH WINE ROUTE

This is the most established route, with well over 100 estates and farms to choose from, almost all of which are reached via the three major roads radiating from the town center. Note that it's worth double-checking opening times if you're traveling over the weekend.

ALONG THE R306   Heading southwest out of town, one of the best-known farms is 300-year-old **Neethlingshof** (② **021/883-8988;** Mon–Fri 9am–5pm, Sat–Sun 10am–4pm; summer closing times 2 hr. later), worth visiting just for the pleasure of driving up its gracious pine-lined avenue and tasting the Noble Late Harvest. Once there, however, you may find the experience relatively commercial. To reach **Zevenwacht** (② **021/903-5123;** Mon–Fri 8:30am–5pm, Sat–Sun 9:30am–5pm)—one of the prettiest wine estates in the country, with a manor house on the edge of a tranquil lake and views all the way to the ocean, but pretty mediocre wines—take the M12 to Kuilsriver.

ALONG THE R44   Many of the loveliest wine estates are off the road running north to Paarl. Your first stop should be the beautiful **Morgenhof** to sample the merlot and chardonnay (② **021/889-5510;** Mon–Fri 9am–5pm, Sat–Sun 10am–5pm, earlier closings in winter), followed by **L'Avenir** (② **021/889-5001;** Mon–Sat 10am–5pm) to try the Pinotage. The turnoff for tiny **Muratie ★★★** (② **021/865-2330;** daily 9am–5pm), one of the most authentic and least commercial estates, is next. It's a must not only for its berry-rich red wines and port, but for the satisfying ambience of the estate; it's where you'll find the oldest building in the Stellenbosch area (1689). Next is **Kanonkop ★★** (② **021/884-4656**), for more famous reds; the equally acclaimed **Warwick ★★** (② **021/884-4410**); and **Le Bonheur** (② **021/875-5478**)—all on the road to Paarl. Before you hit Paarl, however, don't miss **Babylonstoren ★★★** (② **021/863-3852**), the sensational revival of an 18th-century farm and providing perhaps the best accommodation and dining anywhere in the region. If you don't stop for brunch or lunch at the excellent **Babel ★★★** restaurant, be sure to ask for a **tour of the garden ★★★**—or simply check in for the night (see below).

ALONG THE R310   This is the road to take for the most dramatic views along the **Helshoogte Pass,** which links Stellenbosch with Franschhoek. Before ascending the pass, though, consider first detouring off the R310 into Ida's Valley and heading for **Rustenberg ★★★** (② **021/809-1200;** Mon–Fri 9am–4:30pm, Sat 10am–1:30pm). This gorgeous estate is renowned for its red wines, as well as its peaceful and beautiful setting, with a historic manor house contrasting with a tasting center and state-of-the-art milking parlor. Once on the Pass, your first stop should be **Neil Ellis ★★** (② **021/887-0649;** Mon–Fri 9:30am–4:30pm, Sat 10am–2pm), where tastings happen in a gorgeous new winery (opened Dec 2010) built with rammed earth walls and showcasing a minimalist aesthetic. Next up is **Tokara,** where olives are grown and pressed alongside the vineyards; brunch or lunch here at the gorgeous **DELIcatessen ★★ ☺** (② **021/808-5950;** Tues–Sun 9am–3:30pm), as memorable for the views as for the fresh, open design (and wonderful children's play area). The deli's shop is open until 5pm; in April and early May it's usually possible to arrange to watch the olives being pressed—call ahead for a private tasting. On the other side of the road, **Delaire Graaff ★★★** is simply the most spectacularly situated estate in the Winelands, resuscitated and relaunched in 2009 by diamond dealer and art patron, Laurence Graff. With two restaurants, immaculate lodgings (reviewed below), a spa, tasting lounges, gallery-quality displays of art—huge canvases and monumental sculptures—against a backdrop of superlative architecture, and matchless views. You may find it hard to tear yourself away, but it's worth getting to carbonneutral **Bartinney ★** (② **021/885-1013;** Mon–Fri 8am–5pm) just next door—the wines being produced by award-winning winemaker, Therese de Beer, are superb. You can continue all the way over the pass and—at the T-junction—either turn right and press on to Franschhoek, or left (and then left again) to reach three more impressive farms: **Vrede en Lust ★**, for excellent wines and great country cooking (restaurant: ℂ **021/874-3991**); **Babylonstoren ★★★**, for its cutting-edge gardens (R10 self-guided tour) and stunning daytime restaurant, Babel (reviewed below); and **Backsberg ★★** (ℂ **021/875-5141**). From here, a round trip takes you back to Stellenbosch via the R44.

WHERE TO STAY
On the Outskirts of Stellenbosch
Don't think of the Winelands as a series of towns and villages as much as one vast overlapping area, with many of its best lodgings are in rural or countryside environs between two villages. The two options reviewed below are possibly our favorite places to stay in the entire Winelands region, and they're very convenient for Stellenbosch, Franschhoek, and Paarl—if you can bear to tear yourself away.

Babylonstoren ★★★ 📷 Superlatives trip off the tongue. Like the biblical legend for which it's named, this "Tower of Babylon" conjures up mystery, mystique; a chic rural retreat centered on a showstopper garden with over 300 edible plants. By day, the gardens are visited by the curious and hungry (you're encouraged to pick your own ingredients); at night you have the farm to yourself. There are walks, cycle routes, a dam for canoeing, a massive, elevated farm-style pool, vineyards, and a library. Suites are extraordinary, designed by style maven Karen Roos (who, together with her media tycoon husband, owns the estate). The best are the large whitewashed cottages nearest the garden—glass-walled cubes have been attached with state-of-the-art eat-in kitchens. Both sophisticated and unpretentious, offering pampered country life with spellbinding views. As one guest remarked: "This place makes me want to be a better person"—come and be reinvented.

Klapmuts/Simondium Rd., Franschhoek. www.babylonstoren.com. ℂ **021/863-3852.** Fax 021/863-1727. 12 units. High season R4,270 double; R5,935–R6,405 2-bedroom suite (3–4 guests). Low season R2,970 double; R4,150–R4,480 2-bedroom suite (3–4 guests). Rates include breakfast, laundry, minibar, garden tours, and certain activities. Stay 4 nights pay for 3. MC, V. **Amenities:** Restaurant (**Babel** p. 158); deli; lounge/library; bikes; canoes; pool; spa. *In room:* A/C and fans, TV, fireplace, hair dryer, heated towel rack, library, music system/MP3 docking station, kitchen (6 cottages only), underfloor heating, free Wi-Fi.

Hawksmoor House ★★★ ⚜ An old Cape Dutch manor house meticulously restored and decorated with an eclectic mix of contemporary classic and antique furniture, lending a gracious, sensuous boho texture to the grand-scale spaces. You're invited to treat it as your own country home—a down-to-earth atmosphere where you truly let your hair down (and forgive some of the vagaries of farm living, such as occasional power or water outages, and relaxed service). Bedrooms are appealing and cosseting (some with fireplaces), but do explore the 220-hectare (544-acre) wine estate and take in a spectacular array of scenes—views stretch as far as Table Mountain. Only breakfast is served, but your hosts provide the lowdown on the local dining scene and everything else worth investigating. ***Note:*** Hawksmoor is an easy 25-minute drive from Cape Town's city center, so ideally located for both.

Majieskuil Farm, off the R304 near Klipheuwel, around 20km (12 miles) from Stellenbosch; turn left off the N1 and look for the tiny sign. www.hawksmoorhouse.co.za. ℂ **021/884-4815** or 072/367-4788. Fax 021/884-4816. 14 units. Summer R1,950 double; winter R1,500 double. Rates include breakfast and afternoon tea. MC, V. **Amenities:** Dining room; lounge; honor bar; bikes; library; free Internet; pool; wine cellar. *In room:* A/C, TV/DVD (on request), fireplace (in 4), MP3 docking station (on request), underfloor heating (in bathroom).

In & Around Stellenbosch

For better value accommodations, it's worth considering a spot within the historic center—attractions and a great selection of restaurants and shops are then only a short stroll away along the oak-lined streets. Of these, the best options are **Middedorp Manor** and **River Manor** (both reviewed below), but if you're specifically after something with a sense of real history, **Coopmanshuijs** ★, 33 Church St. (www.coopmanshuijs.com; ✆ **021/883-8207;** from R2,150 double in summer) dates from 1713, when it was one of the first grand residences in town. Public areas are stuffed with period-influenced furniture and decor—it's a slightly too cluttered for our taste but there's even a tiny spa and small courtyard pool squeezed in, and you're right in the heart of village life.

Budget hunters may also want to investigate a few lower-priced options: **Roosenwijn Guest House** ★ (www.stellenguest.co.za; ✆ **021/883-3338**) is right next to Middedorp Manor, and offers comfortable rooms tastefully decorated in Afrikaans-Afro chic for between R880 and R1,540 double (depending on the season and room size). Given its location (a 2-min. walk from the center) and the attractive decor, this is one of the best deals in town, but it doesn't have a great pool or any real garden to speak of. Opposite is Victorian-era **Bonne Esperance** (www.bonneesperance.com; ✆ **021/887-0225;** R750–R1,150 double), a warrenlike guest house worth considering only if you can get an upstairs room, specifically nos. 5, 14, or 15.

Beauclair ★★   This historic house—near Stellenbosch's famous Coetzenburg rugby grounds—is filled with antiques and original paintings, yet the overall effect is far from outdated or prissy but rather one of pared down elegance. As is the norm in these mindful conversions of old houses, each room differs, but all have big fat beds bedecked with wonderful linens. One of the superior rooms has a massive balcony overlooking the pool and back garden; but it's room no. 5 that you want: a massive space with a light-filled bathroom and open plan lounge area.

1 Coetzenburg Rd., Stellenbosch. www.beauclair.co.za. ✆ **021/886-7662.** Fax 021/886-8982. 7 units. High season R1,980 classic double, R2,200–R2,420 superior double; low season R1,520 classic double, R1,700–2,070 superior double. MC, V. No children under 12. **Amenities:** Dining room; lounge; pool. *In room:* A/C, TV/DVD, hair dryer, heated towel rack, minibar, underfloor heating (in bathroom), free Wi-Fi.

Delaire Graff Lodges & Spa ★★★   Located on the crest of the Helshoogte Pass (convenient for both Stellenbosch and Franschhoek), this over-the-top boutique hotel—built by billionaire diamond magnate and art collector Laurence Graff—offers privacy in just a handful of "lodges," each a sumptuous suite with large terrace, plunge pool, and the most exquisite view in the Winelands. Tailor-made furniture suggests African safari influence—leather surfaces, wooden decks, raffia, grasscloth, and oversized stitching on a canvas of creams, mushroom, and natural browns. Each room is just steps away from the fabulous spa, and there are two restaurants on your doorstep (and state-of-the-art wine cellars and lavish tasting room). It's decorated with extraordinary local art—Deborah Bell's iconic canoes immersed in pools between huge glass walls, Dylan Lewis's bronze cheetahs, and Kentridges on the walls.

Helshoogte Pass (R310), Banhoek Valley, Stellenbosch. www.delaire.co.za. ✆ **021/885-8160.** Fax 086/626-4403. 10 units. High season R8,800–R9,350 deluxe double, R9,800–R10,400 luxury double. Low season R7,150 deluxe double, R7,950 luxury double. 4-person lodge R16,200–R26,500 depending on season. Rates include breakfast, mini bar, wine tasting, and evening canapés with sparkling wine. 1 child sharing with 2 adults pays R600–R650. AE, DC, MC, V. **Amenities:** 2 restaurants (**Delaire Graff,** p. 159, and **Indochine**); lounges; bar; babysitting; cinema; pool; room service; spa; wine cellar. *In room:* A/C, TV/DVD, butler's kitchen, hair dryer, iPad, minibar, MP3 docking station, heated plunge pool, free Wi-Fi; Owner's Lodge includes fireplace.

Lanzerac Hotel & Spa ★★ ☺ Just under 10 minutes' drive from the town center, this gracious historic manor with outlying rooms and suites is situated amid rolling vineyards and soaring peaks of Jonkershoek Valley; a refined rural choice that will suit those who prefer a more hotel-like ambience, with all the bells and whistles. Entry-level "classic" rooms come with facsimile antiques and plenty of comfortable touches, but for real privacy, opt for a huge suite out in the gardens (some have a pool). Laid back, and sporting vast, rollicking lawns; an exquisite spa (the only "nibbling fish" dermalogical treatments in the province), and old-fashioned service, the Lanzerac is a stalwart and as hotels go the best Winelands choice, but personally we prefer the casual embrace of Hawksmoor's shabby-chic good looks and low-key hospitality not to mention great value (see above).

Lanzerac Rd., Stellenbosch 7599. www.lanzerac.co.za. ℂ **021/887-1132.** Fax 021/887-2310. 48 units. Peak season R3,410 classic double, R4,140 luxury double, R5,780 junior suite, R8,260 suite; value season R2,330 classic double, R2,920 luxury double, R4,080 junior suite, R5,790 suite. Rates include breakfast. Children under 4 stay free, children 5–11 pay R550 if sharing. AE, DC, MC, V. **Amenities:** 2 restaurants; cigar bar; lounge; babysitting; free Internet (near reception); 4 pools (including 1 indoor and heated); room service; spa; wine tasting and cellar tours. *In room:* A/C, TV, hair dryer, heated towel rack, minibar, underfloor heating, Wi-Fi (by voucher, for R89 per 230MB, in a few rooms).

Middedorp Manor ★★★ A hushed retreat from the bustle of the student village, yet all the action is just a short walk from the front door (you're within 4 min. of 10 decent restaurants, in fact). And from the gracious welcome of Maxwell, the self-styled butler, to the attentions of the fluffy house cat, this feels like home from the moment you enter. A few handpicked antiques, yet contemporary; unfussy and pared down. Bedrooms are crisp, tranquil; at night, wooden shutters keep out any noise. The lounges are good spaces in which to unwind, as its the garden with its wild irises, persimmon trees and pretty little pool; by sunset, it fills with birdlife, and out come olives, served with port or sherry. It's small (just four rooms—book no. 1, the largest); perfect if you want to rent a house in its entirety.

16 Van Riebeeck St., Stellenbosch. www.middedorpmanor.com. ℂ **021/883-9560.** 4 units. High season R2,070 luxury double, R2,650 deluxe double; low season R1,260 luxury double, R1,610 deluxe double. Rates include breakfast. MC, V. **Amenities:** Breakfast room; honor bar; lounge; library; pool. *In room:* A/C, TV/DVD, movie library, hair dryer, free Wi-Fi.

River Manor Boutique Hotel & Spa ★★ A few minutes' stroll from the heart of town, this guesthouse comprises two interlinked national monuments on an oak-lined road that follows the course of the Eerste River. It's recently acquired a slightly more contemporary facade—pale gray walls and some up-to-date aesthetic touches in the otherwise Colonial-themed rooms (still graciously outfitted with historical prints, turn-of-the-20th-century trunks, and chunky antique wardrobes offset by bold-colored fabrics). The pools are surrounded by lounger-dotted lawns, and for those who want to escape the sun, deep verandas have comfortable chairs and striped awnings; fragrant with the scent of ripening guavas, the garden twinkles at night with fairy lights. You're best off booking a superior room (no. 16 is a personal favorite).

No. 6–8 The Avenue, Stellenbosch 7600. www.rivermanor.co.za. ℂ **021/887-9944.** Fax 021/887-9940. 18 units. High season R1,300 petite double R1,990 standard double, R2,800 superior double. Green season R960 petite double R1,360 standard double, R1,990 superior double. Rates include breakfast. Children by prior arrangement. MC, V. **Amenities:** Restaurant; bar; lounges; 2 pools; room service; spa. *In room:* A/C and fan, TV, hair dryer, minibar, free Wi-Fi.

Sugarbird Manor ★★ 🍃 Ten minutes from Stellenbosch center, yet countryside bliss is yours as you navigate through the tree-lined gardens culminating in this modern, good-looking guesthouse among the vineyards and protea plantations. Proteas figure large in the spacious manor house—surrounded by 21 hectares (52 acres) of working farmland—from the bulging vases to full-length charcoal portraits and textile designs. Bedrooms are fairly compact, very neat, and frill-free; the superior rooms downstairs have private patios with direct pool access. The upstairs rooms lack balconies, but the view from the bed in room no. 8—across a lawned garden, infinity pool, and gently undulating hills that float off all the way to a backdrop of jagged mountains—is great. If you feel like hanging about, you're free to use the barbecue, and they'll serve breakfast (and lunch) to your room (or the pool). The rural environment demands exploration; biking trails start from your front door.

Protea Heights Farm, Devon Valley Rd., Stellenbosch 7600. www.sugarbirdmanor.co.za. ✆ 021/865-2313. Fax 021/865-2326. 9 units, 3 with shower only. High season R1,200–R1,450 double, R1,700 suite. Low season R1,000 double, R1,200 suite. Rates include breakfast. AE, DC, MC, V. **Amenities:** Dining room; lounge; bikes; pool. In room: A/C, TV, hair dryer, free Wi-Fi.

WHERE TO EAT

In the last few years, Stellenbosch has emerged as *the* Winelands dining destination—although you'll still hear fierce arguments according that honor to Franschhoek. It's a debate worth putting to the test, so come hungry. Stellenbosch certainly offers greater variety and better value. Because there's a year-round buzz, which has a lot to do with the huge seasonal student population, you never want for ambience, which Franschhoek lacks come nightfall. Stellenbosch's dining scene also isn't quite so focused on tourist trade, meaning there's a slightly more authentic cuisine culture.

The last few years have seen an astronomical growth in small, cafe-style eateries right in the heart of the town: Among the best is **Nook Eatery ★★**, 42 Ryneveld St. (✆ 021/887-7703; Mon–Fri 8am–4pm, Sat 8am–1pm, pizza night Fri 6–9pm)–our number-one choice for breakfasts and light daytime dining. They do a wonderful lunch buffet (you pay by weight for whatever's on their organic, free range spread), but also offer burgers, croque monsieur, wraps, sandwiches, and soups. First rate coffee, too. Further along the same road, there's more good atmosphere, vibrant decor, and interesting food at **5 Ryneveld ★** (✆ 021/886-2940; daily 8am–10pm), which has a private cinema space with art-house and cult screenings. Nearby, you can combine browsing for unusual local crafts (no beads or wirework) with superb cakes and quiches (try the butternut and biltong if it's on the blackboard) at **Cinnamon & Silk** (✆ 021/886-7166; Mon–Fri 8:30am–5:30pm, Sat 9am–3:30pm); their baked nougat cheesecake is a winner. Whatever you do, don't miss **De Oude Bank Bakkerij ★★★** (✆ 021/883-2187; Tues–Fri 8am–3pm, Sat 9am–3pm, Sun 9am–1pm), tucked down an alley at 7 Church St. (behind Dorp Street Gallery), where artisanal baker Fritz Schoon (who apprenticed at île de pain in Knysna; see p. 225) turns out gorgeous sourdough loaves, dark rye, and baguettes from a wood-fired oven in a rustic-chic space. The sit-down bakery doubles as a deli, with Lucas Jamon ham (from Prince Albert), several lesser-known wines, preserves, tapenades, and good coffee from a micro-roastery in nearby Kuilsrivier. Grab a seat and choose from the handwritten menu—it's the kind of place where you want to bide your time. Pizza, beer and wine are served on Wednesday and Saturday evenings from 6:30 till 10pm, perhaps accompanied by live music.

For more substantial fare, book early at any of the places reviewed below—many are out of town; most offer sublime views by day. If you'd like the vineyard experience, but not the fine dining atmosphere, then pick up a packed lunch basket at **Warwick ★★** (✆ 021/884-4410; Sun–Thurs 9am–5pm, Fri 9am–6pm), on the

R44, the best Winelands picnic experience available with purpose-made picnic pods around the lake on the estate, or you can head to the viewing deck above the vineyards.

If you want more sophisticated dining in the historic center, there's a decent mix all within walking distance of each other (and possibly from your guesthouse door). In terms of ambience and architectural setting, **The Big Easy** (reviewed below), owned by golfing legend Ernie Els, is on par with the best. Oenophiles should head for **Wijnhuis** (© **021/887-5844**), in the Dorpsmeent Complex on Andringa Street, where you can dine on average Mediterranean-type fare but with plenty of by-the-glass tastings of the region's best wines.

Finally, no overview of Stellenbosch eateries would be complete without a mention of the Pan-African buffet (lunch R195, dinner R250; drinks and 10% service charge extra), served by the face-painted staff at **Moyo** (© **021/809-1133;** daily 11:30am–11pm), on the Spier Estate (a sprawling tourist mecca with hotel, craft stalls, wildlife sanctuaries, and other entertainment): This is a great summer-night option, when the treetops are lit up, the drummers and dancers are writhing in the candlelight, and the Bedouin-tented lounge areas abutting the dining area look their most romantic and inviting. Combining the theatrical with interesting dishes from across the continent, Moyo is a recommended, albeit touristy, night out. Parents with young kids may want to look at lunch Spier's **Eight ★** (© **809-1188;** Tues–Sun 10am–4pm), another lovingly decorated venue for light-to-substantial meals; beneath the trees, there's a play area for children, with squirrels scampering beyond.

AmaZink Eatery ★ 📷 🍴 SOUTH AFRICAN   The most accessible "township" restaurant in the country—close to Stellenbosch—is a collaboration between enterprising local, Loyiso "Roots" Mbambo (also restaurant manager), and award-winning restaurateur Bertus Basson (of Overture fame; see below), who consults on the menu. But, more than anything, it's a chance to experience how many real South Africans (as opposed to tourists and the well-to-do) let their hair down when they head out for hearty grub and easy-flowing liquor: Don't be shy—people here are keen to meet you. Meat (mix and match as much as you want, or order the Khoro platter, which includes sausage, chicken and a lamb chop) is barbequed on big wood-burning fires in an open kitchen, and served with pumpkin fritters, *pap* (a bit like polenta) and *chakalaka* (a spicy sauce that goes with most anything). People are here to have a good time, so the bar is key, and this is one of few township restaurants where wine is available (they even have their own label from a local farm)—be sure to arrange a taxi.

118A Masithandane St. Khayamandi, Stellenbosch. © **021/889-7536.** www.amazink.co.za. Main courses R40–R120. MC, V. Wed 11:30am–11pm; Thurs 6–11pm; Fri 11:30am–late; Sat 11am–late; Sun 11am–3pm.

Babel ★★★ 😊 SOUTH AFRICAN/MODERN COUNTRY   Even amidst so many exquisite Winelands restaurants, this beautiful indoor-outdoor eatery really is a tower of inspiration and fresh ideas. Although it's closer to Paarl and technically associated with Franschhoek's wine route, Babel is even more easily accessed from Stellenbosch, and a convenient add-on to several of its wine routes. Ingeniously, the restaurant concept (dreamed up by South African food doyen Maranda Engelbrecht) turns much of what you know about dining on its head. The menu, changing according to what comes out of the pesticide-free garden, asks you to contemplate what you might like to combine. Salads, for example, are listed by color (green, red, yellow) and then ingredients show up at the table for a DIY mixing session. Organic meats from the region include slow-roasted pork belly glazed with prickly pear and ginger; or lamb cutlets with mint geranium and cavello nero drizzle, beet chutney and ginger salt. Desserts are an experience unto themselves, broken down into flavor categories (sweet, sour, bitter, or savory)—we swoon for Gorgonzola crème brûlée with cabernet sauvignon vinegar syrup. Edgy, this is an astonishingly good addition to the Winelands dining scene.

Babylonstoren, Babylonstoren Rd. (R45). ℭ **021/863-3852.** Reservations highly recommended. Main courses R55–R145. MC, V. Wed–Sun 10am–4pm.

The Big Easy ★ INTERNATIONAL One of Stellenbosch's most dazzling heritage buildings, La Gratitude, is now a bistro co-owned by golfing legend Ernie Els. A wine (and sometimes sports) bar it still manages to be the most stylish restaurant in town, offering tastings most days and a decadent assortment of vintages to pair with dishes from a small menu of average comfort dishes. There's something for all tastes—apparently the millionaires like the burgers, accompanied by astronomically priced wines. Tee off with a dozen west coast oysters with cabernet dressing, or sample the wonderful pan-fried soft-shell crab. Then get stuck into one of the chargrilled steaks, the sesame-encrusted tuna, or slow-cooked lamb shank. The restaurant comprises a warren of elegant dining spaces, cozy lounge nooks, slick bars, and a 10-seat private golf-themed dining room, all serviced by a brigade of coiffed waitstaff, some very eloquent on the subject of wine.

95 Dorp St., Stellenbosch. ℭ **021/887-3462.** www.ernieels.com. Reservations recommended. Main courses R75–R260. AE, DC, MC, V. Mon–Fri 7:30am–11pm; Sat–Sun 8:30am–11pm.

Casparus ★★ ECLECTIC Former Tokara chef Etienne Bonthuys is well known for his love of over-the-top flavor combinations and fiery temperament; he's apparently toned down the latter now that he's working his own kitchen, right on one of Stellenbosch's most historic streets. A former theater cafe has been transformed into a sensation-stirring indoor-outdoor restaurant with moveable walls that slide or swing away completely in summer, letting the dining area merge with the deep, tranquil back garden. The design is inspired as much by Piet Mondrian as by Beijing's Bird's Nest Stadium—an unexpectedly modern space hiding behind an innocent, original early-19th-century facade. As you'd expect from a chef renowned for his experimental ways, the menu is a regularly changing, ever-evolving thing, inspired by seasonal availability, but generally with plenty of seafood starters, and a lineup of meaty mains. Flavors are inventive—although some question his more decadent pairings, such as springbok with lobster sauce—and some of the simpler dishes are wonderfully light and fresh. Save room for something sweet, too—a simple pairing of berries and homemade mint ice cream is the perfect end to any meal. Hopefully, by the time you sit down to dine, teething problems with uneven service will have been resolved.

59 Dorp St., Stellenbosch. ℭ **021/882-8124.** Reservations highly recommended. Main courses R70–R150. AE, DC, MC, V. Tues–Sat noon–3pm and 7:30–10pm.

Delaire Graff ★★ BISTRO High on the Helshoogte Pass this is arguably the best-located restaurant in the region: Facing the Simonsberg and craggy Groot Drakenstein mountains, with vineyard-carpeted valleys plunging away from beyond the terrace on which you're seated, the experience is quite sensational. And if the majestic setting and astonishing vistas aren't enough, there's impressive art at every turn, a gigantic glass-walled winery, and the genius building itself. Meals are a bit of a hit and miss affair however (not ideal given the price), with quite a high chef turnover since opening—if they get the right cook, this will be a winner, so watch this space.

Helshoogte Pass (R310), Banhoek Valley. ℭ **021/885-8160.** www.delaire.co.za. Reservations recommended. Main courses R110–R170, lobster R295. AE, DC, MC, V. Daily noon–2:30pm; Mon–Sat 6:30–9:30pm.

Dornier Bodega Restaurant ★★ ☺ MODERN FARM CUISINE   Housed in a renovated Cape Dutch barn, this is a mellow spot for a languid lunch, wine-fuelled conversation, and unpretentious cooking. Grab a table on the terrace and linger over the views of the contemporary winery against a stunning *fynbos*-clad mountain backdrop. Chef Neil Norman sources wonderful ingredients—some of which grow wild on the Dornier Estate—to prepare nourishing comfort food that's uncomplicated (line fish with licorice ghoo, risotto with prawns and scallops, and game served with seasonal vegetables). There are so many great starters that you may want to make a meal of them. A glass of Donatus white goes exceptionally well with most everything (as does the homemade sparkling lemonade). During the day, kids have a roaring good time in the dedicated play area.

Dornier Wine Estate, Blaauwklippen Rd., Stellenbosch. ✆ **021/880-0557.** www.bodega.co.za. Reservations highly recommended. Main courses R85–R130, crayfish R250. AE, DC, MC, V. Daily noon–5pm; Thurs–Sat 6–9:30pm. Closed May–Sept dinner.

Jardine at Jordan ★★★ CONTEMPORARY COUNTRY   Enjoying George Jardine's dishes is a privilege—he's considered one of the best chefs on the continent (and justifiably so). Passionate about every stage of what ends up on your plate, he grows his own herbs and vegetables, smokes his own fish, and operates a wood-fired oven for enhanced flavor. A few things we've loved: cured trout (from Stanford) with smoked garlic dressing; salt and pepper calamari; deep-fried onion flowers. More hearty fare includes suckling pig baked in the wood oven with honeyed parsnip, braised savoy cabbage, and baby carrots, or line caught hake "grenobloise"—with caramelized onion, braised cavolo nero and butternut. Follow the maitre'd into the cheese room where you choose from various South African artisan cheeses, served with homemade pickles and jams. Views across the farm's small duck-dappled farm dam are of vineyards and mountains. For a serious food journey there's a six-course tasting menu offered twice weekly.

Jordan Wine Estate, Stellenbosch Kloof Rd., Vlottenburg. ✆ **021/881-3617.** www.jordanwines.com. Reservations highly recommended. R225 2-course lunch, R250 3-course lunch; R300 6-course dinner tasting menu, or R500 with paired wines. AE, DC, MC, V. Daily noon–3pm (May–Sept closed Mon) and Thurs–Fri 6:30pm–close.

96 Winery Road ★★ 🍴 MODERN SOUTH AFRICAN/STEAK   This is one of the most unassuming and unpretentious restaurants in the Winelands, yet it has a loyal local following—wine magazine editors and wine farmers included—who appreciate the informal atmosphere; unfussy, delicious food; great wine list; and excellent service (this is one place where waiters really know their wines). The menu changes every 6 months (with daily changes to accommodate fresh, seasonal produce), but established favorites include the "famous" duck and cherry pie (meat roasted in a rich port and black cherry sauce) and a succulent beef burger (topped with brie and sautéed black mushrooms). The dry-aged steaks are legendary. In season, you'd better book way in advance.

Zandberg Farm, Winery Rd., btw. Stellenbosch and Somerset West. ✆ **021/842-2020.** www.96wineryroad.co.za. Reservations recommended. Main courses R85–R145. AE, DC, MC, V. Daily noon–3pm, Mon–Sat 7–10pm.

Overture ★★★ FRENCH   Since this spot picked up a coveted spot in the *Eat Out* top-10 restaurants list in its first year (and retaining its position in 2010), you need to book weeks in advance to experience Chef Bertus Basson's legendary food. Keeping it real is part of the ethos that drives Basson, something of a culinary superhero in these parts; energetic and sailor-mouthed, he keeps a testosterone-fueled kitchen: "We cook like men," he says; rather than messing with anything "new and experimental," he focuses on using the freshest local ingredients (whatever the local market, farmers, and fishmonger supply) to create food that tastes every bit as good as it looks. By adapting the menu daily and eliminating waste—so no part of any animal or vegetable is thrown away—he promises creative choices, with no telling what'll be served; there's no signature dish here. There'll be around seven options and just a couple of desserts, each paired with a delicious wine from the Hidden Valley estate.

Hidden Valley Estate, Annandale Rd. ✆ **021/880-2721.** www.dineatoverture.co.za. Reservations essential. A la carte main courses R110–R135; 4 courses R340, or R455 with wine; 5 courses R400, or R500 with wine; 8-course tasting menu R600, or R750 with wine. AE, DC, MC, V. Tues–Sun noon–3pm; Thurs–Fri 7–9pm.

Rust en Vrede ★★★ INTERNATIONAL   This restaurant has racked up all the major accolades in 2010's *Eat Out* awards, and is climbing steadily up the San Pellegrino list of world's top 100 restaurant (reaching spot number 61 in 2011), so be prepared to get your reservation in well in advance. Menus are stuffed with curious-sounding ideas (cumin cured blesbok, pear and Riesling risotto, kingklip poached in goat's milk), yet they play out without too much fuss—the main focus is on the interesting pairing of flavors. They source meat from their own farm in the Kalahari Desert, and grow their own vegetables and herbs. If you prefer to have a few different options, go for the four-course menu. But, if you'd like to put yourself entirely in the chef's hands, opt for the set six courses—there's always something surprising in the lineup (such as pigeon and fig, with braised bacon, goat's milk, and pistachio cream and a pickled beet purée).

Rust en Vrede Wine Estate, Annandale Rd., Stellenbosch. ✆ **021/881-3757.** www.rustenvrede.com. 4 courses R440; 6 courses R580, or with wine R880. AE, DC, MC, V. Tues–Sun 7pm–late.

Terroir ★★★ INTERNATIONAL   Chalkboard menus are de rigueur in the Winelands and here you find them packed with simple-sounding, exquisitely executed dishes, courtesy of Chef Michael Broughton, one of the country's best. You have to drive through a bland housing estate to get to what is—given the status of its cuisine—a surprisingly rustic space. Once you're seated, the venue fades a bit into the background as the food (prawn risotto, springbok loin, Karoo lamb, white chocolate mascarpone and raspberry tart) comes into full focus. Much is prepared using the wood-burning oven, so you'll pick up a sensuous smokiness on items such as the slow-braised pork belly. Predictably, the wine list features vintages from the estate, most available by the glass.

Kleine Zalze Wine Estate, Techno Park turnoff, Strand Rd. (R44). ✆ **021/880-8167.** Reservations essential. Main courses R152–R196. AE, MC, V. Mon–Sun noon–2:30pm; Mon–Sat 6:45–9:30pm.

Franschhoek

33km (20 miles) E of Stellenbosch; 79km/85km (49/53 miles) E of Cape Town via Stellenbosch/Paarl.

If you plan to concentrate on just one Winelands destination, the prettiest valley by far is Franschhoek (literally, "French Corner"), the land Simon van der Stel gave the French Huguenots fleeing religious persecution in 1688. Closely surrounded by soaring mountains, Franschhoek is so lush a local once compared it to "living in a lettuce," and the genuine sense of being ensconced in a valley—with snow on the surrounding mountains in winter—has always made it feel worlds apart, a homogenous pocket of

European gentility. Its popularity with tourists has seen the main road running through the village's heart transformed into a twee strip of shops and restaurants trading under "Francophile" banners that no longer have anything to do with village life. Still, explore further afield (down side roads or along dirt country lanes), and you understand why it has so many fans. It also boasts the densest concentration of fine-dining restaurants in Africa and excellent accommodations. It's very faux French, however, and some complain that it's just too touristy—at times you can set your watch by the lunchtime arrival of tour buses, and the rivalry between establishments is palpable. While it's much busier and more developed than Tulbagh, Riebeek-Kasteel or Darling (see below), relative to Stellenbosch it's very easy to navigate and offers a comparatively rural atmosphere, with dirt tracks a few blocks from the main road, and glorious views wherever you look. Incidentally, the prison just outside Franschhoek on the road to Paarl and Wellington is the one from which Nelson Mandela was released and made his first appearance on television as he took his first steps to freedom in 1990.

ESSENTIALS

VISITOR INFORMATION   Pick up one of the maps and a regional brochure at the **Information Centre,** on the main road through town (𝄢 **021/876-3603;** www.franschhoek.org.za; Mon–Fri 9am–6pm, Sat–Sun 9am–4pm).

GETTING AROUND   The town is small enough to traverse on foot, but to visit the wine farms, you'll need to hire a car, bicycle, horse, or specialist guide. For the latter, see "Exploring the Winelands," a box on p. 150; for transfers and general tours in the area, contact **Winelands Tours** (𝄢 **021/876-4042**). For wine-tasting expeditions on purebred Arab horses, contact **Paradise Stables** (𝄢 **021/876-2160;** www. paradisestables.co.za; R550 includes wine tasting); to do so by bike, rent one from **Manic Cycles** (𝄢 **021/876-4956;** www.maniccycles.co.za).

THE FRANSCHHOEK WINE ROUTE

EN ROUTE FROM CAPE TOWN   The quickest way to Franschhoek from Cape Town is via the N1. Take Exit 47, turning right on the R44 toward Klapmuts and Stellenbosch, then the R45 to the left marked FRANSCHHOEK. Some of the farms along the way worth looking in on are **Backsberg, Babylonstoren,** and **Vrede en Lust** (see "The Stellenbosch Wine Route," above); this is also where you'll find **Le Bonheur Croc Farm** (𝄢 **021/863-1142**), which runs guided tours every 45 minutes (although, you should know that it's a leather farm more than anything else).

EN ROUTE FROM STELLENBOSCH   If you're coming from Stellenbosch, the quickest route is over the scenic Helshoogte Pass (or R310), linking it with Franschhoek and Paarl. There are enough estates along the way to fill a day (see "The Stellenbosch Wine Route," above), culminating with the beautifully maintained Cape Dutch estate of **Boschendal** ★★ (𝄢 **021/870-4200;** open from around 8:30 or 9:30am to 4:30 or 5pm; wine tastings on Sun only in season [Nov–Apr]). Together with Vergelegen and Constantia, Boschendal is one of the Winelands' most photographed Cape Dutch estates, combining an excellent **manor house museum** (admission R10) with beautiful grounds and great wines. **Boschendal Restaurant** offers an old-fashioned **luncheon buffet** ★★ (𝄢 **021/870-4274;** R240 per person; daily 12:30–3pm; bookings essential) in the manor's original wine cellar: Expect to find a huge table covered from end to end with tasty traditional Cape Malay and South African dishes.

ALONG THE R45 TOWARDS FRANSCHHOEK Just beyond Boschendal, the R310 terminates in a T-Junction at the R45; turn right for Franschhoek, or consider crossing the road into **Allée Bleue,** a huge estate producing award-winning wines, gallons of olive oil, fruit, and herbs. There's a bistro-cafe at the entrance, but you need to penetrate deeper to really appreciate the estate's stunning views of the Groot Drakenstein, Simonsig, and Franschhoek mountains. To do so, book ahead for a **summer picnic ★★** (✆ 021/874-1021; daily 11:30am–3pm). Baskets of fresh country fare are served to tables laid out beneath the oak trees within easy reach of the vineyards and orchards. Back on the R45 towards Franschhoek, the first notable farm worth visiting is **Solms Delta ★★** (✆ 021/874-3937), which has become an essential stop over the last couple of years, not only for the innovative restaurant, **Fyndraai** (reviewed below), but for one of the most informative and lively winetastings in the valley. Over the summer, the estate runs music concerts featuring indigenous music genres, and there's a small museum in the same building where tastings are held. The farm has become an example of community empowerment— the neurosurgeon who bought the estate several years ago insisted that the workers become active partners in the business and the project is a model of transformation.

The next interesting stop is the home of Antonij Rupert Wines, **L'Ormorins ★**, with a luxury wine-tasting experience (✆ 021/874-9045; Mon–Fri 9am–4:30pm, Sat 10am–3pm). Visitors are whisked to the cellar by golf cart and then sit amid an important art collection while hearing about the vintages. There's a standard tasting (R30) with six wines and a port, but the more extensive R70 tasting includes superior vintages and is a must if you're into full-bodied wines. An equally good reason to stop here is Rupert's superlative **Franschhoek Motor Museum ★★★** (✆ 021/874-9000; www.fmm.co.za; R60 adults, R50 seniors and car club members, R30 children 3–12; Tues–Fri 10am–5pm, Sat–Sun 10am–4pm, last entry 1 hr. before close), where you can view and learn about some of the sexiest motorized vehicles ever produced, including many rare models, all in mint condition. The collection of around 300 vehicles spans a century of cars, but the oldest exhibit is an 1898 motorized Beston tricycle. You can't possibly see every car in Rupert's collection—it's so large it has to be rotated; 80 are seen per tour, and there's always an intriguing themed exhibit on the go. Next up, champagne lovers shouldn't miss the Franschhoek home of some of the country's premiere sparkling wines, **Graham Beck ★★** (✆ 021/874-1258; Mon–Fri 9am–5pm, Sat–Sun 10am–4pm), with another architecturally dramatic, high-tech cellar and modern tasting room.

Getting much closer to Franschhoek village, **La Motte ★★** (✆ 021/876-3119; Mon–Fri 9am–4:30pm, Sat 10am–3pm) has been producing wines for 3 centuries (and now it's also under the Rupert family banner). Visit to sample its red wines, but perhaps stay to dine at one of the best restaurants in the valley (reviewed below), or peruse the collection of works by Pierneef in the dedicated gallery, which also hosts exhibitions by assorted contemporary South African artists. Or, opposite La Motte, take the Happy Valley Road turnoff and head for **Môreson** (✆ 021/876-3055; Mon–Sun 11am–5pm); the sauvignon blanc is a good choice for lunch at the estate's relaxed restaurant, **Bread & Wine** (reviewed below), worth visiting for the oven-fresh focaccia alone, served with Mediterranean-style dips. If it's setting you're after, take the Robertvlei Road to **GlenWood** (✆ 021/876-2044; Mon–Fri 11am–4pm, Sat–Sun 11am–3pm in summer) for a beautiful drive and a taste of the estate's fine chardonnays. Back on the main road, pop into **Grande Provence** (✆ 021/876-8600; daily 10am–6pm) to sample the semisweet Angels Tears wine; there's a posh restaurant here, too, as well as a wonderful art gallery and outdoor sculpture garden. Ask if you might be allowed to take a peek at the subterranean cellar, where important guests are hosted for dinner. Just as you reach Franschhoek village, follow signs to **Mont Rochelle** (✆ 021/876-3000; wine tasting daily 10am–7pm), still owned by a descendant of the French Huguenots, for its glorious setting—you can also picnic up here, with luxury food baskets prepared by one of the hotel kitchens (see below).

FRANSCHHOEK PASS ROAD The main road into Franschhoek becomes Huguenot Road and meets a T-junction at the base of the Franschhoek Mountains at the other end of the village. Directly opposite is the **French Huguenot Monument,** erected in honor of the French Protestant refugees who settled here between 1688 and 1700. Turn left to drive the Franschhoek Pass for lunch at **La Petite Ferme**—a must, if you can get a table (see below). Also on the road heading up to the Pass, **Haute Cabrière** (✆ 021/876-8500; tastings R30, Mon–Fri 9am–5pm, Sat 10am–4pm, Sun 11am–4pm) is recommended—and not just for the excellent Pierre Jourdan champagne. Cellar tours (R40 per person) run weekdays at 11am and 3pm, and on Saturday at 11am you can usually witness winemaker Achim von Arnim uncork his bottles by slicing the neck off with a saber; an in-depth tasting and tour follows.

ALONG EXCELSIOR ROAD If instead you turn right at the monument, you'll see a few more options as you feel yourself disappearing into the Franschhoek Mountains: The boutique-style **Boekenhoutskloof ★★** (✆ 021/876-3320) produces internationally acclaimed wines, particularly reds; weekday tastings held 9am to 5pm. Another boutique-style winery to watch for is **Stony Brook,** where tastings are held Monday to Friday 10am to 3pm and Saturday 10am to 1pm; outside these hours, make an appointment for a more informal and personal tasting with owners Nigel and Joy in their home (✆ 021/876-2182). Also along this road is **Café Bon Bon** (see below).

WHERE TO STAY

Franschhoek's property boards have prices quoted in rands, euros, and dollars—proof of its popularity with visitors from all over the world. This tribe—commonly known as Swallows—spend the summers in Franschhoek and then head back to Europe during the sodden winters. They've pumped serious capital into the valley, and as a result, there's no end to lodging possibilities. Besides our top picks in different price categories, reviewed below, also take a gander at the **Owner's Cottage ★★★**, at Grande Provence, which *Harper's Bazaar* considers one of the top villas on earth; rates start at R14,000 for one room in summer, and go up to R42,000 for the whole house over New Year (www.grandeprovence.co.za). If you like the idea of having a place all to yourself (and possibly self-catering), then also take a look at **Explorers Club,** below; the three houses on offer are beautifully decorated, well-kitted, and offer very fair value. Another top choice for a more affordable stay, **La Cabriere Country House ★** (www.lacabriere.co.za; ✆ 021/876-4780) was undergoing a major overhaul at press time; the London-based owner was in the throes of rebuilding, but his new rooms will be larger and swankier than before, so keep an eye on his website.

Auberge Clermont ★★ 🍃 On a working wine, plum, and olive farm, in an old wine cellar, painted cream and offset with baby blue shutters, this inn is inspired by the tastes and colors of Provence—the gardens, redolent with the scent of lavender and roses, are an integral part of this theme; when weather's good, breakfast is served out here, beneath 140-year-old oak trees. Rooms are large and comfortably decorated, yet none of the bedrooms compares with the beautiful and spacious honeymoon suite, as eye-catching as it is elegant. The two loft rooms are also a good choice if you require a greater sense of privacy. A spacious two-bedroom villa with its own kitchen and pool occupies the 150-year-old farmhouse in a formal French garden.

Robertsvlei Rd., Franschhoek 7690. www.clermont.co.za. ℂ **021/876-3700.** Fax 021/876-3701. 7 units. High season R1,800 double R2,100 honeymoon suite, R3,100 villa; low season R1,500 double, R1,650 suite, R2,500 villa. Double and suite rates include breakfast. AE, DC, MC, V. **Amenities:** Dining room/bar; small pool; room service; tennis court. *In room:* A/C, TV, hair dryer, minibar, free Wi-Fi.

Explorers Club ★★★   Jo Sinfield is an explorer and adventurer and it shows in the inventive design of his three fully equipped efficiency cottages, tucked away in the best part of residential Franschhoek—far from the tourist throngs, but an easy walk to the main road. There's not a single bit of faux-French in sight—rather simple, chic interiors with innovative, quirky furniture, bespoke light fittings and assorted collected artifacts from world travels. Biggest is the **Explorers Club,** sleeping up to six adults and four children in wonderfully proportioned bedrooms (of which one occupies a stand-alone cottage on the far side of the large lap pool in the garden with its mini-vineyard). Hidden behind a jungle garden, the **Map Room** is a romantic two-bedroom cottage with a brilliant, big upstairs open-plan living area—rustic chic. For a more refined, contemporary look, choose the **Library.**

Cabriere St., Franschhoek 7690. www.explorersclub.co.za. ℂ **072/464-1240.** 3 units. The Map Room R1,700 double, R2,300 for 4. Explorers Club R2,700 double, R2,900 for 4, R4,200 for 6. The Library R3,500 double, R3,900 for 4 people, R4,900 for 6. No credit cards. **Amenities:** Kitchen; dining area; lounge/fireplace; TV/DVD; movie library; solar-heated pool (Explorer's) *In room:* Fan, hair dryer, underfloor heating, free Wi-Fi.

La Petite Ferme ★★★   Although they've added four equally handsome rooms in the manor house adjacent their fabulous daytime restaurant, the privacy and views afforded by the old Vineyard Suites remain *the* reason for checking in. Particularly lovely is the aptly named Vista suite, also the most private. The estate's vineyards are within touching distance, and beyond are sweeping valley and mountain views, enjoyable from your king-size bed or private terrace with plunge pool. Spacious and graciously decorated, rooms have all the creature comforts. Staff arrange transfers into the village at night, or day tours of the wineries. Some may find the suites a little cut off from the action—at 5pm, the restaurant closes, and staff is now a phone call away—but this level of privacy, in this kind of location, is priceless.

Pass Rd., Franschhoek 7690. www.lapetiteferme.co.za. ℂ **021/876-3016** or -3018. Fax 021/876-3624. 9 units, some with shower only. R1,144 standard manor house double. R1,892 standard vineyard suite double, R2,112 superior vineyard suite double, R2,816 deluxe vineyard suite double. Rates include breakfast. AE, DC, MC, V. No children under 12. **Amenities:** Restaurant/bar (daytime only; see p. 165); small pool; room service. *In room:* A/C, TV/DVD, fireplace, hair dryer, minibar, plunge pool (Vineyard suites), underfloor heating.

La Residence ★★★   Set on a 12-hectare (30-acre) working farm, Liz Biden's opulent boutique retreat is as good as it gets, if money's no object. Tucked away between the vineyards behind the village, virtually on the slopes of the mountains that form part of the views, the theatrically decorated, sumptuous suites are by the best dressed in the valley, each with unique thematic touches (Asian antiques in the smoldering Tang and Tibetan suites; ultrachic designer classicism in Armani; palatial Indian decadence in Maharani) and tremendous attention to detail. Although it's utterly exclusive, there's hardly a hint of pretentiousness, and the attractive spaces are as comfortable as they are eye-catching, and every guest is treated like the celebrities who love this most sumptuous Winelands escape.

Elandskloof Private Road, Elandskloof Farm, Franschhoek. www.laresidence.co.za. ℂ **021/876-4100.** Fax 021/876-2030. 11 units. R8,200–R8,600 luxury double, R8,530–R8,950 superior double. Rates include breakfast, local drinks, laundry, and local transfers (within Franschhoek). Full board rate available. AE, DC, MC, V. **Amenities:** Restaurant; lounges; bar; pool; room service; spa. *In room:* A/C, TV/DVD, hair dryer, minibar (complimentary), free Wi-Fi.

Le Quartier Français ★★★   This swanky inn offers upbeat accommodations paired with excellent dining, a supercentral location, and all kinds of extras (an in-house cinema with gourmet popcorn; complimentary transport within Franschhoek; massage and other treatments available). Without valley views, it's the rooms that cinch it; most encircle a central courtyard with verdant gardens and a large oval pool, and are huge, comfortable, and stylish. The look is audacious, with great attention to detail. Of the "standard" rooms, no. 16 is best (there's a private garden area). Or splurge on the ultra-chichi Four Quarters suites in the modern wing (the loveliest views are from no. 3). Extras include a private butler and an additional heated pool. Suites have a minibar, iPod docking station, and Wii; two have a plunge pool.

16 Huguenot Rd., Franschhoek 7690. www.lequartier.co.za. ℂ **021/876-2151.** Fax 021/876-3105. 21 units. High season: R3,700–R3,900 inn double, R4,750–R4,900 grande double, R4,950–R8,100 suite. Low season: R2,900 inn double, R3,700 grande double, R3,900–R6,500 suite. Rates include breakfast. Children 12 and under stay in pool and house suite loft rooms free of charge. AE, DC, MC, V. **Amenities:** 2 restaurants (**The Tasting Room** and **The Common Room,** p. 167); bar; lounge; cinema; library; 2 pools; room service; wellness center. *In room:* A/C, TV/DVD, movie library, CD player, music library, hair dryer, free Wi-Fi.

Résidence Klein Oliphants Hoek ★★ 🍴   The "Little Elephant's Corner" is a warm, sociable, good-value guesthouse within easy walking distance of the main road, but set at the edge of a classic ornamental garden in the town's old Mission House. An Italian lady with a keen sense of style, Renata is another European who came to Franschhoek, fell in love, and stayed. She's given all the rooms a beautiful overhaul and turned the entire place into a classy boutique retreat. Standard "comfort" and courtyard rooms are just fine, but there are a couple of special spaces, such as the secluded Hidden Missionary Room or the Sundeck Jacuzzi suite, definitely worth splurging on; these have fireplaces and private outdoor areas. A great choice if you want a sense of history, but don't want to blow your budget—and the view from the Victorian veranda overlooking the rose and lavender garden is quite sublime.

14 Akademie St., Franschhoek 7690. www.kleinoliphantshoek.co.za. ℂ **021/876-2566.** Fax 021/876-2766. 8 units. High season R1,380–R1,630 double, R1,820–R2,700 special rooms and suite. Low season R780–R1,140 double, R1,360–R1,640 special rooms and suite. AE, MC, V. **Amenities:** Lounge; bar; library; pool. *In room:* A/C and fan, TV, fireplace (some), hair dryer, underfloor heating (most), free Wi-Fi.

WHERE TO EAT

Despite stiff competition from Stellenbosch, Franschhoek still clings to its self-pro-claimed title as the gourmet capital of South Africa, and there's certainly an astonish-ing choice, given the relatively miniscule size of the village. Several restaurants (notably **The Tasting Room;** see below) are now fixtures on the global foodie map, and Franschhoek is renowned for its produce, particularly its rainbow trout, olives, and handcrafted chocolates; chocoholics should book The Chocolate Experience at **Huguenot Fine Chocolates** (ℂ **021/876-4096**), where you can choose from 45 chocolate varieties (although, if you're looking for chocolate makers rather than chocolatiers, it's worth saving yourself for DV Chocolate in Hermanus). Another local icon is Reuben Riffel, the star of Franschhoek's favorite rags-to-riches success story—and creator of **Reuben's,** 19 Huguenot Rd. (ℂ **021/876-3772;** Mon–Sun

8–10:30am, noon–3pm, and 6–9pm), long a big hit on the main Franschhoek strip. It's now one of three restaurants, so you've more chance of spotting him on television (promoting a local spice brand) than seeing him in his Franschhoek kitchen. A better bet just a few steps away, also on the main road are The Common Room or **Ryan's Kitchen** (both reviewed below). Note that if you're keen to escape starched linen tablecloths you can order a picnic platter from **The Country Kitchen Restaurant** (© **021/876-3000;** R290 feeds two) and sprawl under trees beside the dam. Finally, if you simply want a low-key country-cafe meal in a sublime vineyard setting, head for the terrace at **Café Bon Bon ★★**, just outside the village; La Petite Dauphine, Excelsior Rd. (© **021/876-3936;** daily 8am–4pm, Wed 7–10pm; main courses R62–R135). What started out as a low-key coffee shop became so popular that it was forced to expand and take on ex–La Residence chef Chris Smit. Sit beneath the trees or in the converted 200-year-old cellar, surrounded by artworks (for sale) and fabulous aromas. Start with the fish cakes, and then consider ostrich curry, roasted pork belly, or ostrich shepard's pie with sweet potato mash.

Bread & Wine ★★★ ☺ MEDITERRANEAN Neil Jewell's superlative cooking has established a firm fan base, with foodies driving from all the way from Cape Town not only for the great food but for the relaxing courtyard venue—if you're here in summer, book an outside table. The menu changes regularly, but the risotto of Italian summer truffle, asparagus, and auricchio cheese, made with a generous dash of the wine estate's champagne, is a firm favorite; also look out for the heavenly char-grilled tuna, served with lime pickle crushed potato, prawn bisque, and tomatillo tempura. Save space for the exceptional fresh-baked breads—you can purchase more at the estate's "farm grocer," along with Neil's famous cured meats.

Moreson Wine Farm, Happy Valley Rd., Franschhoek. © **021/876-3692.** www.moreson.co.za. Main courses R95–R160. AE, DC, MC, V. Daily noon–3pm.

Fyndraai ★★★ CONTEMPORARY CAPE Sean Schoeman's "food of origin" has been a work in progress over the last few years, with dishes that draw on culinary traditions relevant to our past, making use of little known local ingredients, and make them palatable and interesting for the discerning modern diner. Although it's dotted with names you need the back-page glossary to interpret, it's fun discovering that *katballetjies*—literally "little cat balls"—are in fact the tiny bulbs of a licorice-flavored plant, for example. Many of the flavors come from the farm's own indigenous herb garden. Save room for a slice of traditional milk tart, or delicious lavender and *boegoe*-flavored crème brûlée. There's a choice of spaces: Sit beneath the trees or on the terrace for views of the mountains across the lawns and vineyards, or head inside and dine above glass-covered excavations of the original foundations. Or, order a picnic and find a private spot along the river—bring swimming clothes.

Solms Delta Wine Estate, R45. © **021/874-3937.** www.solms-delta.co.za. Main courses R89–R122; picnic R135 per person. AE, DC, MC, V. Daily 9am–5pm.

Le Quartier Français Tasting Room/Common Room ★★★ INNOVATIVE/ BISTRO **The Tasting Room** has long been the best fine dining destination in Franschhoek—and in 2011 was the only South African restaurant to earn a place on the San Pellegrino top 50. Executive Chef Margo Janse experiments like a true adventurer, pushing the boundaries with local ingredients and unexpected pairings, such as coffee-roasted warthog loin. She makes a point of taking inspiration from indigenous ingredients, even using *Amasi* in her confit goat, served with cauliflower and braised horseradish. It's one of the world's great multi-award-winning restaurants, and in season you need to reserve months in advance (or stay at the hotel). If Tasting Room is full, or you don't want to blow the restaurant budget on one meal, Janse also oversees the menu at **The Common Room** right next door. It's an excellent choice: Considerably more laid-back, open throughout the day, it's ideal for tapas-style dining, or for heavier (and delicious) signature dishes like the chicken cooked in a wood-burning pizza oven, or free-range fillet with a buchu-infused béarnaise sauce.

16 Huguenot St. ⓒ **021/876-2151.** Common Room tapas R25–R40, main courses R135–R180. Tasting Room R620 for 5 courses with wine; surprise menu R770, or R1,150 with wine. AE, DC, MC, V. Common Room daily 7am–late. Tasting Room daily 7–9pm.

Pierneef à La Motte ★★ MODERN CAPE   Named in honor of one of South Africa's great artists, this vineyard restaurant also pays tribute to so-called "Boerekos" (Afrikaans for "farmer's food"), and with it the use of aromatic spices and lots of meat, including less popular animal parts such as pig cheeks, pig brain, and sheep's head. Having done his time at Michelin-starred restaurants in Europe, Chef Chris Erasmus now dreams up intriguing combinations in the large open-counter kitchen here—prawn and biltong salad, spare rib risotto (paired with succulent springbok shank), smoked pork belly with almond-flavored prawns, ostrich neck gnocchi, and roast loin of wildebeest (gnu) with honey and turnip gratin. Vegetarian choices are limited, though the risotto of cashews, chili and roasted pepper sounded inviting. Bank on overindulging on desserts—why choose between butternut and lavender panna cotta and the honey ice-cream with hazelnut soup?

La Motte, off the R45. ⓒ **021/876-8800.** Main courses R75–R160. AE, DC, MC, V. Tues–Sun 9am–5pm, Thurs–Sun 7–9pm.

Ryan's Kitchen ★★ CONTEMPORARY SOUTH AFRICAN   "Keep it local and keep it real" seems to be the catchphrase for Chef Ryan Smith, who did a tour of duty in high-profile European restaurants in the '90s and now brings an international slant to his inward-looking menu. Smith doesn't believe in overly elaborate, pretentious food, and he prefers indigenous and seasonal ingredients to exotic produce—fine food, without the fuss. Together with his Russian wife, Svetlana (who manages the front of the house), Ryan operates a cozy dining space, and is constantly in view behind the counter of his tiny, home-style kitchen. By day, it's a casual bistro where you can get light meals (mielie risotto, vetkoek with curried lamb, or even a genuine Durban bunny chow), but at night, candles flicker on the tables and the mood is utterly romantic.

12 Huguenot St. ⓒ **021/876-4598.** www.ryanskitchen.co.za. Lunch main courses R55–R65; dinner R175 for 2 courses, R195 for 3 courses; set menu R295, or R495 with wine. MC, V. Tues–Sun noon–2:30pm and 6:30–9:30pm.

THE OVERBERG & WHALE COAST

During the 17th century, the Dutch settlers saw the jagged Hottentots Holland mountain range as the Cape Colony's natural border, beyond which lay what they called Overberg (literally, "Over the Mountain"). Today this coastal area—wedged between the Cape Peninsula and the garden route, with mountains lining its northern border and the ocean on its south—encompasses a vast patchwork of grain fields, fruit orchards, and fynbos-covered hills. The region is also home to several interesting wine routes, producing wines that display the unique characteristics of its specialized terroir.

Known as "the graveyard of ships," this rugged coastline is pounded by both the Atlantic and the Indian oceans, which meet at **L'Agulhus,** Africa's most southerly point. East of this point is **Arniston** (Waenhuiskrans, to locals), a bleak fishing village overlooking a magnificent turquoise bay, and **De Hoop Nature Reserve,** which vies with the garden route's Tsitsikamma as the most beautiful coastal reserve in South Africa.

The Overberg Coast is also a sanctuary for the southern right whales that return in increasing numbers every spring to mate and nurse their young off the aptly named "Whale Coast." The towns of **Hermanus** and De Kelders, both of which overlook Walker Bay, and Koppie Alleen in **De Hoop Nature Reserve,** are considered the best locations for viewing these strangely elegant 60-ton, callus-encrusted cetaceans.

There are two main routes to Hermanus, unofficial capital of the Overberg: the **N2,** which cuts over the mountains by way of **Sir Lowry's Pass** and then passes through the wine- and apple-growing **Elgin Valley** (also the quickest way to reach the garden route); and the slightly more circuitous and cliff-hugging **Coastal Route,** at parts as scenic as Chapman's Peak and highly recommended.

En Route: Two Wine Estates & Elgin Valley

From the city, the N2 takes you past the airport and straight to Somerset West, a town with some of the country's priciest real estate despite the town ranking as one of the dullest on the planet. However, **Vergelegen ★★★** ("Far Location"; ✆ **021/847-1334;** daily 9:30am–4pm; call for tour times) is a must-see wine estate, marred only by the fact that you need to drive all the way across the sprawled-out town to get there. Built by reprobate Willem Adriaan van der Stel (who took over from his father as governor of the Cape in 1699), the project was a serious abuse of his power, as he built it on land that did not actually belong to him and used Dutch East India Company slaves and resources to compete with local farmers. He was sacked in 1707, and the farm was demolished and divided. Today this beautifully restored wine estate, surrounded by gorgeous gardens, is known to be Mandela's favorite, as well as the only one to host Queen Elizabeth II and the Clintons during their respective state visits. The estate restaurant, **Lady Phillips** (✆ **021/847-1346**), serves fine meals in a wonderful atmosphere; in summer, the alfresco **Rose Terrace** is glorious for a relaxed meal. Another worthwhile Somerset West destination, and a great contrast to the centuries-old Vergelegen, is the modern glass and concrete box called "cellar in the sky" at **Waterkloof ★★** (✆ **021/858-1491**). The views alone—the vineyards sweeping below, and all the way across False Bay—are unforgettable. Waterkloof is just beyond Somerset West itself, above impoverished Sir Lowry's Pass Village. From here, you can reach the Overberg either via the coast, turning toward it at Gordon's Bay (see below) or traverse Sir Lowry's Pass over the Hottentots-Holland mountains, depositing you in the fertile Elgin Valley. A mere 60km (37 miles) from Cape Town, Elgin Valley is a personal favorite: the prettiest, most authentically rural wine-growing valley within close proximity of the city, and well worth an overnight stop if you're keen to get off the beaten track. It also has a clutch of wine farms—the region is said to produce some of the best sauvignon blancs in the country (prioritize your visit to include stops at **Iona ★★★** ✆ **028/284-9678** and **Oak Valley ★★★** and **South Hill ★** (✆ **021/844-0033**) to sample them—but is best known for its apples—the valley produces 65% of South Africa's export crop (and it's home to Appletiser, the

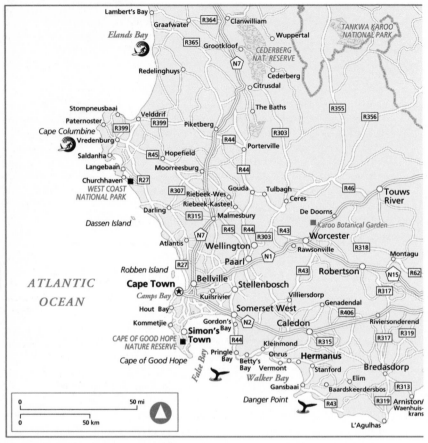

world's number one sparkling apple juice). It's also here that South Africa's first *methode cap classique* fermented cider, Terra Madre Pommes Classique, is produced. If you're here in summer, look out for music concerts held at the **Paul Cluver Amphitheatre ★★★** (www.cluver.com has the lineup), the loveliest performance space in the country, with an outdoor stage and tiered seating built beneath soaring ghost gum trees; buy tickets well in advance (some of the country's top bands and musicians appear here in riveting close-up), bring blankets and cushions, and definitely make plans to overnight at **Old Mac Daddy ★★★** (www.oldmacdaddy.co.za; 𝄐 **021/844-0241;** R975-R1,200 per trailer; R1,750–R2,100 six-person villa). This "luxury trailer park" consists of 13 imported vintage Airstream trailers mounted on a hillside and then individually decorated by different artists. The resulting bedrooms provide the sensation of sleeping inside an art installation, a dramatic counterpoint to the crisp, pine-fresh minimalism of the attached lounge, with its massive foldaway glass walls and sweeping valley views. If Old Mac Daddy is full (and you really need to book well

Surfing

Whale watching

ahead), then opt to stay at **South Hill** ★ (www.southhill.co.za; ✆ **021/844-0033,** or 021/421-1367 reservations; from R900 per room), a super guesthouse on a wine estate, with the valley's best restaurant bang on your doorstep: **Gordon Manuel @ The Venue ★★★**; at R165 for two courses, also a good value. There's also a pool, a comfy lounge (with fireplace), and a kitchen where you're welcome to cook. Rates start at R900 per room.

The Coastal Route: Gordon's Bay to Hermanus

You can reach Hermanus in about 80 to 90 minutes via the N2 (which takes you right through the gorgeous Elgin valley; see above), but the coastal route, which adds another 20 to 30 minutes to the journey and snakes along the sheer cliffs of the Hottentots Holland mountains as they plunge down to the oceans below, is the recommended route if you not including Elgin in your trip (or you could save the coastal stretch for the return from Hermanus). To take it, head for **Gordon's Bay,** an easy

40-minute drive from Cape Town on the N2, and take the coastal road (R44) out of town. Keep an eye out for **whales** and **dolphins** in **False Bay** as you descend the cliffs and bypass the river mouths and rocky outcrops broken by small sandy coves oft shaded by ancient milkwood trees.

Having crossed the Rooiels River (named for the red alder trees that grow in the riverine bush up the gorge), you head through fynbos-covered hills passing the Buffels River and the sprawling holiday village of **Pringle Bay.** While Pringle isn't in itself a beautiful village, the coastline and mountain views are lovely, and it's in a UNESCO World Nature Reserve. If you're hungry, stop at the clearly signed **Hook, Line and Sinker ★★** (✆ **028/273-8688;** Thurs–Sun lunch, Wed–Sun dinner) thoroughly unpretentious, with newspaper-covered tables and fresh, fresh seafood—it's popular and seating is limited so reservations are a good idea). Or stop at **Lemon and Lime Deli** (✆ **028/273-8895**) to pick up some treats such as smoked snoek pâté and a loaf of its famous bread, and press on. Just past Pringle Bay, where the R44 cuts inland past the Grootvlei marshlands, is a less traveled detour to **Cape Hangklip,** pronounced *hung*-clip—literally, "Hanging Rock" (just check that the road is open before you leave Pringle Bay). This 460m-high (1,509-ft.) wedge of rock was often mistaken for Cape Point, which incidentally is how False Bay came by its name. After skirting three lagoon-type lakes—estuaries blocked by coastal dunes—you reach **Betty's Bay,** home to a remarkable number of ugly vacation cottages, one of only two land-based colonies of jackass penguins (the other is in Cape Town), and the secluded, beautiful **Harold Porter National Botanical Garden** (✆ **028/272-9311;** Mon–Fri 8am–4:30pm, Sat–Sun 8am–5pm; R16). Take one of four trails up the mountain to the **Disa Kloof Waterfall** (duration 1–3 hr.) to appreciate the beauty of the Cape's coastal fynbos.

The R44 now heads northeastward in the direction of Caledon, while the road to Hermanus branches eastward from the inland side of the Palmiet Lagoon. This is called the R43; take it and keep an eye out for the R320 turnoff, which will take you past the vineyards of the **Hemel-en-Aarde** (Heaven and Earth) valley. Here you can go on wine tastings at the small but excellent selection of farms that make up the **Hermanus Wine Route** (see "What to See & Do," below), stopping for lunch along the way (see "Where to Eat," below).

Hermanus

With a backdrop of mountains, a large lagoon and long white beach, deep rock pools, and a wealth of coastal fynbos, **Hermanus** was destined to develop into one of South Africa's premier vacation resorts—and that was before the whales began attracting aficionados all over the world to what is billed as the best land-based whale-watching experience in the world. Humpback, Brydes, and Minke whales make occasional appearances, but the bay is essentially frequented by southern right whales—in recent years, as many as 2,000 whales have followed the annual migration from Antarctica to flirt, mate, and calve in the warmer waters off the southern Cape coast.

Whales aside, there are numerous **wine farms** in the nearby Hemel-en-Aarde Valley; you'll also find the chance to experience a **close encounter with a great white shark** (see "Shark-Cage Diving," on p. 129) in Gansbaai, take walks on **beaches and cliff paths,** and set off on a number of **good trails** in the Walker Bay and Fernkloof nature reserves. With Hermanus as your base, the **picturesque villages** of Stanford, Arniston, and Elim are only a short drive away, or you could escape the relatively jammed streets of Hermanus and bed down in one of several stunning eco-reserves nearby, and treat the tourist town as the day trip (see "More Whale Coast Destinations," below).

ESSENTIALS

VISITOR INFORMATION The **Hermanus Tourism Bureau** is at the Old Station Building, at Mitchell and Lord Roberts streets (✆ **028/312-2629;** www. hermanus.co.za; all year Mon–Sat 8am–5 or 6pm, Aug–Apr Sun 10am–2pm).

GUIDED TOURS For an insight into the greater community, take a walking tour of the Hermanus neighborhood of Zwelihle, the first black township established in the Overberg, with Wilson Salukazana, a registered guide and proprietor of **Ubuntu Township Tours** (✆ 073/214-6949). **Walker Bay Adventures** (✆ **082/739-0159**) runs kayaking trips in the Walker Bay whale sanctuary for R300 per person (2 hr.); you can also kayak across the lagoon for wine-tasting beneath Mosaic Farm's milkwood trees for R450 per person. Call **Fernkloof Nature Reserve** (✆ **028/313-0819;** www.fernkloof.com) to find out about specialized fynbos tours. Wine lovers will enjoy an introduction to the Hemel-en-Aarde Valley's many wine farms and tasting rooms: contact Cape Wine Academy–accredited **Percy Tours** (✆ **072/062-8500;** www.percytours.com) for details. Two-hour tours start at R350 per person. See "Staying Active," earlier in this chapter, for **guided horseback riding** excursions. Also see "Whale-Watching," below, for boat operators with permits.

WHAT TO SEE & DO

The sweeping 30km (19-mile) curve of **Grotto Beach** can be seen from most vantage points of Walker Bay. This is a great family beach, made for long walks and swimming. Closer to town, **Voëlklip** is a popular swimming beach where the hip youth hang out; the closest beach, **Langbaai** (pronounced *lung*-buy, meaning "Long Bay"), offers the best bodysurfing, though currents can render it hazardous.

Fernkloof Nature Reserve (✆ 028/313-0819) overlooks the town and offers more than 50km (31 miles) of hiking trails and great views of Walker Bay. The reserve shelters the rare and endangered Roridula gorgonias, the world's largest carnivorous plant, which can reach up to 2m (6½ ft.).

Whale-Watching

A protected species since 1946, the once-threatened southern right whale is Hermanus's single biggest draw. In season one can clearly view the whales in action—breaching, logging, spouting, fluking, lobtailing, and spyhopping—sometimes at a distance of only 10m (33 ft.), from the craggy cliffs that run along the town's shoreline. For the best sightings, take the 12km (7.5-mile) cliff path from New Harbour east to Grotto Beach and the lagoon. Beware of the waves—in 2000 a visitor was swept off the rocks and drowned. Also recommended are the terraces above the Old Harbour, where there's a public telescope. Bringing your own binoculars is highly recommended.

Hermanus is very proud of the fact that it is the only town in the world to have a "whale crier": During whaling season, the crier walks the town streets from 10am to 4pm, blowing a kelp horn in a sort of Morse code to alert the town's inhabitants to the presence and whereabouts of whales. If you don't understand the code, never mind; he also wears a sandwich board and carries a cellphone—he can be contacted directly for reports of the latest whale sightings; at press time the position was up for grabs, so call the museum (✆ **028/312-1475**) for his number.

HEAVEN ON EARTH: THE hermanus WINE ROUTE

Wineries comprising the Hermanus Wine Route are almost all located on the R320, or **Hemel-en-Aarde** ("Heaven and Earth") **Road**, which runs virtually the length of the narrow valley, home to one of the world's top ten chardonnays and a clutch of award-winning pinot noirs. The oldest and most respected wineries are **Bouchard Finlayson ★★★** (*(C)* **028/312-3515;** tastings Mon–Fri 9:30am–5pm, Sat 9:30am–12:30pm) and **Hamilton Russell ★★★** (*(C)* **028/312-3595**). The latter for many years enjoyed the dubious distinction of producing South Africa's most expensive wines—sample the chardonnay and pinot noir here (for free; Mon–Fri 9am–5pm, Sat 9am–1pm) and you'll discover why (be warned, though—you'll be hard-pressed to walk away without a purchase). Another chardonnay you'll want to take home is the one produced at **Ataraxia ★★★** (*(C)* **028/212-2007;** www.ataraxiawines.co.za; Tues–Fri 9am–4pm and weekends 10am–3:30pm), an estate that's taken the industry by storm (*Decanter* called this a "Top 10 New World Chardonnay Producer" in 2009); it's much farther inland, in the most elevated part of Hemel-en-Aarde, with a hair-raising approach—but the destina-tion is definitely worth it. If, once in the valley, you find you don't want to leave, consider spending the night at another beautiful wine estate: **Sumaridge** (*(C)* **028/312-1097;** www.sumaridge.co.za), which has wine tastings (Mon–Sun 10am–3pm), a restaurant, and an effi-ciency guesthouse (R700 double). At the start of the route, **Hermanuspieters-fontein ★★** (*(C)* **28/316-1875;** www.hpf1855.co.za) gained serious recogni-tion in 2010 when Bartho Eksteen was crowned Diners Club Winemaker of the Year; the farm also hosts a **weekly food and wine market** (*(C)* **083/388-8239;** Sat 9am–1pm), where among many other products you can sample the country's only "bean to bar" chocolate, from Hermanus chocolate makers, **DV Artisan Chocolate** (*(C)* **028/316-4850;** www.dvchocolate.com). You can also sample this rich, flavorful chocolate at **Newton Johnson Wines ★★** (*(C)* **087/808-1616;** Mon–Fri 9am–4pm, Sat 10am–2pm), where it can be paired with vin-tages from the estate, and even features on the menu of the estate restaurant, **Heaven** (see "Where to Eat," below). For an expert introduction to Hemel-en-Aarde's wines, contact **Percy Tours** (see "Guided Tours," above).

For assured up-close encounters, consider boarding a boat with a license to approach the whales (up to 50m/164 ft.). Plan on paying around R850 per adult, children under 5 travel free, while older children are eligible for discounted rates. Some of the longest-running operators are **Ivanhoe Sea Safaris** (*(C)* **082/926-7977**), boasting some 8,000 close approaches to southern right whales over the years, and **Southern Right Charters** (*(C)* **082/353-0550**), with 12 years of experience.

Shark-Cave Diving

You are picked up from your guest house (in Hermanus or Cape Town) and taken to **Gansbaai,** a coastal town some 30km (19 miles) east of Hermanus (180km/112 miles from Cape Town). After a debriefing, boats head out to Dyer Island and nearby Geyser Island, favorites of the jackass penguin and seal breeding colonies, whose pups are an all-time-favorite great white shark snack—so much so that the channel between the islands is nicknamed Shark Alley. The better operators claim not to bait the sharks, but rather use chum (a mixture of tuna blood and seawater) to lure the predators by means of a scent trail (this practice remains contentious, but the contribution toward research that your outing funds is incontrovertible). Certainly you stand an excellent chance of seeing one from the cage (or the boat, if you prefer to keep your distance). The going rate in 2011 was R1,750 per person and included your hotel transfer, a buffet breakfast, a half-day at sea on a customized catamaran/boat, wetsuit and snorkeling equipment, a lecture on white sharks, packed lunch at sea, tea, and return transfer. Note that you don't need any diving experience to descend in the cage—you use a mask and snorkel.

There are quite a few vying for your money, but the two operators with the best environmental credentials are **White Shark Projects ★★★** (✆ 028/384-1774 or 076/245-5880; www.whitesharkprojects.co.za), one of the longest-running and most respected (the company was instrumental in getting the white shark protected under South African law and was the recipient of the 2004 SKAL International Ecotourism Award), and **Marine Dynamics ★★★** (✆ **028/384-1005;** www.shark watchsa.com), also internationally recognized for responsible tourism; the latter also offers excellent whale-watching trips in which a marine biologist will take you within 50m (164 ft.) of southern right whales migrating along this coastline.

WHERE TO STAY

Hermanus itself is not a particularly attractive town—away from the sea, it resembles any sprawling city suburb—but it has a certain buzz, and offers a huge variety of places to stay and dine. If you're watching your budget, **House on Westcliff** (www. westcliffhouse.co.za; ✆ **028/313-2388;** R600–R900 double) offers cheery, cheap-as-chips garden rooms. Pluses are the shady garden, sheltered pool, and location (just across the street from the coastal path, and near the new harbor). Also on Westcliff Road (at no. 84), **Harbour Vue Guest House** (www.harbourvue.co.za; ✆ **028/312-4860;** from R900 double) has four neat, comfortable rooms, including two with sea views; decor is old school. On the other side of town in Voelklip, a stroll away from a tiny, sheltered swimming beach, **Hermanus Beach Villa** (www.hermanusbeach-villa.co.za; ✆ **028/314-1298;** R840–R1,100 double, R960–R1,560 suite, breakfast included) offers sea views from balconies attached to each of its compact (but great value) rooms and suites. Given the prices, it's very popular, so book well ahead. If you like modern uncluttered spaces **Selkirk House** is a techno-modernist's dream (it's almost entirely automated), with bland contemporary furniture and chrome and packed stonewalls. It's backed by indigenous bushland on Hermanus Heights, so not walking distance from the sea but you can enjoy panoramic wraparound views from the rooftop; book number 1 for the room with the best all-round views (www.selkirk house.co.za; ✆ **028/312-4892;** R1,100–R1,700 double).

Right in the center of town is the relaxed **Auberge Burgundy ★** (www.auberge. co.za; ✆ **028/313-1201**), where standard rooms start at R1,180 double. Those with balconies and ocean views are your best bet—although the garden options aren't half bad, either. There are a few larger rooms, as well as a penthouse with three double rooms, for R2,950. Just be aware that this area gets unbearably busy in prime season, so noise can be a problem. Breakfast is just across the road at the Burgandy restaurant (see "Where to Eat," below). Avoiding the noise problem altogether is Burgundy's sister guesthouse, **Ocean Eleven ★★**, 11 Westcliff Rd. (www.oceaneleven.co.za; ✆ **028/312-1332;** R2,100–R2,600 double), a Cape Cod–style house on the cliffs above the ocean. In fact, the only sound you're likely to get here is from the waves

If you'd prefer a more rural option with an architecturally charming streetscape (from this point of view, Hermanus is horribly bland), and you don't mind being on a lagoon rather than at the sea, base yourself in the village of **Stanford** ★★, a 15- to 20-minute drive beyond Hermanus. Thanks to planning strictures, the village has retained its historical integrity and, popular with Cape Town's creative types, now boasts a number of lovely places to eat and stay. Best among these is Mosaic Farm (p. 182), outside the village along a dirt road leading to a private reserve. But Stanford is only the tip of the iceberg for travelers in search of seclusion (or even isolation). There are a number of tiny villages and amazing nature reserves as you head deeper into the Overberg—and you'll have your pick of places near the sea, or sequestered among hills smothered in carpets of thick, fragrant fynbos (see "More Overberg & Whale Coast Destinations," below).

crashing against the rocks below. Despite the name, there are only 10 rooms, and those in the main house have original architectural features, such as teak floors and high ceilings—there are also plenty of tall windows to make the most of the view, which can be admired from every room. There is also an apartment sleeping four, which goes for R3,700. If money is no object, the most luxurious accommodations options are listed below.

Auberge Provence ★   Set on the cliffs overlooking Walker Bay, just meters from the whale-watching path that meanders above it, this Provençal-style guesthouse features superb original artworks (including Angus Taylor metal sculptures) and is centered on a central courtyard pool. Interiors are smart, with large stone fireplaces for winter; the exterior features a rustic stone facade, heavy wooden shutters, and wrought-iron balconies. Bedrooms are spacious, tastefully furnished, and very comfortable: You can luxuriate in bed while watching the whales, snug under goose-down duvets. It's close enough to the convenience of the village, but you'll have to get in your car to get to the beach.

25 Westcliff Dr., Hermanus. www.aubergeprovence.co.za. ✆ **028/312-1413.** Fax 028/312-1423. 5 units. Summer R2,190 double, R2,890–R3,090 suite; winter R1,590 double, R2,190–R2,390 suite. Rates include breakfast. AE, DC, MC, V. **Amenities:** Lounge; babysitting; library; pool. *In room:* TV, hair dryer, minibar, heated towel rack, underfloor heating, free Wi-Fi; suites have plunge pool or Jacuzzi.

Birkenhead House ★★★   A glam boutique hotel located right on the sea, this is owned by the same couple who brought us Royal Malewane (p. 354) and La Residence (p. 165). Decor is eclectic—French baroque meets 21st-century modern—with white and cream a great contrast to the blue horizons. The public spaces are gorgeously over-the-top (massive gilded mirrors, French antiques, chandeliers), but not all bedrooms are created equal. The top choices are nos. 1 and 2, with the only unobstructed sea views, but the showstopper effect happens on the large public terrace seemingly floating above the sea, flanked by Hermanus's best swimming beaches. Right next door is the child-friendly **Birkenhead Villa** ★★★. The ambience is even more relaxed and intimate, and although you're not immediately on top of the seafront, the bedrooms all have some ocean view (nos. 1 and 4 have the best) and radiate class and comfort. Service and cuisine standards are also faultless.

7th Ave., Voelklip, Hermanus. www.birkenheadhouse.com. ✆ **028/314-8000.** Fax 028/314-1208. **Birkenhead House:** 11 units. R5,080–R5,500 double, R6,700–R7,250 luxury double, R8,030–R8,650 superior double, R66,745–R72,090 entire house. No children under 12. **Birkenhead Villa:** 5 units. R8,030–R8,650 double (includes 2 children under 12 sharing in family room). Rates include all meals, local beverages (excellent house wines), laundry, and local transfers (within Hermanus). AE, DC, MC, V. **Amenities:** Restaurant; bar; lounges; concierge; library; 3 pools (includes 1 at Birkenhead Villa); room service; spa. *In room:* TV/DVD, movie library, music library, hair dryer, heated towel rack, minibar, MP3 docking station, underfloor heating, free Wi-Fi.

The Marine Hermanus ★★★   Situated on the craggy cliffs close to the town center, this hotel is the grand dame of Hermanus (built in 1902), with wonderful views of Walker Bay and its whales. It's old-fashioned in many ways, which can be seen as a blessing (or not), depending on taste and age. Some rooms are a little floral and "done" for certain tastes, others are more blandly contemporary, but the location and graciousness of age are unbeatable. It's worth spending a little more for a luxury room with an ocean view (be specific when booking, unless you don't mind facing the pool courtyard). Guests can relax in the beach-chic lemon- and cream-colored lounge or the comfortable wicker-furnished sea-facing bar—or put on your bathrobe and head for an invigorating swim in the tidal pool below the cliffs.

Marine Dr., Hermanus. www.marine-hermanus.co.za. ✆ **028/313-1000.** Fax 028/313-0160. 42 units. High season R4,200–R4,400 double, R5,350–R6,600 luxury double, R7,350–R8,800 suite; low season R2,600 double, R3,500–R3,950 luxury double, R4,650–R5,800 suite. AE, DC, MC, V. Children under 12 accommodated by arrangement in low season. **Amenities:** 2 restaurants (including **Seafood at the Marine,** p. 178); bar; lounge; babysitting; concierge; heated saltwater pool; room service; spa; wine cellar. *In room:* A/C, TV/DVD player, movie library, hair dryer, minibar, heated towel racks, underfloor heating, free Wi-Fi.

Mosselberg on Grotto ★★ ☺   Kick back and whip off your shoes: You're here to relax and enjoy breathtaking proximity to an amazing stretch of white beach. This sleek guesthouse is designed by an award-winning South African architect who knows how create great indoor-outdoor flow and make the most of spaces and views. It has just a few rooms around a central courtyard with a gorgeous pool, and homey lounging (and play) areas. With direct access to the famous cliff path that leads you to expansive Grotto Beach, this is one of the few upmarket options in Hermanus to welcome children. The pool isn't fenced off, but there's a playroom with a pool table and board games to keep youngsters occupied if the weather turns. Most glam is the spacious **Southern Right** suite **★★★**, with perfect sea views, balcony, fireplace, polished sandstone bathroom, and dressing area-cum-meditation room.

253a 10th St., Voelklip, Hermanus. www.mosselberg.co.za. ✆ **028/314-0055.** 5 units. R1,370–R2,900 double, R1,670–R3,100 junior suite, R2,070–R3,500 suite. Rates include breakfast. MC, V. **Amenities:** Dining room (excellent dinners); lounge; honesty bar; babysitting; pool; free Wi-Fi (in most public areas). *In room:* Fan, TV, hair dryer, minibar, heated towel racks, underfloor heating.

WHERE TO EAT

Hermanus offers a plethora of dining options in every possible category. And, if you're prepared to drive a bit, there are many more wonderful places at nearby wine farms and in the neighboring village of Stanford, a mere 20km (13 miles) away.

In Hermanus

In Hermanus itself, you'll almost certainly want a sea view while taking in its bounty. Few restaurants in the world can beat the location of **Bientang's Cave** (✆ **028/312-3454;** daily 11:30–4pm; Fri–Sat 7–9pm; reservations essential)—a cave in the rocks literally just above the sea—but don't expect great meals or service. A better bet if you're in this area (near the old harbor) is all-day **Burgundy** (© **028/312-2800**), opposite the old harbor. The oldest building in town (the stone-and-clay cottage was built by a Swedish boat builder in 1875), it has a large terrace overlooking the bay and offers simple, reasonably priced fare (seafood mains R60–R140; seafood platter R240). With its tables and chairs spilling out of a pretty store selling organic soap and homewares, **The Bistro at Just Pure** ★★ (© **028/313-1193**; www.justpure bistro.co.za; daily 8am–5pm) is a perfect all-day dining spot with the sea views from beneath an umbrella on the verandah, or soak up the atmosphere of the scented emporium within: the place is packed with evidence of artisan creativity (and its skin and body products are must-buys); food and coffee are excellent (scrumptious salads) and they offer free Wi-Fi.

But if you really want to savor delectable food with waves crashing all around you, join the locals at **Harbour Rock** ★★ 🍴 (© **028/312-2920**; www.harbourrock. co.za; daily 12:30–3pm and 6:30–10pm or later; main courses R90–R130). There's a good sushi menu alongside the range of fish, shellfish, and meat options, and wine suggestions are included for all mains. And if you really want to hang with locals, the next-door pub is where you'll meet them—the same menu is offered, albeit in less salubrious surrounds.

Quayside Cabin ★★ ☺ SEAFOOD Grab a table in this rustic, part-converted shipping container overlooking the fishing boats and bustle of the new harbor, and you'll be surrounded by contented locals digging into the freshest, most succulent seafood in town (it's off-loaded right next to you, after all). As owner-chef Mike says, they must be doing something right: Quayside has been singled out as one of the country's coolest seaside restaurants, lauded for its wine list and praised by locals. They're famous for deep-fried calamari, but do try the creamy *perlemoen* (abalone) casserole with a dash of sherry or the magnificent curry "hotpot." Service is attentive; the decor is a casual tangle of fishing nets, puppets, and dangling stiletto heels.

Lower Slipway, New Harbour. © **028/313-0752.** Reservations recommended. Main courses R90–R125. MC, V. Summer daily noon–4pm and 7pm–late; winter (May–Aug) closed Sun–Tues nights.

Hermanos ★★★ SPANISH/STEAKHOUSE In an old fisherman's cottage, bedecked with nudes commissioned from a local artist, this lovely newcomer may not have sea frontage, but excellent culinary credentials. Chef Wayne Spencer has worked at Monaco's Michelin-starred The Mandarin and, at La Residence where he cooked for Elton John. Now, with a restaurant of his own, he serves comfort food—rib-eye steak, hot-rock fillet, baked line fish, herb-marinated lamb rump—done really well. Prices are reasonable, with just one gigantic steak—a humungous rump with all the trimmings—going for R250. Spencer keeps things local, sourcing from farms within a small radius of his kitchen.

3 High St. © **028/313-1916.** www.hermanos.co.za. Most main courses R78–R130. DC, MC, V. Mon–Sat 6pm–late.

Seafood/Pavilion at the Marine ★★★ SEAFOOD Considered the best seafood restaurant in the Overberg, Seafood at the Marine is a slick hotel bistro. Many old favorites still feature on the menu, which injects creativity into the local bounty—unpretentious staples such as fishcakes and a Cape Malay seafood bunny chow (curry in hollowed-out bread), as well as Rich Man's Fish and Chips, served in the *Financial Mail*. The biggest drawback is that much of the restaurant is without a sea view (although there is a small annex, off the hotel lounge, where you can look at the ocean)—this is compensated for, somewhat, by the open, semi-interactive kitchen. Down the other end of the hotel, though, its sister restaurant, **Pavilion at the Marine ★★★**, makes more of the location (but is strangely only open for dinner): With its checkered black-and-white floor and smart update of the 1920s architecture (sea views are through great big archways), it's a gorgeous place to eat.

The Marine Hermanus, Marine Dr. *C* **028/313-1000.** Reservations recommended. Seafood: main courses R140–R420, seafood platter for 2 R850; 2 courses R195; 3 courses R230. AE, DC, MC, V. Daily noon–2:30pm and 7–9:30pm. (Pavilion only open Sept–Apr Tues–Sat 7–9.30pm.)

Around Hermanus

STANFORD Foodies in search of superfresh organic ingredients, innovatively combined and presented with unpretentious home-style flair, should head to this quaint, tidy village, just a few clicks east of Hermanus. Here, Mariana and husband Peter tend to their vegetable garden as carefully as to their guests at **Mariana's Home Deli & Bistro ★★** (*C* **028/341-0272;** Thurs–Sun lunch; no children under 10; no credit cards). If Mariana's is full (it is sometimes booked up over a month in advance), another gem to root out is **Havercroft's ★** (*C* **028/341-0603;** Fri–Sat from 7pm, Sun lunch from 12:30pm; no credit cards). It's just a handful of tables in a tiny ramshackle cottage surrounded by rambling moonflowers and way-ward irises, and the menu is tiny and eclectic—but a decadent Sunday lunch roast is a sure thing. With its deli counter and owner-chef Jero beaming from ear to ear behind it, **Graze Slow Food Café ★★**, 21 Queen Victoria St. (*C* **082/491-8317;** www.grazecafe.co.za) is the place to grind to a standstill and indulge in a long Medi-terranean-style lunch. A blackboard menu is inspired by his Italian wife and produce comes from their own farm. The only drawback is infrequent opening hours (Fri 9:30am–4pm; Sat 9am–4pm), although occasionally dinners are served, too.

HEMEL-EN-AARDE VALLEY Alternatively, head west, turning into this sub-lime wine route, where the sought-after farming community is capitalizing on its superb 360° vistas (and dire global wine trading conditions) by diversifying into res-taurants. The best of these is **Heaven ★★** (*C* **072/905-3947;** www.newton johnson.com; Tues–Sun 10am–5pm), on the Newton Johnson Winery. The view is indeed heavenly, and the menu—changing almost daily, depending on what's avail-able—is excellent. Signature dishes include the deep-fried "blooming onion" with tandoori chicken filling, and the steak, cooked to perfection by owner-chef Bruce Henderson. Incidentally, Bruce is famous for his other venture, **B's Steak-house** (*C* **028/316-3625**), which you'll pass on the way here and that naturally also serves excellent steaks. There is also the swanky, see-and-be-seen **Temptation Restaurant ★★** (*C* **028/313-2007;** open Wed–Mon from 10am for lunch) at La Vierge, where you can taste the estate's fine, steely green sauvignon blancs and enjoy French-country meals in a glass-fronted bubble with dramatic views. From La Vierge, the dirt road continues to **Creation** (*C* **028/212-1107**), another estate turning out interesting wines, where the eponymous luncheon venue (Mon–Sat 11am–3pm; Sun 11am–2pm) provides sustenance to accompany award-winning vintages (the pinot noir is justifiably renowned). Deeper into the countryside is laid-back **Mogg's Coun-try Cookhouse ★★** (*C* **028/312-4321;** Wed–Sun 12:30–2:30pm). Having passed all (and hopefully sampled a few) of the Hemel-en-Aarde wineries along the way, you'll find this colorful cottage at the end of a bumpy dirt track—a thoroughly rustic venue (a reincarnated laborer's hut) where mother-and-daughter team Julia and Jenny serve three choices per course from a menu that changes weekly; everything is homemade, from the cauliflower soup to the baked lemon yogurt tart. It's warm and friendly, and you can bring your own bottle of wine at no extra charge—and there's loads to keep children occupied.

More Overberg & Whale Coast Destinations

Continue straight through Hermanus, and you soon pass the quaint village of **Stanford ★★**. Turn in here for a selection of good eateries (see "Where to Eat—Around Hermanus," above), loads of antiques stores, and a compelling village atmosphere. Stanford is usually bypassed by thrill-seekers heading for **Gansbaai,** the world's shark-caging diving capital (see below); beyond Gansbaai, though, things get more interesting (and decidedly less mainstream). Follow signs along a dusty, corrugated dirt road to **Baardskeerdersbos,** a minute speck on the map, where a few dilapidated farms and unsuccessful attempts at gentrification do little to salvage the impression of a community struggling to emerge from a forgotten era. Just before Baardskeerdersbos, however, the **Farm 215** eco-retreat is among the most idyllic spots to stay anywhere in the region (reviewed below). It's far more refreshing than hotel-like **Grootbos ★** (www.grootbos.com; ✆ **028/384-8000**), which is nearer Gansbaai (and the sea) and similarly surrounded by fynbos, but emphasizes overt luxury (and a hefty price-tag; R2,940–R7,950 double) over real nature-inspired solitude. Beyond Baardskeerdersbos, tiny, idiosyncratic **Elim ★★**, clearly signposted off the R319, is definitely worth seeing if you're more interested in getting off-the-beaten-track to really worthwhile spots. Established as a Moravian mission station in 1824, the town remains relatively unchanged architecturally and is still inhabited by descendants of the original Moravian church members, who make their living from harvesting fynbos, and now, tourism. Incidentally, Elim soil produces gorgeous flinty dry sauvignons (although, ironically, the town itself is dry), so white wine lovers should heed signs pointing the way to **Strandveld Vineyards** (✆ **028/482-1906**), between Elim and Cape Agulhas: It's the southernmost winery in Africa, best known for it's easy-drinking First Sightings range (those under the Strandveld label are more exclusive).

Two nearby coastal destinations well worth visiting are the village of **Arniston** and **De Hoop Nature Reserve ★★★**. To reach either, follow signs from Elim to Bredasdorp, or you can reach them more directly from the N2. Arniston is predominantly only a stopover if you want to take a side trip south to Africa's southernmost tip, **L'Agulhas,** which is where the Indian and Atlantic oceans meet. Barring the interesting fact of its location, the place itself is pretty unremarkable, unless you wish to view the wreck of the freighter *Meisho Maru* 38 or visit the oldest lighthouse on the coast. Built in 1848, the **Lighthouse Museum** (✆ **028/435-6078**) houses a licensed restaurant (daily 9am–late), but for superb views of the oceans and their clandestine meeting, book a table at nearby **Agulhas Country Lodge** (✆ **028/435-7650**).

Arniston, a combination of the small fishing village of Kassiesbaai and a collection of weekend getaway homes for Capetonians, is lapped by a startling turquoise sea and surrounded by blindingly white sand dunes. Don't be panicked by signs for WAENHUIS-KRANS—Arniston, named after a British ship that wrecked here in 1815, is also officially known by this, its Afrikaans name, which refers to the limestone cave that is big enough to house (*huis*) a wagon (*waen*). For centuries, the local fishermen have been setting out at first light to cast their lines and returning at night to the quaint lime-washed, thatched cottages clustered on the dunes overlooking the sea. These dwellings, some of which date back 200 years, have collectively been declared a national monument and are picture-postcard pretty, though doubtless less romantic to live in. You can wander through the sandy streets of the **Kassiesbaai community** ★ on your own or visit with the local community guide (✆ 073/590-2027). To overnight at Arniston, your best bet is the **Arniston Spa Hotel,** which enjoys a great location overlooking the turquoise sea (sea-facing rooms go for R1,300–2,350 double, including breakfast; www.arnistonhotel.com; ✆ 028/445-9000).

The gorgeous **De Hoop Nature Reserve** ★★★ (✆ 028/425-5020; entry R30 per person) has what many consider to be the best whale-watching spot on the entire coast, a huge beach dune appropriately called Koppie Alleen (Head Alone). But most visitors are here to explore one of the most beautiful coastal reserves in the world: 51km (30 miles) of pristine white beach dunes, limestone cliffs, rock pools, wetlands, coastal fynbos, and no one to disturb the peace but zebras, several species of antelopes, and more than 260 species of birds. Inside the reserve, there are limited routes (you can drive to the beach or accommodations), so the reserve is best explored on foot (there are four trails; make sure you do part of the Coastal Trail, as well as the Coot or Heron Vlei Trail). Note the reserve hours (7am–6pm); visitors intending to overnight should report to the reserve office no later than 4pm on the day of arrival, or call ahead if you are running late.

WHERE TO STAY & EAT

De Hoop Nature Collection ★ ☺   This is a wonderfully peaceful 36,000-hectare (88,920-acre) slice of nature and ideal for parents with young children—there are antelope, birds, and flowers to identify, huge sand dunes to roll down, and endless coves and small rock pools to explore. Accommodations are in whitewashed farm-style houses dotted around the reserve; the original ones have been a little spruced up (though architecture and fittings remain basic), and newly added cottages have a few extra features. All are comfortable, although you'll have to share ablutions (and kitchens) if you choose to stay in one of the rondawels at the Opstal. Try for Koppie Alleen, all alone near towering dunes, or the Opstal Vlei Cottages, perfect for birders. The old Melkkamer Manor House and the two stone Melkkamer cottages nearby (one of which is electricity free) are perfect if you want added privacy and historical ambience. Most options are efficiency units, but there is a shop, and the Fig Tree Restaurant offers mediocre meals (which can be delivered to the Melkkamer cottages). Do however bring something to barbecue; each cottage has its own outdoor cooking facility, most under milkwoods. Those accommodated in the stone Melkkamer Vlei and Foreman's cottages (across the vlei from the Opstal) can request meals at the Melkkamer Manor House.

✆ **028/542-1254,** or 021/422-4522 or 086/133-4667 reservations. www.dehoopcollection.co.za. 30 units. Rondawels R650 double; cottages R1,485–R1,980 for 4 people; larger cottages R1,980–R7,200. Camping from R250. AE, MC, V. **Amenities:** Restaurant; babysitting; bike tours; hiking trails; tennis courts (own racket required). In room: Kitchen (in all cottages), no phone.

Farm 215 ★★★   Floating in a sea of fynbos amid empty skies and blissful silence, this is a genuine off-the-grid eco-paradise. By day you're surrounded by paradisiacal views stretching off in every direction; at night, watch for the occasional flash from a far-off lighthouse at Danger Point or look up at the star-studded sky. There are three huge rooms in the main house (close to the lounge-bar-restaurant and lap pool), but rather choose one of the free-standing solar-powered fynbos suites. They're cool, contemporary, open-plan spaces with a focus on that epic panorama—an entire wall of sliding glass opening onto a terrace. You can strike out on foot or opt for a horseback excursion—you can ride all the way to an unblemished beach, potentially

The Overberg & Whale Coast

One of the most authentic experiences in the Overberg has to be dining in the heart of the Kassiesbaai community. On a prearranged night, you can delight in pan-fried fish, caught by the local fishermen, and green bean stew, prepared by their wives, and served by candlelight in one of the century-old fishing cottages. The meal costs R135 per person; to book, call Lillian Newman ((C) **028/445-9760** or 073/590-2027), a resident of Kassiesbaai who can also arrange for a guided tour.

watching whales from the saddle and dodging seals on the beach; the horses also have traversing rights within nearby Agulhas National Park. As in heaven, there's not a TV or A/C unit for miles.

Hartebeeskloof and Koudeberg, Baardskeerdersbos. www.farm215.co.za. (C) **028/388-0920.** R1,700–R1,800 homestead suite, R2,600–R2,800 fynbos suite. Rates include breakfast. Minimum 2 nights. AE, MC, V. **Amenities:** Dining room; honor bar; lounge; horseback riding; library; pool; walking trails. *In room:* CD player, fireplace, hair dryer, no phone, free Wi-Fi.

Mosaic Farm ★★   With 933 hectares (2,305 acres) of unspoiled wilderness along the edge of the Hermanus Lagoon, this quiet retreat feels marvelously secluded, yet is just a short drive from Stanford (or Hermanus for that matter), and a fun, bouncy 4X4 drive to a vast white sandy beach backed by humungous dunes. It's also a bird-watcher's paradise, attracting numerous water bird species as well as the rare blue crane, S.A.'s national bird. You can settle in for a few nights of luxury in one of five safari-style glass-and-stone suites set under whispering milkwood trees; these come with outdoor showers and overlook the lagoon and Overberg mountains. Or opt for one of four efficiency cottages (various room configurations) near the original late-19th-century solid stone Spookhuis (Ghost House), now home to a restaurant, wine cellar, and deli.

8km (5 miles) outside Stanford. www.mosaicfarm.net. (C) **028/313-2814** or 082/825-3211. Fax 086/276-3026. 9 units. Lagoon Lodge R2,800 double. Rates include dinner, breakfast, and most activities. Efficiency cottages R800–R1,800 (for 2–4 people; R100–R200 per additional person). MC, V. **Amenities:** Restaurant; deli; lounges; bar; beach excursions (by 4X4); bird-watching; boating; guided walks; kayaks; library; quad bikes; free Wi-Fi in lounge and restaurant; wine cellar. *In room:* Hair dryer, minibar; cottages have kitchens.

RURAL VILLAGE TREATS: TULBAGH, RIEBEEK KASTEEL & DARLING

While their wine routes are less hyped than Stellenbosch and Franschhoek, many of the little agricultural towns that dot the countryside around Cape Town offer opportunities to sample delicious well-priced wines in really pretty surroundings—without the constant stream of tourists.

Tulbagh ★★

130km (81 miles) N of Cape Town; 80km (50 miles) NW of Stellenbosch

Historic Tulbagh—surrounded by the wrinkled peaks of the gorgeous Witzenberg, Obiqua, and Witzenberg mountains—is a wonderful detour. It's nowhere as twee as

Franschhoek or developed as Paarl or Stellenbosch, and the mix of rusticity, Cape Dutch history, and natural beauty offer a sense of genuine escape. Europeans first discovered the valley in 1658, and the first farmers settled here in 1699; the town's Dutch heritage is still celebrated with a Cape Dutch Food and Wine Festival each March or April. There are 36 listed monuments in this tiny town, most fine examples of Cape Dutch architecture, evident in the facades of the restored houses lining Church Street—every one was restored to its original condition after a freak earthquake measuring 6.4 on the Richter scale flattened the town in 1969, and the effect is that of an open-air museum. Stroll the street to study the buildings—panels outside each monument explain the style and origin of the houses, and some of them, converted by residents into boutiques, restaurants, and guesthouses, can be seen from the inside. Surrounded by mountains on three sides, Tulbagh's vineyards are protected from overripening by cool air trapped here at night and within minutes of the historic town center are some impressive wine estates. Established in 1710, **Twee Jonge Gezellen ★** (© 023/230-0680; www.houseofkrone.co.za; Mon–Fri 9am–4pm, Sat 10pm–2pm) is one of the oldest estates in the country. If you find yourself here in January or February, try and book a seat at its Night Harvest dinners. For around R300, you will enjoy a three-course dinner paired with the estate's wines, a cellar tour, and a visit to the vineyards to see the grapes being picked. A biodynamic farm with the region's best Rhône varieties, **Tulbagh Mountain Vineyards** (© 023/231-1118; visits by appointment only) is a young farm but has had time to get the connoisseurs' noses twitching in approval for both its white blend and the Syrah. But it's the artfully executed tasting room at **Saronsberg ★★★** (© 023/230-0707; www.saronsberg.com; tastings Mon–Fri 8:30am–5pm, Sat 10am–2pm; R25) where you're appreciate the stylish space as much as tasting vintages that have been pulling in fistsful of awards; the shiraz and Full Circle blend are probably the most lauded, but the sauvignon blanc, too, demands attention. The modern tasting room has a wonderful outlook and a selection of contemporary South African art. Lastly, an essential stop for shiraz, cabernet sauvignon, and chenin blanc fans is **Rijk's Private Cellar** (© 023/230-1622; www.rijks.co.za; tastings Mon–Fri 10am–4pm, Sat 10am–2pm, call to check on public holidays)—you can also stay the night (see below). For a break from all the tasting, you can explore parts of the valley on a guided horseback ride through the orchards and vineyards with **Tulbagh Horse Trails** (© 023/230-0615; tulbaghhorsetrails@obiekwa.co.za).

ESSENTIALS

VISITOR INFORMATION The local **tourism office,** on Church Street (© 023/230-1375), provides maps and brochures; before traveling, visit www.tulbaghtourism.co.za.

WHERE TO STAY

If you don't mind being some distance out of town, then the finest place to bed down has got to be **India House ★★★**, a knockout efficiency house in the Bastiaanskloof Valley, right at the end of the Bainskloof Pass. It's an unrivaled retreat with superb mountain views, access to the neighboring fynbos reserve, and—besides every possible convenience—gorgeous, artful decoration. The only problem will be finding the motivation to explore beyond the trails and river rock pools on the property. You can cook for yourself or even enlist a personal chef—a private vegetable and herb garden is part of the deal. The house sleeps six and costs around R4,000 per night; to book it, visit www.perfecthideaways.co.za, or call © 021/790-0972.

Besides the places reviewed below, consider first contacting Jayson Clark—his **Cape Dutch Quarters** (www.cdq.co.za) is a central booking service for several efficiency properties in town, as well as B&Bs in historical homes (including the one he runs with his mom; reviewed below). Jayson's passion for Tulbagh is part of the renaissance spirit evident in this quiet village, and he'll set you up with accommodations, dining tips, and sightseeing suggestions. If you'd like to be in a farm-type environment, but Rijk's (below) is a bit too pricey, also consider **Manley Wine Lodge,** Main Winterhoek Rd. (www.manleywinelodge.co.za; ✆ 023/230-0582; R1,100–R1,500 double), which offers good value and neat cottages on a working boutique wine farm. There's a decent country cuisine restaurant and you can visit the small-scale production cellar for tastings. For a bit of novelty, there's also **Vindoux** ★ (www.vindoux.com; ✆ 023/230-0635 or 082/404-7778; R1,200 double in summer), a vast working fruit farm with a handful of cabins built up among the branches of a few trees. After exploring Tulbagh's vineyards, head back here for a signature *fynbos* body wrap at the little day spa, and then ascend to your treehouse (really a pine cabin on stilts) and laze on your terrace or your poster-style queen beds—note that if the wind blows, the noise from the trees will trouble light sleepers. Also available are cheaper **efficiency cottages** (R550 double) as well as a vast three-bedroom **wooden chalet** on stilts (from R1,900 for four people)—it has a small pool and swings for the kids. There's no restaurant, but breakfast and dinner can be ordered to your room. Last, if you're looking for a more hotel-like experience, chain-managed **Rijk's Country House** ★★ is the only five-star guesthouse in the area, and caters successfully to small conferences and weddings. Located just outside town, it's bland in comparison to the B&Bs on Church Street or Vindoux's treehouses, but comfortable enough, with rolling lawns and vineyards spread out directly in front of the main building. Rooms 4 and 12 are slightly more spacious; two-bedroom suites have fireplaces and DVDs (www.africanpridehotels.com/rijks; ✆ 023/230-1006; R2,200–R2,700 double; R2,700, including breakfast) *Note:* If you're looking for real five-star luxury then **Bartholomeus Klip** (reviewed on p. 186) is a very convenient base from which to explore Tulbagh; it's about 30 minutes away.

Tulbagh Country Guest House ★ 🔪 Reserve the massive honeymoon suite at the front of this historic house and you're virtually whipped back in time 200 years,

---

🎁 Where the Boys Are

Unassuming Tulbagh is home to the Cape's best-dressed men-only hideaway, a hot, handsome boutique guest farm called **Shisa!** ★★ (✆ 083/324-4466 or 083/954-4428; www.shisafarm.com). Hosts Joe and Francois have combined their respective talents as architect and photographer to come up with a look you won't find anywhere else in the country: sort of industrial-chic meets Warhol in the bush), while the surrounding landscape provides a genuine farm experience. A bar, lounge, innovative pool, and tanning deck and sauna all provide great opportunities for socializing with other guests (there are just a few rooms, so things can get pretty intimate), and this is a popular out-of-town getaway for Capetonians, so you won't find yourself surrounded solely by tourists. The chic "Afro-Zen" double rooms are beautiful, with vivid color accents, and a good value at R1,100, but we'd recommend the Champagne suite (R1,500).

albeit with modern conveniences at your fingertips. This well-established B&B enjoys a prime setting, among the historic monuments on Church Street. Antique fittings and furniture, vintage artworks, bric-a-brac, and creaking wooden floors contribute to a cozy, homey atmosphere. Breakfasts happen at the communal kitchen table, complete with handed-down china and cutlery, and most of the town's eateries are within spitting distance. There are cheap backpacker rooms, too, and modest efficiency cottages in assorted configurations.

24 Church St., Tulbagh 6820. www.capedutchquarter.co.za. ℭ **023/230-1171** or 082/416-6576. Fax 023/230-0721. 5 units, 1 with shower only. R750–R900 double. Rates include breakfast. AE, MC, V. **Amenities:** Dining room; babysitting; small outdoor pool. *In room* A/C (most), TV, hair dryer, minibar, no phone, free Wi-Fi.

WHERE TO EAT

Sure, Tulbagh is not yet on the culinary map, and it doesn't have any restaurants even remotely approaching the level of sophistication and variety available in Stellenbosch and Franschhoek, but it's all very relaxed and very good value. Be warned that the most famous stop in town, **Paddagang Restaurant,** Church Street (ℭ **023/230-0242**)—where *boerekos* (farmers' food) such as traditional *babotie,* waterlily stew, and roast chicken is served according to time-honored recipes—really has very little (aside from reputation) to recommend it. Rather more difficult to avoid, however, is **Things I Love ★** (ℭ **023/230-1742**), a country deli, bakery, and gift emporium in the heart of the village. Its shelves bulge with local wines, olives, preserves, clothing, and fudge made by the local pastor's wife. The attached restaurant is decorated with all kinds of vintage junk; it's enough just to take it all in, but order from the menu—you won't be disappointed. For home-cooked meals with a bit of an experimental edge, head to **Readers Restaurant ★**, in a mid-18th-century house on Church Street (ℭ **023/230-0087**), where cat-crazy Carol Collins has been turning out satisfying country dishes in her little kitchen for over 14 years. Try the chicken breast stuffed with chocolate, spinach, and feta; ostrich with gooseberry and amarula sauce; deep-fried whole onion; or Carol's exceptional lamb strudel. Just down the road, **29 Church Restaurant ★** (ℭ **082/905-5390;** Tues–Sun 11am–3pm, Tues–Sat 6–10pm) is a newish Belgian eatery turning out an encyclopedic menu that includes mussels, naturally. The only place in town that's open on a Sunday night is **The Olive Terrace ★** at the Tulbagh Hotel, 22 Van der Stel St. (ℭ **023/230-0071;** daily noon–3pm and 6–9:30pm).

You could also sample some of these products at the source: If you've got a sweet tooth, stop at Schoonderzicht Farm and sample Niki de Wolf's Dutch- and Belgian-style **Moniki Chocolates** (ℭ **023/230-0673;** www.schoonderzicht.com)—with memorable flavor variations: Chili and pinotage, or Shiraz truffles with salt and pepper? You can opt to pair wines with her chocolates (R35 for three pairings), or get a crash course in making your own. At **Kimilili** (ℭ **023/231-1503;** www.kimililifarm. co.za), on the Boontjiesrivier Road, off the R46 between Tulbagh and Wolsely, you can taste award-winning organic cheeses—just call ahead (weekdays only).

Riebeek Kasteel ★★

45km (28 miles) W of Tulbagh

While growing slowly more chichi, **Riebeek Kasteel,** just a short drive from Tulbagh (even quicker if you're coming from Darling via the R315; and possible to sidestep both by heading directly from Cape Town on the N7, after which you jump on the R27), is still delightfully rural (yes, those are sheep grazing in that garden), and the streets have retained much of their historical character (the first farms in the area were granted to farmers back in 1704). It's our favorite Winelands village in the Western Cape; estate agents talk about it as the "new Franschhoek" because of its exceptionally quaint atmosphere and the sweeping vineyards and olive grove surroundings—but the architecture is not nearly as twee, and the quirky ex–Cape Town community very different. Despite a population of around 12,000 people, on a quiet day you can perform cartwheels in the empty streets—unless there's yet another film crew in town. The only time things really heat up is during the annual **Olive Festival,** held early in May, when thousands of visitors drop by to sample the Valley's produce. This can also be done all year round at the **Olive Boutique,** 49 Church St. (© **022/448-1368**), or on the **Kloovenburg Wine Estate** (© **022/448-1635;** www.kloovenburg.com), which, according to *Wine* magazine, makes the best olive oil in the country—and good wines too, of course. Also justifiably famous for deep, fruity reds is **Allesverloren** (© **022/461-2320**), the oldest estate in the Swartland area. Riebeek Kasteel is a wonderful example of a small South African town, yet with enough bohemian-style eateries and browse-worthy stores to satisfy any urban cravings.

WHERE TO STAY IN & AROUND RIEBEEK KASTEEL

In addition to our favorites, reviewed below, both **Travellers Rest** (© **022/448-1383;** R695–R795 double) and **Kasteelberg Country Inn** (© **022/448-1110;** R760 double) offer comfortable B&B lodgings (and they serve decent meals).

Bartholomeus Klip ★★★   Near the tiny hamlet of Hermon, about 25 minutes from Riebeek Kasteel but still in the Valley, this luxury country lodge is on a working wheat and sheep farm, and proves a wonderful base from where you can combine a bit of wildlife-viewing (spot bat-eared foxes, blue cranes, a variety of antelope, or the super-rare geometric tortoise on the 4,000-hectare/10,000-acre nature reserve) with wine tastings (in Riebeek Kasteel, Tulbagh, or Paarl). Accommodations are in a restored Victorian homestead, elegantly furnished in period style. There are only five bedrooms; the best by far is the refurbished Orchid suite, which has its own entrance and a private veranda with great views. It's a peaceful place, with little to do but enjoy exceptional food (included in the rate), laze around on loungers—the large, deep, farm-style pool is wonderful—and walk, cycle, or drive through the reserve. Families are welcome at Wild Olive House, a small efficiency farmhouse nearby (adults can arrange to eat at the main house).

Elandskloof Mountains, Hermon (take the BO HERMON turnoff from the R44). www.bartholomeusklip. com. © **082/529-8539** or 082/322-1758 Fax 086/604-8539. 5 units. High season R4,928 double, R5,340 suite; midseason R3,330 double, R4,084 suite. Rates include brunch, high tea, dinner, all game-viewing, and sports activities. AE, DC, MC, V. No children under 16 in main house. **Amenities:** Dining room; bar; 3 lounges; mountain biking; canoeing; game drives and game walks; fly-fishing; pool; windsurfing (on dam). *In room:* A/C, hair dryer.

Kloovenburg Pastorie ★★   The Victorian-era old Dutch Reformed Church parsonage is now a slick-looking, ultra-intimate guesthouse, within strolling distance of the village heart as well as the vineyards. If you don't mind being left to your own devices it's a very romantic retreat, with only three rooms, each done out in a smart contemporary classic style (soothing grays, mushrooms, and whites) with antique furnishings and pretty chandeliers. Ask for suite-size Grape, which has a separate entrance and a wonderful big glass shower. Walking trails start right at the house—

one goes through the vineyards and to the top of Kasteel (castle) mountain, for views of the entire Riebeek Valley.

Corner of Main and Church sts., Riebeek Kasteel. www.kloovenburg.com. ✆ **022/448-1635.** R1,100 double. MC, V. **Amenities:** Lounge; kitchen; pool (planned by mid-2011). *In room:* A/C, TV, hair dryer.

Old Oak Manor ★ ☺ It's not particularly manorlike, but this lovely guesthouse (originally styled by Cape Town–based interior designer Salomé Gunther) is crammed with character (and characters). Its lived-in French Provençal–inspired decor has attracted the lenses of style magazines with well-worn Persians muted colors, and weathered wood all adding to the cozy, lavender-scented atmosphere. Of the four rooms in the house, Tara and Julius have the edge, as they have bathtubs and open onto the pool. A simple miniature garden cottage basks in a corner of the property, but first prize goes to the Loft (it sleeps up to four), in the space above Café Felix, a huge open-plan bedroom-cum-living area with a cloud of a double bed, two singles, and an enormous scented bathroom.

7 Church St., Riebeek Kasteel. www.oldoakmanor.co.za. ✆ **022/448-1170.** 6 units. High season R750 double, R950 luxury double, R850 cottage, R1,600 loft; low season R600 double, R750 luxury double, R650 cottage, R1,250 loft. Rates include breakfast. MC, V. **Amenities:** Restaurant (**Café Felix,** reviewed below); lounge; Internet (on request); pool; room service. *In room:* TV, hair dryer, minibar.

WHERE TO EAT

This is a town where good food is reason enough to stay awhile. A plethora of small cafes, boutiques, wine farms, and restaurants offer excellent country cuisine in casual settings, often with more than a hint of quirkiness. New kid on the dining block is the young and energetic **Auntie Pasti** ★, 16 Sarel Cilliers St. (✆ **022/448-1331;** Sat–Sun breakfast, Wed–Sun lunch, Wed–Sat dinner), which is right next to Bar Bar Black Sheep (see below), with some fantastic tapas and variations of Italian standards.

Bar Bar Black Sheep ★★★ SOUTH AFRICAN Furnished with bright plastic tablecloths and quirky bric-a-brac, it's tucked away amid the colorful boutiques and stores on Short Street. Even on a quiet midweek night, the place buzzes—and rightfully so. This is another menu that changes regularly, but expect South African favorites such as roasted marrow bones, *waterblommetjiebredie,* and *skilpadjies* (lamb's liver wrapped in kidney fat). Meat is central here (although vegetarians will get something very special), and the focus is on honest, excellent tastes—each plate is impeccably finished (the T-bone steak, for example, could come with homemade anchovy butter, mustard mayonnaise, and rosa tomato chutney in which to dunk your fries). Super waitstaff really adds to the experience.

Unit 7 Short St., Main Rd., Riebeek Kasteel. ✆ **022/448-1031** or 076/901-0585. www.bbbs.co.za. Main courses R82–R140. MC, V. Wed–Sun noon–3pm and 7pm–late; Sat–Sun 9am–11am.

Café Felix ★★ COUNTRY Once an old tobacco barn, this uncluttered, airy eatery with a pretty courtyard shaded by oaks has become a bit of a Riebeek Valley landmark. Emphasis is on simple but hearty French-Italian country cuisine, while the wine list offers choice staples (and one or two special finds) from local cellars. The house special, a slow-roasted lamb shank, flies off the menu, but there are plenty of alternatives (such as the seared tuna), and the menu is always changing.

7 Church St., Riebeek Kasteel. ✆ **022/448-1170.** Reservations recommended. Main courses R80–R100. MC, V. Tues–Wed and Fri 8am–3pm and 6–9pm; Sat 8am–9pm; Sun 8am–3pm.

Considered the Western Cape's premiere popular music event, **Rocking the Daisies** ★★★ (www.rockingthe daisies.com) is a weekend of rollicking good fun held in October, on Cloof Wine Estate just outside Darling. Besides attracting some of the country's very best bands to the main outdoor stage, there's an exceptional electronic tent, world music bar, and stand-up comedy stage all running concurrently It's billed as the country's greenest festival—organizers offset carbon emissions by planting trees. The festival draws a huge crowd; you can save yourself the usual bother of camping by reserving a pre-erected tent at the mobile **Kreef Hotel** (www. kreefhotel.co.za; ✆ **082/922-5029** or 082/301-4951), which offers hot showers, simple buffet breakfasts, and a secure site close to all the action, but far from the potential rowdiness of the open camping area.

Darling

A mere hour's drive from Cape Town, this small town attracts its fair share of visitors, particularly when the **Darling Wildflower Show** is on. Usually held during the third weekend in September, the annual event has been running since 1917. Another big September draw is the **Voorkamerfest** ★★★, a 3-day event held toward the beginning of the same month, in which visitors are transported to three mystery destinations on Friday or Saturday night, going into the living rooms ("front room" or *voorkamer*) of Darling residents who have bravely offered their homes as venues, to watch three shortish live performances. The venues are all over town, from farms to township, while acts are brought from all over South Africa and Holland (comedy, drama, music) and there are very few duds.

A good reason to visit at any time of the year is Pieter Dirk Uys's informal theater and restaurant, **Evita se Perron** ★★ (✆ **022/492-2831**; Tues–Sun 10am–4pm), on Arcadia Street. Uys is one of the country's most accomplished satirists, famous for creating the flamboyant stage persona Evita Bezuidenhout, the gray-haired *tannie* (auntie) who, during the Apartheid era, held sway over the imaginary homeland of Bapetikosweti and is now the First Lady of Darling. Uys has made even the most conservative South Africans laugh at the nation's tragic ironies (not an easy task for a man dressed in women's clothing), while always lambasting the status quo. **Evita se Dagkombuis** (literally, "Day Kitchen") serves breakfasts and light meals throughout the day: gay muffins, affirmative tarts, and *koeksisters* (twisted, fried dough plaits doused in syrup). To view pure Afrikaner kitsch, take a wander through her **Boerassic Park,** where garden gnomes keep an eye on plastic flowers and art students have created a monumental Gravy Train, filled with some of South Africa's most loved (and despised) politicians; there's also a more serious collection of artifacts, letters, and images inside, many of which evoke some of the sadness of Apartheid-era South Africa. There are also a few excellent wine estates to visit in and around Darling, of which our top picks are the good-value **Alexanderfontein** for its excellent value sauvignon and merlot, the bold reds at **Cloof,** and superlative whites at **Groote Post.**

If you can't face the thought of driving back to Cape Town, stagger down to the **Darling Lodge** (www.darlinglodge.co.za; ✆ **022/492-3062**; R880 double), a charming Victorian building with six en-suite rooms, local art on the walls, a pool, and a resident wolfhound. For more, visit the local **Tourism Information** office (© 022/492-3361; www.darlingtourism.co.za; Mon–Fri 9am–1pm and 2–4pm, Sat–Sun 10am–3pm), which dispenses maps, details of nearby flower reserves (at their best from around July to early Oct—one of the nicest is the **Tienie Versveld Wild Flower Reserve**), and any other information needed.

THE WEST COAST ★★

For many, the West Coast is an acquired taste—kilometers of empty, often windswept beaches and hardy coastal scrub, low horizons and big skies, lonely tree-lined dirt roads, and distant mountains behind which lie lush pockets carpeted in vineyards make this a truly off-the-beaten-track experience. Most visitors venture up here to catch the spring flower displays that occur in West Coast National Park (60 to 90 min. from Cape Town) anytime from the end of July to early September; the park is also a world-famous birding site. But there are plenty more gems to uncover—such as eating fresh crayfish, with your feet in the sand; living like the lauded gentry at the Melck homestead at Kersefontein; or visiting the gentrified seaside fishing village of Paternoster.

Essentials

VISITOR INFORMATION There's very little reason to visit any of the towns before Paternoster. The **Paternoster Village Tourism** office (© 022/752-2323; Mon noon–5pm, Tues–Fri 9am–5pm, Sat 9am–6pm) is as you enter town, on the right side of the road before the four-way stop.

GETTING THERE From Cape Town, take the N1, then turn north onto the R27. If you intend to travel farther north, say, to Cederberg, and want to get there quickly, take the N7 off the N1; this is the main road north to Namaqualand (the flower region) and Namibia.

GETTING AROUND The only way to explore the area is by car or with a tour operator. **Sun Tours** (© 021/797-4646 or 083/270-5617; www.suntourssa.co.za) offers tailor-made tours with a network of guides in vehicles ranging from Harley-Davidsons to luxury sedans. They charge per vehicle, not per person, which means good value for families or larger groups. From R330 per hour.

GUIDED TOURS For a look at San culture and history (the San, called Bushmen in the past, are Southern Africa's First People), visit **!Khwa ttu** (© 022/492-2998; www.khwattu.org; daily 9am–5pm; tours are set for 10am and 2pm and cost R240 per

5

> ### 📎 Flower Viewing
>
> **For up-to-date information on the best places to view flowers at any given time, contact the Flower Line at © 083/910-1028 (daily Aug–Oct).**

adult, R120 per child), an educational center run by the San themselves, off the R27 en route to Langebaan. San-guided tours include a game-viewing drive and nature walk, a visit to a traditional village, and an introduction to the clicks and tones that are such a characteristic part of San speech.

West Coast National Park ★★

With its magnificent azure water and countless road-crossing tortoises (stay alert when driving), the **West Coast National Park** (© 022/772-2144; R72 in flower season, otherwise R40; daily Apr–Aug 7am–6pm and Sept–Mar 7am–7pm) encompasses almost 30,000 hectares (74,100 acres) of wilderness, as well as a 16×4.5km (10×2¾-mile) marine lagoon, on which the coastal town of Langebaan is situated. Pack a picnic, camera, and bathing suit, and head for one of the picture-perfect coves near Preekstoel and Kraalbaai, where brilliant blue waters gently lap white sands bordered by emerald green succulents. There's also a good chance of spotting whales from July to early November from points overlooking the Atlantic Ocean. The **Postberg** section, which contains zebra, wildebeest, and gemsbok, is open only in August and September from 9am to 5pm, when the flowers are most spectacular. The community at **Churchhaven** (marked by the Anglican church of St. Peter), which was founded in 1863 by George Lloyd, a deserter from an American merchant vessel, has now closed the road running past it; the only way to gain access is to rent one of its basic efficiency cottages (see below). The hamlet enjoys a unique setting on one of the world's greatest wetlands. Overlooking a blindingly white beach and surrounded by salt marshes, the settlement is visited by more than 140 bird species (including the greater flamingo).

There are two entrances to the park: one off the R27, some 100km (62 miles) north of Cape Town, and the other just south of Langebaan. You can see a good deal of it by entering the one and leaving by way of the other, but make sure you visit the **Information Center** at **Geelbek** (✆ **022/772-2799**), on the southern tip of the lagoon—there's a restaurant (see "Where to Eat," below) and several bird blinds near the water.

WHERE TO STAY

If you value peace and quiet and fancy being deep within the reserve, with scant trace of humanity, book one of the fabulous rustic-chic efficiency pads at **Churchhaven ★★★**, a cluster of cottages right on the aquamarine lagoon. Two favorites are **Whaler's Way ★★★**, and the very pretty, impeccably renovated **Morning Mist ★★★**; they each sleep up to six people and go for R2,500 to R5,000 per night depending on season and time of the week. Book through www.perfecthideaways.co.za (✆ **021/790-0972**). The other option (also efficiency) inside the park itself is **Duinebos** (reviewed below), which has the advantage of being close to the Geelbek Restaurant.

Langebaan has grown exponentially over the years: This is no quaint fishing village, but a sprawling town, hugely popular with watersports fans and South Africans during the summer holidays. The only South African–graded five-star accommodations in Langebaan itself is **Harrison's House** (✆ **022/772-0727** or 084/806-6322; R1,100–R1,390 double), a compact boutique guesthouse with a splash pool, small gym, and some great views (the upstairs luxury lagoon room is the one to ask for). No children under 12 are permitted, and if you like your space and want to be closer to the beach, you'd be better off at **The Farmhouse** (www.thefarmhousehotel.com; ✆ **022/772-2062;** peak season R1,500–R2,650 double). If you're on a budget, a good alternative is **Friday Island** ⚓, Main St. (www.fridayisland.co.za; ✆ **022/772-2506;** sea-front-facing units R800–R990). The simple whitewashed rooms (ask for one facing the water) are right on Langebaan beach. There's a young and very friendly vibe (the receptionist will be calling you "lovey" within moments of check-in), and tanned locals frequent the restaurant for calamari steaks and light fare. It's also just moments from our recommended kite-surfing operator (see "Staying Active," p. 145).

Another option is to stay *on* the water. There are two recommended **houseboats** available for evenings spent floating on surreal-blue surface of the lagoon. One of

The West Coast & Side Trips to the Northern Cape

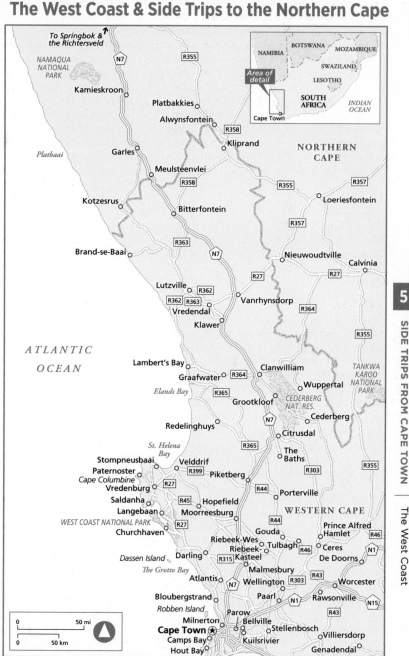

To Springbok &
the Richtersveld

NAMAQUA
NATIONAL
PARK

N7

R355

NAMIBIA · BOTSWANA · MOZAMBIQUE

SWAZILAND

Area of
detail

LESOTHO

SOUTH
AFRICA

Cape Town

INDIAN
OCEAN

Kamieskroon

Platbakkies

Alwynsfontein

R358

Platbaai

Garles

Kliprand

NORTHERN
CAPE

Meulsteenvlei

R358

R355

R357

Kotzesrus

Bitterfontein

Loeriesfontein

R357

Brand-se-Baai

R363

N7

Nieuwoudtville

Calvinia

R27

Lutzville

R362

R362 R363

Vredendal

Klawer

Vanrhynsdorp

R364

R27

R355

ATLANTIC
OCEAN

Lambert's Bay

Graafwater

R364

Clanwilliam

Wuppertal

TANKWA
KAROO
NATIONAL
PARK

Elands Bay

R365

Grootkloof

CEDERBERG
NAT. RES.

Redelinghuys

N7

Cederberg

Citrusdal

St. Helena
Bay

R365

The
Baths

Stompneusbaai

Velddrif

Paternoster

R399

Piketberg

R303

R355

Cape Columbine

Vredenburg

R27

Porterville

Saldanha

R45

Hopefield

R44

Langebaan

Moorreesburg

WESTERN CAPE

WEST COAST NATIONAL PARK

R27

R44

Churchhaven

Gouda

Prince Alfred
Hamlet

R46

Dassen Island

Darling

Riebeek-Wes

Riebeek-
Kasteel

Tulbagh

R46

Ceres

N1

The Grotto Bay

R315

Malmesbury

De Doorns

Atlantis

N7

Wellington

R303

R43

Worcester

Blouberfstrand

Paarl

N1

Rawsonville

N15

Robben Island

Parow

R43

Milnerton

Bellville

Cape Town ★

Stellenbosch

Camps Bay

Kuilsrivier

Villiersdorp

Hout Bay

Genadendal

0   50 mi
0   50 km

5

SIDE TRIPS FROM CAPE TOWN | The West Coast

191

these, the luxurious efficiency **Nirvana ★★** (*©* **021/689-9718**), accommodates up to 24 people on two decks, and costs at least R7,800 per night (for 12 people). A smaller, more rustic boat, is **Larus** (*©* **021/552-0008** or 021/426-4260), which takes up to six passengers and starts at R1,400 (for four people). Visit **www.house boating.co.za** for more details on both.

Duinebos Chalets ★ ◢ Book well in advance for the privilege of staying here in springtime; guests at these simple efficiency chalets are usually the first at the gates of Postberg Wildflower Reserve. The square, flat-roofed, ocher-colored cottages suit the mood of the surrounding fynbos-carpeted wilderness, and even when it's full, it's possible to tap into an away-from-it-all sense of tranquillity. It's no hotel experience but there's a good little pool, sheltered by walls fashioned from small rocks, and each chalet has its own barbecue and full kitchen. Three of the chalets (nos. 9–11) face outward, toward the reserve, and are set slightly apart from the rest, making them more private, but these have only single beds. Based here, you have the park at your fingertips, and if cooking seems like too much effort, Geelbek restaurant is about 1km (½ mile) away.

West Coast National Park, 7km (4½ miles) NW of the park's southern entrance, signposted off the main road. www.duinebos.co.za. *©* **022/707-9900.** 11 units. R530–R650 double, R710–R825 for 4. No credit cards. **Amenities:** Children's play area; pool. *In room:* Fan, fireplace, kitchen, no phone.

Kersefontein ★★ It's one of the most authentic farm-stay experiences in the country—being hosted by Julian, the eighth-generation Melck, in his beautiful Cape Dutch 18th-century farmstead on the banks of the Berg River. It's a 7,000-hectare (17,290-acre) working wheat and cattle farm, and the sense of history is palpable—on the way to the grand dining room, you will pass, for instance, the skull of the last Berg River hippo, shot by Martin Melck in 1876 after it bit his servant; and the aviation-themed pub occupies the old farm bakery. Sleeping quarters are separate from the main house. Choose from two "African" rooms (top choice, with doors opening onto a small private veranda and sweeping lawns), the Victorian suites (with communal lounge and kitchen), an efficiency cottage (a short drive away and blissfully tranquil), or a one-room unit (for singles, in a farmyard building with its own fireplace and oodles of space). Decor is classic and classy, but it's the reality of the working farm outside that stuns. There are two runways here, so you can fly yourself in (or ask Julian, a skilled pilot, to hire a plane and take you for a ride). You'll also find horses for exploration, and the West Coast National Park lies less than an hour away.

18km (11 miles) N of Hopefield. From Malmesbury, take the R45 toward Hopefield (55km/34 miles); take the road to Velddrif for 18km (11 miles) and turn right before the grain silos, crossing the Berg River to reach the farm. www.kersefontein.co.za. *©* **022/783-0850** or 083/454-1025. 6 units. R1,000–R1,900 double. Rates include breakfast. AE, MC, V. **Amenities:** Dining room; bar; lounges; bikes; boats; horse-back riding; library; scenic flights. *In room:* Fan, no phone.

WHERE TO EAT

Meals such as slow-cooked lamb, smoked snoek salad, and ostrich carpaccio are served in the **Geelbek Restaurant** (make a reservation during the busy vacation season; *©* **022/772-2134**) right within West Coast National Park. It's housed in a Cape Dutch homestead built in 1744—but it's unlikely that you'll see flamingos while eating your meal, as suggested on the website. For that, you need to take one of a number of short trails to the bird blinds overlooking the lagoon—this is particularly rewarding in summer, when the blinds can provide views of thousands of migrant waders and flocks of pelican, flamingo, curlew, and sandpipers. There's space for children to roam and playground equipment.

Boesmanland Plaaskombuis ★★ SOUTH AFRICAN/SEAFOOD   If you want to get familiar with South African cuisine, this is one place to learn about traditional *boerekos* (literally farmers' food), although there's plenty of west coast seafood on the menu, too. Set against the beach, with seating on log stumps at simple round tables, this farm kitchen offers eat-as-much-as-you-can buffet-style dining from bubbling *potjies* (iron pots) and fish grilled on open fires. If fish stews and roast lamb don't fill you up in a hurry, the sourdough bread and milk tart will. They also do traditional farm breakfasts.

Langebaan, signs from Club Mykonos casino. www.boesmanlandfarmkitchen.com. ℰ **022/772-1564.** Reservations essential. Lunch or dinner buffet R100–R140. Daily 8:30–10am; noon–2pm and 7–9pm.

Paternoster & Columbine Nature Reserve ★★★

To reach the gem of the West Coast, stay on the R27 past West Coast National Park and Langebaan, and then take the R45 west to Vredenburg. Drive straight through this ugly town and take the 16km (10-mile) road to **Paternoster,** a tiny fishing village that—due to strict development guidelines—retains a classic West Coast feel, with picturesque whitewashed fisherman-style cottages washed by the heady scent of cold seas and kelp, bringing on an instant vacation mood. From relatively obscure gem to becoming *the* place to stay on the West Coast, Paternoster now has dozens of B&Bs, efficiency cottages, and guesthouses, most within easy walking distance of dazzling white beaches (though often windswept), dotted with colorful fishing boats. If you'd like to get out on the water without getting wet (and be warned, the water on this coast is freezing), contact Dianne at **Kayak Paternoster** (ℰ **082/824-8917**). Relaxed, early morning trips venture out to the bird colonies—apart from the chance to see penguins, you may spot whales, dolphins, and seals along the way. Paternoster now also boasts a string of surprisingly good restaurants and a community of artists and designers from up-country who, having sampled the delights of this laid-back coastal hamlet, promptly packed up and moved in. But there still salty long-term locals to keep things real: To meet some, brave a visit to the **Panty Bar** at the **Paternoster Hotel;** you'll be deep in conversation—and up to your eyeballs in lowbrow paraphernalia (mostly bits of underwear left by visitors).

Adjacent Paternoster, the 263-hectare (650-acre) **Cape Columbine Nature Reserve** ★★ (ℰ **022/752-2718;** daily 7am–7pm; day visitors R10) is home to a wide variety of flowers; the best time to visit is obviously spring, but the reserve's superb location is a relief from the rest of the coastline's degradation by developers. You can also climb to the top of the last manned **lighthouse** in the country; views are sublime, and the tower's mechanics are interesting too. There are public campsites (with cold showers) right on the sea at Tietiesbaai (within the reserve), but rather opt for one of the four tiny, A-frame huts at **The Beach Camp** (www.the beachcamp.co.za; ℰ **082/926-2267;** R620 double including reserve fees). It's a rustic backpacker-type setup with communal kitchen facilities, shared showers with hot water, a bar, and proper beds in the huts—you'll have a clear view of the sea just beyond the tips of your toes. Bring hiking shoes.

WHERE TO STAY

With numerous efficiency cottages to choose from, you'll be spoiled for choice if you decide on an extended stay: Options include **Hocus Pocus** (ℰ **022/752-2660** or 083/988-4645; R750–R1,250, sleeps two to four) with its eclectic, cottagey decor, and the very chic three-bedroom **Sugar Shack** ★★ (ℰ **086/162-6539**; R1,300–R2,850 for up to six people), just a short stroll from the beach. The owners of Abalone

House (reviewed below) also have a selection of places in varying price ranges, the quaintest of which is **Kliphuisie** ★ (literally "little stone house"; R740–R950 double), a lovingly preserved fisherman's cottage, perfect for romantic hideaways; visit **www.seasidecottage.co.za** for all the options. Not efficiency, but also rather fabulous, is the homey, colorful **ah! guesthouse** ★ (www.ahguesthouse.com; © **082/ 464-5898;** R900–R1,100 double, breakfast included), which showcases some wonderful decor ideas, including some inventive recycling. Even if you don't stay here, book a meal (see "Where to Eat," below).

Abalone House ★★★ It's the smartest place to stay in Paternoster and yet you'll feel instantly feel at home, relaxed by the boho profusion of eye-catching paraphernalia. A warren of downstairs spaces comprises relaxing nooks, dining rooms, and cozy lounges, including the conservatory-style Orchid Room and a well-stocked library. The place is packed with collectibles—plants, antique birdcages, wooden ducks, real ducks (a pair, living in the garden, occasionally ventures inside), crystal decanters, brass telescopes, polished silverware, cowhides, Persian rugs, and tinkling wind chimes. What might elsewhere feel claustrophobic instead makes you want to kick off your shoes and plunge into one of the sofas, if the neighbor's cat hasn't gotten there first. Bedrooms are uncluttered and luxurious. Although it lacks immediate beachfront proximity, this is made up for with sweeping views afforded by the rooftop terrace (also where the best rooms are situated—ask specifically for a sea-facer up here); sink into the rooftop Jacuzzi and you could spend the day staring at the ocean.

Kriedoring St., Bekbaai, Paternoster. www.abalonehouse.co.za. © **022/752-2044,** or 086/722-7973 reservations. Fax 086/215-1839. 10 units. High season R2,800–R3,000 double, low season R2,200 double. Rates include breakfast. MC, V. **Amenities:** Restaurant; bar; lounges; library; Jacuzzi; small pool. *In room:* A/C, TV/DVD, movie library, heated towel rack, underfloor heating, free Wi-Fi.

The Oystercatcher's Haven ★★ Right on the edge of Paternoster (for now, anyway—new streets are already being laid out nearby), it overlooks massive, sea-swept black boulders and a deserted beach with views down the coast to Columbine Nature Reserve. At press time, the owners were about to dramatically expand one of the rooms (upstairs) to create a suite-size space that will have truly impressive sea views. The breakfast room is a sheltered sanctuary, as are the sun-drenched courtyards and patio.

48 Sonkwas St., Paternoster. www.oystercatchershaven.com. © **022/752-2193** or 082/414-6705. Fax 022/752-2192. 3 units. R1,500 double. Rates include breakfast. MC, V. **Amenities:** Lounge; pool. *In room:* Fan, TV, hair dryer, heated towel rack, minibar, no phone.

Paternoster Dunes Boutique Guesthouse ★★ Book one of the four rooms that face the sea and it's a quick skip from your private patio down a dune into the icy waves. The house centers on a courtyard with compact pool, chaise longues, and huge drapes creating an outdoor lounge effect. Hosts Deon and Gavin are interior designers and it shows: Bedrooms (with small or open-plan bathrooms) are immaculate, done out in an upbeat classical style. They're good for squirreling away, but the upstairs lounge, bar, and deck have such sublime views, you'll want to spend time here, too. Keep an eye out for whales as you toast another sunset; with some luck, Deon will be grilling crayfish on an open fire.

18 Sonkwas St., Paternoster 7381. www.paternosterdunes.co.za. © **022/752-2217** or 083/560-5600. Fax 022/752-2217. 6 units, most with shower only. R1,900 sea-facing double, R1,600 non-sea-facing double. Rates include breakfast. AE, MC, V. **Amenities:** Dining area; honor bar; lounge; small library; heated plunge pool; spa. *In room:* A/C and fan, TV/DVD, movie library, hair dryer, heated towel rack, minibar, no phone, free Wi-Fi.

WHERE TO EAT

Foodies should definitely time their visit to coincide with the opening hours of **Gaaitjie** (reviewed below), one of the best restaurants on the entire South African coast, or make an effort to book for one of the four-course dinners at former Jo'burg chef Arnold Hoon's communal table at **ah!,** 1 Mosselbank St. ★★★ (*℃* **082/464-5898;** R225–R295, depending on whether or not crayfish is involved), though you'll need to book in advance, and in-house guests get preference. Failing that, there are several other very good options, starting with the matchless setting of **Voorstrandt** (*℃* **022/752-2038;** daily 10am–10pm), which is a prime spot day or night (and especially at sunset). This red rustic tin-roof shack is right on the beach—when the sun sparkles off the crescent-shaped beach and ocean, the sense of contentment is almost surreal. The menu lines up casual, unexceptional bistro fare (with plenty of seafood), but if you're here November through April, there's only one thing to order: succulent whole crayfish, served with garlic or lemon butter. Other popular dishes include the Malaysian seafood curry (R98) and the "three-fish dish," line fish caught off this coast. Lacking views or the wave soundtrack is the slightly more formal **Noisy Oyster** ★★ (*℃* **022/752-2196;** Wed–Sat noon–3pm and 6–9pm, Sun noon–3pm; booking essential), which offers more by way of innovation: stuffed and Parma ham–wrapped sardines, wok-tossed baby calamari in chermoula, or Thai green fish curry. And plenty of oysters, of course. It's worth noting that **Blikkie Pizzeria** ★, in a 110-year-old pastel green tin cottage (32 St. Augustine Rd.; *℃* **022/752-2246;** Tues–Thurs noon–8pm, Fri–Sat noon–9pm), received second place in the Global Pizza Challenge within a few months of opening in 2010.

Gaaitjie ★★★ SOUTH AFRICAN   Chef Suzi Holtzhausen is the west coast's culinary darling; her latest restaurant—a cottage on the rocks right on the beach—has switched-on foodies venturing from Jo'burg to sample her ever-changing menu. She's always been big on seasonal, indigenous ingredients, and she's now looking to the shoreline for inspiration (vegetables that grow under sea spray, minor experiments with seaweed), and turning out such scrumptious dishes as chilled pea and fresh crayfish soup; a fragrant stew of black mussels, baby calamari, sweet pepper, and spicy sausage; roasted quail on hot beets; rich chocolate mousse with salt dust. Meat is always on the menu and fabulously prepared, but vegetarians should probably call ahead to let Suzi know. Reserve weeks ahead for a table on the enclosed terrace overlooking the sea, and arrive early to take in the sunset.

Off Sampson Rd., right on the beach. *℃* **022/752-2242** or 083/375-4929. Reservations essential. Main courses R110–R135. MC, V. Thurs-Mon noon–2pm and 6:30-8:30pm.

Saffron ★★★ BISTRO/INTERNATIONAL   Bistro by day, intimate fine dining by night, this studious little in-house restaurant at Abalone House is in the expert hands of Welsh-born chef Darren Stewart, who changes his menu according to what's freshest. Make do with low-key light fare at lunch (club sandwiches; mussels in cream, garlic, and white wine; and beer-battered fish), or prepare for sophisticated, yet unpretentious, evening meals—seared quail breast and confit leg with honey parsnips, endive and smoky raisin jus, or stumpnose with bokkom oil. If it's available, finish with chocolate risotto and orange marmalade ice-cream.

Abalone House, Kriedoring St. *℃* **022/752-2044.** Dinner reservations recommended. Lunch main courses R55–R75. Dinner set menu R265, dinner main courses R90–R130. MC, V. Daily 7am-late.

CEDERBERG

Inland and parallel to the west coast, the spectacular sandstone Cederberg mountains, home to citrus and rooibos tea farmers, march north, affording fabulous hiking among weathered crags. The Cederberg Wilderness Area lies around 200km (124 miles) north of Cape Town—it's a hikers' paradise featuring majestic jagged sandstone mountains that glow an unearthly deep red at sunset; strange-shaped rock formations that dominate the horizon; ancient San (Bushmen) rock-painting sites; burbling streams in which to cool off; a variety of animals, such as baboon, small antelope, leopards, and lynx; and rare mountain fynbos such as the delicate snow protea and gnarled Clanwilliam cedar. You can drive through, but the best way to explore is on foot. In keeping with its "wilderness" designation, there are no laid-out trails, though maps indicating how to reach the main rock features—the huge Wolfberg Arch and the 30m-high (98-ft.) Maltese Cross, as well as to the two main Cederberg peaks— are available.

Essentials

VISITOR INFORMATION   The excellent **Clanwilliam Information Centre** (© **027/482-2024;** www.clanwilliam.info; Mon–Fri 8:30am–5pm, Sat 8:30am–12:30pm) is opposite the old church hall on Main Street. To camp or walk in the Cederberg Wilderness Area, you will need a permit from **Cape Nature,** in Cape Town, before you travel (© **0861/227-362-8873;** www.capenature.org.za)— although day walkers can get permits from the local Information Centre, too. You can't miss Wupperthal's **Tourism Bureau** (© **027/492-3410;** www.wupperthal.co.za; Mon–Fri 9am–4:30pm, Sat 9am–noon), on Church Square, next to Leipoldt House.

GETTING THERE   **By Car**   **Clanwilliam** lies about 2½ to 3 hours drive from Cape Town off the N7; some miles before (approximately 188km/116 miles from Cape Town), you'll see the turnoff for **Cederberg Wilderness Area** (marked Algeria).

The Cedarberg, Clanwilliam & Wupperthal

Covering 710 sq. km (277 sq. miles), the **Cederberg Wilderness Area** is reached via a dirt road that lies halfway between the towns of Citrusdal and Clanwilliam. Of the two, the pretty town of **Clanwilliam** is the more attractive base, with a few attractions of its own, including the country's main rooibos tea-processing factory, the Ramskop Wildflower Reserve, and a spectacular drive to the nearby Moravian mission station of **Wupperthal ★★**. It's worth visiting this isolated rural community just to travel the 90-minute dirt-road trip from Clanwilliam, with its breathtaking views of the twisted shapes and isolated tranquillity of the northern Cederberg. An interesting stop along the way is the **Sevilla Rock Art Trail ★★★**, a wonderful self-guided 2km-long (1.2-mile) trail that visits 10 fine rock-art sites and is an easy, magical introduction to the genre (you'll need a permit and map from nearby **Traveller's Rest** (© **027/482-1824**). Once in Wupperthal, you'll feel lost in time: It looks pretty much the way it did when it was established as a Moravian mission station in the 1830s. In fact, some Wupperthal farmers still use sickles to reap, donkeys to thresh, and the wind to sift their grain.

WHERE TO STAY & EAT

Contact **Cape Nature Conservation** for camping (hikers be warned: visitor numbers are strictly limited, so book early; see "Staying Active," earlier in this chapter) and accommodation hire in the Cederberg reserve (www.capenature.co.za;

© 021/659-3500); ask for **Rietdak,** an efficiency cottage 400m (1,312 ft.) from the river (R530–R800 for up to four people). The best place to stay in Clanwilliam is Blommenberg Guest House (www.blommenberg.co.za; © 027/482-1851; R750–R970 double); it's a simple three-star place, but the warmth of the welcome you get from Eric and Joan and their attention to detail put it in a class of its own. But for all-out luxury, with excellent guided tours of San rock art, you can't beat Bushmans Kloof, northeast of Clanwilliam.

THE GREAT CAPE ROAD TRIP: THE LITTLE KAROO & GARDEN ROUTE

The juxtaposition of the lush Garden Route—its green forests watered by tea-colored rivers that empty into a series of large placid lakes—with the harsh, semi-arid and rugged plains of the Klein Karoo places the journey east of Cape Town firmly among the country's most dynamic travel experiences. A sun-drenched area about 250km (155 miles) long and 70km (43 miles) wide, the Klein Karoo is wedged between the Outeniqua Mountains that separate it from the coastal Garden Route and the impressive Swartberg mountain range in the north. To reach it from any angle, you have to traverse precipitous mountain passes, the most spectacular of which is the Swartberg Pass, connecting the Klein Karoo with its big brother, the Great Karoo. It's great driving country, with vast open spaces, roads that are (for the most part) empty of traffic, and plenty of interesting pit stops and detours.

Historic **Swellendam,** a pretty town at the foot of the Langeberg Mountains, is the perfect halfway stop (for lunch or the night) if you're traveling from Cape Town to the Garden Route directly via the N2. However, a far more rewarding detour involves swinging north from Swellendam and tooling along **Route 62,** absorbed by the vast open landscapes and possibly stopping in small Klein Karoo *dorpies* (villages) such as **Montagu, Barrydale,** and **Calitzdorp,** dwarfed by their surroundings, their Cape Dutch and Victorian buildings slowly transformed by escapees from urban-corporate life into hip and funky stop-offs.

For many, Route 62 culminates in **Oudtshoorn,** the country's ostrich-farming epicenter, with famous subterranean caves and unusual animal encounters, but no Klein Karoo journey is complete without traversing the breathtaking **Swartberg Pass** to the lovely hamlet of **Prince Albert,** with the best-preserved Karoo architecture and enough to keep you entertained for a 2-night stopover.

Our coverage of the **Garden Route**—a marketing epithet derived from the lushly forested visual impression of this narrow coastal strip—commences at the lethargic hideaway village (and slowly growing residential development) of **Wilderness.** The route extends as far as the **Storms River Mouth** in the east; and from the shore of the Indian Ocean to the peaks of the Outeniqua and Tsitsikamma coastal mountain ranges that effectively cocoon the region from the interior. Highlights include the various sections of the **Garden Route National Park,** incorporating the Lakes District and some of the country's loveliest coastline; the **Knysna lagoon** and the surrounding indigenous forests; and **Plettenberg Bay.** This latter offers some of South Africa's best swimming beaches and sublime temperate climate, making it the holiday darling of the moneyed set, which in turn has spawned a hideous urban sprawl. Thankfully all is not lost, as you will still find beautiful *fynbos* and forest environs, especially magical in the area known as the **Crags,** also home to some of the continent's best wildlife sanctuaries. The real garden of the Garden Route, however, is the **Tsitsikamma,** where dense indigenous forests, interrupted only by streams and tumbling waterfalls, drop into a beautiful and untouched coastline.

Aside from its scenic attractions, this coastal belt also takes pride of place on the itinerary for adrenaline junkies, with a rush of activities ranging from the highest bungee jump in the world to riding elephants and cage-diving with great white sharks. The region also boasts a number of private game reserves, but few compare with the well-stocked reserves in the bordering Eastern Cape province. However you devise your driving itinerary (and this chapter is here to help you do just that), make sure you set aside enough time in which the plan is to do exactly nothing. Isn't that what vacations are all about?

STAYING ACTIVE

ABSEILING Take a 45m (148-ft.) abseil (rappel) next to a waterfall in the Kaaimans River Gorge in Wilderness, then canoe out (R365 per person). Call **Eden Adventures** (© **044/877-0179;** www.eden.co.za). Or swim, float, jump, and abseil down Kruis River Gorge with **Tstitsikamma Falls Adventure** (© **044/280-3770;** www.tsitsikammaadventure.co.za). You can also rappel in the Swartberg mountains with **Swartberg Adventures** (© **082/926-9389;** R180 for 2–3 hr.).

BOATING You can cruise the ocean all along the coast; recommendations can be found under each section.

BUNGEE-/BRIDGE-JUMPING The **Bloukrans River bridge-jump** (© **042/281-1458;** R690 per person), 40km (25 miles) east of Plettenberg Bay, is the highest commercial bungee-jump in the world: a stomach-churning 7-second, 216m (708-ft.) free fall. Operators Face Adrenaline hold the Guinness World Record certificates for the most jumps completed in an hour (19), as well as the most jumps in a 24-hour period by one person (101). Open daily from 9am to 5pm.

CANOEING/KAYAKING Naturally, one of the best ways to explore South Africa's Lakes District is via its many waterways. Canoes can be rented throughout the area—contact the local tourism bureau wherever you are. The 2-day **Keurbooms River Canoe Trail ★★★**, near Plettenberg Bay, is unguided and takes you 7km (4¼ miles) upstream through totally untouched vegetation to an overnight hut, where you're assured of total privacy. The hut houses four people; you may need to self-cater. For bookings, call **CapeNature** (© 0861/227/362-8873; www.capenature.co.za). **Eden Adventures** (© 044/877-0179; www.eden.co.za) handles short-canoe rental in Wilderness, for trips up the river culminating with a picnic-perfect waterfall. For sea-kayaking tours of the marine-rich ocean around Plettenberg Bay, contact **Dolphin Adventures** (© 083/590-3405; www.dolphinadventures.co.za). Tours start at R250 for 2 to 2½ hours.

DIVING   There are snorkeling and diving routes in **Tsitsikamma National Park** (© 042/281-1607). Gear and guides can be rented from **Untouched Adventures** (© 073/130-0689) at Storms River Mouth Rest Camp, or from **Pro Dive** (© 044/533-1158) in Plettenberg Bay; ask about Jacob's Reef, another good spot off the Plett coast. **Hippo Dive Campus** (© 044/384-0831) offers equipment and dives in the Knysna area, where there are a number of wrecks to explore; they also arrange snorkeling experiences.

GOLFING   You're really spoiled for choice on the Garden Route, also known as South Africa's "Golf Coast". The almost unrestricted (and unpoliced) development of new courses in the past decade, however, has produced a groundswell of opposition from locals, who fear that the environmental impact of these thirsty lawns for the well heeled is still to be felt.

In George   The original **George Golf Club course ★★** (© 044/873-6116) is a scenic 72-par walk that offers excellent value at R380. By contrast the much-vaunted **Fancourt ★★★**, South Africa's premier golf resort offers visitors a chance to play on their Gary Player–designed Montagu (rated number seven in the country by *SA Golf Digest*) and Outeniqua courses (© 044/804-0205; 18 holes for R795, golf cart R330, caddy R190). The top Links course (18 holes for R1,660) is only open to hotel guests. If you're not up to par, enroll at the **Fancourt Golf Academy** (© 044/804-0190), said to be one of the best in the world; priced from R240 per ½-hour lesson, or R1,200 for an 18-hole personal on-course lesson. Newcomer **Oubaai Golf Course** (© 044/851-1234), part of the Hyatt Regency Golf Resort & Spa, is the first Ernie Els signature course in Western Cape. Located approximately 10km (6¼ miles) from George Airport, Oubaai Golf Course is a championship layout and not surprisingly rated by Els, a two-time winner of the U.S. Open and a British Open title holder, as one of his favorite courses in the world.

In Knysna   Even if you loathe golf, you'll be in awe of the breathtaking views at **Pezula ★★★** (© 044/384-1222; see p. 232). Designed by Ronald Fream and David Dale, it enjoys a glorious location atop the Knysna East Head cliffs. The course boasts a luxury hotel and spa (greens fees R590–R790 for day visitors, R725 for hotel guests). Deeper inland, on undulating hills that overlook the Knysna river and lagoon, is the perfectly groomed Jack Nicklaus Signature Golf Course at **Simola** (© 044/302-9677; www.simolaestate.co.za), which is a little less tricky to play than Pezula. Nevertheless, the course has an interesting configuration: five par-3s and five par-5s (greens fees R590–R750; includes cart and halfway house). The estate is also home to an ultramodern resort-style hotel with spa.

In Plettenberg Bay   If you've worked your way through George and Knysna, you can now choose between the challenging 18-hole course in evergreen surrounds at the **Plettenberg Bay Country Club** (© 044/533-2132; greens fees R390) and the Gary Player–designed **Goose Valley ★** (© 044/533-5082; R520).

HIKING   Garden Route   Truly, a walker's paradise. Mark Dixon's **Garden Route Trail ★★** (📞 082/213-5931 or 044/883-1015; www.gardenroutetrail.co.za), offers a variety of guided nature walks, including beach walks and birding experiences. They offer easy 3- and 5-day coastal walks (luggage portaged) taking you from the forests of Wilderness to Brenton-on-Sea outside Knysna; you'll take in stunning coastline scenes along the way. For serious hikers, the following are worth noting: the clearly marked 108km (67-mile), 7-day **Outeniqua Trail ★** (📞 044/302-5606), which takes you through plantations and indigenous forests (shorter versions available); the 60km (37-mile), 6-day **Tsitsikamma Trail ★★** (📞 042/281-1712 information, or 044/874-4363 reservations), an inland version of the more famous Otter Trail, which includes long stretches of fynbos, as well as forests and rivers; and the 27km (17-mile), 2-day **Harkerville Trail ★★** (also called the Mini Otter Trail, and a good alternative), which features forest and coastal scenery (📞 044/302-5606). Best of all is the 42km (26-mile), 5-day **Otter Trail ★★★**, South Africa's most popular trail. It's a very tough coastal walk, taking you through the Tsitsikamma Section of the Garden Route National Park, past rivers and through indigenous forests, with magnificent views of the coast; its popularity means it must be booked at least a year in advance (📞 012/426-5111; www.sanparks.org). The 3-night **Dolphin Trail** is a luxury trail in the Tsitsikamma, with all luggage portaged; comfortable, fully catered accommodations; plenty of time for lolling in tidal pools; and trained field guides accompanying walkers (📞 042/280-3588; www.dolphintrail.co.za). For those who don't have the time (or energy) for overnight trails, the 10km (6.25-mile) **Pied Kingfisher Trail,** in Wilderness, follows the river through lush indigenous forest to a waterfall; the slightly shorter **Kranshoek Walk,** in the Harkerville Forest, is another great forest environment; and the 9km (5.5-mile) **Robberg Trail,** in Plettenberg Bay, is definitely worth exploring for its wild coastline and whale-watching opportunities.

In the Klein Karoo   Hike the relatively unexplored **Swartberg mountains ★★★** (📞 082/926-9389 or 073/185-9301; www.swartbergadventures.co.za). There are no marked trails where these guys go, and you'll scramble through gorges and swim in cool mountain streams in the shadow of sheer cliffs, before overnighting in caves on the way up some of the highest peaks in the Western Cape. Book well in advance.

HORSEBACK RIDING   In Swellendam   Two Feathers Horse Trails (📞 082/494-8279) offers short or full-day excursions in the Langeberg Mountains.

In Wilderness/Knysna   Cherie's Riding Centre (📞 082/962-3223) offers scenic trails along the Swartvlei Lake and forests, as well as a beach ride (with a light lunch). **Forest Horse Rides** (📞 044/388-4764) takes small groups through the Knysna forests.

In Plettenberg Bay   Contact **Equitrailing** (📞 044/533-0599 or 082/955-0373) to explore fynbos and forests in this area.

MOUNTAIN BIKING   For half- to 8-day mountain-biking tours of various regions covered in this chapter (including the Swartberg pass), contact **Mountain Biking Africa** (📞 082/783-8392; www.mountainbikingafrica.co.za).

In and Around Prince Albert   Cycle the mighty Swartberg Pass—mercifully, downhill. Contact **Lindsay** (📞 082/456-8848), who also organizes the popular Three Passes Tour that takes in Meiringspoort and the Montagu Pass, as well as the Swartberg.

In & Around Wilderness   To tour the foothills of the Outeniqua Mountains (close to George), contact **Eden Adventures** (© **044/877-0179;** www.eden.co.za); the half-day tour also involves some canoeing.

In Knysna   All three of the Diepwalle State Forest trails are ideal for mountain biking, particularly Harkerville, which has four color-coded routes: The Harkerville red route, which includes forest, fynbos, and the craggy coastline, is considered one of the best in South Africa—book early. For more information on trails in the **Knysna State Forests,** contact Jacques at **Knysna Cycle Works** (© **044/382-5153;** www. knysnacycles.co.za), who can supply everything you need including children's bikes).

PARAGLIDING   Wilderness is considered South Africa's best site for coastal flying, and is among the top-five safest training areas on the planet; see p. 129.

QUAD BIKING   Traverse a 14km (8.5-mile) trail between Wilderness and George on four wheels with **Quad Adventures** (© **072/303-9011;** www.quadgardenroute. co.za). They also offer shorter and nocturnal drives as well as 2- to 3-day adventures in the Klein Karoo, or along the Garden Route and Route 62—although nights are spent camping.

SHARK-CAGE DIVING   In Mossel Bay   See box on p. 129.

SKYDIVING   In Plettenberg Bay   You can jump from a plane attached to an instructor and then experience 35 seconds of carefree free fall from 3,000m (10,000 ft.) with **Skydive Plettenberg Bay** (© **082/905-7440;** www.skydiveplett.com). The drop zone is at the local airstrip, and training is limited to a 10-minute briefing.

SURFING   Top spots in this part of the country include **Inner and Outer Pool** and **Ding Dangs** at Mossel Bay, and **Vic Bay** near Wilderness. Or head straight for **Jeffrey's Bay** in the Eastern Cape (p. 256), not too far east of Plett. Call **Surf Shop** (© **044/533-3253**) for rentals in Plett (board R100; wetsuit R50); see chapter 8 for rentals in Cape Town.

TREETOP CANOPY SLIDES ★   A bit like experiencing brief spurts of horizontal flight, this popular adventure activity in the Tsitsikamma forest is loads of fun. Attached to a rope on a pulley system, one glides through the indigenous forests from tree to tree. Breathtaking views, albeit from a slightly hair-raising angle. Contact **Stormsriver Adventures** (© **042/281-1836;** www.stormsriver.com), internationally recognized as responsible tourism operators.

WHALE-WATCHING   Although not as hyped as the Overberg coast (discussed in the previous chapter) the Garden Route is a rewarding base for whale-watching—particularly in Plettenberg's lovely bay, a veritable marine mammal nursery. Remember that there are limited boat-based whale-watching permits issued annually for the entire South African coast, so check your operator's credentials and note that boats are not allowed to approach closer than 50m (164 ft.), though whales are free to approach stationary boats. Recommended companies are discussed throughout the chapter.

WHITE-WATER RAFTING   Felix Unite (© **021/702-9400** or 079/509-9975; www.felixunite.com) runs rafting trips (R475 per person) on the Breede River near Swellendam, but it's pretty tame when compared with the Doring River, considered the best in the Western Cape and running from mid-July to mid-September. Instead of a raft, you get a yellow tube, wetsuit, and helmet for the 5-hour river excursion with **Tsitsikamma Blackwater Tubing** (© **042/281-1757;** www.blackwatertubing.net;

R495), an adventure-filled morning that includes some hiking, rock-jumping, and paddling through the Storms River Gorge.

SWELLENDAM

Swellendam is 220km (136 miles) E of Cape Town

Back in the early 1700s, the Dutch East India Company was perturbed by the number of men deserting the Cape Colony to find freedom and fortune in the hinterland. Swellendam was consequently declared a magisterial district in 1743, making it the third-oldest colonial settlement in South Africa and bringing its reprobate tax evaders once again under the Company fold. In 1795, the burghers finally revolted against this unwanted interference and declared Swellendam a republic, but the Cape's occupation by British troops later that year made their independence rather short lived. Swellendam continued to flourish under British rule, but a devastating fire in 1865 razed much of the town.

Almost a century later, transport planners ruined the main road, Voortrek Street, by ripping out the oaks that lined it, ostensibly to widen it. Two important historical sites to have survived on this road are, at no. 36, the **Oefeningshuis,** built in 1838, and, at no. 11, the over-the-top baroque **Dutch Reformed Church,** built in 1901. The **Swellendam Tourism Organisation** is at 22 Swellengrebel St. (*028/514-2770;* Mon–Fri 9am–5pm, Sat–Sun 9am–1pm).

What to See & Do in & Around Swellendam

Aside from the wealth of colonial-era buildings, Swellendam backs onto the very beautiful **Marloth Nature Reserve ★★**, where trails offer ample opportunity to escape into nature, and there are a number of local artisan enterprises worthy of a visit. **Wildebraam Berry Estate** (*028/514-3132;* www.wildebraam.co.za; Mon–Fri 8am–5pm, Sat 9am–4pm) does tastings of its unique liqueurs (chocolate chili, hazelnut, lemon, and even guava), berry preserves and jars of chili products; Nov–Dec you can also pick your own berries (great fun if you're traveling with kids). In town, at 264 Voortrek St., you can visit **Rain** (*028/514-2926;* Mon–Fri 8am–5pm, Sat 9am–4pm, Sun 11am–3pm), the original store for a range of locally produced bath and beauty products that have now spread to Europe, but started in a small rural factory in Swellendam.

Bontebok National Park ★ 📖 Accessible by car or mountain bike, this is South Africa's smallest reserve, dedicated to saving the once near-extinct and very pretty bontebok antelope, as well as the rare coastal renosterveld fynbos it grazes on. There are no large predators in the park, so good to explore on foot, with some easy walking trails along the lovely Breede River. On the river's banks, **Lang Elsie's Kraal Restcamp ★** (*021/552-0008* reservations) comprises 10 upgraded efficiency wood, stone, and glass chalets (R775 double), suitable for families (four people max). They're comfortable enough, but the setting is the clincher.

7km (4¼ miles) N of town. *028/514-2735.* www.sanparks.org. R50 adult, R25 child. Summer daily 7am–7pm, winter daily 7am–6pm.

Drostdy Museum complex ★★ Comprising the Drostdy, the Old Goal and Ambagswerf (Trade's Yard), Mayville House, and Zanddrift, this is your one-stop architectural history primer. The Drostdy was built by the Dutch East India Company in 1747 to serve as residence for the *landdrost* (magistrate), and features many of the building traditions of the time: yellowwood from the once abundant forests, cow-dung and peach-pit floors, elegant fireplaces, and, of course, Cape Dutch gables. The Drostdy also houses an excellent collection of late-18th-century and early-19th-century Cape furniture in the baroque, neoclassical, and Regency styles.

Swellengrebel St. ⓒ **028/514-1138.** www.drostdymuseum.com. R30. Mon–Fri 9am–4:45pm; Sat–Sun 10am–3:45pm.

WHERE TO STAY

Augusta De Mist ★★   Set within 1.5 hectares (3¾ acres) of lush, jungly gardens, new owners Michel and Henk have done a superb overhaul of this gorgeous early-19th-century country house, and along with the personal attention they give every guest, have turned Augusta into one of the best places to stay in town. For privacy, choose one of the suites and cottages in the gardens (the tastefully furnished Arum and Agapanthus cottages, with reed ceilings and fireplaces, are particularly good), but if you've a love for history opt for a suite in the original Cape Dutch manor house, supposedly where the eponymous Augusta spent a night in 1803. Henk does a combination of inventive and traditional South African meals (biltong soup, locally sourced lamb shank, malva pudding) on select nights.

3 Human St., Swellendam. www.augustademist.com. ⓒ **028/514-2425.** 7 units. R1,000–R1,100 heritage double; R1,100–R1,500 garden suite; R1,150–R1,500 heritage suite; R1,150–R1,700 garden cottage. Rates include breakfast. Children 2 and under free, under 12 R350, under 18 R400. MC, V. **Amenities:** Restaurant (limited days), lounge, well-stocked library, wine cellar; outdoor saltwater pool; spa treatments. *In room:* A/C (in most), TV/DVD (in most), bar fridge, fireplace (in most), hair dryer.

Bloomestate ★★   This slick, spacious retreat will suit travelers who prefer a more contemporary design to the Cape Dutch that otherwise predominates here. The Dutch owners have brought a cool, citrus-fresh look to a spacious property with abundant landscaped gardens and a bit of luscious jungle with a Jacuzzi perched above a pond thick with lily pads. Rooms are modern, with furniture by some interesting designers, vibrant color combinations, and cubist inspiration; pity they are all right next to each other given the size of the grounds. But there are lovely outdoor lounging areas, and a stylish lounge in shades of lemon, lime, and gray.

276 Voortrek Rd., Swellendam 6740. www.bloomestate.com. ⓒ **028/514-2984.** Fax 028/514-3822. 7 units. Summer R1,300–R1,600 double; winter R970–R1,100 double. AE, MC, V. **Amenities:** Breakfast room; lounge; honor bar; open air Jacuzzi; heated saltwater pool; spa treatments. *In room:* A/C, MP3 docking station, free Wi-Fi.

De Kloof Luxury Estate ★★   It's one of many national monuments in town, but behind De Kloof's whitewashed walls are some cool, contemporary spaces, filled with Asian and African artifacts (collected by Marjolein when she worked in West Africa and China). Set in spacious grounds complete with golf putting green and driving range, it's walking distance to the center of town—that's if you don't get too side-tracked by the idyllic setting and tranquility of the pool. Some of the luxury rooms are so beautifully situated that we prefer them to the deluxe options, though they lack bathtubs and have a little less space; all feature good beds, and glorious rainfall showers. Those on a luxury treasure hunt should opt for the double-story honeymoon suite, with a waterbed and vast fireplace.

8 Weltevrede St., Swellendam 6740. www.dekloof.co.za. ⓒ **028/514-1303.** Fax 028/514-1304. 9 units. R1,200–R1,590 luxury double; R1,400–R1,790 deluxe double; R2,000–R2,500 suite; from R1,600 family suite, with up to 3 children at discounted rates. Rates include champagne breakfast. AE, DC, MC, V. **Amenities:** Restaurant, multiple lounges, including cigar lounge in winter; mountain bikes (free); room

service; spa/exercise room; golf driving range and putting green (free); large outdoor pool. *In room:* A/C, TV, hair dryer, movie library, minibar, heated towel racks, underfloor heating, Jacuzzi (suite only), fireplace (suite only), free Wi-Fi.

Schoone Oordt ★★   Just a stroll away from the museums, this carefully restored Georgian-fronted country house (with Victorian filigree) offers accommodation in spacious rooms and a comfortable, relaxed atmosphere. If you have the funds to spare, opt for the more private honeymoon suite, with its view of wilder gardens and a stream. Inside the rooms, antiques—restored by the owner—add character to the quality fixtures; hanging potted plants, colorful wildflowers, and individually chosen artworks add to the personal touch. Service is sincere and spot-on; you'll have breakfast in a broad sun-splashed conservatory up at the main house—signature items include poached nectarine and perfect eggs Benedict.

1 Swellengrebel St., Swellendam 6740. www.schooneoordt.co.za. ✆ **028/514-1248.** Fax 028/514-1249. 9 units. Summer R1,850 luxury double, R2,250 honeymoon/family suite; winter R1,100 luxury double, R1,650 honeymoon/family suite. Rates include breakfast. AE, DC, MC, V. **Amenities:** Breakfast room, lounge w/bar; outdoor pool. *In room:* A/C, TV/DVD, fireplace, fridge, hair dryer, heated towel racks, underfloor heating in bathrooms, free Wi-Fi.

WHERE TO EAT

There's a range of dining possibilities in town, including one world-class Italian that is something of a must-experience if passing through this part of the world: **La Sosta** is reviewed below. The **Old Gaol ★★** (✆ **028/514-3847;** daily 8:30am–5pm, dinner Tues–Sat from 6:30pm, summer only) justifiably tops the lunch lists, and not only for it's new tree-bedecked setting opposite the town's pretty Dutch Reformed Church on Voortrek Street. The menu features South African dishes such as *bobotie,* oxtail, Cape-style (Malay) curries, and homemade chicken pie, and they still bake traditional *roosterkoek* (bread) over the coals. Children have their own outdoor play area and a special menu. Leave room for a slice of one of their home-baked cakes—their *melktert* (milk tart) is baked in a copper pan and quite legendary.

La Sosta ★★★ ITALIAN   Milanese couple Cristiana and Giovanni serve unforgettable food at this unassuming, pared-down space that spills directly from the side of the customized kitchen in their thatched home, built in 1838. Giovanni meets, greets, charms, and serves, while Cristiana cooks, giving a modern edge to honest Italian dishes learned from her mother and grandmothers. Tuna bressaola (slightly smoked Sicilian-style carpaccio) is a must-order, as are any of the perfectly al dente pastas; even the caprese salad is special—mountains of mozzarella and ultra-juicy tomatoes doused in peppery olive oil. There's typically always at least one game dish, such as kudu filet, but prepared in the Italian way. Everything's fresh (fish especially) and marvelously simple—but the flavors are on a grand scale.

145 Voortrek St. ✆ **028/514-1470.** www.lasostaswellendam.com. Main courses around R105–R135, 4-course tasting menu R270. MC, V. Daily 7pm–late; closed Sun–Mon Aug to mid-Dec; closed Mon mid-Dec to Mar; closed May–July.

Sabine's Drostdy Restaurant ★★ BELGIAN/INTERNATIONAL   Step inside this heritage-listed building (the oldest in town, built in 1757) on a busy night (when it's open, it's full) and you'll find half the town's population tucking into hearty meals, and sizzling cuts of steak being raced out of the kitchen or filet flambéed in brandy right in front of whooping diners. Adventurous Sabine left Europe more than 22 years ago, arrived in Swellendam for a holiday, and stayed. She also makes great breakfasts and offers a tapas menu during the day (a very good cold meat and cheese platter), but signature dishes include her lamb casserole, Malay chicken curry, and Belgian apple tart. For something truly out of the ordinary, try her African soup, a fruity, curried soup made with banana.

Swellengrabel St. ℂ **028/514-3825** or 082/770-4719. Dinner reservations essential. Main courses R65–R135. MC, V. Wed and Fri–Sat 10am–5pm; Sun–Tues 10am–midnight. Closed June–July.

ROUTE 62 ★★★

South Africa's most enchanting road trip is highly recommended for its empty roads, spectacular mountain scenery, vineyard valleys, small-town architecture, and wide-open plains. With no detours or stops, this scenic route—also known as "the longest wine route in the world"—could add a mere 90 minutes to your overall itinerary; but if you value the journey as much as the destination, you'll factor in at least 2 to 3 nights along the way. If you like things a little quirky, and keen to meet interesting South Africans at their most welcoming and enthusiastic, this is one detour not to be missed—or rushed.

The Best of Route 62

One-horse **Ashton** marks the official start of the R62, kicking off with the 10km (6¼-mile) **Cogmanskloof Pass ★**, which deposits you in **Montagu,** a fruit- and wine-growing town at the foot of the Langeberg Mountains. It's a reasonable stopover if you're driving from Cape Town (or any of the nearby Winelands or Whale Coast towns) and although the town itself is rather nondescript, the soaring brick-red mountains surrounding it are balm for the soul. There's also plenty of fine Victorian architecture to amble past, and many arrive to take a therapeutic dip in the nearby **hot springs** (ℂ 023/614-1150), a constant 109°F (43°C), bathing in them is a sensory pleasure that's marred by the aesthetic ruin brought about by the resort that grew around the springs. Open daily from 8am to 11pm, for R40 to R60 per person.

From Montagu, the road east wends its way through a mesmeric semi-arid landscape, passing a succession of sleepy settlements, offbeat produce stands, and wine estates, the craggy mountain ranges a constant undulating background. One of the Western Cape's two proper Big 5 game reserves—the luxurious **Sanbona**—is found here, but is really only a worthwhile stopover if you're willing to spend at least 2 nights; it encompasses a vast (54,000-hectare/133,380-acre), seriously beautiful terrain and to explore it all *and* take in sufficient wildlife requires a bit of time (and money). Further along, you can sample the fruit of the vine at **Joubert-Tradouw** (ℂ 028/572-1619), a boutique winery, where you can take lunch at the deli-style eatery before a walk through the orchards, or spend the night at its B&B. After this you soon find yourself in **Barrydale,** a popular escape for the Cape gay community, and located in a narrow valley beneath the Langeberg Mountains. An essential stop is the unassuming but reputable **Clarke of the Karoo ★** (ℂ 028/572-1017; daily 7:30am–4:30pm), which feels like a cross between a roadside diner and an urbane deli, its shelves packed with good-looking local produce (such as preserved quail's eggs, red onion marmalade, and luxurious chocolate sauce). Owner Mike Clarke dabbles in creative cooking, but there's always Karoo lamb curry, Karoo lamb burger, and—for more adventurous palates—Karoo oysters.

Next up, **Calitzdorp** apparently shares climatic similarities with Portugal's Douro Valley and has made a name for itself as the country's "Port Capital," though disputes over the use of the "port" designation means the wine names are modified to become

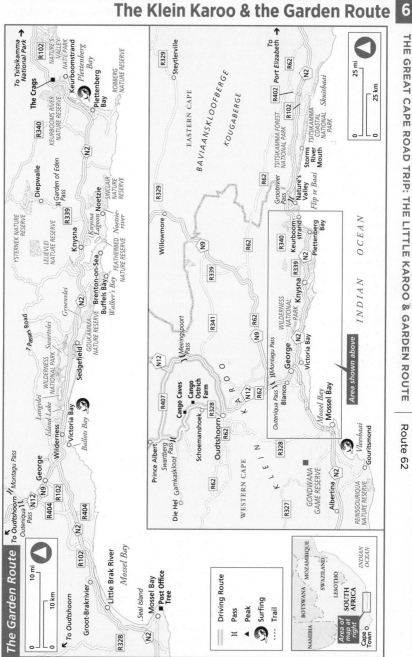

known more specifically as "Cape Tawny Port" or "Cape Vintage Port" and the like. Don't miss a tasting at **Boplaas** (© **044/213-3326**) and **Die Krans** (© **044/213-3314**), or slip down the side streets to discover its historic buildings and idiosyncratic eateries like **Die Handelshuis,** 2 Geyser St. (© **044/213-3172**), decorated like the Karoo version of a roadside diner with vintage kitsch and nostalgic memorabilia, but attached to a beauty salon and contemporary art gallery. Around the corner, **Karoo Life** (© **044/213-3217**) is a small hotel painted in autumnal colors and the best place in town to dine—preferably on its vine-covered terrace, although the Karoo-kitsch interior is very cozy when the winter cold descends. From here, you could easily walk to at least six different cellars; for more, visit **Calitzdorp Tourism,** 3 Voortrekker Rd. (© **044/213-3775**) or check out www.calitzdorp.co.za. If you end up staying the night (recommendations below), don't miss the nightly 6pm organ recital in the pretty sandstone church—the organ is rated the best in the country.

From Calitzdorp, you can drive directly to Outdshoorn (following the R62), but a recommended detour is to slip through the vale at the foot of the majestic Swartberg range, and then ascend the twists and switchbacks of the Swartberg Pass to spend a night in the Groot Karoo town of Prince Albert—highly recommended (see later in this chapter)—before continuing south to Oudtshoorn, and on to the contrasting pleasures of the Garden Route.

Where to Stay, On & Off Route 62

Of **Montagu's** many B&Bs, **Aasvöelkrans** ★★ (www.aasvoelkrans.co.za; © 023/614-1228; R750–R800 double, with breakfast), is the most interesting—a fantastically eccentric and arty space that's part stud farm, part urbane retreat, with a gang of chickens roaming the grounds, horses in the adjoining paddock, and clever design choices and works by local artists. There are just a handful of individually decorated and much-loved rooms, and your host will point you toward hiking trails that start right across the road on a stud farm at the foot of the Langeberg Mountains. To mingle with locals and listen to golden hits played on a baby grand piano, choose a room in the Carrington Villa at the Art Deco **Montagu Country Hotel** (www.montagucountryhotel.co.za; © **023/614-3125;** R1,550 double, including breakfast). Somewhat isolated, yet just 3km (1¾ miles) outside of town (off the R62) is **Les Hauts de Montagu** ★ (www.leshautsdemontagu.co.za; © **023/614-2514;** R1,200–R1,700 double, including breakfast), a guesthouse offering 10 Provençal-style bedrooms in five cottages on the grounds of a 19th-century Cape Dutch homestead. Set within a 600-hectare (1,483-acre) indigenous garden, it includes commanding vineyard and mountain views and a tiny chapel (sadly, dinner is no longer served here, meaning you need to drive to town to eat).

Further along is **Sanbona Wildlife Reserve** ★★ (www.sanbona.com; © 028/572-1365 or 041/407-1000; R8,470–R9,500 double, including all meals, games drives and select drinks) a 54,000-hectare (133,437-acre) private sanctuary sheltering the Big 5 (some of which are quite elusive) in a unique and magnificent terrain. Offering comprehensive game drives through Klein Karoo scenery that makes for a very different safari experience from other reserves in the country, Sanbona is very beautiful, if you like arid landscapes. There are three camps to choose from, the best of which is the secluded **Dwyka Tented Lodge** ★★★, comprising nine canvas-topped stone cottages arranged along a dry riverbed at the base of a steep ravine (for the best views, book no. 8—no. 1 is the most secluded). Each one has a deck and private plunge pool, and they're designed to take full advantage of the dramatic rock mountain view—you'll spot black eagles, baboons and klipspringers (a small, cute rock-jumping antelope) from your room; massive sliding doors fold away to make sure you can keep an eye on the scene no matter what you're up to. Also luxurious are the six very large, plush suites at **Tilney Manor,** although the atmosphere will better suit older travelers; while **Gondwana Lodge,** which welcomes children, is quite hotel-like and conventional.

For significantly less money you could stay in nearby Barrydale; the grape-colored **Barrydale Karoo Hotel** (*C* **028/572-1226;** R700–R1,200 double) reopened under new ownership in 2010, after a period of neglect. It's an old hotel, but locals and bikers (and probably a few real ghosts) haunt the downstairs bar. Your best bet here are the luxury garden suites (R1,000–R1,500). Beyond Barrydale (about halfway to Ladismith), you need to be alert to spot the turnoff (unmarked) that leads to Ashley and Andre's three farm cottages at **Wolverfontein ★★** (www.wolverfontein.com; *C* **028/551-2277;** from R300 double), a farm established in 1890 on the banks of the Touws River. Two cottages are efficiency, while the third, Moreson Manor, offers B&B accommodation for up to four people. Decor is Karoo-inspired and tongue-in-cheek, and guests get to experience some true outback isolation in a mesmeric setting—at night, don't neglect the star-painted sky.

Calitzdorp Country House ★★ (www.calitzdorpcountryhouse.co.za; *C* **044/213-3760;** R1,400–R1,800 double, including breakfast) is one of the smartest lodging options anywhere on Route 62, with a pretty location (just outside town), lovely views across vineyards, and stylish, individually designed rooms. The owners are collectors who have compiled an amazing collection of Asian, Victorian, Cape, Zanzibari, Cameroonian, and even French classical pieces. If you really want to spoil yourself, sign up for their five-course dinner. Back in town and considerably cheaper, but with everything you need for a good slumber, is **Port Wine Guest House,** 7 Queen St. (www.portwine.net; *C* **044/213-3131;** R640–R800 double), in a large, thatched 1830 homestead with a big pool, pleasant garden, and patios shaded by vines.

PRINCE ALBERT & THE SWARTBERG PASS ★★★

Prince Albert, an 18th-century Karoo town that lies 100km (62 miles) north of better-known Oudtshoorn, is the Cape's most charming *dorpie* (little village), with well-preserved Cape frontier architecture and a uniquely contained atmosphere. It can be reached as an easy day trip from Oudtshoorn (or even Wilderness), but if you feel like spending a romantic night under a star-spangled sky, you'd be well advised to stay. In fact, plenty of travelers from around the world have stumbled in, fallen head-over-heels with the low-key atmosphere and irrigation canal–lined streets, and never left, which accounts for the innate sophistication of village life here. Despite the steady but slow influx, its touristic nature has not detracted from its charm, and there are a wealth of great places to stay and dine, and much to fill your days, too. But for many, the greatest highlight of a visit here is simply traversing the Swartberg Mountains to get there.

Tip: If you're pressed for time you can reach Prince Albert directly (about 3½ hours) from Cape Town via the N1, spending the night (or two) here before traversing the Swartberg Pass to Wilderness and the rest of the Garden Route.

A Breathtaking Drive: The Swartberg Pass ★★★

To reach the **Swartberg Pass ★★★**, a 27km (17-mile) gravel road built more than 100 years ago by master engineer Thomas Bain, you can follow a direct route from Calitzdorp (described under "Where to Stay," below, and bypass Oudtshoorn) or travel via Oudtshoorn to take the R328 that heads north of the town (also known as Cango Valley Rd.). About 1km (a little more than a half-mile) before the road terminates at the Cango Caves, you'll find a turnoff to the west, signposted PRINCE ALBERT. This marks the start of the pass, which soon begins its steep ascent. By the time you reach the summit, you will have enjoyed stupendous views of the Klein Karoo, which lies some 1,220m (4,002 ft.) below. Stop to gird your loins, for the journey has only just begun. The northern descent is hair-raising—10km (6¼ miles) of zigzags, serpentines, twists, and steep gradients on a narrow dirt road with nothing between you and the abyss but a good grip on the wheel. (You'll note a turnoff to the west that will take you to **Die Hell (Gamkaskloof) ★★★**. This is another magnificent drive, particularly memorable if you're a fan of fynbos, but unless you overnight in one of the rudimentary Cape Nature cottages, you'll have to return the way you came—the road is very slow going. Set aside most of the day for this detour.)

The road continues to twist and turn before finally winding its way out of the Swartberg. At this point, you can either go to **Prince Albert** or turn back into the mountains and return to Oudtshoorn via Meiringspoort. To return to Oudtshoorn, take the road back to the Swartberg Pass, keeping an eye out for the R407, which takes you east through Meiringspoort—another spectacular drive, though views now are up: The **Meiringspoort Pass ★** is a natural ravine created by an ancient river course, and features soaring cliffs and spectacular rock formations. The 25km (16-mile) paved road follows and crosses the river several times as it winds along the floor of the gorge.

To explore the area on foot, Erika Calitz and CapeNature offer **The Donkey Trail ★★** (© 083/628-9394; www.donkeytrail.com; R3,000 per person all inclusive) a guided 4-day, 26km (16-mile) hiking trail from Groenfontein (15km/9.3 miles from Calitzdorp) over the Swartberg and into Die Hel; your gear is transported by rescued, rehabilitated donkeys.

WHERE TO STAY EN ROUTE TO THE SWARTBERG PASS ★★★

The dirt road detour between Calitzdorp and the start of the Swartberg Pass (the most direct route to Prince Albert), is a wonderful off-the-beaten track journey taking you to some amazing rural retreats. If you're ready for a bit of off-the-grid solitude, head for either **Boesmanskop** or **The Retreat at Groenfontein** (both below)—reached via dirt roads and located in small, remote valleys with breathtaking views yet close enough to Calitzdorp, Prince Albert, and Oudtshoorn to explore each on day trips.

Boesmanskop ★★★ 📷 This rank's as one of the most authentic and fabulous farm-stay experiences in South Africa. Squeeze through a narrow, densely overgrown, winding driveway and find yourself at the doorstep of a welcoming, inimitable host. Tinnie Bekker might be off milking cows, hanging tobacco, or feeding ostriches, but once you step inside your room, the short wait for him will have been worth it. Tinnie is a farmer by trade, but as an interior designer he's a natural, and the vast suite he's put together above his pool room is one of our favorite places to bed down anywhere. You can wander the farm—ducking between the vineyards or losing yourself in one of Tinnie's jungly secret gardens—or plunge into the long, black pool. Tinnie leaves you to do what you want, but after serving dinner (he's a talent in the kitchen, too) is happy to converse, so coffee in the lounge, decorated with Cape Dutch antiques and artworks (many by his extensive collection of talented friends), is a must.

Kruisrivier, 31km (19 miles) NE of Calitzdorp; follow signs off R62 btw. Oudtshoorn and Calitzdorp. www. boesmanskop.co.za. © **044/213-3365.** 2 units. R1,000 double. Rates include breakfast and dinner. No credit cards. **Amenities:** Dining room; lounge; pool. *In room:* Fridge, hair dryer, no phone.

The Retreat at Groenfontein ★★

If you believe that real luxury is a star-filled sky, with no noise or light pollution and crystal-clear air, you'll find that here, along with numerous mountain trails and rock pools. Reached via a long, bumpy but satisfying drive along a scenic dirt road that end in this secluded valley, with nothing in it but a Victorian farmhouse, floating above pretty gardens, and a warm welcome from your hosts, Marie and Grant. Make sure you book one of their four garden suites, and all you'll want is to relax on your veranda and gaze at the sublime Swartberg mountain views. If you crave solitude and walks to pristine streams, this is the perfect place—you'll get a serious sense of being in some kind of final frontier territory here. Dinners, served communally, are convivial, with free-flowing conversation and plenty of wine. There isn't a plethora of servants, and the decor isn't anything you'll find in a design magazine, but the atmosphere is homey and warm.

Groenfontein, 20km (12 miles) NE of Calitzdorp; follow signs off R62 btw. Oudtshoorn and Calitzdorp. www.groenfontein.com. © **044/213-3880.** Fax 086/271-5375. 8 units. R1,420–R1,820 double. Rates include breakfast and dinner. DC, MC, V. **Amenities:** Dining room; lounge; bar service; hiking trails; free Internet; library; pool. *In room:* Fireplace (in some), hair dryer, no phone.

Prince Albert ★★★

Your jaw will no doubt still be hanging wide open by the time the Swartberg spits you out some 5km (3 miles) short of Prince Albert, the ultimate cool Karoo *dorpie*, and the most romantic and sophisticated of them all. Aside from the quality of the light and air, the village is an architectural gem, with almost all the buildings preserved and maintained in their original 19th-century form—you can learn a great deal about the various building styles (and much more besides) during a highly engaging dusk **Ghost Tour ★★★** that winds through town with **Ailsa Tudhope** (© **023/541-1211;** www.storyweaver.co.za; R50), a superb storyteller and authority on everything from the history to the intriguing social dynamics of this small community. Besides exploring the farms, restaurants, and quirky shops, you can go for an adrenaline-charged **cycle down the mighty Swartberg pass.** World adventurer Lindsay will provide the bikes and drive you to the top (© **082/456-8848**). Or, for splendid Karoo vistas, head off on one of the **trails up the *koppie*** immediately behind the town; also a spectacular spot for star-gazing, so be sure to contact **Astro Tours ★** (© **072/732-2950;** www.astrotours.co.za; R150) to get a handle on the star-dappled canopy. On weekends, artist-gallerist Hennie Boshoff runs a highly recommended 90-minute **Art After Dark** tour ★★ (© **023/541-1366** or 083/267-2436; R50; from 6pm) of his sculpture garden and art house-cum-living museum, **Villa Kruger** (www.azazel.com/villakruger). It's an intriguing insight into the creative world of a wide range of artists—tours are limited to 12 people and last around 1½ hours; English tours happen each Saturday (and include a glass of wine). By day, make an appointment to visit the state-of-the-art olive press, showroom, and tasting room at **Prince Albert Olives ★★**—you'll come away with a good understanding of the award-winning stuff they're producing here (beautifully packaged, too). Also a great treat is a trip to the local fig farm, **Weltevrede ★★** (© **023/541-1229**), in a sublimely beautiful

One good reason to find yourself in lively Prince Albert is to sign up for a course at **African Relish** ★★★ (© 023/541-1381; www.africanrelish. com), a cooking school in the heart of the village. Here, a state-of-the-art kitchen serves as the hub for various culinary experiences, as well as tours that combine cooking with other diversions, such as cycling, or learning to blend wine. Courses may be designed to specific interests, or themed, or even driven by big personalities (such as

BBC food celebrity Reza Mahammad or Franschhoek's Reuben Riffel). The school regularly operates as a restaurant where delicious meals are prepared in the open kitchen (partially a result of courses run that day). The whole experience is very convivial—co-owner Jeremy Freemantle, who relocated here to start the school, is fascinated by the provenance of food and the culture around Prince Albert, and his knowledge and passion shows. (Also see "Where to Stay," below.)

valley (some 25km/16 miles from town). The family-run farm is mostly off the grid, using gas, sun, and wind. Make an appointment for a personal tour of the orchards and to see how various fig products are prepared and packed—don't neglect to eat at least one fresh fig straight from the tree; harvesting happens January through May—the rest of the year you'll have to make do with the dried version, which are delicious. There are three guest cottages (from R400 double) kitted for self-catering, but it's possible to prebook breakfasts and dinners.

Cheese lovers should stop at **Gay's Dairy** (© 023/541-1703) to taste the produce from Gay's lovely herd of Guernseys, while wine lovers with a sweet tooth must make a point of stopping at **SoetKaroo** ★★★ (56 Church St; © 023/541-1768), a tiny vineyard in the center of town, where Herman and Susan Perold produce a delicious Red Muscat d'Alexandrie, a traditional dessert wine, bottled in gorgeous decanters. The other wine you'll be seeing regularly during your stay is produced at **Bergwater Vineyards** (© 023/541-1703; Mon–Fri 9am–4:30pm, Sat 10am–3pm), on the road to Meiringspoort, where you can enjoy a relaxed tasting in the stone-wall cellar. They also produce olives, and brandy is distilled in a traditional copper pot kettles. Finally, there's much to be learnt from the entrepreneurial conservationists at **Renu Karoo** ★★, a 100-hectare (247-acre) desert farm under the protection of CapeNature on which they run 2-hour 2km (1.2-mile) nature walks (R80 per person, or R200 for just two people), talking you through the geology of the 250-million-year-old rocks and inland sea that once existed here, and introduce you to the idiosyncrasies of just some of the 4,500 plants found in the Karoo—it's amazing to learn how the various endemic species cope with the arid conditions. Loads to do, and you haven't even been near the **Fransie Pienaar Museum** (© 023/541-1172; R10; Mon–Fri 9:30am–12:30pm and 2–4:30pm, Sat 9am–12:30pm, Sun 10:30am–noon) in the center of town yet. Go—it's good.

If there's anything more you need to know, **Prince Albert's Tourism Information** is clearly signposted at 109 Church St. (© 023/541-1366; Mon–Fri 9am–6:30pm, Sat 9am–1pm); or contact Lindsay at **Dennehof** (© 023/541-1227 or 082/456-8848; lindsay@dennehof.co.za).

WHERE TO STAY

Prince Albert has some excellent deals, and hospitality levels are high. Besides the wonderful places reviewed below, one of the best deals in town is the gorgeous, three-bedroom cottage **Vergeet-My-Niet** ★, 8 De Beer St. (℃ 023/541-1069 or 083/316-4015; R500–R660 double). Tucked away on a quiet street but within walking distance of restaurants and museums, it's filled with lovely furniture and has a great fireplace, a garden, and a dam with geese. Another excellent efficiency option is **Cactus Blue** ★★★ (www.explorersclub.co.za; R950 double, R1,400 for four people), a fabulously designed two-cottage refuge designed for three couples, and packed with true class (and a sense of fun) and lots of modern luxuries (plunge pool, TV/DVD with movie library, and full kitchen with washing machine and dishwasher) to sweeten the deal.

African Relish ★★★ 🔥 A choice of four characterful efficiency cottages—two contemporary units are right on the village's main drag, while the other freestanding Karoo-style houses date from the 1800s and are virtually out in the sticks, a few minutes' drive away. The latter are particularly enchanting, with their own windmills whirling away in your Karoo garden, and hens pecking away at the ground. These cottages have good kitchens, and comfortable lounging area, indoors and outside (no pools but there is A/C). Decor is Karoo chic—quirky antiques, offbeat collectibles, vintage magazines, old-school porcelain, and artworks set against a white palette. Check-in is at the innovative cooking school; you're escorted to your door with a bottle of the local vino and jar of olives, and told all there is to do—step inside and instantly realize you want to extend your stay.

Reception at 34 Church St., Prince Albert. www.africanrelish.com. ℃ **023/541-1381.** Fax 023/541-1386. 4 units. R1,100 double, or R1,500 for 4 people. MC, V. **Amenities:** Restaurant, lounge; cooking school; tours, excursions, and cooking courses arranged. *In room:* A/C, fireplace, hair dryer, kitchen, no phone.

Dennehof Guesthouse ★★ 🔥 A tranquil oasis in an 1835 farmstead on the outskirts of the village, this winning retreat includes the oldest surviving building in town. Park your car behind the manually operated gate and jump on a bicycle to explore the town; Ria and Lindsay (who, incidentally, offers some of the finest—and most exciting—tours of the region and the Swartberg Pass) are exceptional hosts, and will point you towards the best the town has to offer. Genuine Karoo hospitality, complemented by good looking, character-filled rooms done out in various very personal, idiosyncratic variations on "Karoo chic"—art, converted collectibles, and pretty antiques fill the spaces as much as the warmth of your hosts. Without hesitation, book the gorgeously renovated Wagon Shed with it's romantic outdoor bathroom. Breakfast on a wooden deck hovering above one of the famed *leiwater* water channels, is another reason you'll be longing to return to Prince Albert.

20 Christina de Wit St., Prince Albert. www.dennehof.co.za. ℃ **023/541-1227.** Fax 023/541-1124. 7 units. R770–R1,040 double, R860–R1,040 honeymoon suite. Rates include breakfast. AE, MC, V. **Amenities:** Lounge; dinners on request in winter; honor bar; bikes; pool; free Wi-Fi in main house. *In room:* A/C, fireplace (in most), fridge (in most), hair dryer, no phone.

De Bergkant Lodge ★★ In a Cape Dutch national monument (but with most rooms in the new Georgian-style extensions), with lovely antiques, two large saltwater swimming pools, an outdoor "star bath," and even a wellness center, De Bergkant is certainly the most upmarket guesthouse in the village, with the most spacious rooms (courtesy of them being custom-built rather than renovated) and a general air of well-bred gentility. It's a good, well-run spot, with great facilities, but we feel it lacks the warmth and personality of our other top choices in town.

5 Church St., Prince Albert. www.debergkant.co.za. *©* **023/541-1088.** 9 units. R1,000–R1,600 double. AE, DC, MC, V. No children under 12. **Amenities:** Breakfast room, lounge, honesty bar; 2 large outdoor pools; star bath. *In room:* A/C and fans, TV, fridge, hair dryer, underfloor heating.

WHERE TO EAT

By day, **Prince Albert Country Store,** 43 Church St. (*©* **023/541-1053**), is a great place to browse for antiques and collectibles, then settle in for a wholesome lunch on the porch overlooking the back garden. Owners William and Colleen Penfold have the gift of the gab and love to share tales about their produce and their town. If the Olive Branch (below) or the restaurant at the cooking school, African Relish ★★, isn't open, our favorite dinner spot, with its emphasis on fresh local ingredients, and a convivial setting, is **Gallery Café ★★** (*©* **082/749-2128;** main courses R75–R128; dinner only) is pulling in compliments. Peruse the chalkboard on the veranda of the Seven Arches building (the restaurant is upstairs), and make a reservation (if it's warm, ask for a table on the veranda overlooking Church St., otherwise you're between walls packed with art). There are plenty of meat options and—scarce in the Karoo—some decent vegetarian options, too. Plus delectable homemade ice cream. If The Olive Branch (below) or the restaurant at the cooking school, **African Relish ★★**, isn't open, you could dine at the Café or opt for classic Karoo fare (traditional *bobotie*—lightly curried ground beef cooked in a savory egg custard and served with yellow rice, Karoo lamb pie, chicken pie, or Karoo leg of lamb, followed by sticky malva pudding or steamed lemon pudding) in the **Karoo Kombuis ★**, 18 Deurdrift St. (*©* **023/541-1110;** dinner Mon–Sat; main courses R65; no credit cards; BYOB)., though standards have been slipping here in recent months, with far too much prepared in advance and served with little love.

The Olive Branch ★★★ [image] SOUTH AFRICAN INNOVATIVE   Sometimes the best experiences break the mold completely—and who ever said restaurants have to behave like restaurants. Self-styled chef and food innovator Bokkie Botha came to the kitchen by way of his love of eating (including forays into various three-star Michelin restaurants). Now his twice-weekly eatery is an essential stop for anyone interested in food: He prepares three courses (four choices for each course), interspersed with interesting in-betweeners (such as chilled beetroot consommé with sour cream, vodka and pomegranate seeds) and finished off with local cheeses and macaroons. Expect delicious slow-roasted leg of Karoo lamb, venison, and wonderful vegetables, many of which he grows himself, alongside his own herbs, in the garden alongside the restaurant. Innovative food aside, Bokkie loves spending time sourcing top local wines, with plenty of well-priced vintages on offer.

Mark St. bokkieb@iafrica.com. *©* **023/541-1821** or 082/892-7222. R220 per person. No credit cards. Open 2 nights per week only; call or e-mail ahead to find out when.

OUDTSHOORN: OSTRICHES & OTHER ANIMALS

Oudtshoorn—unofficial center of the Klein Karoo—is largely known for its ostrich farms, of which the earliest date from the early 1800s, when the introduction of wire fencing and successful seeding of sweet Lucerne first made the large-scale domestication of these flightless birds possible. But it was only when Victorian fashion victims developed an insatiable appetite for ostrich feathers around 1880 that the town really took hold, with land values in the Oudtshoorn area shooting up overnight. At the height of the feather boom, the so-called feather barons built lavish town houses where they would occasionally overnight before returning to their marble-floored farmhouses, architectural curiosities, these are worth seeking out (see "Feather Barons & Ostrich Palaces" box below). For more about the town's fascinating history, visit the **CP Nel Museum,** corner of Baron van Rheede Street and Voortrekker Road (*©* **044/272-7306;** R15 includes Le Roux Town House entry; Mon–Sat 9am–5pm). Located in a handsome sandstone building this old-fashioned museum has many exhibits relating to Oudtshoorn's boom period; it also houses a synagogue and exhibits relating to Oudtshoorn's once-large Jewish community—in fact, Oudtshoorn was often derisively referred to as Little Jerusalem by those envious of the success of the feather merchants, most of whom were Jewish. **Arbeidsgenot ★** (meaning "The Pleasure of Work"), 217 Jan van Riebeeck Rd. (*©* **044/272-2968;** R15 adults, R10 children; Mon–Fri 9am–noon and 2–4pm) is not a feather palace, but the humble abode of C. J. Langenhoven, author of South Africa's first national anthem (the second half of its current one), and his family home from 1901 to 1950. It's an authentic house museum, not least because everything has been left as it was when the man penned his novels and poems. It's a tranquil place to spend a half-hour, although you need to call ahead to check if anyone is available to let you inside.

Animal lovers (and parents with kids) interested in up-close encounters with fascinating species are spoilt for choice in Oudtshoorn. Aside from visiting an **ostrich farm** or the **Cango Wildlife Ranch,** or booking a **Meerkat Adventure** (all reviewed below), you can meet elephants at nearby Buffelsdrift (see "Where to Stay," below) with the trained pachyderms of the **Oudtshoorn Elephant Company.** Either book an **Elephant Experience** (R210) in which you feed them and spend time watching them perform trained maneuvers (such as kicking a soccer ball), you get to "arm wrestle" (or trunk wrestle), and get a short briefing on some of their most curious physical and behavioral attributes. For a more personal interaction, opt to go on an **Elephant Walk Safari,** or an **Elephant Ride** (R550 adult, R275 child for either). (It's worth noting that there is strong, mounting opposition in certain conservation circles to the use of these superintelligent creatures, built to migrate over huge distances, as tourism attractions kept in relative captivity; the debate is far from over.) It's also possible to book a (rather tame) **game drive** at Buffelsdrift (R350 adult, R175 child).

For more information visit the **Greater Oudtshoorn Tourism Office** (*©* **044/ 279-2532;** www.oudtshoorn.com; Mon–Fri 8am–5:30pm, Sat 9am–1pm; corner of Baron van Rheede and Vorrtrekker streets.

The Cango Caves ★★ ☺ The **Cango Caves** were first explored in 1780 by a local farmer who was lowered into the dark, bat-filled chamber, which is now named in his honor. The **Van Zyl Hall,** 107m (351 ft.) across and 16m (52 ft.) high, has some incredible million-year-old limestone formations, including the Organ Pipes. A second chamber was discovered in 1792, and a century later the caves opened as a tourist attraction. Regrettably, they were damaged in the 1960s and 1970s, when the floors were evened out with concrete; ladders, colored lights, and music were installed; and a separate entrance was opened for "nonwhites" (who had tours at different times).

Today the caves enjoy a slightly more respectful treatment, with wardens fighting an ongoing battle to keep the limestone formations from discoloring from exposure to lights and human breath (although their running commentary is a tad irritating). There are two tours to choose from: the hour-long standard tour, which departs every hour and visits six chambers; and the 90-minute **adventure tour,** which covers just over 1km (a little over a half-mile), some of which must be crawled (under no circumstances tackle this if you're overweight or claustrophobic; have heart, knee, or breathing problems; or are not wearing sensible shoes—it's slippery in places).

Approximately 30km (19 miles) from town on the R328. ✆ **044/272-7410.** www.cangocaves.co.za. Adventure tour R80; standard tour R64. Daily 9am–4pm; last tour departs 3:30pm. Closed Dec 25.

Cango Wildlife Ranch ★ ☺ Affording an opportunity to see rare creatures up close, it's hard not to be won over by this animal park, not least as the ranch is involved in breeding programs to help build up cheetah, Bengal tiger, and other endangered species numbers. Entrance fees include an hour-long guided tour, and allow you to wander on wooden walkways through the "Valley of the Ancients" passing various tropical species, plus crocodiles, lemurs, and a pair of pigmy hippos (hugely endangered, these are now virtually nonexistent in the wild). Besides the opportunity for those over 16 to stroke white tiger cubs or relaxed cheetahs (and kids over 10 to pet very young cubs, if available), the ranch's key claim to fame is the only **crocodile cage diving** facility on the planet (children from 10 years can participate with an adult). You'll be lowered into a clear, heated pool that contains five full-grown crocs—they promise you'll get close enough to see their toenails.

Off the R328, en route to the Cango Caves. ✆ **044/272-5593.** www.cango.co.za. High season R110 adults, R65 children 4–13; winter R95 adults, R55 children; children under 4 free. Big-cat encounters R160–R300; crocodile cage diving R280. Daily 8am–4:30 or 5pm.

Meerkat Adventures ★★★ ◙ ☺ You need to be up before the crack of dawn to spend time with Oudtshoorn's most intriguing mammals: Meerkats (also known as suricates) have starred in *National Geographic,* BBC, and Discovery Channel documentaries, but meeting them in person is far more satisfying. Devey Glinister is the conservation-obsessed wildlife rehabilitation expert who took over where charlatan Grant McIlrath (of Meerkat Magic—a private enterprise said to have defrauded tourists who prebooked nonexistent tours) left off. Confirm details of your tour with Devey the night before; it's a pre-dawn meeting outside Oudtshoorn, followed by tea and then a short walk and brief wait at one of the meerkat mounds, waiting for the ridiculously cute and amazingly gregarious creatures to emerge. Observing them as they go about their early morning routine (soap opera antics combine with sentry duty and sun-worshipping—the meerkats literally need to solar-charge their batteries for the day!) and hearing about the complexities of their personal/social lives is thoroughly rewarding. *Note:* Unless you are the only people on the tour, this is only suitable for children aged 10 and over who are patient and well behaved.

De Zeekoe Reserve, Oudtshoorn. ✆ **084/772-9678.** www.meerkatadventures.co.za. deveyg@gmail. com. R600 per person. Tours start at sunrise (5:30am in summer, later in winter) and must be reserved and confirmed in advance.

Moooi @ Jamstreet ★★★ Given the anonymity of Oudtshoorn's town sprawl, this quirky bohemian sculptural garden with a strong environmental focus is the most attractive man-made creation for miles. An evolving, living artwork, the former dairy farm is filled with clever ideas, including a labyrinth made from 6,252 recycled wine bottles (based on the Byzantine mosaic floor of San Vitale in Ravenna, it's unique in the world) and a stylishly curated gallery with paintings on the walls and sculptures

It was the ostrich that put the Klein Karoo on the map: During the late 19th and early 20th centuries, when the world decided that ostrich feathers were simply the hautest of haute, Oudtshoorn, where the first ostriches were farmed, found itself crowned the feather capital of the world. Local ostrich farmers, known then as "feather barons," became millionaires overnight, building themselves luxurious "ostrich palaces," clearly identifiable by their sandstone turrets and other baroque touches. The best preserved of these (albeit not the grandest) is the **Le Roux Townhouse** (Mon–Fri 9am–1pm and 2–5pm), a mini mansion on High Street. Built in 1909, the interior features some original pieces dating from the Le Roux family's heyday, but the majority of the furnishings—imported from Europe between 1900 and 1920—have been bought and placed *in situ* by the **CP Nel Museum,** where you can see photographs of many of the "palaces" that were knocked down. (Fortunately, more survived than were knocked down.) Though most are closed to the public, they're worth walking or driving past; pick up a map from the tourism office but don't miss **Pinehurst,** on Jan van Riebeeck Street, now part of a teachers' training college, and the elegant **Mimosa,** on Baron van Reede Street. Sadly, the boom went bang in 1914, with the outbreak of World War I. The profitable trade in feathers never really recovered, with fickle Dame Fashion seeking her postwar inspiration elsewhere, but in the last few decades the ostrich has experienced a huge surge in popularity—for those who haven't yet tried it, it's a delicious and low-fat alternative to beef, and bears absolutely no resemblance to chicken.

filling out the troughs where cows would once have fed. Everywhere you look, there's something eye-catching and artfully arranged. And that's over and above the gang of geese that patrols the grounds, the outdoor amphitheater (which hosted Smokie during the 2011 Arts Festival), the pretty little cafe, and the boutique selling out-of-the-ordinary keepsakes and collectibles. The outdoor men's latrines are worth a special look (don't let the warning signs put you off). Moooi is incidentally an intentional misspelling of the Afrikaans word *mooi,* meaning pretty, and pronounced *moy.*

Rooiheuwel Rd., Oudtshoorn. ✆ **082/510-0516.** www.jamstreet.co.za. Free entry. Mon–Sat 9am–4pm.

Tantinki ★★   An easy stop on the way to Moooi, and essential if you want to taste award-winning, naturally low-fat, preservative- and colorant-free goats' milk cheese. Sonja Ferreira has been farming goats for 13 years and likes to describe her methods are "primitive." She produces 14 cheeses in 17 different styles, as well as 10 flavors of fudge (exported to the U.K.), and a fantastic goats' milk ice cream. She also offers 2-day cheese-making courses in which you can learn to prepare five cheeses, and take home a culture kit. Note the excellent **fresh produce market** every Saturday morning.

45 Langenhoven Rd. ✆ **083/340-5820.** Mon–Fri 8am–5pm; Sat 9am–1pm

Visiting an Ostrich Farm

The ostrich remains the primary source of income for Oudtshoorn, with thousands flocking to see, touch, eat, and (yes) even ride the giant birds. There are some 400 ostrich farms. Highgate (incidentally, the biggest ostrich farm in the world), Safari, Oudtshoorn, and Cango all vie for the tourist buck—R60 to R70, to be

Every March and April, Oudtshoorn hosts the **Klein Karoo National Arts Festival (KunsteFees) ★★★**, one of the biggest and best cultural festivals in South Africa. If you are booking well in advance it's worth spending a few nights to catch a few shows and shop for crafts, but be warned that the best places to stay are often booked a year in advance. Contact the Tourism Bureau for more information (*(C)* **044/279-2532; www.oudtshoorn.com**).

exact—offering more or less the same 45- to 80-minute tour. These include an explanation of ostrich farming (from incubation to tanning), guided tours of the farm, the opportunity to sit on an ostrich and stand on its eggs, and an ostrich derby. All offer meals with ostrich on the menu (you usually need to prebook). Of the farms, **Cango Ostrich Farm ★** (*(C)* **044/272-4623;** daily 8am–4:30pm), on the road to the caves, is far away the best, not least because of its location overlooking the beautiful Schoemanshoek Valley. It's also smaller and more intimate than the others. Visitors take a brief walk from one process to the next rather than being driven around a large farm, and you meet an ostrich that enjoys human affection, and get a look at emus, so you can spot the differences. Finally, while you can sit on an ostrich and go for a brief, adrenaline-pumping sprint around the yard, the birds (which do not sweat and have a tough time regulating temperature) are not raced here, saving you the embarrassment of this circus display, which is also potentially injurious to the animals. The 45-minute tours (R65 adults, R35 children aged 6–17) take place daily from 9am to 5pm; reserve ahead and enjoy a lunch or dinner served in restored laborers' cottages with great views overlooking the valley.

WHERE TO STAY IN & AROUND OUDTSHOORN

With the exception of **Rosenhof** (reviewed below), most of our top choices are located outside Oudtshoorn. **La Plume ★★** (www.laplume.co.za; *(C)* **044/272-7516;** R1,280–R1,650 double), a Victorian guesthouse on a working ostrich and cattle farm offers very comfortable accommodations, rich with antiques, gilt-framed oil paintings, choice fabrics, feathers, candelabras, and lots of personal style. Particularly good are the honeymoon and superior suites. Dinners (R195) are sumptuous affairs with good Karoo cuisine, and farm tours (R150) are available. Heading out of Oudtshoorn in the other direction, you come to the one horse town of De Rust, where you'll find one of our favorite budget lodging options, the homey and personable **Riverside Accommodation ★**, 29 Schoeman St. (hamptonh@mweb.co.za; *(C)* **044/241-2110** or 083/291-0519; R500 double), offered by chef Niekie Eksteen and jeweler Soan Jacobs, the amicable owners of De Rust's best eatery (the **Village Trading Post;** see "Where to Eat," below). Guest rooms are filled with character—exposed brick walls, huge mirrors, poster beds, and what he calls "from-the-heart decor"—and they also open on to a pool and lush views of mountains that rise from the edge of the garden. It's a blissful little spot to hide away from the world; the rate includes a brilliant Trading Post breakfast.

Buffelsdrift Game Lodge ★ ☺   Offering a tiny taste of what it's like to be on a real safari, this 3,000-hectare (7,413-acre) "mini reserve" sans predators offers a toned-down version of what you get in Kruger. Not by any means in terms of game viewing, but the safari-style accommodations are novel if you haven't slept in them elsewhere: spacious en-suite tents, tastefully furnished and built on the edge of a dam. There are no doors, keys, or locks, and instead of TV, you roll up the canvas flaps to reveal a gorgeous scene. Book a "superior"—nine tents ranged along the edge, so you're likely to see game ambling down for a drink while you're doing the same on your deck (nos. 7, 8, and 9 are closest to the game area). The lodge offers morning and evening bush safari drives, where the focus is on plants and the environment as well as animals; you should see buffalo, rhino, giraffe, and zebra, as well as plenty of antelope. No "wild" elephants but you can walk or feed tame rescued youngsters that live near the lodge.

Off R328, 7km (4¼ miles) N of Oudtshoorn, on the way to Cango Caves. www.buffelsdrift.com. ✆ **044/272-0000.** Fax 086/523-8345. 25 units. High season R2,590 double, R3,066 waterfront double; low season R1,512 double, R2,002 waterfront double. Children aged 3–12 pay R378–R767 if sharing with 2 adults. Rates include breakfast, dinner, and choice of 2 activities (game drive, elephant feeding, or horseback safari). Noninclusive rates available. AE, DC, MC, V. **Amenities:** Restaurant; bar; lounge; game drives; helipad; horseback riding; pool; room service; spa treatments; walking trails; free Wi-Fi (in restaurant and bar). *In room:* A/C, hair dryer, minibar.

De Zeekoe ★ ☺ A 2,000-hectare (4,940-acre) working farm (ostriches, cattle, sheep, and springbok, as well as alfalfa fields) offering a choice of accommodation, this is a great base if you're intrigued by the idea of Meerkat Adventures: Guests here get a discount, and since the little critters live on De Zeekoe's nature reserve the dawn wake-up call isn't so painful. The compact two-bedroom timber **efficiency cabins** near an active dam (perfect for bird-watching from your porch) are a rustic option for families (though not ideal for toddlers). Five minutes down the road is the restaurant, a wonderful pool, and a variety of slick, modern accommodations at Main House, of which nos. 12 and 13 (deluxe units) have the best views. For better value, the luxury rooms, also at the Main House, aren't huge but still have verandas and reasonably tasteful decor.

Off the R328, 9km (5½ miles) SW of Oudtshoorn. www.dezeekoe.co.za. ✆ **044/272-6721.** Fax 044/272-8534 19 units. R940 standard double, R1,180 lake cabin double, R1,360 luxury double, R1,720 deluxe double, R1,900 superior double; 30% less in winter. Rates include breakfast. AE, DC, MC, V. **Amenities:** Restaurant; bar; bikes; canoes; farm tours; horseback riding; pool. *In room:* A/C, TV, hair dryer, minibar; lake cabins include kitchenette.

Jamstreet ★★★ 🔌 ☺ It's a bit out of town, but it's gorgeous, luxurious, and an absolute bargain. On a farm-turned-outdoor gallery and amphitheater, this red, handsomely renovated Karoo cottage has three rooms (with space for three couples or a large family) and is fully equipped for a self-catered stay. Hide-covered headboards, curtains made of recycled bottle tops, a bathroom clad almost entirely in corrugated iron—imaginative creativity is everywhere in this vibrantly decorated space, along with most everything you need for a comfortable stay, including a barbecue, small pool, and pair of ostriches patrolling an adjacent patch of land. *Note:* At press time, Danie and Wim were converting four former laborers' cottages into electricity-free guest suites with similar facilities and the same sense of boho panache.

Rooiheuwel Rd., 4.5km (2¾ miles) from Oudtshoorn. www.jamstreet.co.za. ✆ **082/510-0516.** 1 unit (more planned). R850 for the cottage or R350 per person. No credit cards. **Amenities:** Restaurant (daytime only); gallery. *In room:* A/C, hair dryer, kitchen, plunge pool.

Rosenhof Country House ★★ This is the most upscale place to stay in Oudtshoorn itself: a lovely, calm oasis furnished with selected works by a wide range of famous South African artists, a wellness center, and in springtime, a rose-filled garden that saturates the air. Rooms are built around a courtyard, each with its own entrance.

Though each has a different theme, they share the most important characteristics: space, beautiful linens, well-sprung beds, and elegant, if rather old-fashioned. Tucked behind trees and hedges is a large pool—a necessity during the searing summer heat (book one of two cottage-suites for your own private pool, fireplace, and Swartberg views). Dinners are a five-course affair (R270) served in the original 1852 homestead, with herbs fresh from the garden; staff is excellent.

264 Baron van Reede St., Oudtshoorn 6620. www.rosenhof.co.za. © **044/272-2232.** Fax 044/272-3021. 14 units. High season R3,100–R3,300 double, R4,200–R4,400 suite; low season R2,250 double, R3,100 suite. Rates include breakfast. AE, DC, MC, V. Children by prior arrangement only. **Amenities:** Dining room; bar; lounge; art gallery; gym; pool; room service; sauna; spa treatments. *In room:* A/C, TV, hair dryer, heated towel rack, minibar, free Wi-Fi.

WHERE TO EAT IN & AROUND OUDTSHOORN

Oudtshoorn has two excellent restaurants; in addition, if you want to hang with the locals in a friendly, unpretentious (and very well-priced) casual environment serving healthy portions and good flavors, head straight for **Bello Cibo ★**, 146 Baron van Rheede St. (© **044/272-3245;** Mon–Sat 11am–10pm). They serve Italian standards, but there's ostrich and venison, too. For a light (and fabulous) lunch, **Moooi @ Jamstreet** (see above) deserves as much acclaim for its carrot cake and salads as for the artworks in the adjacent gallery. And, if you're traveling between Oudtshoorn and Prince Albert via the Meiringspoort Pass, time your hunger for a pit stop at the **Village Trading Post ★** (© **044/241-2110** or 083/291-0519; daily 8am–3 or 5pm) on the main road through De Rust; probably the best reason to slow down rather than zooming through the one-horse town. Plenty of good old-fashioned food, including traditional *boerekos* lunches on a Sunday, hearty burgers, marinated biltong salad, and fat omelets, and designed like a crazy, boho museum, packed with vintage eye-candy and a glitzy art garden at the back—you can buy anything here, including the table you're eating at.

Jemima's ★★ SOUTH AFRICAN INNOVATIVE   Long rated the best restaurant in the Klein Karoo, this Oudtshoorn restaurant is still in the capable hands of Pierre and Debbie Malherbe, although that doesn't mean they're always there. You'll still find good traditional South African fare with innovative twists, such as Cape Malay babotie with Cape gooseberry chutney, a Karoo lamb platter with a "drunken apricot" in muscatel jus, and the "Three Tenors"—ostrich, venison, and beef, with three sauces. Still a good choice but somewhat overtaken by Kalinka.

94 Baron van Reede St., Oudtshoorn. © **044/272-0808.** www.jemimas.com. Main courses R60–R180 dinner. AE, DC MC, V. Daily 11am–3pm and 6pm–late.

Kalinka ★★★ SOUTH AFRICAN CONTEMPORARY   With more by way of culinary adventure, this cozy, stylish restaurant is located in a sandstone house on the main road. Russian-born, big-eyed Olga concocts innovative meals with flair and charm; besides a reputable Vodka selection and—on occasion—caviar pancakes, the menu has a strong South African focus. The African trio of springbok, kudu, and ostrich will satisfy any adventurous meat cravings, or try the quail in honey soy sauce, served on roasted butternut risotto, or pork filet stuffed with basil and cheese and wrapped in bacon. Kalinka believes in uncomplicated dishes, relying more on using the best-possible local ingredients, and the results are often genius.

93 Baron van Reede St., Oudtshoorn. © **044/279-2596.** www.kalinka.co.za. Main courses R75–R170 dinner. MC, V. Daily 6–10pm. Closed June–July.

WILDERNESS & ENVIRONS ★★★

Wilderness is 461km (286 miles) E of Cape Town and 73km (45¼ miles) S of Oudtshoorn

Set around the mouth of the Touw River, Wilderness marks the western end of a chain of lakes that stretches some 40km (25 miles) east, most of which are part of **Garden Route National Park.** Officially, the narrow coastal strip that forms the Garden Route starts a little farther west, in the rural town of Heidelberg, but it's here in Wilderness—far from the sprawling suburban and industrial developments of **Mossel Bay** and the nondescript town of **George**—that you start to understand why this coastline is so popular.

Wilderness itself is hardly untamed, but it's an interesting mix of unfettered dune-backed beach, mountain rock face, protected nature reserve, and a growing rash of ugly residential and leisure property development, with a highway that whips directly through, just behind the beach. However, none of this takes away from the ease with which you can disappear into forest or slip off along a seemingly deserted length of coast, and despite the best efforts of developers, Wilderness remains the smallest and by far most tranquil of the coastal towns along the Garden Route. If you enjoy the low-key vibe of a true getaway destination, Wilderness—effectively surrounded by the national park—is then the best base on the Garden Route if you'd prefer to unpack for a few days and explore, rather than hop from place to place. It's just a short (20-min.) drive from well-marketed (but very touristy) Knysna, while the popular 'burb-like town of Plettenberg Bay is just under an hour away; even Oudtshoorn and Prince Albert are easily experienced as a day trip from here.

ESSENTIALS

GETTING THERE **By Air** You can fly to **George Airport** (✆ **044/876-9310**) daily from the major centers (including Cape Town, Johannesburg, and Durban) with **SAA** (✆ **044/801-8434**) and its subsidiaries; other airlines servicing George (from Johannesburg only) are **1Time** and **Kulula.com.**

By Car Wilderness is approximately 4½ hours from Cape Town on the N2. We highly recommend following Route 62 (earlier in this chapter), and pausing in Prince Albert or Oudtshoorn and environs.

By Bus The intercity buses (**Intercape, Greyhound, Translux,** and **Baz Bus**) travel from Cape Town along the Garden Route to Port Elizabeth. See chapter 13 for regional numbers.

WHAT TO SEE & DO

The best way to see Wilderness is from above, preferably attached to ace paragliding instructor Jan Minnaar of **Cloud Base ★★★** (✆ **082/777-8474** or 044/877-1414; www.cloudbase.co.za). Tandem flights afford 15 to 20 minutes (R550) of prime coastal soaring—you launch from a spot known as Map of Africa, and on a clear day can see the Knysna Heads. Flying conditions are particularly good from August to May, and in September there's every chance of spotting whales and dolphins from the air. Jan also does training: A basic license paragliding course requires 7 days of flying (so count on being here for 10–12 days; training is weather dependent and costs R8,500)—or you can take a 1-day introductory course (R1,000). It's a good idea to contact Jan a few days ahead of your arrival; ask him to schedule your flight for the first good-weather day that you're in Wilderness (or Knysna). Experienced pilots can rent equipment.

Ugly Mossel Bay, about an hour west of Wilderness, was the site of the first European landing on the South African coast, when Bartholomieu Dias, having battled a fearsome storm, tacked in for water and safety in 1488. **The Bartholomieu Dias Museum Complex** (✆ 044/691-1067) comprises a collection of historic buildings, of which the **Maritime Museum,** Market St. (Mon–Fri 8:15am–5pm, Sat–Sun 9am–4pm; R10, or R25 with ship access), is arguably worthwhile. It relates the early Portuguese-seafaring history (which is a bit text heavy) and houses a life-size replica of the caravel in which Dias set sail in 1487—it's hard to imagine going where no man has gone before in something that looks like a large toy. The ship on display was built in Portugal and sailed from Lisbon to Mossel Bay in 1987 to commemorate the 500th anniversary of Dias's arrival on southern Cape soil. Outside the Maritime Museum is the **Post Office Tree,** South Africa's first post office. In 1501, the first of many sailors sent his mail by leaving a letter stuffed in an old boot and tied to what the city founders claim is this particular milkwood tree. Soon this became an informal postal system, with letters picked up by passing ships and distributed accordingly. But frankly, for most the only reason to pull in to Mossel Bay is to get close to an ocean-going apex predator: White Shark Africa ★★★ (✆ 082/455-2438 or 044/691-3796; www.whitesharkafrica.com) is the only shark-cage diving operator in town, so your encounter with a great white is likely to be less crowded than in Gansbaai. Cost is R1,300 per adult and R550 for children for a 4-hour trip, including breakfast and a light lunch; the same rate applies for viewing from a boat only. If it's any consolation, you'll get a 25% reduction in the unlikely event that you don't see a great white.

Down on the ground, Wilderness is all about getting close to nature. Although the beaches along this stretch are magnificent, strong currents regularly claim unsuspecting and inexperienced swimmers. You're better off floating in the waters of the **Serpentine,** the waterway that links Island Lake, Langvlei, and Rondevlei to the Wilderness lagoon. Don't be put off by the tea-colored water or frothy bubbles; these are caused by plant oxides and oxygenation, and the water is perfectly clean. One marvelous way to experience the beach is at night with Judy Dixon; she offers a **Moonlight Meander** ★★ (✆ 044/883-1015; wwwgardenroutetrail.co.za), but only on full and new moon evenings when she shines a flashlight into rock pools and introduces you to a world you never imagined existed.

You can explore the area on foot on a number of trails that take from 1 to 4 hours to walk, or cover some 15km (9¼ miles) of inland waterways in a canoe; a popular outing is a 45-minute canoe trip up the river, followed by a hike to the waterfall. **Garden Route National Park** (✆ 044/877-1197; R80 per day) issues trail maps (for canoeing information; see "Staying Active," earlier in the chapter). For more details, contact the **Wilderness Tourism Information Bureau** (✆ 044/877-0045; www.wildernessinfo.co.za; Mon–Fri 8am–5 or 6pm, Sat 9am–1pm).

WHERE TO STAY

Wilderness is always peaceful—even in peak season—and conveniently situated within striking distance of the Klein Karoo and day trips to Knysna and environs. But nothing good stays secret in an area this popular, and as a result there's been an explosion in accommodations options, particularly on the beach. This includes the first five-star boutique hotel, appropriately called Views (www.viewshotel.co.za; © **044/877-8000;** high season R3,140–R12,800 double; low season R2,080–R7,360 double). Certainly the most luxurious hotel on the Wilderness beach, it does have splendid views and a great wellness spa (though you can stay elsewhere and book a treatment here). However, we feel it is a little overpriced given the other beachfront (and lagoon) options reviewed below, none of which involve a 152-stair climb down (and up from) the beach. If you do stay, pay the premium for a sea-facing room—those looking toward the mountain include a gas station in the foreground.

The Dune Guest House ★★   With the constant roar of ocean and wide-open views right from your bed, you'll have little doubt as to why you're here. Grab the beach bag (prepacked with towels, bat, and ball), and head down the short boardwalk onto an almost solitary beach that stretches as far as the eye can see. Gary (an artist and former basketball player from Switzerland) has created a homey B&B with genuine beach house sensibility, right down to the displays of shells and carved fish. While your room is well appointed and very comfortable, things are effortlessly laid back; you're received like a visiting friend rather than a paying guest, and encouraged to get barefoot. There's a big efficiency apartment for families, but don't miss out on Gary's very special breakfast.

31 Die Duin, Wilderness 6560. www.thedune.co.za. ©/fax **044/877-0298.** 5 units. High season R1,200–R1,400 double, R1,650 apt.; low season R800–R1,000 double, R1,100 apt. Rates include breakfast. MC, V. Children by prior arrangement only. **Amenities:** Honest bar; lounge; pool. *In room:* Fan, TV, CD player, hair dryer, heated towel rail, minibar, underfloor heating, free Wi-Fi.

Moontide Guest Lodge ★★ 🗡 ☺   Located right on the lagoon banks, with floating decks, this lovely guesthouse is one of the best value options on the Garden Route; a stylish barefoot, glamorously boho hideaway. The thatched homestead, with distinctively decorated suites in a bird-filled garden, is set among 400-year-old milkwood trees, and all rooms have entrances that lead out into semiprivate or private seating areas. Built on stilts among the trees with glorious views, the aptly named Treetops is not the largest, but is the most private and has a lovely outdoor shower. Very spacious Milkwood has a second bedroom in the thatched loft; masks, textured fabrics, and art instill a bit of Afro-chic character. Also popular is two-bedroom Stone Cottage, with large private patio, and Moon River, which opens onto the extended viewing deck and plunge pool, and has a mezzanine children's room. Owner Maureen is extremely helpful, from restaurant bookings to planning excursions.

Southside Rd. (at the end of the cul-de-sac), Wilderness. www.kalinka.co.za. © **044/877-0361.** Fax 044/877-0124. 9 units. High season R900–R1,440 double; low season R600–R700 double. Rates include breakfast. AE, MC, V. **Amenities:** Dining room; lounge; boat; pool; free Wi-Fi in lounge (with limited room access). *In room:* TV, hair dryer, minibar.

Ocean View ★★★   Despite the prickly reception from the Dutch manager, we recommend this seafront option as the best-looking beach house in town—at least if you like your architecture super-contemporary and spaces very pared down. Built over multiple levels, with different mezzanines, lounging spots, and just a few steps down to the beach, Ocean View opened only at the end of 2010, so everything is spanking new, and the uncluttered spaces and glass walls invite both light and gorgeously framed ocean views. Despite the austerity of the straight, clean lines and dark wood trim (and yes, some might find it too cold or bland), there are a few quirky touches—

If you don't have time to go on a real safari in the Eastern Cape or north, yet you're after a genuine wilderness experience with an authentic deep-in-the-bush vibe, the best Big 5 reserve (along with Sanbona, the desert reserve off the R62) is **Gondwana ★★** (www.gondwanagr.co.za; ℂ 044/697-7002), about 45 minutes from George Airport. Rehabilitated from former cattle and sheep farms, the 11,000-hectare (27,182-acre) *fynbos* reserve has 13 domed "Kwena Huts," designed as a kind of postmodern (and ultrasmart) variation on traditional African dwellings. These in turn are arranged in a horseshoe pattern (resembling a Khoisan *kraal*) overlooking a valley at the foot of the Langeberg Mountains. The setting is magical, and designers have made efforts to match this scenic splendor with luxuriously laid-out open-plan suites. Each round hut has a straw roof with skylight, walk-in closet, open shower, and a stove fireplace.

They also have huge glass doors to let in loads of light and excellent views, and the tub is angled for views of the Langeberg and Outeniqua mountains (which, incidentally, are the last visible evidence of the Gondwanaland split—they include the oldest rock on the planet). Elsewhere at Gondwana there are luxury villas, but these are nowhere near as charming as the huts. Although you could easily spend the entire day ogling the view from the pool on the lip of a ridge above the valley, there's plenty more to keep you occupied, including spa treatments, horseback safaris, fishing, mountain biking, and picnics in the bush. And you do see plenty of game here—there's a single lion pride, eight elephants, and the rare desert black rhino. Children can join a "Junior Ranger" program with their own specialized game drives. Cost is R7,200 to R8,500 double, including all meals, local beverages, and two game drives per day.

a life-size cow watches over the downstairs lounge, for instance, but the real wow is the views, enjoyed from every bedroom. Much better value than Views, the nearby boutique hotel.

39 Die Duin, Wilderness. www.theoceanview.co.za. ℂ**044/877-0137.** Fax 044/877-0141. 7 units. Summer R1,500–R1,800 double; winter R1,000–R1,200 double. MC, V. **Amenities:** Dining room; lounges; bar; pool. *In room:* A/C, TV, underfloor heating, free Wi-Fi.

WHERE TO EAT

It's said that if you remove your shoes before entering a restaurant in Wilderness, you must be a local—we're not suggesting you do this, but it's worth following the locals to their favored eateries. In the center of Wilderness, Roxanne and Cheri—known to everyone here as **The Girls ★★** (ℂ 044/877-1648; Tues–Sun 6–11:30pm, closed June)—serve a great, slightly experimental menu, with vast numbers of fresh prawns and good seafood (try the Cajun calamari steak), but also some good steak and venison. The location is less than spectacular—right next to a gas station in the shadow of the N2—but this doesn't deter regulars (which includes new visitors who go on the first night and then return the very next), because service is good and the food is delicious and great value. For die-hard carnivores, there's **Joplin's ★★**, a timber shack-bar (part of Pirate's Creek; look for the turnoff from the N2, just after the Wilderness turnoff; ℂ **072/292-4247**) that calls to mind a Southern diner in the style of *True Blood*. Rose (the one with the rose behind her ear) is the owner-chef, and she serves only one dish: steak (rump, T-bone, fillet, or sirloin) topped with a fried egg (a Portuguese tradition) and served with a side order of fries, though if you call ahead, Rose will prepare a vegetarian or fish option. For more average fare, the pizzas at **Pomodoro** (℡ 044/877-1403; daily 8am–11pm; near The Girls) aren't bad, as the full tables and constant buzz attest. Also casual, but in a far more attractive setting (walking distance to the beach), and occupying what was once the Wilderness Railway Station, is **Beejuice Café** (℡ 073/975-9614; Wed–Mon 8am–9:30pm, Tues 8am–6pm). There's a blackboard dinner menu with a small selection of South African specialties, but this is really a lovely little place for breakfast, or easygoing lunches of sandwiches and tapas.

For a finer dining experience, reserve your place at **Serendipity** (below).

Serendipity ★★★ 🍴 INTERNATIONAL/MODERN CAPE This fine-dining spot, tucked into a residential street on the river's edge, has bagged loads of awards, yet it's the experience—not the accolades—that proves the point here. Despite its haute credentials, it's very much a family affair: Lizelle is the extraordinary ex–Prue Leith chef; husband Rudolf is front-of-house; and the venue, a house on the banks of the lagoon, is Lizelle's parents' guesthouse. Lizelle changes the five-course set menu regularly, but expect fresh locally procured ingredients, combined with creativity and skill: Breyani stuffed quail with spring onion mash; beet and maize rice risotto with roasted mushrooms, porcini foam and lemon zest mascarpone; or rosemary-crusted lamb rack served with chickpea and pearl barley ragout. Even the baked milk tart has a twist—it's scented with cinnamon and comes with blueberry frozen yogurt. And the palate-cleansing honeybush and witblits slushie is an instant crowd-pleaser.

Freesia Ave. (off Waterside Rd.). ℡ **044/877-0433.** www.serendipitywilderness.com. Set menu R299. AE, MC, V. Mon–Sat 7pm–late (closed for a month in winter).

KNYSNA

500km (310 miles) E of Cape Town, 43km (27 mile) E of Wilderness, and 280km (174 miles) W of P.E.

Knysna used to be a sleepy village inhabited only by a handful of hippies and wealthy retirees, but the last decade has seen a tourist boom that has augmented numbers substantially—nowhere is this more evident than on the congested main road that runs through town. Genuine locals will tell you that the cluttered town center has nothing to do with Knysna, and to find its true heart you need to explore the outlying areas and back roads. Knysna remains the emotional heart of the region, with a resident population that actually lives here year-round (unlike Plett, which turns into a ghost town in winter). Its raison d'être is the large tidal lagoon, around which the town has grown, and the towering sandstone cliffs (called The Heads) that guard the lagoon's narrow access to the sea. The eastern buttress has unfortunately been developed, but this means you can now overnight and play golf surrounded by spectacular sea and fynbos vistas, while the western side remains untouched—a visit to the Featherbed Nature Reserve should be high on your list of priorities. And, of course, it's in the forests around Kynsna that the soul truly finds sanctuary.

Essentials

VISITOR INFORMATION The **Tourism Information Bureau** (℡ 044/382-5510; www.visitknysna.co.za; Mon–Fri 8am–5pm, Sat 8:30am–1pm; hours are extended Dec–Jan) is at 40 Main St. For emergencies on the water, contact the **National Sea Rescue Institute** (℡ 044/384-0211 or 082/990-5956).

THE STATE OF KNYSNA'S forests & elephants

The founder of Knysna (pronounced *Nze*-na) was George Rex. In 1802, at the age of 39—having shocked the Cape community by shacking up with a woman "of color"—he purchased the farm, which included the whole basin containing the Knysna lagoon. By the time of his death in 1839, he had engaged in a number of enterprises, the most profitable of which was timber, and had persuaded the Cape authorities to develop Knysna as a port. Knysna's development and the decimation of its forests were well underway. That any forests escaped the devastation of the 19th century is thanks to far-sighted conservation policies introduced in the 1880s, and today Knysna has the largest areas of indigenous forests left in South Africa. The Knysna elephants have fared less well. Attempts to augment their numbers by relocating three young cows from Kruger National Park failed miserably when it was discovered that the last remaining Knysna elephant was also a female and the surviving cows were subsequently relocated to the Shamwari game reserve in the Eastern Cape. Today you can still see elephants in Knysna, but they are in an Elephant Park, which recently got some bad press when Harry trampled one of his handlers, crippling him, and adding to the ongoing debate about whether it is defensible to use elephants as tourist attractions.

GETTING THERE & AROUND   Knysna is 70km (44 miles) from the airport in **George** (see "Wilderness: Getting There," earlier in this chapter), where you can rent a car. For a fun way to get around (not to mention avoid Knysna's seasonal traffic congestion), rent a mountain bike (see "Staying Active," earlier in this chapter). For a taxi, call **Benwill Shuttle** (✆ **083/728-5181** or 044/384-0103).

GUIDED TOURS   For customized nature walks and tours, contact **Howard Butcher** (✆ **072/018-1333** or 044/388-4671; howard@walkwild.co.za), who covers everything from birding and fungi, to entomology, musical township tours, and unraveling complex ecosystems. He is also an accomplished bush pilot and can put together itineraries that cover the country when time rather than money is your primary consideration. All excursions, from half-day walks to full itineraries, are planned to suit your time and budget; prices start at R200 per person per hour for short outings (minimum cost R600); the longer your itinerary, the more cost-effective it becomes.

BOAT TOURS   For a gentle, informative, and fun boat tour of the lagoon, with an on-board tasting of fresh oysters, and a close-up look at the oyster beds and the Heads, join the **Kysna Lagoon Oyster Tour** ★ (✆ **082/892-0469;** www.knysnacharters.com; R330 adults, R60 children under 12), which sets off each day at low tide and lasts 1½ hours. The **Featherbed Company** (✆ **044/382-1693**) runs trips to the nature reserve of the same name (see "The Top Attractions," below). With comfortable seating and a restaurant/bar on board, the floating double-decker **John Benn** (✆ **044/382-1693**) offers a 90-minute trip on the lagoon that costs R130 for adults (R65 children), meals and drinks extra. R265 buys you a ticket on their **catamaran**—the only yacht licensed to go through the Heads (although only when weather and conditions permit); the same trip at sunset (with a sundowner platter and drinks included) costs R520. Featherbed also offers trips on its paddle cruiser (R160 lunchtime cruise), which offers a buffet-style dinner cruise for R370. For sailing trips, contact **Springtide Charters** (© 082/470-6022; www.springtide. co.za) to charter the hand-built luxury yacht *Outiniqua* for one of various exclusive cruises, including breakfast, all-day, sunset, dinner, or overnight cruises.

SPECIAL EVENTS Knysna gets very busy during the annual **Pink Loerie Mardi Gras,** a gay pride event held for a few days in late April and early May, and even busier during the **Knysna Oyster Festival** held in July. Incidentally, it's not just about consuming oysters—there are a number of physically challenging events, including the popular Forest Marathon, trail runs through Featherbed Nature Reserve, and a cycle tour. **Gastronomica,** a culinary celebration now forms part of **Naturally Knysna,** a new multitiered annual festival scheduled to launch in October 2011; it'll also include a local music festival and a festival celebrating green issues.

What to See & Do in Knysna

Besides the top attractions listed below, one of the first things first-time visitors are usually encouraged to do is take a drive to the **Knysna Heads ★★**, where you can walk right up to the lagoon mouth and watch skippers gingerly navigate the treacherous surf. Stop for tea (or fab fish and chips) with a view at the **East Head Café ★** (© 044/384-0933; much better than slicker-looking Cornuti across the parking lot), and then check out the rare Knysna seahorse at the small NSRI aquarium—this fragile endemic is endangered by the ongoing development in and around the lagoon.

Exploring the forests is another major drawing card (see below), as are **lagoon-based activities;** several companies run boat trips on the lagoon, home to 200 species of fish and a major supplier of oysters—expect to see these on almost every Knysna menu. (For ferry and sailing options, see "Boat Tours," above.) If you've an interest in history (or historical architecture), pick up the **Heritage Building Walk** leaflet from the tourism office. Produced by the Knysna Historical Society, it's a self-guided walking tour of 20 points of interest in the town, and does much to remove the sinking sensation that this has become an overdeveloped tourist trap.

Another local product worth trying is the beer. **Mitchell's Brewery,** Arend Street (© 044/382-4685), produces four types of unpasteurized "live" ales, the best of which are Bosun's Bitter and Forrester's Draught. You can either take a 10-minute tour and tasting (R50; Mon–Fri 10:30am or 3pm; tastings only 9:30am–4:30pm) or sample them with your meal at most Knysna eateries. Ask for directions or a list of outlets from the Tourism Bureau, or combine oyster- and beer-tasting with a lagoon trip by boarding the **John Benn Ferry** (© 044/382-1693) and heading for the bar. To reach the closest beach, you'll need to head west to **Brenton-on-Sea,** an endless stretch of sand 16km (10 miles) from Knysna, or, better still, east for **Noetzie Beach ★★★**, some 11km (6¾ miles) from town. It's a steep walk down to this beautiful little beach, but a small, very swimmable estuary spilling out into the ocean and five over-the-top crenellated castles overlooking the beach make it more than worthwhile. Knysna lagoon's **Bollard Bay,** accessed from Leisure Isle, is excellent for small kids a lagoon-lapped beach, with safe swimming in the shallow waters.

Last but not least, Knysna offers some of the best shopping this side of Cape Town; you'll even find an outlet for New York leather designer to the stars **Aldo Kleyn**—the man who created the leather coats worn in *The Matrix*—in Thesen Harbour Town (© 073/299-0598), along with a number of other places you'll likely want to pillage.

The exception to this, with its super-sophisticated take on African-influenced house-wares and local crafts, is **Am-Wa,** corner of Waenhout Street and Vigilance Drive, Knysna Industria (© **044/382-3186**). Using sustainable raw materials—such as springbok and nguni cowhides—they produce a wide range of original (and unique) functional designs, manufacturing everything from ottomans to purses, on par with anything you'd find in the best of Cape Town's design shops. If you're here on a Saturday, consider taking a morning drive to the nearby coastal village of Sedgefield, where the weekly **farmer's market** is among the best in the country.

THE TOP ATTRACTIONS

Featherbed Nature Reserve ★★   This privately owned nature reserve on the western head of Knysna is a Natural Heritage Site and home to the endangered blue duiker antelope. Guests are ferried over and then ascend the head in a large open-topped vehicle to enjoy magnificent views of the lagoon, town, and ocean. You're then led down through milkwood forests and coastal flora onto the cliffs and coastal caves on the 2km (1.2-mile) **Bushbuck Trail** (you can also drive down), before being served a buffet lunch beneath the milkwood trees (not included in the 2:30pm tour). *Note:* The reserve's peace is seriously compromised during Knysna's busiest season, when additional trips are made, and up to 100 visitors are accommodated at any one time, and its star rating drops.

Ferry leaves from Municipal Jetty, Remembrance Dr., off Waterfront Dr. © **044/382-1693.** www.knysna featherbed.com. 4-hr. tours run at 10am, 11:30am, and 12:30pm, and include lunch; R420 adults, R200 children 11–15, R90 children 4–10. 3-hr. tours run at 8:30am and 2:30pm; R295 adults, R40–R100 children.

Knysna Forests ★★   These last pockets of indigenous forest, now part of the Garden Route National Park, are some distance from town: **Goudveld State Forest** is 30km (19 miles) northwest of Knysna, while **Diepwalle** is some 20km (12 miles) northeast. Goudveld is a mixture of plantation and indigenous forest, making Diep-walle, with its ancient yellowwoods, the better option for the purist. Look out for the emerald Knysna Loerie and the brightly hued Narina Trogon in the branches. Diep-walle has three excellent color-coded circular trails, all 7 to 9km (4.2–5.5 miles) long (the red route is recommended because it features the most water).

Diepwalle: Take the N2 east; after 7km (4¼ miles), turn left onto the R339 for 16km (10 miles) before taking turnoff to Diepwalle. Goudveld: Take the N2 west, turn right into Rheenendal Rd. © **044/302-5606.** R12 to walk; R25 to cycle. Daily 7:30am–4pm.

Living Local Community Experiences ★★   Knysna may be one of the best places in the country to interact with people living away from the gentrified spotlight of traditional tourism. With a focus on getting a feel for local culture, there are several accompanied, informative tours can take you into the townships and shantytowns that sprawl across the hills behind Knysna (ironically, ensuring that the poorer com-munities enjoy some of the finest views in the area). A stand-out experience is a visit to the **Judah Square Rastafarian Community,** the largest Rastafari community in the country. Your dreadlocked guide, either Zeb or Maxi, will detail the history and spiritual philosophy behind Rastafarianism, giving you some personal insight into their way of life, detailing the notion of a universal humanity, and a fairly strict moral code. On certain days, you can also participate in certain ceremonies (they're wel-coming and don't mind if you photograph activities, but mostly want to share their view of the world with you), and there's overnight accommodation (perhaps at the **Jah Works B&B;** © **083/502-2229**) and a chance to feast on vegetarian cuisine. If you're here in July, don't miss the annual **Rasta Earth Festival ★★**, which cele-brates the Earthday (birthday) of Emperor Haile Selassie as well as Emancipation Day (commemorating the abolition of slavery), and includes a 2-day music festival. ℭ **044/382-5510** or 044/382-6960. www.knysnalivinglocal.co.za.

Where to Stay

Prices vary depending on season—most places specify low, high, and peak seasons. Peak season (to be avoided) is usually from mid-December to mid-January, while even the short-lived low season (May–Aug) incorporates the very busy Knysna Oyster Festival, when rates will briefly skyrocket. In the heart of Knysna, **Inyathi Guest Village,** 52 Main Rd. (www.inyathi-sa.com; ℭ **044/382-7768;** R620–R720 double, including breakfast), attracts a younger visitor with a great combination of value and inoffensive taste. Despite its location just off the horribly busy main road, with tourist information and dining options within close walking distance, Inyathi maintains a sense of privacy. Innovatively laid out around a courtyard, many of the double-bedded timber cabins feature beautiful stained-glass windows, and most have a luxurious slipper bathtub. While the rooms are decorated with charm and creativity, they are relatively small—not the sort to lounge around in all day. If you don't want to spend a lot of money, but staying in the perennially mobbed town doesn't appeal, then why not relive the '60s at **Peace of Eden** (www.peaceofeden.co.za; ℭ **044/388-4671** or 072/528-5859), a motley collection of efficiency cabins (R550–R950 for four people in the two-story unit), safari tents (R300–R450 double), and a small traveler's lodge for backpackers. It's part farm, part forest, part recording studio, with a tranquil hippie vibe and zero pretense—located far from the crowds, 15 minutes away from town off Rheenendal Road. Owned by nature lovers Jen and Howard, the cabins—often booked by South African bands here to utilize the studio—are comfortable and cozy, and ideal if you prefer the countryside, love riding horses, or just want to laze in a hammock.

Closer to the action, chichi Thesen Island has become the new heart of Knysna (though old locals and hippies would certainly disagree!), with the lagoon at your doorstep and plenty of restaurants within walking distance. If the **Lofts** and **Turbine** (see below) are both full, look into renting an apartment, cottage, or villa through **Thesen Islands Destinations ★★** (www.theislands.co.za; ℭ **044/382-7550**), the official short-term rental agent.

If you can do without the views and don't mind being ensconced in a homey envi-ronment with lots of personal touches and casual-chic decor—not to mention a leafy garden with a pool—then take a look at good-value **Stannards Guest Lodge, ★** 22 Fraser St., Hunters Home (www.stannards.co.za; ℭ **044/384-0778**), which has standard double rooms from R890 in high season. It's very much a B&B-style hands-on operation, but Hélène and Patrick have perked the rooms up with bright fabrics and tasteful African crafts. All rooms have private entrances, but if you value your independence, they also have two well-equipped efficiency cottages (R620–R980 double, R930–R1,530 for four people), with all the comforts you really need, includ-ing a fireplace (ideal in winter).

If you like the idea of being at a resort surrounded by undulating fairways, but find **Pezula** (reviewed below) out of your league, or are a keen golfer, then consider **Simola ★** (www.simolaestate.co.za; ℭ **044/302-9600**). Situated high on a hill behind Knysna with sweeping views, a Jack Nicklaus Signature golf course, and a spa, Simola offers comfortable rooms at relatively down-to-earth prices. The one-bed units (not to be confused with the cupboard-size standard rooms) have their own fully equipped kitchens (R1,800–R3,190 double, with breakfast). And while accommodations at Pezula are more luxurious, Simola's golf course is more highly rated.

To experience a different side of Knysna, look into spending a night in a local township at a warm and welcoming family-run B&B; you can contact Knysna Tourism's **Glendyrr** (ℂ **044/382-5510**) for more information, or visit the website of **Living Local Community Experiences** (see "The Top Attractions," above).

Belvidere Manor ★   In a picture-postcard-cute suburb to the west of town, this historic manor house (with creaky floorboards and an intimate bistro) has a variety of detached cottages on its manicured lawns, sweeping down to the water's edge; they're decidedly bland (with none of the personality of Phantom Forest, or its magical setting) but the original lagoon suites are spacious, tastefully decorated, and fully equipped for cooking. Despite wavering service, it's a peaceful retreat, best suited to travelers who will enjoy wandering the suburbs lanes. Meals are served either on the veranda of Belvidere House, a national monument, or in the authentic pub.

Duthie Dr., Belvidere Estate, Knysna 6570. www.belvidere.co.za. ℂ **044/387-1055.** Fax 044/387-1059. 28 units. High season R1,950–R2,200 double; low season R1,540–R1,900 double. Rates include breakfast. AE, DC, MC, V. No children under 10. **Amenities:** Restaurant; bar; lounge; pool; room service. *In room:* Fan, TV/DVD, fireplace, hair dryer, heated towel rack, kitchen, Wi-Fi (R30 per ½ hr.).

Falcon's View Manor ★★   Set high up on Thesen Hill, overlooking the lagoon and surrounded by peaceful gardens, this guesthouse offers a gracious retreat from the hustle and bustle of town. The 1899 Manor House features a wraparound veranda and elegant sitting room, as well as garden- or lagoon-view rooms on the upper level. The main house has been spruced up with funky Modern art, and the six bedrooms upstairs have a fairly contemporary look (lagoon-facing room no. 4 gets our vote for decor, size, and views, while no. 8 has a plush red velvety ambience and great big bathroom). If you prefer lawns to views, opt for one of the luxurious garden rooms, where the big bedrooms, each furnished in muted modern colors and huge sleigh beds, lead out onto private terraces overlooking the gardens (part jungle, part cultivated) and pool. Come sunset, there's nothing better than to idle on the front veranda's comfy cane armchairs, admiring the grandstand views of the entire lagoon spread out before you like theater.

2 Thesen Hill, Knysna 6570. www.falconsview.com. ℂ **044/382-6767.** Fax 044/382-6430. 9 units. High season R1,470–R1,780 manor double, R2,100 garden double; mid season R1,200–R1,470 manor double, R1,780 garden double; low season R940–R1,150 manor double, R1,470 garden double. AE, DC, MC, V. **Amenities:** Dining room; lounges; bar; pool; room service. *In room:* A/C and fan, TV, hair dryer, minibar (garden rooms), heated towel rack, underfloor heating (garden rooms), free Wi-Fi.

Kanonkop House ★★   For one of the best views in town, book the aptly named Paradise Room. This haven of sumptuous comfort floats above a forested slope, with vistas stretching across the entire lagoon to the Heads—to be enjoyed from the balcony, your bed, and even the elevated tub. This room was in such demand (don't bother with the back rooms overlooking the pool) that owner Chris Conyers added two more below it: Sunbird (chic in subdued grays) and Forest (fittingly themed and theatrical in execution) also offer fresh, individual decor, a plethora of personal touches, and more magnificent views. Chris and his family will ply you with sundowners and advice, and they assume responsibility for your total experience in Knysna, so expect a thoroughly warm welcome and very personal, hands-on introduction

Escape the seasonally congested streets of Knysna by staying on the lagoon itself, cruising the waters with **Lightley's Holiday Houseboats** (www.houseboats.co.za; ✆ **044/386-0007**). You need no experience to skipper—just switch on and "drive" (navigational video, charts, maps, and instructions are supplied, and the 45-min. check-in includes a detailed introduction to your floating home), and at night you drop anchor in one of seven sheltered bays. You can fish for dinner from your boat or chug along to Thesen Island where (by arrangement) you can dock at the jetty and head out for a meal; you can even stop by the Featherbed Nature Reserve. Houseboats come equipped with everything: stove, fridge, hot and cold water, chemical toilet, CD players, a cellphone if you don't have one, electric lights, crockery and cutlery, and barbecues—just remember to pack towels, keep an eye on tide timings, and don't run out of fuel. **Leisure Liners,** which sleep up to four people, go for R940 to R2,100 double, but you may want to splurge on a better-looking six-sleeper **Aqua Chalet.** *Note:* The houseboats are far from posh; if you'd prefer a more luxurious boating experience, with own skipper and chef, charter the three-bedroom, 15m (50-ft.) luxury yacht *Outiniqua* (www.spring tide.co.za; ✆ **082/470-6022**).

to local life. Not only that, but they've got genuine eco-credentials—even their superb ultra-luxe toiletries are chosen to ease water recycling.

6 Cuthbert St., Kanonkop, Knysna. www.kanonkoptours.com. ✆/fax **044/382-2374**. Fax 044/382-2148. 5 units. High season R3,390 double with view, R2,390 double no view; low season R1,860 double with view, R1,420 double no view. Extra person pays R600 if sharing with 2 adults. Rates include breakfast and local drinks. AE, DC, MC, V. No children under 10. **Amenities:** Bar (complimentary); lounge; bikes; boating (sunset cruise); golf (reduced rates at Pezula and Simola); kayaks; library; pool; wakeboarding; waterskiing. *In room:* A/C, TV/DVD, CD player, music library, fishing, hair dryer, MP3 docking station, heated towel rack, underfloor heating, free Wi-Fi.

The Lofts ★★ Not even a decade ago, Thesen Island was a derelict sawmill and timber yard, and this old boatbuilding shed stood forlorn and neglected at the water's edge. Now Thesen is the trendiest address in Knysna, crammed with many fine eateries, great retail spaces, and hundreds of Cape Cod–style townhouses attached to private moorings. Built into one end of the resuscitated Boatshed, The Lofts is one of the best places to stay in Knysna. Not only is it diagonally above **île de païn,** Knysna's most celebrated bakery-cum-casual-restaurant (effectively your dining room), but accommodations are spacious, very modern, and comfortable; most have big balconies, and the three open-plan lagoon suites are literally above the water (ask for the suite in Tower 3—it sports a wraparound balcony and the most extensive view).

The Boatshed, Thesen Island, Knysna. www.thelofts.co.za. ✆ **044/302-5710**. Fax 044/302-5711. 15 units. Summer R1,690–R2,000 loft double, R2,070–R2,440 lagoon double, R2,400–R2,840 2-bedroom suite (4 people), R2,280–R2,690 villa double; winter R1,170 loft double, R1,280 lagoon double, R1,800 suite (4 people), R1,430 villa double. Children pay R100–R360 if sharing with 2 adults. Rates include R70 breakfast voucher per person. AE, MC, V. Children by arrangement. **Amenities:** 3 lounges; honor bar; plunge pool; spa. *In room:* A/C, TV, hair dryer, minibar, Wi-Fi (R20 per 100MB).

Pezula Resort Hotel & Spa ★★   Atop the Knysna East Head cliffs on an undulating links course, this is among the most luxurious choices in Knysna, with a plethora of facilities and activities. Tiptop accommodations are matched only by the effortless access to the beautiful semiprivate Noetzie beach (they transport you, and then treat you to refreshments at one of Noetzie's famed faux castles)—all reasons why it lands on so many "Best Of" lists. It's modern by design, with plenty of de rigueur stone and dark slate, Bali-inspired architecture, and adorned with lots of South African art. After a hand massage at check-in, you're shuttled to your suite by golf cart: There are four units per freestanding block, spread around the grounds above manicured golfing lawns; the markup on the more spacious and elegant superior suites are worth it.

Lagoonview Dr., Pezula Estate, East Head Cliffs, Knysna. www.pezula.com. © **044/302-3333.** 78 units, plus 5 villas, and 2 private castles. High season R6,440–R7,510 double, R14,860–R15,810 presidential suite, R13,620–R15,810 villa; low season R5,180–R5,480 double, R12,410 presidential suite, R10,950 villa. Children under 12 stay free if sharing with 2 adults. Rates include breakfast and general spa access. AE, DC, MC, V. **Amenities:** Restaurant (**Zachary's,** p. 235); lounge; cigar lounge; bar; archery; beach excursions; bikes; canoes; children's activity center; fishing; golf; helicopter rides; horseback riding; library; room service; pétanque (boules); 2 heated pools (indoor and outdoor); spa; 4 tennis courts; walking trails. *In room:* A/C, TV/DVD, fireplace, hair dryer, heated towel rack, minibar, free Wi-Fi.

The Phantom Forest Eco-Reserve ★★★   If you're looking for a more back-to-nature "luxurious safari treehouse" experience, look no further. Overlooking the Knysna River, this is a genuine eco-friendly retreat; meandering boardwalks connect the public spaces to the privately located suites, stashed away in the forest canopy. Classic suites comprise a double-volume bedroom with stupendous view, a sitting area leading out to a small, elevated deck, and a large bathroom. The newer Upper Tree suites have additional luxuries such as spa tubs on the edge of their enormous decks, so you can bathe in the forest; the Moroccan Suites are done out in dazzling colors. The food is incredible (see "Where to Eat," below), and you don't really want to leave once you've arrived—besides, you have to leave your car at the foot of the hill and wait for a transfer vehicle to traverse the steep road, an experience that greatly adds to the feeling of being cocooned, enhanced by an unforgettable setting, special architecture, and jaw-dropping views.

Off Phantom Pass, 7km (4¼ miles) from Knysna. www.phantomforest.com. © **044/386-0046.** Fax 044/387-1944. 14 units. High season R3,750 classic double, R4,000 Moroccan double, R4,450 Upper Tree double; low season R3,100 classic double, R3,400 Moroccan double, R3,550 Upper Tree double. Rates include breakfast. AE, DC, MC, V. No children under 12. **Amenities:** Restaurant; bar; bikes; canoes; 2 pools (beautiful views); spa and sauna; walking trails; free Wi-Fi in lodge. *In room:* Fan, hair dryer, heated towel rack, minibar, spa bath (some), underfloor heating in bathroom.

Rockery Nook ★★★ 🎁   Tucked away on the Knysna Heads, neighboring some enormous vacation houses on the water's edge in Millionaires Row, this small collection of personally styled efficiency digs are among the Garden Route's best-kept secrets. Behind the walls of this stucco-and-stone beach house, with sash windows framed by blue shutters, you'll find super-chic Provençal-style interiors with an arty mix of local paintings, crystal chandeliers, and antique armoires. For families booking a long-stay holiday, the multi-level Main House (with seven bedrooms) is ideal, with a fully equipped kitchen, a dining area with a huge table, as well as an airy, sea-facing lounge. Oyster Nook and Lovers Nook, two lovely little apartments just a few steps away from the lagoon, are decorated with the same unique character and flair. Lagoon beach access is instantaneous. Booking procedures can be quite casual: Reconfirm details before arrival.

George Rex Dr., The Eastern Heads, Knysna. www.rockerynook.co.za. ☎ **082/820-9246.** Fax 011/646-9278. 3 units. Main House R6,000–R8,800 (sleeps 15); Lovers Nook R1,200–R1,600 double; Oyster Nook R1,050–R1,400 double. No credit cards. **Amenities:** TV, kitchen, free Wi-Fi.

The Turbine Boutique Hotel and Spa ★★

A modern, funky hideaway with an urban sensibility, this is design-concept hotel for younger travelers. A functioning turbine power station until 2001, the generators and original wood boiler now form part of the Pop-inspired decor—bright primaries and modern artworks give the building a fresh atmosphere, while the location, right in the heart of the Thesen Islands development, is ideal for quality shops, restaurants, and boat launches. Rooms are sleek, comfortable, and subtly inspired by the colors, moods, and textures of the lagoon environs. Views are sometimes lacking, though, and standard rooms on the small side—book a suite with a balcony if you want to avoid feeling hemmed in (a corner suite if possible).

TH36 Sawtooth Ln., Thesen Islands, Knysna. www.turbinehotel.co.za. ☎**044/302-5746.** Fax 044/302-5747. 24 units. High season R2,390 double, R2,790–R3,190 suite; low season R1,990 double, R2,390–R2,790 suite. Rates include breakfast. **Amenities:** Restaurant; lounge; bar; art gallery; library; pontoon barge; pool; room service; spa; wine cellar. *In room:* A/C, TV/DVD, movie library (R25 per title), hair dryer, heated towel rack, Internet (cable supplied; 100MB free), kitchenette (in suites), minibar, MP3 docking station.

Under Milkwood ★★ ☺

This timber "village," set under centuries-old milkwood trees, with cobbled streets running past a higgledy-piggledy muddle of bungalows to a sandy beach and the lagoon, is charming. It's also convenient, with the Knysna Heads and restaurants within walking distance. Each two-bedroom chalet has a fully equipped kitchen and an open-plan lounge, a sun deck, and barbecue facilities. Front chalets have direct beach access (these are pricier, but not only is the location enviable, they afford more privacy than the cheaper middle chalets, for example). The hillside chalets offer the best value but require climbing stairs. If cooking isn't your thing, there are three rooms in the small B&B—Paquita, with its expansive balcony overlooking the lagoon, is an excellent choice.

13 George Rex Dr., The Heads, Knysna. www.milkwood.co.za. ☎**044/384-0745.** Fax 044/384-0156. 14 units. Chalets: High season R2,670–R3,860 (up to 4 people); low season R990–R1,765 double. Extra person pays R85–R125 if sharing with 2 adults. B&B rooms R610–R1,400 double. DC, MC, V. **Amenities:** Babysitting; canoes; paddle-skis. *In room:* Heater and fan, TV, hair dryer, heated towel rack, kitchen.

Villa Afrikana ★★

A modern conversion of a multilevel Spanish-style villa in the hillside neighborhood of Paradise, all six rooms overlook the lagoon. Each is a large, swanky, minimalist space with a clean, chic aesthetic that emphasizes the views—modern artworks and animal hides add a dash of color and texture—and the vistas simply improve the higher up in the house you go. Each room is unique, but our favorite is top-floor Noetzie (the best view, a spa bath, and a fireplace), while even Materolli—the only one without a balcony—has epic views from its corner position, and boasts the best bathroom. The whole house (including the kitchen) is available for you to make yourself at home—there's a formal dining room, but light meals can be served wherever you want them. Hands-on, unobtrusive hosts supply reliable advice.

13 Watsonia Dr., Paradise, Knysna. www.villaafrikana.com. ☎/Fax **044/382-4989.** 6 units. High season R2,100–R2,500 double; low season R1,700–R1,900 double. Rates include breakfast. MC, V. No children under 12. **Amenities:** Dining room; lounge; honor bar; room service. *In room:* A/C and fan, TV/DVD, hair dryer, underfloor heating (in bathroom), free Wi-Fi.

Oysters by the Dozen

Knysna is renowned for the oysters its estuary produces, and the **Knysna Oyster Company** (Thesen Island; ℂ **044/382-6941; www.knysnaoysters.co.za**), founded in 1949, is still the least pretentious place to order them (R78–R183 for 12).

Where to Eat

Knysna has a host of choices, and where you dine might have more to do with where you find yourself when hunger strikes. Aside from those reviewed below we'd like to highlight **Cruise Café** (ℂ **044/382-1693**), conveniently located near the Featherbed Company, and overlooking the lagoon. It's unpretentious, airy, and good value. If you're in the Knysna Waterfront, **34 South** (ℂ **044/382-7331**) is fairly mediocre but the seafood is fresh and the place is always buzzing. On Main Road, head straight for **Olive Tree** (ℂ **044/382-5867**); it's owned and managed by Ellen, and everything on her menu is a hit. And naturally, if you're exploring the Heads, the best place to dine is **East Head Café ★★★** (ℂ **044/384-0933**). At press time, it's the top choice in Knysna, and given the views (it's a kind of beach shack wedged into the rocks and overlooking the Knysna heads), reliable meals (fish and chips are famous), and laid-back child-friendly atmosphere (there's a dedicated play area for kids), hardly surprising. It gets really busy in season so get here early, or book well in advance.

Firefly Eating House ★★ 🍴 ASIAN This is one of our favorite Garden Route restaurants. It's not just the venue—a tiny dining room with rich red walls and a small outside garden patio lit up with fairy lights—or the fiery, delicious food, but the sense that you have stumbled onto something fragile. Self-taught mother-and-daughter chef team Dell and Sanchia escaped the Jo'burg rat race and took a chance by opening a restaurant so intimate (they started with just four tables) that it seemed like financial suicide. But when genuine passion translates into such tantalizing flavors, failure is not an option. Whatever else you order, make sure you have the *bobotie* spring rolls; for the rest, you can count on the spot-on menu descriptions, complete with hotness ratings for the curries. When you reserve (and you *must*), ask specifically for armchair seating.

152A Old Cape Rd. ℂ **044/382-1490**. www.fireflyeatinghouse.co.za. Reservations highly recommended. Main courses R80–R90. No credit cards. Tues-Sun 6-10pm.

île de païn ★★★ BREAKFAST/LIGHT MEALS Atkins dieters, be warned: When Austrian chef-patron Markus Färbinger bakes, bread is all you'll want to eat. Whether it's his potato bread, fluffy croissants, fragrant focaccia, crispy ciabattas, or signature *companion* (half-wheat, half-rye sourdough made with a 300-year-old starter dough), Markus reminds you that supermarket fare is bland and forgettable. Partner Liezie Mulder oversees a scrumptious menu of breakfast and lunch items prepared from painstakingly sourced ingredients (in season, don't miss the toasted baguette with figs, Gorgonzola, rocket, and balsamic reduction). You sit at long wooden tables under the trees or inside the bakery, from where you can choose from daily sandwiches, salads, soups, light grills, and sweet treats.

10 The Boatshed, Thesen Island. ℂ **044/302-5707**. www.ildepain.co.za. Breakfast dishes R30–R58; lunch meals R35–R89. AE, MC, V. Tues-Sat 8am-3pm; Sun 9am-1:30pm. Closed part of May and Aug.

The Phantom Forest ★★★ PAN-AFRICAN It's worth dining here just for the primal forest atmosphere and views in this stunning eco-reserve (see "Where to Stay," above). Residents enjoy first dibs on tables, though, so book in advance, and then get here early enough to order a predinner drink, and watch as the enormous sky changes into its sunset hues, reflected in the lagoon waters below. There are two venues: a six-course table d'hôte dinner served in the **Boma,** featuring a soup, a choice of four starters, sorbet, a choice of four main dishes, cheeses, and a choice of desserts—all in all, one of the best meals you'll have in South Africa. With demand outstripping chair space in summer, you can also opt for **Chutzpah,** an intimate, semicasual Moroccan-themed venue up at the pool, where colorful cushions, sunken lounges, and hookahs set the tone. Five-course platters are prepared with spices mixed in-house—expect a huge variety of flavors. Both venues afford a romantic experience and are worth the wait for the elevator up from the base of the hill.

Phantom Pass Rd. (C) **044/386-0046.** www.phantomforest.com. Reservations essential in high season. Boma set dinner R290. AE, DC, MC, V. Daily from 7pm. Latest arrivals 8pm.

Sirocco ★★ FUSION/SEAFOOD   A pared-down, modern-chic atmosphere prevails; by day there are wonderful views with natural light streaming in; by night, the sleek, minimalist look is accompanied by glowing panels of lime green. Service is quick, seafood is generally excellent, and dishes a whole lot less pretentious than the polished modern aesthetic might lead you to imagine. Sirocco is best known for its prawns, but they also produce a mean bouillabaisse, and the day's line fish is always a good bet. Arrive in time to take in the sunset, accompanied by colorful cocktails and a menu packed with good choices. Lighter fare is available in the afternoon.

Thesen Harbour Town. (C) **044/382-7196.** www.sirocco.co.za. Main courses R68–R135; crayfish and seafood platters subject to availability. AE, DC, MC, V. Daily noon–10pm.

Zachary's ★★ SOUTH AFRICAN CONTEMPORARY   New York–born chef Geoffrey Murray is a serious Slow Food devotee. His dishes invariably celebrate the freshest seasonal fare he can find (organic greens come from the on-site garden and he's developed a special relationship with many local farmers, so gets in amazing produce). He grills a mean fillet of matured Karan beef, and the organically farmed Karoo lamb (perhaps with pomegranate, eggplant, lamb manti, yogurt, and sumac) is superlative. There's usually a grilled game cut (impala with blueberries and cocoa, or springbok loin with butternut, smoked bacon popcorn, chestnut, and celeriac puree), superfresh line fish, and a memorable vegetarian option (the gnudi is a triumph, as is anything done with mushrooms). If you can't decide from the a la carte selection there's a daily-changing "Farm to Table" set menu promoting local producers—it's an excellent value, too.

Pezula Resort Hotel & Spa, Pezula Estate, Lagoonview Dr., East Head Cliffs. (C)**044/302-3364.** www.zacharys.co.za. Reservations essential. Main courses R125–R195, "From the Farm to the Table" set menu R175. AE, DC, MC, V. Daily from 7pm.

PLETTENBERG BAY, THE CRAGS & TSITSIKAMMA

Plett is 32km (20 miles) E of Knysna, and 210km (130 miles) W of Port Elizabeth

Several miles of white sands, backed by the blue-gray outline of the Tsitsikamma Mountains, curve languidly to create **Bahia Formosa** (Beautiful Bay), as the Portuguese sailors who first set eyes on it named it. Over the years, its beauty has inevitably drawn an ever-increasing string of admirers; some 50,000 of Jo'burg's wealthiest individuals descend on the seaside town of **Plettenberg Bay** (or Plett, as its known locally) every December, augmented by mostly inebriated Cape Town graduates here to celebrate the end of school at the annual "Plett Rave". But in the off-season, when most vacation homes stand empty, a far more laid-back atmosphere prevails. Though some find the ghost town unsettling, the empty beaches certainly make up for it, as does the scenic splendor of the lush environment and mountains silhouetted in the near distance. Sadly, money and taste seem to enjoy an inverse relationship; huge monstrosities line most of the beachfront, particularly Robberg Beach, with the exception being the less-developed far-western edge, bordering the **Robberg Nature Reserve,** which occupies a beautiful rocky peninsula that shelters a large seal colony.

East of Plett, the inland area from Keurbooms River to the Bloukrans River is known as **The Crags ★★★**. This offers an altogether different experience, with a serene countryside atmosphere and sophisticated and lovely lodgings. Although without beach views, it shelters several world-class opportunities to eyeball some rare and fascinating creatures at close quarters, and taste one of the country's most talked about sparkling wines. About an hour farther east, across the provincial border into the Eastern Cape, the **Storms River Mouth ★★★** is the focal point of the **Tsitsikamma forest belt.** Besides trying some of the best-loved multiday hiking trails in the country, you may choose to simply contemplate the magnificent beating of Indian Ocean waters against jagged coastal rock.

What to See & Do in Plettenberg Bay & The Crags

There's not much to do in Plett itself but laze on the beach. **Lookout** beach is on the eastern side and was the most popular, but most of it has been washed away in a ferocious storm that pounded the coast a few years back. The much smaller **Central Beach,** dominated by the timeshare hotel Beacon Isle, is the area from which most of the boats launch, leaving **Robberg,** on the west, as the current swimmer's favorite, or the far less utilized (but not quite as safe from a swimming point of view) **Keurbooms,** to the far east. Plett is blessed with two estuaries, with the Keurbooms River in the east by far the larger and least spoiled. You can access the **Keurbooms River Nature Reserve ★★** (© 044/533-2125; daily 6am–7:30pm in summer, 7:30am– 5:30pm in winter; R25 picnic fee) only by water—it's definitely worth paddling upstream to view the lush vegetated banks and bird life; keep an eye out for Knysna loeries, kingfishers, and fish eagles. A canoe and permit will run you R60 (R90 for a double canoe); both are available at the gate kiosk at the slipway. There is also a highly recommended overnight canoe trail in the reserve—see "Staying Active," at the beginning of the chapter. For R120 per adult (R60 children under 12), you can head upstream without lifting a finger by joining **Keurbooms River Ferries** (© 083/254-3551; departs from slipway). Daily scheduled trips, which last approximately 2½ hours, take place at 11am, 2pm, and 5pm, and include an optional 30-minute walk or picnic (bring your own food or preorder; pack a bathing suit)—they also rent out self-drive motor boats. Farther east lies **Nature's Valley,** a tiny hamlet on a wide, deserted sweep of beach, and beyond this **Storms River Mouth,** both in the **Tsitsikamma National Park ★★★**—a must on any Garden Route itinerary (see below).

Most of the interesting items on your to-do list are in and around The Crags—several **world-class animal sanctuaries** are based here (the best are reviewed below), and you'd be remiss for missing a trip to **Bramon Wine Estate ★** (© 044/534-8007; www.bramonwines.co.za), which is also where you'll find one of our favorite

Garden Route restaurants. Despite its distance from the traditional grape-growing areas, Bramon produces the country's only 100% sauvignon blanc Cap Classique. At press time, **Nyati** (© 082/771-9370 or 044/534-8007; www.jjj.co.za) was in the process of relocating its **mapoer-based liqueur distillery** from **Buffalo Hills** (a predator-free game reserve) to The Crags; after seeing how the distinctive (and, at 60% alcohol, quite potent) bush-style spirit is distilled, you'll be able to taste a few of these unique liqueurs (made using different fruits, such as gooseberry, marula, blueberry, and even strawberry and chili). Don't underestimate the strength of the straight mampoer shots. The Crags also has its own **Elephant Sanctuary** ★★ (© **044/534-8145;** daily 8am–5pm; R325 for an hour), which is close to the other animal centers, and a more intimate affair than Knysna Elephant Park (below), since there's no driving around. (Again, it's worth noting that some conservationists feel that elephants and other wild animals should not be used as tourist attractions, regardless of the circumstances of their birth or rescue, as it creates a market and may in some way distress animals that are not inclined to be pets.)

On the other (western) side of Plett, you can catch one of three daily flying displays at **Radical Raptors** ★★ ☺ (© **044/532-7537** or 083/382-2417; www.radical raptors.co.za; R60 adults, R40 children aged 3–12; Tues–Sun 11am, 1pm, and 3pm), a rehabilitation center for injured birds of prey. Flying sessions involve a variety of non-releasable birds (including a jackal buzzard, African goshawk, and spotted eagle owl), that you're unlikely to see at such close quarters—never mind perched on your very own gloved fist.

Finally, for insight into life beyond the beachfront mansions and ugly postmodern architecture, join a **township tour** ★★ (© 044/533-5083; www.oceanblue.co.za; R150) of **Qolweni,** a Xhosa neighborhood where you'll visit a child-care center (funded by the tours), a shebeen, a *spaza* shop, and a local home, meeting a variety of residents along the way—you'll possibly also meet a local sangoma (traditional healer) and be entertained by children singing. The tour also stops at a township backpackers where it's possible to overnight (R200 for dinner, bed, and breakfast). For more information, you could visit Plett's **Tourism Bureau,** located in Melville's Corner Shopping Centre (© **044/533-4065;** www.plettenbergbay.co.za; Mon–Fri 9am–5 or 6pm, Sat 9am–2pm, Sun 9am–1pm), but there's nothing they can tell you that your host won't.

Knysna Elephant Park ★★ ☺   This "safari," undertaken in 4WD vehicles that depart from reception every half-hour, affords you an opportunity to touch the elephants that roam the 80-hectare (198-acre) "reserve," and if you purchase a bucket of food (for R30) you get to feed them, too. The park now has 12 elephants, most of which were born in Kruger and have been returned—according to the park's promoters—to "the home of their ancestors." Having met the rescued elephants you then walk with them (with the tips of their trunk in the palm of your hand) to a spot where they're taken through a bit of a routine, performing tricks and generally demonstrating their intelligence as their handlers issue instructions.

Off N2, 9km (5½ miles) W of Plett, and 22km (14 miles) E of Knysna. ©**044/532-7732.** 45- to 60-min. tour R190 adults, R100 children 6–12; daily 8:30am–4:30pm, departure every ½ hour. Exclusive sunrise/sunset walk R1,250 adults, R650 children; departures 6:30am and 4:30pm. Elephant rides and walks R815 adults, R390 children; departures 9:30am, 10:30am, 3pm, and 4pm. Advance booking essential.

Monkeyland & Birds of Eden ★★★ ☺   When Richard Branson wants advice on how to care for rare primates on one of his private islands, he approaches the folks at **Monkeyland**—it's known in international circles not only because it's the first place of its kind on earth but because of its devotion to primates. Many here have been saved from laboratories or rescued from nefarious (illegal or simply uncaring) pet handlers; here, a dozen or so different species roam free within a vast indigenous forest, giving visitors a chance to observe—with the aid of a knowledgeable ranger—the behaviors of rare, endangered, or critically vulnerable primates, including white-handed gibbons and lemurs. It's mesmerizing. Next door, three more primate species—bush babies, the miniature cotton-top tamarin, and a family of golden-handed tamarins—share facilities with the feathered species at **Birds of Eden.** This is another sanctuary showcasing such a dazzling array that you could easily spend half a day just staring out across the 2½-hectare (6-acre) enclosed dome. A variety of living conditions are exactingly simulated in the largest free-flight aviary in the world, pro-tecting around 3,500 birds. You wander unguided, at times virtually suspended midair as you follow the canopy walk with birds passing overhead and below. Situated within walking distance of one another, these are two extraordinary facilities for compro-mised animals to live relatively normal lives, albeit in environments that contributes to greater awareness of the plight of animals and birds threatened primarily by the illegal pet trade. Children will love it; so will you.

The Crags (signposted off N2, 16km/10 miles E of Plett). ✆ **044/534-8906.** www.monkeyland.co.za or www.birdsofeden.co.za. Admission to either is R125 adults, R63 children aged 3–12; admission to both is R200 adults, R100 children. Daily 8am–5pm.

Robberg Nature Reserve ★★★   This rocky peninsula on the western side of the bay offers fantastic whale-watching opportunities as you stretch your legs on a 9km (5.5-mile) trail to **the Point,** usually teeming with roosting gannets, terns, and cormorants. The going gets very rocky, so wear good shoes; also use sun protection and avoid hiking during high tide. There are shorter trails, including the 2-hour **Wit-sand Circuit,** which goes past the **seal colony,** and the ½-hour **Gap Circuit.** Pick up a map from the gate.

Follow signs off Airport Rd.; the gate is 8km (5 miles) SE of Plett. ✆ **044/533-2125** or -2185. Admission R25 adults, R12 children. Daily 7am–5pm (8pm in Dec–Jan).

Tenikwa ★★★   Len and Mandy Freeman's wildlife awareness center offers a rare opportunity to meet South Africa's seldom-seen smaller cats, including caracal, serval, leopard, African wildcat, and cheetah. A 1-hour tour takes you into enclosures where the animals live; if they're in the mood, you can interact with them. Rescued penguins and seabirds also receive shelter here, and there's a walkway overlooking an open area where meerkats play out their daily soap opera. Note that Tenikwa is a rehabilitation center; animals currently being rehabilitated are not exposed to visitors (that would defeat the purpose), only captive-born animals that will never survive the wild. The highlight here is the opportunity—at sunrise (7:30am) or sunset (4:30pm)—to join the cheetahs on their exercise walks, spending around 1½ hours with the cats. You can also spend a full day with the cheetahs, working in the rehab center.

Forest Hall Rd., The Crags. ✆ **044/534-8174.** www.tenikwa.co.za. Guided tours R150 adults, R70 chil-dren aged 6–13. Sunrise and sunset cheetah walks R400. Cheetah walk and guided tour combo ticket R450. Crazee Cat Day R1,400. Closed shoes and pants are recommended; no fur, tassels, or scarves to be worn. No children under 1½m (4 ft. 11 in.) on cheetah walks. Daily 9am–4:30pm.

WHERE TO STAY IN & AROUND PLETTENBERG BAY

As in Knysna, Plett's prices vary markedly, dropping considerably after summer (defi-nitely try to avoid Dec–Jan, when the place is mobbed). Our top choice remains **The**

With whales and dolphins regularly doing the rounds in Plett's well-sheltered bay, a permanent seal colony clinging to the rocky cliffs at Robberg Nature Reserve, and an abundance of cormorants, gannets, terns, and other sea birds amassed along the coast, you should make every effort to join a **marine safari ★★★** in the mammal-rich bay, which is an important nursery and also the country's first national marine park. Apart from the Bryde whale, the Indo-Pacific humpback, and the bottlenose and common dolphins that feed in the bay year-round, Plett enjoys seasonal visits from southern right, humpback, and killer whales during their annual migration (July–Oct). Even if you're unlucky enough not to see one of the seafaring giants, the trip out to sea with views back toward the shore, is always sublime. It's worth booking with a boat licensed to approach the whales up to 50m (164 ft.)—only 11 permits for such encounters are granted in the entire country. One of them belongs to fair-trade-accredited **Ocean Blue ★★★** (℃ **044/533-5083;** www.oceanadventures.co.za); one of the longest-running operators in town, its business also contributes to upliftment projects in the local community. Tours last around 2 hours and cost R400 (out of whale season) or R650 (July–Nov); proceeds benefit whale and dolphin research and conservation. If you prefer to use your own muscle-power, they also run **sea kayaking trips** (R250 for 2–2½ hr.), which typically go past the seal colony, or beyond the bird colony at Keurbooms River mouth. A noisier way to view Plett's marine mammals is by air. **African Ramble** (℃ **044/533-9006;** www.aframble.co.za) offers half-hour scenic flights in the area from R1,600 (for two people); note that you can also charter their 5- to 18-seater planes to any of the private game lodges in the Eastern Cape.

Grand, but for those who like the service, fine dining, and facilities one expects from a Relais & Châteaux hotel, book at **The Plettenberg ★★** (www.plettenberg.com; ℃ **044/533-2074;** R2,600–R4,400 standard double, R3,950–R6,600 sea-facing double, R4,650–R8,800 suite). Situated on a hill overlooking Lookout Beach with views of a sandy arc of beach stretching away toward Keurbooms and the blue-gray mountains beyond, this hotel has a fantastic vantage point, but not all rooms take advantage of this (specify a "Lookout Beach view;" no. 18 is a perfectly sized corner unit), and the hotel is also split up on two sides of the road. It does have a classy restaurant (**Sand,** see "Where to Eat," below), a spa, and two exclusive-use villas (from R11,550). Be warned, though, that the idyllically situated infinity pool in front of Sand—perfect for watching surfers bob and glide on the nearby waves—also takes the brunt of any wind sweeping up from the sea.

At the other end of the price spectrum, we love the rusticity and weathered feel of **Stone Cottage ★★**, at Harker and Odland streets (www.stonecottage.co.za; ℃ **044/533-1310;** from R600 double with kitchen), an old shack (with rooms also in a newer building built in the same style) languishing amid indigenous gardens just a few minutes' walk from Central Beach. If you favor unfussy decor—family heirlooms and antiques, whitewashed walls plastered with vintage photographs, Victorian bathrooms, ancient doors, curious hand-me-downs, and loads of character—this will suit. You can choose a fully outfitted efficiency unit (the Oupa Jannie Cottage has three bedrooms, and a reed-enclosed al fresco shower) or a space with kitchenette, or a room without any kitchen facilities at all. There's a lovely wooden deck and great sea views, and the manager is an ace in the kitchen, able to conjure up lunch or dinner with just a few hours' notice.

In Plettenberg Bay

The Grand ★★★ Homey, quirky, timeless—this remains the most romantic, tastefully cozy place in town. On the high street (close to everything, and walking distance to the beach), it's all about easy living. Three rooms face the pool courtyard in addition to the original four huge upstairs suites, with their impressive views; each very individually decorated. All lean toward a witty, luxuriously bohemian feel, including extralong, extrahigh king-size beds (requiring footstools); in room no. 6, the freestanding tub is placed, altarlike, in front of shuttered doors that open onto views of Lookout Beach. For a little extra romance—and your own pool—book the Bath House, which has side-by-side Victorian bathtubs. Head downstairs to be plied with drinks around the pool or in the lounge areas, and be sure to book a table at the restaurant, where candles and single red roses are jammed into empty bottles, and everywhere you look another piece of antique, fantasy memorabilia, or tongue-in-cheek artwork demands attention.

27 Main Rd., Plettenberg Bay. www.thegrand.co.za. © **044/533-3301.** Fax 044/533-4247. 8 units. R1,300–R3,000 double. Rates include breakfast. MC, V. No children under 16. **Amenities:** Restaurant; bar; lounges; library; pool; room service; minispa; free Wi-Fi. *In room:* Fan, TV/DVD, movie library, hair dryer, no phone.

Milkwood Manor ★ 🍃 A modest, dignified guesthouse with a great location, Milkwood Manor was once tucked away amid dense trees, but massive floods changed the course of the Keurbooms River, and now the Manor is drenched in light and sunshine and perched literally meters from the river mouth (the flood also washed away the pool and parking lot); you can watch fresh water meet the sea from your bed, and launch a kayak for the short paddle to a long stretch of virtually private beach. The Georgian-style building is decorated with a subtle Eastern flavor, and rooms are comfortable, if not huge (beds are queen-size or twins). Be sure to claim a room with a view of the sea and lagoon; no. 2 is a winner (although a twin). Out back is a gate onto the river, a terrace, and the on-site restaurant—if you wish the owner will provide an insider's perspective on Plett over breakfast.

Salmack Rd., Keurbooms River Mouth, Plettenberg Bay. www.milkwoodmanor.co.za. © **044/533-0420.** Fax 044/533-0921. 11 units, some with shower only. High season R1,800 lagoon- and sea-facing double, R960 inland-facing double; low season R1,300 sea/lagoon-facing double, R760 inland-facing double. Rates include breakfast. MC, V. No children under 8. **Amenities:** Restaurant; lounge; kayaks; free Wi-Fi. *In room:* Fan, TV, hair dryer, no phone.

Southern Cross Beach House ★ 🍃 You cannot help feel the pull of the ocean at this family-run B&B-style timber beach house. Done out in pale-pink and white, it stands out in concrete-dominated Plettenberg—an American Colonial seaboard-style home that's one of very few guesthouses built right on the beach; a timber boardwalk leads through the vegetated dunes to the sand. Located on the western side of Robberg Beach, close to the reserve, the beach here is pretty deserted and provides an excellent sense of escape. Rooms are tasteful and compact—like the rest of the house, they are decorated predominantly in cool whites with an occasional touch of black or natural wood. The owners live upstairs (where the best views are); all the guest rooms are built around a grassy courtyard, so none enjoy a sea view, and unless you close your doors and window shutters, they lack privacy.

2 Capricorn Ln., Solar Beach, Plettenberg Bay. www.southerncrossbeach.co.za. ✆ **044/533-3868.** Fax 044/533-3866. 5 units. High season R1,550–R1,990 double; low season R1,390–R1,750; low season R990–R1,390 double. Rates include breakfast. AE, DC, MC, V. **Amenities:** Lounge; honor bar. *In room:* TV, hair dryer, no phone, free Wi-Fi.

Around Plettenberg Bay

Besides the above, Plett's best accommodations are outside of town, surrounded by indigenous bush and forests and beautiful gardens, with cliff- or riverside settings— or, in the case of **Singing Kettle,** right up against the edge of a beach (Keurboom-strand) less mobbed than any of those in Plett proper. Besides these reviewed below, there are two good-value options worth looking at, both a few miles before the Plett turnoff. **Fynbos Ridge** ★ (www.fynbosridge.co.za; ✆ **044/532-7862;** from R2,400 double) is a small, private floral reserve with enthusiastic owners who offer five B&B rooms in the Cape Dutch–style manor house, a studio apartment, and three newly refurbished freestanding cottages (efficiency); there are two good walking trails here, and a pathway through the jungly bush leads to the secluded pool with views stretching across the forest toward distant mountains. Also in a Cape Dutch homestead is **Laird's Lodge** ★ (www.lairdslodge.co.za; ✆ **044/532-7721;** R1,660–R2,600 double, including breakfast), which is run like a small, very personal hotel (17 rooms, all with a private terrace) with plenty of cozy lounges, a wine-tasting room, and a sun-bathed breakfast courtyard; interiors are stylish and the grounds leafy and neat.

Emily Moon River Lodge ★★

Built among milkwood trees and overlooking a wetland valley ringed by distant mountains, Emily Moon combines an unbeatable location with Indo-Afro-chic styling. Set on the Bitou River just outside Plett, this is the perfect romantic getaway, a quiet sanctuary that's great for honeymooners and birders. The secluded lodges, individually decorated with real flair and with a strong focus on comfort, has a private living area leading onto a private deck, which overlooks the wetland below. They're the kind of rooms you can easily spend the whole day in, but it's worth heading to the restaurant, which spills out of another beautifully boho indoor-outdoor space and merges with semisheltered pockets of lounging space around one of the pools—views from here are lovely, too. Be warned that they're expanding; the most recently added suites don't have such full-on views.

Bitou River, Plettenberg Bay. www.emilymoon.co.za. ✆ **044/533-2982.** Fax 044/533-0687. 10 units. High season R2,540 double, family suite R2,480 plus R450 per child; low season R1,440 double, R2,000 family unit. Rates include breakfast. AE, DC, MC, V. No children under 8. **Amenities:** Restaurant (**Emily's,** p. 245); sushi bar; bar; bikes; canoes; 2 pools; free Wi-Fi in restaurant. *In room:* Fan, TV, fireplace, hair dryer, heated towel rack, minibar, underfloor heating.

Hunter's Country House ★★★ ☺

With its bulging bookshelves, mounted trophy horns, bundles of cut flowers, oil paintings of country scenes, hand-carved wood furnishings, and the sweet aroma of the previous evening's fires, this century-old converted farmhouse conjures up a more genteel time. Still, the bedouin tent-covered chill-out lounge and wooden decks outside are terribly chic, and loaded with inviting cane and wicker seating—also awfully chichi is the private dining room with its silver-flecked Ralph Lauren wallpaper. Sleeping quarters are very private, in charming cottages set in manicured, butterfly-filled gardens, each individually furnished with antiques, and with its own fireplace and private patio and piece of garden. Very much aimed at families, with an informal dining area, a Teen Scene room complete with darts and pool table, and a preschool teacher to keep the little ones occupied.

10km (6¼ miles) W of Plett, off the N2. www.hunterhotels.com. ☎ **044/533-5533.** Fax 044/533-5973. 18 units. High season R2,500–R4,240 double, R4,500–R7,900 suite, R3,990–R6,280 family suite (2 adults, 2 children); children under 10 pay R475–R750 if sharing. Low season R1,880–R2,160 double, R2,850–R3,500 suite, R3,175 family suite; children under 10 stay free. Rates include breakfast. AE, DC, MC, V. **Amenities:** Restaurant; dining room; bar; lounges; children's facilities; concierge; library; massage; pool; room service; free Wi-Fi in lodge. *In room:* A/C, TV, fireplace, hair dryer, minibar, pool (in suites), undercarpet heating.

Tsala Treetops Lodge ★★★   Step out of your car and through the oversized, hand-carved doors of the lodge, and you enter another world, beautifully decorated with tribal artifacts, plush furnishings, and cozy, nooklike lounging spaces tucked between the bookshelves, African antiques, fireplaces, and glass walls affording views of the surrounding forest. Listen for monkeys gamboling through the canopy as you follow your hosts along elevated boardwalks through thick foliage, a journey culminating in either a private glass and timber "treehouse" or plush stone-and-timber two-bedroom villa-in-the-sky, complete with state-of-the-art kitchen, and a pair of en suite bathrooms with an outdoor shower. With every imaginable convenience, the safari-inspired lodgings all have double-volume lounges surrounded by generous decking, and fabulous forest views from every vantage (villa 17 and suite 10 have best views; nos. 1, 3, and 6 are also top choices).

10km (6¼ miles) W of Plett, off the N2. www.hunterhotels.com. ☎ **044/532-8228.** Fax 044/532-5587. 16 units. High season R5,990–R7,220 double, R7,940–R8,780 villa (4 persons); low season R3,800 double, R5,200 villa (4 persons). Rates include breakfast. AE, DC, MC, V. No children under 10 in suites, or under 8 in villas. **Amenities:** Restaurant (**Zinzi,** see p. 245); dining room; bar; lounges; concierge; library; massage; room service; free Wi-Fi in lodge and restaurant. *In room:* A/C and fan, TV/DVD/CD, movie library, music library, fireplace, hair dryer, heated towel rack, kitchen (villas only), minibar, plunge pool.

WHERE TO STAY IN & AROUND THE CRAGS

Fairview ★★ 🏷 ☺   Living up to its name, this gracious Cape Dutch–style family home is set above a forested valley—you can book it either by the room or as one gorgeous entity. The mood is one of out-of-time elegance: Bird-and-floral wallpaper adorns the master bedroom, and a sitting room and dining area are furnished with antiques, vintage reading matter, a piano, and crystal decanters, plus views of the Outeniqua Mountains from the patio. The gardens were created by the owner, who wrote her book *In a Country Garden* here—the style (like that of the house) is that of a romantic bygone era, and yet with the spacious dimensions of a more recent construction. A complete getaway, with a kitchen in which to make yourself at home.

The Crags, 12km (7½ miles) E of Plett on the N2, signposted to the left. www.fugitives-drift-lodge.com. ☎ **082/832-1895,** or 034/642-1843 reservations. Fax 034/271-8053. 3 bedrooms in main house and separate 3-bed cottage. High season R800–R1,400 double, R1,600 main bedroom double; low season R640–R1,120 double, R1,180 main bedroom double. Children under 16 pay R320–R480 if sharing with 2 adults. Rate includes breakfast (except Dec 15–Jan 15). AE, DC, MC, V. **Amenities:** Lounge; TV/DVD; movie library; barbecue; kitchen; pool. *In room:* Fan, hair dryer, underfloor heating, free Wi-Fi (main bedroom, sporadic).

Hog Hollow Country Lodge ★★★ ☺   Overlooking the dense indigenous forests that drop away below the lodge and carpet the Tsitsikamma Mountains beyond, Hog Hollow offers charm, comfort, privacy, and pampering. Both duplex and simplex suites are recommended: fold-away doors lead out onto private balconies or decks with hammocks and chairs to enjoy the views. (The six "forest" luxury suites are slightly bigger, but two are a fair walk away.) You're welcome to dine alone but it's very convivial joining the set table—an informal dinner party that is almost always a success. Everything is done in a special, personal way that keeps it real, and very memorable. Children get special treatment, too: toy boxes, milk, and a gingerbread man at bedtime, and great babysitters. If you want an exclusive family retreat, there's a marvelously kitted Villa about 400m (1,312 ft.) from the main lodge (for up to four guests; R7,920 including breakfast).

Askop Rd., The Crags; 18km/11 miles E of Plett, signposted off the N2. www.hog-hollow.com. ©/fax **044/534-8879.** 16 units. R3,040 double. Children 2–12 pay R760 if sharing with 2 adults. Rates include breakfast. MC, V. Closed for a month in winter. **Amenities:** Dining room; bar; lounge; babysitting; library; pool; sauna. *In room:* Fan, emergency cellphone, CD player, music selection, fireplace, hair dryer, heater, minibar, free Wi-Fi (erratic, but available in lounge).

Kurland ★★★ ☺ Surrounded by paddocks, polo fields, and duck-filled dams, this gracious estate, with just 12 rooms, is the country's premier polo destination and the best option on the Garden Route if you don't mind foregoing a sea view. Located in the beautiful rose gardens, rooms are huge (each with a living area, some with private plunge pools) and filled with character; decorated in authentic English country-manor style, with antiques, bookcases, oil paintings, and bouquets. Ten suites have loft rooms, with pint-size furnishings for children—there are also two extra pools for youngsters, a dedicated playroom, special adventure-style outings—and everyone loves the Shetland ponies. The beach is a bit of a drive, but you probably won't want to leave the grounds, content to simply soak up the relaxed, cultivated ambience. The dreamy little spa is very popular, and there's a 700-hectare (1,700 acre) estate to explore, so grab a pony (or bike) and go. Best of all, despite it's grand air, it's not in the least stuffy.

Off N2, The Crags; 19km (12 miles) E of Plettenberg Bay. www.kurland.co.za. © **044/534-8082.** Fax 044/534-8699. 12 units. High/peak season R3,400–R7,800 double; low season R2,500–R3,400 double. Children under 5 free if sharing, children 5–12 free except in peak season; R1,100 children 5–12 sharing in peak season; R725–R1,250 children 13–16 sharing. Rates include breakfast. AE, DC, MC, V. Closed June. **Amenities:** Dining room; lounges; bar; babysitting; children's activity room; bikes; horseback riding; library; 4 polo fields; 3 pools; quad bikes; room service; spa; floodlit clay tennis court; free Wi-Fi in library. *In room:* Fans, TV, fireplace, hair dryer, minibar, plunge pool (in superior suites).

Singing Kettle Beach Lodge ★ 🗡 ☺ A gorgeous location bang on the beach, with short walks to seclusion—that's what makes this unpretentious, suitably beach-themed inn just perfect. Decor is of the pine-and-laminate-floor variety, but very comfortable, and each room has a balcony with deck furniture to enjoy the lovely sea and beach views. Your hosts also supply everything you need for the beach—towels, umbrellas, even Boogie boards. Besides the fact that it really is right on the beach, and appropriately casual for a family hotel, it's small—only two spacious deluxe suites (able to accommodate four) with equipped kitchenette, and four standard double rooms with small overtures to self-sufficiency (toaster, fridge, microwave, that sort of thing), although you'll no doubt want to hang out at the convivial restaurant **Enrico,** downstairs.

Main St., Keurboomstrand. www.singingkettle.co.za. © **044/535-9477.** Fax 044/535-9478. 6 units. High season R1,200–R1,320 double, R1,800–R1,900 suite; low season R920–R1,100 double, R1,380–R1,500 suite. Rates include basic health breakfast. AE, MC, V. **Amenities:** Lounge; babysitting. *In room:* Fan, TV, fridge, hair dryer, kitchen or kitchenette, free Wi-Fi.

Tamodi Lodge & Stables ★★ 🗡 On a gravel road between Keurbooms Beach and the highway, this superbly situated lodge is intimate and exclusive, with stunning views: Step out onto the wooden deck—up on stilts high above the Matjies River—

and in front of you emerald indigenous forests cover vast undulating valleys, with the silhouetted Outeniqua Mountains the distant horizon. It's a huge thatched building, with lots of packed stone, wood and glass, local artworks, bonsais, and African fabrics. Enormous doors (made from recycled railway sleepers and Rhodesian teak) lead to comfortable, luxurious rooms with big glass walls and sliding doors opening onto a private deck with epic views. Book the Honeymoon suite, a huge space with carved four-poster bed, enormous walk-in wardrobe, and outdoor shower. Part of a natural conservancy (warthogs, baboon, and bushbuck do visit) and also a working equestrian farm with a riding school, the grounds include unfenced dams and effortless access to nature. It's close to Bramon wine estate, and the excellent Italian restaurant **Enrico's** is a short, easy drive. Or you can investigate the wine cellar downstairs.

Keurboom Heights; off the N2, 10km (6 miles) from Plett (turn right at the Vodacom cellphone tower). www.tamodi.co.za. ☎ **044/534-8071** or 082/551-9313. Fax 044/534-8703. 3 units. High season R1,500 double, R1,950 honeymoon suite; low season R1,240 double, R1,500 honeymoon suite. Rates include breakfast. AE, DC, MC, V. **Amenities:** Dining room; 4 lounges with fireplace; honor bar; bikes; boma (outdoor fireplace); horseback riding (by arrangement; experienced riders only); library; pool; wine cellar. *In room:* TV, hair dryer, heated towel rack, underfloor heating, no phone, free Wi-Fi.

WHERE TO EAT

It's the location rather than the food that draws people to **Lookout Deck** (☎ **044/533-1379**). Right on the beach, with awesome views across the ocean to the Tsitsikamma Mountains stretching beyond, this is probably the best-placed restaurant on the Garden Route. Enjoy a sunrise breakfast on the upstairs deck, or get here for sundown and try the Lookout's famous wild oysters, picked off the Plett coast. Sipping sundowners at Lookout Deck is a hard act to follow, but if you tire of the semi-attired *Baywatch*-type babes and bums tossing back Mermaid's Orgasms and Beach Affairs, there's room to move on, preferably to one of the fully reviewed restaurants below.

However, if you're in the mood for pizza with a sea view, head for **Cornuti Al Mare ★** (☎ **044/533-1277**). You can't miss it—it's to the left of the hill you have to drive down to get to Central/Robberg beach, and the facade and balcony are covered in hand-painted tiles and mosaics. Better still, for the best beachside option, take a drive to **Ristorante Enrico ★** (☎ **044/535-9818**; daily noon–10pm, closed May and 4–6pm in peak season), located beneath **Singing Kettle Beach Lodge** (p. 243), right on Keurbooms beach (a few minutes' drive east of Plett center). The eponymous Roman owner has his own boat (with a fishing charter business) ensuring that he always has the freshest seafood—so opt for line fish baked with olive oil, white wine, and garlic. He's also developed a light two-layer pizza called Farcita, definitely worth trying. Foodwise, it's a great deal better than Lookout Deck, and the beach and ocean views really are wonderful. Back in town, the name on everyone's lips at press time was **Scotty's Restaurant & Bar ★★**, Treilage House, 82 Longships Dr. (☎ **044/533-4945**; Wed–Sun 9:30am–late), for its good vibe and fresh, wholesome bistro-style food (and decent portions). Most vegetables are from Scott Rattray's own garden, and the menu is overhauled daily. If you're after a fine-dining experience within listening distance of the ocean (and, if you're early enough, exceptional sea views, too) you'd be hard-pressed to beat a table at pale-hued **Sand at The Plettenberg ★★** (☎ **044/533-2030**). Its Garden Route Origins tasting menu, a five-course feast that showcases local produce (including Bitou Bay seafood and Outeniqua-farmed ostrich stew), can be enjoyed with wines chosen to complement each item (it'll run you R365, or R545 with wine). It's romantic, but not quite as alluring as the elegant boho decor and easy bonhomie at **Grand Café ★★** (see above), where the food may not be quite so flash, but the drinks flow freely and the concise newspaper-style menu of popular comfort dishes (sugared salmon, mussels and chips, filet béarnaise, and such, or pizza, pasta, and salad) hits the mark.

If you're prepared to head a bit out of town, two of the best-looking spaces hereabouts include **Emily's** (reviewed below) and, in the other direction, **Zinzi ★** (© **044/532-8226**), which serves bistro-style fusion cuisine in a spacious room overlooking the leafy grounds at Tsala Treetops (see above). Zinzi is very relaxed: You eat on oversize furniture (ottomans, wingbacks, cushions), surrounded by flickering candles, upbeat lounge tunes, and a sophisticated display of African artifacts. The food, too, looks to the north of Africa as well as the Mediterranean; be warned however: Being child friendly (they get their own menu), Zinzi is not the most romantic choice.

Bramon ★★★ 🍴 TAPAS   In a black, white-shuttered house set against the vineyards, this fresh, upbeat country kitchen, located a way out of town, churns out delicious flavors. It's cheerful indoors, but everyone wants to be outside—especially at the tables tucked between the vines. You place your order by ticking off your choices: Great-sounding salads (avo and roast Parmesan; biltong and strawberry), and a big variety of mezze-style plates—springbok carpaccio, chicken kabobs, Spanish meatballs, smoked trout filet, pickled fish—served with fresh-baked bread. You can compile your own cheese platter, or go for the coastal oysters served with Champagne sorbet (R14 each). Save room for the tapas-style homemade ice-cream selection, or try champagne and strawberry cheesecake. Relaxed and vibrant, with staff as bubbly as the sparkling wine.

The Crags. © **044/534-8007.** www.bramonwines.co.za. Salads R35–R55; mezze items R10–R38. DC, MC, V. Daily 11am–5pm.

Emily's ★★ SOUTH AFRICAN/FUSION   Routinely named by many Plett locals as their favorite place to eat: On a deck overlooking the Bitou River, the assemblage of bric-a-brac and African artworks creates an interesting visual foreground, while the views provide one of the most disarming backgrounds. There's a slight Asian influence on the menu (a great sesame-encrusted seared tuna with wasabi mash and wok-fried greens, as well as roast Peking duck), but you might also find Italian-inspired prawn and mussel *cartoccio* (a tinfoil baked pasta parcel) among the hearty local steaks on offer. By day, there's good-value sushi from **Katy's Palace Bar,** above the main pool, around which there are pretty lounge areas to enjoy a drink as the sun sinks before you sit for dinner. You'll surely want to linger, so check it out as a place to stay.

Emily Moon River Lodge, Bitou River, Plettenberg Bay. © **044/533-2982.** www.emilymoon.co.za. Main courses R75–R135. AE, DC, MC, V. Tues–Sun noon–2:30pm; daily 6pm–late.

Nguni ★★ MODERN SOUTH AFRICAN   Named after a South African cattle breed, this black-and-white-styled restaurant with low ceilings and thick, uneven whitewashed walls (once a fisherman's cottage) is the most inspired dining venue in Plett proper. At night, paraffin lamps set a cozy, romantic mood, but when the sun is out you'll want to sit beneath the vines on the white wicker chairs outside. Owners Jacqui and Natalie offer traditional South African dishes, often with a twist—babotie spring rolls, Cape Malay curries, chicken bunny chow (curry in a hollowed-out half-loaf), ostrich "hot dogs" (with sweet potato chips), and—during summer—hearty game steaks, such as springbok with a porcini mushroom and sherry sauce.

6 Crescent St. © **044/533-6710.** www.nguni-restaurant.co.za. Main courses R65–R165. AE, DC, MC, V. Mon–Fri 9am–late; Sat 6pm–late; may close over weekends outside high season.

6 Nature's Valley, Tsitsikamma & Storms River Mouth

Starting from just beyond Keurboomstrand in the west, the easternmost part of the Garden Route National Park consists of a narrow coastal belt extending some 80km (50 miles) along one of the most beautiful sections of the southern Cape coastline, and includes a marine reserve that stretches 5½km (3½ miles) out to sea. The craggy, lichen-flecked coastline is cut through with spectacular river gorges, and the cliff surrounds are carpeted in fynbos and dense forest. The Otter Trail, which takes in the entire coastline, is South Africa's most popular trail, which gives some indication of its beauty (see "Staying Active," earlier in this chapter).

It's divided roughly into two sections: The lovely **Nature's Valley Section** (R50 adult, R25 children) in the west, and the easterly **Tsitsikamma Section,** incorporating Storms River Mouth, a breathtaking intersection of rocky gorge and ocean, strung with footbridges. There is no direct road linking them, but it's well worth taking the detour off the N2 and visiting both, though Storms River Mouth is the more awesome sight of the two. To reach Nature's Valley, the only settlement in this part of the park, take the scenic R102 or Groot River Pass. Visit the ever-helpful Beefy and Tish, who run a local information center from the **Nature's Valley Restaurant, Pub and Trading Store** (✆ 082/395-1605; beefy@xnets.co.za) and can help with anything from a weather report to local B&B or efficiency accommodations options—they have rentable digs of their own, too.

To visit **Storms River Mouth** ★★★, take the marked turnoff, some 60km (37 miles) from Plettenberg Bay, and travel 10km (6¼ miles) toward the coast. (**Note:** Do not confuse Storms River Mouth with Storms River Village, which is just off the N2 and has nothing much to recommend it, except that the popular canopy tour begins here, and there's the '60s-obsessed retro diner **Marilyn's,** which hosts The Elvis Festival Africa each year.) The gate is open 24 hours, and the entry fee is R100 per adult, and R50 for kids from 2 to 16. You can eat at the on-site **restaurant** (✆ 042/281-1190), situated at the beginning of the walk to the Storms River Mouth—despite having one of the best locations on the entire Garden Route, right on the sea, though, it features pretty standard institutional fare. A better option is to call ahead (as early as possible) and book a table at **Fynboshoek Cheese** ★★★ (✆ 042/280-3879), and then head off farther east along the N2 to find it. It's one of those great surprise culinary destinations where you can enjoy wonderful fixed-menu lunches made and grown by resident cheese maker Alje van Deemder. There are only 20 seats (food is prepared for the number of people expected), and it's difficult to find (with no signs), so confirm directions when you book. If, after you've filled up on some fine cheese-inspired dishes, you're in the mood for an animal-related excursion, head a short way farther east to visit the **Tsitsikamma Wolf Sanctuary** (✆ 021/657-5859; R30 adult, R15 children under 10, night tours R250; Mon–Sun 8:30am–4pm), where five packs of wolves and cross-breeds are provided safe haven. It's not a petting zoo, but a chance to learn a bit about animals that most people assume don't occur in this part of the world—here because someone stupidly thought they'd make neat pets.

EXPLORING THE TSITSIKAMMA & STORMS RIVER MOUTH

Fair-trade-accredited **Stormsriver Adventures** (✆ 042/281-1836; www.storms-river.com) offers activities in and around the park, including **canopy tours** ★★★, where you slide along steel cables 30m (98 ft.) above the forest floor—a delightful

📷 3, 2, 1, Bungeeeeee!

If Plett's views aren't enough to take your breath away, remember that the world's highest bungee jump is only a 15-minute drive east on the N2. For R620, you can have the rare privilege of free-falling for 216m (708 ft.) off the Bloukrans Bridge, and then watch yourself doing it all over again on video (see "Staying Active," at the beginning of the chapter).

experience and, judging by the surrounding grins, one enjoyed by both the very young and fairly old. With no roads connecting sites of interest, most of your exploring here will happen on foot. The easiest and most popular walking trail is the 1km (.5-mile) boardwalk, which starts at the visitor's office, and winds its way along the mountainside, providing beautiful glimpses of the sea and forest, and finally descending to the narrow mouth where the dark waters of the Storms River surge into the foaming sea. This walk also takes you past the appropriately named **Mooi (Pretty) Beach,** a tiny cove where the swimming is safe, though the water can be very cold. Once at the mouth, don't miss the excavated cave, with its displays relating to the Khoi *strandlopers* (beachcombers) who frequented the area more than 2,000 years ago. You can cross the suspension bridge that fords the mouth and climb the cliff for excellent ocean views, though it's steep going. To explore the otherwise inaccessible gorge, catch the *Spirit of the Tsitsikamma* ★, a boat that departs from the Tsitsikamma restaurant from 9:30am to 3:45pm every 45 minutes for a half-hour journey upstream. The trip costs R66 per person. To find out more about the various trails, pick up a map from the visitor's office (✆ **042/281-1607**) at the rest camp. Hours are from 7am to 6pm daily. There is also a snorkeling and scuba-diving trail; for equipment and a guide, contact **Untouched Adventures** (✆ **073/130-0689** or 078/871-1952) at Storms River Mouth rest camp, where you can also ask about the **Kayak & Kloof** trip that they run up the river mouth (R380).

WHERE TO STAY & EAT

The Fernery ★★ ☺   If the institutional vibe of the government-owned Restcamp (below) puts you off, this is a wonderful alternative, although cut off from the national park itself, and attached to a busy fern export farm. You're not close to the river's mouth, but views are dramatic. If you can, book one of twelve efficiency chalets—the best of these (Porcupine and Francolin, Otter and Jacana) feel pretty private. They feature cowhide rugs on pine floors, dark wood fittings and white wood walls—a full kitchen, barbecue facilities, and oodles of space, two lounges, oversized bathrooms with double showers, and plunge pools on huge decks above the valley. Or, for serious cliff-edge sensation, bag a luxurious room (honeymoon suite is best) at the intimate lodge (remodeled in 2010), taking advantage of the sensational position above the Sand Drift Gorge and the rock cliffs plunging into the ocean. The B&B chalets are older and less spacious, but fine for a night or two. You can hear the roar of the surf even in the little restaurant, with plenty of glass inviting in the views.

Forest Ferns Estate, Bluelilliesbush, Tsitsikamma. www.forestferns.co.za. ✆ **042/280-3588.** Fax 041/394-5114. 17 units. R1,260 garden suite double, R1,700 luxury suite double, R1,900 honeymoon suite double, R1,760–R2,600 family chalet (sleeps 4), R1,260 B&B chalet double. MC, V. **Amenities:** Restaurant; bar; lounge; bikes; fishing; hiking trails; 2 pools; sauna. *In room:* TV, hair dryer, minibar (or kitchen).

Storms River Mouth Restcamp ★ 🌶 South African National Parks is not about to win any architectural awards, but Storms River is its best attempt. Almost all the units enjoy good sea views, but the 11 semi-detached chalets located literally spitting distance from the sea (nos. 13–15 are up on a hill) take first prize. The symphonic rush of pounding surf is ongoing and invigorating (unless you're a light sleeper), and each has a lounge, kitchen, and veranda facing the surf. You can head off into the forest or walk the rocks; at low tide, the rock pools reveal a treasure trove of shapes and colors. If you're going to have all your meals at the restaurant, consider staying in the forest huts, particularly nos. 1 and 2, which overlook a burbling stream, but remember that the cabins are sweltering hot in peak summer and you share ablutions. Far better to book one of the isolated honeymoon cottages—or family cottages numbered 9 and 10—which are also right on the ocean. If you don't mind a short, steep walk up from the restaurant and sea, there are a couple of elevated "guest cottages" (sleeping eight), with luxuries such as DVDs and slightly better decor.

Garden Route National Park, Tsitsikamma Section. www.sanparks.org. ✆ **042/281-1607,** or 012/428-9111 reservations. 84 units. R375 forest huts double; R675 forest cabin double; R1,095 for family cottage; R690 ocean-side double; R735–R795 chalet double; R995 honeymoon cottage double; R1,215 family cottage (4 people); R2,370 guest cottage (4 people). 10% discount May–Aug. AE, DC, MC, V. **Amenities:** Restaurant and bar; shop. *In room:* TV (in some), kitchen (in most), no phone.

THE EASTERN CAPE: GAME RESERVES, SETTLER TOWNS & UNRIVALED COAST

7

The country's second-largest province has a sun-drenched coastline that stretches for 800km (496 miles), from the lush Garden Route to subtropical KwaZulu-Natal. Its hinterland comprises rolling green hills, vast scrubland plains, and craggy mountains. A decade ago, the Eastern Cape was rarely included in international travel itineraries; most of its best attractions, such as the Wild Coast and pretty Graaff-Reinet, are well off the beaten track. But the large-scale and ongoing rehabilitation of vast tracts of fallow farmland into game sanctuaries has transformed the region into a must-see destination for many, not least because these game reserves enjoy the additional advantages of being malaria free and easily accessible—a mere 45 to 90 minutes by car from the capital city of Port Elizabeth.

Besides **Addo Elephant National Park,** there are a dozen or so private game reserves, with accommodations as luxurious as their Kruger counterparts, and excellent game rangers on hand to unravel the mysteries of the prickly, low-lying scrubland terrain—quite different from the classic picture-postcard landscape of Africa. However, the sparseness of the vegetation means you never feel hemmed in: The vistas are huge, and the opportunities to see game are excellent. The area has its own strange, rugged beauty: You'll treasure such sights as a moonlit euphorbia forest, looking more like props from a sci-fi moonscape, or an entire hillside ablaze in orange aloe blossoms.

The Eastern Cape is also steeped in history: This is the birthplace of some of the country's most powerful political figures, the most famous of

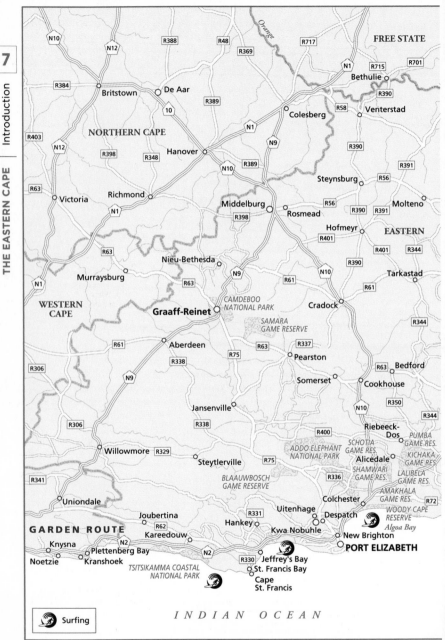

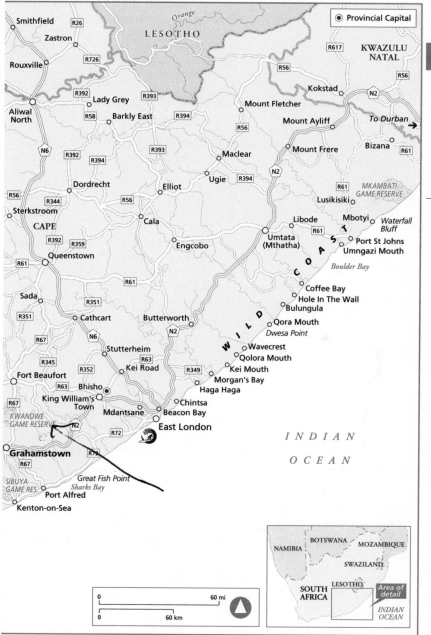

whom are Steve Biko and Nelson Mandela. And **Port Elizabeth** was a crucial center of the anti-apartheid movement, with a notoriously deadly security police in close attendance. Today, township tours provide an insight into Port Elizabeth's role in South African history, as well as an authentic introduction to traditional Xhosa rites and ceremonies.

Look beyond the inharmonious modern development, and you'll see much colonial-era architecture; moving north into the thirstlands of the **Karoo,** you will find vast, uninhabited plains with such atmospheric names as the **Valley of Desolation,** near **Graaff-Reinet,** the Eastern Cape's oldest settlement. If you like unpopulated spaces, small towns, and picturesque architecture, this is a highly recommended detour, possibly on a self-drive tour between the Garden Route and Gauteng. Alternatively, opt to explore the coastal attractions, from surfing the perfect wave in Jeffrey's Bay to exploring the aptly named **Wild Coast,** where you'll find the country's most unspoiled beaches and time-travel to arguably the most authentic rural African experience in the country.

PORT ELIZABETH

763km (473 miles) E of Cape Town; 1,050km (651 miles) SW of Johannesburg

The approach to Port Elizabeth, referred to by locals as P.E. and now part of the sprawling Nelson Mandela Metropolitan Municipality, is somewhat depressing. Factories alternate with brown brick houses on the freeway into town, the ocean breeze is colored by the stench of smokestacks, and a network of elevated highways has effectively cut the center of the city off from the sea. But that's only half the story.

For most, Port Elizabeth is simply an entry or departure point—usually for a trip up or down the Garden Route, or to visit one of the nearby malaria-free game reserves. Thanks to the relaxed atmosphere—more town than city in many respects—and easy access to some seriously appealing beaches, not to mention the availability of quality accommodations and its emerging restaurant districts, it can make a relaxed and unexpectedly stylish pit stop for a night or so. It's also laced with unexpected gems—the oldest opera house on the continent is here, and there's an abundance of Victorian architecture, much of it now at the heart of a bustling Africanized market. Take a township tour that covers some of the capital's political history, hang out on Humewood Beach, or amble along the Donkin Heritage Trail to get a sense of P.E.'s settler past. If you're not spending the night in a game reserve, P.E. is a good base for an easy day trip into one of the nearby reserves—though this is unlikely to be as satisfying as spending a few nights in the bush under a star-spangled sky.

Essentials

VISITOR INFORMATION Nelson Mandela Bay Tourism dishes out maps and flyers at the **Donkin Reserve Lighthouse Building** (© **041/585-8884;** Mon–Fri 8am–4:30pm, Sat–Sun 9:30am–3:30pm) at Belmont Terrace, central P.E; another office is at **The Boardwalk** (© **041/583-2030;** daily 8am–7pm), opposite Hobie Beach, on Marine Drive, in Summerstrand. Or visit www.nmbt.co.za before traveling.

GETTING THERE **By Car** P.E. is on the N2, which runs between Cape Town (7 hr. away; through the Garden Route) and Durban.

By Air **Port Elizabeth International Airport** (© **041/507-7319,** or 086/727-7888 flight information) is 4km (about 2½ miles) from the city center. **SAA** (© **041/507-1111;** www.flysaa.com) and **British Airways** (© **041/508-8000**)

The 1820 Settlers: Deceit, Despair & Courage

The Industrial Revolution and the end of the Napoleonic wars created a massive unemployment problem in Britain. With their underpopulated colony in southern Africa under threat by the indigenous tribes, the British authorities came up with the perfect solution: Lured by the promise of free land and a new life, 4,000 men, women, and children landed at Algoa Bay in 1820, more than doubling the colony's English-speaking population. Many were tradesmen and teachers with no knowledge of farming, and they were given no prior warning of their real function: to create a human barrier along the Fish River, marking the eastern border of the Cape Colony. On the other side of the river were the Xhosa (easiest to pronounce as *Kho*-sa). The settlers were provided with tents, seeds, and a few bits of equipment, and given pockets of land too small for livestock and too poor for crops. Pestilence, flash floods, and constant attacks by the Xhosa laid waste their attempts to settle the land, and most of them slowly trickled into the towns to establish themselves in more secure trades. Thanks in no small measure to their stoic determination, Port Elizabeth is today the biggest coastal city between Cape Town and Durban, and the industrial hub of the Eastern Cape, with road, rail, and air links to every other major city in South Africa.

connect P.E. with Johannesburg, Cape Town, and Durban, as does no-frills airline **Kulula.com** (© 086/158-5852). No-frills **1Time.co.za** (© 041/507-7392; www.1time.aero) flies in from Johannesburg and Cape Town. There is an ATM in the passage connecting the terminals, and metered taxis wait outside, or call **Hurter Cabs** (© 041/585-5500) for an airport transfer.

By Bus Greyhound, Intercape, Baz Bus, and **Translux** all connect P.E. with Johannesburg, Cape Town, and Durban. (See "Getting There" in chapter 13 for more.)

By Train The national mainline train runs between Johannesburg and Port Elizabeth; for details, call **Shosholoza Meyl** (© 087/802-6674), which operates an overnight Tourist Class (meaning no-frills basic sleeper) train departing Johannesburg at 1:15pm every Wednesday, Friday, and Sunday. (See "Getting Around" in chapter 13.)

GETTING AROUND **By Car** The best way to explore the Eastern Cape is with your own wheels. **Avis** (© 041/501-7200), **Budget** (© 041/581-4242), **Imperial** (© 041/581-4391), and **Tempest** (© 041/581-1256) all have desks at the airport.

By Taxi Hurter Cabs (© 041/585-5500) has a 24-hour taxi service. Socially responsible **Calabash Tours** (© 041/585-6162; www.calabashtours.co.za) offers private transfers to any of the safari destinations in the Eastern Cape.

By Air Contact **John Huddlestone** (© 041/507-7343 or 083/653-4294) for a helicopter trip to any of the reserves or an aerial tour of the city.

GUIDED TOURS OF PORT ELIZABETH & BEYOND The best general-interest tours in the city and the province are offered by **Alan Fogarty** ★★★ (© 041/367-4820 or 072/358-4634; www.alantours.co.za), a *fundi* (expert) on everything from wildlife to history, with an unbridled passion for the Eastern Cape—he has over 3 decades of experience (and is the chairperson of the Eastern Cape Field

Guide Association). Alan puts together city and township tours (R375 per person), and safaris to the best wildlife parks—and he'll show you a side of the Wild Coast (discussed later in this chapter) that will take your breath away. Anything from a half-day to a 3-week excursion is possible, tailor-made to your preferences and personal interests, and particularly brilliant if you prefer making a few discoveries the guidebooks fail to mention. Alternatively, orient yourself with one of the P.E. City Tours offered by **Ezethu Tours** (📞 **041/463-2570**); there's a 4-hour morning or a 3-hour afternoon excursion that takes in a number of the best cultural sights. For specialized township tours, see "What to See & Do," below.

[Fast FACTS] PORT ELIZABETH

Area Code   Port Elizabeth's area code is **041.**

Auto Repair   Call **AA Breakdown** (📞 **083/843-22**).

Emergencies   For an **ambulance,** call 📞 10177; **general emergencies,** call 📞 107; **National Sea Rescue Institute (NSRI),** call 📞 041/507-1911; **Police Flying Squad,** call 📞 10111; or **police,** call 📞 041/394-6740. The best private hospital is **Greenacres** (📞 041/390-7000).

What to See & Do

Note that Addo National Park is only 45 minutes from the city; it offers various safari options (like riding an elephant, described later in this chapter) that are easily part of city excursions.

TAKING A TOWNSHIP TOUR ★★★   To gain real insight into the city, contact fair-trade-accredited **Calabash Tours** (📞 **041/585-6162;** www.calabashtours.co.za) about its excellent 3½-hour Real City Tour (R420). It starts in the city center and looks at Port Elizabeth's history and the forced removal of residents out of the city to "coloured" and black townships. For an even more interactive experience, take its early evening Shebeen Tour (R500; daily 4–7:30pm), which includes some of the township drinking houses (called shebeens).

A WALK THROUGH SETTLER HISTORY   If you're interested in P.E.'s early history, take the 5km (3-mile) **Donkin Heritage Trail,** a self-guided walk marked with a blue staggered line that takes you past 47 places of historical interest in the old Hill area of central P.E. You can pick up a map from the tourism office in the Donkin Lighthouse Building, which is in the **Donkin Reserve,** located below Belmont Terrace and Donkin Street—a quaint row of Victorian houses collectively declared a national monument.

If you'd prefer to walk with a guide, **Rose Trehaven** (📞 **041/583-2584**) offers **historical walks** as well as **evening ghost tours** with a focus on mysterious tales and hauntings that have beset parts of the city.

> ### 💬 Rites of Passage
>
> It is not unusual to pass young men covered in white clay on the road—in rural as well as urban areas of the Eastern and Western Cape. These are Xhosa initiates, teenage boys who are about to learn the customs of their clan, culminating in the ancient but controversial practice of removing the foreskin (without anesthetic) to mark their transition to manhood.

The Crushing of Black Consciousness

Take a detour from the Heritage Trail and visit the sixth floor of the otherwise charmless building located on 44 Strand St.: This is where Steve Biko—the charismatic black-consciousness leader of the 1970s—died while being interrogated by the security police. This, combined with the Soweto uprising, led to the imposition of the arms embargo by the U.N. Security Council. Until the Truth and Reconciliation Commission hearings, the official version of events was that Biko slipped and fell, and no one was ever arrested. You can visit the room in which Biko was interrogated; it houses items relating to the man and his past.

THE RED LOCATION MUSEUM ★★★ This fascinating museum shares its name with the township that surrounds it—Red Location was named after the color of rusted corrugated iron and was home to many famous anti-apartheid activists. The museum (which has won much praise in architecture circles) is made up of 12 unmarked, rusted "memory boxes" within a larger exhibition space; each is home to a collection of memories or stories—the spaces between are for reflection. Exhibitions focus on local heroes of the struggle against apartheid, music and jazz, trade unions, sport, cultural life, and much more; some of the exhibits have a strong oral narrative component. Find it on the corner of Olof Palme and Singaphi streets, New Brighton (℃ **041/408-8400;** Mon–Fri 9am–4pm, Sat 9am–3pm). Admission is R12 per adult.

EXPLORING THE BEACHFRONT Enjoying an average of 7½ hours of sunshine a day, and lapped by relatively warm waters, Port Elizabeth beaches see a lot of action. The first crescent is **King's Beach.** A safe swimming beach, it has good family facilities, including the **McArthur Baths Swimming Pool Complex** (℃ **041/582-2282**), which stretches south to **Humewood Beach,** the best swimming beach, and is proud of its Blue Flag status. Opposite you will find **Bay World Museum Complex** (℃ **041/584-0650;** daily 9am–4:30pm; R25), which houses a snake park and a museum featuring fossils, scale reconstructions of shipwrecks, and a display on the Xhosa. A little farther along is the beachfront entrance to the **Boardwalk Casino and Entertainment World,** with loads of restaurants and shops, a cinema, and, of course, a casino—but it's soulless. To escape the crowds, keep traveling the beachfront road until it becomes Marine Drive, and then take Sardinia Bay Road to visit the big dunes of **Sardinia Bay**—this is a great picnic spot and walking beach, with warm waters. Declared a marine reserve, it's the start of the **Sacramento Trail ★**, an 8km (5-mile) coastal walk.

COASTAL CRUISE Get out to the **St. Croix Island marine reserve** to see the world's largest colony of endangered African penguins (around 20,000); one of the most amusing bird species on the planet. You can set off with **Raggy Charters** (℃ **041/378-2528;** www.raggycharters.co.za) for an Algoa Bay sundowner cruise, or to explore the islands and spot humpback whales, which mate and calve within Nelson Mandela Bay (June–Aug, and Oct through early Jan).

J-BAY: HOME OF THE perfect WAVE

Situated 75km (47 miles) west of Port Elizabeth, Jeffrey's Bay is an easy detour on the way to or from the Garden Route, particularly if you feel like stopping for lunch on the beach. Follow the signs to Marina Martinique and you'll find the rustic **Walskipper**(✆ **042/292-0005** or 082/800-9478); order a plate of prawns, calamari, mussels, scallops, and crab sticks (about R165), but don't expect finesse—meals come on enamel plates, with chunks of freshly baked bread, and waiters are, more often than not, barefoot.

Considered one of the top three surfing spots in the world, J-Bay (as it's affectionately known to locals) shot to international fame in the 1960s cult movie *Endless Summer*, which featured the break at Supertubes, the fastest and best-formed break on the South African coast, as well as Bruce's Beauties, a rare right-point break you'll find a little farther west, at the quiet coastal hamlet of Cape St Francis. For lessons, call veteran surfer **Andrew Moon** at the **Wave Crest Surf School** (✆ **073/509-0400;** R200 for 2 hr., includes board and wetsuit). If you decide to stay, make sure you're right on the sea, because J-Bay is architecturally a fright. The best places to stay include the aptly named **On the Beach,** 32 Waterkant St. (www.onthe beachjbay.co.za; ✆ **082/527-9414**),

which has guesthouse rooms and suites for R900 to R1,360 double (insist on a sea view, which most have; the Seagull, Beach and Oyster suites are best), and two efficiency apartments, each sleeping four people (R1,500–R2,000 per night); and the pricier **Diaz 15** (www. diaz15.co.za; ✆ **042/293-1779;** high season R2,200–R3,700 double; low season from R1,870 double), comprising two- and three-bedroom apartments, a three-bed penthouse, and a superior suite, located right on the beach; nos. 2, 3, 5, and 10 have the best sea views. You'll find a more appealing atmosphere (and much classier lodgings) in **St Francis Bay ★★**, a small coastal town a 20-minute drive west of J-Bay. The best option is **The Sands @ St Francis** (www. thesands.co.za; ✆ **042/294-1888;** R3,240–R4,360 double), which has just five bedrooms. Travelers on a budget could consider the laid-back **Sandals** (www.sandalsguesthouse.co.za; ✆ **042/294-0551;** R1,200–R1,685 for a standard double); it has good facilities, chilled Afro-Caribbean style, and 10 comfortable rooms with private decks or patios—and is just a couple of blocks to the beach. For more information, contact the **J-Bay Tourism Office** (✆ **042/293-2923;** www.jeffreysbay tourism.org).

Where to Stay

Overlooking Donkin Reserve, the **King Edward Hotel** (www.kingedwardhotel. co.za; ✆ **041/586-2056**), one of the oldest hotels in town—built in 1903—has been given a new lease on life after being bought by the shah of Dubai and given a thorough makeover. While some of the character has been stripped away, there's still plenty of evidence of a former, glitzier era—gracious architecture, stained-glassed windows, internal archways and fountains, and Art Nouveau touches. No two rooms are alike, but be aware that some of the entry-level units (R900 double) are quite basic, with pitifully small (shower only) bathrooms; the sea-facing luxury suites (R1,635) are suitably stylish and have private balconies, however. Be warned, though, that they cater to conference groups, so it can fill up.

Hacklewood Hill Country House ★★ This gracious Victorian home has been artfully converted, with none of the generous spaces of the original compromised. Calling it a country house is rather presumptuous—it's 4 minutes from the airport, and *very* much in the heart of the city. It's also a bit of a haunt for VIPs visiting P.E., which can be annoying when they seize everyone's attention. The entire house is furnished with period pieces, with colors and fabrics evincing fine, but resolutely old-fashioned taste. Their bathrooms may be the clincher, though. Each is bigger than most hotel rooms and is furnished with the same care as the bedrooms: Victorian tubs set center stage, with deep armchairs in which to laze after you've soaked.

152 Prospect Rd., Walmer, Port Elizabeth 6065. www.hacklewood.co.za. © **041/581-1300.** Fax 041/581-4155. 8 units. High season R3,200–R3,450 double; low season R2,670 double. Rate includes breakfast. AE, DC, MC, V. No children under 8. **Amenities:** Restaurant; bar; cigar lounge; airport transfers (R85); pool (saltwater); room service; tennis court; wine cellar. *In room:* A/C, TV, hair dryer, minibar (on request), free Wi-Fi.

Joy of Art ★ 🖌 If you like getting the inside scoop on the city you're visiting, you'll hear it firsthand from hosts Mike and Daniel, who clearly love their city. This is also good value, and some distance (but an easy drive) from the city, meaning that it affords views that make it feel as if you're in the countryside, with views of the ocean beyond the nearby stud farms. It's a contemporary B&B-style experience, with very comfortable, spacious, and individually designed bedrooms (each themed on a different artist, with tribute paintings by Daniel, an artist himself); a big lawn, and an open-plan lounge-dining area and kitchen that feels more like home (with family pets) than a guesthouse. Ask for an upstairs suite with private balcony facing the sea.

2257 Milkwood Ave., Lovemore Park, Port Elizabeth. www.joyofart.co.za. © **041/368-7140.** Fax 086/684-4832. 7 units. R900 double. Rate includes breakfast. AE, DC, MC, V. No children under 14. **Amenities:** Dining area; lounge; pool. *In room:* Fan, TV/DVD, movie library, CD, Jacuzzi (in 3), microwave, minibar, free Wi-Fi.

Radisson Blu Hotel ★★ Right across the road from Summerstrand's Pollock beach, this slick business hotel offers well-appointed rooms, with sea views from every room. Entry-level rooms are compact and—like the entire hotel—sleek, modern, and modular (pale gray walls, open-plan bathrooms, wired for business). The higher up you go, the better the views. With every intension of being P.E.'s social hub, the hotel punts its in-house Italian (and Tabú lounge), as well as its Camelot spa and opportunity to abseil down the side of the building (unique in South Africa); while you have everything you need at your fingertips, you're also conveniently close to surfer-studded beaches, shops, and the Boardwalk complex. If you like things anonymous, and don't mind conference groups traipsing through the foyer, it's a very good option.

Corner Marine Dr. and Ninth Ave., Summerstrand, Port Elizabeth. www.port.elizabeth.radissonsas.com. © **041/509-5000.** Fax 041/509-5001. 173 units. R1,480–R1,580 superior double; R2,060–R2,160 business double; R2,900 junior suite; R4,045 presidential suite. Rates include 2 children sharing. AE, DC, MC, V. **Amenities:** Restaurant; lounge; bar; abseiling; gym; pool; spa. *In room:* A/C, TV/DVD, hair dyer, minibar, free Wi-Fi.

Shamwari Townhouse ★★★ Easily the plushest urban accommodations in the city, this Art Deco–style boutique hotel has raised the bar dramatically since it opened in 2008—and they've now added a second house. Übermodern, the dramatic public spaces are a treasure trove of original South African art, sumptuous period-inspired decor, glitzy wallpaper, and fine furnishings. Guest suites are on a grand scale, and all have a private balcony or small garden to enjoy balmy summer evenings. There's an impressive spa, fine dining in the Jazz Room, and the striking Salon Privé, with its

Fornasetti wallpaper and the second-largest collection of single malts in the country. The in-house mini-cinema is modeled on that of England's Prince Charles. A no-expense-spared polished, sophisticated hotel—but service not always up to par.

5 Brighton Dr., Summerstrand, Port Elizabeth. www.shamwaritownhouse.com. ℂ **041/502-6000,** or 041/407-1000 reservations. Fax 041/502-6001. 10 units. R2,950 double. Rates include breakfast. AE, DC, MC, V. **Amenities:** Restaurant; multiple lounges; bar; babysitting; cinema; gym; library; heated outdoor pool; spa; wine cellar (with private dining). In room: A/C, TV/DVD, hair dryer, minibar, free Wi-Fi.

Singa Lodge ★★   Designed a bit like an intimate resort, with earthy colors, sensual textures, and a gorgeous garden, Singa offers an appealing mix of Eastern and African elements: The individually decorated and privately situated suites are rich with screens, mosaics, hand-stenciled wallpapers, and embroidered silks. They differ in size and atmosphere, but no. 1 is a beauty with green-washed concrete floors, a massive mosaic studded shower, fireplace, and vast amounts of bright, warm space; while no. 8 (the smallest) has a lovely Asian feel. Good dining, a sexy outdoor lounging area, a reading room with a respectable collection of single malts and cigars, and the location (in laid-back Summerstrand, close to lovely Pollock Beach) is just perfect.

Corner 10th Ave. and Scarbourough Dr., Summerstrand, Port Elizabeth. www.singalodge.com. ℂ/fax **041/583-3927,** or 086/111-2485 reservations. 12 units. R2,400 luxury suite, R3,000 executive suite. Rates include breakfast. AE, DC, MC, V. Children by arrangement. **Amenities:** Restaurant; bar; lounge; gym; library; pool; room service. In room: A/C, TV/DVD, hair dryer, minibar, MP3 docking station, free Wi-Fi.

The Windermere ★★ 𝄞   One road back from King's Beach and a stone's throw from McArthur Pools, this was the first guesthouse in P.E. to embrace the modern boutique-hotel aesthetic, with customized fittings and furniture throughout, much of it designed by Haldane Martin, one of the country's top designers. Luxury rooms are huge, with oversized bathrooms to match; the look is pared down, sleek, and comfortable. Book one of the upstairs rooms for views—particularly room no. 9, which has a great sea vista from its balcony. Plenty of room to unwind here: plump sofas, assorted indoor and outdoor lounging areas, and a neat bar decorated with Mandela-era election posters—and the staff is particularly personable and helpful.

35 Humewood Rd., Humewood, Port Elizabeth 6001. www.thewindermere.co.za. ℂ **041/582-2245.** Fax 041/582-2246. 9 units. R1,500 double. R500 per child sharing. Rates include breakfast. AE, DC, MC, V. **Amenities:** Dining room; lounge; bar; gym access; plunge pool; room service. In room: A/C, TV/DVD, movie library, CD, music library, hair dryer, minibar, free Wi-Fi, underfloor heating in bathroom.

Where to Eat

P.E.'s latest (and trendiest) dining district is **Richmond Hill**—until just a few years ago a derelict near-slum populated by drug-dealers and prostitutes. Now you can dip into a very pleasant cafe culture (with infinite opportunities for people-watching) not to mention some good surprises for foodies, the best of which is **Flava ★★** (ℂ **041/ 811-3528**; Tues–Sun noon–3pm, Tues–Sat 6–10pm). "I cook from my heart," says owner-chef John, a former butcher who fell into the food business 20 years ago, and finally has his own kitchen where he invents interesting dishes and makes efforts to offer perhaps the best unpretentious food in the city. Prawns are pan-fried in sweet lemon grass, honey, and chili; filet is flambéed in brandy with green peppercorn sauce; burgers are made with beef, lamb, honey, and four different pestos and then smothered with Roquefort, bacon, and brie. And he crafts extraordinary salads, such as anchovy and camembert, with balls of crème fraîche, honey, and nuts. Around the corner, among a bunch of good-looking, well-peopled eateries, **Deli Street Café ★★**, 24 Lutman St., Richmond Hill (ℂ **041/582-2157;** Mon–Fri 7:30am–3:30pm, Sat

7:30am–2:30pm), feels as cozy and comforting as apple pie—you could easily spend all day just watching the regulars breezing in and out between the mismatched tables and chairs, old wooden crates, cushions made from recycled hessian sacks, chalked-up menus, and interesting artworks (much of it for sale). There's plenty to imbibe while you people-watch: salad niçoise, lamb wraps, handmade pasta with shrimp, chili, and ginger. A chirpy, cheerful space with good coffee, too.

If you prefer considerably more formal, nearby **Nosh ★**, 1 Cooper St. (© **041/ 582-2444**), is where P.E.'s fashionable set like to see and be seen over roast impala loin with chocolate chili sauce or roast duck drizzled with honey and oyster sauce. In an old house in Walmer, Joel Malkinson's semiposh **Wicker Woods ★★**, 50 Sixth Ave. (© **041/581-1107;** Tues–Sat 7pm–late), is touted by many locals as their absolute favorite, with an upmarket-but-relaxed ambience and exceptional food to match. There's a slightly more family-geared atmosphere at adjoining sister restaurant, **Mangiamo ★★**, not least due to its superb pizza. Also in Walmer, architecturally eye-catching **Amaze,** corner of Main Road and Sixth Avenue (© **041/581-0776;** Mon–Sat noon–3pm and 6–10:30pm), is a wood-clad rectangular box that begs investigation; inside things are quite minimalist. It's new enough to still have tongues wagging—and worth getting the opinion of a local for word of current food quality. Menu offerings cater to most tastes: confit duck, pork glazed with honey and Van der Hum liqueur, filet with jalapeño sauce, and fresh line-caught fish with butternut mash. For a serious fine dining experience (and we mean you need to dress for the occasion), book a table at **The Jazz Room ★** (at superexclusive Shamwari Townhouse, reviewed above); you can choose a two- or three-course meal (R160 or R220) or the five-course tasting menu (R350), but don't expect much by way of vegetarian dishes. The other fine hotel restaurant to try is **Ginger ★** (© **041/583-1220;** www. ginger-restaurant.co.za), at The Beach Hotel, right next to the entrance of the Boardwalk Casino and Entertainment Complex (which features an abundance of bland eateries). Ginger's seared scallops on leek and sherry risotto is a memorable starter.

Closer to the water—right on the beachfront, in fact—a favorite for both ocean- and people-watching (surfers, joggers, sea-kayakers, and strollers) is the aptly named, supercasual, and very family-friendly **Blue Waters Café ★**, The Boardwalk, Marine Dr. (© **041/583-4110;** daily 8am–11pm). It's totally unpretentious—grab a seat on the terrace for views of the endless comings and goings on the beach and promenade below (or inside near the fireplace in winter)—and give in to the efficient, personable attentions of your server.

Finally, if you're in the mood for something with a bit of zing, follow the locals to laid-back **Natti's Thai Kitchen ★★**, Park Lane (© **041/373-2763;** dinner Tues– Sat), where Natti (assisted by her surfer husband, Mark) has been warming palates with her authentic, sometimes-fiery cuisine for over a decade. It's definitely not fancy, but if you're hip to its personal, boho charm (and don't mind barefoot servers), you'll love it.

ADDO & NEARBY PRIVATE GAME RESERVES

Addo's main entrance is 72km (44⅖ miles) N of Port Elizabeth

The nearest and biggest Big 5 game reserve in the province (45 min. from P.E.'s center), and the only one in which you can self-drive (guided trips also available), **Addo Elephant National Park ★★** (© **042/233-8600;** www.addoelephantpark. com; R140 per day; daily 7am–7pm) was proclaimed in 1931 in order to protect the last remaining Eastern Cape elephants. From 11 elephants roaming a mere 20 sq. km (7¾-sq.-mile) parcel of land, there are now around 540 in a vast 180,000-hectare (445,000-acre) habitat. Addo's extends from Darlington Dam in the Karoo all the way to Woody Cape on the coast, including the island of St Croix (home to an estimated 20,000 endangered African penguins) and Bird Island (home to the largest gannet-breeding colony in the world). But it's essentially for the big land-based beasts that people come: Addo has the densest concentration of elephants in Africa. They're in evidence year-round, but the most attractive time of the year to visit is spring, when the harsh Eastern Cape bushveld is softened with flowers and herds can be seen standing in carpets of yellow daisies. Other animals to look for are the black rhino, buffalo, lion, hyena, zebra, red hartebeest, eland, kudu, bushbuck, warthog, and—on a guided trip—a few endemic species such as the flightless dung beetle, found almost exclusively in Addo. Fences separate some parts of the reserve, limiting the full Big 5 to a relatively concentrated area around the main rest camp and central areas. In 2010 the fence between the main area and the southerly Colchester section was dropped, meaning there's considerably more room to explore.

If you want to get really close to the pachyderms, look into booking an **Addo Elephant Back Safari** (www.aebs.co.za), a 3-hour experience that includes walking with elephants that were saved from hunting by the Knysna Elephant Park, getting to know them and their handlers, and taking a short ride to the watering hole. The cost is R875 to R995 per person (including lunch), with three safaris daily. Wear pants and comfortable walking shoes. They're signposted on the road to Addo's main entrance.

Where to Stay & Eat

Addo was the first national park to offer **concessions** to private operators, thereby ensuring that the park had a few luxury alternatives to the more basic and crowded rest camp. If you're prepared to splurge, we'd put our money on the utterly sublime **Gorah Camp** (reviewed below); however if you're looking for family-geared accommodations, you may prefer the gracious, homey **RiverBend Lodge** ★ (www.river bendlodge.co.za; ☎ **042/233-8000;** R3,900–R7,200 double, including all meals and activities), which is situated within the 17,000-hectare (41,990-acre) private Nyathi concession. Eight luxury rooms in a farmhouse-style atmosphere are complemented by superb cuisine and personal attention. RiverBend's **Long Hope Villa** is a three-bedroom 1940s farmhouse with a private chef, situated 500m (1,640 ft.) away from the main lodge (R10,000–R15,000 per night for four guests). Both are very child friendly, ideal for families wanting to spend time together rather than pack the kids off on separate game drives.

If these prices give you pause, you can stay **outside the park** and either take a tour or drive yourself. In this case, **Elephant House** (see below) is probably the best option in the region; it's also the closest to Addo's main entrance. An extremely reasonable B&B for those on a budget is **Halstead Farm** (www.halsteadfarm.com; ☎ **042/233-0114;** from R750 double, including breakfast); the two rooms are individually decorated with a colonial character and they open onto lovely gardens—there's also a pool, and you're a 10-minute drive from the park. Farther into the Sundays River Valley, off the Kirkwood Road, is **Hitgeheim Country Lodge** (www. hitgeheim.co.za; ☎ **042/234-0778;** R2,500–R3,100 double including breakfast). It's surrounded by a minireserve with some game, and with its spectacular views, luxurious chalets, fine food and wine, and amenable hosts (Archie also arranges 4-hr. game-viewing trips into Addo with a specialist; R650 per person), it is a very good, if fairly pricey, option.

GAME DRIVES & BIG 5 day trips

To ensure the best sightings, head for the watering holes (pick up a map at the entrance), or take a private tour to get off the beaten track. Three-hour guided game drives in open-topped vehicles are also provided by the park. These are not as good as heading out with a private operator (such as **Alan Fogarty ★★★**; ✆ 041/367-4820 or 072/358-4634; www.alantours.co.za), but they're cheap—just make sure it's in one of the smaller vehicles (you can pre-book on ✆ 042/233-8657; addogame drives@sanparks.org, but payment must be made at the Game Drives Office in advance). There are six drives through the day (mostly R220): at sunrise, morning, midday, midafternoon, sundown (R310), or at night (R250), which is the only time to view the nocturnal activities of such carnivores as the black-backed jackal and bat-eared fox.

Two good alternatives to Addo are Amakhala and Pumba, both on the road to Grahamstown. First up is the turnoff to **Amakhala ★** (✆ 046/636-2750; www.amakhala.co.za), the nearest private Big 5 reserve, offering day trips for R980. It's only 50 minutes from P.E.; safaris leave at 11am in winter and noon in summer; they include game drives, a picnic lunch, and a river cruise. Farther along, only 15 minutes from Grahamstown (about 70 min. from P.E.), you'll see the Alicedale/Pumba turnoff: Park at the Day Safari Arrivals Centre for **Pumba ★★** (✆ 046/603-2000; www.pumbagamereserve.co.za), or call from P.E. and arrange a transfer. Pumba is a 6,500-hectare (14,820-acre) reserve but also boasts white lions (a genetic mutation) and cheetahs. The day safari comprises a 2½-hour game drive to the boma restaurant, where you will be served a meal before embarking on a brief game drive back to the Arrival Centre. Day safaris depart at 7am and 4pm in summer and 10am and 3pm in winter, and cost R960 for adults and R630 for children (over 8 only).

Schotia (✆ 042/235-1436; www.schotia.com), a tiny (1,700-hectare/4,199-acre) reserve east of Addo, offers a 6-hour experience (beginning at 3pm) in which you're likely to see one of the reserve's lions, as well as rhinos, giraffes, and hippos. The drive costs R660 and includes supper around the fire. For R1,320, you can include a morning game drive through Addo to view buffalo and elephant (neither of which occurs in Schotia), with transfers from P.E. (pickup 9am), or the Addo area (10am), and lunch included.

Addo Main Camp ★ 🗡 ☺ This is a great budget option, with something to suit everyone (as long as you're not expecting fabulous décor or architectural smarts); the object is to put you right in the park, and often staring at the grazing animals from your very own verandah. Game drives depart from here and most of the camp is encircled by the game-rich wilderness, just beyond the elephant-resistant Armstrong Fence. A restaurant serves basic, filling meals—chicken, fish, steaks, and a few traditional dishes like *umcabosi*, a mix of spinach and pap (maize porridge). Alternatively, specify whether you want a semi- or fully equipped kitchen or shared cooking facilities. The simplest cabins (with shared kitchen) go for R550, and there's a cluster of five (cheaper) tents (with fridge, heater, and fan) for real safari vibe. Better, though, are the comfortable efficiency cottages with bush views (often with elephants wandering through); the rondawels (with views of the floodlit waterhole); the two-bedroom guesthouses (with kitchens and TV); and chalets nos. 17 to 24 and 29 to 38, which all have good park views. If you're keen on dawn drives, you can be in the game-viewing area within minutes of dragging yourself out of bed. *Note:* **Camp Matyholweni** (📞 **041/468-0916**), a newer rest camp with comfortable efficiency cottages, operates at the southern (Colchester) entrance to the park, much closer to the beach. Its drawback is the lack of facilities such as restaurant or shop, but these are a short drive away.

Addo Elephant National Park. www.addoelephantpark.com or www.sanparks.org. 📞 **042/233-8600,** or 012/428-9111 reservations. 65 units. R420 tent double, R550 forest cabin double, R900 cottage/chalet/rondawel double, R1,100 family chalet (4 people), R2,575 guesthouse (4 people). Daily conservation fee R140 adults, R70 children. AE, DC, MC, V. **Amenities:** Restaurant; fuel station; game drives; hiking trails; horseback riding; pool. *In room:* A/C (in some), fan, TV (in some), kitchen or kitchenette (most), no phone.

Elephant House ★★ This luxury colonial-safari lodge is located just a few minutes' drive from Addo's entrance. The quality of accommodations and public areas help make up for the fact that you're not actually in a reserve. Rooms feature Persian carpets, old prints, and other heirlooms, while lounges and verandas are filled with soft, cozy sofas, plenty of reading matter, and a tranquil atmosphere. There are two pools to wallow in and the lodge offers a wide variety of safaris (Addo game drives are R650) and tours if you're not keen on driving. *Note:* There are also six good-value B&B cottages—**The Stables**—in a field adjacent the lodge, plus a restaurant and wine bar blessed with massive log fireplaces and chandeliers, and another pool.

Off the R335, 8km (5 miles) from the main entrance to Addo. www.elephanthouse.co.za. 📞 **042/233-2462.** Fax 042/233-0393. **Elephant House:** 8 units. High season R2,400 double; low season R1,500 double; R500 per extra person sharing. **Stables:** 6 cottages. High season R1,400 double; low season R1,100 double; R300 per extra person sharing. Rates include breakfast. AE, DC, MC, V. **Amenities:** Restaurant (at Stables); dining area; bar; lounges; babysitting; game drives; 3 pools; room service; TV/DVD library; free Wi-Fi in TV lounge. *In room:* A/C, hair dryer, minibar.

Gorah ★★★ Grasslands, game, and big skies stretch out before you in delicious, deep silence at Gorah, punctuated only by animal grunts and the sounds of grass being chewed (clearly audible through the canvas walls of the 11 elegant thatched tents at 2am). Small wonder that this is one of our top three safari destinations in the Eastern Cape (the others being Kwandwe and Samara). The lack of electricity (it is solar powered and has strong green credentials) adds to the experience: The camp comes into its own at night, when winking lanterns and candles illuminate the colonial-era lodge (Gorah House was built in 1856) but are no match for the dazzle of stars overhead. A water hole a stone's throw from the lodge veranda provides downtime game-viewing of exceptional quality; drives will top up any sightings you may have missed. This is a true retreat, and the care and attention to detail brought to every aspect of your experience, combined with the exceptional surroundings, make it hard to beat.

Turn right off the R335 just after passing Addo village and follow the dirt road for 10km (6¼ miles) to Gorah's gate. www.gorah.com. 📞 **042/235-1123,** or 042/233-2462 reservations. Fax 042/235-1124. 11 units. High season R9,840–R12,700 double; low season R6,700 double. Children 10–16 sharing with 2 adults pay R1,320–R2,480. Rates include meals, nonalcoholic beverages, and game drives. AE, DC, MC, V. No children under 10. **Amenities:** Dining areas; lounges; boma; horseback riding; library; pool; free Wi-Fi. *In room:* Fan, heater, in-house phone.

PRIVATE GAME RESERVES NEAR & BEYOND ADDO

The rehabilitation of huge tracts of farmland to their natural state has meant that there are now quite a number of private wildlife preserves within striking distance of Addo. The name most easily recognized is **Shamwari** (reviewed below), which draws big-name celebrities and high-rollers, but the finest safari experience in the Eastern Cape, offering a choice of lodges and impeccable guiding, is **Kwandwe** (reviewed below). Aside from these top-end choices there are four more reserves with various lodgings that might better suit your pocket.

Offering the widest array of accommodations (under various owners) is the 18,000-acre (7,284-hectare) **Amakhala Game Reserve** (www.amakhala.co.za; *C* **046/636-2750**), a mere 45 minutes from P.E and with excellent game viewing. Amakhala has ten distinct lodging options, ranging considerably in terms of luxury and price tag. At the top end is the intimate and family-friendly **Hlosi** (reviewed below), and the beautifully designed **Safari Lodge ★★** (R5,360–R7,160 double, all-inclusive), with accommodations in 11 thatched and luxuriously appointed ocher-colored thatch-topped suites inspired by the architecture of Mali. Also attractive are the five free-standing voluminous tented units at **Bush Lodge ★** at Reed Valley (R5,760–R8,360 double, all inclusive), each handsomely kitted out with stove fire, lovely stone tub, and doors that fold away on to a small deck with plunge pool and double shower perfectly poised for animal watching; the only drawback is that you have to drive to the main game-viewing area. If you're on a budget, you can't beat Amakhala's **Carnavon Dale** (R2,960–R4,160 double), a historic Edwardian-style settler farmhouse from 1857. Or, if you want nothing but canvas between yourself and the bush, there's **Woodbury Tented Camp** (same rate), which is basic, family-managed, and situated just across the valley from the site of the first dinosaur fossil discovery in South Africa.

Aside from **Blaauwbosch Private Game Reserve** (www.blaauwbosch.co.za), a 5,000-hectare (12,350-acre) reserve that is much farther north and closer to the Karoo desert, which is fairly unremarkable in terms of accommodation and price, there are two smaller reserves worth considering, both close to the settler town of Grahamstown: the 6,000-hecatre **Pumba Private Game Reserve** (reviewed below) and nearby 7,500-hectare (18,533-acre) **Lalibela Private Reserve.** Pumba only has two camps, but Lalibela has quite a few options, not all operated by the same companies but all traversing much the same area. Of the Lalibela options our first preference is for **Kichaka Lodge ★** (www.kichaka.co.za; *C* **046/622-6024;** R6,900–R8,500 double), which is tucked away on the northeastern part of Lalibela. The lodge centers on a large deck above an infinity pool hovering above a vast waterhole in which resident hippo, Harry, wallows all day. Wooden boardwalks lead to 10 thatched stone cottages, each with own plunge pool; other than the horrid laminate-wood flooring, they're very luxurious, built on three levels, affording lazy views from the beds. If this seems pricey (bearing in mind that all meals, most beverages, and game activities are included), you may find **Idwala Lodge** (www.idwalalodge.com; *C* **046/622-2163;** R3,900–R7,300 double) more attractive, particularly in winter when plunge pools and the like are irrelevant. Located on the western border of Lalibela, it's less luxurious but tiny and intimate (only four secluded chalets), and offer unpretentious good value particularly in winter. The oldest camp in the Lalibela reserve is the eight-unit **Mark's Camp** (www.lalibela.co.za; high season R4,330–R6,500 double; low season R3,000–R4,500 double). Here the focus is definitely on families with a full children's entertainment program and your own full-time nanny included in the price; perhaps not ideal for families wanting to actually spend time together but ideal if for full-time mothers or fathers desperate for a real break.

However, staying in any one of these small reserves, with their relative proximity to highways and towns, is incomparable after a stay at Kwandwe.

Hlosi Game Lodge ★★ ☺ Game-viewing starts before you arrive; then you're welcomed with hot chocolate and Amarula, and an invitation to feel right at home. With its double-sided fireplaces and homey arrangement of bar, lounges, and dining areas, a children's room packed with books, toys and PS2, and decks looking out across the grasslands, the main lodge is a comfortable space in which to schmooze; you'll see plenty of animals come to drink at the nearby watering hole, and elephants slurp water from the pool. Suites are cute thatched cottages with polished stone floors and luxurious appointments, right down to the body butter and scrub in the bathrooms. Family suites have some fun extras, including outdoor shower and Jacuzzi, and cupboards filled with children's games. In fact, children are treated like minor royalty here, with all kinds of activities laid on (including a camp out with ranger-led storytelling and marshmallows around the fire). *Note:* If you like the sound of this, but want something more suitable for romance, check out nearby **Bukela ★★**, which has space for just four couples and is tucked away in a valley.

Amakhala Game Reserve, R342 Alexandria/Karel Landman Rd., signposted off the N2. www.lionroars. com. © **042/235-1133,** or 041/581-0993 reservations. Fax 041/502-9429. 6 units. R7,790 double. Children pay R1,950 if sharing with 2 adults. Rates include all meals, most local beverages, games drives, and snacks. AE, DC, MC, V. **Amenities:** Dining room; bar; lounges; pool; free Wi-Fi. *In room:* A/C, TV, fireplace, hair dryer, Jacuzzi, minibar, underfloor heating

Kwandwe ★★★ Kwandwe is our top choice of the Eastern Cape reserves: From the moment you pull in at the (supposedly haunted) colonial-era ostrich farm manor house for check-in and welcome drinks, you feel at home and at ease. And it doesn't hurt that you're surrounded by devastatingly gorgeous vistas crammed with game ("the lion breed like rats here," jokes one ranger), and consistently turning up unusual sightings—nocturnal oddities such as aardwolf and aardvark (antbear) are regularly seen. Covering 22,000 hectares (54,362 acres), it has the added benefit of 30km (19 miles) of Great Fish River frontage—a big contrast to the typically arid Eastern Cape environment. The massive reserve has two main lodges, the original being **Great Fish River Lodge,** which looks as though it had been furnished for Karen Blixen: Persian rugs, antiques, hand-stitched damask linen, cut-glass decanters, African spears, and old-style hunting prints—all very *Out of Africa.* Each suite enjoys fabulous views (even from the Victorian tub), thatched viewing decks, and private plunge pools. The more modern (and slightly less formal) **Ecca Lodge,** with its contemporary corrugated iron and stone gabion architecture set on rolling slopes, is unusual and surprising—the lines between indoors and outside are blurred, and the modern suites are enormous and airy. In addition, there is **Uplands Homestead,** a gracious 1905 farmhouse accommodating six, and **Melton Manor,** a lovely house full of quirky, homey luxuries and accommodating eight; Melton's suites can also be rented individually.

25km (16 miles) N of Grahamstown, signposted off the R67; from the N2, take the R67 FORT BEAUFORT turnoff and follow for 19km (12 miles), turning left onto a gravel road at the Kwandwe sign; the gate is 5km (3 miles) on. www.andbeyond.com. © **046/603-3400,** or 011/809-4300 reservations. Fax 011/809-4511. **Great Fish River Lodge:** 9 units. **Ecca Lodge:** 6 units. High season R13,870 double, midseason R9,610 double, low season R7,760. **Uplands Villa:** R18,195–R29,080 exclusive use. **Melton Manor:** R20,790–R33,570 exclusive use; high season R11,190 double, midseason R8,910 double, R6,930 double. Rates include all meals, local beverages, game activities, and laundry. AE, DC, MC, V. No children under 12 at Great Fish River Lodge. **Amenities:** Dining areas; bar; lounges; boma; bush walks; game drives; room service. *In room:* A/C, hair dryer, minibar, plunge pool, free Wi-Fi.

THE EASTERN CAPE | Addo & Nearby Private Game Reserves

Shamwari Private Game Reserve ★★ ☺ The first big Eastern Cape reserve to be restocked with game, Shamwari has hosted a string of famous guests, from Tiger Woods to Brad Pitt. It's a little commercial in comparison to Kwandwe (and Samara, see "Camdeboo," below), but the quality of the game viewing and the rangers' knowledge at this 27,000-hectare (66,718-acre) reserve is beyond reproach. The reserve has a variety of lodges to choose from, all distinctive (but not all equally desirable). Aimed at the top-end market are **Eagles Cragg** ★★, comprising nine junior suites (and a spa) in a forested gorge, and **Lobengula Lodge** ★, with six suites. Eagles Cragg suites all have massive foldaway glass doors leading to private viewing decks with plunge pools, indoor-outdoor bathrooms, lavish interiors, but you can't help feeling that they've missed the point with all the marble, sweeping staircases, and overly showy ethnic-chic decor that disconnects you from the bush. Infinitely better—to our minds, at least—is **Bayethe** ★★★: Comprising 12 immaculate en-suite luxury canvas, brick, and thatch tents with wonderful views from your private deck and plunge pool, it certainly offers the most authentic bush experience. Designed specifically with young families in mind is the fairly modest **Riverdene,** a converted farmhouse with nine mediocre rooms reached via rather bland passageways—all very child-friendly and safely fenced. Parents seeking more luxury (at a marginally higher price) can opt for **Sarili** ★, a more recently built thatched villa overlooking the Bushmans River; it is more exclusive and has an appealing contemporary air, but not all rooms have views. **Bushmans River** (an original 1860 settler farmstead) is the most intimate, but with only four rooms sells out quickly, so book well ahead. Popular with older clientele is **Long Lee Manor,** a beautifully furnished pink Edwardian property built in 1910 and still accommodating guests in a rather overt colonial style. It is large and quite hotel-like, looking out over the reserve rather than feeling immersed in it.

72km (45 miles) NE of P.E.; follow the N2 toward Grahamstown for 65km (40 miles), turn left at the Shamwari sign on to the R342 (gravel), turn right at the Shamwari sign. www.shamwari.com. ✆ **042/203-1111,** or 041/407-1000 reservations. Fax 041/407-1001. High season R9,000–R11,900 double; low season R8,470–R11,500 double. Some lodges close for low season. Rates include all meals, selected beverages, and game drives. AE, DC, MC, V. **Amenities:** Dining room; bar; lounges; airport transfers; babysitting; bush walks; game drives; pool. *In room:* A/C, TV (some), hair dryer, minibar, free Wi-Fi or Internet.

Pumba Water & Bush Lodge ★★ ☺ While considerably smaller than Kwandwe (and a touch cheaper), Pumba boasts five different biomes, making game viewing a treat. Of the two lodges, your best choice is probably **Pumba Water Lodge** ★★—thatched chalets with packed stone exteriors, all overlooking Lake Kariega, linked to central open-plan communal areas by wooden walkways. Interiors are expansive and pretty, with wooden floors, indoor and outdoor showers, and a pool on your private timber deck. Of the entry-level "Impala" rooms, no. 6 is the one to pick, or go for no. 9 if you want a superior (gigantic) "Gemsbok" suite. Parents should pick **Msenge Bush Lodge,** which is visibly fenced off, making it safer for children, who also receive special treatment here.

20km (13 miles) W of Grahamstown. www.pumbagamereserve.co.za. ✆ **046/603-2000.** Fax 046/603-2001. **Pumba Water Lodge:** 12 units. High season R9,080–R11,760 luxury double, R9,980–R13,540 superior double, R11,360–R15,300 suite. Low season R6,840 luxury, R7,520 superior, R8,200 suite; R1,500–R5,880 extra person. **Msenge Bush Lodge:** 11 units. High season R9,080–R11,760 luxury double, R9,980–R13,540 family suite; low season R6,840–R11,760 double; R1,500–R2,160 extra person. AE, DC, MC, V. Children under 8 by prior arrangement. **Amenities:** Dining areas, lounges; bar; bush walks; fishing; game drives; pool; spa. *In room:* A/C and fan, fireplace, plunge pool, free Wi-Fi.

Private Reserves on the Sunshine Coast

These two beach vacation towns are popular with locals during the summer season and an easy drive on the R72 from either Port Elizabeth or Grahamstown. They offer a host of outdoor activities, including golf, horseback-riding, and water sports, but the main attraction for overseas visitors are the game reserves in the area. Nearest the coast at Kenton-on-Sea, and the most relaxed, is **Sibuya** (reviewed below), which is designed for a truly intimate relationship with nature at very reasonable prices. Neighboring **Kariega Private Game Reserve** (www.kariega.co.za; 𝒞 **046/636-7904**) has four lodges; prices suit both those seeking luxury and budget-beating families. The 9,000-hectare (22,240-acre) reserve is in the Kariega River Valley, an 80-minute drive from the P.E., and near the beaches of Kenton-on-Sea. Of the four, **River Lodge** (R5,600–R7,900 double all-inclusive) is the most luxurious: The thatched suites, some of which are grouped in a double-story block, ramble along the Bushman's River—units 8, 9, and 10 are farthest from the main building and thus more private. Besides the normal game drives, this lodge also offers river trips and fishing. **Ukhozi Lodge** (R5,200–R7,500 double, all-inclusive) has a wonderful rustic feel, and the 10 suites all have private plunge pools, but **Kariega Main Lodge** (R4,400–R6,300 double, including meals and game drives) offers better value for families, with 21 spacious timber chalets, each with its own viewing decks. Some come with plunge pools at no extra cost, so make sure to book these in advance. The final option is **The Homestead,** a private sole-use house with five rooms, its own chef and ranger, and a secluded position in a remote part of the reserve for extra privacy and those who want a more flexible schedule. It's all yours from R17,000 to R23,000 per night.

Oceana ★★★ It is out of the way, but this überswanky establishment, owned by Texan Rip Miller, is worth traveling for. The position is out of this world: A central thatch and stone lodge floats over coastal forest and a golden, deserted beach that stretches as far as you can see. Four private, luxurious ocean suites linked by wooden boardwalks enjoy the same outlook, as do rooms in the main lodge. Staff go out of their way to personalize this Afro-chic safari-beach house experience. While Oceana is a reserve with a wide variety of antelope (and rhino), there's no 5am wakeup call: Arrange to go on game drives, walks, relax in the spa, or visit the magnificent beach, just as you please. This no-rules approach also applies to dining: Enjoy formal meals, or request a barbecue or beach picnic. For families or friends traveling together there's the exclusive-use Ocean House, a real retreat.

Right off the R72, 7km (4¼ miles) east of Port Alfred. www.oceanareserve.com. 𝒞 **083/616-0605.** Fax 086/602-3767. 8 units. Ocean suites R9,000 double; lodge suites R8,000 double; private house from R18,000 for 4 people. Rates include meals, local beverages, and activities. MC, V. **Amenities:** Dining room; bar; lounges; bush walks; fishing; game drives; game room; horseback riding (on the beach); pool; room service; spa; wine cellar. *In room:* A/C, TV/DVD, movie library, hair dryer, minibar, no phone, free Wi-Fi.

Sibuya Game Reserve ★ 🔪 ☺ Prepare for a very authentic bush experience in a unique environment: Despite its proximity to the coastal village of Kenton-on-Sea (where you hop aboard a boat for the 30-min. trip to your lodge), Sibuya offers total immersion in an unspoiled wilderness. There's no other game reserve in the country with as much navigable river, so game drives are mixed with activities on the water (even beach trips are possible). Home to the Big 5, these 3,000 marvelously diverse hectares (7,413 acres) are thick with plants, and have genuine "Land Before Time"

THE EASTERN CAPE   Addo & Nearby Private Game Reserves

appeal. Sibuya comprises two separate eco-friendly tented camps tucked into a riverine forest and virtually invisible from the outside; **River Camp** is smaller and very child-friendly (activities keep them busy all day), and the elegant safari design works to let as much of the outside in—big roll-up canvas flaps and walls of glass through which to peer into the forest. **Forest Camp** has twice as many tents, but they're all very secluded, reached via circuitous timber boardwalks—when you roll up the bathroom walls, it's as though you're genuinely outside, and some have swingbeds near the river's edge from where you can watch elephants on the opposite bank.

Kenton-on-Sea; river transfers from the Kenton jetty. www.sibuya.co.za. 📞 **046/648-1040.** Fax 046/648-1443. **River Camp:** 4 units. **Forest Camp:** 8 units. High season R4,990 double; low season R4,500 double. Children aged 3–12 pay R1,125–R1,248 if sharing (River Camp only). Rates include all meals, beverages, and activities. AE, DC, MC, V. **Amenities:** Dining area; bar; lounge; boating; bush walks; fishing; game drives; small library.

CAMDEBOO, GRAAFF-REINET & NIEU BETHESDA

254km (158 miles) NW of Port Elizabeth; 837km (519 miles) S of Johannesburg

The Great Karoo holds a very special place in our hearts, with its vast stretches of semi-arid nothingness, sheep and game ranches interrupted by far-off *koppies,* monumental rock formations, sheer cliffs and craggy gorges. At its heart, is **Graaff-Reinet,** South Africa's fourth-oldest town, and one of few large settlements surrounded by a nature reserve, **Mount Camdeboo National Park.** A good stopover if you're driving between Johannesburg and the Garden Route, the town boasts some 220 national monuments, while the immediacy of the enveloping Camdeboo plains makes for a mystifying setting, demanding at least 2 days of your time. While you could devote a morning tracking down the town's architectural gems, the real highlight is a trip to the nearby **Valley of Desolation,** coupled with a safari at one of the private game reserves in the shadow of the Camdeboo's exquisite **Sneeuberg** mountains range, the second-highest range in the country. And definitely make time set off north through this landscape to find one of the world's best examples of outsider art in nearby **Nieu Bethesda,** a time-trapped hamlet possessing considerable charm.

Essentials

VISITOR INFORMATION   **Graaff-Reinet Tourism** (📞 049/892-4248; www.graaffreinet.co.za; Mon–Fri 8am–5pm, Sat 9am–noon) is at 13A Church St.

GETTING THERE   By Car   From Johannesburg, travel south on the N1, then take the N9 south at Colesberg to Graaff-Reinet. From Port Elizabeth, take the R75 north, a 3-hour drive. (If by chance you find yourself traveling on the N10 from Cookhouse to Craddock—a much longer trip—make sure to stop at the Daggaboer farm stall, a haven of hospitality, homemade ginger beer, pickles, and venison pie.)

GETTING AROUND & GUIDED TOURS   The easiest and best way to explore the town is on foot or by bicycle. For guided tours of the town and environs and bicycle rentals, contact **Karoo Connections Tours ★** (📞 049/892-3978; www.karooconnections.co.za). They provide town and township tours; trips to the Valley of Desolation, Bushman rock art, and the Owl House; and game-viewing drives in the Camdeboo National Park. They also can provide information on horseback-riding and hiking tours, and they run half- and full-day tours to the superb under-the-radar **Mountain Zebra National Park,** a little-known but lovely game preserve.

What to See & Do

With more national monuments than any other South African town, the streets of Graaff-Reinet are a pleasure to stroll. Incorporate an informal walking tour with a visit to at least one of the four buildings that comprise the **Graaff-Reinet Museum** (© **049/892-3801;** Mon–Fri 8am–5pm, Sat–Sun 9am–2pm; admission R25). Of these, **Reinet House,** a stately Cape Dutch home facing Parsonage Street, is by far the most interesting. Built in 1812 as the Dutch Reformed Church parsonage, its large, airy rooms display period furniture, a collection of antique dolls, and various household objects. Within walking distance, the **Old Library Museum,** on the corner of Church and Somerset streets, houses a collection of fossilized Karoo reptiles that inhabited the area more than 200 million years ago. Also worth a look is the slightly scrappy but still evocative exhibition on the life of Robert Sobukwe, the founder of the Pan Africanist Congress, which broke away from the ANC in 1958. Sobukwe spent years on Robben Island and was buried in Graaff-Reinet, his hometown. Other buildings worth noting are the stately **Dutch Reformed Church,** 1 block up from the Old Library Museum, which dates from 1886, and the delightful **Graaff-Reinet pharmacy,** a typical Victorian pharmacy that still operates at 24 Caledon St. Also stop by the **Pierneef Museum,** Middle Street (© **049/892-6107;** Mon–Fri 9am–12:30pm and 2–5pm, Sat and Sun 9am–noon), where the artist's impressive Johannesburg Station Panels are now on display. Viewed with suspicion for years because of perceived ties to Afrikaner nationalism, Pierneef's characteristic, stylized landscapes are garnering renewed appreciation lately—and you may recognize some key South African landmarks (such as the Valley of Desolation or Knysna Heads) from your travels. Last, see another side of Graaff-Reinet on a walking tour of **uMasizakhe Township:** Isaac Mashoeng of **Ingomso Future Township Tours** (© **083/559-1207;** mashoengisaac@yahoo.com; R120 for 2 hr., including transport) will share its history and introduce you to locals, with visits to a kindergarten, library, clinic, church (on Sun), and a local home to taste some homemade food—you'll also hear about traditional Xhosa feasts and ceremonies, such as initiation, weddings, and burials.

CAMDEBOO NATIONAL PARK ★★★

Graaff-Reinet lies in the center of this extraordinary-looking 19,000-hectare (46,950-acre) protected area, the highlight of which is the **Valley of Desolation ★★★.** Sunset is the best time to visit, when the dolomite towers that rise some 800m (2,624 ft.) from the valley below turn a deep red, and the pink light softens the Camdeboo plains. The short, 1.5km (1-mile) Crag Lizard walking trail that starts at the parking lot is a good introduction to the landscape. On your return, watch for the endangered mountain zebra—this is one of its last remaining habitats. All in all, the park hosts 43 mammal species; the entrance to the game-viewing area is off the same road as the Valley of Desolation, the R63.

Valley of Desolation is 14km (8½ miles) from Graaff-Reinet, signposted off the R63. © **049/892-3453.** www.sanparks.org. R60 adult. Daily 6am–7:30pm.

NIEU BETHESDA & THE OWL HOUSE ★★★

Nieu Bethesda, 50km (31 miles) north of Graaff-Reinet, is a typical Karoo *dorp* (small rural town) with unusual charm; such modern-day luxuries as electricity are relatively recent phenomena, and donkey carts still ply the dusty streets, but the main attraction is the **Owl House and Camel Yard ★★★,** on New Street (© **049/841-1603;** www.owlhouse.co.za). In her late 40s, after the deaths of her parents, Helen

Martins became obsessed with transforming her house into a world of her own making, a project that was to absorb her for the next 30 years. She was obsessed with light: The interior features large reflecting mirrors to maximize this, and every conceivable surface is covered with finely crushed glass, with colors creating large patterns, including a favored sunbeam motif. In the candlelight, the interior glitters like a jewel. Martins's inner vision spread into her backyard, enveloping her in a mystical world of glittering peacocks, camels, mermaids, stars, shepherds, sphinxes, towers, and serpents. Immortalized in the award-winning play and movie *Road to Mecca* (starring Kathy Bates), the house is one of the world's most inspiring examples of Outsider Art. Tours are held from 9am to 5pm daily; admission is R30.

Tea and light meals are available daily at **The Karoo Lamb** (✆ **049/841-1642;** daily 7am–after dinner), on the corner diagonally opposite the Owl House. There is no official tourism bureau, but owners Ian and Katrin can assist with just about anything—they also sells all kinds of Karoo crafts and deli goodies. Or head for the **Two Goats Deli** (✆ **049/841-1602;** daily from 10am—but call ahead to check), which makes its own goat's cheeses and serves a delectable range of bread, cheese, salamis, and preserves for lunch—plus, it shares premises with the Sneeuberg brewery, which means ales are on tap and plentiful.

Where to Stay & Eat

Reviewed below, **Aa'Qtansisi** is our top pick in town, but you'd do well to also set aside at least 2 nights at one of the private game reserves a short distance from Graaff-Reinet, where the terrain forms a humbling backdrop to opportunities to track cheetah on foot. A reasonable B&B with a lovely garden is **Buiten Verwagten** (www.buiten verwagten.co.za; ✆ **049/892-4504;** R750–R900 double); choose the Victoria room with its lovely brass bed, or the honeymoon room with its cedar floors and easy access to the pool. There's also a spa for those in need of pampering. It may not look inspiring form the outside, but one of the most sociable places in town for a good meal is **Pioneers** (✆ **049/892-6059;** opening hours vary, so call ahead), which serves hearty, satisfying meals, as well as unlikely dishes such as tripe, ostrich carpaccio, and baby beef Bombay. Other consistently agreeable dining options include **Coldstream** (✆ **049/891-1181**) and the amiable **Kliphuis** (✆ **049/892-2345**), a stone cottage with tables indoors and out, a fine collection of hats, and a wide-ranging menu with plenty of venison and lamb. Many foodies—including some famous South Africans—arrive in Graff-Reinet with just one thing on their minds: dinner at **Gordon's Restaurant** ★★, Andries Stockenström Guest House, 100 Cradock St. (✆/fax **049/892-4575;** www.asghouse.co.za), a rather special (and expensive; R300 per person) affair involving very exciting recipes and lots of free-range, organic, and often personally foraged or grown produce. Linger over slow-cooked Karoo-inspired meals as Gordon talks you through the process with eland and kudu trophies watching from the walls of the covered courtyard. Never content with "ordinary," Gordon serves port and biltong soup, kudu pâté, springbok filet infused with garlic, and scrumptious spring rolls, perhaps stuffed with wild hare with whiskey and honey, arugula, raisins, and muscatel (a dessert wine). In winter, Gordon also puts together "cooking adventures" ★★ in which you accompany him as he procures ingredients for dinner, join him in the kitchen, and then taste the rewards of his hard work.

Aa'Qtansisi Guesthouse ★★ Built in 1852, Graff-Reinet's slickest guesthouse was once a school attended by South African billionaire Anton Rupert. Now, between high ceilings and thick walls, its cozy spaces are decorated with antiques and original artworks, and Pierre and Ria provide personally researched knowledge on where to eat and what to see. Bedrooms feature high Zanzibari beds (footstools provided), piled with cushions and done out in interesting fabrics, and with specially made toiletries. There's lots of carved wood, and bathrooms have ball-and-claw tubs and glassed showers. All the rooms have a unique flavor but do take a look at Bus Stop No. 1 (the most distinctly South African), nicknamed the "Slave Quarters," which celebrates local history with antique newspaper clippings, cushions covered in *Drum* magazine covers, coffee sacks turned into cushion covers; it has a private entrance near the pool.

69 Somerset St., Graaff-Reinet 6280. www.aaqtansisi.co.za. © **049/891-0243** or 082/783-4520. Fax 086/617-1216. 6 units. R900–R1,000 double. Rates include breakfast. AE, DC, MC, V. **Amenities:** Dining room; lounge; honor bar; plunge pool; free Wi-Fi (around the house). *In room:* A/C, TV, hair dryer,

Mount Camdeboo ★★ 🐾 One of the best-value options in the Eastern Cape, this private reserve offers a majestic setting at the foot of the Sneeuberg mountain and luxurious accommodations in three Cape Dutch manor houses (each with its own pool, period inspired decor, and modern conveniences) as well as one ultraromantic **Honeymoon Suite** in a 300-year-old stone cottage that in another era was a police gatehouse (bag it if you can). Throughout, exclusivity is seamlessly integrated with genuine home-from-home atmosphere. Only **Camdeboo Manor,** an early-19th-century farmhouse, is shared with other guests—and even that has just four rooms, each with poster beds, raw silk, reed ceilings, and decor that fittingly draws on settler heritage, translated into a wonderfully luxurious, updated idiom. Like the main lodge, the sole-use **Courtyard Manor** and **Hillside Manor** are ranged along a seasonal river, and the surrounding Karoo and mountain vistas are (as at Samara) simply astonishing. This is not Big 5 territory (although there's plenty game, including are cheetah, rhino, and buffalo), but besides game drives, you can enjoy guided walks, rock art, visits to historic battle sites, and stargazing.

Take the R75 from Graaff-Reinet, then the R63 turnoff left to Pearston, then left onto Petersberg Rd., and follow signs. www.mountcamdeboo.com. © **049/891-0570.** Fax 049/892-3362. 5 units, plus 2 exclusive-use villas. Camdeboo Manor and Honeymoon Suite R4,000 double, Courtyard Manor and Hillside Manor minimum R8,000 for 4 people. Children aged 4–12 pay R1,000 if sharing with 2 adults. Rates include all meals, local beverages, and game activities. MC, V. **Amenities:** Dining rooms; lounges; bush walks; game drives; high-speed Internet; pool. *In room:* A/C, TV, hair dryer, minibar, underfloor heating.

Samara Private Game Reserve ★★★ 😊 This is not a Big 5 reserve, but after Kwandwe it's our top pick for game-viewing in the Eastern Cape, with huge, mercurial skies above a surreal landscape of wide-open plains and soaring peaks, and the Camdeboo mountainscape providing an ethereal backdrop to impeccable accommodations and excellent service. Once 11 different once-overgrazed farms, this 28,300-hectare (69,931-acre) wilderness is home to over 60 mammal species and offers the chance to get ridiculously close to free-roaming cheetah. You have a choice of two sumptuous lodges, or a rustic generator-powered **Mountain Retreat** (private; from R8,800 for four, including all meals); your choice comes down to taste. The serenely colonial **Karoo Lodge,** with its corrugated green roof and wraparound veranda, is in the vernacular style of old Karoo towns, surrounded by rugged vistas—choose one of the free-standing Victorian-style Karoo suites with outdoor shower and amazing views. **The Manor** is recently built, with a more modern, Afro-chic look and feel, clean lines and abundant use of white—it feels more like a family home. By day you are treated to a choice of build-your-own adventures, exploring the reserve's rare topographical diversity, and at night as you're plied with drinks and good food, you stare up at an ebony canvas, thick with stars. Or you can head off with your ranger for a night of camping in the bush.

20km (13 miles) SE of Graff-Reinet, signposted off the R63; take the R75 from Graaff-Reinet, then the R63 turnoff. www.samara.co.za. ℭ **049/891-0880,** or 049/891-0558 reservations. Fax 049/892-4339. **Karoo Lodge:** 8 units. R9,600 Karoo/Camdeboo suite, R7,600 lodge suite, R3,900 Sibella suite; low season R6,000 Karoo/Camdeboo suite, R4,800 lodge suite, R3,000 Sibela suite. **The Manor:** 4 units. High season R9,600 double, from R19,200 for 4 people; low season R6,000 double, from R12,000 for 4 people. Children aged 3–14 pay 50% if sharing with 2 adults. Rates include all meals, game activities, and local beverages. AE, DC, MC, V. **Amenities:** Dining room; bar; lounge; pool; free Wi-Fi. *In room:* A/C, hair dryer, minibar, spa treatments.

THE WILD COAST ★★★

The northernmost section of the Eastern Cape stretches 280km (174 miles) from just north of East London in the south to the mouth of the Mtamvuna River, bordering KwaZulu-Natal. The coast is lush and sparsely populated, with innumerable rivers spilling into large estuaries; waterfalls plunging directly into the ocean; coastal, dune, and mangrove forests; long, sandy beaches; rocky coves; and a number of shipwrecks, all of which have earned it the name Wild Coast. This region was part of the former *bantustan* (homeland) Transkei, where any Xhosa that weren't of economic use to the republic were dumped, and as such it has suffered from overgrazing and underdevelopment and is one of the poorest areas in South Africa. Despite this, the people are very hospitable, and exploring this region will provide you with one of the most unaffected cultural experiences available to visitors in South Africa. Note, however, that much of the coastline is difficult to access—dirt roads are pitted with deep potholes, there is virtually no public transportation, and accommodations options are limited. The exceptions to this are the coastal towns of **Coffee Bay** and **Port St Johns,** and the coast south of **Qhorha Mouth** (also known as Qora Mouth); at the southernmost end of the Wild Coast, one of the most scintillating and flawless beaches is **Cintsa,** where lovely **Prana,** a new luxury lodge and spa is tucked behind the dunes.

The only way to reach these coastal towns is via the N2, which cuts through the middle of the hinterland, passing through unfenced green valleys dotted with traditional Xhosa huts and the old Transkei capital, Umtata, now called Mthatha. The only real attraction here is the **Nelson Mandela Museum** (ℭ 047/532-5110; www.nelsonmandelamuseum.org.za; Mon–Fri 9am–4pm, Sat 9am–noon; free admission). Madiba, the clan name by which Mandela is affectionately known, was born near Qunu. The museum is situated in the Bhunga Building, a gracious colonial structure that once housed municipal offices, and comprises several rooms that have been filled with Mandela memorabilia, among them gifts from respectful statesmen, adoring children, and various other admirers. Excellent displays, including posters, videos, and photographs, record the life and works of Africa's greatest statesman.

Essentials

VISITOR INFORMATION The **Eastern Cape Tourism** office in Umtata/ Mthatha can give you information on the Wild Coast. Call ℭ **047/531-5290** or visit www.ectourism.co.za (office hours are Mon–Fri 8am–4pm). Alternatively, contact **Wild Coast Holiday Reservations** (ℭ **043/743-6181**; www.wildcoastholidays. co.za; meross@iafrica.com) in East London, or Ukhenketho **Tourism Port St Johns** (ℭ/fax **047/564-1187**). For information on Wild Coast nature reserves (of which Mkambati—also spelt Mkhambathi—is recommended; don't miss the Horseshoe Falls), contact central bookings at ℭ **043/742-4451.**

GETTING THERE & AROUND **By Plane** The closest main airport to the southern Wild Coast is East London; there are flights here from Cape Town with SAA and 1Time. **SAA** flies to Mthatha (closest airport to Port St John) from Johannesburg 5 days a week, and connects on to East London and Port Elizabeth once a week.

By Car The N2 runs the length of what used to be called the Transkei, with roads to the coast leading southeast off it. Most roads to the coast are unpaved, some are badly marked, and all are time-consuming. Look out for livestock on the road, and don't travel at night.

By Bus The **Baz Bus** (see chapter 13 for regional numbers) travels from Port Elizabeth to Durban, with stops at Coffee Bay and Port St Johns.

By Foot & on Horseback **Wild Coast Meander** ★ (ℭ **043/743-6181**; www. wildcoastholidays.co.za) offers a 6-day hike that covers 55km (34 miles), from Qho-rha Mouth to Morgan Bay, accompanied by guides and porters from the local community. Hikers ford rivers and traverse isolated beaches, but nights are spent in a hotel. Six days, including accommodations, meals, and transfers from the East London airport, costs R6,136 per person for a group of four, R7,972 per person for just two people. Prices decrease for larger groups, and there is also a shorter, 3-day version. The same people run the **Pondo Walk** ★, which uses Mbotyi as a base (see "Where to Stay & Eat," below). You'll go on up to four different guided 1-day trails ranging from 13 to 26km (8–16 miles)—two along the coast and two inland—over 4 days. You'll land back at Mbotyi every night, so no camping required; costs incurred cover accommodation (R1,290–R1,590 double per night) and R200 to R400 per day for a guide. The 3- to 6-day **Amadiba Trails** (ℭ **039/305-6455**; www.amadiba adventures.co.za) is a camping trip completed on foot or on horseback and canoe. You will be accompanied by a local guide, and meals may be enjoyed with members of the local community. Trails (R1,160–R1,710 for 4–6 days by foot, or R2,320–R3,420 for 4–6 days on horseback) start at the Mzamba Craft Village, opposite the Wild Coast Casino, near the border between the Eastern Cape and KwaZulu-Natal.

Where to Stay & Eat

Until recently, quality accommodations on the Wild Coast didn't really exist (although there are some lovely old-fashioned hotels aimed at families)—that's changed since the opening of the luxurious **Prana Lodge** (reviewed below) in a coastal forest behind the dunes at Chintsa. Its proximity to East London (a 40-min. drive from the airport) also makes it one of the most accessible spots along this majestic coastline. Elsewhere, though, the unfettered natural surroundings and opportunity to connect with an out-of-time pocket of Africa will make up for a dip in luxury levels. At remote and difficult-to-access **Bulungula** (reviewed below), in particular, it's worth slipping off the radar. At **Qhorha Mouth,** a river carves its way through forested hills to the sea; here you will find **Kob Inn** (www.kobinn.co.za; ✆ **047/499-0011;** sea-facing doubles and suites are R1,320–R1,980, with all meals included), a child's paradise with trampolines, a pool, volleyball, and canoes—plus mountain bikes and a 6km (3.7-mile) trail along the coast for older nature lovers. The 45 simple rooms are in thatched blocks; request the honeymoon suite for maximum comfort.

Another option worth highlighting, much farther up the coast (best approached from the KwaZulu-Natal side), is **Mbotyi River Lodge** ★ (www.mbotyi.co.za; ✆ **039/253-7200;** sea-facing rooms R1,350–R2,450 double, dinner and breakfast included), which has basic thatch bungalows or timber cabins with balconies or patios (ask for a sea view; "upgraded" rooms also have air-conditioning and TVs, and specify if you want a bathtub). Don't expect too much in terms of luxury or decor, but the surroundings are exquisite—activities include walks, bird-watching, horseback-riding, fishing, mountain biking (bikes can be rented), and, of course, spending time lapping up sunshine on the pristine beaches and exploring the tidal estuary and surrounding waterfalls. Children are welcome and babysitting services are available.

Bulungula Lodge ★ 🥾 📷   Time travel to a tranquil, unspoiled coastal paradise where Xhosa villagers live a simple rural existence, and a perfect, wild beach stretches forever in either direction. Bulungula is far from luxurious, but its charms are so rare and authentic that it really shouldn't be reserved for backpackers. At the end of a heavily rutted, convoluted dirt road (allow up to 3 hr. off the N2), a peaceful rural community co-owns and manages this solar-powered lodge where you stay in traditional *rondawels* (round huts), share rocket-heated showers, and discover what makes the local Xhosa people tick. It's a fabulous place to strike out on foot, ride horses on the beach, or spend hours in a fire-heated forest bath. And when the sun slinks away, you're surrounded by pitch black, with a star-slathered sky above. Children from the village beat out drum rhythms around the fire before you dish up your simple, hearty meal from large pots in the communal kitchen. Returning to a simpler way of life may take some getting use to, but once you've settled into the languid pace, you won't want to leave.

Bulungula, 15km/9½ miles W of Mthatha on the N2, and then follow detailed directions (on the website) covering 103km/64 miles from the turnoff. www.bulungula.com. ✆ **047/577-8900** or 083/391-5525. 5 huts, 3 tents, 5 small dorms; all with shared shower. R300 hut double, R280 tent double. MC, V. **Amenities:** Restaurant; honesty bar; lounge; cultural tours; horseback riding. *In room:* No phone, massage.

📷 **The Serengeti of the Seas**

Every year, from around mid-June to July, South Africa is host to what has been touted as "the greatest dive show in the world" by *National Geographic,* when the sea along the wild coast appears to "boil" as some three billion sardines, accompanied by migrating humpback whales and hundreds of predators (dolphins, sharks, seals, cormorants, and gannets), move from the cold Atlantic waters to the warm, subtropical Indian ocean. It's a migration to rival that of the Serengeti and a must on every serious diver's do-before-I-die list. Most packages run for 8 days, with divers based at Mbotyi River Lodge, on the Wild Coast (best accessed from Durban; see above). Alternatively, simply catch one of the daily charters from Shelly Beach in KwaZulu-Natal and witness the migration from the boat. Contact www.oceansafrica.com or www.sardinerun.net.

Prana Lodge ★★ On a 7-hectare (17-acre) estate, tucked into a gorgeous, semi-wild tropical garden behind immense dunes that loom over a 21km (13-mile) stretch of pristine beach, this is the Wild Coast's only high-end hideaway, a true battery recharger with a balance of barefoot back-to-nature beachcombing and manmade luxuries. To get to the beach you'll need to tear yourself away from the authentic Thai spa, cool lounging areas at the pool, butler-style service, and smart freestanding cottages, each with own enclosed garden, plunge pool and urban luxuries. A wooden boardwalk leads you to the summit of a steep dune; there's a deck where you can chill out on beanbag chairs, cocktail in hand, or plunge into the soft sand and cruise the shore. And if all the pampering and relaxation gets too much, there's game viewing at nearby Inkwenkwezi Private Game Reserve—your hosts will make all arrangements, or assist with surfing, hiking, riding, tennis, golf, fishing, or bird-watching.

Chintsa East, Wild Coast. www.pranalodge.co.za. ✆ **043/704-5100.** Fax 043/704-5110. 7 units. High season R2,500–R3,000 double; low season R2,000–R2,500. Rates include breakfast; all-inclusive and dinner-inclusive rates available. MC, V (credit card payments incur 2½% surcharge). Children under 12 by arrangement. **Amenities:** Restaurant; bar; lounge; babysitting; library; pool; room service; spa; Wi-Fi (in library). *In room:* A/C & fan, TV/DVD, movie and music library, CD player, fireplace, hair dryer, minibar, plunge pool.

Umngazi River Bungalows & Spa ★ ☺ If you want to sample the subtropical pleasures of this untamed stretch of coast without roughing it, this is the Wild Coast's best-loved family resort—although its size and popularity detract somewhat from the experience of being in an unfettered wilderness. Umngazi is in its own nature reserve, overlooking an estuary and beach, and flanked by dense coastal vegetation. With a safe lagoon, boats for hire, river trips, waterskiing, spa treatments, snooker, a host of babysitters, and a separate toddlers' dining room, it offers the perfect family vacation. The en-suite bungalows are basic thatch-topped upgrades of huts that are synonymous with the Transkei; all have outdoor showers—it's definitely worth requesting a sea-view unit (nos. 41–43 are choice). Better still: the more luxurious hillside Ntabeni suites, with wonderful river and sea views. Note that service is far from attentive.

Umngazi River mouth, 90km/56 miles E of Mthatha. www.umngazi.co.za. ✆/fax **047/564-1115.** 69 units. R1,450–R1,980 bungalow double; R1,860–R2,080 river mouth double; R2,040–2,320 honeymoon cottage; R2,750–R3,300 Ntabeni suite. R185–R625 per child sharing. Rates include all meals. AE, DC, MC, V. **Amenities:** Dining room and children's dining room; lounges; bar; babysitting; bikes; birding; boating; children's play area; fishing; guided walks; internet (limited access); saltwater pool; spa; tennis court. *In room:* Fan, minibar (suites only).

AFRICA'S BIG APPLE: JO'BURG

For many, Johannesburg, with its heady blend of First and Third worlds, is the most exhilarating city in Africa. An uncontained urban sprawl at the center of Gauteng—the country's smallest, most densely populated province—it is also the springboard into the animal-rich nature reserves that lie a mere 4- to 6-hour drive beyond its business-driven borders. It's not a tourist destination per se, but there's no denying that the city itself has definite draws: the second-largest city in Africa, where the continent's major financial deals are struck, Jo'burg is a throbbing urban metropolis constantly transforming itself, an eclectic home to the socially vibrant and sassy. Still, most leisure travelers simply use Jo'burg as a gateway. If that's why you're here, that's fine; this chapter will help you make the most of your sojourn, regardless of its length.

THINGS TO DO   Gauteng was literally built on gold—its name, translated from Sotho, means "Place of Gold"—and mining is still an important source of GDP. You may, as many tourists do, choose to descend a mine shaft, but Jo'burg's real draw gets deeper under the skin. Anyone wanting a real understanding of what the country endured and transcended in the last century should make a visit to the award-winning **Apartheid Museum** a top priority, one of the most thought-provoking museums in the world. It's location, south of the city, makes it possible to combine with a tour of **Soweto,** once South Africa's largest "black township," a city within a city, where much of the country's history was written. Today it is inhabited by some five million people, almost all of whom are still black—an enduring legacy of the country's separatist history—and renowned for its warm welcome.

ART & CULTURE   If the litmus test of a society is the art it produces, then Johannesburg is in roaring good health, with public art commissioned across the city (and not just, as it used to be, in areas frequented by well-heeled whites) and the increasing international acclaim local artists are gaining, best showcased in the annual **Jo'burg Art Fair.** Then there are developments like **Arts on Main** in downtown Jo'burg, which—with the maxim: *"Where the artists are, others will follow"*—is leading to the exciting regeneration of an otherwise blighted area and the relocation of the best commercial galleries into an "Art District," located walking distance from each other on **Jan Smuts Avenue,** discussed in more detail under "Shopping," later in this chapter. (And if your taste runs more to fashion and crafts, then visit the boutiques in nearby **Rosebank malls** and **African Craft Market,** where you can shop for artifacts from across the continent.)

DINING   Unlike Cape Town, Johannesburg is not known for its fine dining scene, but it's varied, and you will find every major nationality's cuisine represented within easy reach of the accommodation recommendations below. Most restaurants are located in malls, which offer a greater sense of security but not much by way of romance. So we've recommended the best places to dine al fresco, including **Fourth Avenue, Parkhurst's Dining Strip** where tables spill out onto the street in between shops—hardly Paris but understandably popular.

NIGHTLIFE & ENTERTAINMENT   For live old-school jazz and blues tunes, The **Blues Room** in Sandton, **Katzy's** in Rosebank, and **Kippies** in Newtown are your best bet; for more contemporary live sounds, head for **Bassline,** also in Newtown. Newtown is incidentally home to the iconic **Market Theatre,** while nearby **Braamfontein** is Jo'burg's official theater district; it's also where the überswanky **Randlords** is situated, on the 22nd floor of an apartment block, affording dizzying views of the surrounding cityscape. If you'd rather watch Jo'burgers *at* play, the **Hyatt Piazza, The Zone,** and **The Firs**—interconnected Rosebank malls and within walking distance from each other—are bustling with Jo'burgers on the *jol* (pronounced *jawl,* meaning "good time"). It's a short drive from here to **Moloko,** another cool Rosebank club that's popular with a hip crowd. If you're based in Sandton, **Taboo** is where the stylish strut their stuff. But bear in mind that Jo'burgers are (like all big city animals) notoriously fickle—what's in today is old hat tomorrow. To find out where the city's gregarious are congregating now, speak to your host, or better still, an age-appropriate barman or waiter; alternatively read the nightlife sections of the daily newspaper *The Star,* or the weekly *Mail & Guardian*—and keep your ears and eyes open for any sign of a **Balkanology** party, courtesy of Cape Town's hippest crew. Then get down and have a *jol!*

JOHANNESBURG & ENVIRONS

Johannesburg is 1,402km (869 miles) NE of Cape Town; Tshwane is 58km (36 miles) N of Johannesburg

Johannesburg, Jo'burg, Jozi: Ever evolving, this vibrant city throbs to a heady, relentless beat, fueled by the tremendous sociability of its inhabitants. Jozi's diverse population is a considerably better reflection of South Africa's burgeoning hegemonic spirit than you'll encounter anywhere else in the country, with the new "black diamonds," as the black wealthy elite are referred to, injecting flash and style into the clubs, bars, and restaurants in this city's more cosmopolitan areas.

But it wasn't always like this. Less than 150 years ago the "gold capital of the world" was rolling bushveld. This was to change dramatically when a prospector named George Harrison stumbled upon what was to become the richest gold reef in the world in 1886. Within 3 years, these nondescript highveld plains had grown into the third-biggest city in South Africa, and soon Johannesburg, or eGoli, as it came to be known, would become the largest city south of Cairo. It took only a decade for Jo'burg's population to exceed 100,000, and by 1897 it was producing 27% of the world's gold. The speed at which it grew was due in part to the power and greed of such men as Cecil Rhodes—whose diamond mines in Kimberley provided the capital

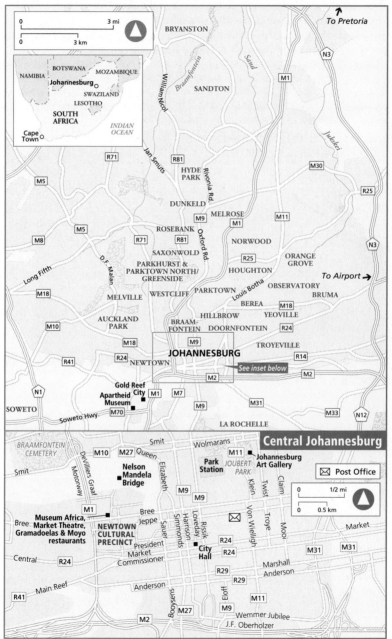

to exploit the rich gold-bearing reefs of the Witwatersrand—and to the availability of cheap labor. Along with other "randlords," as the most powerful consortium of mining magnates was known, Rhodes founded the Chamber of Mines in 1889, which created policies regarding recruitment, wages, and working conditions. In 1893, it institutionalized the "colour bar," which ensured that black men could aspire to no more than manual labor—the precursor of apartheid.

By 1895, the ever-expanding mining settlement far outnumbered the original Boer settlers, who had fled here from what they felt to be the oppressive policies of the British in the Cape. Disgruntled by this secondary "invasion," Botha, president of the then South African Republic (ZAR), denied these *uitlanders* (foreigners) the vote and refused to develop an infrastructure to support mining activities. Four years later, the ZAR and Britain went to war, and in 1902 Britain annexed the republic. The British Empire relinquished its hold in 1910, when the Union of South Africa was proclaimed, but for the millions of black migrant laborers who toiled below the earth, working conditions remained relentlessly harsh. By 1946, more than 400,000 black people were residing in and around Jo'burg; in August that year, 70,000 African Mineworkers Union members went on strike over living and working conditions—to no avail, despite the death of 12 men and injuries to more than 1,000.

During the 1950s, Johannesburg's uniquely black urban culture was given a name. "Kwela" had its own jazzy sounds, heard in the *shebeens* (drinking houses) of Sophiatown, and a slick, sophisticated style, as evidenced in the pages of *Drum* magazine. But this was also the decade of forced removals, when thousands were dumped into the new suburbs of Soweto, and, consequently, a growth phase for the African National Congress (ANC), which in 1955 proclaimed its Freedom Charter—the basis of the current constitution—in what is now known as Freedom Square.

But it would be another 2 decades before the black majority revolted. On June 16, 1976, police opened fire on school students demonstrating against the forced use of Afrikaans as a teaching medium, and sparked a nationwide riot. This was finally crushed in 1978 but not for long: South Africa's black youth had declared war on apartheid and set about making the country ungovernable. Student activism escalated during the 1980s and came to a head during the early 1990s, when political parties jostled for power after Nelson Mandela's release from prison. Some townships were reduced to utter chaos, with a mysterious "third force" (later proven to be state funded) pouring fuel onto the flames. Political peace finally came with the 1994 elections, and Jo'burgers returned to their primary pursuit: making money.

For many, however, this remained an elusive goal. The many years of chaos and growing unemployment spawned a crime wave that, in turn, bred a culture of fear. Walled neighborhoods, burglar bars, security guards, and guard dogs are still common sights, particularly in the northern suburbs, but Jo'burg has undergone a fundamental change in attitude in the past few years, culminating in the hugely successful hosting of the 2010 World Cup. With the advent of various community initiatives, entire neighborhoods have managed to largely eliminate criminal activity, while on an individual level there are few city dwellers more savvy (no Jo'burger would be caught dead with his car doors unlocked, for instance, and handbags are always kept in the trunk). With vigilance becoming second nature rather than an effort, Jo'burgers have moved on, and fear has been replaced with a burgeoning pride, not least at the development of the city's infrastructure. Nowhere is this more evident than when boarding the multibillion-rand new Gautrain, the gleaming new rapid-rail transport system that takes you from the airport to Sandton in 15 minutes; by the end of 2011 the system will extend to Rosebank and Pretoria.

With so much more to see in Southern Africa, there is a natural temptation to rush your Jo'burg experience, but if you have any real interest in the country's recent history, and indeed how far we've come, you'll spend a few days, visiting the art galleries and museums, and mingling in restaurants and bars with a sophisticated, wealthy black middle class that continues to shape the character of a city that for so long was a bastion of white power and control. Jozi may not be the most beautiful, but it is certainly the most happening city in sub-Saharan Africa, much beloved by those tapping into its energy, and pouncing on its opportunities—given a few days, you may feel the same.

Essentials

ARRIVING

BY PLANE Most flights to South Africa arrive at Johannesburg's international airport, known as **O.R. Tambo International Airport** (© 011/921-6911 or 011/390 3909; 086/727-7888 for flight time inquiries; www.acsa.co.za), Africa's busiest hub and now a world-class experience, with excellent restaurants and shops, and gleaming halls and slick finishes thanks to a R3-billion overhaul. Note that even if you have been checked through to another South African destination, you must pick up your luggage and clear Customs continuing to your connecting flight. The **Gauteng Tourism Authority** has a branch in the airport's International Arrivals hall (© 011/390-3614; daily 6am–10pm). Foreign exchange is available 24 hours and there are many credit card–friendly ATMs in the arrivals hall.

The **Gautrain,** South Africa's first-ever rapid rail system, links the airport to Sandton Station between 5:30am and 8:30pm; tickets cost R100 per person one-way and are easy to purchase with a credit card at machines located at the entrance (you will need to buy a R10 "gold card" here, onto which your ticket purchases are loaded; the card is valid for 3 years). The train runs every 12 minutes during peak periods; every 20 to 30 minutes when it's off-peak (such as weekends or the middle of the day; you can see the exact schedule online at www.gautrain.co.za; © 0800/428-87426). From here you can ask your hotel to arrange a pickup, or there will be taxis outside the station.

If you prefer the convenience of a door-to-door service from the airport (or your arrival falls outside Gautrain hours) you can prebook a taxi or shuttle for the 30- to 40-minute drive to the northern suburbs. Taxi lines queue up directly outside the exit, and drivers will approach you as you walk through Customs; however at the risk of sounding paranoid, I'd avoid getting into a vehicle with a total stranger. Either get your hotel or host to arrange the transfer, or prebook with a company so that you are met as soon as you clear Customs; if you'd like assistance withdrawing foreign currency from an ATM on arrival, you can also then ask the driver to show the way.

AIRPORT TRANSFERS/TRANSIT **Monane's Shuttle** (© 072/251-5156 or 083/770-5757; monashuttle@yahoo.com) is a small independent operation offering transfers to Sandton/Rosebank area for a standard R350 (every additional passenger R50). Alternatively, slick outfit **Ulysses** (© 082/233-3320; www.ulysses.co.za) offers reliable and efficient transfers to Sandton for R400 (R440 for two, R480 for three, and so on). For more comparative quotes contact the companies listed on www.johannesburgtransport.com/taxi.htm.

Crime used to form the mainstay of conversation among Jozi's both privileged and poor. Today this is no longer the case—though the fortresslike barricading of homes in the wealthier suburbs is a reminder that for some the easiest way to make it is to take it. Crime statistics show improvements, but visitors are strongly urged to keep on their toes. Carjackings are less common, but keep your car doors locked while traveling and windows up. Don't leave valuables in plain sight in the car, even when you're in it (travel with handbags and cameras in the trunk); this way you avoid a "smash and grab" incident. Generally speaking, be alert at traffic lights; pay attention to what's going on around you. Don't get suckered into stopping your vehicle for strangers; scams involving mock accidents and breakdowns are designed to lure unsuspecting Samaritans. If you sense a potential threat, keep in mind that crossing against a red light—carefully, of course—is allowed.

Generally speaking, inconspicuous consumption is the order of the day: People who have nothing worth stealing are less likely to attract criminals. Don't carry or wear anything of obvious value (though some say it's worth carrying a small sum of cash to satisfy a demand), and try not to look completely lost. Soweto is poorly signposted and it's not a great idea to get lost here, so for now it's still a good idea to explore it with a guide. Hillbrow, Berea, and Yeoville remain no-go areas unless you're accompanied by a guide who is totally familiar with the area and prepared to walk tall. If you are ever mugged, don't protest—hand over the goods or money and walk away.

If this sort of talk makes you nervous, remember that if you booked one of the lodging options recommended below—situated in Jo'burg's safest areas—your chances of becoming a victim of crime are minimal.

Note that if you are merely in transit but wish to see the Apartheid Museum (or visit any other Jo'burg attraction) you can hire the services of a driver/guide from **Wilro Tours** for a 3-, 5-, 7-, 9- or even 12-hour "Go As You Please" tour (www.wilro tours.co.za; ✆ **011/789-9688**). This means you set the pace and the itinerary (they also make suggestions if required). A pickup from the airport to view the Apartheid Museum and delivery back to the airport takes about 5 hours—it costs around R2,000 for one person; R2,135 for two persons; R2,200 for three persons, and so on.

BY TRAIN   If you have to recover from jet lag (or simply have a penchant for being rocked to sleep), I can think of nothing better than trundling to Cape Town by train, particularly on the legendary **Blue Train** ★★ or the even more luxurious **Rovos Rail** ★★★. Alternatively, you may choose to return to Jo'burg this way. Both roll in to **Tshwane** (Pretoria, equidistant from the airport with Jo'burg) from Cape Town (taking around 28 hr.). Rovos also operates other luxury trips throughout the country and as far afield as Dar es Salaam; see "Getting Around" in chapter 13. If you like the romance of rail but find the Rovos and Blue train too steep, look into booking a **Premier Classe** compartment, traveling between Johannesburg and Cape Town and Durban respectively. These budget deluxe trains are operated by **Shozoloza Meyl,** South Africa's main-line passenger services, and offer single-berth compartments, two-berth passenger compartment, and four-berth family compartments (✆ **087/802-6674;** www.premier-classe.co.za; R1,010–R2,210 per person one-way depending on route and date). **Warning:** Because Johannesburg's **Park Station** is a major center for people arriving from all over Africa, the consequent rich pickings for criminals have made it a hot area, so watch your belongings when you arrive, and prebook a transfer to your host/hotel (see "By Plane," above).

BY CAR   Traveling by car in Johannesburg can be nerve-wracking, but armed with a good map not impossible once you have grasped the location of a few main arteries connecting all the major areas of interest. In fact it will liberate you to fully experience the city. However, if you're here for just a few days it is probably advisable to choose accommodation that has restaurants and shops within walking distance (most of our recommendations do), and/or use taxis for the duration of your stay.

VISITOR INFORMATION

Visit www.joburgtourism.com or call © **011/214-0700** for Jo'burg specific information or queries. Another useful website, with up-to-date information on Jo'burg's museums and galleries, is www.joburg.org.za. The **Gauteng Tourism Authority,** covering both Jo'burg and Tshwane, has its **head office** opposite the Market Theatre in Newtown (1 Central Place, corner of Jeppe and Henry Nxumalo sts.); alternatively, to find the nearest office to you, visit www.gauteng.net or call © **0860/428-8364.**

Getting Around

BY CAR   Aside from the **Gautrain,** public transport remains sketchy and, after hours, nonexistent. Getting around Johannesburg is best done by car, but driving is not recommended for the fainthearted: Jo'burg drivers are notoriously impatient, and you will need a map and an innate sense of direction. If you're comfortable with driving, all the major car-rental companies are represented here. You can rent a chauffeured vehicle with Wilro Tours by booking one of its 3- to 12-hour **"Go As You Please" tours,** where you set the pace and itinerary (www.wilrotour.co.za; see "Airport Transfer/Transit"), or give Oupa a call (see below).

BY TAXI   Taxis generally don't cruise the streets (though they do hang around stations and hotels), but you'll probably have to call rather than flag one. **Rose Radio Taxi** is one of the longest-running outfits, a one-stop call center that represents more than 200 owner-driven vehicles of varying quality (charging R280–R350 from the airport to Rosebank and Sandton; © **011/403-9625** or 086/182-2942; www.rose taxis.com). One of the most delightful drivers in town is the genteel **Oupa** (pronounced *Oh*-pah, meaning "Grandpa"); call him directly at © **074/112-3944** or 082/680-5910 to check his availability and rates for any transfer or even full day. Or try **Maxi Taxi** (© **011/648-1212**). In Tshwane, call **Rixi Mini Cabs** (© **012/325-8072**) or **SA Taxi** (© **012/320-2075**). Charges are around R11 per kilometer.

Guided Tours

Apartheid Museum & Soweto Tours ★★★   The most popular tour in Johannesburg is a trip around Soweto, discussed in more detail later in this chapter (see box on p. 296), and the best attraction is the Apartheid Museum: en route to Soweto, this is an easy enough add on (though not many operators offer this). Soweto is a fascinating place, home to some of the most momentous turning points of recent South African history, but to truly understand the miracle of South Africa you need to spend around 3 hours at the Apartheid Museum before moving on to see some of the actual sites where history played out. Wilro Tours offers scheduled tours incorporating both destinations (as well as Jhb/Constitution Hill) or you can book one of its

"Go As You Please" tours, where you set the pace and itinerary—choose between 3, 5, 7, 9, and 12 hours (www.wilrotours.co.za)—pickup and drop-off can be direct from the airport or your hotel. Five hours will cost one person around R2,000; add around R100 for every additional person.

Cradle of Humankind Tours ★★ 🏛 **Palaeo-Tours** (✆ 011/726-8788; www.palaeotours.com; by arrangement only) offers fascinating trips to some of the key sites in what has become known as the Cradle of Humankind, declared a World Heritage Site in 1999 for the significant paleoanthropological discoveries made in the area since 1966. The Cradle, home to human ancestors who lived here some 3 million years ago, made headlines in 2003 when a new dating technique (called burial cosmogenic dating) revealed that the Little Foot skeleton, found in 1997, is 4.1 million years old—one of the oldest in the world. You can visit the **Maropeng Visitor Center ★★★**, touring its 2,500 sq. m (26,910 sq. ft.) of exhibits (with an underground boat ride; great for kids) on your own very successfully. But with Palaeo-Tours you will have a guide who is a paleoanthropology scientist or Ph.D. student who not only explains the history of evolution but takes you to working excavation sites in the Cradle. Tours cover the history of archaeology, as well as some of the philosophical aspects of the appearance of humans. The area is about an hour's drive from the city, and both half- and full-day tours include a short game drive en route at the Rhino and Lion Park. Foodies should reserve a table at **Roots ★★★**, one of the best restaurants in Gauteng, located at the stylish **Forum Homini Hotel ★★** (✆ 011/668-7000; www.forumhomini.co.za).

Art Tour ★★ Chavi Caplan's **Afrocentric Tours** (✆ 082/969-3938; www.afrocentricsa.co.za) helps introduce visitors to the city's vibrant art and design. She'll pick you up from your hotel at around 9am and take you to four galleries in Rosebank's Art District before hopping over to Milpark's charming mixed-use development, **44 Stanley** (see "Shopping," later in this chapter). Lunch is at **Arts on Main ★★★** in downtown Johannesburg, where Kentridge and other artists and galleries have studios. Persuade her to lengthen the tour to show you some of the public art that is dotted around the city, and possibly a trip to the Standard Bank gallery in Braamfontein. Tours run first and last Saturday of every month (around R300 per day); private tours by arrangement.

[FastFACTS] JOHANNESBURG & TSHWANE

Airport See "Arriving," earlier in this chapter.

American Express The most convenient office is in Rosebank on the ground floor at The Zone (✆ 011/880-8382). Hours are Monday to Friday from 8:30am to 5pm and Saturday from 9am to 1pm. There is also an office in Sandton City shopping center, upper level (✆ 011/883-9009). For lost or stolen cards, refer to the help number on the back of the card or call ✆ 086/032-1555 and follow the voice prompts. **Lost Visa or MasterCard** (✆ 080/032-1222).

Area Code Johannesburg's area code is **011**. Tshwane's code is **012**.

Remember to add 27 and drop the 0 if you are using your cellphone from home; thus, to call the airport you would dial + 27 11 921 6911, but if you have a local SIM card or using a local landline you would dial 011 921 6911.

Climate Days are usually sunny, with averages of 70°F (20°C). Even winter days are generally mild (May–Aug), though frost often occurs at night, so make sure you have warm layers to peel off as the temperature rises during the day. Be warned that summer is typified by afternoon thunderstorms; your host/hotel should be able to provide you with an umbrella.

Drugstores Drugstores are known as chemists or pharmacies in South Africa. Ask your host or concierge for the closest pharmacy. Hospital drugstores tend to keep the longest hours; if you're in Rosebank, visit the pharmacy in the **Netcare Rosebank Hospital** (✆ 011/328-0500). To find the nearest Netcare hospital pharmacy to you contact its call center at ✆ 0860/638-2273.

Embassies & Consulates Note that almost all embassies are located in Tshwane (http://embassy.goabroad.com/embassies-in/south-africa): **Australia,** 292 Orient St., Arcadia (✆ 012/423-6000); www.southafrica.embassy.gov.au; **Canada,** 1103 Arcadia St., Hatfield (✆ 012/422-3000; www.pretoria.gc.ca); **Ireland,** Tulbagh Park, 1234 Church St., Colbyn (✆ 012/342-5062; www.embassyireland.org.za); **United Kingdom,** 255 Hill St., Arcadia (✆ 012/421-7500; www.britain.org.za); **United States,** 877 Pretorius St., Arcadia (✆ 012/431-4000; southafrica.usembassy.gov); **Zambia,** 1159 Ziervogel St., Arcadia (✆ 012/326-1847/54; www.zambiapretoria.net); **Zimbabwe,** 798 Merton St., Arcadia (✆ 012/342-5125).

Emergencies Dial ✆ 10111 for flying-squad police. Dial ✆ 999 for an ambulance, or perhaps more reliably, ✆ 082-911 for emergency medical assistance. Call ✆ 011/3755-911 for the City of Johannesburg's Emergency Connect line, 24-hour emergency services relating to all life-threatening situations, including ambulances, fire engines, and metro police. For tourism-related inquiries dial ✆ 087/803-4636.

Hospitals Find the closest **Netcare Hospital,** South Africa's biggest private hospital group, with 31 in Gauteng alone. The staff, medical practitioners, trauma unit, and equipment at these hospitals are equal to the best in the world. If you're in Rosebank, contact **Netcare Rosebank Hospital** (✆ 011/328-0500); to find a particular specialist or the nearest hospital, call ✆ 0860/638-2273 or visit www.netcare.com. If you want a doctor to visit you in your hotel room, ask your host or concierge to contact **Doctors on Call.**

Post Office Post office service is generally poor; ask your hotel or guesthouse to deal with any postal items. To post large items, contact FedEx (✆ 011/923-8000) or DHL (✆ 0860/345-000).

Where to Stay

Given that you don't want to be catching a taxi every time you want to move, we have focused our accommodation recommendations on options that are either connected to malls or walking distance from a few restaurants and shops, with the exception of a few that are just brilliant value—a saving that even a large number of cab trips won't dent!

Essentially the best options sprawl along a south-north axis of suburbs connected by **Jan Smuts Avenue.** We start with **Westcliff** and **Parktown,** two of the city's oldest suburbs, with gracious turn-of-the-20th-century homes and gleaming new corporate HQs on large greened plots, and a few minutes from **Braamfontein** and the old city center. Westcliff and Parktown blend into **Saxonwold** and **Parkwood,** similarly sought after but predominantly residential suburbs providing easy access to neighboring **Rosebank** and its chi-chi malls and burgeoning art district, as well as **Parkhurst** (great for dining) to the east. The brand-new **Melrose Arch** with its cafe-style streets lies a short hop west of Rosebank; the sophisticated shops and restaurants of **Hyde**

Park mall and neighboring suburb of **Craighall Park** lie a few minutes north of Rosebank. In essence these are all minutes by car from each other, but in terms of having shopping and restaurants within walking distance of your accommodations, we have clustered them as follows: Westcliff & Surrounds; Rosebank & Surrounds: Hyde Park & Surrounds and Melrose Arch & Surrounds.

Beyond this city keeps sprawling in an almost seamless development northward to Pretoria, but these suburbs (Bryanston, Fourways, and so on) are not usually of interest or are too far from tourist draws to interest your average short-hop leisure traveler.

Tips: Don't delay making arrangements for the Johannesburg leg of your trip. While it is not a popular leisure destination, business demands are huge, and at certain times of the year rooms book out fast. Note that most hotel rates fluctuate daily depending on how full they are; rates are usually best on weekend nights, so it may be worth timing your stay for a Friday and Saturday. Recent years have seen a burgeoning guesthouse sector in Jo'burg, offering well-equipped rooms, often leading onto lovely gardens, with hands-on hosts to help you navigate the city—at much better rates than hotels. We would far rather bed down in one of these than in a bland cookie-cutter room in a large hotel with impersonal service, so we have increased the recommendations in this sector.

Note that there are some interesting new inner city options—part of the new-generation interest in the beating heart of the "real" city. Once abandoned to slum-lords, the old city center and adjoining Newtown and Braamfontein are enjoying a reemergence as the young and hip—bored with bland suburban streets with their high walls and hidden lives—are moving in with attitude, injecting the old city with creative energy. If you're adventurous and want to get under the skin of where the city is going, you'll stay at Life on Main's **12 Decades Art Hotel** (www.mainstreetlife. co.za/art-hotel), a hip budget efficiency hotel where various young artists were each given a room to "decorate" with a set decade in order to trace the city's history. It's a few steps from Arts on Main, with a couple of dining options to choose from, but it's a pretty hard-core stripped-down choice.

WESTCLIFF & SURROUNDS

If you're looking for a quieter, more mature, "old money" environment, you'd do well to locate yourself in these well-established, leafy suburbs that offer a great respite from the concrete that typifies much of Jo'burg. This is also where you'll find the best leisure hotel in the city and a great value guesthouse, both reviewed below.

Best For: Great central location—majority of tourist draws lie a few minutes south (Constitution Hill and Court; Market Theatre; Civic Theatre; Arts on Main; Origins Museum); a few minutes north lies glitzy Rosebank.

Drawbacks: Not walking distance to shops and restaurants. (The Westcliff offers a complimentary shuttle to malls.)

Recommended Restaurants Within Walking Distance (Daytime): Franco's (54 Tyrone Ave.; ℂ **011/646-5449;** www.francoforleo.co.za) is an unpretentious family-run, family-friendly trattoria, with standard Italian menu. It has a great atmosphere, and it is very popular with locals; tables are a little too close together. See Moyo review below—the Zoo Lake branch is a short drive away.

Expensive

The Westcliff ★★★ 📷 ✨ In a city built for business, this is a welcome relief and by far our favorite Johannesburg hotel: a pink "village" clinging to the steep incline of Westcliff ridge (you park at reception and are shuttled up along winding cobbled lanes) with all you expect from an Orient Express hotel. Hanging on the lip of the large infinity pool, the green suburbs of northern Johannesburg are spread out before you; as dusk approaches, the sky turns pink over the endless forested canopy; with luck elephants from the zoo lumber into view below. Surreal and simply splendid. Each room and suite is uniquely positioned (insist on a room with a view) and sized, but understated elegance is the order of the day, and the marble bathrooms are a real treat. Best breakfast in town.

67 Jan Smuts Ave., Westcliff 2193. www.westcliff.co.za ℂ **800/237-1236** in the U.S., or 011/481-6000. Fax 011/646-3500. 115 units. Best available rate fluctuates btw. R1,900–R3,830 for Luxury Room; R2,970–R4,900 Junior Suites; R4,870–R17,300 for Studio/Luxury/Presidential Suites. Add R220 per person for breakfast. Children 12–18 pay 50%. AE, DC, MC, V. **Amenities:** 2 restaurants; lounge-bar; airport transfers; complimentary scheduled shuttle service to Rosebank, Hyde Park, and Sandton malls; babysitting; golf club privileges; DVD library; gym; swimming pools; room service; excellent spa; tennis court. *In room:* A/C, TV/DVD, hair dryer, minibar, Wi-Fi (complimentary) and ADSL.

Moderate

93 on Jan Smuts ★★★ 🎁 Central, and yet tucked away in attractive gardens, this revamped 1929 mansion is genuine grand "Old Money" Saxonwold, offering plush suites (enormous), and personal service. Aside from the resident chef who prepares exquisite meals at times that work for you, Karen, the owner, has personally inspected the city's museums, galleries, shopping, and offbeat experiences. Despite proximity to the main arterial road through suburban Johannesburg (and easy access to most of the metropolis), this is a hushed, soothing environment—ideal if you need to cool off after a day of negotiations, or after a long flight. With hosts who have applied their own extensive travel experience, every imaginable need has been thought of.

93 Jan Smuts Ave., Saxonwold. ℂ **011/646-5016.** Fax 086/681-6797. 5 units. R3,000 double. Rates include breakfast. AE, DC, MC, V. **Amenities:** Dining room; bar service; lounge; library; pool. *In room:* A/C, TV/DVD, hair dryer, heated towel rack, minibar, MP3 docking station, underfloor heating, free Wi-Fi.

ROSEBANK & SURROUNDS

Rosebank is the fastest growing commercial precinct in Johannesburg, and combines interconnecting indoor malls with outdoor areas that allow for a more cafe-style shopping experience than Sandton. With leafy Parkwood and Saxonwold neighboring it, Rosebank also has a more residential feel than the concrete high-rises of business-orientated Sandton.

Best For: A wide variety of shopping experiences as well as accommodation options, from hotels to beautiful boutique guesthouses and the most popular B&B in the city. Gautrain Station (a modern multi-level station that opened in 2010) makes airport transfers a pleasure. This will also mean direct pedestrian access between Sandton and Rosebank malls.

Drawback: It may be the preferred mall area, but that doesn't mean it's beautiful.

Recommended Neighborhood Restaurants: The selection in the new Firs extension/Hyatt Piazza is excellent: There's fashionable **Koi** for sushi and dim sum, **Kuzina** (www.kuzina.co.za) for authentic Greek fare, and **Doppio Zero,** a very successful chain serving Mediterranean-inspired dishes (including thin-based pizzas). In The Firs proper there's **The Grillhouse,** Rosebank's stalwart steakhouse, with black leather banquette seating, plenty of dark timber and brickwork, and lots of meat cuts (not suitable for vegetarians). Neighboring this is **Katzy's,** Rosebank's live blues and jazz venue (visit www.katzys.co.za to see who's playing when you're in town). Note that The Grillhouse offers a complimentary shuttle that will pick you up from guesthouses in the neighborhood. **Cranks** (Rosebank Mall, off Cradock Ave.) is recommended for a fun evening out if you feel like Thai or Vietnamese in an offbeat atmosphere where hands-on chef-owner Eric Sangschloury produces reasonably authentic dishes for the loyal locals who have followed him here from Melville.

Very Expensive

The Hyatt Regency ★★★
A good bet if you want to be in Rosebank's most happening hotel, walking distance great restaurants and shops—all in a fairly secure environment. Having enjoyed an ambivalent reception on opening about a decade ago (the hotel has a pretty hideous facade), we found that the Hyatt has done much to redeem itself. It hosts cool local acts in the bar, a sexy restaurant and spa, Sunday braai (barbecue) on the terrace, and the recent development of the very successful Hyatt Piazza, the adjacent restaurant-lined square that leads seamlessly to The Firs (one of the interlinked Rosebank malls). These prescient moves have elevated it into pole position as the best five-star hotel in Rosebank, popular with local captains of industry. Rooms are classic plush business quality. (If you like the sound of this but are watching your budget, see neighbor Holiday Inn review below.)

191 Oxford Rd., Rosebank, 2196. www.johannesburg.regency.hyatt.com. ✆ **011/280-1234.** Fax 011/280 1238. 244 units. Best available rate fluctuates. R2,850–R6,800 double; R3,200–R7,000 club room (private-access top floors); R6,000–R30,000 suite. AE, DC, MC, V. Amenities: Restaurant; lounge; bar; butler (club and suites); airport transfers (R595); gym; limousine service; pool; room service; spa. In room: A/C, TV, hair dryer, iPod docking station, minibar, free Wi-Fi.

Expensive

Clico Guest House ★★
Located in Rosebank's residential quarter, yet within walking distance of the mall (daytime only; a taxi at night is advisable), this intimate guesthouse is a great destination for foodies (just remember to book for dinner in advance). Owner-chef Sean does not offer a standard menu but cooks according to available produce, current inspiration, and your particular dietary requirements; even strict vegans leave his table happy. From the well-stocked honesty bar to the friendly staff, the atmosphere is very relaxed; it's a discreet, cozy place with attention to detail that includes good quality filter coffee and fresh milk in your room, quiet minibar, and a private outside area leading from every room.

27 Sturdee Ave., Rosebank. www.clicoguesthouse.com. ✆ **011/252-3300.** Fax 086/636-8770. 7 units R1,975 double. Rates include breakfast. AE, DC, MC, V. **Amenities:** Dining room; lounge with honor bar; airport transfers (R350; R110 to Gautrain); pool. In room: A/C, TV, DVD/VCR player, hair dryer, minibar, stereo, free Wi-Fi.

The Parkwood ★★★
This boutique-style guesthouse is one of our favorite places to stay in the city, offering large, luxurious rooms (more stylish than most five-star hotels), the personal touch of hands-on owner Sarah Shonfeld, and a super location: a 10-minute walk to or from Rosebank's shopping district (again, best done by day). With a natural eye, Sarah has created a great integration of indoor and outdoor spaces, marrying natural materials with luxurious fabrics to create a soothing stylish retreat. It's clearly a recipe for success: The place has doubled in size, without losing its original character. There are two skinny lap pools, and plenty of outdoor nooks to unwind in. Unlike The Peech or Clico, The Parkwood has no in-house restaurant, but the Grillhouse offers a complimentary shuttle.

72 Worcester Rd., Parkwood. www.theparkwood.com. ✆ **011/880-1748** or 082/442-7605. Fax 011/788-7896. 16 units. R1,700 standard double; R1,900 luxury double; R2,050 executive double. Rates include

breakfast. AE, DC, MC, V. **Amenities:** Dining room; lounge; airport transfers (R310); doctor on call; gym; library; pool; refreshment station. *In room:* A/C, TV, DVD/VCR, hair dryer, minibar, stereo, underfloor heating, Wi-Fi (free).

Moderate

Holiday Inn Rosebank ★★ ☺ 🍴   Given that it enjoys the exact same location as the Hyatt Regency—it also offers direct access to Rosebank's connected malls (both The Firs and The Zone)—and is brand-spanking new, this is a great deal, especially on weekends. Long associated—in this country at least—with nasty budget amenities, naff decor, tiny rooms, and even tinier bathrooms, the Holiday Inn's Rose-bank hotel (opened 2010) is clearly trying to break the mold with public spaces that could even be described as glamorous (velvet chairs; glass-walled waterfall; interest-ing wallpaper choices). Rooms (some connected) are bland but offer all the comforts. Ask for a room with shower only unless you don't mind showering in the bathtub. Note Wi-fi charges are ridiculously high.

The Zone Oxford Road, Rosebank, 2196. www.holidayinn.com ✆ **080/099-9136** or 011/218-6000. Fax 011/218-6001. 244 units. Best available rate fluctuates btw. R1,400–R1,600 Mon–Thurs; R1,050 Fri–Sun queen/twin. R1,800–R2000 Mon–Thurs and R1,550 Fri–Sun king. R2,500 Mon–Thurs; R1950 Fri–Sun king deluxe. AE, DC, MC, V. **Amenities:** Restaurant; bar; babysitting; airport transfers; fitness center; pool; room service. *In room:* A/C, TV, hair dryer, iPod docking station, minibar, Wi-Fi (R1 per minute).

Inexpensive

Cotswold Gardens ★ 🍴   A home from home, ideal for anyone who feels intimi-dated by the idea of Jo'burg, and wants discreet but caring hosts to guide them. Guests (many repeat) love the cosseted atmosphere, where hands-on owners Janine and Mike look after you like a long-lost relative, providing comfortable en-suite rooms (two with kitchenettes; all with views of the lovely garden), and spoiling them with the kind of personal attention you just won't get in a hotel. You'll feel safe and pro-tected, and their advice—what to do, where to eat, how to get there—is based on an intuitive understanding of you, combined with faultless knowledge of their city. It's walking distance from Rosebank mall (daylight), but Janine will help arrange any transfers or tours. (The Grillhouse also offers comp transfers from here.) Breakfasts are excellent.

46 Cotswold Dr., Saxonwold 2196. www.cotswoldgardens.co.za. ✆ **011/442-7553** or 082/829-3336. Fax 011/880-6285. 6 units. R900–R1,100 double B&B (rates depend on size). No children under 14. AE, DC, MC, V. **Amenities:** Breakfast room; personal concierge-style service; pool. *In room:* TV, undercarpet heating, hair dryer, complimentary Wi-Fi.

Ilali ★★ 🍴   Hidden behind an anonymous, secretive wall, this guesthouse is a genuine respite; put together in the manner of boutique or gallery, it showcases owner Hannia Weber's passion for detail. She's renovated a garden-shaded 1950s home, and filled it with local art and design as well as quality linens, mattresses, and ultra-luxu-rious bathrooms. She's well connected and can put you on to anything, from the best yoga studios to good local theater and the best art dealers and nearby restaurants. Although officially in Parktown North, with all its lovely eateries, it's a mere 15-min-ute walk to Rosebank's shops and restaurants, and the Gautrain station, too.

19 Chester Rd., at 3rd Ave., Parktown North. www.ilaligh.co.za. ✆ **082/567-5142.** 5 units. R800–R950 double. Rates include breakfast. MC, V. **Amenities:** Dining room; lounge. *In room:* TV, free Wi-Fi.

MELROSE ARCH & SURROUNDS

Melrose Arch and Melrose are near to Rosebank, so a reasonably central choice.
Best For: Nervous travelers. Gated Melrose Arch offers super secure environment, with controlled access, 24-hour closed-circuit TV, security guards, and a host of

cafe-style restaurants around two "piazzas". It's pretty at night when the fairy lights that festoon the trees cast a festive atmosphere over everything.

Drawback: By day it's a bit like a set from some weird reality TV show—with its pastiche design, clinically neat semi-pedestrianized streets, and shiny new traffic lights.

Recommended Neighborhood Restaurants: Orient is a highly rated restaurant serving Asian meals in a stylish setting on the square (see review under "Dining," below). Opposite is **JB's Corner** (*©* **011/684-2999**), serving cheap and cheerful pub-style grub and drinks to the locals who populate the outdoor tables all day long, while neighboring **Moyo's,** serving African cuisine, is more upmarket (see review). Don't miss the sidewalk cafes on the nearby piazza, around the corner from the square.

Very Expensive

Melrose Arch ★ Self-proclaimed "hip hotel," with outsize decor items that recall the stagelike sets of the Schrager-Starcke age (only with less panache), Melrose Arch is useful for an overnighter if you want the anonymity of a hotel combined with the safety of the outdoor cafe style that typifies the controlled access Melrose Arch development. The quirky decor could grate the truly style conscious (nasty illustrations in large gilt frames are particularly offensive), but we definitely like the selection of DVDs that come (already categorized by theme) with every room (make sure you book a pool view). Public spaces are fun and classier than the rooms (great pool area), and good for people-watching. Service is patchy.

1 Melrose Sq., Melrose Arch, Johannesburg 2196. www.africanpridehotels.com/melrosearchhotel. *©* **011/214-6666.** Fax 011/214-6600. 118 units. Standard room R2,275–R3,970 double; price fluctuates depending on availability. Superior room costs R300 more; executive room costs R500 more. AE, DC, MC, V. **Amenities:** Restaurant; bar; airport transfers (R490); DVD library; gym access; library; pool; room service; surround sound music and TV room. *In room:* A/C, TV/DVD, hair dryer, minibar, free Wi-Fi.

Expensive

The Peech Hotel ★★ A clever conversion of a beautiful old home, with the accommodation set in double story blocks in a tree-filled garden, this fab little hotel offers all the pleasures of staying in an independent (personally managed by the charming James Peech) along with the kind of services/facilities you expect from a big corporate. Aside from this, they take responsible tourism seriously (the latest recycling methods; solar-powered fountains; Bokashi composting; Fairtrade in Tourism accreditation). Rooms are lovely, each with small private garden terrace or balcony, and feature large bathrooms (and the softest linen); rooms in the original house are personal favorites. The bistro, spilling out onto the garden terrace, is another highlight—a good thing, as it's a bit too far to walk to Melrose Arch restaurants.

61 North St., Melrose. www.thepeech.co.za. *©* **011/537-9797.** Fax 011/537-9798. 16 units. R1,200–R2,500 double, depending on best available rate. Rate includes breakfast. AE, DC, MC, V. **Amenities:** Restaurant; bar; airport transfers (R465); discounted gym access; library; pool. *In room:* TV, hair dryer, iPod station, free Wi-Fi.

Fire & Ice ★ Another brand-new hotel that opened for the World Cup, and not bad to look at if you like a bit of theatrical decor. It's just around the corner from Melrose Arch Hotel (within the gated development, offering the sense of security that Melrose Arch does), but is pitched at the slightly less affluent corporate client. It sometimes has rooms at half the price of Melrose Arch—do check both online though, as prices fluctuate. Personally I'd rather be at The Peech, but then you need a car or a cab.

Whitely St., Melrose Arch. www.proteahotels.com. © **011/218-4000.** Fax 011/218 4001. 197 units. R1,500–R2400 double. Rates do not always include breakfast; if not head out to JBs. AE, DC, MC, V. **Amenities:** Restaurant; bar; airport transfers (R410); pool. *In room:* TV, hair dryer, Wi-Fi (limited complimentary).

HYDE PARK & SURROUNDS

North of Rosebank is Hyde Park and adjoining Craighall Park, which has a number of good-value guesthouses, the best of which we've reviewed below.

Best For: Hyde Park is much smaller than either Sandton or Rosebank, making it easier to navigate, with classy boutiques, and an elegant array of restaurants.

Drawbacks: Unless you stay at the Southern Sun you'll need to rent a car or use taxis to get around.

Recommended Neighborhood Restaurants: Craighall Park guesthouses are not within walking distance from the mall but **Corner Café** (Corner Buckingham and Rothesay aves.; © **011/880-2244**) is the local hangout, and serves very good food. Restaurants in the mall worth checking out are **Santorini** for Greek fare, **Willoughby's** for sushi, and **Life** (© **011/325-4350**) for delicious light meals and pizzas.

Moderate

Southern Sun Hyde Park ★ 🗡 Incredible as it sounds, one of the best things to do in this new hotel is watch the traffic as it edges slowly north after closing bell on weekdays. You could also, of course, join the local suits for after-work drinks—the pool-bar terrace area is a very sociable gathering spot, with more views toward the far-northern suburbs and a tangle of busy roads. Or, this being a city of mall rats, there's direct access (take the elevator or stairs, and follow signs) into the chichi Hyde Park shopping center onto which the hotel is grafted—cinemas, shops, a great bookstore, and a surfeit of restaurants await (although the best place to eat is the in-house Italian). Existing primarily with businessfolk in mind, the hotel offers best value over weekends. Bedrooms, otherwise, are standard-issue and rather boxy.

1st Rd, Hyde Park. www.southernsun.com. © **011/461-9744.** 132 units. R1,100–R1,530 standard double, R1,195–R1,640 superior, R1,961 deluxe, R2,332 executive, R3,700 suite. AE, DC, MC, V. **Amenities:** 2 restaurants (including **Bice**); bar; lounge; room service. *In room:* A/C, TV/DVD, hair dryer, minibar, MP3 docking station, Wi-Fi (R1 per minute; R80 per day).

Liz@Lancaster ★ 🗡 Located a short driving distance from Hyde Park mall (10 min. to Rosebank malls), this combines exceptional value with hands-on personal attention and great amenities. Liz offers the most comprehensive in-room information we've ever seen—beyond what to do and where to eat, her attention to detail is extreme: she even tunes the radios in every room to a preselected stations, leaving an explanation of what and who the stations appeal to. She also has an in-house driver, which takes an enormous amount of stress out of transfers (R30 to Parkhurst restaurants; R45 to Rosebank). Most rooms include a fully equipped kitchenette and dining table, enclosed private courtyard, along with every possible other amenity. Corner Café is 2 blocks away.

79 Lancaster Ave, Craighall Park. www.lizatlancaster.co.za. © **083/229-4223** or 011/442-8083. 7 units. R700–R900 double. **Amenities:** Lounge/dining room; breakfast patio; airport transfers (R380); pool. *In room:* TV, DVD player, hair dryer, underfloor heating, Wi-Fi (complimentary).

SANDTON

It's a 15- to 20-minute drive north but you can see Sandton City's high-rise office blocks and towers from miles away. This is the brash new business heart of Jo'burg;

its gleaming Convention Centre a prime destination for business travelers, serviced by a string of five-star hotels within walking distance of each other.

Best For: The greatest concentration of retail outlets in the huge indoor underground mall (a bit of a rabbit warren); opposite is the mall around piazza-style Nelson Mandela Square. The Gautrain Station means you can now reach Sandton within minutes of clearing Customs, regardless of traffic. The two hotels below are 50m to 60m (164–197 ft.) from the station.

Drawbacks: A very built-up environment.

Recommended Neighborhood Restaurants: Bukhara is a good North Indian restaurant, while **WhangThai** is one of the best Thai restaurants in the city. Carnivores in search of well-aged steaks should head straight for **The Butcher Shop & Grill.** Don't miss sundowner drinks and tapas on the pool terrace of the **Sandton Sun** hotel—one of the rare al fresco spaces to relax in Sandton, offering reasonably elevated city views, and popular with locals.

Expensive

Da Vinci ★★★ 💼 If style is important, and you want to be in the heart of Sandton City, the boutique-style Da Vinci is unbeatable. A monochromatic palette (only black and white throughout) makes for possibly the prettiest hotel rooms in the country (unless, that is, your taste runs to frilly and floral). The opulence is as restrained as the palette—this is not the ridiculous oversized chairs and massive chandeliers that currently typify "designer," but a classy, cool retreat from an otherwise brash, brassy city. Attention to detail is subtle but sustained: Every artwork (black and white of course) is an original. Sandton City—both the Mall (directly opposite) and the Nelson Mandela Square Mall (direct extension)—are at your feet, with a plethora of restaurant choices and labyrinthine shopping. Staff is warm, welcoming, attentive.

2 Maude St., Sandton. www.davinci.legacyhotels.co.za. © **011/292 7000.** 221 units. R3190 (10% off for online booking). R3430–R3720 deluxe double; R3,800 executive; R4,950 1-bedroom suite; R7,210 2-bedroom suite; R21,390 presidential. Rates include continental breakfast. AE, DC, MC, V. **Amenities:** Restaurant; bar; airport transfers (R500); chauffeur service; gym; pool; room service; spa. *In room:* TV, hair dryer, minibar, Wi-Fi (free).

Moderate

Garden Court 🏷 ☺ This large hotel combines a good Sandton City location—adjacent to the Convention Centre and a short stroll from the malls—with great value. Rooms are small and old-fashioned (tiny bathrooms; shower over bathtub) but clean; the public spaces are easy on the eye. Larger rooms are furnished with two double beds, ideal for families that don't mind sharing a bathroom, and a steal at R1,300. The hotel is popular, so book early and don't expect superfast service at the ever-busy reception.

Corner West and Maude St., Sandton 2010. www.southernsun.com. © **011/269-7000.** Fax 011/269 7100. 444 units. R900–R1,300 double. Rates include breakfast. AE, DC, MC, V. **Amenities:** Restaurant; bar; airport transfers (R350-400); pool; room service. *In room:* A/C, TV, hair dryer.

Where to Eat

Johannesburg offers a thoroughly eclectic mix of dining possibilities: Just about every national cuisine is represented, so if you have a particular craving, simply ask your concierge or host to point you in the right direction, or opt for one of the restaurants within walking distance that we've highlighted in "Where to Stay" (above).

However, if you want a truly special dining experience, grab a cab to DW Eleven-13 Restaurant or Cube (both reviewed below). The latter is located in one of the city's two best dining districts: **Parktown North** and the adjoining **Parkhurst** (both in easy striking distance from Rosebank, Melrose Arch, Hyde Park, and environs); DW Eleven-13 is just north of Parkhurst.

Locals who prefer dining al fresco to artificially lit malls flock to buzzing **4th Avenue Strip in Parkhurst ★★★**, not only for its great selection of sidewalk restaurants and coffee shops, but also for its specialty stores—mostly in decor collectables and antiques. Restaurants on 4th Avenue that we highly recommend are **The Attic ★** (✆ 011/880-6102; 24 4th Ave.), owner managed by Tom Hughes and featuring a menu of Asian and French-inspired cuisine enjoyed by its predominantly trendy following. **Bistro Vine ★★** (✆ 011/327-4558; Shop 24E, 4th Ave.), a French-style bistro owner-managed by Daniel Vine, is recommended for its consistency—of both service and food. Across the Avenue is trendy **Espresso,** more often than not the busiest bit of pavement, but not necessarily filled with people who care about the quality of their food. If you are a coffee aficionado, rather head to tiny, cozy **4th Avenue Coffee Roasters ★**, 4th Ave., Parkhurst (✆ 011/447-4648), a great place for a pick-me-up shot of caffeine. **Nice on Fourth ★** is also recommended, this time for its warm, down-home atmosphere and light wholesome lunches.

Another good al fresco shopping-lunch combination is the *très* trendy **44 Stanley Avenue complex ★★★** (www.44stanley.co.za), headquarters of the burgeoning Milpark loft district that lies about 15 minutes south of Parkhurst. With a mix of some 20 to 30 carefully selected stores (see "Shopping—Flea Markets to High-End Crafts," below) in renovated industrial spaces, you're looking at a manageable afternoon or morning's browsing. Grab a sandwich at **Vovo Telo Bakery ★**, the city's first artisanal bakery (✆ 082/458-0352), or a coffee with a clear conscience from Bean There, serves freshly roasted, fair trade coffee sourced from all over Africa. The courtyard seating outside **Salvation Café ★★** (✆ 011/482-7795) is a good place to do lunch. Food is organic wherever possible, and meats are free-range and free of hormones; the wine list also boasts organic and biodynamic products. Open Tuesday to Sunday 8am to 4pm.

Last, for those who think that malls are for rats, head to nearby **Bamboo Centre ★**, in Melville (about 5 min. from 44 Stanley Ave.; corner of Rustenberg and 9th sts.). This is a tiny shopping complex centered around one of our favorite restaurants: **Service Station ★★** (✆ 011/726-1701; daily 8am–4:30pm). It's a totally unpretentious busy deli-style restaurant, where you help yourself to a buffet of great-looking salads, Mediterranean mezze, and delicious quiches, all paid for by weight (extremely good value); the ice creams, all home made, are to die for.

PARKHURST & PARKTOWN NORTH

Cube Tasting Kitchen ★★★ CUTTING EDGE   Award-winning chef Dario de Angeli is Jo'burg's celebrity chef, and true to form recently opened Cube to critical acclaim lauding it as "the most exciting thing to happen to the Johannesburg restaurant scene in years." This is by no means your usual night out: inspired by the molecular gastronomy practiced by the likes of Blumenthal and Adria, dinner starts promptly at 7, takes 4 hours, and consists of 14 to 20 courses. The menu changes every 6 weeks and has included everything from caramel-apple–foie gras popcorn to deconstructed nicoise salad. Talented Dario personally introduces every course—a culinary journey of foams and gelees set to radically alter the otherwise rather staid taste of Jo'burg diners. There are only 30 seats, so book.

Shop 5, 17 4th Ave., Parktown North. ✆ **082/422-8158.** Reservations essential. R450. AE, DC, MC, V. Tues–Sat 7pm–midnight.

DW Eleven-13 ★★★ INTERNATIONAL   The approach is mildly off-putting—another Jozi hot spot flanking a shopping center parking lot. But step inside and a buzzing atmosphere and service means you're quickly absorbed in melt-in-the-mouth quail, seared foie gras, deeply flavorsome artichoke soup, butternut risotto, super-tender steaks (aged rib-eye and chips, with a bone marrow sauce), and a strong desire to sip cocktails and high-caliber wines all night long. Considered one of the top 10 restaurants in South Africa (the only Jo'burg contender to make the cut), Chef Marthinus Ferreira (who trained under British culinary icon Heston Blumenthal) has created the kind of agreeable, high-end bistro fare that satisfies gourmands as well as creatures of habit looking for a relaxing place to return to day after day.

11–13 Dunkeld West shopping center, at Jan Smuts and Bompas sts., Dunkeld. 🕭 **011/341-0663.** www. dw11-13.co.za. Main courses R110–R145. AE, DC, MC, V. Tues–Sun noon–2:30pm; Tues–Sat 6:30pm–9:30pm.

La Cucina di Ciro ★★ 🏠 ITALIAN   Ciro Molinaro's three-star Michelin experience in France's Loire region simply rekindled his talent for home-cooked Italian fare, which he has been dishing up to his loyal patrons here for years. Ciro—the "Ciroprac-tor" ("Taste bud manipulation and stimulation," as the sign at the door reads)—is usually present, and a charming host. The menu changes regularly, depending on what's in season or looks good in the market, but the focus is fresh ingredients, with plenty of vegetarian options. A typical savory concoction is the sweet-potato-and-onion pancake topped with sautéed prawns with leeks and sherry. The restaurant style is rustic chic; in summer, be sure to book a table on the pavement and enjoy the balmy highveld temperatures.

43 47h Ave., Parktown North. 🕭 **011/442-51876.** www.lacucinadiciro.co.za. Reservations advisable. Main courses R60–R150. AE, DC, MC, V. Mon–Sat 9am–10pm.

MELROSE

Moyo ★★ ☺ MODERN PAN-AFRICAN   More than a restaurant, Moyo is an experience, particularly at night, when music, dance, and other entertainment are on the menus. Now with three branches in Jo'burg (the others are in Newtown and Zoo Lake), it's touristy but incredibly popular, even with locals. The Melrose Arch venue is spread over different levels with an African-themed decor that includes burning fires outside when it's cold, and couches to sprawl on pre- or postdinner. Most menu and buffet items including *tagines, potjies,* and bunny chow (choice of meat rolled into a brioche roll) are African, some reworked to suit a Western palate; food is interesting to the uninitiated but nothing that serious foodies will write home about. For lunch we particularly like the Zoo Lake venue, a lovely place to spend the afternoon with kids (there are often activities arranged for them), with a deck furnished with deep sofas overlooking the lake, and a veritable gallery of African artworks and artifacts. There's a second location at Zoo Lake Park, 1 Prince of Wales Dr., Parkview (🕭 **011/646-0058**).

The High St., Melrose Arch. 🕭 **011/684 1477.** www.moyo.co.za. Reservations recommended. Main courses R60–R155. AE, MC, V. Daily 11am–11pm.

Orient ★★ ASIAN   With its superslick interior, world-class dim sum, and security-conscious location, Orient is a popular choice for businessmen clinching deals in Melrose Arch. Among a wide-ranging Thai/Vietnamese/Japanese/Chinese menu that includes all the usual favorites (including satays; spring rolls; spicy soups; red, yellow, and green curries; and pad Thai), interesting alternatives abound—Hong Kong Pears, Chi Chee Gao, Bang Bang Duck (this latter particularly good), and Grilled Banana

Fish, to name a few. And if that's not enough to tempt you, they also make fairly good sushi.

The High St., Melrose Arch. ℰ **011/684-1616.** Reservations recommended. Main courses R44-168. AE, DC, MC, V. Daily noon–10:30pm.

SANDTON

Assaggi ★★★ 🍴 ITALIAN   You can smell the truffle oil as you enter this always hopping-full restaurant, and your mouth starts to water. Assaggi is also owner-chef-managed (always the best!) by Luciana Righi, who creates some of the best pasta dishes (all homemade) in the city, as well as a range of expertly cooked Italian veal dishes. Aside from the truffle pasta, don't miss the asparagus and Brie lasagna. Great service. The atmosphere—noisy, happy patrons everywhere you look—totally makes up for the unprepossessing location.

Post Office Centre, Rudd Road, Illovo. ℰ **011/268-1370.** Reservations essential. Main courses R60-R130. AE, DC, MC, V. Tues–Sat noon–2pm; Mon–Sat 6:30–9pm.

CITY CENTER

Gramadoelas ★★ SOUTH AFRICAN   For more than 40 years, Eduan Naude and Brian Shalkoff have fed royals, rock stars, presidents, and visitors from all over Africa in their marvelously cluttered restaurant in the Market theater in Newtown's Cultural Precinct. It's useful if you're going to see a show, and keen to try some S.A. classics like mopani worms (*masonja*); *umnqusho*, a mixture of braised beef shins, beans, and maize (said to be Mandela's favorite dish); traditional lamb stews or mild Cape Malay vegetarian, fish, and meat curries (babotie, the delicately spiced mince curry, is excellent). Although six king-size Mozambican prawns will dent your wallet (R190), most dishes are under R100, and there are regular buffets showcasing an array of African dishes.

Market Theatre Complex, Bree St., Newtown. ℰ **011/838-6960.** www.gramadoelas.co.za. Main courses R80–R190. Buffet R250. AE, DC, MC, V. Tues–Sat noon–3pm; Mon–Sat 6:30–11pm.

What to See & Do
THE TOP ATTRACTIONS

Apartheid Museum ★★★ 📷   Many visitors passing through this world-class museum find themselves emotionally unsettled by its meticulous and inspired chronicling of apartheid history. Your journey through the modernist concrete structure begins when you are given an entry pass labeling you as either white or nonwhite (and entering accordingly); you wander through galleries of massive identification cards emphasizing the dehumanizing aspect of racial profiling. A life-size photograph of an all-white race classification board greets you, as do newspaper reports about the board's ridiculous methods (such as sports preferences). It's an emotionally taxing start to a journey that grows in intensity as the history of South African racial segregation and resulting political turmoil is played out in vivid photographs, well-researched textual displays, and gut-wrenching, harrowing video footage. Besides paying tribute to the triumphs of black political leaders and white liberals who contributed to democracy, several installations and spaces evoke the dreadful horrors of apartheid rule, like the bleak hangman's nooses symbolizing the number of political prisoners executed during apartheid rule until as late as 1989. You can also lock yourself in one of three tiny solitary confinement cells that would have serviced prisoners facing lengthy periods of detention without trial. It's exhausting, but by far the most satisfying experience you'll have if you have any real interest in the history of this country, and its miraculous rebirth. Allow 3 hours.

Northern Pkwy. and Gold Reef Rd., Ormonde. 6km (3¾ miles) south of city center. ℂ **011/309-4700.** www.apartheidmuseum.org. Admission R50 adults, R35 children (not suitable for children under 11). R5 guided tour (book in advance). Tues–Sun 9am–5pm. Closed Easter Friday and Christmas Day.

Arts on Main ★★ Part of the much-anticipated revamp of the inner-city, this is a big mash-up of galleries and design/artist's studios (including William Kentridge) spread through various spaces in a converted (and expanding) industrial precinct. You can catch a cutting-edge experimental exhibition in one room, and cross over into another fitted with super-stylish photographs, or browse for pricey, gorgeous T-shirts. The court-yard cafe attracts Jo'burg's boho sort; great for a drink or cuppa tea—ask for directions to the nearby art house cinema where regular events and special screenings are held and there's another relaxed cafe-eatery where you can meet and mingle with a younger arty crowd. Don't miss the groovy **food market** held here every Sunday ★★★.

264 Fox St. www.artsonmain.co.za

Constitution Hill ★★ On a hill overlooking the inner city, this is Jo'burg's answer to Cape Town's popular Robben Island attraction, and is billed as a living tribute to the country's enshrined freedoms and human rights, housing South Africa's architec-turally provocative **Constitutional Court,** where you can view artworks or—in the spirit of transparency—even attend court hearings. Like Robben Island, this is the site of a prison—the notorious 19th-century **Old Fort,** commonly known as **Number Four,** where 100 years of South African history played out; both Nelson Mandela and Mahatma Gandhi were detained here, as well as some notorious criminals like Daisy de Melker. The guided tour includes Number Four, now home to an exhibition that attempts to unearth the notion of criminality. A work in progress, Constitution Hill centers on **Constitution Square,** a central piazza, where you'll find two stair-wells that belonged to the original "Awaiting Trial Block" of the prison; a wall here is filled with a range of comments made by South Africans as the country attained freedom. Tours (90 min.) depart every hour, but we recommend the private tour which costs only R15 more per person.

Constitution Hill, Braamfontein. ℂ **011/274-5300.** www.constitutionhill.org.za. Tours R30 adults (R45 special tour); R15 students and children under 13. Night tours (group only; last Thurs of every month) R80. Mon–Fri 9am–5pm; Sat 10am–3pm. Last ticket sold at 4pm.

Hector Pieterson Memorial & Museum ★★ If you haven't time to visit the Apartheid Museum, this is an essential stop on your Soweto tour. Erected in memory of the 1976 student protest against Bantu education in general and specifically the enforced medium of education (Afrikaans), when police opened fire on hundreds of Sowetan schoolchildren armed only with placards, it offers a window on the anger, fear, aggression, and grief of that year. The concourse leading to the entrance is marked by olive trees symbolizing peace and beautiful columns, with each piece of slate meant to represent one of the children who died in the uprising. Inside the immaculate, modern space are emotionally compelling displays: Video footage of the momentous event and numerous photographs taken by the talented Peter Man-gubane and Sam Nzima. Included is the infamous shot of Hector Pieterson—one of the young boys who was shot—being carried by a young man whose face is contorted in disbelief and pain. Hector's sister runs alongside, her mouth a silent wail of grief. The police reported 59 dead; the actual toll was thought to be closer to 500. Children turned on their parents, something hitherto unheard of in traditional society, and

In 1938, the secretive Afrikaner *Broederbond* (brotherhood) organized a symbolic reenactment of the Great Trek and sent a team of ox wagons from Cape Town to Pretoria (now Tshwane) to celebrate its centenary. By the time the wagons reached Pretoria, more than 200,000 Afrikaners had joined, all of whom camped at Monument Hill, many of them in traditional garb, where the foundation stones for a monument were laid. Ten years later, the **Voortrekker Monument ★★** (✆ 012/325-7885; www.voortrekkermon.org.za; daily 8am–5pm; R40 adults, R20 children) was completed, and the Afrikaner Nationalist Party swept to power. This massive granite structure, sometimes compared irreverently to a large Art Deco toaster, is a fascinating example of 1930s monumental architecture, and dominates the skyline at the southern entrance to Tshwane. Commemorating the Great Trek, particularly the Battle of Blood River, fought on December 16, 1838, the monument remains hallowed ground for many Afrikaners. Every year on that date, exactly at noon, a ray of sunlight lights up a central plaque that reads WE FOR YOU SOUTH AFRICA. The *we* refers, of course, to Afrikaners—in the marble frieze surrounding the lower hall depicting the Trek and Battle, you will find no carvings of the many black slaves who aided the Boers in their victory. The museum below has memorabilia relating to the Great Trek. Most interesting is the "female" version of the monument frieze—huge tapestries depicting a romanticized version of the Great Trek's social events; they are the perfect foil to the Afrikaner men: ladies plaiting threads while the men wrest with stone in the monument. For guided tours contact Arend Posthuma at ✆ **012/326-6770.** With the best views of South Africa's administrative and diplomatic capital, the classically inspired **Union Buildings ★★**, Meintjieskop Ridge, Arcadia (✆ 012/325-2000), are probably the best-known creation of prolific British Imperial architect Sir Herbert Baker. The buildings—the administrative headquarters of the South African government, and office of the president since 1913—are generally considered his finest achievement. The office-block wings are said to represent the British and Afrikaner people, linked in reconciliation by the curved amphitheater. Again, African "natives" were not represented, nor allowed to enter the buildings, except to clean. So the visitor can just image the scenes of huge emotional jubilation in the gardens and buildings on 1994 as South Africans witnessed the inauguration of Mandela, and African praise-singers in traditional garb exorcised the ghosts of the past. Visitors can walk along Government Avenue, the road that traverses the facade, but only those on official business may enter.

destroyed everything they could that belonged to municipal authority—schools, post offices, and the ubiquitous beer halls. The police retaliated with brutal assaults, arrests, and killings. It took them months to control the unrest, which spread throughout the country's youth, but the battle had been lost as hundreds of children left the country to join the banned ANC's military wing, while the others resolved to make the country ungovernable.

Hector Pieterson Sq., corner of Khumalo and Pela sts., Orlando West, Soweto. Museum: Maseko St. ✆ **011/536-0611,** -0612, or -0613. Admission R25; R5 students and seniors. Mon–Fri 10am–5pm; Sat–Sun 10am–4:30pm.

Dispossessed of their land during the 1800s and further reduced to virtual slavery by taxation, thousands of black men were forced to find work in the minefields of eGoli. As more and more settled in inner-city slums, the segregationist government's concerns about the proximity of blacks to white suburbs grew until, in 1930, a solution was found. A farm 18km (11 miles) to the southwest of Johannesburg was designated as the new "township," and blacks living in and around the city were served with eviction papers. It would now take 3 hours to get to work. There were as yet no roads, no shops, no parks, no electricity, no running water. Public transport and policing were hopelessly inadequate. Not surprisingly, most people refused to move, but in 1933 the government declared the Slums Clearance Act and forcibly evicted blacks from the inner cities. Defeated, the new homeless moved in, and Soweto, acronym for the South Western Township, was born.

Today enduring rural poverty means that Soweto remains a magnet for millions searching for a better standard of living, but what makes the sprawling township so interesting is that—unlike the inner city, deserted by whites and only now showing real signs of regeneration—the inhabitants of Soweto have remained emotionally invested in their home, despite the fact that it was forced on them, and the hardship they endured here. Many middle-class and wealthy

blacks still feel more at home here than anywhere else, making South Africa's densest city-within-a-city home to record producers and shebeen queens, multimillionaires and the unemployed, murderers and Nobel Peace Prize winners. And as Soweto's earning capacity grew, so did its spending channels culminating in the opening of **Maponya Mall** (named after the developer Richard Maponya, Soweto's first millionaire and highly respected businessman), where a whole new generation of glam-setters could finally fork out on global brands and Westernized fast food in a mall located in their own backyard. While shack dwellers are still steadily being relocated to more substantial brick abodes, properties in upmarket Diepkloof Extension 1 (colloquially known as Diepkloof "Exclusive" or "Expensive") now include mansions worth millions, plenty of unwieldy satellite dishes, and even a four-star hotel, **Soweto Hotel on Freedom Square** (www.sowetohotel.co.za). Although many houses are now protected by security companies, it's tough community justice that seems to keep crime at bay: So terrifying is the prospect of being punished by community vigilantism that petty burglars have been known to turn themselves over to official police, and the few *umlungu* (whitey) inhabitants of Soweto say they feel safer here than in the suburbs.

In fact, few white South Africans ventured here prior to 2010, but all that

Johannesburg Art Gallery ★★ Predictably, the city's first gallery was financed with the sale of a diamond. In 1904, Lady Phillips, wife of the first chairman of the Rand Mines Company, sold her 21-carat ring to purchase three paintings by Wilson Steer. Over the next 5 years, she wrangled money from her wealthy connections to purchase more artwork and commissioned Sir Edwin Lutyens to design the elegant building that now houses her collection. Ignore the rather dull Flemish and Dutch collections for by the Brenthurst Collection of African Art, comprising curios plundered by European explorers in the 19th century, and later collections of traditional southern African artworks. Happily, despite ignoring black talent during the apartheid

changed with the FIFA Soccer World Cup, when Soweto saw a massive upgrade of facilities and transport as well as the building of **Soccer City,** the stadium that hosted the opening game of the tournament. Prior to this Soccer City also hosted a seminal rugby game which saw thousands of white Afrikaners partying up a storm with Sowetans, surprised and elated by the warm welcome Sowetans are in fact famous for.

Soweto is not easy to navigate, so is still best visited accompanied by a knowledgeable guide, who will not only give a real sense of its history, but help you understand its ongoing evolution. Most operators cover similar ground: the **Mandela Museum,** where Madiba once lived; a stop at the **Hector Pieterson Memorial** (reviewed above); a drive down **Vilakazi Street,** the only street in the world to have housed two Nobel Prize winners; **Freedom Square,** where the ANC's Freedom Charter was proclaimed to thousands in 1956; the **Regina Mundi Church,** the "Parliament of Soweto," where the bullet-marked walls are witness to ex-security-police brutality and the bustling Baragwanath Taxi Rank, opposite the largest hospital in the Southern Hemisphere, Chris Hani Baragwanath Hospital.

Bongani Ndlovu of **Soweto.co.za** ★★ (also their website address, where you can book your tour; ✆ **011/326-1700**) is intelligent, highly knowledgeable, and great fun to tour with, Ndlovu should be requested specifically. A full-day tour, with a pickup in Rosebank, costs R850 and includes a stop at Constitutional Hill before heading to Soweto for various stops, lunch, and all museum charges. If you're up for a party, ask about nighttime shebeen tours, usually limited to weekends. (This operator is highly involved in community projects, so your ticket fee will help change lives.) Note however that you need to be four persons minimum; also that you can do this tour from (and back to) the airport. *Caveat:* The downside of driving around in a bus armed with a camera is the sense that you are treating people like animals in a reserve. You can avoid this entirely by instead taking a 2-hour or 4-hour bicycle tour with **Soweto Bicycle Tours** ★★★ (www.sowetobicycletours.com) offered by either the dynamic Lebo or Phillip from **Lebo's Soweto Backpackers.** Both are excellent guides, and you don't have to be particularly fit (it's about a 15-min. walk from Vilikazi street and the Hector Pieterson Museum). This is not only perfectly safe, but a far friendlier way of interacting with the locals, who appreciate the face-to-face interaction. Lebo will arrange for you to be picked up from your hotel or you can extend the adventure and spend the night in what used to be Lebo's family home, operating as a backpackers since 2003.

years, the gallery now also has a good selection of South Africa's most renowned, including sculptures by Venda artist Jackson Hlungwani and paintings by Helen Sebidi, Alfred Toba, and Gerard Sekoto. For more representation of contemporary artists, you'd do well to try galleries such as **The Premises** (at the Civic Theatre), **Standard Bank Art Gallery** (also in Braamfontein; Corner Simmonds and Frederick sts.) or the **Goodman Gallery** (in Parkwood); the latter is a commercial gallery in the Art Precinct on Jan Smuts—for more recommended galleries, see "Shopping—Flea Markets to High-End Crafts," below.

Klein St., Joubert Park. ✆ **011/725-3130.** Free admission. Tues–Sun 10am–5pm.

Maropeng Visitor Centre ★ ☺ Located in the Cradle of Mankind, about an hour northwest of Johannesburg, Maropeng chronicles the story of human evolution. It's a bit out of the way, and not in the same class as the Origins or Apartheid Museum, but it's a fun thing to do with kids due to the interactive nature of many the exhibits, as well as the underground boat ride (which adults will find a bit tacky). Nearby are the **Sterkfontein Caves** (buy a combined ticket if you want to visit these), where the actual discoveries—fossils of our ancestors said to date back more than 3 million years—were made.

R24, off R563, Kromdraai, Magaliesberg. ℂ **014/577-9000.** www.maropeng.co.za. Admission R115 adults, R65 children (free for under 4s). Combined ticket R190 adults, R110 children. AE, MC, V, DC. Open daily 9am–5pm; last boat ride 4pm.

Origins Centre ★★ This museum has evolved out of the University of Witwatersrand's Rock Art Institute, and the focus is (a little zealously) on showing that racial and cultural differences between various groups of people are largely superficial, as we are all unified by a genetic thread that traces humankind back to a common ancestor in—you guessed it—Africa. It also posits that human beings are united by their unique ability to engage in symbolic thought and cultural exchange. Much of the investigation around this human cultural proclivity is dealt with through the center's extensive focus on the San tribe, whose supposedly primitive way of life is examined in a range of fascinating films, handsome displays, and quality commentary. Of particular interest are details of the mystical San spirit world, typically entered by means of shamanic trance dances. You'll need at least 90 minutes to tour the center, with the aid of the audio guide provided; afterward, you can browse for excellent but pricey African crafts in the gift store while you decide whether to apply for a DNA test to trace your ancestral origins: The test is done at the nearby National Health Laboratory Services, also in Braamfontein.

Enoch Sontonga Ave., Braamfontein. ℂ **011/717-4700.** www.origins.org.za. Admission R75 adults, R35 children under 12; includes audio guide. V. Open daily 9am–5pm but sometimes closed for functions; call ahead.

Shopping

FLEA MARKETS TO HIGH-END ARTS & CRAFTS

Johannesburg attracts people from all over the continent with one sole purpose: to shop in the second largest city in Africa. Of the more than 20 malls, the best are located in **Sandton City ★** (the biggest selection), **Hyde Park ★★** (for its chichi selection and stylish restaurants), and **Rosebank ★★★**, comprising **Zone@Rosebank, The Firs,** and **Rosebank Mall.** Of these, Zone is great for fashion divas, while Rosebank Mall offers the greatest variety of shopping experiences, from boutiques to informal craft and food markets, and also home to the city's best art house cinema (www.cinemanouveau.co.za). Rosebank also has outdoor areas that interlink the three malls, which breaks the monotony of concrete. Note that Rosebank is also home to the burgeoning Art District on Jan Smuts Avenue (not really walking distance from the malls).

If you think malls are for rats, for a truly enjoyable shopping experience with a selection of individual-owned shops in a laid back atmosphere, we recommend a morning browsing the 44 Stanley Avenue complex in Milpark followed by an hour or so at the nearby Bamboo Centre. Or head to Parkhurst's 4th Avenue for lunch, then browse the predominantly housewares and decor shops there (don't miss **amoeba ★**,

Shop 2, corner of 4th Ave. and 7th St.; ℭ **011/447-5025**). **On Saturdays** the Jozi Food Market takes place at Parkhurst's Pirates Sports Club, 4th Avenue Extension, from 8:30am to 1:30pm (ℭ **076/469-8995**).

44 Stanley Avenue ★★★ 🏢   Milpark's 44 Stanley Avenue complex (ℭ **11/482-4444;** www.44stanley.co.za) is great for browsing; delightfully free of crowds and hassle. The lineup—selected for the unique stock they carry—will keep you engrossed for hours, and there are some lovely laid-back places to eat. You'll find whimsical and fantastic garments at **Just** (ℭ **011/482-9836**), showcasing the work of some 30 local fashion designers; top quality handmade crafts and collectibles from all over Africa (ethically sourced, of course) at **Craft Unlimited** (ℭ **011/482-9409**); unique beautifully crafted (much of it custom-made) jewelry items from **Sirkel** (ℭ **011/726-2365**); great gear in natural fabrics at **Lunar** (ℭ **011/726-5558**); hand-selected books from **L'Elephant Terrible** (ℭ **072/617-7343**); and the wonderfully funky **Dokter and Misses** (ℭ **072/259-2328**), showcasing contemporary local design (clothing, jewelry, stationery, housewares, and so on).

Bamboo Centre ★★   Wander into **Tinsel** ★ to look at the beautifully displayed jewelry, then on to **Black Coffee** ★★★, fashion and accessory label of Jacques Van Der Watts, one of Jo'burg's most successful and funky fashion designers. **Love Books** offers a selection of books clearly selected by someone who really does love them.

   Tip: **Black Coffee** can also be found in Arts on Main in downtown Jo'burg, where a **Food Market** ★★—held every Sunday—attracts a hip and trendy crowd to snack on delicious finger foods and sip bubbly and beer under the olive trees.

Rosebank   Young fashion divas looking for affordable "where did you get that?" designer items need to head straight for the **Zone@Rosebank** (ℭ **011/788-1130;** www.thezoneatrosebank.co.za). Start by browsing **The Space** ★, lower level (ℭ **011/327-3640**); if you simply want a cool T-shirt emblazoned with retro-style South African icons or examples of silly local humor, pop into **Big Blue** (ℭ **011/880-3994**), a clothes-shop-cum-novelty-store that's ideal for gifts. Nearby, at **Sowearto** ★ (ℭ **011/447-7004;** www.sowearto.co.za), you can browse through some innovative and funky Afro-chic garments and limited accessories from the studios of happening local designers; the range is funky. Also in the Zone is the **Young Designers Emporium** (ℭ **011/327-4268**) with clothing ranges from some of S.A.'s up-and-coming talents. Upstairs is **Musica Megastore** (ℭ **011/788-1087**), where staff can point you to the African music section. Don't blindly trust their suggestions, however; ask to listen to a few selections before you swipe your credit card. Note that The Zone is also home to **Woolworths,** a seemingly staid national department store but very useful as a one-stop shop selling reasonably priced (and much of it locally designed) clothing (you can uncover some real gems here), as well as underwear, bathing suits, jewelry, cosmetics, housewares items as well as good food. For a full listing of the 120 shops by category housed in **The Rosebank Mall,** visit www.themallofrosebank. co.za. If you're looking for safari-style gear, or simply haven't packed enough cool cotton clothing or warm winter fleeces, visit **Cape Union Mart** (ℭ **011/422-1961**).

   Rosebank's "Art District" is centered on Jan Smuts Avenue. Of the galleries here don't miss the **Everard Read Gallery** on Jellicoe Avenue, if only to see the inside of this striking sculptural structure, and the nearby **Goodman Gallery.**

Johannesburg After Dark

THE PERFORMING ARTS

Braamfontein is considered the theater precinct, with nearby Newtown bringing up the rear. The **Johannesburg Civic Theatre,** Loveday Street, Braamfontein (© **011/877-6800;** www.showbusiness.co.za), is one of the largest and most technologically advanced theaters in the country; this is where large-scale musicals, operas, dance, and orchestral music are performed. The **Wits Theatre Complex,** corner of Jorissen and Station streets, Braamfontein (© **011/717-1372**), attracts a wide variety of local and international theater talent, including good dance productions; quality varies, so be informed. Another option worth investigating, also in Braamfontein, is the relatively new **Alex Theatre** (36 Stiemens St.; www.thealex. co.za). The **Market Theatre,** 56 Margaret Mcingana St., Newtown (© **011/832-1641;** www.markettheatre.co.za), is famous for having spawned a generation of protest theater and is likely to have a good selection of local talent. For current listings for all these venues and more, check out the daily "Tonight" section in *The Star* and the weekly *Mail & Guardian* (www.mg.co.za). Tickets can usually be booked and bought by phone; call **Computicket** (© **083/915-8000,** 083/131, or 011/340-8000; www.computicket.com; Mon–Sat 8am–8pm).

THE CLUB, BAR & MUSIC SCENE

In a city where work is everything, social interaction is an important distraction. You'll discover a seemingly endless selection and variety of bars, pubs, clubs, and downright sleazy drinking holes. If you like to club- or bar-hop, several areas have a concentration of options but many of the larger clubs are in otherwise missable neighborhoods and require some driving to reach. For up-to-the minute news of what's hot and what's happening, navigate to **www.jhblive.com**, an excellent site with reviews of most of Jozi's entertainment spots and information on upcoming events.

Northern Suburbs

The Blues Room ★★ In the heart of Sandton, this upmarket nightclub serves up live blues, jazz, fusion, comedy, and even rock 'n' roll or comedy for an older crowd; slick, safe, and well run. Village Walk Mall, corner of Rivonia and Maude sts., Sandown, Sandton. © **011/784-5527.** www.bluesroom.co.za. Cover varies

Cocoon Lounge ★★ Appealing to an upmarket elite, this is a handsome "champagne, cigar, and cocktail bar," in the same building as high-altitude Taboo (see below), making it the ideal place to get yourself in the mood. The designer-chic look includes walls smothered in lengths of wood and sleek, glamorously lit bars and banquettes in shades of black. Shop 8, 24 Central Centre, Fredman Dr. and Gwen Lane, Sandton. © **011/783-2316.** www.cocoonlounge.co.za.

Moloko Bar Lounge ★★★ Discerning yet welcoming (provided you meet the door policy: dress for success and certainly no under-25s), with Jozi's most gorgeous locals draped around the contemporary lounge-bar decor (it's hidden in Rosebank's self-proclaimed Design District). This is an intimate venue where you get to meet a mixed, upmarket slice of Jo'burg society. The music is laid back and groovy (R&B, hip-hop, gentle house, and a few Latino rhythms); open Thursday to Saturday only. 160 Jan Smuts Ave., Rosebank. © **082/458-0675.** www.molokojoburg.com. Cover varies.

Taboo ★★ This is the quintessential Jozi hangout for unabashed hedonists—unflinching excess is on display in an indoor-outdoor multilevel club where the emphasis is on stalking beautiful creatures of the opposite sex. Dress the part or you'll

A *Who's Who* of Music Superstars

If you're a **jazz** aficionado, some names to watch for are Gloria Bosman, African Jazz Pioneers, Feya Faku, the Sheer All Stars, Andile Yenana, Sipho Mabuse, Lulu Gontsana, Bheki Mbatha, Khaya Mahlangu, Barney Rachabane, Oscar Rachabane, Octavia Rachabane, Herbie Tsoaeli, McCoy Mrubata, Zim Ngqawana, Louis Mhlanga, Linda Kekana, Moses Khumalo, and Pops Mohamed. **Kwaito** acts to look for are Brothers of Peace (BOP), Mandoza, Mafikizolo, Zola, M'Du, Mzekezeke, Kabelo, Mapaputsi, Bongo Maffin, and Mzambiya.

be left out on the street down below. 24 Central Centre, Fredman Dr. and Gwen Lane, Sandton. © **011/783-2200.** www.taboo.co.za.

Tokyo Star ★★   Sino-Zen-inspired decor has replaced the earlier tongue-in-cheek pop culture–defined identity of this former Melville haunt. It's adopted a classier, slightly more grown-up persona (and they've added a cafe). You still have great fun on the dance floor, bopping to an eclectic, fun-fueled selection of tracks by DJs who aren't afraid to plunder a library of old and new tunes. Shop 1, Comtec House, 26 Gleneagles Dr., Greenside. © **084/208-0236.** www.tokyostar.co.za.

Newtown/City Central

Bassline ★★   This is probably still Jozi's most popular live-music venue. Attracting an assortment of top local acts and low-key legends from farther afield, the lineup ranges from jazz, blues, and rock bands to hip-hop and world artists. Many a groovy evening features spectacular talents from around Africa; look for appearances by South African sensation Freshly Ground. 10 Henry Nxumalo St. © **011/838-9145.** www. bassline.co.za. Cover varies.

Randlords ★★★   Catch the dedicated elevator up 22 floors to this fashionable rooftop bar in Braamfontein, and you're given a serious taste of just how chichi and exclusive Jozi can be. Delectable tapas accompany the cocktails, but it's the crowd of devil-may-care beauties with money to burn that will really leave you breathless. The views of the surrounding neon-lit cityscape are pretty memorable too. Southpoint Towers, De Korte and Station sts., Braamfontein. © **011/489-1930.** www.randlords.co.za. Cover R250, unless you're on the guest list.

Shikisha Bar ★★   This bar hosts various events on weekends, some better than others (includes local little-known films). If the Politburo are down for a session, get there and meet some of Jozi's coolest cats. Miriam Makeba St., Newtown. Cover varies.

BIG-GAME COUNTRY: KRUGER NATIONAL PARK & PRIVATE RESERVES & CONCESSIONS

9

Most first-time visitors to Africa imagine a place where vast plains of bush savanna and thicket teem with game, rivers are swollen with honking hippos and lurking crocodiles, dense indigenous jungles shroud twittering birds, horizons shimmer with heat, and the nights are lit only by stars and crackling campfires. And despite the sophistication of its cities, South Africa offers all of the above—along with the most luxurious (or most affordable) Big 5 safaris on the continent. It's quite simply an essential experience: Watching wild animals, dangerous and untamed, moving through beautiful, untouched habitats brings about a deeply satisfying sense of belonging; a feeling of wholeness. It's why so many of us crave regular sojourns in the wilderness.

Blessed with some of the largest tracts of wilderness on the continent, the region has seen this rich heritage expand even further with the stabilization of political relations. Fences between South Africa and parks in neighboring Mozambique, Botswana, and Zimbabwe have fallen away to create one of the largest conservation areas in the world, unfettered by the constraints of human borders.

These areas, rich in big game—where you will also find an unprecedented concentration of the most luxurious lodges in Africa, as well as the continent's most affordable camps—are located in the landlocked provinces of the Northwest (bordering Botswana), and the eastern provinces

Mpumalanga & the Limpopo Province

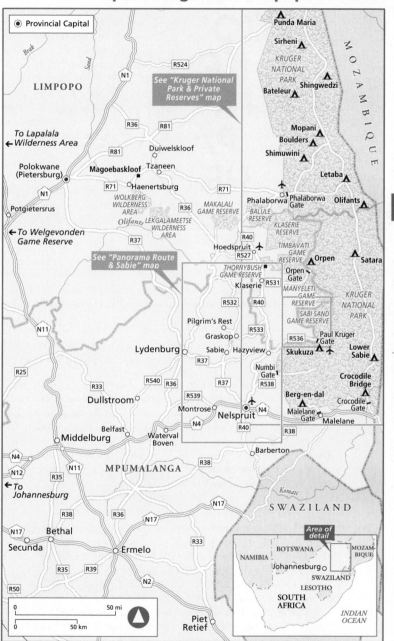

303

of Limpopo and Mpumalanga. The latter two together form the northeastern corner of South Africa and share one of the continent's most famous game reserves, Kruger National Park.

Here too lies the Escarpment (aka Northern Drakensberg), carpeted in a mosaic of indigenous and plantation forest and offering road trips with breathtaking views: the spectacular Blyde River Canyon; the lush subtropical gardens of the legendary Rain Queen; Stone Age sites that recall the rich indigenous precolonial cultures; and boomtowns that tell of Mpumalanga's short but turbulent gold rush. But the primary destination in this region remains Kruger National Park and the private game reserves that surround it. Kruger's budget facilities and well-maintained roads make this the most affordable and accessible safari to independent travelers on limited budgets. By contrast, the exclusive private game reserves that run along the park's unfenced border, as well as the selection of recently created private concessions within the Kruger, are reputed to hold the most luxurious safari lodges and camps on the continent, and it's true. Aside from the exclusivity and luxuriousness of the accommodation, the game-viewing—in open-topped vehicles that are driven off-road by knowledgeable guides—is superlative. Spend a few nights at any one of them, and you are virtually guaranteed truly close-up encounters with the Big 5 animals (lion, leopard, rhino, elephant, and buffalo), an experience that comes highly recommended, despite the steep price tag.

Of the private reserves surrounding Kruger, Sabi Sand is the best internationally known destination, thanks predominantly to its virtually guaranteed leopard sightings and the big-name players located on it, such as Mala Mala, Londolozi, and Singita. But another reserve that is enjoying a deserved increase in prominence is Madikwe, the Big 5 game reserve that lies northwest of Johannesburg, which enjoys the additional benefit of being malaria free. Leopards are more elusive here, but you stand an excellent chance of seeing wild dogs, Africa's most endangered predator. Many of the privately owned and managed lodges and camps here—all sharing the same traversing rights across the entire reserve—offer rates that are better value than those surrounding Kruger, making this arguably the best-value luxury safari destination in South Africa.

(**Note:** For a comparative overview of these reserves, as well as those in Kwazulu-Natal, and Eastern, Western, and Northern Cape, see the box in this chapter as well as p. 337.)

STAYING ACTIVE

The activities listed below are offered outside the game reserves themselves (where game drives and walks are included in the price). If you're looking for a one-stop advice and booking shop for activities and tours in the southern part of this area (Sabie/Hazyview/Panorama Route), a great place to look (and book) is **www.big5 country.com**, which lists absolutely everything—including the slightly more sedate (click on "Things to Do" and on the province of Mpumalanga, then "Continue" under "All Areas" and "All Activities")—from Archery in Graskop and Boat Rides on Blyde River, to Bush Walks in Sabi Sands, Caving by Candlelight in Sabie, and Ziplining in Hazyview. All fees are included on the site. Or visit their office in Hazyview at the Rendezvous Tourism Centre on Main Street. Alternatively, contact **Induna Adventures** (© **013/737-8308;** www.indunaadventures.com) a high-energy outfit located 10km (6¼ miles) outside Hazyview and focusing solely on adventure activities in the area (including mountain biking, river rafting, quad biking, kloofing, abseiling, horse trails, tubing, ziplines, and paintball).

In the northern part of this area (Tzaneen/Magoebaskloof), the best one-stop shop for a great variety of adventure activities is **Thaba Metsi** (www.thabametsi.com).

We include details of a few of the more interesting adventure options below.

AERIAL CABLE TRAIL/CANOPY TOURS ★★ ☺ If you haven't yet experienced the thrill of a canopy or cable trail, make sure you plan a morning near Sabie, and book with **Skyways** (**ℂ 013/737-8374;** www.skywaytrails.com; R450 mornings only; all ages). On the longest aerial "foofy-slide" tour in Africa, you zip along an exhilarating 1.2km (¾ mile), whizzing high above the canopy of the last remaining natural forested valleys along the Sabie River (takes about 3 hr.). In Magoebaskloof there is a similar setup—equally exhilarating and same price; contact www.magoebaskloofcanopytour.co.za.

BALLOONING 📷 Take off just as the sun rises over the Sabie River Valley—unforgettable moment—and float over the lush foothills of the Escarpment for approximately an hour, then alight for with a glass of champagne and breakfast at a nearby lodge with your pilot who will present you with a flight certificate. Based 10km (6¼ miles) from Hazyview, **Balloons Over Africa** (**ℂ 013/737-6950;** www.balloonsoverafrica.co.za; R2,890) prides itself on its expertise, safety record and general attention to detail.

ELEPHANT RIDING/EXPERIENCES ★ Kapama Private Reserve offers **elephant-back safaris** at its luxury tented flagship, **Camp Jabulani** (**ℂ 015/793-1265;** www.campjabulani.com), or you can be picked up from your lodge or hotel and come to the reserve for your 90-minute ride (pickup arranged with Big 5 Country costs R2,100–R2,600). If you drive there it will cost you R1,775 (see "Driving the Panorama Route" box, below, for directions and details). No children under 12 are allowed. There are also two elephant sanctuaries in Hazyview that offer cheaper "elephant experiences" (touching, walking, riding); both are apparently equally good, though we visited **Elephant Whispers.** Inquire with Big 5 Country for a pickup, or head there yourself—it's off the R40 near Hazyview (www.elephantwhispers.co.za). **Elephant Sanctuary** (www.elephantsanctuary.co.za) is off the R536 near Hazyview, next to Casa do Sol Hotel. Most people love the experience and it is a great privilege to be this close to such gentle, intelligent giants, but it's a little zoolike to our taste. In fact, the growth in this industry has not been without controversy, as human-habituated elephants require extensive feeding and sensitive care, and should not be sourced just to feed tourist interests. None of the elephants in the above-mentioned places have been purposefully removed from the wild; always inquire elsewhere into how and where the elephants were rescued.

ENDANGERED WILDLIFE TOUR ★★ Visit two conservation centers—**Moholoholo Rehabilitation Centre** near Hoedspruit and the **Hoedspruit Endangered Species Centre.** The former is a nonprofit organization that works to rehabilitate (if possible) or offer long-term care for abandoned or injured wild animals while the latter is one of the foremost research and breeding centers in S.A., dedicated to preserving the gene pool of endangered animals such as cheetah. This is a surefire way to get up close to animals you are unlikely (or very lucky) to see in the wilds (visitors can even touch one of the cheetahs, the cat that has the most "petlike" tendencies), and at the same time support two very worthwhile causes. Rates depend on operators, but you're looking at between R750 and R950 (depending on numbers;

Golfing in big-game country is not to be taken lightly—a golfer at Hans Merensky was trampled to death by an elephant that had broken through the fence from neighboring Kruger because she tried to confront it. Golfers at the clubs that are also home to wild animals should heed the warning signs posted at water hazards and elsewhere. Should you encounter a large mammal or predator, remain still, then back away quietly—under no circumstances should you run.

you will be picked up from your lodge; see Big 5 Country for more). It's obviously cheaper and less-time consuming to visit just one center, in which case opt for Hoedspruit Endangered Species Centre, but they do offer very different experiences. You can also visit either one or both on your own steam which will represent a significant saving (see details in "Driving the Panorama Route" box, later in this chapter).

GOLFING IN THE WILDS   This region is famous for combining golf with wildlife—where else do you get to sign an indemnity form before you can play? You'll certainly have to do so before teeing off at the 9-hole **Skukuza** course ((*C* **013/735-5543** bookings;   www.sanparks.org/parks/kruger/tourism/activities/golf_course.php)—it is unfenced, and wild animals wander the greens at will. More wild golfing experiences await at the exclusive 18-hole course at **Leopard Creek Country Club ★★★** ((*C* **013/791-2000;** www.leopardcreek.co.za), co-owned by Jack Nicklaus and Gary Player. Besides the resident leopard, crocs and hippos lurk in the aptly named water hazards, and the clubhouse is considered the best on the continent. To play here, you'll have to book into the nearby **Buhala Game Lodge** ((*C* **013/792-4372;** www.buhala. co.za). Private game lodges that can also arrange access are Jock Safari Lodge, Lukimbi, Singita, Sabi Sabi, MalaMala, Lion Sands, Leopard Hills, Ngala, and Londolozi. A good (and far less pricey) alternative is the 18-hole **Hans Merensky ★★** ((*C* **015/781-3931**), which borders Kruger and is often visited by its wildlife (see box below). You can either book into the **Hans Merensky Hotel & Estate** (www.hansmerensky.com) or combine with a safari and book into luxurious **Makalali** (also reviewed later in this chapter), a private game lodge that lies just under an hour away.

HORSEBACK RIDING   A selection of horseback and pony trail rides for beginner, intermediate, and experienced riders can be booked through Big 5 Country (see contact details above), ranging from 15 minutes to 3 hours, and including night rides in the African bush. Better still, book a horseback safari with **Horizon Horseback Adventures & Safaris** (www.ridinginafrica.com). Horizons caters for riders of all abilities, offering various riding experiences in their 15,000-hectare (37,050-acre) reserve in the Waterberg mountains, from riding with plains game to playing polocrosse (a fusion of polo and lacrosse) and mustering cattle. Guests are hosted in a lodge on the edge of a cliff overlooking a beautiful lake with the plains beyond. Costs are around R2,000 to R2,400 per night per person all-inclusive. The same company can arrange horse trail rides in Botswana and on the Eastern Cape coastline. Another great outfit is **Wait A Little** (www.waitalittle.co.za), offering riding safaris in Makalali Reserve. You can meet their horses online, but the organizers will match you with a horse to suit your temperament and ability. Accommodation is in their intimate tented camp or Makalali or Garonga (see reviews of these two lodges later in chapter).

KLOOFING/CANYONEERING This is always a lot of fun, combining hiking with swimming and sliding through pools, deep in the gorge between Mac Mac Pools and Mac Mac Falls. Bring shoes that can get wet but will give you a good grip. The scenery alone is worth it. Costs around R300 to R520 per person, depending on route or duration.

OPEN VEHICLE SAFARIS If you are doing a self-drive safari but want a break from being the driver, or simply want to be in an open-topped vehicle with the wind in your hair, there are various operators offering either a 6-hour morning or 6-hour afternoon game drive, or a 10-hour full-day safari. We'd opt for the 6-hour morning game drive; if you are traveling with family or friends, charter the whole vehicle (this will cost around R2,500–R2,700). Individual bookings for morning game drives range between R650 and R990 per person (depending on operator and whether you are already in the park). You can also arrange for a morning safari in Sabi Sand (R900 per person) Again, inquire with Big 5 Country for the full range of options, but Elephant Herd Safaris come recommended.

SAFARIS ON FOOT Lodges and camps in and around Kruger all offer **bush walks** where you will be introduced to rudimentary tracking skills; the use of plants and trees in medicine as well as bird and insect identification. And yes, you may encounter one of the Big 5 animals. If you're not staying in Kruger but want a morning walking safari in the park, contact Big 5 Country, which will arrange this in Kruger (R690–R710 per person) or Sabi Sand (R850–R900). Dedicated hikers who want more than just a few hours' stroll should look at booking into **Plains Camp at Rhino Walking Safari** (Southern Kruger). Sharing a border with MalaMala Game Reserve, this massive 12,000-hectare (29,640-acre) "restricted wilderness" concession allows no off-road game drives. The focus at the four-unit tented Plains Camp is then firmly on walking, and guests are also given the opportunity to overnight at the camp's "sleep-out digs," deep in the bush (70 min. on foot from Plains Camp), where tents have been erected on decks high up on stilts at a watering hole (www.isibindi.co.za; R5,100–6,440 double per day). Kruger National Park has excellent-value **3-day walking trails** in various locations throughout the reserve (R3,675 for 3 days), as well as a backpack hike (all described in the "Kruger" section), while **Ngala,** a tented camp in the Timbavati reserve, offers walking safaris for the well-heeled (see "Where to Stay & Eat" under "Private Game Reserves," later in this chapter).

EN ROUTE TO BIG-GAME COUNTRY

Getting to the Kruger area by air from Johannesburg is pretty straightforward and dealt with in detail in the next (Kruger) section, but flights are relatively expensive, particularly if there's more than one of you, and if you are driving within Kruger you will need to rent a car there anyway. Add to this the fact that the route takes as little as 5 hours, is easy to follow, much of it scenic—dropping, usually quite spectacularly, from the highveld plateau of Gauteng to the lowveld—with plenty of possible pit stops, and traveling by car becomes an increasingly attractive proposition.

If you do opt for the road, there are essentially three routes. With limited time, the **direct route** between Johannesburg and the entrance gates to southern Kruger/Sabi Sand is a comfortable 5-hour drive on the N4, a smooth toll road in excellent condition. Ask your lodge to fax you exact directions from the airport, but essentially you leave Jo'burg's OR Tambo airport and take the R21 north to Pretoria, then take the N12 which joins the N4, main artery to Mozambique. Pass Witbank and Middelburg and Belfast (you'll turn toward Dullstroom at Belfast if you are due in one of the central gates or reserves; see "Driving the Panorama Route," later in this chapter). Keep traversing the N4, following the signs to Nelspruit (the unattractive capital of Mpumalanga), looking out for the R40 turning, north to White River. Note that just after White River, you'll find **Casterbride Centre,** and opposite it, **Bagdad Centre.** Casterbridge is spread around a series of interlinked, shady courtyards with lots of shops, a theater, a local history and car museum, and even an art house cinema. It's a great place to stop and stretch your legs and grab a bite to eat, with a choice of restaurants: For informal light meals we like **The Courtyard Café and Delicatessen** (✆ 013/750-2102) or, if you prefer a more sophisticated dining experience **Magnolia** (✆ 013/751-1947) is your best bet. Alternatively, if you're looking for a little more local action, **The Fez** (✆ 013/750-1253) has been a popular hangout for many years. The Fez is located in Bagdad, the small center directly opposite Casterbridge.

From White River you simply keep traveling north on the R40 to Hazyview where you will find signs to Kruger's southern gates (R536). All in all it's a pleasant, easy drive, and the environs become scenic within 2 hours of leaving Johannesburg (though the towns are unattractive).

If you have the time, and you enjoy a road trip, there are two alternatives to this direct route. The first is the more popular route, principally because it gives the same easy access to the southern Kruger/Sabi Sand gates but via the **Panorama Route ★★★**—a spectacular half-day drive described below. **Pilgrim's Rest ★** is an optional side trip. This journey will definitely warrant an overnight stay at one of the many places that lie between 3 and 4 hours away from Gauteng (we've recommended a great selection below).

The second route is slightly longer (bank on an additional hour) but in parts even more scenic, with far less development and generally a great deal more atmospheric: hence the fact that the **Letaba/Magoebaskloof area ★★** is also known as "Land of the Silver Mist" and "Garden of the Rain Queen." It may not boast as many attractions as the Panorama Route but most of the drive is glorious head-clearing stuff, and it will take you past a real gem: Kings Walden (reviewed below) well worth the detour, and our favorite resting place en route to Kruger.

This is the most popular route to big-game country, with roads taking you past seemingly endless pine and eucalyptus plantations, interspersed with pockets of tangled indigenous jungle, plunging waterfalls, and some breathtaking views of the plains. A 4-hour drive from Gauteng, it's an easy escape for Johannesburg's ever-harassed city dwellers, desperate to breathe fresh air and drive around with unlocked doors. Unfortunately, the air is not always that fresh; Mpumalanga's industrial activities are responsible for one of the highest acid rainfalls in the world. This is compounded during the dry winter months, when veld fires are often rife, coloring the air with a hazy smog. While this is one reason to consider traveling via the Letaba/Magoebaskloof area, nothing matches the magnificent view of the lowveld plains from the aptly named **God's Window,** or watching the Blyde River snake through the floor of the eponymous canyon 700m (2,296 ft.) below—both experienced on the aptly named Panorama Route. In addition, the region's popularity makes for a plethora of great accommodations, with surrounding plantation forests and farms offering superb settings.

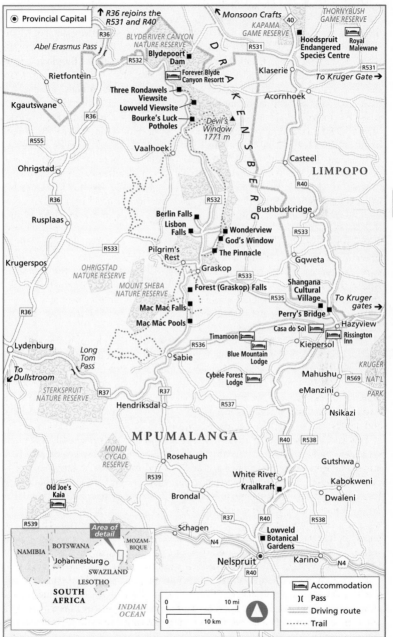

- Provincial Capital

↑ R36 rejoins the R531 and R40

↖ Monsoon Crafts

THORNYBUSH GAME RESERVE

KAPAMA GAME RESERVE

R36

Abel Erasmus Pass

BLYDE RIVER CANYON NATURE RESERVE

R532

Blydepoort Dam

Rietfontein

Forever Blyde Canyon Resortt

Klaserie

Hoedspruit Endangered Species Centre

Royal Malewane

R531

To Kruger Gate →

Three Rondawels Viewsite

Lowveld Viewsite

Acornhoek

Kgautswane

R36

Bourke's Luck Potholes

Devil's Window 1771 m

D
R
A
K
E
N
S
B
E
R
G

R555

Vaalhoek

Casteel

LIMPOPO

Ohrigstad

R36

R532

Berlin Falls

Bushbuckridge

R40

Rusplaas

Lisbon Falls

Wonderview

God's Window

R533

Pilgrim's Rest

The Pinnacle

Gqweta

R533

Krugerspos

OHRIGSTAD NATURE RESERVE

Graskop

Shangana Cultural Village

R535

To Kruger gates →

R36

MOUNT SHEBA NATURE RESERVE

Forest (Graskop) Falls

Mac Mac Falls

Perry's Bridge

Lydenburg

Long Tom Pass

Mac Mac Pools

Timamoon

Casa do Sol

Hazyview

Rissington Inn

To Dullstroom

STERKSPRUIT NATURE RESERVE

R37

R37

Sabie

R536

Blue Mountain Lodge

Kiepersol

Mahushu

R569

KRUGER NAT'L PARK

Hendriksdal

Cybele Forest Lodge

R537

eManzini

Nsikazi

MPUMALANGA

MONDI CYCAD RESERVE

Rosehaugh

R40

R538

Gutshwa

R539

White River

Kraalkraft

Kabokweni

Old Joe's Kaia

Brondal

R37

Dwaleni

R539

Schagen

R40

R538

Lowveld Botanical Gardens

R531

BOTSWANA

MOZAM-BIQUE

N4

Nelspruit

Karino

N4

NAMIBIA

Johannesburg

SWAZILAND

LESOTHO

SOUTH AFRICA

INDIAN OCEAN

Area of detail

Accommodation

)(Pass

Driving route

Trail

0 — 10 mi
0 — 10 km

9

BIG-GAME COUNTRY

En Route to Big-Game Country

Getting There

Depart the N4 when you reach the cool heights of Belfast, turning north onto the R540 to **Dullstroom.** The promise of landing a 6- to 7-pounder in the well-stocked dams and streams of the highveld's best trout-fishing region makes Dullstroom a popular weekend getaway for urban South Africans. At 2,012m (6,599 ft.) above sea level, this is also the highest town on the Escarpment—expect bitterly cold evenings in the winter, and don't be surprised to find fires lit even in midsummer. If you're feeling hungry at this time (Dullstroom is about 3 hr. from Johannesburg) there are plenty of restaurants lining the main street (see recommendations below), all a better bet than the eateries you'll find in Lydenburg, the next town on your route. Lydenburg, or "Place of Suffering," was founded by a party of depressed Voortrekkers who, having lost a number of loved ones to a malaria epidemic in nearby Ohrigstad, retreated to its mosquito-free heights in 1849. Happily, Lydenburg proved to be a misnomer, and today the town has a substantial center, though there's little to see beyond some really interesting examples of pioneer architecture. The town is also known for a famed archaeological find: the **Lydenburg Heads,** seven ceramic masks that date from the 5th century and were discovered in the late 1950s. You can see replicas of the heads (the originals now reside in the South African Museum in Cape Town) at the **Lydenburg Museum** (✆ **013/235-2213;** www.lydenburgmuseum.org.za), situated in the **Gustav Klingbiel Nature Reserve,** 3km (1¾ miles) out of town on the R37. Guided tours are by appointment only; call ahead. Hours are Monday through Friday from 8am to 4pm, Saturday and Sunday from 8am to 5pm; free admission.

From Lydenburg, the R37 east takes you down the **Long Tom Pass ★★**—at 2,150m (7,052 ft.), the second-highest mountain pass in South Africa. It was named after the Creusot siege guns that the Boers lugged up the pass to try to repel the British forces during the Second Anglo-Boer War (1899–1902). These guns, or cannons, were known as Long Toms because of their extended necks, which could spit a shell 9.5km (6 miles). Near the summit of the pass, at the **Devil's Knuckles,** a Long Tom replica commemorates the 4-day battle that was fought on this mountainside in 1900—the original cannons were destroyed by the Boers to prevent them from falling into British hands. You can still see the holes blasted by the cannons as the Boers retreated down the **Staircase,** a series of hairpin bends that zigzag down the pass.

Sabie's Gold-Digging Roots

Sabie (pronounced *Sah*-bee) dates from 1871, when a few friends, picnicking at the Lower Sabie Falls, were showing off their marksmanship skills. Bullets chipped the rocks behind the mock targets, revealing a glint of gold, and prospectors promptly followed. The initial boom was short lived, though the mining industry was still to transform Sabie. The first commercial trees, intended for mine props, were planted in 1876 and today form the heart of what are claimed to be the largest man-made forests in the world. To date, more than 400,000 hectares (1 million acres) have been planted with pine and eucalyptus, and many of these are destined to prop up shafts in the mines that run deep below Gauteng's surface; tree-huggers can find out more at the **Forestry Museum** (✆ **013/764-1058;** Mon–Fri 8am–4:30pm, Sat 8am–noon; R10 adults, R5 children).

Continuing east along the R37, passing the turnoff south for Hendriksdal, you come to the small forestry town of Sabie.

Sabie is only 55km (34 miles) from the nearest Kruger gate, but to get to the Panorama Route you will now take the R532 runs north to **Graskop.** (Pilgrim's Rest, a restored gold-mining village, lies another mountain pass away and warrants a separate visit of at least a half-day, excluding travel time.) Graskop is the gateway to the **Panorama Route,** a continuation of the R532 as it curls along the rim of the Escarpment, with lookout points along the way that provide relatively easy access to some of the most panoramic views in Africa (see "Driving the Panorama Route," below). Once past the canyon lookouts, the final descent to the lowveld follows the Abel Erasmus Pass to **Hoedspruit,** which offers easy access to Kruger via the centrally located Orpen Gate, and also lies very close to the private Timbavati, Thornybush, Kapama, and Manyeleti private game reserves. From Hoedspruit, you can also head south to **Hazyview** for access to the Paul Kruger, Phabeni, and Numbi entrance gates to southern Kruger, or to Sabi Sands Reserve, or to complete a loop returning to Sabie or Graskop.

Where to Stay & Eat

As mentioned, Dullstroom's popularity as a weekend escape for Jo'burgers has meant that it sustains a fairly good dining scene, and this is a good place to stop for lunch, assuming you're hungry. Restaurants come and go here but **Fibs** (Lesedi St.; ✆ **013/254-0059**), located in an old general store and famous locally for its pizzas, deserves a medal for longevity. Alternatively push on through to the next town, to one of the most authentic pit stops in the region located on Lydenburg's main road: **Vroutjies** (meaning "Little Women") **Coffee Shop** (✆ **013/235 3016**) serves a mean apple tart and baked cheesecake, as well as decent line of light meals including sandwiches, quiches, baked potatoes, and burgers.

As you drop to the Lowveld there is more choice and less that stands out. Certainly your will dine well at all the lodges described below, and nonresidents are welcome at all of them. **Blue Mountain Lodge** near Sabie is perhaps the top choice for a special romantic occasion (make sure to get here before dark to enjoy a drink on the deep verandas overlooking the lush, manicured gardens), with close runner-up the Relais & Châteaux **Cybele Forest Lodge.** But for a really laid-back gregarious atmosphere, with no pretensions and really good food (not to mention ease of access), head for **Rissington Inn** (✆ **013/737 7700**) just outside Hazyview. The menu is plain but extensive (even a few great vegetarian options) and firmly comfort; most of the dinner entrees, such as tarragon trout, cost R80 to R110, making it the best value for quality home-cooked fare on the Escarpment. It seats only 35 and is often packed with locals, so book in advance.

If you're near Graskop, **Harrie's Pancakes** (✆ **013/767-1273;** daily 8am–5pm) is a great lunch pitstop. The original Harrie's (he's opened four more outlets since flipping his first pancakes here almost 2 decades ago), and it remains consistently good: thick crepes are filled with interesting combinations, such as trout fillet and horseradish, for example, or butternut with feta and roasted pepper sauce, or green fig preserve with pecan nuts and cream.

Last, if you're interested in sampling traditional African fare accompanied by some super singing and dancing by local Shangaan people, book a Lunch Tour or Evening Festival at the nearby **Shangana Cultural Village ★★** (✆ **013/737-7000;** www. shangana.co.za; R353 near Hazyview; open daily, depending on tour bookings). It's very touristy but unexpectedly enjoyable as a night's entertainment, particularly if you haven't experienced the moving sight of African dancers belting it out elsewhere.

DRIVING THE panorama route

This drive takes you past the Blyde River Canyon, the largest, deepest canyon in the country, as well as the sheer 1,600m (5,248-ft.) drop from the Escarpment to the warm lowveld plains shimmering below. Hot air rising over this wall generates the heavy mists and high rainfall that, in turn, create the unique montane grasslands and riverine forests of the Blyde River Canyon Nature Reserve, which starts just north of Graskop before broadening out to include the Blydepoort Dam, 60km (37 miles) north. To complete the Panorama Route as a circular trip (approx. 160km/99 miles), stopping for most of the view points and returning to either Sabie or Graskop, you should set aside a day.

As you follow the tour below, refer to the "Panorama Route & Sabie" map earlier in this chapter for more information.

To drive this route, take the R532 north out of Graskop before turning right on the R534. The first stop is the **Pinnacle**—a thin, tree-topped, 30m-tall (98-ft.) quartzite rock that juts below the view point. **God's Window ★★★**, 4km (2½ miles) farther, which offers the first view of the open lowveld plains, is more impressive. (Wonderview is a variation of this and can be skipped if you're pressed for time.) The looping R534 now rejoins the R532. Turn left and look for the sign if you want to visit **Lisbon Falls,** which drops 37m (121 ft.). To continue on to Blyde River Canyon, turn right onto the R532, taking in the 48m (157-ft.) **Berlin Falls** on the way. (While pretty enough, neither are worth it if you are planning to include Vic Falls in your itinerary!)

Back on the R532, head north for **Bourke's Luck Potholes** (*©* **013/761-6019**). Here gold-digger Bourke predicted that he would strike it lucky, but he found nothing in these large scooped formations, carved by the movement of pebbles and water in the swirling whirlpools created by the confluence of the Blyde and Treur rivers. Bourke was not the last person to be disappointed by the Potholes—it's a long walk to look at them, and they reveal very little. Nor does the visitor center, which, in addition to some dry displays on the geology of the area, features a few dusty stuffed animals. The lichen trail is very easy and good for children. Gates open from 7am to 5pm; admission is R25.

Some 20km (12 miles) north is the lookout for the **Three Rondawels ★★★**, by far the most impressive stop of the entire trip. The name—which refers to the three circular hut-shaped outcrops that are more or less opposite the lookout—does nothing to describe the humbling size of what beckons. A sheer drop threatens to pull you off the precipice; thousands of feet below, the Blyde River snakes its way through the canyon to the tranquil Blyde Dam, embraced by green mountains. Beyond, the great lowveld plains shimmer in the distance.

Tip: If you're feeling thirsty, drop into the **Forever Blyde Canyon Resort** (the turnoff is a couple of miles north past the Three Rondawels and clearly signposted; *©* **013/769-8005**), which offers another angle on the Three Rondawels from its terrace; it's no foodie haven however, so don't go much beyond a toasted sandwich order. (If you'd like to take a look at

Blue Mountain Lodge ★★   This is a very romantic place (albeit a little resort-like, despite its relatively small size), very luxe and comfortable, and the hands-on GM Reinhardt works hard to ensure every expectation is met. The best accommodation option is to book one of the Victorian suites: Separate cottages are set below ponds, palms, a pool, a dining terrace, and a grand staircase that sweeps down to

the resort's very basic budget efficiency lodging, go to www.foreverblydecanyon.co.za—ask for a cottage with a view.)

From here, you will descend the **Abel Erasmus Pass** before passing through the J. G. Strijdom Tunnel. Approximately 20km (12 miles) from here is the turnoff for **Monsoon Gallery** (📞 015/795-5114), off the R527. Located in a 1.6-hectare (4-acre) lush garden, Monsoon carries a selection of African crafts, but stock is often limited; you can also enjoy a light meal at the adjacent **Mad Dogz Café** (📞 015/795-5425).

At this point, you can stay on the R527, heading east for **Hoedspruit,** if you wish to enter the Timbavati private game reserve, the central Orpen gate or head for the (Eastgate) airport. Alternatively you can take one of two detours—look for the turnoff to the budget **Forever Swadini Resort** (📞 015/795-5961; www.foreverswadini.co.za). From here, you can take a 90-minute boat trip on the Blyde Dam to see the mouth of the canyon and look up at the Escarpment towering above (www.blydecanyon.co.za; R95 per adult, R60 children 2–8; best to book 📞 072/260-4212). Or take the R531, which takes you past **Moholoholo Rehabilitation Centre** (📞 015/7955 236; www.moholoholo.co.za; R100 tour; R50 kids) to join the R40 lower down. At this junction you can turn north and travel a few miles (on the R40) to Kapama, a fenced private reserve and site of the popular **Hoedspruit Endangered Species Centre ★★** (📞 015/793-1633; www.wildlifecentre.co.za), also known as the "Cheetah Project," and a classier outfit than Moholoholo.

This is also the pickup point for Kapama's **elephant-back safaris ★★★**. The latter is well worth considering. For R1,775, you get to be transported through big-game country on the back of one of these lumbering giants and learn more about this most intelligent of species. The Cheetah Project is equally educational but less exhilarating. Guided tours (daily every hour 8am–3pm; R130 adults, R60 children 6-12) kick off with a video presentation, after which you are driven through the center by a ranger, sighting cheetahs, wild dogs, rhinos, and various bird species. At 90 minutes, the tour is a tad long, and although several of the cheetahs raised here have been successfully released into the wild, it still feels a little like a large, comfortable zoo. However, it is the one place where you can see the so-called king cheetah, a rare variant whose striking semistriped coat is associated with an unusual recessive gene.

Turn back south on the R40 and you can enter central Kruger via Orpen Gate (the closest to the Satara Rest Camp), or to travel to the Manyeleti or northern Sabi Sand reserves via Gowry Gate. Keep going south on the R40 to reach the turnoff for southern Kruger gates and/or Sabi Sand gates (in Hazyview).

To return to Graskop, keep following the R40 south to Klaserie, then follow the R533 from Bosbokrand, climbing Kowyn's Pass to Graskop. (**Note:** The R40 between Hazyview and Acorn Hoek, can be unsafe to travel at night, when animals wander at will. During daylight, you're more likely to be pulled over for speeding, so take it easy either way.)

more immaculately manicured lawns. Aside from the suites are the decadent manor houses—these are essentially single-occupancy luxury villas, private and very spacious, and come with their own staff. The Quadrant rooms (ex-stables) are very average. Food is another reason the lodge still enjoys a good reputation, despite no longer seemingly an independent concern (always a worry).

Take the Kiepersol turnoff, 28km (17 miles) east of Sabie on the R536, and follow for 4km (2½ miles) before turnoff. www.bluemountainlodge.co.za ✆ **013/737-8446.** Fax 013/737-6917. 15 units. Summer season (Sep–Apr): Victorian suites R3,370 double (Ballentine suite R4875); manor houses R6500; Quadrant rooms R2,225 double. Winter season: Victorian suites R2,800 double (Ballentine R4075); manor houses R5,400; Quadrant rooms R1825 double. Rates include breakfast. AE, DC, MC, V. No children under 12. **Amenities:** Restaurant; bar; large pool; room service; Wi-Fi in reception area. *In room:* A/C, hair dryer, minibar.

Buhala Country House ★ 👔   Buhala is a great alternative to staying inside the Kruger if you'd prefer more luxury (better dining, spa therapies, and so on) and intimacy (only 10 rooms), without the huge price tag of a private reserve lodge. In fact, Buhala is effectively part of the Kruger, located as it is on the banks of the Olifants (facing into Kruger): Elephants and hippo are regular visitors. It's only 10 minutes to the Malelane Gate, and besides, Buhala has its own open-topped vehicle to take you on game drives. This is also a top choice for golfers; guests at Buhala may play Leopard's Creek, arguably the most exclusive golf course in South Africa. Do check out unpretentious Rissington for an even better value near-Kruger experience (without the reserve views however, or amenities).

Turn-off from N4 (past Nelspruit and Malelane village). www.buhala.co.za. ✆ **082/940-8630.** 10 units. R2,266–R2,750 double; R3,565 suite. Rates include breakfast. Dinner around R200. AE, DC, MC, V. No children under 10. **Amenities:** Restaurant; bar; game drives in Kruger with Buhala's ranger; golf at nearby LC; spa; swimming pool; tennis. *In room:* A/C, hair dryer, minibar (Elephant Suites only).

Casa do Sol ★ ☺   A charming Mediterranean-style resort village, complete with cobbled streets, white stucco walls, and terra-cotta roof tiles, set in award-winning tropical gardens behind which stretch 500 hectares (1,235 acres) of indigenous bush. Casa do Sol was established in 1968 and still retains a vaguely 1970s feel, despite ongoing renovations and upgrades. The double suites are ideal for families—ask for one upstairs and you'll enjoy views of the valley and estate from the private patio. An all-around excellent family resort, with a good ambience, though it doesn't offer the well-bred intimacy of lodges such as Blue Mountain or Cybele, or the privacy of Timamoon.

P.O. Box 57, Hazyview 1242. Off the R536, 39km (24 miles) east of Sabie and 5km (3 miles) west of Hazyview. www.ahagroup.com ✆ **013/737-8111.** Fax 013/737-8166. 54 units. Summer: Casa R1,920 double; Villa R2,230; double suite R2,420; additional person over 12 R450. Winter: Casa R1,710 double; Villa R1,960; double suite R2,340. Children under 12 stay free in double suite, which can accommodate 2 kids; R250 for their meals. AE, DC, MC, V. **Amenities:** Restaurant; bar; babysitting; fishing; horseback riding; 2 pools; room service; tennis court (all-weather); free Wi-Fi in bar area; wildlife trails to view antelope. *In room:* A/C, TV, hair dryer, minibar (in villas and suites).

> ### 📎 Stock Up on the Way to Kruger
>
> If you're traveling on the Sabie-Hazyview road, stop at **The Windmill Wine Shop** (✆ 013/737-8175; Mon–Sat 9am–5pm) to snack on a tapas platter or stock up on deli fare (cold meats including local smoked trout, South African cheeses, pickles and olives, fresh bread) as well as local craft beers or Cape wines—a picnic to enjoy on your veranda in a Kruger Park rest camp.

Cybele Forest Lodge & Health Spa ★★★   With more character than most of its competitors, Cybele (pronounced Sigh-*bee*-lee) has been offering Jo'burgers a respite from the rat race for more than 30 years. Even Capetonians would travel north just to relax in the subtropical surroundings and sample the legendary cuisine served by what is now recognized as a Yellow Shield member of Relais & Châteaux. It's lost a little of its personal hands-on management over the years, but the beauty of the 120-hectare (296-acre) grounds remain lovely, and it manages to combine a wonderful sense of being marooned in nature with real luxury. The suites offer everything from private heated pools to fireplaces (some even in the bathrooms), but you'll be very comfortable in the garden cottages too. The terrific spa features two hydrotherapy baths and offers everything from facials to African Rungu & Calabash massages.

Off the Spitskop turnoff of the R40, 28km (17 miles) east of Sabie on the R536. Alternatively, follow signs off the R40 btw. Hazyview and White River. www.cybele.co.za ✆ **013/764-9500.** Fax 013/764-9510. 12 units. Summer: R3,700–4,300 cottage; R4,980–R7,990 suite. Winter: 2,740–R3,190 cottage; R3,690–R5,910 suite. Rates include breakfast. AE, DC, MC, V. No children under 10. **Amenities:** Restaurant; bar; gym; hiking trails; horseback riding; free high-speed Internet; pool; spa; trout fishing (tackle provided). *In room:* A/C, fans, TV/VCR, fireplace, hair dryer, minibar, private heated pool (in suites), stereo.

Numbela Exclusive Riverside Accommodation ★ 🍴 🎒 ☺

With just three charming cottages on a rambling 80-hectare (200-acre) estate with a river running through it, this will suit you if you like being left alone (along with good value) and don't need lots of amenities. All the cottages are neat as a pin: Thatched River Cottage (sleeps two or three) is right on the river, with whitewashed walls and artifacts collected by the original owners from travels through Africa. Yellow Wood is slightly bigger (sleeps four) and elevated, but also has its own sandy river beach and comes with outdoor shower. Tin House has four bedrooms and is efficiency only; suits larger groups. Owner-host Tracey Nepten lives on the adjoining property and will ensure you find your way to the waterfalls and trails, and recommend restaurants. Breakfast is served on your cottage patio but must be booked in advance. It's unpretentious and charming, but there's no on-site restaurant.

20km (16 miles) north of Whiteriver, off R40 to Hazyview. www.numbela.co.za. ✆ **084 491 2708.** River R900–R1,000 double. Yellow Wood R1,000 double. June–July and Easter/Christmas surcharges apply. Children under 12 by arrangement. **Amenities:** Efficiency units; running/walking trails; river swimming. *In room:* Fireplace, hair dryer, fully equipped kitchen, barbecue, CD with music.

Rissington Inn ★ 🍴 ☺

We love owner-run establishments that offer hands-on personal attention, and Chris Harvey's presence looms large in this comfortable, thatched lodge, just 10 to 15 minutes from Kruger's Phabeni Gate. What it lacks in style it more than makes up with warmth; a really laid-back space, ideal for young people traveling in a group, families, or anyone gregarious looking an informal place with vibe (for romantic privacy, rather head to Numbela's River Cottage or Timamoon, depending on budget). Euphorbia, Ivory, Baobab, Mahogany, and Kigelia have views; the Garden suites are more private. The two hillside suites are ideal for extended families/large groups, each with two bedrooms (sleeping 5; 10 in total) a spacious sitting room, sun terrace, and shared usage of an additional pool.

Hazyview. Follow signposts off R40. P.O. www.rissington.co.za ✆ **013/737-7700.** Fax 013/737-7112. 16 units. R1,000 standard double; R1,520 superior double; R1,780 Garden suite; R1980 hillside double, each additional adult R495. Children R190. Rates include breakfast. AE, DC, MC, V. **Amenities:** Restaurant; bar; library; pool; room service; Wi-Fi in main area (free). In room: TV (in hillside suites only), hair dryer.

Timamoon ★★★

If you want to truly get away from it all, with absolutely no disturbances, Timamoon's six thatched "lodges," each located a few minutes' drive from one another, is where you can wander around naked. Kruger lies just 40 minutes away, but you'll be hard-pressed to leave your well-appointed, secluded, and spacious lodge, furnished with artifacts that the owners have collected from years of travel throughout Africa. Each features an en-suite bedroom (one has two bedrooms) with four-poster king-size beds draped in mosquito netting, decks with private plunge pools, luxurious bathrooms, and outdoor showers. Moon River is the honeymoon suite, but Full, New, and Blue Moons all enjoy similar spectacular locations on the lip of a gorge, overlooking dense forested slopes through which the Sabie River cascades (Amber and Many Moons are not on the lip). One drawback here is that there's no phone (bring your own) or room service; you'll also have to drive to reach the restaurant—a charming candlelit stilted room.

24km (15 miles) east of Sabie, turn off from R536; follow signs for 3km (1¾ miles). www.timamoonlodge. co.za. *℡* **013/767-1740.** Fax 013/767-1889. 6 units. R3,800–R6,000 depending on lodge or time of year. Rates include breakfast and dinner. AE, DC, MC, V. No children under 16. **Amenities:** Restaurant. *In room:* Hair dryer, high-speed Internet, minibar (on request), plunge pool.

Pilgrim's Rest ★★

Located 35km (22 miles) north of Sabie, Pilgrim's Rest was established in 1873 after Alex "Wheelbarrow" Patterson discovered gold in a stream flowing past what would become one of the first gold-rush villages in South Africa. Having struck out on his own to escape the crush at Mac Mac, he must have been horrified when within the year he was joined by 1,500 diggers, all frantically panning to make their fortunes. A fair number did, with the largest nugget weighing in at 11kg (24 lb.), but by 1881, the best of the pickings had been found, and the diggings were bought by the Transvaal Gold Mining Estates (TGME). Development tapered off fast, and the deserted village, looking much as it did in the early 1900s, was later declared a national monument.

If you're looking for historical accuracy, then you'll find Pilgrim's Rest's streets are a great deal prettier than they would have been in the at the turn of the 20th century, and the overall effect, from the gleaming vintage fuel pumps to flower baskets, is a sanitized, glamorized picture of life in a gold-rush town. However, its history makes it more authentic than a theme park, with a few poignant spots, the best of which is the evocative **Pilgrim's Rest Cemetery ★★**. Besides the headstone simply inscribed ROBBERS GRAVE—the only tomb that lies in a north-south direction—the many children's graves are moving testimony to how hard times really were, and the many nationalities reflect the cosmopolitan character of the original gold-rush village. Just below is the humble **St. Mary's Anglican Church,** overlooking the main street as you enter town.

Most of the historical buildings line the single main street in what is commonly called "Uptown," including the **Tourist Information Centre (*℡* 013/768-1060;** www.pilgrimsrest.org.za; daily 9am–4pm); the center is clearly marked on the main street; staff will supply town maps as well as tickets to the museums, and will book tours for you. Architecture along the main street is classic colonial Victorian: Walls are corrugated iron with deep sash windows, and corrugated-iron roofs extend over large shaded *stoeps* (verandas). If you're feeling hungry or wish to overnight you can do so at the **Royal Hotel,** a heritage hotel with some of the very rooms that have been accommodating guests since 1873 (www.royal-hotel.co.za); certainly don't leave town without visiting the hotel's **Church Bar ★**: The tiny building used to be a church in Mozambique before it was relocated here, answering the prayers of the thirsty Pilgrims of Mpumalanga. The three museums in town (the **Dredzen Shop and House Museum,** the **News Printing Museum,** and the **House Museum**) can all be visited with a single ticket sold at the Tourist Information Centre (R12). None of these house museums feel particularly authentic; furnishings and objects are often propped haphazardly and look much the worse for wear. The **Alanglade Museum ★** (R20), located in a forested grove 1.5km (about 1 mile) north of town, is a little more interesting. Once the home of the TGME's mine manager and his family, the furnishings, while not originally their belongings, are of the era and provide some sense of the lifestyle and strange claustrophobia of living in an isolated forest near a gold-rush town in Victorian times. The hourly tours run from 11am to 2pm Monday through Saturday, and must be booked half an hour in advance from the Pilgrim's Rest Tourist Information Centre. You can also try your hand at **gold panning** (R12) in the Pilgrim's Rest stream, though your chances of finding anything of value? Fat, or slim!

The Magoebaskloof Route

If you are planning to visit central or northern Kruger, or simply want to take a route through a much greener, less developed region, head north on the N1 Toll Road (credit cards accepted throughout) and don't stop until you get to Polokwane, a 330km (205-mile) drive that should take approximately 3 hours. From Polokwane (a city that offers absolutely no reason to stop) you head due east on the R71 to Haenertsburg.

If you have time, pop into the **Cheerio Gardens** (✆ 015/276-4924) just outside Haenertsburg, best visited when the trees are in full bloom (usually in Oct). Alternatively, stay on the R71 to **Magoebaskloof** or take the R528 loop through **George's Valley** to Tzaneen. Both routes are rewarding: winding mountain passes that offer dramatic views of dense forests and large still lakes. The steeper gradients of the R71—you will drop 56m (180 ft.) in under 6.5km (4 miles) as you wind down the Drakensberg Escarpment to the subtropical lowveld—swing the balance somewhat in its favor. Look out for the turn off marked HOUTBOSDORP, which takes you on a 12km (7.5-mile) route into the **Woodbush State Forest,** the largest area of indigenous forest in Limpopo. The **Debengeni Falls** lie just east of here and are reached by following the road that finally returns to the R71 via the De Hoek State Forest. After to the turnoff to Debengeni and De Hoek the woodlands change into subtropical plantations of avocado, banana, mango, paw paw, nuts, kiwi, and litchi, and rolling hills of soft green tea bushes. If you've never visited a tea estate a stop at **Pekoe View Tea Garden** (✆ 015/305-4999) and the Sapeko Tea Estate is highly recommended, if only for the view. If you turn south at the T-junction with the R36 you will get to Tzaneen in a few minutes; turn north, toward Duiwelskloof, and you can visit the home of Modjadji, the Rain Queen, but note that this circular route will add 100km (60 miles) to your journey.

An Easter Pilgrimage to Moira

While traversing the R71, keep an eye out for the huge Star of David etched onto a hill overlooking a small settlement some 30km (19 miles) from Polokwane. This marks the Zion City Moira headquarters of the African Zionist Church, the biggest Christian congregation in South Africa. An estimated three million members make the annual pilgrimage to Moira every Easter—so the week preceding is not to the best time to be on the R71, dodging brimful minibus taxis careering to Moira, their drivers on a mission from God to get as many members as possible there by Good Friday.

Tzaneen marks the transition from Escarpment to Lowveld; travel for another hour east on the R71 and you'll reach Phalaborwa, one of the Kruger's central gates, ideal if you are on your way to Letaba or Olifants Rest Camps (or the Hans Merensky Golf Club; see "Staying Active," earlier in chapter). Alternatively, if you take the R36 that runs southeast from Tzaneen, you'll access the lodges in Makalali, Timbavati or Manyeleti, or enter Kruger via the central Orpen gate.

Tzaneen itself is an unassuming town servicing the predominantly farming community that surrounds it, with its principal draw being the small but interesting ethnographic collection at the **Tzaneen Museum ★** (*©* **083/280-4966;** Mon–Fri 9am–4pm; Sat 9am–noon). Just outside Tzaneen on the R71 you will find the headquarters for **Kaross Studios** (*©* **015/345-1458;** www.kaross.co.za), the award-winning hand-embroidered textiles you will find in just about every craft boutique in the country. They serve light lunches here, but if you're feeling tired and hungry it's time to head for the lofty heights of nearby **Agatha ★★**, located 15km (9 miles) south of Tzaneen, and get "on board" the beautiful Kings Walden.

Kings Walden Garden Manor ★★★ 📖   Magical, mystical, romantic. Famous for its gardens, Kings Walden has developed—under the management of Sophie and Steven—into a relaxing, comfortable place to stay, rather than just a tourist attraction. Service is sincere and warm; cuisine excellent, but it is the location that is the showstopper. Floating 1,050m (3,444 ft.) above sea level, the garden has been laid out to suggest a ship setting sail into the skies with the grounds falling away on three sides and the grand "decks" providing dramatic views of the undulating lowveld. Trees, walls, and statuary are covered in moss and lichen—testimony to the damp conditions that often prevail when clouds descend on the gardens. This serves only to heighten the garden's ethereal, romantic beauty, as do well-positioned ponds and mirrors. Kruger's closest gate is 75 minutes away, making this an ideal place to catch your breath en route, but you'll wish you had time to stay longer.

Old Coach Rd., Agatha. www.kingswalden.co.za. *©* **015/307-3262.** 6 units. R1,350 double; children 60%. Rates include breakfast; dinner R225. AE, DC, MC, V. **Amenities:** Dining room; lounge; pool. *In room:* Fireplace, hair dryer.

KRUGER NATIONAL PARK ★★★

Southern (Malelane) gate 428km (265 miles) NE of Johannesburg; northern (Pafuri) gate 581km (360 miles) NE of Johannesburg

The Kruger is simply one of the greatest wildlife destinations in Africa, along with the Masai Mara and Serengeti in East Africa, or Chobe and Okavango in Botswana. Proclaimed by South African president Paul Kruger in 1898, it is one of the largest wildlife sanctuaries in the world, stretching 381km (236 miles) from the banks of the Crocodile River in the south to the Limpopo River in the north, and covering almost 2.5 million hectares (6.2 million acres). In addition to this is the 150,000-hectare (370,500 acres) stretch of privately owned land flanking the Park. Home to South Africa's most famous game lodges and camps, these private reserves are owned by groups of freehold landowners and concession-holders with traversing rights, and with no fences between Kruger, a public (government-owned) park, and the private reserves, animals are able to follow natural migratory routes. While it makes no difference to the animals whether they are on public or private land, your experience will be radically different. Book the national park accommodation, and you have essentially signed up for a self-drive safari on demarcated, mostly paved roads; staying in very, very basic bungalows or huts (or tents); in camps the size of small resorts; eating canteen-style food (or cooking yourself, by far the better option). Stay in a private reserve (or one of the private concessions within the park) and you will enjoy the finest close-up Big 5 experience in Africa, driven off-road, often virtually within touching distance of animals, and cosseted in the most unbelievable luxury, with meals and drinks that will have you feeling like a goose being prepared for foie gras.

Regardless of whether you opt for a private lodge or a public rest camp, you cannot fail to be impressed with the sheer diversity of life the Kruger sustains. Sixteen eco-zones (each with its own geology, rainfall, altitude, and landscape) are home to more than 500 bird species and 147 mammal species—more than any other reserve in Africa, including an estimated 2,000 lions, 1,000 leopards, 6,200 white and 350 black rhinos, 12,500 elephants, and 25,000 buffaloes. Cheetah, African wild dog, spotted hyena, zebra, giraffe, hippo, crocodile, warthog, and some 21 antelope species also roam Kruger's open plains and waterways. The rich flora varies from tropical to subtropical; almost 2,000 plant species have been identified, including some 450 tree and shrub species and 235 grasses. The opportunity to see wildlife is superb—many people report seeing four of the Big 5 (the most elusive being the leopard) in a day, and some are lucky enough to see them all. Don't count on this; rather, set out to enjoy the open roads, undulating landscape, and countless species you will encounter along the way.

For those looking with a little culture to temper the abundance of nature, Kruger also has a number of archaeological sites, the most interesting being the Thulamela Heritage Site, a 16th-century stone-walled village overlooking the Luvuvhu River in the north. Others include the Stone Age village at Masorini, and more than 170 documented prehistoric rock painting sites, the most accessible being found at the Crocodile Bridge hippo pool, in the private concession leased to Jock Safari Camp, and along the Bushman and Wolhuter trails. Historical sites relating to early European explorers and Kruger's beginnings are also dotted throughout the park.

But excitement over the Kruger's incorporation into transfrontier conservation initiatives has to some extent been tempered by ongoing concerns over the disputes before the country's Land Claims Commission, charged with returning land appropriated from its original owners under apartheid governance. Thus far, two of these claims have been settled in a manner that has had all-round benefits. The first land claim to be awarded was that of the Makuleke clan, which received ownership of the Pafuri area, now known as Makuleke Contractual Park. Two lodges have been built on the property, The Outpost and the Pafuri Tented Camp, as well as a wilderness school called Eco Training. The second land claim, in which a stretch of land to the south of Numbi Gate has been awarded to the Mdluli clan, has also become a win-win situation. It now operates as a concession called Mdluli Game Reserve, and is the site of a tented camp and field guide training academy run by a safari company called Untamed Africa (www.untamed.co.za)—again proving that sustainable land development can benefit both local communities and nature conservation.

Essentials
ARRIVING
BY PLANE To get to Kruger by air you will have to fly into Johannesburg first. With limited time, fly to the commercial airport nearest to your lodge and arrange for the lodge to do the road transfer (up to 3 hr. depending on location) or the airstrip nearest your lodge. There are incidentally regular "scheduled" shuttle charters

Kruger National Park & Private Reserves

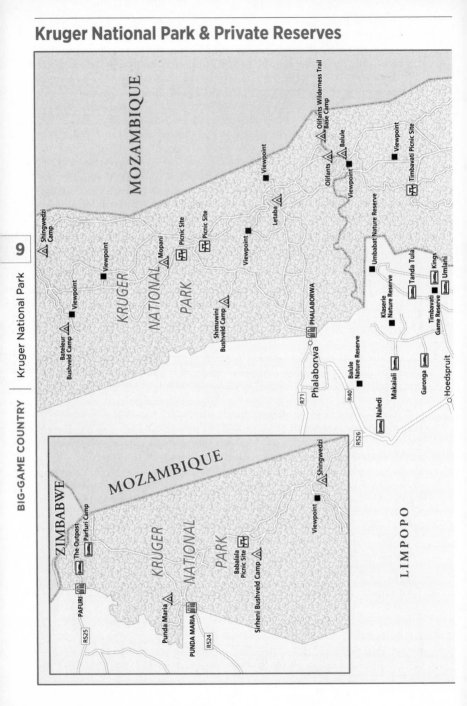

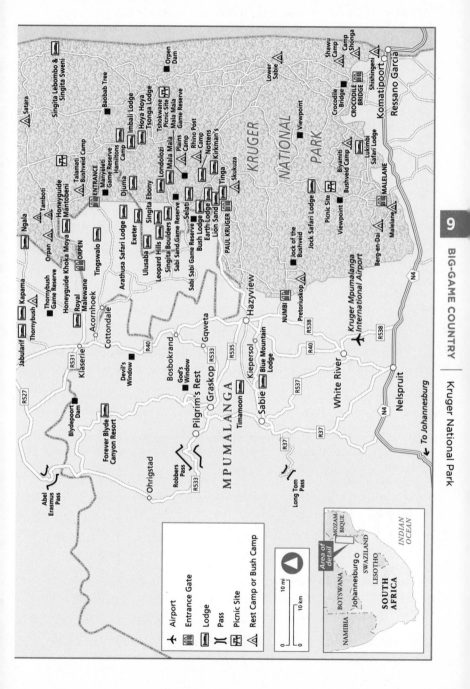

(routings and departure times vary from day to day depending on guests) into Sabi Sand private reserve and Skukuza airstrip in Kruger National Park; inquire directly with your lodge or contact Federal Air (www.fedair.com), as these are often not a great deal more expensive than commercial flights (at press time you could for instance fly into Sabi Sand for R3,900 round-trip) and very convenient. Alternatively, to check out the commercial flights, know which is the closest to your choice of lodge: There are three main airports in the Kruger vicinity (see below); for price comparisons, check www.saflights.co.za (KMIA is closest to Jo'burg and the busiest route to Kruger, and therefore the least expensive).

In brief the three commercial airport locations are as follows:

Kruger-Mpumalanga International Airport (KMIA): Located just outside Nelspruit, the provincial capital, this is the busiest by far (still sometimes referred to as Nelspruit Airport), serviced by three airlines (SAA, Kulula, and British Airways, inevitably Kulula offers the best deals; at press time around R950 round-trip) and is ideal to enter the gates to southern Kruger or Sabi Sand.

Hoedspruit Airport (**HDS** in Hoedspruit) is ideal to enter southern or central Kruger, or Manyeleti or Timbavati. Only SAA fly here and you are looking at around R2,200 at press time.

Phalaborwa Airport (**PHW** in Phalaborwa) is ideal to enter central Kruger (on your way to Letaba or Olifants Rest Camps) or the lodges in Makalali or Garonga. Only SAA flies to this, the least busy airport, and you're looking at close to R3,000 at press time.

BY CAR The park has 10 entrance gates, with the southern gates a comfortable 5- to 6-hour drive from Johannesburg or Pretoria. Reaching the northern gate via Letaba could take as long as 7 or 8 hours. The closest gate, Malelane, is 428km (265 miles) from Johannesburg, while Pafuri (the farthest) lies around 580km (360 miles) northeast. The southern gates are **Malelane, Crocodile Bridge, Numbi, Phabeni,** and **Paul Kruger.** The central gates: **Orpen** and **Phalaborwa.** The northern gates: **Punda Maria, Giriyondo** (from Mozambique), and **Pafuri.** Allow enough time to reach the park; entrance-gate hours (see "Fast Facts: Kruger National Park," below) are strictly enforced. For easy access, officials recommend the newest gate, **Phabeni.** You will need to pay a park entrance fee at whichever Kruger National Park gate you enter (see below) as well as at any of the Private Reserve gates (inquire from your lodge; Sabi Sand R110 per vehicle at press time).

VISITOR INFORMATION All inquiries and applications should be made to **South African National Parks (SANParks): www.sanparks.org**. If you need to make contact via mail the address is P.O. Box 787, 643 Leyds St., Muckleneuk, Tshwane, or call ✆ **012/428-9111;** fax 012/426-5500; Mon–Fri 7:30am–5pm, Sat 8am–1pm). You can also phone the park directly at ✆ **013/735-4000** or 013/735-4246. Accommodation and campsites at all public rest camps within the park can also be booked by e-mail or telephone, but it's far easier and more efficient to use the very user-friendly and almost instantaneous online booking service on the SANParks website, which is pretty self-explanatory. The park's headquarters is situated at Skukuza Rest Camp, located in the southern section, on the banks of the Sabie River (see later in this chapter).

GETTING AROUND By Car If you have flown in and need to rent a car, contact **Avis** (www.avis.co.za), with desks at all three airports (Kruger-Mpumalanga International Airport; ✆ **013/750-1015**); Hoedspruit Airport (✆ **015/793-2014**);

Phalaborwa Airport (℡ **015/781-3169**), as well as at Skukuza, main camp in the Kruger (℡ **013/735-5651**). **Budget** (www.budget.co.za) operates from the Kruger-Mpumalanga Airport (℡ **013/751-1774**) and Phalaborwa Airport (℡ **015/781-5404**). It's exciting to explore the park at your own pace in a rental car, but at least one guided game drive in an open-topped vehicle is recommended (see "Guided Game Drives & Walks," below). Note also that the park has opened 4- to 5-hour **4x4 Adventure Trails** that take you right off the beaten track into areas previously off-limits, but you will have to rent a 4WD vehicle to complete these. Sign up for these from Pretoriuskop, Satara, Phalaborwa Gate, Punda Maria, and Shingwedzi. The Planning Trails are weather-sensitive, so they must be booked on the same day.

When to Go

First off, Kruger's affordability combined with its efficient maintenance standards means that it is very, very popular, particularly the best camps, so when you go may very well be determined by availability. Book as early as you can (though you cannot book more than 11 months in advance). Certainly each season has advantages. Between October and March, when summer rains (often in the form of dramatic thunderstorms) have transformed the dry landscape into a flowering paradise, the park is alive with young buck and migratory birds, but at the same time, temperatures can soar above 105°F (40°C), dropping to 68°F (20°C) in the balmy evenings. The dense, junglelike foliage hides game, and the malaria risk is at its highest. In the winter, when water is scarce and the plant life recedes, animals are easier to spot, especially at water holes and riverbeds. Because this is the most popular season, however, be prepared to share your sightings with other motorists. The days are warm, but temperatures can drop close to freezing at night, and units are not heated. Try to avoid going during the school holidays, particularly in winter, when the park really is packed to capacity.

[FastFACTS] KRUGER NATIONAL PARK

Admission Hours   For the Park   Entrance gates open from January to February from 5:30am to 6:30pm, March from 5:30am to 6pm, April from 6am to 6pm, May to July 6am to 5:30pm, August to September 6am to 6pm, October from 5:30am to 6pm, and November to December from 5:30am to 6:30pm. If you are going to be traveling late best to double check these times online.

For the Rest Camps Camps are fenced off to protect residents from predators. The gates to these follow the same hours, except in the summer months (Nov–Jan), when they open an hour earlier (4:30am). If you're changing rest camps, try not to travel more than 200km (124 miles), to ensure you get to your new camp before gates close. Operating hours for camp receptions are usually 7am

until half an hour after gate closing time; shops are typically from 8am to a half-hour after camp gates close, though they are shorter at some smaller camps; restaurants 7 to 10am, noon to 2:30pm, and 6 to 10pm.

Bank & ATM Networks There is a bank and ATM at Skukuza; it's a good idea to get cash here if you haven't already done so outside the park. (While you can pay by card for most anything, cash for a drink at a picnic site shop is useful, and all fuel must be paid for in cash.) There is also a proper ATM at Letaba. Most of the shops in other camps have mini-ATMs, but these don't always have cash, so don't wait until your wallet is empty before trying one of them.

Driving Rules   Unlike private game reserves, where rangers are free to drive off road, everyone at Kruger drives on roads; the public drives on approved roads only. The speed limit is 50kmph (31 mph) on paved roads, 40kmph (25 mph) on gravel roads, and 20kmph (12 mph) in rest camps. If photographs of fatally maimed animals don't help ensure that these speeds are adhered to, speed traps do. Stay in your vehicle unless you're at a designated picnic site.

Fees   SANParks charges a **daily conservation fee** for each person entering the park; 2012 fees for overseas visitors are R192 per adult and R96 per child per day. If you plan to spend more than 6 nights in Kruger or visit other national parks in South Africa, look into purchasing a **Wild Card** (valid for 1 year), which provides free access to all national parks. At press time, a Wild Card cost R325 for an individual, R535 for a couple, and R640 for a family.

Fuel   Every main rest camp has a fuel/gasoline station. You must pay in cash or with a local petrol card—no credit or debit cards are accepted. (Note that bush camps don't have gas.)

Internet & Phone
Camps with Internet cafes are Skukuza, Lower Sabie, and Berg-en-Dal. Most of the main camps have cell-phone reception, but the bushveld camps and roads usually don't.

Malaria   While certain areas of Kruger are soon to be removed from the list of malarial areas, the risk of infection remains, and it is a disease you really want to avoid. The highest risk is between October and May, during which time a course of prescription antimalaria drugs is advised (for more information, see chapter 13).

Medical Emergencies
There is a doctor in Skukuza (☏ **013/735-5638** or 082/557-9210). If you need help during the night, drive to the camp gate and beep your horn. The closest hospitals are in Nelspruit, Hoedspruit, and Phalaborwa. Of these, I'd head for Nelspruit Medi-Clinic, a 260-bed multidisciplinary private hospital and part of one of the largest, most respected private hospitals groups in Africa (☏ **013/759-0500**).

Money/Traveler's Checks/Credit Cards   South African rands, traveler's checks, Visa, MasterCard, Diners Club, and American Express are accepted. Foreign currency can be exchanged at all rest camps.

Reservations   The easiest way to book rest camp accommodations is on the user-friendly website www.sanparks.org. However, preference for choice units is given to written applications (this includes e-mail) received 11 months in advance. Pay your deposit as soon as possible to ensure the booking—this can be done over the telephone or Internet with a credit card.

Rules   Park rules are printed on the entrance permit—read it. Park officials do not have a sense of humor when it comes to breaking the rules.

Safety   Don't let the paved road fool you—once you've left the safety of your fenced-off rest camp, you really are in the wild. *Under no circumstances* should you leave your vehicle unless you're at a designated site (see "Designated Pit Stops & Picnic Sites," below, or get a map from a rest camp shop). One ranger who left his game drive to "relieve" himself didn't survive to do up his zipper, so make sure to take care of any bathroom business before leaving camp. When in camp, try not to be frightened by spiders and other small insects you may encounter; unlike mosquitoes, they can do you no harm. Snakes are a rare occurrence in camps; if you do spot one, alert reception. (See chapter 13 for more safety tips on safaris.)

Exploring the Park

SANParks officials make no bones about the fact that their main concern is wildlife; *Homo sapiens* are a necessary nuisance. Although an effort is made to service visitors' needs, such as providing escorted game drives (highly recommended unless you're going on to a private game reserve), and the park's stated intention to support conservation through tourism, the rules (such as gate-opening times) are inflexible, staff can be bureaucratic, accommodation is basic and in some cases threadbare (though clean), beds are for the most part single, and, because services are geared toward the South African efficiency market, you're pretty much expected to toe the line. However, there is talk of the development of two hotels, one in Skukuza and the other in Malelane, which has many objecting to the commercialization of the park, while others are hoping for a little more 21st-century luxury at (hopefully) an affordable price.

THE LAY OF THE LAND

Despite its many defined eco-zones, to the untrained eye, much of the park looks the same. A major portion is covered with a large shrublike tree called mopane. You'll find the most variation in the south and very far north of the park—old bush hands, in fact, divide the park into three distinct regions: The south they call the "circus"; the central area, the "zoo"; and the north, the true "wilderness." These are apt descriptions, particularly in the winter months, when the human and animal population soars in the water-rich south, while the less-accessible north remains a calm oasis.

Southern Kruger, aka "circus," supports some of the richest game concentrations in Africa, which in turn attracts the most people. The busiest—and often very rewarding—road linking Skukuza to Lower Sabie Rest Camp is often referred to as **Piccadilly Highway,** and motorists have been known to virtually jostle each other to get a better view of lions and even create traffic jams around great sightings. It's the best part of the park for spotting rhinos (very common btw. Lower Sabie and Crocodile Bridge), leopard, and spotted hyena, and also hosts good concentrations of lion, elephant, and buffalo.

The **central area** still features a wide variety of species, particularly around Satara Rest Camp, where open plains frequently reward with good sightings and cheetah. A little more laid-back, with fewer camps, but with a reputation for the highest concentration of lions, this area continues to attract its fair share of tourists, though not in the same numbers as Skukuza or Lower Sabie.

Most of the 13,000-odd resident elephants are found north of Olifants rest camp, but mile after mile of dense mopane scrubland makes even these huge animals difficult to see. The **northern part** of the park is probably not the best destination for a first-time visitor, unless you're a bird-watcher or it's combined with a sojourn in the south. But this remote wilderness area has definite advantages for real bush lovers, not least because you will share the experience with far fewer people. As you travel farther north, the mopane is broken by the lush riverine vegetation of the Shingwedzi, the baobab-dotted sandveld, fever-tree forests, and, finally, the tropical flood plains that lie between the Luvuvhu and Limpopo rivers. This northernmost part of the park is in fact at the crossroads of nine of Africa's major ecosystems, and the countryside is full of contrasts and the most prolific birdlife in the park: This region is *Birdlife S.A.*'s top destination in the country. Spend at least 5 days in the Kruger—ideally, longer—if you include the north in your itinerary.

BETTER WILDLIFE-VIEWING FOR THE SELF-GUIDE safari

1. **Purchase a detailed map** that indicates all rivers, dams, dirt roads, and lookout and picnic points. These are available at all rest camp shops and entrance gates. The comprehensive *Prime Origins Guide to Exploring Kruger* is highly recommended to those who want to take a self-drive safari; you will also find plenty of inexpensive introductory booklets for sale at all the park shops.

2. Between picnic spots there are no restrooms, gas stops, or shops, so **plan your journey along the way** and make sure you have something to drink and eat in the car, should you wish to stay with a sighting for some time.

3. **Be there at the right time.** The best times to view wildlife are in the early morning and late afternoon; animals don't move much in the heat of the day. Set off as soon as camp gates open (4:30–6:30am, depending on the season).

4. You're bound to bump into something if you **follow a river.** Always stop on bridges when crossing (traffic allowing) and look for crocodiles, herons, water monitors (lizards that can grow up to 3m/10ft.), hippos, and so on. Certain bridges, particularly those over the Letaba and Olifants rivers, allow you to get out of your vehicle—but please *exercise caution.* In winter, you're almost always assured of seeing animals at a water hole or dam; just park your car and wait.

5. **Spot a spotter.** A stationary car with binoculars pointed in a certain direction is an obvious clue. It is not considered bad form to ask what they have spotted (but you're unlikely to get a polite answer if you obscure their view).

DESIGNATED PIT STOPS & PICNIC SITES

The designated sites dotted throughout the park are the only places visitors are allowed to get out of their vehicles. Maps, available at the entry gates and all rest camp shops, will indicate where these are located, as well as the types of facilities each has. (These may include restrooms, boiling water, barbecue grills, seating, shade, telephones, educational displays, and shops staffed by attendants who sell wood, hot refreshments, and cold drinks.) The best-equipped and most popular sites are **Nkulu** (on the Sabie River btw. Skukuza and Lower Sabie), **Afsaal** (under a giant jackalberry tree on the main road btw. Skukuza and Malelane), and **Tshokwane** (near the three-way junction of the road connecting Skukuza and Lower Sabie to Satara, and named after an elephant bull that used to frequent the area). The shops here sell everything from scones to brandy. Less busy, with good game- and bird-viewing opportunities, are **Orpen Dam,** an elevated picnic spot overlooking the water, east of Tshokwane; and **Pafuri,** the best picnic site in the park, but located in the far north.

GUIDED GAME DRIVES & WALKS

Even if you're driving yourself, a guided game drive in an open-topped vehicle is a good way to get oriented, as experienced guides identify animals so you don't have to look them up in a book. During peak season, the major rest camps (Skukuza, Lower

6. **Appreciate the rare.** Most first-time visitors want to check off the Big 5, but it's worth finding out more about other species. Sighting a wild dog becomes that much more exciting when you know there are fewer than 400 left in the park.

7. **Bring a good pair of binoculars** and drum up some enthusiasm for the vegetation—that tree you stop to admire may reveal a leopard.

8. **Drive slowly**—sharing the shadow of the tree you just whizzed past could be a pride of lions. (The recommended speed for viewing is 25kmph/16 mph.)

9. Dirt roads give a great sense of adventure, but **don't shun the paved roads:** Besides being quieter, less dust makes for tastier grass verges.

10. **Consult the animal-sightings board** at your rest camp reception area—many animals are territorial and don't cover huge distances. Some experts advise that you concentrate on a smallish area, getting to know the movements of the animals, rather than driving all over the park.

11. Animals have the right of way on the roads. If a group of elephants is crossing, **keep a respectful distance,** switch the car off, and wait. If you're lucky enough to spot a black rhino (which has a hooked lip rather than the wide, square lip of the white rhino), be *very* wary.

12. **Never feed the baboons and monkeys** that hang out at picnic sites; this is tantamount to signing their death warrant, as they then become increasingly aggressive and have to be shot.

13. Most important, **be patient.** The only way you'll ever witness a kill, or any interesting animal interaction, is by watching a situation unfurl.

Sabie, Satara, Berg-en-Dal) provide these in large 23-seat vehicles; the only way to avoid potential noise and obstructed views is to book one of the less popular main camps (such as Mopani) out of season or stay at one of the recommended **bush camps,** where drives take place in open-topped 10-seaters (See "Where to Stay & Eat," below).

The best option, offered almost everywhere, is a **sunrise drive ★★** (R190 per person at rest camps, R250 at bush camps), which departs any time from 4 to 6am (30 min. before gates open). The 3-hour **sunset drives ★** (same price), departing 2 hours before the gates close, are as popular as the sunrise drives. You can also book these at the entrance gates, meaning you don't have to overnight here to experience this, and you'll be accommodated on a 10- or 23-seater, depending on numbers. However, the 2-hour **night drive ★** (same price; only at Bateleur; Letaba; Mopani: Olifants; Punda Maria; Satara; Shimuwini; Shingwedzi; Sirheni; Talamati), departing 2 hours after the gates close, is the one to make sure you're on as—outside the concession areas—this is the only way to see the Kruger at night, giving visitors an opportunity to view the nocturnal activities of such animals as bushbabies, porcupines, civets, hyenas, honey badgers, and aardvarks. Be warned, however, that nocturnal animals are shy, and on a bad night, sightings can be frustratingly rare (and with no passing scenery, extremely dull); it this happens, it's worth trying again for the following night. You can book any of these drives when making your accommodations booking—particularly advisable for early morning and night drives, and essential during school vacations (every province has different dates, but they tend to fall in June–July, Sept, Dec–Jan, and Apr).

To appreciate one of the country's more authentic culinary experiences, you may enjoy a **bush braai,** offered by the Kruger's main camps. These barbecues under the stars are a sociable way to conclude late-afternoon game drives; inquire at your camp reception about availability, booking and price.

Sitting in a vehicle for the duration of your safari will undermine a full experience of the bush, so do also consider booking a **morning walk ★★★** (R365 per person), which usually last 3 to 4 hours with a maximum of eight people, offered at most rest camps and bushveld camps. If you don't mind the heat, **afternoon walks** (R285) are another option offered at the bigger rest camps.

BIG GAME ON FOOT: WILDERNESS TRAILS ★★★

These 3-night, 4-day trails (R3,675 per person for the duration), catering to a maximum of eight people, offer an opportunity to experience the real essence of the African bush in Kruger at an extremely affordable rate. Although you are unlikely to see as much big game on foot (and you may spend a lot of time hoping you don't), and you won't get as close to most animals as you can in a vehicle (animals don't associate the smell of gasoline with humans), you will be introduced to the trees, insects, and animals that make up the surrounding bush under the protection of an armed and experienced guide. The emphasis is on reconnecting with the wilderness in some elemental way rather than ticking off species, but guides are armed for a reason.

As yet, there has never been a human fatality on any of the Kruger trails, and considering the caliber of the guides on hand, it is unlikely to ever occur, but do follow their instructions—given at the start of each trail—closely.

The locations of the base camps—comprising thatched A-framed two-bed huts with reed-walled, solar-heated showers and a shared flushing toilet—have been selected for their natural beauty. Note that unlike the trails offered in KwaZulu-Natal's Hluhluwe-Umfolozi reserve, you'll return to the same base camp every night. Besides bedding, towels, cutlery, and food, the park supplies rucksacks and water bottles. Drinks (which you must supply) are kept cold in gas fridges. Age limits are 12 to 60 years, and a reasonable degree of fitness is required—you will be covering from 8 to 15km (5–9¼ miles) a day.

You have seven trails to choose from: The **Napi, Bushman,** and **Wolhuter** are all situated in the southwestern section, known for white rhino, granite hills, and Bushman rock paintings. The **Metsi-Metsi,** which overlooks a small waterhole, and the **Sweni,** which overlooks the marula and knobthorn savanna, are in the central area, known for its lions. **Olifants Trail ★,** which overlooks the perennial Olifants River, west of its confluence with the Letaba, is particularly scenic and one of the most popular. **Nyalaland,** situated in the pristine northern wilderness among the sandveld's fever tree and baobab forests, is a favorite of birders. But even if you're not a birder, the vegetation and views more than make up for the relative lack of game. Reservations often need to be made well in advance; you can check availability for all trails departing up to a year ahead (and make bookings) at **www.sanparks.org**.

Hard-core wilderness enthusiasts who are very fit and want to experience a "hard" hike rather than the relaxing standard wilderness trails should sign up for the 3-night

Olifants Back Pack Trail or **Mphongolo Back Pack Trail.** These are fairly grueling—you walk to a new overnight spot every night, set up camp unaided, and carry all provisions in (and out), including your own tent (R1,930). Olifants is also the camp to book into if you want to tackle a **Mountain Bike Trail** in the park, with the recommended morning trails costing R435. Afternoons, when it's hotter, are 3 hours long and cost R240. Places are limited to six participants per trail (reservations should be made 2 days in advance at Olifants; © **013/735-6606** or -6607) and are led by two qualified and armed field guides; bikes and other gear provided. Three routes are available, graded according to difficulty and technicality (the Hardekool Draai trail is recommended for beginners).

Last, bear in mind that early morning and evening guided walks for a maximum of eight people are offered at most camps for those eager to walk, but not particularly far.

Where to Stay & Eat

Kruger National Park has 12 Rest Camps (large sprawling camps, some the size of a small suburb), five Bushveld Camps (more intimate), two Bush Lodges (for groups), five Satellite Camps (basic), and two Sleepover hides (one of the most private options). The largest are the Rest Camps, offering reasonably priced but very basic efficiency accommodation (as well as campsites), swimming pools, reasonably stocked grocery and gift shops, ATMs, and mediocre restaurants. Note that the emphasis is squarely on functionality rather than on chic design or luxurious facilities, like bathtubs or double beds.

If you're not prepared to shell out for the luxury lodges within the Kruger (located in privately held concessions) or the private reserves adjoining the park, but you want a level of pampering absent from the Kruger rest camps, then a good option is to stay in one of the hotels or guesthouses situated on Kruger's periphery, and enter the park daily. Only 10 minutes from the Phabeni Gate, **Rissington Inn** is a recommended option, while **Buhala Country House** is practically part of the Kruger (fenced into the park, as it is located right on the Crocodile River that snakes its way through the southern Kruger boundary); for reviews of these see "The Escarpment & Panorama Route: Where to Stay," earlier in this chapter.

PARK REST CAMPS

The SANParks Rest Camps, though somewhat institutional in atmosphere, are difficult to fault when it comes to their primary objective of providing a base from which to explore one of Africa's truly great wildlife sanctuaries. However they are not to everyone's taste. While many South Africans share a certain nostalgia in coming back year after year to find the same impala-lily and bird fabric on every curtain, cushion, and bed; *Custos Naturae* stamped on every sheet; and the kudu crest embossed on every soap; Kruger camps display little in the way of architectural or decorative flair. That said, the (mostly en-suite) accommodations—situated in camps scattered throughout the park—are scrupulously clean, and, for the most part, very cheap; in fact, they offer astonishingly good value when compared to park accommodation anywhere else in Africa. They are also remarkably varied, with four or five accommodations types located in various options, including rest camps, satellite camps, bushveld camps, and bush lodges (the latter suitable only for groups). Of these, the **Bushveld Camps** are highly recommended—with only 7 to 15 units in each, they offer more privacy than the large rest camps (Skukuza, the largest, has more than 200 units, as well as a landing strip, a 9-hole golf course, a bank, and two restaurants, to mention just a few of the camp's facilities). You will have to do your own cooking, however, when the camp gates are locked at night—only the main rest camps have restaurants. But if you don't mind cooking (get a bush barbecue going; you can purchase your meat from a nearby rest camp shop), you'll be treated to a more intimate atmosphere; even game drives in the Bushveld Camps are always in smaller 10-seat vehicles

Other than these the most popular accommodations in Kruger are the main **Rest Camps,** which offer a variety of options (in order of luxury: huts/safari tents, bungalows, cottages); of these, Skukuza, Lower Sabie, Satara, and Olifants are the most popular. All units are sparely furnished and semiserviced: Beds are made and floors are swept; you're not really supposed to leave the dishes, but staff will wash up—do please leave a tip (around R10–R15 per day should do). Water is scarce, so "en suite" usually means flushing toilet, sink (often in the bedroom), and shower, though in recent upgrades the basin has finally become part of the bathroom. The bigger Rest Camps are like small suburbs and are designed to encourage interaction among guests (units are close together and often emulate the old Voortrekker *laager,* a circle, facing inward), so there is little privacy. Try to book a river-facing unit (assuming there is one) or check to see whether you can book a perimeter unit; these face into the bush, albeit through a fence, and cost only slightly more for the slightly heightened sense of privacy.

The three- to six-bedroom "guesthouses" represent the top accommodations option in each Rest Camp. It's well worth investigating these if you're traveling with friends, as they are usually situated in the best location in the camp and offer the most privacy and small luxuries like bath tubs.

It's really best to plan at least one barbecue, cooked in front of your bungalow, which is what most local visitors do. This doesn't require much advance organization, as all accommodation units have their own fridge and barbecue, and the main Rest Camps all have shops selling basics such as milk, bread, butter, cheese, spreads, dishwashing liquid, tea, canned products, cereal, cold drinks, lighters, and wood, along with a selection of fresh or frozen meats and a variable range of fresh vegetables. That said, epicureans are advised to shop at a supermarket in one of the Escarpment or Lowveld towns before entering Kruger. The wine selection in the camp shops is surprisingly good—if you don't know what you're looking for and just want an everyday table wine, choose one of the Nederburgs, an old standby.

If you can't be bothered to cook, all the larger camps also have dining facilities. Although the food served at these chainlike eateries is not going to win any culinary awards, it's good value, filling, and caters to a great array of tastes and needs, including vegetarians and diabetics—and standards and service have greatly improved since management was outsourced a few years ago. Hours and prices at the Tree Restaurants vary slightly from one camp to the next, but most are buffet with breakfast typically costing R100 per person, lunch R130, and dinners around R170. The cheaper Wooden Banana Snack Bars are open from 7am to 9pm and serve a variety of salads, pasta dishes, burgers, toasted sandwiches, and other dishes in the R40 to R70 range. There are also Boma Braais at most of the large rest camps, serving three kinds of barbecued meats with a selection of salads and breads.

If you're traveling during peak summer, especially with kids, think twice before booking into a camp without a swimming pool. Facilities for travelers with disabilities are available at Crocodile Bridge, Berg-en-Dal, Lower Sabie, Skukuza, Satara, Olifants, Letaba, Mopani, Shingwedzi, Pretoriuskop, and Tamboti.

Note: Star ratings for Kruger camps below are relative to **each other** and not in any way an indication of equality to ratings provided elsewhere in the book; compare any rest camp to a lodge in a private reserve or concession and the rest camp would have no stars.

Berg-en-Dal ★ SOUTH Modern facilities and proximity to Malelane Gate make Berg-en-Dal (like Skukuza) ideal for first-night orientation before heading deeper into the park. It's a relatively rest camp (meaning it was built in the 1980s), and thus rather different than its older counterparts, offering accommodation in prosaic brick bungalows set amid attractive indigenous gardens. Besides being ideal habitat for leopards and rhinos, the granite hills around Berg-en-Dal are the only place in Kruger where gray rhebok and mountain reedbuck occur, and the terrain offers some relief from the mostly flat bushveld elsewhere in the park. Try to book a perimeter unit (code BA3U on the website) for the opportunity to spot wildlife through the fence, or one of the spacious family cottages or exclusive guesthouses (particularly no. 26). Each unit has an enclosed patio and braai area, offering a sense of privacy lacking in most other camps. A walking trail within the camp leaves the river and follows a narrow path through dense bush, where Braille signs are set out to guide the visually impaired past plants and animal skulls on display. The dam sees much wildlife activity, although you may have to sit on one of the benches and wait for it: Crocodiles lurk—and hunt—in its waters, and water birds are always around.

Enter through Malelane Gate, southern Kruger. www.berg-en-dal.co.za. ℭ **013/735-6106/7.** Fax 013/735-6104. 88 units. Bungalows R800–875 double; additional child/adult R86/172. Family cottages R1,475 for 4 people; additional child/adult R145/290. Guesthouses R2,775 for 4 people; additional child/adult R252/504. **Amenities:** Restaurant; auditorium; bush braais; bush walks; camping; fuel; game drives; Internet access; pool.

Letaba ★ CENTRAL This rest camp is set in elephant and buffalo country, just where the mopane terrain starts to become monotonous. The location, along a large bend of the Letaba River, sees plenty of activity, particularly in the winter. The nearby Engelhardt and Mingerhout dams are also excellent game sites, and the gravel road that follows the Letaba River is worth exploring. Always a favorite with Kruger aficionados, Letaba now has a swimming pool and upgraded visitor facilities. Unfortunately, very few of the units have views, but the restaurant has one of the best; it's worth planning a visit to eat lunch here while watching various plains animals wandering down for a drink. Accommodations are in thatched units set in gardens grazed by resident bushbuck and shaded by well-established apple leaf trees, acacias, mopane, and lala palms that support a prolific birdlife. Bungalows on the perimeter

---

Water (and 500 Pounds of Plants) for Elephants

An elephant consumes up to 200kg (480 lb.) of vegetation daily; a herd thus has a huge, potentially destructive impact on the landscape. This is why elephant numbers need to be controlled, by either culling or translocation. Elephants are extremely sensitive animals, however, and actively mourn the death of a family member, performing intricate burial ceremonies. When clans reunite, they make a great show of affection, "kissing" (probing each other's mouths with their trunks) and trumpeting their joy. To find out more about this amazing species, book a 90-minute **elephant safari** or stay at **Camp Jabulani.**

fence (booking code BG2U or BG3U) are the pick. Better still, the pricier Fish Eagle and Melville guesthouses have good views and plenty of space. Furnished safari tents are a budget alternative but the bathrooms and kitchen facilities are shared.

Enter through Phalaborwa Gate, central Kruger. www.sanparks.org/parks/kruger/camps/letaba.
ⓒ **013/735-6636.** Fax 013/735-6662. 125 units. Safari tents R400–R470 double (shared ablutions). Bungalows en suite R725–R780 double (shared kitchen) or R780–R880 (with kitchen). Some can accommodate an additional child/adult R86/R172. Guest Cottages R1,500–R2775 for 4 people; additional child/adult R145–R504. **Amenities:** Restaurant; bar; bush braais and breakfasts; elephant hall; fuel; game drives and walks; pool; shop.

Lower Sabie ★★ SOUTH Overlooking the Sabie River, with large lawns and mature trees, this is among the most pleasant in Kruger, particularly if you bag a waterfront bungalow (booking code BD2U, BD3U, or BD3UZ). There are also 24 good-value East African–style safari tents, all with twin beds, en-suite shower and toilet, and an outdoor "kitchen" (hot plate, fridge, barbecue)—but, again, book one with a riverside view (booking code LST2UZ), a real bargain. Every unit has a braai, but unless you have a kitchen, you will have to rent cutlery and crockery, available for a small fee from reception. Once again, there is no privacy, as most units share walls. Stroll along the paved walkway that overlooks the Sabie River at night with a flashlight: The red eyes you light up probably belong to hyenas, lured by the smell of barbecuing meat. Just about every animal has been spotted drinking along the riverbanks, and at night you'll fall asleep to the grunting of hippos. Lower Sabie has a plum location for game-viewing, at the junction of three of the park's most consistently rewarding roads: the H4-2 to Crocodile Bridge (excellent for rhinos), the H4-1 to Skukuza (bird-rich riparian forest that's also prime elephant, buffalo, and leopard territory), and the H10 to Satara (elephant, rhino, lion, and cheetah regulars). With two dams nearby, Lower Sabie also provides an excellent base for observing wetland birds.

Enter through Crocodile Bridge or Paul Kruger Gate, southern Kruger. ⓒ **013/735-6056.** Fax 013/735-6062. 119 units. Huts, tents, bungalows with communal facilities: R375, R625, R790 double. Safari tents R680 double. Bungalows R830–R870 double. Family bungalows and guesthouse and family cottages R1,470–R2,775 for 4 people. **Amenities:** Restaurant; fuel; game drives and walks; Internet; pool.

Olifants ★★ CENTRAL On a cliff top 100m (328 ft.) above the banks of the Olifants River, with views of the vast African plains that stretch beyond to the hazy Escarpment, this smallish camp is a great favorite. The bungalows along the camp's southwest perimeter (booking codes BBD2V, BD2V, and NGU2; the latter with no kitchen) are the most private and have spectacular views of the river and the animals that drink there, watched by basking crocodiles, while eagles wheel above, searching for prey—it's almost worth rearranging your trip around their availability. One feels less caged in here than at Kruger's other camps; the sudden drop below Olifants' bungalows means that no perimeter fence is required, and the expansive views are totally uninterrupted. Like many of the Kruger units, the veranda incorporates both kitchen and dining area. (***Tip:*** Do not leave food out here; groceries must be kept under lock and key from thieving baboons, hence the lock on the fridge.) Families note that there are two-bedroom bungalows with river views, and this camp has the best guesthouses in the park, with 270-degree views.

Enter through Phalaborwa Gate, central Kruger. ⓒ **013/735-6606.** Fax 013/735-6609. 109 units. Bungalows with best view of river R980 double; other bungalows R720–R830 (communal kitchen), or R940–R960. 4-bed bungalows R1,030–R1,100 double; R86/R172 additional child/adult. 8-bed guesthouses R2,800 for 4; R252/R504 child/adult. **Amenities:** Restaurant; bush braai; fuel; game drives and walks; trails (hiking and mountain biking).

Punda Maria ★ 🏕 NORTH   Very few people have the time to travel this far north, just one of the reasons why Punda Maria—near the Zimbabwean border—is the number-one choice for wilderness lovers. Built in the 1930s, this small thatched and whitewashed camp retains a real sense of what it must have been like to visit Kruger half a century ago, with communal kitchen facilities and old-style architecture. In 2004, the camp added seven fully equipped safari tents in a great location (well worth booking) and a much-needed pool. The area does not support large concentrations of game, but it lies in the sandveld, where several springs occur, and borders the lush alluvial plains, making it a real must for birders. A nature trail winds through the camp, and the surrounding area is scenically splendid. Make sure you head north to the Luvuvhu River, the only real tropical region of the park, and one of the top birding destinations in southern Africa. Overlooking the Luvuvhu, **Thulamela Heritage Site** protects the remains of a large stone city built in the 16th century after Great Zimbabwe was abandoned. A little farther east along the river is the most beautiful picnic site in Kruger, **Pafuri,** which lies under massive thorn, leadwood, and jackal-berry trees, where the colorful Narina trogon is resident and water is constantly on the boil for tea. The camp offers guided morning expeditions to both these sites.

Enter through Punda Maria Gate, northern Kruger. ℂ **013/735-6873.** Fax 013/735-6894. 31 units. Safari tents R735 double; bungalows R735–R775 double (R660 with communal kitchen). Family bungalow R775 double; R86/R172 additional child/adult. Family cottages R1500 for 4 people; R145/R290 additional child/adult. **Amenities:** Restaurant; bird hide; bush braais; fuel; game drives and walks; pool; shop; trails (4WD).

Satara ★ CENTRAL   The second-biggest and one of the four most popular camps in Kruger (the others being Skukuza, Olifants, and Lower Sabie), Satara is located in one of the finest game-viewing areas in the park. The rich basaltic soils support sweet grasses that attract some of the largest numbers of grazers, including buffalo, wilde-beest, zebra, kudu, impala, and elephant. These, in turn, provide rich pickings for the park's densest lion and cheetah populations—spend 2 to 3 days here, and you are almost certain to see both. Just as well the game-viewing is so good, because the set-ting and housing at Satara camp itself are rather disappointing: five massive *laagers,* each 25-rondawel strong, with verandas all facing inward. The best options are the perimeter units (booking code BD2V), though the view to the bush is through an electrified fence. That said, the camp now has a pool and a new day visitor center (convenient for those who stop here for lunch); it's also one of only two camps that offer the luxury of a deli. *Tip:* The H7 to Orpen Gate is especially good for cheetahs and lion; the loop to Gudzani Dam and Nwanetsi Picnic Site via the S100 and H6 is famously beautiful, with wonderful river views in summer, and plentiful game in winter; while the Tshokwane area south of Satara is said to have the highest concen-trations of lions in southern Africa.

Enter through Orpen Gate, central Kruger. ℂ **013/735-6306.** Fax 013/735-6304. 166 units. Bungalows R785–R1,210 double; R86/R172 additional child/adult. Guest cottages R1,525 for 4 people; R145/R290 additional child/adult. Guesthouses R2,800–R3,075 for 4 people; R252/R504 additional child/adult. **Amenities:** Restaurant; bush braais; deli; fuel; game drives and walks; pool; trails (4x4).

Skukuza ★★ SOUTH   Just east of the Paul Kruger Gate, you will find Skukuza, so-called "capital" of Kruger, accommodating some 1,000 people in prime game-viewing turf—top roads include the H1-3 north to Satara and the loop to Lower Sabie via the H4-1 and S30/128. This is an ideal spot for first-time visitors, though it would be a pity if this were your only experience of the park, because it really is like a small

TRACKER tips

Of course, you can't expect to know in a few days what professional trackers have gleaned in many years of tracking animals or growing up in the bush, but nature does provide myriad clues for the amateur tracker.

1. **Look for "hippo highways."** Hippos don't pick up their feet when they move; they drag them. So if you see a trail of trampled grass leading to a water hole, it's likely a hippo has been going back and forth from the water (where it stays during the heat of the day) to the grass it feeds on. Don't tarry on a hippo highway; once they set off on their well-trodden paths, very little will stop them.

2. **Use your nose.** Elephant urine has a very strong scent; waterbucks have a distinctive musky smell.

3. **Train your vision.** Vultures wheeling above may indicate the presence of predators, as may fixed stares from a herd of zebras or giraffes. A cloud of dust usually hovers over a large herd of moving buffalo. And, of course, paw prints provide vital information, not only to what has passed by (you should purchase a wildlife guidebook to recognize the differing imprints), but how recently it was there. This latter skill takes years of experience to hone.

4. **Examine trees.** Bark and branches sheared off trees or trees rubbed raw are evidence that elephants have passed by—they eat the bark and use trees as scratching posts. And certain trees attract specific species—giraffes, for example, love to browse the mopane.

5. **Listen to the sounds of the bush.** The lead lioness makes a guttural grunt to alert her pride. Baboons, monkeys, squirrels, and birds give raucous alarm calls in the presence of predators. Kudus bark when frightened.

6. **Look for droppings and dung.** Elephant dung is hard to miss—extralarge clumps full of grass and bark—while a trail full of fresh black, pancakelike dung marks the passing of a herd of buffaloes. A good wildlife guidebook will have illustrations of many species' dung.

7. **Watch bird behavior.** Follow the flight of oxpeckers and you're likely to locate a herd of Cape buffalo; oxpeckers survive off the ticks and other insects that cling to the buffalo hide. Cattle egrets dine on the insects and earthworms kicked up by grazing herbivores.

town, with two restaurants, a bank, a post office, a doctor's office, a deli, an Internet cafe, and three pools. Besides the people and cars, there is the noise of the occasional plane landing, though this doesn't seem to distract the many visitors strolling along the wide walkway that follows the course of the Sabie River. Accommodations are in a range of thatched en-suite units, the best of which are the luxury riverside bungalows (booking codes LR2E and LR2W; avoid the "semi-luxury," which are not good value), which were rebuilt after the 2000 floods and offer great river views, as well as luxuries such as a double bed, fully fitted kitchen, and satellite TV. All other units have fridges on their small verandas, some with hot plates and cooking equipment. Furnished East African–style tents are available for the budget-conscious, but you have to share bathrooms and kitchen facilities with the hordes of campers and RV drivers who descend on the camp, particularly in June/July and December/January.

Enter through Paul Kruger or Phabani Gate, southern Kruger. ☎ **013/735-4152.** Fax 013/735-4054. 238 units. Safari tents R390 double. Ordinary bungalows R790 (communal kitchen) to R855 double; luxury riverside bungalows R1,505 double. Guest cottages R1,470 for 4 people; R145/R290 additional child/adult. Guesthouses R2,775 for 4 people; R252/R504 additional child/adult. **Amenities:** 2 restaurants; bar; deli (w/Internet cafe); airport; bank w/ATM; braai; doctor; fuel; game drives and walks; 9-hole golf; library; 3 pools; post office; shop.

OTHER CAMPS

Among the other main camps, **Mopani** (☎ **013/735-6535/6;** from R770 for a bungalow; R870 for a bungalow with view) is the most modern in Kruger, with a lovely setting on the Pioneer dam, untamed bush gardens, and relatively large bungalows. Try to book one of the popular units with dam views (nos. 9–12, 43, 45, 47–54, and 101–102), but even if this fails, there are plenty of decks and the bar from which to enjoy the sunset. The one drawback with Mopane is that game-viewing in the surrounding mopane woodland is somewhat hit and miss, but the camp still makes a good stopover en route between the central Kruger and the far north. The other option in northern Kruger is **Shingwedzi** (☎ **013/735-6806;** two-bed bungalows with own toilet and kitchenette go for R725 to R750; note that there are two bungalows (booking code BD2D) with double beds if you're on a budget honeymoon or romantically inclined to prefer sharing your bed. Shingwedzi is a medium-size rest camp yet far quieter than most comparably sized camps, due its remote location in prime elephant territory. Game-viewing along the Shingwedzi River can be superb, and the riparian forest between the camp and Kanniedood Dam ranks among the best areas in the park for birding.

Farther south, **Orpen** (☎ **013/735-6355;** R815 double for a bungalow), one of the Kruger's smallest camps, with only 15 units, also enjoys a reputation for fine sightings—lions, cheetahs, and wild dogs are regularly seen in the area. However, for a more atmospheric accommodation experience it is far better to book its satellite camp, **Tamboti ★★**, which is Kruger's answer to the East African safari tent, and one of the park's unsung gems. Tamboti comprises 40 tents, each with two to three beds, tucked away among apple leaf, jackalberry, and sycamore fig trees on the banks of the Timbavati River (R930 fully equipped tent with double bed; R400 double with communal ablutions and kitchens). Book well in advance, though, as the camp is both small and very popular because of its location and the privacy of the tents, every one of which has a view; animals, particularly elephants, are attracted by the promise of water. Do bear in mind that, as a satellite camp, it has no restaurant or staff.

Another low-key gem, ideal for true bush aficionados who wish to forego luxury, is the tiny satellite camp of **Balule ★** (☎ **013/735-6606**), set near the banks of the Olifants River between Olifants and Satara rest camps. There are just six three-bed huts here, at the bargain price of R280 for two (R394 for three), using common shower blocks. The rusticity of Balule is underscored by the lack of electricity, and the nearest shop, restaurant, and filling station are at Olifants, which is also where you need to check in (you can also do so at Satara), so stock up on food, firewood and candles while you are at the Rest Camps.

Note: Two Rest Camps we definitely don't think are worth considering: **Crocodile Bridge** (☎ **013/735-6012**) because it's much too close to civilization, across the river from the farms that neighbor Kruger, where you might as well be, with a better view looking back at the park. The second is **Pretoriuskop** (☎ **013/735-5128**), Kruger's oldest camp, which is popular but only 8km (5 miles) from the Numbi Gate. Most people press on to Berg-en-Dal, deeper in the bush.

BUSHVELD CAMPS

The five bushveld camps are much smaller than the major rest camps and as such provide a greater sense of being in the bush. They have no restaurants or shops, however, so you must do your own cooking, and any last-minute shopping will have to be done at the nearest rest camp. On the plus side, most of the en-suite units are more spacious than rest-camp options and feature well-equipped kitchens with braai (barbecue) spots. Only residents are allowed to travel the access road, which makes this an excellent place to get away from it all. Best of all, the game drives are in vehicles that accommodate 8 to 10 people. You pay a little more for the seclusion (rates are all quoted for four persons regardless of how many people use it), but it's still good value given the greater privacy even if you are only two (and excellent value if you are more).

The centrally located **Talamati ★★★**, close to the Orpen Gate (© **013/735-6343;** 14 units at R1,330–R1,750 for two to four persons), and southern **Biyamiti ★★★**, close to the Malelane Gate (© **013/735-6171;** 15 units at R835–R965 for two, or R1,610 to R1,765 for one to four), are the most popular, located as they are in Kruger's game-rich areas, and easily accessed.

Shimuwini, Bateleur, and Sirheni are all in the northern section of the park. **Shimuwini ★★**, which is reached via the Phalaborwa Gate (© **013/735-6683;** R1,225–R1,415 for four), and **Sirheni ★★**, halfway between Shingwedzi and Punda Maria (© **013/735-6860;** R1220 for four), both have scenic waterside settings that attract a variety of game and birds, and offer night drives. **Bateleur ★★** (© **031/735-6843;** R1440 for four) is the oldest bushveld camp and the most intimate, with only seven thatched units rather than the usual 14 or 15. The closest gate to Bateleur is Phalaborwa. *Tip:* If you are traveling in a large group or as a family with teenage kids, or you just want assured privacy, it is worth asking about the two bush lodges: **Roodewal** (44km/28 miles north of Satara) and **Boulders** (25km/15 miles south of Mopani) comprise separate sleeping units connected via boardwalks to communal living areas. Booking one of these lodges (Roodewal enjoys the better setting) will give you the ultimate in 21st-century luxury: peace and privacy at a fraction of the cost of renting an entire lodge in the private reserves that abut the Kruger. The rate is R2,465 and R4,715 for the first four persons, respectively; each additional person costs R370. The lodges sleep a maximum of 19 and 12 persons, respectively.

For more information on all of the above, inquiries and applications should be made to **South African National Parks (SANParks): www.sanparks.org** (see "Visitor Information," earlier in this chapter).

CAMPING

Billed as a "rustic campsite," **Tzendse,** on the banks of the eponymous river, is the best place to pitch your tent. The only "pure" campsite, with no built accommodations, reception area, or electrical outlets, this is by far the most serene and scenic campsite in the park, with open-air communal showers. Reception is at Mopani. Campsites are also available at most of the main Rest Camps (**Balule, Berg-en-Dal, Crocodile Bridge, Letaba, Malelane, Maroela, Lower Sabie, Pretoriuskop, Punda Maria, Satara, Shingwedzi,** and **Skukuza**). Campers share bathrooms (shower/toilet blocks) and kitchens, and have access to all rest-camp facilities. Every site has a braai (barbecue), and many also have electricity; you will need to bring in all your own equipment, however, including a tent. Camping costs R58 per person, with usually a maximum of six per site. (If you want to camp without having to pitch

BIG-GAME COUNTRY | Kruger National Park

An exciting night, and the most private you'll have within the Kruger National Park confines, is to spend it in one of the two **sleeper hides** (term for private cabins in South Africa): **Shipandane,** situated 3km (2 miles) south of Mopani camp, on the Tsendze River, and **Sable Dam** hide, near Phalaborwa Gate. Bird hides by day, they are transformed into primitive dwellings 30 minutes before the gates close. Each comprises a boma with barbecue, a sleeping area (minimum two persons; maximum six), and a chemical toilet. With the presence of water comes game: Large buffalo herds and elephant bulls frequent these areas, often meters from where you sleep, and this is the closest you'll get (outside a few select private lodges such as Umlani)

to wild, dangerous animals without the presence of an armed ranger. It's a highly recommended experience if you like your nature untainted by noise and the presence of other people, but it's not for the fainthearted. There is no electricity (you are supplied with a chargeable lamp) or running water, you will have to make your own bed (pick up bedding and keys from Mopani camp and Phalaborwa Gate, respectively), and you will have to bring your own food, wood, and water (cutlery and crockery supplied). The perimeter is fenced, and under no circumstances—unless you have a suicidal streak—should you leave the enclosure at night. The cost is R445 for the first two people and R214 per additional adult, R107 per child.

9

BIG-GAME COUNTRY | **Kruger's Private Reserves & Concessions**

a tent or lug bedding across the world, a number of camps have furnished and equipped safari tents. Most are reviewed above—the best option is Tamboti, a satellite of Orpen.)

KRUGER'S PRIVATE RESERVES & CONCESSIONS

The difference between a visit to a Kruger Park rest camp and a private lodge is so big as to be almost incomparable. The luxurious accommodations afford supreme privacy and luxury, with unfenced accommodations that make the most of the bushveld environs. And visitors are taken in open-topped and elevated Land Rovers to within spitting distance of animals by Shangaan trackers and armed rangers, who give a running commentary on anything from the mating habits of giraffe to the family history of a particular lion. Animals in these reserves, particularly Sabi Sand, are so used to being approached by vehicles that they almost totally ignore them. You can trail a leopard at a few feet without it so much as glancing backward. Two-way radios between rangers, many of whom are allowed to traverse on each other's land, ensure good sightings, although these can be somewhat marred when three or sometimes four vehicles (the maximum lodges allow) converge on the same spot.

The 2- to 4-hour game drives take place in the morning and again in the late afternoon and evening, with stops in the bush for a hot drink and snack in the morning (particularly in winter) and cocktails in the evening. It can be bitterly cold in the winter, and you may opt instead for an escorted walk after breakfast—another service included in the rate.

It's 5am. The phone rings. It's the lodge manager. He politely asks how you slept, then requests that you not leave your room as planned. There has been a leopard kill meters from your chalet. He apologizes for the inconvenience and informs you that an armed ranger will be along shortly to escort you to the dining room for coffee before you depart on your early morning game drive. This seldom happens, but every so often it does. Lodges in private reserves are not fenced off from predators, so you are advised to exercise extreme caution—under no circumstances are guests of any age to walk about unaccompanied after dark.

In addition to pursuing animals off-road through the African bush, these private reserves offer unfenced accommodations of luxuriously high standards. Equally high end is the cuisine. As all meals are included in the rate, this is certainly not the time to go on a diet. Breakfasts are served late (after the morning game drive, which usually ends btw. 9 and 10am), so some lodges prefer to skip lunch altogether and serve a high tea at 3pm, with quiches, sandwiches, and cakes. From there, you depart on a 3- to 4-hour evening game drive, traveling with a spotlight once it's dark, tracking nocturnal creatures on the move. You will more than likely be expected to dine with your game-drive companions and ranger (if this is a problem, alert the staff in advance, and alternative arrangements will be made). Dinners feature grilled or roasted meat, giving visitors an opportunity to taste at least one species spotted earlier that day—kudu, springbok, impala, and warthog are particularly popular. Lodges cater to dietary requirements but require advance warning, as supplies take time to arrive in the bush. If you're a vegetarian or keep kosher or halal, notify the lodges prior to your arrival. Almost every lodge rotates dinners from their dining room to the ever-popular open-air *boma* (an open-air enclosure lit with a large fire), and some even offer surprise bush dinners, with a game drive concluding at a serene spot where tables have been set up under trees or in a riverbed.

The drawback to all this? A hefty price tag. If you've come to South Africa to see big game, however, it's definitely worth delving a little deeper into your savings and spending at least 2 nights in a private game reserve, preferably three. Prices (which are often quoted in U.S. dollars and include all meals, game drives, bush walks, and most of your bar bill) vary considerably (from season to season, for example), and it is possible to find more affordable options, the best of which are described below. Alternatively, some of the private concessions within Kruger—notably Rhino Walking Safaris and Shishangani—offer a near-comparable wildlife experience at a far lower price (see "Private Concessions Within Kruger," above).

Note: If you're driving, you'll pay an admission fee at the entrance gates of some of the private reserves. Not all accept credit cards so carry about R300 in cash which should cover two adults and vehicle (R20–R80 per person; R100–R120 per vehicle), with the leftover change amount dependent on which reserve you're entering.

Where to Stay & Eat

You can expect to find some of the finest lodges in the world within and abutting Kruger, offering the last word in unabashed luxurious accommodation and producing meals that far exceed your expectation of a bush kitchen catering for a relatively small

Sabi Sand Game Reserve

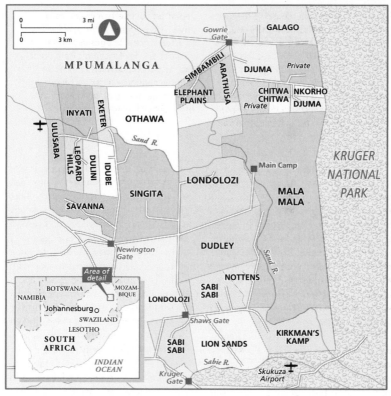

amount of guests. Because lodges and camps need adequate warning to stock up on fresh produce (remember, all meals as well as game activities are included in the rates below), special dietary requirements need to be planned well in advance. And despite the steep price tags, the best are extremely popular, so booking ahead is essential. Although winter is often the best time to view game, many lodges experience a seasonal drop-off and reduce prices from May to September (though sadly not as much as they used to). Naturally it is also worth looking online for special packages, and the longer you stay the stronger your negotiating power.

PRIVATE CONCESSIONS WITHIN KRUGER

Modeled on the successful government program in Botswana, the Kruger concessions were awarded to various safari companies for a 20-year period in 2000, on the condition that camps should in no way disturb the environment. Competition for these contracts was understandably stiff, and the standard of accommodation at most concession lodges is comparable to their luxurious counterparts in Sabi Sands and other top private reserves, and the experience very similar, with game drives in open vehicles and, in some cases, guided bush walks.

Besides looking at the pros and cons of booking a camp in one of the new **private concessions within the Kruger** (discussed under the same heading below), you'll need to consider the major private reserves that border one another and Kruger's southern and central section. The most famous are, from south to north, **Sabi Sand, Manyeleti,** and **Timbavati.** None of these reserves are fenced off from the others or Kruger, which allows a seamless migration of animals through an area roughly the size of Massachusetts—and growing bigger every year. Each of these three reserves features the Big 5 (lions, leopards, elephants, rhinos, and buffaloes). Each private reserve has a number of luxury lodges or camps that share traversing rights on land, thereby increasing the range of their vehicles. Many also report major sightings to the other reserves. In fact, with a cumulative 6 hours of every day spent tracking game, you will almost certainly see four of the Big 5 (the usual exception being the elusive leopard) during a 3-night stay. Bear in mind that you will enjoy yourself a great deal more (and irritate your ranger less) if you spread your focus to include an interest in the myriad species that make up life in the bush. The reserve characteristics are briefly as follows:

Sabi Sand ★★★, a 66,000-hectare (163,020-acre) reserve that encompasses the southern lowveld, is the most game-rich area in the country, and where your chances of getting up close to leopard are the best in Africa. It's hardly surprising, then, that this has become known as the continent's most exclusive reserve, with the largest number of luxury camps, including such legendary properties as MalaMala, Londolozi, and Singita, all of them overlooking the Sand River. In fact, the life-giving Sand River is a good indicator of camp, with the best located in the eastern section of Sabi Sands, closest to Kruger. Camps located on the far western section have light pollution at night from the human settlements on the Kruger border, a pity if you have flown halfway across the world to experience one of the largest wilderness areas on the planet.

During the apartheid era, when black people were not allowed to vacation in Kruger, **Manyeleti ★**—the 23,000-hectare (56,810-acre) reserve just north of Sabi Sand—was considered "their" reserve, and a visit to the original Manyeleti Rest Camp makes the most basic Kruger camp look like a luxury option. Officially, it's actually still a public reserve but within which private companies operate a few key concessions. Its border with Kruger Park is unfenced, so animals can roam freely between the reserves. Some very luxurious lodges—such as **Tintswalo ★** (*✆* 011/464-1208 or 015/793-9013; www.tintswalo.co.za)— have opened their doors in the Manyeleti, with rates comparable to Sabi Sand; not ideal given that you don't enjoy the same virtual guaranteed leopard sightings, and (unlike Sabi Sand, Timbavati, Thornybush, and Balule) operators in Manyeleti are restricted in the areas in which they may drive off-road in pursuit of game. Good-value Honeyguide (reviewed below) is however well worth it and our top Manyeleti choice, particularly if you're keen on a more authentic bush experience, with semi-luxury tents and a laid back atmosphere.

Just north of Manyeleti is **Timbavati ★★**, the 65,000-hectare (160,500-acre) reserve located

9

BIG-GAME COUNTRY | Kruger's Private Reserves & Concessions

alongside Kruger's central section. Timbavati offers a comparable game experience to the much-vaunted Sabi Sand, but the vegetation is less arresting (lots of scrubby mopani bushes; less water), and rhinos are relatively scarce. However, animals are almost as habituated to vehicles here as at Sabi Sand, and you can get within a few feet of large predators. The main reason to choose Timbavati over Sabi Sand is that it has far fewer camps and fewer people, and the rates are generally friendlier—particularly at Umlani, one of the most authentic bush experiences in the area.

Bordered in the north and west by Timbavati, the 14,000-hectare (34,580-acre) **Thornybush** game reserve is currently still a fenced reserve, thereby curtailing animal migration. It does boast a high percentage of lions, but the thicket-type vegetation is not always as conducive to sightings of varied species. The best reason to choose this reserve is Royal Malewane, a lodge that offers unbelievably luxurious accommodations and superb style; suites that are on par with Singita Ebony. Other private reserves in the region worth considering are **Balule,** another "island" (entirely fenced) Big 5 reserve, located just north of Hoedspruit and created only 15 years ago when the farm owners decided to drop the game fences between their farms. Balule has since grown into a 35,000-hectare (86,450-acre) reserve and enjoys the advantage of having the perennial Olifants River flowing for approximately 20km (12 miles) through the center. It also has the best value for money lodge in the entire Kruger: Naledi, reviewed below. **Makalali,** another Big 5 reserve that lies within striking distance of Kruger's central

Phalaborwa Gate, is another island reserve worth considering. Farther north, and cut off from Kruger, it extends over 26,000 hectares (64,220 acres) and with the introduction of buffalo in 2008 is now a proudly Big 5 reserve (though leopard sightings here, as in everywhere but Sabi Sand, are rare). The area is also of geological interest, with quartz rock crystals strewn throughout the area. **Kapama,** another "island" Big 5 reserve, is included predominantly for those interested in an elephant-back safari.

Visitors unwilling to risk malaria and eager to view wild dog should visit **Madikwe ★★★**, a 75,000-hectare (185,250-acre) Big 5 reserve in the northwest, with a variety of excellent camps and lodges that give those abutting Kruger a run for their money—these are discussed in more detail later in this chapter. Then there is also the 40,000-hectare (98,800-acre) **Welgevonden ★★** reserve, which has the Big 5 but the rather major disadvantage of not allowing vehicles off-road to get closer, but is only a 4-hour drive north of Johannesburg.

Note: Outside of this region (and therefore this chapter) the Big 5 reserves worth considering are **Tswalu Kalahari Reserve ★★** a desert reserve in the Northern Cape, suited to those who love a real sense of space, and KwaZulu-Natal's **Phinda ★★** and **Mkuze Falls ★**, with subtropical vegetation and abundant birdlife (p. 389). If you can afford the time (and they don't come cheap), then every attempt should be made to combine a South African reserve (or reserves) with a sojourn in Botswana's **Okavango Delta ★★★**— the "original Eden" (p. 425).

Within most of these concessions guides can theoretically drive off-road to track or view animals from a close-up perspective, but the strict procedures imposed by Kruger authorities severely limit the number of sightings where this is permitted. Your experience could be compromised by heavy rains in summer, which means you can't go off-road or, in some cases, even use internal game-viewing roads. Also, the animals are not always as acclimatized to vehicles as those in the private reserves. As a result, the Kruger concessions tend to offer rather erratic game-viewing and do not promise the almost guaranteed full house of Big 5 sightings associated with Sabi Sand, which makes them less suitable to the typical first-time safarigoer. On the plus side, the Kruger concessions tend to have more of a wilderness feel, and game drives are less frantically oriented toward chasing the Big 5. Guides tend to concentrate on whatever animals they might chance upon, rather than following radio alerts to other vehicles' sightings. As such, the ideal combination, budget permitting, would be to follow a few days of intensive Big 5 game-viewing in Sabi Sand (or another private reserve) with a more relaxed sojourn at one of the Kruger concessions.

Which concession? Broadly, the best in terms of overall lodge/wildlife experience is (unsurprisingly) Singita, but it is priced accordingly. We also rate Rhino highly for the general experience (though it's more orientated toward walking safaris) and Shishangani/Shawu/Shonga (SSS), Lukimbi, and Imbali for wildlife sightings. SSS is especially good for rhino, Lukimbi for lion, Imbali for lion and cheetah. In addition to the top concessions reviewed below, another option is the upscale **Tinga Private Game Lodge** (www.tinga.co.za; © **013/735-8400**), which operates two luxury camps: **Narina** and **Legends,** both on the Sabie River, in the vicinity of Skukuza) and recently taken over by More Hotels (which manages the lovely Lion Sands). Grand without being overly decadent, Narina offers space and privacy and is the more remote of the two; each unit has a private lounge, a large bathroom with double showers, and its own heated plunge pool. It's pricey (from R12,000–R15,800 double), so check for online specials and compare with other lodges in this area (southern Kruger, on river) before booking.

The most singular of the Kruger concessions, set in the far north, is **Makuleke Contractual Park,** which comprises the 23,600-hectare (58,292-acre) wedge of land between the Luvuvhu and Limpopo River. This area was incorporated into Kruger in 1969, when its 1,500 Makuleke residents were forcibly evicted at the hands of the apartheid government. In 1998, the Makulele people won the first land claim in Kruger, but instead of resettling the land that was returned to them, they opted to develop it for tourism and contract game management to the national park. Today two private lodges (Pafuri Camp and The Outpost; see below) lie within the concession, and local people contribute to the daily running of both, a landmark exercise in sustainable development. Also known as the Pafuri Triangle, Makulele has the highest biodiversity of any part in the Kruger, with more than 75% of the park's species occurring in just 1% of its surface area; it's also the one part of the park with a truly tropical ecology. The area is legendary among South African birdwatchers for the presence of several rarities, including Pel's fishing owl, racket-tailed roller, crested guinea-fowl, and triple-banded courser. It is also noted for several non-wildlife landmarks, notably the lush yellow fever forest running toward Crooks Corner near the confluence of the two rivers, the spectacular Lanner Gorge, and the 16th-century Thulamela Heritage Site. However, general game-viewing in Makulele can be rather slow and large predators are scarce, making it more attractive to dedicated wilderness enthusiasts and bird-watchers than to safari neophytes.

Note that if you are approaching one of these camps in your own vehicle, you will need to enter the nearest Kruger gate in a timely manner, generally 2 hours before they close (see gate times above) and pay an entry fee (currently R45–R120 per person).

Hamiltons 1880 Tented Camp ★★ 🛥 This is the most upscale of three camps in the 10,000-hectare (24,700-acre) Imbali concession, which lies in the game-rich acacia woodland between Skukuza and Satara, an area renowned for its dense populations of lions and other large predators. Set in lush riparian woodland along the seasonal Nwatsitsonto River, it comprises six luxury en-suite tents, all furnishes with king-size four-poster beds dressed in crisp white linen, privately located on stilts with wooden floors, with viewing decks and an outside shower with view. Tents are linked via raised timber walkways to the open tented lounge and dining room and pool. Hamilton's size makes it an ideal camp for anyone wanting to escape the rat race. The nearest gate for access to Hamilton's is Orpen, 50km (31 miles) away.

P.O. Box 196, Skukuza, Kruger Park. www.hamiltonstentedcamp.co.za. ☏ **11/516-4367.** 6 units. R7,330 double, including meals and activities; excluding drinks. AE, DC, MC, V. No children under 11. **Amenities:** Dining/bar area; boma; bush walks; butler/room service; game drives; pool. *In room:* A/C, fans.

Jock Safari Lodge ★★ ☺ A warm, convivial camp, elegant and tasteful, yet without pretensions of grandeur. The large thatched bungalows, situated for maximum privacy, each feature great bushveld views, large bathrooms with tubs and indoor/outdoor showers, own *sala* (shaded outdoor pavilion) overlooking the river, and there are fireplaces for winter. The lodge is in the south, at the confluence of the Mitomeni and Biyamiti rivers, where herds of antelope and elephant gather to cool off and quench their thirst. At 6,000 hectares (14,820 acres), this is Kruger's smallest concession, a bit of a drawback, but made up by density of game. If you're looking for a more secluded experience, book one of the three suites at Little Jock Lodge; 1km (⅔ mile) away. Honeymooners should book room no. 1; families opt for room nos. 2 and 3, which are right next to each other. Little Jock shares a communal pool and has its own staff, including chef and ranger; the only reason to go to the main camp would be for Internet or spa treatments.

P.O. Box 781, Malelane 1320. www.jocksafarilodge.co.za. ☏ **041/407-1000.** Fax 041/407-1001. 12 units. R8470–R9,000 double. Rate is all-inclusive except for imported wines and spirits. Children under 4-11 sharing with parent pay 50%. AE, DC, MC, V. **Amenities:** Dining area; bar; babysitting; boma; bush walks; game drives; Internet; "kids on safari" program; pool; room service; shop; valet (on request); wellness center. *In room:* A/C, hair dryer, minibar.

Lukimbi Safari Lodge Situated in the far south of the park, Lukimbi enjoys exclusive traversing rights across a 15,000-hectare (37,050-acre) area that supports good populations of lion, elephant, black and white rhino, and the occasional wild dog. The terrain is also more suited to off-road driving than most concessions. The split-level dining and sitting area overlooks the permanent pool and animals that come to drink there. The spacious rooms are spread widely along the riverbed for privacy and reached via a raised wooden walkway where the wildlife can pass under unimpeded. Despite the excellent game-viewing, Lukimbi's decor and design leaves a lot to be desired when compared to similarly priced concession lodges, and thus seems overpriced. It's 25km (16 miles) from Malelane Gate.

P.O. Box 2617, Northcliff, 2115. www.lukimbi.com ☏ **011/431-1120** or 013/635-8000 direct. 16 units. R9,000–11,000 double, all-inclusive. Discounted rate for children under 12. AE, DC, MC, V. **Amenities:** Dining room; bar; bush walks; DVD library; game drives; free Internet; library; pool; satellite TV; wine cellar. In room: A/C, minibar.

The Outpost ★★   Cantilevered out of a rocky mountainside, The Outpost is an modern minimalist lodge set atop a hill in the Makuleke Contractual Park, the most untouched region of northern Kruger, a good 120km (74 miles) from the nearest town (7-hr. drive from Jo'burg/OR Tambo airport). The 12 en-suite guest "spaces" are constructed of steel, canvas, and aluminum, and are completely open to the elements except for the rock face they appear to grow out of. The unparalleled unscreened 180-degree views of the Luvuvhu floodplain—a richly textured terrain of ancient baobabs, thorny acacias, and lush palms—are spectacular (best from "space 12"). Design may be a little cold and hard edged for those wanting a more classic bush experience (if so, nearby Pafuri Camp is a better bet, and far better value). In fact it's rather pricey given that it is hard to get to (unless you fly in, which adds to the price), doesn't include drinks (a small quibble but it seems a tad ungenerous) as well as the fact that despite the amazing biodiversity, certain species (such as leopard) are less easily spotted than in the more crowded southern Kruger.

P.O. Box 786064, Sandton 2146 www.theoutpost.co.za. ℂ **011/245-5704.** 12 units. R8,300–R10,900 double, all-inclusive. Check website for special offers. No children under 10. AE, DC, MC, V. **Amenities:** Dining room; bar; bush walks; game drives; library; pool; wine cellar. *In room:* Eco-friendly cooling system, minibar.

Pafuri Camp ★★ 🍃 ☺   Managed by Wilderness Safaris, southern Africa's most influential safari operator, this archetypal bush camp has an unpretentious atmosphere and a magnificent location on the forested banks of the Luvuvhu River. Accommodation is in luxury standing tents (including six family tents) with secluded river views in two separate areas, connected by a 2km-long (1.2-mile) raised wooden boardwalk that affords great birding opportunities and allows game—especially the lovely nyala antelope—to wander through unimpeded. It is the only other camp, besides The Outpost, in the vast Makuleke Contractual Park, so you feel—and are— surrounded by a vast tract of wilderness. It's off the beaten track (7 hr. drive from Jo'burg), but it ranks among the most affordable concession lodges in the Kruger, ideal for birders, and makes a good add-on to a Wilderness itinerary to Namibia or Botswana, where this company dominates.

P.O. Box 5219, Rivonia, 2128, South Africa. www.wilderness-adventures.com ℂ **011/257-5111.** 20 units. From R3,200 double (dinner bed and breakfast). R600 additional child. Game activities R200 per activity per person. AE, DC, MC, V. **Amenities:** Dining room; bar; bush walks; game drives; library; 2 pools; river safaris; wine cellar.

Rhino Walking Safaris ★★ 🍃   This award-winning private concession shares a border with MalaMala Game Reserve, renowned for its lush vegetation and the density of its game, particularly leopard. Although the area is a massive 12,000 hectares (29,640 acres), it is a restricted wilderness concession, meaning that off-road game drives are not allowed. Instead, the focus is on game walks and luxury sleep-outs, which are a welcome break from the monotony of most other safari lodge schedules. There are two small lodges: the more traditional **Rhino Post,** which gives visitors a choice between game walks and drives, and the exclusive four-unit tented **Plains Camp,** where you'd better be prepared for a cumulative 4 to 5 hours of bush walking per day. Guests also have the opportunity to overnight at the camp's "sleep-out digs" deep in the bush (70 min. on foot from Plains Camp), where tents have been erected on decks high up on stilts at a watering hole. You need carry only a few clothes and toiletries; all other necessities are provided. Back at Rhino Post, accommodations are neat and functional. Set on raised wooden decks with private terraces overlooking the Mutlemuve River, the thatched guest rooms have canvas walls that allow the sounds

By the 1940s the lumbering rhino—arguably the most prehistoric-looking large mammal on the planet—had been hunted to virtual extinction within the Kruger area, and was only reintroduced (with animals relocated from Hluhluwe-Imfolozi Game Reserve in Kwazulu Natal) in the late 1960s. The first (100 white rhinos) were reintroduced to southern Kruger. For many years the slow-growing population remained rooted in the south, particularly around Crocodile Bridge. As numbers increased, they gradually colonized the central and northern parts, as well as the adjacent private reserves, and today the greater Kruger is estimated to hold between 6,000 and 8,000 white rhino, or some 35% to 40% of the global total. The Kruger has thus been instrumental in the white rhino's IUCN Red List status rising from Endangered to Near-threatened over the past 2 decades. Kruger also supports a population of around 300 black rhinos, descendants of the fewer than 100 individuals reintroduced between 1971 and 1998. This represents between 5% and 10% of the global black rhino population, but even so, sightings of these are scarce, with the area around Pretoriuskop and Crocodile Bridge offering the best chance of a glimpse of this thicket-loving creature.

However, this rosy outlook has begun to darken as rhino poaching within the park has reached epidemic proportion: from a handful annually, to—in 2010—a shocking 333. By April 2011, 144 rhinos had been slaughtered in Kruger. Police believe the poaching to be the work of cartels that sell rhino horns in Asia, where they're valued as an aphrodisiac and other so-called medicinal qualities for around $2,000 apiece. Many South Africans, horrified by the numbers (as well as video footage of a rhino that survived having its face ravaged, and the vet crying as he tried to describe the pain it must have been in before he euthanized it) have been galvanized into protest. Given that rhino horn is purely keratin, the exact same substance found in human nails and hair, a campaign call went out in April 2011 for South Africans to donate their nail clippings and send them to the embassies where rhino horn is illegally marketed. Watch the video on www.youtube.com/watch?v=iUGtrLB_k_U.

of the bush to penetrate at night; bathrooms feature tubs, double basins, and an outdoor shower. Public areas are elegant and simple, with wood and packed-stone walls, and an inviting glass-walled wine cellar.

Reservations: P.O. Box 1881, Jukskei Park 2153. www.isibindi.co.za. ✆ **011/467-1886.** Rhino Post 8 units. R5,100–R5,700 double. Plains Camp 4 units. 3 nights (1 night Rhino Post and 2 Plains Camp) R7,790–R8,610 double. Rates include all meals and game activities. AE, DC, MC, V. No children under 12 at Plains Camp or on bush walks. Children under 12 pay 50% if sharing. **Amenities:** Dining area; bar; bush walks; game drives; gym; Internet; library; pool; wine cellar. *In room:* Hair dryer, minibar (Rhino Post only).

Singita Lebombo & Sweni ★★★ 📷 Step into your suite at Lebombo and you are in the most stylish camp in Africa; the last word in designer safari, luxuriating in the camp that helped Singita (and Africa) receive numerous awards, while gracing its way into the pages of coffee-table tomes. **Sweni,** named for the beautiful river over which its six fabulous suites look, is its more intimate neighbor. Both lodges feature the best in modern design: Dramatic wraparound glass walls and massive glass sliding doors open onto outdoor showers and private balconies where you can sleep out in summer, and home-grown modern furniture created by local craftspeople working in concert with funky young designers. The whole effect is more Afro-Euro chic boutique hotel than game lodge, but the views are pure bush and very relaxing. Rooms are stocked with board games and treats to occupy you between meals (which are superb, and accompanied by a top-notch selection of Cape wines). Lebombo is lighter, brighter, and quite dramatic in its proportions, while Sweni is more intimate and has a homier atmosphere. Between Lebombo and Sweni is Singita's "Village," comprising a spa, state-of-the-art gymnasium, wine-tasting facilities, and some great shopping. Situated in a 15,000-hectare (37,050-acre) concession bordered by Mozambique, the camp is elevated on a sheer cliff, with views of the Lebombo Mountains and surrounding bushveld plains. Game-viewing is possibly the best of any of the Kruger concessions, with the added bonus that off-road driving is seldom a problem.

P.O. Box 23367, Claremont 7735. www.singita.co.za. ℂ **021/683-3424** or 013/735-5500. Fax 021/671-6776. Sweni 6 units. Lebombo 15 units. R23,750 double all-inclusive (except champagne and spa treatments). No seasonal discounts. AE, DC, MC, V. Children over 10 only. **Amenities:** Each lodge has dining areas; bar; lounges; boma; bush walks; game drives; Internet; library; pool; room service; wine cellar. (The Village: art gallery; craft and gift stores; gym; spa; wine-tasting venue.) *In room:* A/C, hair dryer, minibar.

IN SABI SAND

Djuma ★★   Djuma **Vuyatela** is a vibrant lodge that combines modern Euro elements with more traditional African textures and design, and offers untrammeled access to more than 9,000 hectares (22,230 acres), 7,000 hectares (17,290 acres) of which it owns, making it one of the largest landowners in the Sabi Sand Reserve. Because there are only three camps within Djuma (the other is Cheetah Plains, separately owned), you'll share your game-viewing with very few others. Aside from Vuyatela (comprising just eight thatched chalets, each with a generous bedroom, dressing room and bathroom, separate lounge, and large private deck with small plunge pool and shower) there is **Galago,** an efficiency single-unit lodge; a good value option if you are traveling as a group. Djuma can be accessed only via the northerly Gowrie Gate, a very awkward destination, reached via miles of harrowing dirt road, so you should definitely consider flying in with a fly-in package arranged through the lodge.

P.O. Box 8034 White River 1240. www.djuma.com ℂ **013/735-5118.** Vuyatela 8 units. Galago 5 units. Vuyatela R9,000 double. Rates include all meals and drinks, and game drives/bush walks. Galago R9,500 for entire camp sleeping up to 10, including game drives but not meals. Children under 12 pay 50%. AE, DC, MC, V. **Amenities:** Dining room; bar/lounge area; aquarium; boma; bush walks; game drives; gym; library with high-speed Internet and Wi-Fi (in Vuyatela); massage (in Vuyatela); pool; room service in Vuyatela). *In room:* A/C, hair dryer, minibar (in Vuyatela).

Exeter River/Dulini/Leadwood ★★   Argentine owner Stephen Saad transformed the three lodges in the Exeter stable (**River Lodge ★★**, **Dulini ★**, and **Leadwood Lodge ★★★**) into high-end, design-conscious, Afro-chic hideaways, then handed over management to the excellent &Beyond team (formerly CC Africa), one of the top safari outfits in Africa. Each of the three lodges has its own staff complement and public spaces. Aptly named River Lodge is the closest to a bush experience, but this does not mean you'll have to forgo private plunge pools, inside and outside showers, and luxurious living quarters. Large glass walls and huge screened doors look out onto views of the river. Shades of ocher and clay, taupe, and teak bring a slick, sophisticated look to the huge double-volume lounges. Dining areas are huge, magnificent open-sided rooms with views of the nearby Sand River—a beautiful place to drink and dine. Dulini has the advantage of being slightly smaller, with only six guest suites, but for the most exclusive privacy book one of the four huge Leadwood suites, in stone "cottages" with fireplaces. Game traversing area is 10,000 hectares (24,700 acres), shared with other concessions.

&Beyond, Private Bag X27, Benmore 2010. www.andbeyondafrica.com. ✆ **011/809-4300.** Fax 011/809-4400. 18 units. River Lodge 8 units. Dulini 6 units. Leadwood Lodge 4 units. River Lodge and Dulini: high season R13,300 double; midseason R10,670; low season R9,260. Leadwood high season R16,580 double; midseason R12,100; low season R11,090. Rates include all meals, game drives, bush walks, and most drinks as well as laundry. AE, DC, MC, V. **Amenities:** Dining room; bar; boma; bush walks; game drives; gym; pool; wine cellar (in Leadwood). *In room:* A/C, hair dryer, minibar, plunge pools.

Kirkman's Camp ★★ ☺ 📷 If you'd prefer, Blixen-like, to be based in a turn-of-the-20th-century homestead, then Kirkman's—originally a hunting lodge, built in the 1920s—is a top choice, not least because of &Beyond's focus on delivering 100% on the guest experience. The camp retains a strong colonial flavor, with double French doors and huge sash windows opening onto deep veranda and rolling green lawns—very different from the majority of lodges (where thatch and/or canvas is de rigueur). Cottages are grouped in two-unit bungalows built in the Victorian style; rooms are perfectly functional but not luxurious; maintenance is not quite up to standard. However, the staff (a happy, laid back group) make this a ★★★ experience: Game drives unexpectedly end up at "breakfast pizza" stations (replete with bottles of ice cold champagne), parents with kids on a game drive could round a corner to find someone waiting with ice creams, and the singing and dancing in the boma at night will have you stomping along. Meals are of the best served in Kruger. Traversing rights are quite small (currently 3,000 hectares/7,410 acres), shared with Lion Sands.

&Beyond, Private Bag X27, Benmore 2010. www.andbeyondafrica.com. ✆ **011/809-4300.** Fax 011/809-4400. 18 units. R7,560–R10,790 double, including all meals, game activities, most drinks, and laundry. AE, DC, MC, V. Children stay in adjacent rooms (not connected); rates on request. **Amenities:** Dining area; bar; boma; boules and croquet; bush walks; children's activities for game drives; game drives; games; Internet and Wi-Fi area; lounge; massage; pool; room service; tennis. *In room:* A/C, hair dryer.

Leopard Hills ★★ Like Ulusaba (Virgin billionaire Richard Branson's neighboring lodge), Leopard Hills is elevated on a ridge that offers stunning views of the plains, only in more stylish surrounds. Game-viewing is also very good, traversing, some 10,000 hectares (24,700 acres) of the western sector of the Sabi Sand, though it's shared with a quite a few (including Ulusaba and Exeter) and as a result, this sector sees a fair amount of traffic (sightings are limited to a maximum of three vehicles). You can enjoy the views from virtually everywhere, the public areas, the spa, as well as from five of the well-proportioned suites (specify a suite with savanna views), which are tasteful and generous, with wraparound glass frontages opening onto private sun decks, each with its own small rock plunge pool. The muted cream, white, tan, and brown African-themed decor is executed with a mixture of rough untreated timber, bamboo, concrete, sisal. A fully stocked wine cellar, fine cuisine, and very well-maintained library with a cozy fireplace complete the picture. If an elevated location isn't going to float your boat I'd opt for the better-value Exeter River or Leadwood, or Lion Sands River.

P.O. Box 612, Hazyview 1242 www.leopardhills.com. ✆ **013/737-6626.** Fax 013/737-6628. 8 units. R15,800 double. AE, DC, MC, V. Children stay on request. **Amenities:** Dining area; bar; lounge; boma; bush walks; game drives; gym; Internet; library w/TV and DVD/VCR/CD players; pool; room service; spa treatments. *In room:* A/C, hair dryer, minibar.

Lion Sands ★★★ This family-owned concession is the location of one of our favorite lodges, thanks to the cool, classy decor; riverside setting; a choice of pools (sun or shade); friendly staff; huge (again, beautifully decorated in shades of cream) rooms with the best-stocked minibar/coffee stations; extensive bathrooms (egg-shaped stone tub, and an outdoor shower in own garden) and great game viewing. With only 3,500 hectares (8,645 acres) to traverse, you might expect Lion Sands to be slim on sightings. But given its location on the game-dense banks surrounding the Sabi River, you are unlikely to leave disappointed (see the monthly percentages on their website). If privacy is key, book one of the Ivory Suites: Morning tea (the game drive wake-up call) is delivered through a service hatch, you have your own lounge with every room and in-room spa treatments on tap—ideal for honeymooners or celebs, though for a little more you could be at Singita where the real celebs (for a reason) are luxuriating. Lion Sands also has a beautiful single-use villa, 1933 Lodge.

P.O. Box 30, White River 1240. www.lionsands.com. ✆ 013/735-5000. Fax 013/735-5330. Reservations: P.O. Box 2667, Houghton 2041. ✆ 011/484-9911. River Lodge 20 units. Ivory Lodge. 6 units. River Lodge high season R11,560–R13,880; low season R9,350–R11,220. Ivory Lodge R19,000 double. AE, DC, MC, V. No children under 12 at Ivory. **Amenities:** Dining area; lounge bar; boma; board room; bush walks; clay pigeon shooting; game drives; lectures (nature and stargazing); library; pools; spa treatments; Wi-Fi; wine cellar. *In room:* A/C, hair dryer, minibar. (In Ivory: CD player, fireplace, heated plunge pool, telescope; Wi-Fi.)

Londolozi ★★★ ☺ Londolozi is one of the most famous camps in Africa; indeed, having set the standard for accommodations, cuisine, and game-viewing activities, it became the model for all subsequent luxury lodges in southern Africa. For many years the flagship for the safari outfit &Beyond, the Varty family resumed management of the lodge a few years back and brought several changes, such as the Lion Cubs Den, at the time the first program aimed at fostering bush knowledge among children, custom-designed around each individual child's interests but offering a diverse array of activities, from starting a fire with a couple of sticks and pancake cooking in a termite mound oven, to learning how to dive a Land Rover or wallowing in the mud. Boyd Varty also offers special 5-day "healing and personal development" retreats, devised in conjunction with Martha Beck; there is also a specially designed vehicle for photographic safaris. It's a big lodge (32 units) but divided into five separate camps strung alongside the Sand River, all within walking distance of one another but serviced by their own public spaces and staff, and sharing some 14 000 hectares (34,580 acres). **Founders Camp** is the most laid-back, family-friendly and a personal favorite; adjacent **Pioneer Camp** is effectively a sprawling luxury family home accommodating eight adults and six children. **Varty** is good for families (two connecting suites) as well as couples, while stylish **Tree Camp** and **Private Granite Suites,** the latter comprising just three suites built right into the river (two have private plunge pools that drop onto the boulders that form the Sand River banks, close enough to the river that you can hear it running while lying in bed), are best for honeymooners or couples who don't want to be disturbed. With a staff to guest ratio of three to one, service is impeccable, but at this level our money is still on Singita.

P.O. Box 41864, Hyde Park 2024. www.londolozi.co.za. ✆ 011/280-6640, or 011/280-6655 for reservations. Fax 031/735-5100. Founders Camp 10 units. Varty Camp 10 units. Pioneer Camp 3 units. Tree Camp 6 units. Granite Suites 3 units. Founders R12,980–R13,900; Varty R11,800–R13,900; Pioneer R19,000; Tree R19,000; Granite R21,000. All double rates include all meals and game activities, and most drinks. Rates drop from 4th night, and further from 6th night. Children under 12 sharing pay 50%. No children at Tree Camp or Granite. **Amenities:** Each camp offers its own dining area; bar; babysitting; boma; bush walks; children's programs for various ages; game drives; pool; room service; wellness center including massage and yoga; Wi-Fi (in certain areas only). *In room:* A/C, hair dryer, minibar, plunge pool (not all suites at Founders).

MalaMala ★★★ ☺ This legendary reserve pioneered the Sabi Sands–style photographic safari back in the 1960s, and today it still delivers an unbelievable wildlife experience, with close up encounters that will leave even the most amateur photographer satisfied. This will not suit younger chic travelers demanding stylish decor, but MalaMala remains *the* top destination in the greater Kruger for those whose priority is superlative game-viewing. It's the largest single private reserve in the region—extending over 13,300 hectares (32,850 acres), it shares a 19km (12-mile) unfenced border with Kruger and boasts 20km (13 miles) of frontage either side of the perennial Sand River. Traversing rights are reserved only for MalaMala guests (up to 60) accommodated across its three camps, which make for a very low vehicle density and far more relaxed atmosphere for game-viewing than elsewhere in Sabi Sands. The Big 5 were recorded on all but 25 days in 2010, with an average of four separate leopard sightings per day—an impressive record. The veteran **Main Camp** is a determinedly unpretentious and trend-resistant setup: Accommodation is in large, simply decorated cottages with two en-suite bathrooms, each with river or marsh views; public spaces haven't changed in decades. There is less overture to decadence on drives (you must request sunset drinks or coffee stops if you want these); here it's all about the game; as such, there are no restrictions to time—you can stay out all day if you wish. **Sable Lodge** is part of Main Camp, using the same rooms but with a smaller and more exclusive common area aimed at small groups. **Rattray's on MalaMala** is their luxury option: just eight classically styled cottage-size suites, each with a timber deck with tiny plunge pool, an outside shower, and a private garden overlooking the Sand River.

P.O. Box 55514, Northlands 2116. www.malamala.com. ✆ **011/442-2267.** Fax 011/442 2318. Main/Sable Camp 28 units. Rattray's 8 units. Main camp $1,250–$1,300 double, $1,400–$1,450 suite, $340 rate for children sharing; Sable $1,550 double, no children under 12; Rattray's $1,850–$1,900 double. No children under 16. Rates include all meals and activities; excludes drinks. AE, DC, MC, V. **Amenities:** Dining area; bar; boma; bush walks; game drives; Internet/library; massage room; pool; room service. *In room:* A/C, hair dryer (minibar, plunge pool, Wi-Fi in Rattray's only).

Notten's ★ ✦ The closest thing to a budget experience in Sabi Sand, this family-owned and run camp offers good value given the superb wildlife area it is located in—you get the same game-viewing as some of the neighboring properties at half the price! Accommodation is in eight separate cottages, each totally individual as the lodge has grown organically, and some overlook the lovely grassy plain that the public spaces do; this plain has seen plenty of game action over the years. Decor is comfortable and unpretentious; it's a place to put your feet up and make yourself at home. Food is similarly honest, home-style cooking. There is a lovely pool—long enough to do laps in. Families can choose from one family room or the triple room, but note that children under 6 are not accommodated unless the lodge is booked as a whole.

P.O. Box 622, Hazyview 1242. www.nottens.com. ✆ **013/735-5105.** 8 units. R4,200–R6,700 double, depending on season. Rates include all meals, game drives/bush walks, most drinks, and laundry. 30% discount for children 6–12. AE, DC, MC, V. **Amenities:** Dining room; bar/lounge area; boma; bush walks; game drives; pool. *In room:* A/C.

Sabi Sabi ★ ☺ With more than 3 decades in the safari business, Sabi Sabi offers a slick operation, with three very different lodges. **Earth Lodge** is clearly its attempt to build thoroughly modern lodge, built from "earth" for the new millennium. But architecturally it fails, as you are dwarfed and virtually overpowered by concrete overhangs and thick concrete walls. The pretty new decor certainly helps, but our preference is still for the original (but far less exclusive) **Bush Lodge.** Public spaces here are wonderful, with lived-in colonial splendor the order of the day; actual rooms are very hotel-like though, and units are too close together for privacy. But if you are traveling with young kids there is a fun "school", a well-equipped preparatory class-room and play area, manned by Ashleigh Todd, a qualified primary school teacher, who prepares activities for youngsters to play-educate. Alternatively there's the exclusive **Little Bush Camp** (formerly Londolozi's Safari Lodge), which offers six luxury rooms on a dry riverbed, or the eight-unit **Selati Lodge,** named after the famed turn-of-the-20th-century railway line that ran through the area, and decorated with vintage railway memorabilia. As for the game-viewing, Sabi Sabi matches any other property in Sabi Sands when it comes to the Big 5, and its lodges enjoy exclusive traversing rights, but over a far smaller area (6,500 hectares/16,060 acres) catering to almost twice the bed capacity than Mala Mala, so you will see many more vehicles.

P.O. Box 52665, Saxonwold 2132 www.sabisabi.com. © **011/447-7172.** Fax 011/442-0728. Bush Lodge 25 units. Selati Lodge 8 units. Earth Lodge 13 units. Little Bush R11,000 double; Bush Lodge R13,000 double; R17,000 suite; Selati R13,400 double; R14,490–17,000 suite. Earth Lodge R17,000 double; R34,000 suite. Rates include all meals, local beverages, game drives, and bush walks. AE, DC, MC, V. No children under 13 at Selati or Earth. Special rates for children apply. **Amenities:** Dining area; bar; boma; bush walks; children's "Elefun" center; game drives; Internet (Bush and Earth); pool; room service. (Earth and Bush Lodges also offer spa, small gym, Internet center, and wine cellar.) *In room:* A/C, hair dryer, minibar. (Presidential suites come with a Land Rover and ranger; at Earth, they'll throw in a butler.)

Singita Ebony & Boulders ★★★ ☺ Frommer's has rated Singita as the best in the country since it first opened, and awards and accolades for Luke Bailes's sumptuous lodge just kept flooding in. While you might find it difficult to leave your room at other lodges, here it is virtually impossible. But move you must, for the quality of the game-viewing is superlative. Singita enjoys semiexclusive traversing rights to more than 18,000 hectares (44,460 acres), and the best rangers in the business will look after you. Sabi Sands Singita comprises two totally separate lodges, **Boulders** and **Ebony,** both built on the Sand River, but each so different you'll feel like you're in an entirely new lodge. Suites in the contemporary-style Boulders Lodge are the size of a small house; Ebony Lodge features the same standard of luxury, service, and privacy, but the decor has an African colonial theme. A Relais & Châteaux lodge, Singita offers superb dining at all meals; wine tastings (largely South African wines) in Boulders' handsome wine cellar are popular ongoing events. The Singita staff approach is intuitive intelligence, and the vibe is happy, free of snootiness. For those traveling with children, the family units at Boulders and Ebony provide the kind of memories that truly are priceless.

P.O. Box 23367, Claremont 7735. www.singita.co.za. © **021/683-3424** or 013/735-5456 direct. Fax 021/683-3502. Ebony Lodge 12 units. Boulders Lodge 12 units. R23,750 double, all-inclusive (except French champagne). No seasonal discounts. AE, DC, MC, V. **Amenities:** Dining room; bar; lounge; bush walks; game drives; gym; high-speed Internet; library; room service; home and curio shop; spa; 12,000-bottle wine cellar. *In room:* A/C, hair dryer, minibar, private pool.

Ulusaba ★ Ulusaba, owned by Sir Richard Branson, lies in the far west of Sabi Sands, where its aura of exclusivity is undermined somewhat by the fact that it shares traversing rights with a half dozen other properties, and borders the human settle-ments on the western fence line. There are two camp locations: Rock Lodge has the better one, high atop a hill, with panoramic views across the acacia-studded plains running eastward to Kruger. Decor is much improved since Branson first took over, but it's still pretty pedestrian—you're definitely here for the views, and the master suites with their jaw-dropping views and plunge pools are pretty grand. Safari Lodge has a more conventional setting in riparian forest running along a seasonal water-course. It makes ample used of organic material and stilted walkways that evoke

Tarzan's jungle. The latest suites (walking distance from Rock Lodge), named Cliff Lodge, are huge two-bedroom units, elevated on stilts with own pool—when booked as sole use it accommodates a maximum of five adults and four kids; ideal for families. Ulusaba attracts plenty of funky people drawn by the prospect of staying as a kind of houseguest in a rakish billionaire's lodge, and the emphasis is very much on having fun, but we think there are probably better places to spend your money.

P.O. Box 71, Skukuza 1350, South Africa www.ulusaba.virgin.com. © **011/325-4405.** Safari Lodge 10 units. Rock Lodge 10 units. Cliff Lodge 2 units. Safari: R9,500–R19,200 double. Rock R13,800–R19,200. Cliff Lodge R12,600–R13,650. Rates are all-inclusive. AE, DC, MC, V. Children welcome; inquire into rates. **Amenities:** Dining area; bar; lounges; boma; bush walks; children's room w/TV, DVDs, computer, and board games; game drives; gym; Internet; library; pool; room service; star observatory; wine cellar. *In room:* A/C, hair dryer, minibar, Wi-Fi (in some areas), plunge pool (in some suites), Wii (Cliff Lodge).

IN MANYELETI

Honeyguide Tented Safari Camps ★★ 🍴 ☺ Honeyguide's tented camps offer an authentic African safari experience, in tents that have all the luxuries of a room, great game-viewing—all in all the most exceptional value, particularly during the low season. Relaxed safari chic comes close to describing the informal minimalism of **Mantobeni Tented Camp,** with its Morris chairs, leather couches, cotton sheets, old-style lanterns, and damask linen evoking *Out of Africa.* Guests are accommodated in East African–style tents, set on raised wooden decks with lovely concrete bathrooms featuring double showers and partially sunken tubs. Set in a riverine forest, most of the 12 tents overlook a dry riverbed or the water hole; it's a good idea to reserve tent no.1, which enjoys more privacy and is likely to be farther away from loud neighbors. The central lounge/dining and lazing area is sparsely furnished, and tents can become hot in summer, when guests head for the narrow, elegant pool. Early morning drums alert you to the dawning game drive, and tea is brought to your tent—a luxury even the most upmarket camps don't always offer. Five minutes away, the 12 en-suite tents at Honeyguide's **Khoka Moya Tented Camp** offer almost exactly the same experience, but the tents (this time set on concrete slabs) are slightly more spacious, and the somewhat more elegant bathrooms don't have tubs. Khoka Moya's more contemporary furnishings include large plush ottomans and beanbags around the fire. Most important, Khoka Moya allows children, making it great for families, while Mantobeni is more suitable for romance.

P.O. Box 786064, Sandton 2146. www.honeyguidecamp.com. © **011/341-0282.** Fax 011/341-0281. Mantobeni 12 units. Khoka Moya 12 units. High season R7,600 double. Low season (Mar 1–June 30) R5,000. Includes all meals, drinks, and game activities. No children under 12 at Mantobeni; children 2–12 sharing with adults pay 50% at Khoka Moya. AE, DC, MC, V. **Amenities:** Dining room; bar; lounge; boma; bush walks; game drives; pool; Wi-Fi. *In room:* Fan.

IN KAPAMA

Camp Jabulani ★★ 📷 This is the top lodge in Kapama—a fenced "island" private reserve near Hoedspruit that harbors all the Big 5 but is best known for its elephant-back safaris, an activity that offers a unique giraffe's-eye view over the African bush and its inhabitants. The nighttime elephant-back trips, silent below a glittering African night sky (Jabulani is perhaps the only place in the world to offer a nocturnal elephant safari) are truly wondrous. The camp itself is opulent, with Relais & Châteaux cuisine and accommodation in six spacious and beautifully decorated wood, stone, and thatch cottages, all with private deck and plunge pool, carved into a patch of riparian forest alive with monkeys and birds. There is also a new Villa, with its own dedicated chef, ranger, and vehicle to cater to families. Game drives, bush walks, and visits to the associated Hoedspruit Endangered Species Center are all available, but the stars of the show are the elephants, which consist of the young male Jabulani, hand-reared after being orphaned at the age of 4 months, and a herd of 12 adolescents rescued from Zimbabwe.

R40, 5km (3 miles) south of Hoedspruit. P.O. Box 25745, Monument Park, 0105. www.campjabulani.com. ☏ **015/793-1265.** 6 units. R15,000–R16,000 double. Rates include meals, game drives, guided bush walks, and elephant activities. Villa R41,250–R44,250. No children under 12 unless the entire camp is reserved. AE, DC, MC, V. **Amenities:** Dining room; bar; lounge; bush walks; children's "Team Tusker" program; clay pigeon shooting (by request); elephant activities (safaris and stable visits); game drives; hot-air ballooning (by request); Wi-Fi in public areas; library; massage. In room: A/C, fan, hair dryer, minibar, plunge pool.

IN TIMBAVATI

Gomo Gomo Game Lodge (www.gomogomo.co.za), with its face-brick walls and cheap tiled floors, is not going to be featured in the pages of a glossy design mag anytime soon, but it's worth a mention for the good-value rate alone: R3,420 double during the winter months and R3,800 during the summer (Aug–Apr)—excellent, given that this includes all game activities (two drives and a bush walk daily) and all your meals. The game-viewing—over a 6,000-hectare (14,800-acre) area—offers every chance you'll see the same amount of game as someone staying at Royal Malewane, at a fraction of the price. However, the overall experience is incomparable.

Kings Camp ★★ This is an ideal place if your idea of "roughing it" is letting the butler have the afternoon off. While Tanda Tula (reviewed below) provides a more authentic bush experience, accommodations at Kings Camp are pure luxury (better value than &Beyond's main Ngala camp, reviewed below, or lodges of a similar standard in Sabi Sands). Actually, it's hardly a "camp" at all; the large, private thatched chalets are arranged at the edges of a well-tailored lawn with a pool and various cozy and comfortable lounge-cum-viewing-areas. On your personal terrace, you can sip martinis or lounge on a hammock just meters from the animal-rich Timbavati bush, while in your suite you're cocooned in luxury. Rooms are air-conditioned and spacious; bathrooms are large, with his-and-hers outdoor showers. Upon returning from a grueling early evening of tracking leopard, lion, and buffalo, your room will be filled with an herbal scent and your bath drawn piping hot. Note that they too have a sole-use Villa for families or groups (up to eight) traveling together.

Seasons in Africa, P.O. Box 19516, Nelspruit 1218. www.kingscamp.com. ☏ **013/755-4408.** Fax 013/752-5842. 11 units. High season R9,800 double. Midseason R9,200 double. Low season (May–Sept) R8,000. Honeymoon suites R9,790–R11,600. Rates include all meals, game activities, and most drinks. Children under 12 pay 50% if sharing with 2 adults. AE, DC, MC, V. **Amenities:** Dining room; bar; lounge/viewing deck; babysitting; bush walks; doctor; game drives; gym; library; pool; room service; shop; therapy tent; TV. In room: A/C, hair dryer, minibar.

Ngala Tented Safari Camp ★★★ ☺ &Beyond (formerly CC Africa) is one of southern Africa's premier safari operators, with a variety of camps and lodges working to varying standards, but always with a strong (successful) emphasis on spoiling guests with thoughtful, unexpected touches. In Timbavati they own Ngala: one of the largest private reserves in the Timbavati, it delivers a superb bush experience, with only two camps to share 14,000 hectares (34,580 acres) of land, and providing one of the best game-viewing experiences outside of Sabi Sand. Of the two camps we highly recommend **Ngala Tented Safari Camp,** comprising just six deluxe en-suite tents on the banks of the Timbavati River. It's a little cheaper, but **Ngala Main Camp ★★,** with its thatched cottages that are a little cramped and too stacked on top of one another, is not in the same class as the tented camp, unless you're nervous, a novice, or parent of small kids, wanting the security of a small gracious hotel-like camp in the bush.) *Note:* Ngala also offers highly recommended tailor-made walking safaris, dining and sleeping under the stars for 2 nights, for R6,120 per group per night plus individual lodge accommodation rates.

Private Bag X27, Benmore 2010. www.andbeyondafrica.com or www.ngala.co.za. ✆ **011/809-4300.** Fax 011/809-4315. Tented Camp 6 units. Main Camp 21 units. Tented Camp R8,450–R13,900 double. Main Camp R7,220–R9,440 double. All rates include meals, game activities, and most drinks. Children under 11 pay 50%. AE, DC, MC, V. **Amenities:** Restaurant; boma; bar; lounge; babysitting; game activities; pool. *In room:* Hair dryer.

Tanda Tula ★★   One of the very first luxury tented camps to open in the South African bush, and still one of the best. The 12 tents are all privately situated, each with its own furnished *stoep* (veranda); try to reserve tent no. 1 for the best view (or no. 10 as an alternative). Because the surrounding bush is dense and rooms are not as luxurious as its competitors', you're more likely to spend time in the elegant and comfortably furnished open-sided lounge and dining area, which leads out onto the lawns and pool. This is where drinks and lunch are served, and at night a huge fire blazes, although dinner is served in the adjacent boma. Weather permitting, breakfasts are served in the bush, and braais (barbecues) take place regularly on the riverbed. Tanda Tula means "To Love the Quiet," and the team does everything possible to ensure that you can do just that. Game drives cover a potential 20,000 hectares (49,400 acres), providing Tanda Tula with access to the largest area in Timbavati, and you'll likely spot at least three of the Big 5 in 1 day. *Note:* Tanda Tula also offer a highly recommended overnight walking safari, with 2 nights in camp and 2 nights dining and sleeping under the stars on an elevated platform overlooking a productive waterhole, for R6,800 to R5,400 per person per night depending on group size.

P.O. Box 32, Constantia 7848. www.tandatula.co.za. ✆ **021/794-6500.** Fax 021/794-7605. 12 units. High season (Dec–Mar) R9,870 double; low season May–Sep R7,600 All rates include meals, game activities, and drinks. AE, DC, MC, V. No children under 12. **Amenities:** Dining area; bar; lounge; boma; riverbed braais; bush breakfasts; bush walks; game drives; pool. *In room:* Fan, hair dryer.

Umlani Bushcamp ★ 🍴 ☺   Offering one of the most authentic bush experiences in Africa, Umlani ("Place of Rest") is not luxurious (accommodations are in thatched, reed-wall en-suite rondawels, two of which sleep four) but remains a favorite. Aside from the fact that it's relatively affordable, the absence of electricity makes the experience at night, when flickering candles and lanterns light the camp, deeply romantic. It has no formal gardens and very few staff, and is all in all a really relaxed camp, the kind of place where you sit with your toes in the sand listening to the sounds of the bush (rather than the hum of the pool filter) or swing in the hammock hoping a predator won't come padding down the dry Nshlaralumi riverbed. Hosts are laid back, and every effort has been made to retain a sense of what it's like to camp in the middle of the bush; there's even a stilted treehouse overlooking a water hole, where you can spend the night with only the sounds of nocturnal animals—highly recommended. Umlani is small, but with traversing rights to parts of Tanda Tula, it covers 10,000 hectares (24,700 acres) and regularly has great sightings.

P.O. Box 11604, Maroelana 0161. www.umlani.com ✆ **021/785-5547.** Fax 0866/968518. 8 units. R6,050 double. Children under 12 R1,512. 3-night special including shuttle transfer from Jo'burg R15,460 double. Rates include all meals, most drinks, game drives, and bush walks. AE, DC, MC, V. **Amenities:** Dining room; bar; boma; bush breakfasts; bush walks; game drives; library; microlighting and ballooning by arrangement; pool.

IN THORNYBUSH

Royal Malewane ★★★   It's difficult to imagine that anything would be too much trouble for the gracious staff at Liz Biden's much-lauded luxury lodge, which puts up a very strong fight with Singita as *the* ultimate luxury safari destination in Africa (though Singita's location in the more game-dense Sabi Sand is hard to beat, not to mention it's East African camps in Grumeti, adjoining Serengeti). Elevated walkways are the only link between the palatial units, set on stilts right in the midst of the bush, each with a huge open-plan bedroom/sitting room with fireplace and equally enormous bathroom. Whether you're lying draped in Ralph Lauren linen in the antique canopied king-size bed or luxuriating in the elegant claw-foot bathtub or huge open shower, floor-to-ceiling windows provide wonderfully unobscured views of your private outdoor terrace, with outside shower and gazebo and, beyond that, the bush. The chefs John Jackson conjures up remarkable meals, including a sumptuous Bedouin-themed affair served in the bush, but don't be surprised if, immediately after dessert, you're whisked away on an impromptu game drive, prompted by roaring lions. For the ultimate honeymoon or getaway destination, you won't find better than the palatial Royal and Malewane Suites, where up to four guests can enjoy the same unfettered luxuries visited upon regulars Elton John and Bono, including the personal attentions of a private butler, private chef, and masseur. With traversing rights on 11,500 hectares (28,405 acres) and some of South Africa's top trackers, the lodge offers excellent game-viewing opportunities—elephant and lion are easily seen within the hour.

P.O. Box 1542, Hoedspruit 1380. www.royalmalewane.com. © **015/793-0150.** Fax 015/793-2879. 6 units. R22,500 double; Royal and Malewane suites R60,500 for 4 people. Rates include all meals, local beverages, game drives, and bush walks. AE, DC, MC, V. **Amenities:** Dining room; lounge/bar; aromatherapy; boma; bush and theme dinners; bush walks; game drives; gym; library; massage; room service; spa w/heated lap pool; Wi-Fi. *In room:* A/C, hair dryer, minibar, plunge pool; Wi-Fi. (Royal and Malewane suites include TV, CD/DVD player; iPod docking station; full kitchen; private chef and butler; masseuse; Royal suite includes laptop, fax/printer; Wi-Fi.)

IN BALULE

Naledi Bush Camp ★★ 🍴 ☺   Naledi, located in the relatively new Balule reserve, is hands down the best value for money safari your money can buy. It's not as stylishly decorated as the top-end lodges but the price is incredible: You're paying just a bit more than it costs to be in one of Kruger's basic huts, in a crowded camp, yet here you are staying in one of only three privately located suites (two sleeping four), in relative luxury (Leadwood even has its own private plunge pool!), enjoying delicious meals and being taken on game drives and bush walks by a passionate, knowledgeable guide. Sleeping a maximum of eight guests means you are assured of personal attention, and personal is exactly what it is. Naledi is family owned and managed: Everyone—from Kim who prepares (with the wonderful Sam) your three-course meals, to her husband, Kjell, who takes you on your game drives—is part of the family, and by the time you leave you will feel as if you are too. Public spaces are elevated and multileveled, with great views of the water hole and surrounding plain, and plenty of nooks to retreat to and enjoy the luxury of utter privacy and luxury, surrounded by miles and miles of untouched bush.

Naledi Bushcamp, Hoedspruit. www.naledigamelodge.com © **015/793-3374** or 086/686-1870. 3 units. R3,110–R3,500 double, depending on suite. Rates include all meals and game activities; excludes drinks. Children 3–12 pay 50%. AE, DC, MC, V. **Amenities:** Dining areas; lounge/bar; boma; bush walks; game drives. *In room:* A/C, hair dryer, plunge pool (Leadwood only).

IN MAKALALI

Makalali Game Lodge ★★ ☺ ⚡   Makalali means "Place of Rest" in the local Shangaan language, and you can expect plenty of it in what *Tatler* magazine once voted the Most Innovatively Designed Hotel in the World. Aiming for a sensual bush experience with something seemingly inspired by Antoni Gaudí, it combines architectural styles from all over Africa—shaggy East African roof thatching adorns mud and stone walls, while rugged North African–inspired turrets create a mythical village palace sensibility. Makalali consists of four camps—each with its own swimming pool, boma, and lounge and dining area—situated on various points of the Makhutswi River, which flows for approximately 8 months of the year. Rooms are huge and totally private; each features a fireplace as well as a *sala*, joined to your hut via a boardwalk, where you can arrange to have a romantic dinner. Try to book a room in the uniquely situated camp 4, where the rooms are most dispersed and you reach your public areas via a swing-bridge. Don't get stuck with room no. 3 in camp 4 (adjacent the staff village) or room no. 4 in camp 1; the latter is too close to the kitchen. Makalali offer a 2-day "wildlife mini-rangers" course for kids ages 6 and older. While you relax by the pool, they spend a couple of hours a day learning basic bush survival skills with a qualified ranger.

P.O. Box 809, Hoedspruit 1380. www.makalali.co.za. © **015/793-9300.** 4 camps, each with 6 units. R5,000. See website for special offers. Rate includes meals, game activities, and laundry. Children under 12 sharing R800. AE, DC, MC, V. **Amenities:** Each camp includes dining area; bar; lounge; boma; babysitting; bush walks; game drives; Internet; massage; kids program (R330 per child); pool; room service. *In room:* A/C, fans, hair dryer.

Garonga ★   Garonga's approach to the bush experience is more "soul safari" than big game. The lodge is part of the Makalali Conservancy (reviewed above), but the emphasis here is as much on "re-earthing" the senses as tracking animals. This is the perfect place to end a frenetic vacation, with no scheduled game drives imposed on you—an easel, pencils, and small Zen garden are placed in your room, and an aroma-therapist is on standby to further help de-stress you. Situated on raised platforms along a dry riverbed, the six standard units have low adobe walls, topped by a vast tent of cream canvas. King-size beds are swaddled in white muslin, and a large hammock swings above every deck. For those who'd love a soak in the wilds, the staff will set up a private bush bath with candles and bath salts; there is also a sleeping platform on stilts 20 minutes from camp for the more adventurous. **Little Garonga** comprises three luxurious suites, one with pool, and all sharing own public spaces; this is ideal for those traveling in a group/extended family of four to eight.

P.O. Box 737, Hoedspruit 1380. www.garonga.com. © **087/806-2080.** Fax 011/447-0993. 7 units. R5,100–R6,400 double, depending on season. Little Garonga R19,400–R24,000 for 6 adults depending on season. (Inquire if you only require 1 suite.) Children R1,885–R2,125. No children under 8. Children sharing 8–15 pay 50%. Rates include all meals, drinks, game activities, and laundry. AE, MC, V. No children under 12. **Amenities:** Dining area; bar; boma; aromatherapy; bush walks; game drives; library; pool; reflexology; Wi-Fi. *In room:* Hair dryer. Hambledon suite: A/C, minibar, plunge pool.

THE WATERBERG & WELGEVONDEN RESERVE

Approximately 350km (217 miles) N of Johannesburg

The Waterberg, a 150km-long (93-mile) mountain ridge that rises dramatically from the bushveld plains to 2,085m (6,839 ft.) above sea level, is substantially less populated than the big-game country that lies to the east of the Escarpment, in and around

Kruger. With no major roads and only one town (Vaalwater) within a 15,000-sq.-km (5,850-sq.-mile) area, the region is almost totally devoid of humans, making it one of most pristine wilderness areas in the country. It also offers a more varied terrain within a smaller area, with majestic mountainscapes and rocky ravines, grassed valleys, and lush riverines. **Welgevonden Reserve,** a magnificent 40,000-hectare (98,800-acre) wilderness that encompasses much of the Waterberg, is the most accessible Big 5 reserve in the country: a mere 2½-hour drive from Johannesburg; the reserve is also malaria free. Add to this the mountainous landscape and lack of congestion when compared with some of the private game reserves around Kruger, and the relatively good-value rates, and it becomes a very appealing choice indeed. However, the reserve has very strict guidelines, to protect the more fragile environment. Vehicles are not allowed off-road, for example (it takes too long for the tracks to "heal"), which can be a major drawback and extremely frustrating if you spot a lion walking 100m away. It also makes leopard sightings very, very rare. But the landscape is arresting, and the intimacy of the small lodges is most conducive to relaxing, so we cover a few options in brief below.

9 Essentials

Welgevonden Reserve has four landing strips. Your lodge will arrange the 1-hour charter from Johannesburg airport, or make the 2½-hour journey by car to the Welgevonden's main entrance (if you are driving, park at the entrance gate and wait for your lodge to pick you up; ask for the lodge to fax or e-mail a map).

Where to Stay & Eat

The intimate stone-and-thatch **Makweti Safari Lodge** ★ (www.makweti.com; R4,400–R9,000, depending on season/unit), was one of the first lodges to open in Welgevonden, and still one of the most attractive options in the reserve. Beyond the low-key and tasteful use of African artworks and artifacts, the layout emphasizes privacy (only five generously proportioned chalets, most with king-size beds, small verandas on stilts, some with plunge pools), and the setting is fabulous, on a rocky ravine at the edge of a verdant valley. The beautifully presented meals are accompanied by fine South African wines from less commercial estates and, weather allowing, are served in the boma. Guests at small, intimate **Mhondoro Lodge** ★—offering good value at R6,700 (www.mhondoro.com)—are made to feel well and truly at home. And what a lovely, unassuming home: Like Makweti, it was built to blend harmoniously with the landscape; you almost don't notice the handful of stone and thatch structures until you're right on top of them. The decor is classic safari: all muted earth tones and natural fibers, and selectively chosen African artworks. The four guest chalets (one sleeps four) are all free-standing and private; furnishing is understated plush. Very personally owned and run by Ant and Tessa Baber, **Ant's Nest & Ant Hill** (www.waterberg.net; R5,800–R8,300 double) are two "bush homes," this time located in Waterberg reserve, which has over 40 species of game (but no lion or elephant). These are great family destinations, particularly those who like horseback riding: you can choose your steed from a herd of over 60 horses, enough to suit all ability of rider. It also has impeccable green credentials. While the bush homes will suit families or groups traveling together, the horseback riding safari experience is also open to individuals, and inexperienced riders are provided with lessons. Ant's Hill accommodates 12 persons in four chalets (the family unit sleeps six); Ant's Nest has six luxurious en-suite bedrooms that accommodate a maximum of 12 guests. Since March 2011, the Ant Collection has also taken over tourism in the 40,000-hectare (100,000-acre) **Lapalala Reserve** (www.lapalala.com), ideal for hikers wanting 100% seclusion. Aside from these, it's always worth looking into possible specials from **Clearwater Lodges** (www.clearwaterlodges.co.za; © **021/889-2034**): their **Kudu Lodge ★★** is set in the middle of a large, open, short-grass savanna, often surrounded by grazing antelope, zebra, and rhino. Each generously sized chalet has a deck from which you can enjoy the passing parade at the nearby watering hole. At R4,580 double, all-inclusive, the rate during winter (May–Oct) is an excellent value (summer: R8,780).

MADIKWE GAME RESERVE ★★★

Over the past decade Madikwe—only proclaimed in 1991, when it was the recipient of the largest game-translocation exercise in the world—has been making serious inroads on the Southern African safari market, and with good reason. Located right on the Botswana border, this 75,000-hectare (185,250-acre) reserve—slightly bigger than either Sabi Sand or Timbavati—is prime game-viewing turf. The area has highly diverse eco-zones—bordered by the Dwarsberg Mountains in the south and the Marico River in the east, the reserve's rocky hills, perennial rivers, seasonal wetlands, acacia bushveld, savanna grassland, and Kalahari's desertlike sandveld allow it to support a huge array of animal species. That said it is not in the same league as the Sabi Sand in terms of game densities, leopard sightings in particular. While pretty enough it also does not have the lush riverine forests and wide grassed riverbanks that typify Sabi Sand. But on the plus side Madikwe is malaria free and boasts the second-largest elephant population in the country (and many of them delightfully frisky); most importantly, visitors are virtually assured of seeing wild dogs here: exhilarating to watch when hunting, this is Southern Africa's most endangered predator, and why Madikwe is seen as a good add-on to Kruger, or alternative. The other major difference between Madikwe and its Kruger counterparts is the massive traversing area that every lodge has access to. Unlike Sabi Sand and to a lesser extent Timbavati, where traversing rights are bartered and bought, won and lost, leaving the large landowners sitting pretty while the smaller concession owners scramble to share their land without losing their advantage, every lodge in Madikwe has access to the entire 75,000 hectares (185,250 acres). Effectively this means that the couple paying R22,000 per night could have the same game-viewing experience as a couple paying R3,200 a night, though that would assume that the rangers are equal, when no doubt the better ranger is the one being paid the higher salary at the higher-end lodge. However, the democratic arrangement is rather pleasing, and everyone is very sensitive about sharing sightings—as soon as a Big 5 (or other interesting animal) sighting is discovered, it is called in by radio (which explains why the viewing is so good despite the lower density of game) and no more than three vehicles at any particular sighting keeps the experience low key (though you may end up queueing for wild dog, as you wait for the first-in vehicle(s) to leave).

Commercial expansion over the last few years has been rapid, seeing construction of a host of new-generation lodges here, yet Madikwe remains large enough to satisfy visitors craving solitude on game drives (particularly if you're not chasing specific species)—something the smaller lodges adjoining Kruger can't always deliver.

Essentials

Madikwe is some 280km (174 miles) northwest of Johannesburg. There are daily flights to the reserve from Johannesburg (occasionally two flights); your lodge will arrange air transfers (it's a 45-min. flight). If your time is limited, fly, but the road journey is recommended, with a possible overnight stop in the Cradle of Humankind (the best hotel here is www.forumhomini.com), which lies en route. A direct journey by car should take between 3 and 4 hours from Johannesburg; most lodges will arrange a road transfer, meeting you off the flight at the airport. It's an easy road trip, with classic big African skies, and you don't hit dirt roads until you're inside the reserve itself. However, which gate you enter through will be determined by the proximity of your chosen lodge; ask for a map and details if you're driving yourself. Note that it gets very hot in summer and, surprisingly, cold in winter. The best times to visit are at the beginning (Nov) or the end (Apr) of the season, when temperatures are more temperate. Visiting during the winter months (May–Oct) represents substantial savings; simply pack a few ultrawarm layers. ***Note:*** There is a R50 per person per day reserve entrance fee (children R20), as well as a new government levy of about R10 for the upliftment of the previously disadvantaged local communities. Make sure these are included in the rate (entrance fees usually aren't) or you can settle the amount at your lodge.

Where to Stay & Eat

Besides the following options, there are two super-luxury lodges we'd like you to view online if you're planning a special occasion (and have a large budget to play around with). **Molori ★★★** offers no-holds-barred opulence (real antiques; Philippe Starck rim-flow bathtubs; Fendi daybeds; crystal chandeliers), and the kind of seclusion celebs and politicos escape to when they need a rejuvenating dose of African bush (John Travolta and his family flew in with their counselors after the death of his son; Raila Odinga, prime minister of Kenya, was here around the time his country was embroiled in postelection violence; Kate Moss recently spent quality time with her daughter and friends). Riana and her husband, Greg, are the warm, hands-on managers of this glamofari destination; with virtually no money spent on marketing, all traffic is generated by word of mouth—but when the mouths are the likes of Colin Cowie, those words clearly carry a lot of weight. Take a look at it on www.molori.com; rates are available on request, but you're looking at a starting price of around R22,000 per night all-inclusive.

Another special occasion venue is **Mateya Safari Lodge ★★★** (www.mateya safari.com), with only five superluxurious suites, offering a great sense of privacy, excellent service standards, and a highly rated wellness center. That said, the rate is pretty steep: R15,000 double (R11,000 during Aug–Sept low season); personally we'd rather book into Jamala.

Impodimo Lodge ★★   Located in the less busy western Madikwe, Impodimo is an unpretentious lodge that gets all the basics right. The decor exudes well-bred comfort and with two separate suites (with own pool and public spaces) and just eight well-proportioned chalets (including generous bathrooms with outside showers), it offers peace and exclusivity. If you're lucky enough to have Matt as your ranger, you are in for some excellent game-viewing, with new facts about every animal and plant that crosses your path. Unlike some of the fancier lodges that look like film sets, the public spaces invite lounging about, and blend in so well with the natural environment that animals wander through the camp regularly (the pool is often used as a drinking hole by the elephants that frequent this part of Madikiwe). It's also relatively

Madikwe is proudly home to the first wholly owned community safari lodges to be developed in South Africa: **Buffalo Ridge,** an elevated eight-unit lodge that affords grand views of the thornveld plains of Madikwe, is owned and run by the Balete community; its sister lodge on the eastern edge of Madikwe, **Thakadu River Camp ★★,** is managed and owned by the Molatedi people. Both communities have enlisted the aid of the Madikwe Collection to help with promotions and safari logistics. The only tented camp in Madikwe, **Thakadu ★★** (www.thakadurivercamp.com or www.madikwecollection.com; © 011/805-9995 or 082/926-7373; R6,200–R6,900 double; children sharing R1,725) is set within the riverine forest that lines the banks of the Marico River; each of the 12 tented suites has a viewing deck and views of the river. It's also a great choice for families (four of the tents have sleeper couches), with special programs for kids. And finally it's good to know that you're helping a community that has taken the initiative to create employment opportunities and negotiate a substantial stake in the profits. (Incidentally, the Madikwe Collection is also partnering with **De Hoop Nature Reserve** [see p. 181], South Africa's most beautiful coastal reserve, so it's worth inquiring into packages that combine a trip here, too.)

good value (particularly May–Sept): Rates are a quarter of those for Mateya (and half those for Makanyane), but you'll have the same game experience and want for nothing. Meals are not up to the standard of the rest of the lodge, and this is also one of those where the ranger dines with you almost every meal—if you are wanting privacy, state upfront (when booking) to avoid awkwardness.

Madikwe West. www.impodimo.com. © **018/350-9400** or 083/411-7400. 10 units (includes 2 suites; Deluxe sleeps 4 adults; Family sleeps 4 adults and 2 children). High season: R7,370 double; R20,500–R22,500 suite. Low season (May–Sept) R5,500 double. Children sharing pay 50%. No discounted rates for suites. Rates include all meals and game activities; excludes drinks. AE, DC, MC, V. **Amenities:** Dining area, bar, lounge, boma; babysitting; game drives; massage. *In room:* A/C, hair dryer, minibar.

Jamala Madikwe Royal Safari Lodge ★★★ 🎁 🍴 This is hands down our favorite lodge in Madikwe, with sumptuous accommodation in five huge privately located villas; superb, gentle staff; hands-on personal attention from the owners; sublime cuisine and an overall sense of decadence and generosity that has you feeling totally pampered and spoiled within 24 hours of arrival. Every guest is treated like royalty; nothing is too much trouble, and given the small team, the attention to detail is just amazing—clearly a result of the passion the owners have for their lodge, the bush, and their guests. Shaun is a charming, funny host; his more reticent partner, Rodney, who takes care of much of the back of house detail, the perfect foil. Both are very cognizant of guests' need for privacy and provide plenty of it, but if you indicate a desire for company, theirs is excellent. All this, along with the great game viewing—even from their comfortably furnished viewing deck (what Shaun calls the "sofa safari")—is what keeps so many of their guests coming back. We certainly can't wait.

P.O. Box 451, Molatedi, Madikwe. www.jamalamadikwe.com. © **082/929-3190** or 082/927-3129. 5 units. R11,000 double, including all game activities, meals, and most drinks (great wine selection). No children under 16 unless camp is booked as a whole. **Amenities:** Multiple dining areas; lounge-bar; bush walks; game drives; library; viewing deck. *In room:* A/C, hair dryer, minibar (well-stocked), plunge pool, Wi-Fi.

Mosetlha Bush Camp 🔥 Budget travelers looking for professional guided game-viewing, based in a no-nonsense eco-camp with minimal environmental impact—one that will make you feel okay to sit around the campfires with bare feet in the dust—you can breathe a sigh of relief. Mosetlha is perhaps the most authentic bush camps left in Big 5 territory: a breath of fresh air, given that virtually every other concession holder's dream is to re-create an urban sanctuary in the bush (and charge for the privilege). Here accommodation is very, very basic: raised, partly open-sided wooden cabins, sharing three toilet/shower complexes (non-flushing) situated among the cabins (potties provided for middle-of-the-night emergencies). There is no electricity, and water is heated with a donkey boiler; home-style cuisine, prepared in the traditional bush style on the open fire, is equally no-nonsense. This is a rustic no-frills experience, but you get to see the same amount of game (there are four excellent ranger-trackers) as you would if you were spending 10 times more at one of Madikwe's chi-chi lodges. Note that they cannot process credit cards in the camp, so bring cash for tips and drinks (which are, like everything else, very reasonably priced). Mosetlha was changing ownership at time of writing.

P.O. Box 78690, Sandton, 2146 South Africa. www.thebushcamp.com. ©/fax **011/444-9345.** 9 units. R3,200 double. Rate includes all meals, game activities, and emergency evacuation insurance. No children under 8. AE, DC, MC, V. **Amenities:** Dining area; lounge/bar area; boma; game drives and walks.

Madikwe Safari Lodge ★★ ☺ High on style and low on pretense, this lodge—comprising separate camps—has drawn inspiration from the turreted anthills that dot the Madikwe landscape, with packed earth, stone, huge leadwood branches, and thatch to fashion a series of organic living spaces. Interiors are filled with interesting artifacts from around Africa, including some quirky tongue-in-cheek touches. It's the type of safari lodge that makes you want to explore the property as much as the wildlife, which often appears right out front. If you're traveling with children, you'll probably be stationed in West or South Camp, where guest rooms are larger and have sleeper couches. East Camp is the largest in terms of capacity (seven rooms); North Camp, with only four suites, is the one for romance. No matter where you're stationed, you'll enjoy a great sense of privacy: Separated from each other by fat stone walls, the rooms open onto expansive views of the bush, which begins at the edge of your wooden deck (with private plunge pool, outdoor shower, and lounge chairs). At the time of writing it was rumored that &Beyond had lost the concession rights, and the lodge due for new management; check online to ensure that the standards are as high as they were under &Beyond, and whether rates have been retained.

Private Bag X27, Benmore 2010. www.andbeyond.com. © **011/809-4300.** Fax 011/809-4315. 20 units total. High season R9,910. Midseason R7,990. Low season R6,650 double. Rates include all meals, beverages, game drives, and laundry. AE, DC, MC, V. **Amenities:** 3 separate camps, each with own dining area, bar, lounge, boma; babysitting; children's programs; game drives; library; massage. *In room:* A/C, hair dryer, minibar, plunge pool.

Makanyane Safari Lodge ★★ Each suite at this private game reserve along Madikwe's eastern border has huge wraparound glass walls that not only allow you to feel immersed in the bush, but afford picturesque views of the river where animals come to drink in early morning. You can spend your entire day lazing on your bed, watching the comings and goings of thirsty wildlife from your private lounge-deck or enjoying an in-room massage. Of course, then you'd miss out on the excellent game drives; game is plentiful and the lodge is frequently visited by all sorts of animals: At the main lodge, pachyderms also cross the river to try to drink from the infinity pool at the edge of the large, stilted terrace, partially canopied by thorn trees that grow straight through the wooden deck. A good choice if you want a more impersonal experience than Jamala offers.

Krokodildrift 87KP, Madikwe Game Reserve. P.O. Box 9, Derdepoort 2876. www.makanyane.com © **014/778-9600.** Fax 014/778-9611. 8 units. High season (Sept–Apr) R11,200 double. Low season (May–July) R9,200 double. Rates include all meals, most beverages, game drives, and walks. Visit the website for package rates. AE, DC, MC, V. **Amenities:** Multiple dining areas; wine cellar; bar; lounge; sala; bush walks; curio shop; doctor on call; game drives; gym; Internet facility; library; pool; spa; Wi-Fi. *In room:* A/C, hair dryer, minibar.

Morukuru ★★ ☺   With just three sole-use villas on its own 2,000-plus-hectare (4,940-acre) private reserve abutting Madikwe, exclusivity and privacy (there are never any other guests besides you and those you choose to accompany you) make this a great retreat for families or friends keen to really reconnect. Perched under trees on the banks of the Groot Marico River, the two original "bush villas" (referred to as the Lodge and the Owner's House) are huge, each with its own lounge, kitchen, indoor and outdoor dining areas, and infinity pool hanging over the river. Personally we prefer the decor and styling of the new villa, **Farm House,** with its modern take on the traditional homestead, and greater sense of space (with rolling green lawns, and set within a 100-hectare/247-acre fenced-in area, so kids can play at will or you can walk/jog without fear of bumping into large animals). As you have your own chef, own butler, nanny (if needed), and a private safari guide and tracker, there is no schedule and absolutely no pressure; you can do whatever you want and pretty much set your own itinerary. The small staff complement is permanently at your beck and call; ask if you'd prefer to be alone. Unless you're exceptionally gregarious, this is pure, unadulterated bliss. If you are a group of four or more, the low-season rates in Farm House represent excellent value.

Reservations office is in the Netherlands. www.morukuru.com © **31/229/29-9555.** Fax 31/229/23-4139. Owner's House with 2 bedrooms sleeps 4. Lodge with 3 bedrooms sleeps 6 adults and 4 children. Farm House with 5 bedrooms sleeps 10. Owner's House R16,540 (low season R11,540) for 2 persons; additional R5,775–R8,275 per person depending on season. Lodge and Farm House R23,100 for 4 persons (low season R15,400 for 4); each additional person R3,850–R5,775 depending on season; child (under 16) R1,925–R2,890. Rates include all meals, most beverages, game drives, walks, laundry, and meet-and-greet personal airport transfers. MC, V. **Amenities:** Multiple dining areas; bar; lounge; boma; kitchen; babysitting; bush walks; bush dinners; butler; dancing (traditional, on request); doctor on call; game drives; golf (on request); library (book, CD, DVD, Wii); pool; spa and gym visits (on request); Wi-Fi; wine cellar. *In room:* A/C, hair dryer.

9

BIG-GAME COUNTRY

Madikwe Game Reserve

KINGDOM OF THE ZULU: KWAZULU-NATAL

10

Demarcated in the west by the soaring Drakensberg Mountains, its eastern borders lapped by the warm Indian Ocean, densely vegetated KwaZulu-Natal is often described as the country's most "African" province. Its subtropical latitude translates into long, hot, sticky summers, and balmy moderate winters, while the warm Mozambique current ensures that the ocean is never more than a couple of degrees cooler than the air. These sultry conditions have long lured the region's landlocked neighbors, making it the most popular local seaside destination in the country, resulting in a tide of condominiums, timeshares, and gated resort communities, ruining, at least for nature lovers, the coastal belt south of the Tugela River.

In the center of this development is **Durban,** among Africa's busiest ports. With a truly cosmopolitan mix of African, Indian, and colonial cultural influences, it possesses a unique energy that spawns some of the continent's most creative trendsetters, and a beach-loving mindset that has birthed some of the world's top surfers. Still, most international travelers come for the region north of the Tugela River, known as **Zululand**— where the amaZulu rose to power during the early 19th century under the legendary ruler Shaka. Ethnic traditions still play a major role here, and visitors can witness *sangoma* initiation rites or the annual reed dance, attended by thousands of Zulu virgins and their king. Zululand is also home to the majority of the KwaZulu-Natal game reserves, including Africa's oldest wildlife sanctuary, **Hluhluwe-Umfolozi,** and one of the country's finest private reserves, **Phinda.** This is one of the few places in the world where you can track a pride of lions or walk with black rhino in the morning, then spend the afternoon cruising for hippos and crocs along the lush waterways of **iSimangaliso Wetland Park,** or diving the rich coral reefs off Sodwana Bay. It's well worth making time to join the privileged few who have explored the rich marine life and pristine coastline even farther north, diving or snorkeling off beautiful **Mabibi** or **Rocktail Bay.** More intrepid nature lovers should head to **Kosi Bay** in the far northern corner of the province, where the swamp and raffia palm forests afford great birding.

The **Midlands,** with its fine country lodgings and definitive arts and crafts "Meander," leads up into what is surely the pride of place for those who enjoy walking: the soaring **Drakensberg Mountains,** or uKhahlamba, "Barrier of Spears," as the amaZulu called them. The site of more than 35,000 ancient San rock paintings—thought to be the most densely concentrated on the African continent (including the famous Game Pass Shelter, the "Rosetta Stone" of Bushmen paintings)—the Drakensberg was declared a World Heritage Site in 2000, garnering international attention for southern Africa's most majestic mountain scape.

With most of the region's top sights within a 3- to 4-hour drive from Durban's gleaming new international airport, the diversity of the province is wonderfully accessible. And with its laid-back bustle, warm swimmable ocean, and abundant rumors that the city will be jostling for a place as Olympic host city in 2020, Durban may eventually give Eurocentric Cape Town a run for its money.

STAYING ACTIVE

BIRD-WATCHING   Three of South Africa's best bird-watching destinations—St Lucia/iSimangaliso, and the Mkhuze and Ndumo reserves—are located here, and there's enough variety to keep twitchers endlessly entertained. With various self-drive routes and over 600 recorded species, the popular **Zululand Birding Route** (✆ **072/277-7254;** www.zbr.co.za) is an online resource providing links to local guides and detailed information on how to tackle a bird-oriented trip. If you prefer someone else to show you the way, contact Leon at **Lawson's Birding and Wildlife Tours ★★★** (✆ **013/741-2458;** www.lawsons.co.za), which operates throughout southern Africa but includes the important KZN reserves (such as Ndumo and Mkhuze, discussed below) in its fully catered, tailored bird-watching safaris.

A 4-hour drive north of Durban, **Mkhuze Game Reserve** (✆ **035/573-9004**) is connected to the coastal plain via the Mkhuze River, and also has 430 species of bird on record (as well as a variety of game). Maps are issued at the reception office—look for the three bird hides at Nsumo and Nhlonhlela Pans, where you can picnic and watch the non-stop spectacle on the waterway. You can overnight in chalets and en-suite tents (limited facilities include a small restaurant serving simple pub-grub-style dishes; a shop stocking basic food supplies and liquid refreshments; and a swimming pool—essential during the hot summer months). Mkhuze is reached via the N2 (take the Mkhuze Village turnoff; the Emshopi Gate entrance is 28km/17 miles farther). Even farther north, on the border between KwaZulu-Natal and Mozambique, **Ndumo Game Reserve** (✆ **035/591-0058**) has some 430 species, and is often compared with the Okavango Delta in Botswana, with numerous pans and yellow fever tree forests, wetlands, and reed beds teeming with more than 60% of South Africa's birdlife. There's a camp here with seven twin-bed chalets shaded by overhead marula trees (and cooled by air-conditioning). Guests share an ablution block and there's a shared kitchen—bring your own food, and the camp cook can prepare your meals. Mercifully, there's also a pool. Expect to pay R40 per person to enter each park, as well as R40 for your car. For more information on either park, visit www.kznwildlife.co.za; to book accommodation call ✆ **033/845-1000.**

CANOPY TOURS ★★★   Two different canopy tours—in which you're attached to a series of wire slides by means of high-tech harnesses—are available in the Drakensberg region. Splendid views and a sense of exhilaration as you float above ancient forests, gushing waterfalls and fairytale streams. Closest to Durban, the **Karkloof**

Canopy Tour (📞 033/300-3415; www.karkloofcanopytour.co.za) in the Midlands offers exhilarating speeds and forest canopy views; the **Drakensberg Canopy Tour** (📞 **036/468-1981** or 083/661-5691; www.drakensbergcanopytour.co.za) operates in the Central Drakensberg near Cathkin Peak and Champagne Castle; you whizz along 12 slides through the Blue Grotto forest, taking in unusual views of waterfalls and launching from platforms attached to sheer cliff faces. Both tours last around 2½ hours and cost R450 per person.

DIVING ★★★   A popular activity along this coast is diving with sharks—without the cage. **African Dive Adventures** (📞 **039/317-1483;** www.africandiveadventures.co.za) offers a variety of ways in which to spend time in the water with the underwater predators; most popular is diving with ragged tooth sharks (and also Zambezi and tiger sharks, depending on season) at Protea Banks, rated by many as the best shark diving spot on earth. Baited cageless tiger shark dives with full equipment rental cost R1,150 (2–3 hr.); you can also snorkel with the tigers for R600 (equipment included). A regular dive is R540. Situated within the iSimangaliso Wetland Park, **Sodwana Bay** is generally considered the top diving spot in the country, with coral-covered reefs inundated by tropical fish; nearly all shark species have been spotted here, and there have been at least three recent photographed sightings of coelacanths (115m/378 ft. below the surface). **Reefteach ★★** (📞 **082/339-6920;** www.reefteach.co.za) is recommended for quality dive tuition (R3,000 for the Open Water course, including equipment, but not lodging); they will also arrange suitable catered or efficiency accommodation. Various outfits offer packages that include accommodation. **Coral Divers** (📞 **033/345-6531;** www.coraldivers.co.za) has en-suite cabins (R1,340 double, including dinner and breakfast) and reasonably priced dives and equipment hire; introductory diving courses cost R800, or R3,995 for the PADI-accredited Open Water course (with 5 nights tented accommodation). **Sea Escapes** (📞 **083/459-4222** or 082/853-2905; www.seaescapes.co.za) also offers up to advanced level diving courses, with assorted lodging options (an Open Water course with all gear and 5 nights in a cabin costs R3,850 per diver).

FLY-FISHING ★★★   Stay at Hartford House (p. 398) in the Midlands and engage the services of **Wildfly,** one of the country's premiere fly-fishing outfits, which offers master class tuition on the guesthouse estate. Make arrangements in advance, though.

HIKING ★★★   The **uKhahlamba Drakensberg mountain range** is a hiking mecca. Of the many trails traversing the Drakensberg (and, really, you're unlikely to be disappointed by any of them), we highly recommend the **Giant's Cup Hiking Trail ★★★**, located in the Cobham area. This 3- to 5-day self-guided, clearly marked hike takes you past caves with San paintings, crystal-clear rivers, pools, and deep grass valleys. You overnight in basic huts along the way (R75 per person per night). Alternatively, if you have only a day, try the **Sentinel Trail,** connecting the Royal Natal and Cathedral Peak Parks. Bookings are managed by KZN Wildlife (www.kznwildlife.com).

Within the 66,000-hectare (163,020-acre) **Hluhluwe-Umfolozi Reserve,** between the White and Black Umfolozi rivers, is a 25,000-hectare (308,750-acre) wilderness untouched by human beings. Uncharted by roads, it's accessible only on foot. The five **wilderness trails ★★★** here are considered the country's best, superior even to those in Kruger. They offer the best opportunity to appreciate the silence and solitude of the wilderness, refreshing visitors physically, mentally, and spiritually.

Most popular is the 3-night **Base Camp Trail,** based in the tented Mndindini Trails Camp. Hikers share ablutions (showers and flush toilets). There's a fridge for BYO drinks, and you carry only daypacks with your personal effects, water, and lunch. Cost is R3,952 per person, excluding the R110 per day conservation levy. The cheaper 2-night (with option to extend to 3 nights) **Short Wilderness Trail** is based around a more basic satellite camp; showers are buckets, and toilets consist of a spade, match, and paper; cost is R2,180 per person, excluding levy. The extended version costs R3,200. Hard-core nature lovers or those ready for a life-changing experience should opt for a 3- or 4-night **Primitive Trail,** a return to the original pioneering tradition, in which you walk to a new campsite every night, carry your gear, and sleep under the stars (note that a fair degree of fitness is required for this trail); cost is R2,220 to R2,685 per person. Trails run mostly from March to mid-November (to avoid the worst of the heat) and are fully catered (including all equipment, bedding, and food); they do, however, require a minimum of four individuals to go out on the trail as scheduled. If this quota isn't booked, the trail will be canceled and payments refunded. You have the option, however, to pay the minimum charge for four people, to ensure the trail takes place. For inquiries or bookings, call *©* **033/845-1067** or 033/845-1000 (e-mail trails@kznwildlife.com); or visit www.kznwildlife.com.

SURFING   **Learn 2 Surf** (*©* **083/414-0567;** www.learn2surf.co.za) is your best bet for making contact with top instructors; their Durban outfit offers lessons at Addington Beach, near uShaka Marine World (which, incidentally, is where you'll find lessons and gear for most watersports). **Safari Surf Shop** is Durban's most reputable surfboard manufacturer, so head there if you want to pick up a customized board, any related gear, or advice; they're at 6 Milne St. (*©* **031/337-4231;** www. safarisurf.com). Good surf spots around the city are North Beach and the adjacent Bay of Plenty. Check out Green Point, the Spot, Warner Beach, Baggies, and Cave Rock; the latter has an excellent right reef break but is a little farther out of town. New Pier is extremely popular, very crowded, and competitive.

DURBAN

1,753km (1,087 miles) NE of Cape Town; 588km (365 miles) SE of Johannesburg

The Union Jack was first planted in Durban's fertile soil in 1824, a year after George Farewell fortuitously happened upon its harbor. It was only after the fledgling settlement was formally annexed in 1844, however, that the dense coastal vegetation was gradually consumed by buildings with broad verandas and civilized with English traditions such as morning papers, afternoon tea, and weekend horse racing.

Sugar was this region's "white gold," yielding fortunes for the so-called sugar barons. The most famous was Sir Marshall Campbell; today his home, housing the Campbell Collection, is one of Durban's star attractions, and tourists still travel along the broad beachfront promenade in the two-wheeled "rickshaws" (hand-pulled by primped and preened faux "Zulu warriors") he introduced to the city in 1893. The world's voracious appetite for sugar was responsible for the strong Indian strain in Durban's architecture, cuisine, and customs—during the 19th century, thousands of indentured laborers were shipped in from India to work the sugar plantations, and today Durban is said to house the largest Indian population outside of India.

South Africa's third-largest city, Durban attracts the lion's share of South Africa's domestic tourists and offers a completely unique atmosphere. On the surface is the creeping sense of decay typical of tropical places, in which the constant presence of humidity brings about a kind of torpor. Yet beneath the surface, the city pulsates with promise—and not only among real estate agents exhilarated by the urban rejuvenation that happened for the World Cup in 2010. The upgrade—one which many residents say has salvaged the best parts of the city (notably its beachfront) from the brink of tip-heap status—includes the installation of the sculptural Moses Mabhida Stadium. Within walking distance of the ocean, it is connected, via the revamped Golden Mile promenade, to the uShaka Marine World, home to one of the world's best aquariums. Along the way, there are countless opportunities to unfurl your beach towel, plant your umbrella, gawk at surfers, jog, in-line skate, cycle, or amble. The beachfront stretch ranks among the country's most diverse people-watching zones, where the Shembe may be conducting a baptism while surfers look for the perfect wave, or a group of Hindus may be lighting clay votive lamps while a Zulu *sangoma* tosses in an offering to the ancestors.

Durban has always been a beach-lover's idyll, but besides churning out bronzed beauties and many of the world's top surfers, there's also a sense of pride in birthing some of the country's best creative talents, producing traditional pottery and beadwork as well as cutting-edge fashion and interior design. As a hub of multiculturalism, Durban cooks, and it's certainly worth joining Street Scene for one of their insightful tours of the city, or into the outlying townships. The bubbling markets of Warwick Triangle will startle and surprise: Indian dealers trade in everything from spices and sari fabrics to fresh fish and meat, while Zulu street hawkers ply passersby with anything from haircuts to *muti*—baboon skulls, bits of bark, bone, and dried herbs—used to heal wounds, improve spirits, ward off evil, or cast spells. It is a bizarre and wonderful city, a truly African city, undergoing its own full-tilt renaissance.

Essentials

VISITOR INFORMATION There's a **tourism information counter** in the arrivals hall at the airport but best to make your travel arrangements at the Tourist Junction, 160 Monty Naicker St., where **Durban Tourism** (✆ **031/304-4934;** www.durbanexperience.co.za; Mon–Fri 8am–4:30pm, Sat 9am–2pm) is located, as well as a branch of **eZemvelo KwaZulu-Natal Wildlife** (aka KZN Wildlife) and **Tourism KwaZulu-Natal.** To make the most of your time here, contact **Street Scene Tours ★★★** (✆ **031/368-5909;** www.streetscenetours.com) and sign up for at least one of its innovative city or township tours.

GETTING THERE By Plane King Shaka International Airport (DUR; flight information ✆ **086/727-7888;** general inquiries ✆ **032/436-6585;** www. kingshakainternational.co.za) opened on May 1, 2010, and is located 35km (22 miles)—35 minutes—north of central Durban. Currently Emirates flies here from London (via Dubai), and offers some very good online deals. From here you can then fly directly on to Cape Town, or stay for a few days. The airport is just moments from the N2 Highway, making onward journeys north or south very straightforward; access to Zululand's key destinations, including its Big 5 reserves, requires minimal effort. A general number for metered taxis servicing the airport is ✆ **032/436-6035.**

By Train Shosholoza Meyl (✆ **087/802-6674;** www.shosholoza-meyl.co.za) runs overnight Tourist Class (very basic sleeper; R260) services from Johannesburg (departures Wed–Mon 6:30pm), pulling into Durban Station on NMR Avenue the following morning (at 7:21am). The relatively luxurious **Premier Classe** (deluxe sleeper; R1,010) runs only on Fridays, departing Johannesburg at 6:20pm, and arriving in Durban at 8:30am the next day.

Central Durban

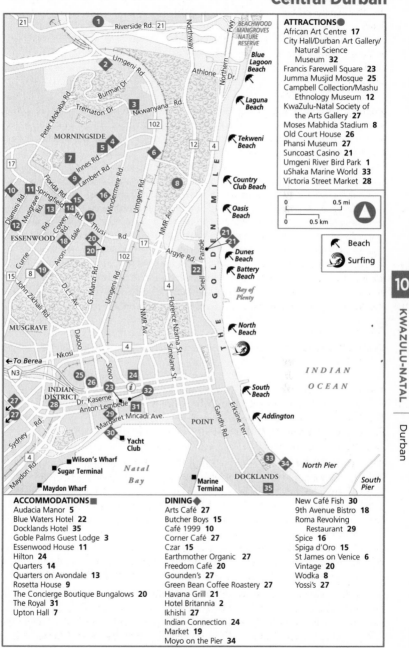

ATTRACTIONS ●
African Art Centre **17**
City Hall/Durban Art Gallery/
    Natural Science
    Museum **32**
Francis Farewell Square **23**
Jumma Musjid Mosque **25**
Campbell Collection/Mashu
    Ethnology Museum **12**
KwaZulu-Natal Society of
    the Arts Gallery **27**
Moses Mabhida Stadium **8**
Old Court House **26**
Phansi Museum **27**
Suncoast Casino **21**
Umgeni River Bird Park **1**
uShaka Marine World **33**
Victoria Street Market **28**

0   0.5 mi
0   0.5 km

🏖 Beach
🌊 Surfing

ACCOMMODATIONS ■
Audacia Manor **5**
Blue Waters Hotel **22**
Docklands Hotel **35**
Goble Palms Guest Lodge **3**
Essenwood House **11**
Hilton **24**
Quarters **14**
Quarters on Avondale **13**
Rosetta House **9**
The Concierge Boutique Bungalows **20**
The Royal **31**
Upton Hall **7**

DINING ◆
Arts Café **27**
Butcher Boys **15**
Café 1999 **10**
Corner Café **27**
Czar **15**
Earthmother Organic **27**
Freedom Café **20**
Gounden's **27**
Green Bean Coffee Roastery **27**
Havana Grill **21**
Hotel Britannia **2**
Ikhishi **27**
Indian Connection **24**
Market **19**
Moyo on the Pier **34**

New Café Fish **30**
9th Avenue Bistro **18**
Roma Revolving
    Restaurant **29**
Spice **16**
Spiga d'Oro **15**
St James on Venice **6**
Vintage **20**
Wodka **8**
Yossi's **27**

Since democratizing, road names have continued to be a political issue. Some cities have been quicker to rename certain roads—especially those honoring colonialism and Eurocentric history or remembering Apartheid heroes. Durban saw a wave of sudden and unexpected name changes in 2010, a move attributed largely to local city manager Mike Sutcliffe. The initial response, notably from white people who feel they weren't consulted on the process, has tended to focus on the unnecessary expense involved, not to mention the choice of unfamiliar names (many of them belonging to unsung heroes of the revolution) and overly long and supposedly difficult-to-pronounce names. Some of these name changes have radically upset certain groups, and there has been a very vocal outcry—as well as some low-level vandalism—against names that some find offensive (one 'hood was horrified to discover a road renamed in honor of an Apartheid-era bomber who'd been responsible for the death of local residents) and others find irrelevant (a road named after Che Guevara?). Speak to anyone who lives here and you're likely to hear strong opinions on the matter. Finally, it's worth knowing that although everyone calls the metropolis Durban, the city now falls within a greater metro region designated eThekwini. We've provided both old and new names wherever possible in this chapter.

By Bus Country-wide operators **Greyhound, Intercape,** and **Translux** (see chapter 13 for contact information) all arrive and depart at the station complex, while the **Baz Bus** does drop-offs at hostels.

By Car The N2 from Cape Town runs parallel to the coast as far as Zululand; the N3 from Johannesburg meets the N2 at Durban.

WHEN TO GO The best time to visit is from February to mid-May, when the majority of domestic tourists have returned inland; increasingly, though, these months are becoming the hottest. Temperatures range from 61°F to 73°F (16°C–25°C) in winter (May–Aug) and 73°F to 91°F (23°C–33°C) in summer (Sept–Apr).

GETTING AROUND **By Car** A number of companies have desks at the airport, including **Avis** and **Budget**—there's no telling which will be cheapest on any given day, so shop around; it's worth comparing rates with **Value Care Hire** (© 086/143-7483; www.valuerentalcar.com). For cheap deals, call **Windermere Car Hire** (© 031/312-0339 or 082/454-1625) or **Comfort Car Rentals** (© 031/368-6563). Be sure to get a contract with unlimited mileage. *Warning:* Durban drivers may be the worst in the country—there's a serious lack of discipline on the roads. Be forewarned that lane changing is sudden, indicator lights are seldom used, and traffic circles (which are numerous) are badly negotiated. Keep your wits about you.

By Bus The CBD, beachfront, and Berea are serviced by three **People Mover** bus routes (© 031/309-5942; www.durbanpeoplemover.co.za), which operate between 5am and 10pm daily (until 9:50pm on Sun); pickups are at 15-minute intervals, and tickets cost R4 (day passes available). Less reliable (and not as safe) are the blue **Mynah** buses covering routes between Durban and its suburbs; you can catch the **Umhlanga Express** (© 082/268-0651) to Umhlanga Rocks.

By Taxi   **Mozzie Cabs** (☎ **086/066-9943**; www.mozzie.co.za) and **Zippy Cabs** (☎ **031/202-7067** or -7068; www.zippycabs.co.za) are both reputable taxi operators. **Super Shuttle** (☎ **0860/333-4444** or 082/903-0971) offers a personalized transfer service to any destination in KwaZulu-Natal.

GUIDED TOURS   Highly recommended is **Street Scene Tours ★★★** (☎ **031/368-5909**; www.streetscenetours.com), which has put together a variety of in-depth excursions around Durban, or into the townships on the fringes of the urban center. Each tour is themed to give it a focus that sets it above the mundane, and you'll appreciate the variety of stops on any given route. They'll also tailor a tour for you.

On Foot   **Historical Walkabout** and **Oriental Walkabout ★★** tours (both R100) can be arranged through **Durban Africa** (☎ **031/304-4934**). Book the day before.

By Boat   Get up early and join one of the **boat trips to the shark nets ★★★** run by the **KwaZulu-Natal Sharks Board.** Currently the most viable protection for swimmers, these controversial nets are responsible for the deaths of hundreds of sharks, as well as rays, dolphins, and endangered turtles; the Board tags and releases any live animals caught (around 600 sharks are caught annually, and of these 80 are released). Passengers get to see the meshing teams checking the nets for captured sharks (and any other unfortunate creatures that might have been caught), and there's often opportunistic whale- or dolphin-spotting along the way; seeing the city from this angle, witnessing activity in and around the harbor, and abundant birdlife all make this excursion very worthwhile. Departures are usually around 6:30am from Wilson's Wharf; you must book in advance as minimum numbers apply (☎ **082/403-9206**; www.shark.co.za; R250 per person). **Adventures Extreme Ocean Safaris** (☎ **082/960-7682**; www.kznwhale.co.za) offers licensed boat-based whale-watching, launching from Shelley Beach, about an hour south of Durban; the 90-min. boat trip also goes to the shark nets, and typically includes dolphin-viewing. For a more thrilling waterborne outing, contact **Ocean Ventures** (☎ **086/100-1138**; www.ocean ventures.co.za), which runs ocean-riding safaris aboard its rigid inflatable boats that launch from Umhlanga Rocks and uShaka (Vetchies) Beach (at uShaka Marine World). These are high-speed, adrenaline-chasing trips, but may include lucky sightings of whales, sharks and dolphins; private charters are available and they do ocean-kayaking trips, too. For many more boating options, visit **www.durbancharterboat association.co.za**.

Sangomas at Dawn

The Durban beachfront and its warm and inviting ocean is a mecca for all walks of life: Stroll along a Durban beach at dawn, and you may see a group of Zulu *sangomas* (traditional healers), their beads and buckskin adornments covered in brightly colored cloth, wading into the ocean to collect seawater to be used in *muti* (traditional medicines) to protect crops. An estimated two-thirds of South Africans regularly consult *sangomas,* and even large pharmaceutical companies are tapping into their knowledge of the medicinal properties of plants; the *muti* industry is believed to be worth well over R2 billion a year. Later in the day, you might spot the same *sangomas* at Warwick Junction, the largest *muti* market in Southern Africa, where the assortment of medicines offered for sale is simply staggering.

By Air   Legend Aviation (📞 **031/563-5065;** www.legendaviation.co.za) offers a variety of trips, from a 30-minute flight along the coast as far as Ballito, to 75-minute trips as far as the Tugela River mouth; they also welcome any suggestions.

CITY LAYOUT   **The **city center encompasses the buildings and memorials surrounding Francis Farewell Square, as well as the **Indian District**—the latter is now very seedy and best explored with a guide (see above)—and the **"Golden Mile,"** a long stretch of beachfront that forms the eastern arm of the city. Running south from Blue Lagoon Beach, it terminates in Durban's **Point,** where touristy (but child-friendly) uShaka Marine World leads the regeneration of this previously underutilized harbor area. Stretching eastward from here is **Margaret Mncadi Road** (formerly **Victoria Embankment,** or simply the Esplanade); running at more or less 90 degrees to the Golden Mile along the harbor's edge, it forms the city's southern border. This is where you will find the run-down BAT Centre (overlooking the Small Craft Harbour) and, a little farther along, Wilson's Wharf. On the western outskirts of the city lies **the Ridge,** as Durbanites refer to the wealthy colonial-era suburbs, like **Berea,** with elevated views of the city and harbor. Most of the city's best guesthouses and many restaurant and nightlife hubs are here, so it's a good place to be based. If you'd prefer to be on the ocean, **Umhlanga Rocks** or even **Umdloti** (Oomshlow-tea)—once uncrowded seaside villages bordered by cane plantations and near-jungle, but now developed northern suburbs—are the enclaves to be.

[FastFACTS] DURBAN

Area Code   Durban's area code is **031.**

Emergencies   For an **ambulance,** call 📞 **10177** and ask to be taken to the casualty unit at **Entabeni Private Hospital** (📞 **031/204-1300**). Staff will also treat non-emergencies. Another good option is **St Augustine's Hospital,** 107 JB Marks (Chelmsford) Rd., Glenwood (📞 **031/268-5000**). **Police:** 📞 **031/300-3333; Flying Squad:** 📞 **10111; SAP Tourist Protection Unit:** 📞 **031/368-4453;**

Fire Brigade: 📞 **031/309-4341; NSRI** (sea rescue): 📞 **031/361-8567; Rape Crisis:** 📞 **031/312-2323.**

Pharmacy   Late-night pharmacies include **Medicine Chest** (📞 **031/305-6151**), 155 King Dinuzulu (Berea) Rd., and **Day-Night Pharmacy** (📞 **031/368-3666**), 9A Nedbank Circle, corner of Mahatma Gandhi (Point) Rd. and Dr Pixley Kaseme (West) St. (the latter has free delivery).

Safety   Malaria has not been reported in Durban

for more than 50 years, but if you plan to travel into northern Zululand, a course of antimalarial drugs is advisable (p. 450). Like any large city where a large percentage of the population is poor, Durban is troubled by street crime. The display of wealth is unwise anywhere in the city or beachfront, and visitors are advised to do their explorations of these areas during the day.

Weather   For a weather report, call 📞 **082/231-1603.**

Exploring the City

CITY CENTER   **For an excellent overview of the city and its myriad, diverse parts, contact **Street Scene Tours ★★★ (📞 **031/368-5909,** 071/887-3079, or 083/995-8002; www.streetscenetours.co.za); Richard and Sthembiso offer an excellent "alternative" tour (from R400 per person) which starts in the lavish residential suburbs overlooking the city, and then descends into its heady bowels. You'll explore the bustling markets around Warwick Junction, including the *muti* market where *sangomas* prescribe traditional cures that include snakeskin and multifarious allegedly medicinal plants—it's the biggest traditional medicine market in Southern Africa. Let your guides know beforehand if you'd like to set up a consultation with a traditional healer. Their tour allows plenty of time for you to observe and absorb the intoxicating sights, sounds, and smells—and then you'll dine in one of the city's popular Indian eateries and sample the best coffee in town, too. Street Scene also runs a Society Tour that is more about discovering cafe culture and emerging Durban design—and there's a Nightlife tour which can be tailored to meet your particular after-hours predilections. **Durban Tourism** (*©* **031/304-4934**) also offers walking tours (see "Visitor Information," above) in the city center.

Alternatively, if you're looking to explore a number of architectural icons and museums at your own pace, start at nearby **City Hall,** a stone-for-stone replica of Belfast's City Hall, built in 1910. The first floor houses an outmoded **Natural Science Museum** (*©* **031/311-2256**), where an array of very dead-looking animals is useful only as a crash course in wildlife identification (mildly helpful if you're heading out on safari). One floor up, you'll find the **Durban Art Gallery** (*©* **031/311-2264;** Mon–Sat 8:30am–4pm, Sun 11am–4pm; free admission), sometimes with quite provocative exhibitions (look out for the **Red Eye** multimedia arts festival, held here in Sept). Back in the 1970s, this was the first national gallery to recognize African crafts as art, and today it has arguably the most representative collection of traditional and contemporary South "Africana" art in the country (see "Discovering Zulu History," p. 386). East of the City Hall, facing Samora Michel (Aliwal) Road, is the **Old Court House,** home of Durban's local-history museum (*©* **031/311-2233;** Mon–Sat 8:30am–4pm, Sun 11am–4pm; free admission). The oldest surviving public building in Durban (erected 1866), this is a lovely example of the Natal Verandah style and today houses a rather dry collection of exhibits that focus on 19th-century history. Mahatma Gandhi was a regular visitor, and a few of his artifacts are housed here.

If you're specifically interested in Durban's prolific deco architecture (and the uniquely Asian-influenced deco style that's also found here), visit the website of the **Durban Art Deco Society** (www.durbandeco.org.za); you can access an online brochure detailing the most interesting buildings with maps and good explanations. There's also an online virtual tour.

THE GOLDEN MILE BEACHFRONT   The Portuguese explorers who first laid eyes on Durban's beachfront described it as "sands of gold"—a moniker that has stuck long after the high-rises and concrete promenades dwarfed the beaches. Today, following a multimillion-rand upgrade and reburbishment of the entire area, there's a string of efficiently managed—and clean—beaches, backed up by broad promenades and all kinds of kitschy leisure activities. A stroll from one end to the other will reveal which of the dozen or so beaches are preferred by which Durban tribe, and clear signs designate which are approved for bathing, which are suitable for surfing, and which are currently safe (determined by tidal activity, water quality, and shark activity, if any). Certain beaches are the domain of fishermen, while centrally located **North Beach** is the traditional quintessential meeting of kitsch and cool, haunted by fresh-faced surfers and watched by diners in casual food joints at the promenade's edge—unfurl your towel and join the sun-worshippers, or grab an ice-cream and cruise the strip. The northerly **Bay of Plenty, Battery Beach,** and **Suncoast Beach** tend to attract the holiday crowds. The latter beach is overlooked by the eponymous super-kitsch Deco-style **Suncoast Casino & Entertainment World**—which, aside from the casino, contains cinemas and restaurants, including the popular **Havana Grill**

A VIEW FROM THE basket handle

The most obvious and talked about change to the Durban skyline has been the arrival of the **Moses Mabhida Stadium,** which sprung up just north of the city center in preparation for the 2010 FIFA World Cup tournament; during the Cup it was arguably the most celebrated and admired new stadium, attracting praise not only for its architectural beauty but for clever proportions that allow spectators (in certain seats) to enjoy a simultaneous view of the ocean, cityscape, and game on the field. The stadium connects cleverly with the city, too, with a long, wide glistening pedestrian mall leading up to the southern entrance. It also offers plenty of opportunities for visitors to get involved even on non-match days. The unusual basket-handle design comes with a funicular-style **SkyCar** (Mon–Sun 9am–6pm, last trip 5:30pm; R50 adult, R25 children under 12) which transfers passengers up to the stadium's highest point in 2 minutes; excellent 360-degree views of the city and Indian Ocean await. It's also possible to walk up to the top via the 550 steps built into the other side of the

handle (**Adventure Walk;** Sat–Sun 10am, 1pm, and 4pm; R80); or you can ascend 450 steps before throwing yourself from one of the supporting beams attached to a bungee cord to experience the world's first and only sports stadium swing (and the biggest swing on the planet). It's known as **Big Rush** (✆ **031/332-3250;** www.bigrush.co.za; daily 9am–5pm; R595), and you'll jump from a height of 106m (348 ft.), swinging out in a 220m (722-ft.) arc beneath the stadium's arch. If you're more interested in what's going on inside the stadium than the views from above it, there are **behind-the-scenes tours** (of which the "professional tour" is longer and more detailed, and includes entry to the one of the change rooms, the presidential atrium, and other usually off-limits parts of the arena, including insight into some of the unusual artworks commissioned for the stadium); these depart regularly. Whatever else you do, if there's an opportunity to **catch a game** here, do; for more information on any of these activities or events hosted at the stadium, visit www.mosesmabhidastadium.co.za.

and Winebar, which has a deck area a stone's throw away from the sea (see "Table with a Sea View, Please" box, p. 382); nevertheless, the casino complex represents the apex of tastelessness in a city with so much more to offer than the fast-food and Day-Glo on display here. Located to the far north of the Golden Mile, at the estuary mouth, is **Blue Lagoon,** where fishermen stand all day and teens gather for romance and mild debauchery at night. Nearby is **Umgeni River Bird Park** (✆ **031/579-4600**), good for kids, with more than 300 species from around the world housed in large aviaries, and planted with palms, cycads, and other tropical plants.

THE POINT & HARBOUR AREA   The star attraction here (particularly for families) is **uShaka Marine World** ☺ (✆ **031/328-8000;** www.ushakamarineworld. co.za), located at the southernmost end of the Golden Mile. Set over 16 hectares (40 acres), this waterfront theme park incorporates sea and fresh water, a re-creation of a 1920 cargo ship, lush indigenous vegetation, and a state-of-the-art aquarium: Sea World (daily 9am–5pm, some activities closed Mon–Tues; R130 adult and R99 children)— one of the world's five biggest, boasting the largest collection of sharks in the Southern Hemisphere. There are also dolphin and seal stadiums, a shark cage (in which you can dive with the predators for R150), a snorkel lagoon, and a "Wet 'n Wild" world—slides and rides to keep the kids happy for the entire day. And uShaka is justifiably proud of the fact that every drop of water pumped into its system returns cleaner than when it came in. For grown-ups, the star attraction here is **Moyo on the Pier ★**, a breezy bar hovering above the water (see "Table with a Sea View, Please" box below).

Farther south, the resuscitated **Docklands** area has been reclaimed from the prostitutes and drug lords; it's now dotted with new and renovated buildings as gentrification sets in.

Swinging inland, along the northern edge of Durban's vast harbor, you can stop by the **Small Craft Harbour** (off Margaret Mncadi), where you can have a meal at **New Café Fish** at the nearby **Yacht Mole;** for more harbor activity, head to nearby **Wilson's Wharf,** Durban's tacky, miniature waterfront complex, replete with bars and restaurants overlooking the very active harbor.

BEREA   This gracious old suburb is home not only to much of Durban's elite (as well as the house occupied by the president and visiting dignitaries), but also where you'll find the **Campbell Collection ★★**, 220 Gladys Mazibuko (Marriott) Rd. Housed in Muckleneuk, the neo–Cape Dutch home that sugar baron Sir Marshall Campbell built for his family in 1914, it gives one a great sense of what it must have been like to live in colonial splendor high up on the ridge, with sweeping views from the upstairs rooms of the harbor below. Tours take in the gracious gardens and the Cape Dutch furniture and artwork collected by Campbell's son (whose private hunting farm became what is today the private game reserve MalaMala), as well as the extensive Africana library and ethnological artifacts collected by his daughter, "Killie" Campbell. Killie was a voracious collector of traditional utensils, ornaments, art, musical instruments, sticks, and various items of beaded clothing (don't miss the necklace of British redcoat buttons worn by Zulu warriors as a sign of bravery). Today her collection, known as the **Mashu Ethnology Museum,** occupies Muckleneuk's original kitchen, and is one of the country's finest groupings of African artifacts. You could spend hours just plying through the 300-odd images of different tribal groups painted by Barbara Tyrrell. Tours of the collections and the museum are by appointment only (✆ **031/207-3432;** http://campbell.ukzn.ac.za; R20 per person).

UMHLANGA & THE NORTH COAST   The most popular (and developed) seaside suburb on the North Coast, **Umhlanga Rocks** (pronounced *Oom*-shlung-ga) is a 20-minute drive north of the city center. Originally part of Marshall Campbell's sugar estate, it is now simply an extension of Durban, with safe swimming areas and plenty of accommodations and leisure options. It also has its own visitor center: **Umhlanga Tourism Information Centre** (✆ **031/561-4257;** www.umhlanga tourism.co.za; Mon–Fri 8:30am–5pm, Sat 9am–1pm), on Chartwell Drive. Besides the beach, the one place worth visiting, particularly for parents, is the office of the **KZN Sharks Board** (✆ **031/566-0400;** www.shark.co.za; R35 adults, R20 children 4–12). This is one of the most prestigious centers for shark research in the world, and after a (slightly dumbed-down) 20-minute film presentation about these awesome predators, there is a shark dissection (aimed squarely at youngsters, but not recommended if you're in any way queasy) in which one of the specimens caught in the nets (up to 14 species swim off this coast) becomes part of a kind of educational stand-up comedy routine. Presentations happen Tuesday through Thursday at 9am and 2pm, and Sunday at 2pm. Far better: Catch a Sharks Board **boat ride** to observe firsthand how the meshing crews go about servicing the shark nets (see "Guided Tours—By Boat," above).

To experience the real virtue of the North Coast these days, you really need to head farther up the coast, away from the overwrought development that has transformed Umhlanga from village to suburb in the last decade. Just a few minutes away, the small and still relatively village-like (albeit lined with vacation apartments) coastal resort of **Umdloti,** is still an option for a less manic vacation (with easy beach access and a couple of good places to eat).

If you're looking for truly uncrowded beaches, head farther north still, beyond overdeveloped Ballito to one of the coast's more rudimentary villages, such as **Blythe-dale** (roughly 25km/16 miles north of Ballito and 70km/43 miles north of Durban), which has a lovely beach; some 13km (8 miles) farther, the tiny hamlet of **Zinkwasi,** between a subtropical beach and the lagoon, is the least developed beach resort on the North Coast and marks the end of the so-called "Dolphin Coast".

Shopping for African Crafts & Design

The **African Art Centre ★★★**, opposite Quarters Hotel, at 94 Florida Rd. (© **031/312-3804;** www.afriart.org.za; Mon–Fri 8:30am–5pm, Sat 9am–3pm, Sun 10am–3pm), is the best place to browse for woodcarvings, ceramics, beadwork, baskets, tapestries, rugs, fine art, and fabrics sourced from craftsmen and artists located throughout the province. This nonprofit organization has a knowledgeable, helpful staff—they can tell you about the artists and their creations. Proceeds are reinvested in the development of local talent. If this whets your appetite, a visit to the **Kwa-Zulu-Natal Society of the Arts (NSA) Gallery ★★★**, 166 Bulwer Rd., Glenwood (© **031/202-3686;** www.nsagallery.co.za; Tues–Fri 9am–5pm, Sat–Sun 10am–4pm), is a must. The excellent exhibitions feature artists from different cultural and ethnic backgrounds and include paintings, mosaics, beadwork, and embroidery. The adjacent shop has a wide variety of visual arts, including works by master craftspeople, and the area has become a dining hub (including the NSA's alfresco Arts Café), so time your visit to coincide with lunch. Also well worth a look (although without quite the same variety offered), is the **Phansi Museum** (see "Touring the Phansi with Princess Phumzile" box, above) which has a small, selective crafts shop, where you can choose between quality contemporary designs and special difficult-to-source collectibles.

Where to Stay
DURBAN CITY

Hotels line the city center's beachfront: Most are pretty tacky. Bargains are to be had, however, and if you're up for a bit of time travel, the **Blue Waters Hotel**, 175 Snell Parade, Durban (www.bluewatershotel.co.za; © 31/327-7000; R337–387 per person double, including breakfast) is an interesting choice. You can bag a deluxe seaview room for R774 to R1,094 including breakfast. Rooms are bland and modern, but with its iconic location near the northern end of the Golden Mile (directly across from Suncoast Beach), and a '70s lounge, bar, and indoor pool straight out of a David Lynch movie, it doesn't lack for character. If you're looking for genuine comfort and value, you're better off in a great guesthouse on what is sometimes referred to as "The Ridge": not to be confused with Umhlanga Ridge, this is the Glenwood-Berea-Morningside belt, old-money suburbs with views overlooking the city and harbor. Here, **Essenwood House** (see below) is our top pick, but another good option is homey **Rosetta House,** 126 Rosetta Rd., Morningside (www.rosettahouse.com; © 031/303-6180; R990–R1,050 double, including breakfast), owned by a lovely couple who really take you under their wing—perfect if you don't mind the company,

Taking a tour through Glenwood's **Phansi Museum,** 500 Esther Roberts Rd. (📞 **031/206-2889** or 083/450-3270; www.phansi.com), is a wonderful experience—not only because you learn about many different indigenous cultures, but because self-styled "curator" and guide Phumzile Nkosi regularly breaks into song, or performs brief vignettes during the tour. There are moments when her voice will bring a tear to your eye, or make you want to dance. Housed in the former home of Esther Roberts, Durban's first female anthropologist, Phansi (pronounced *Punzi*) means "the place beneath" or "basement," because that's where the museum's eclectic collection started out—in the underbelly of this Victorian-era national monument. Today, it's jam-packed with thousands of artifacts, traditional costumes, and genuine oddities such as grass penis-covers worn after circumcision, supplied by elderly ladies, and known as "passion killers." King Shaka's troops, Phumzi quips, wore these during battle. You'll see a red hat made from human hair that is attached to the wearer's head and non-detachable, and a doll carried by 21-year-old virgins to let guys know they're available. The museum includes 30 life-size marionette puppets adorned in ceremonial dress—these were exhibited to great success in Manhattan in 2008/2009. Descended from Swazi royalty, Phumzile is a power-house of knowledge on southern African cultures, and while you could spend a week listening to her, she'll tailor the tour to meet your time pressures. Start or end your visit with strong coffee and a toasted sandwich in Phumzi's *spaza*-style cafe, **Ikhishi** (literally "kitchen"), and ask about the regular live music performances that are held here in the evenings—this may be a chance to catch a show that's very special. The museum is open Monday to Friday 8am to 4pm (weekends by appointment); tours cost R40 adult, R30 children under 16.

and it's only 2 minutes from buzzy Florida Road. If being within walking distance of Florida Road's restaurants is important, urban hipsters opt for well-priced **The Concierge** (reviewed below). If for some reason you need to be more central (or close to the Convention Centre), the two best business city hotels are **The Royal ★** (www.theroyal.co.za; 📞 **031/333-6000;** R2,360 double, R2,720 suite), a classic with a reputation for good service, or the super-dull **Hilton** (📞 **031/336-8100;** from R1,233 double), which neighbors the conference center.

Audacia Manor ★★ Audacia evokes a sense of opulent colonial history, using rich fabrics, dark antique-style mahogany furniture, and original Oregon pine floors, the designers have successfully achieved a rich, clubby atmosphere. Guest rooms are divided between the Manor House and the Coach House; the latter have four-poster Victorian beds, spa baths, and indoor-outdoor showers in private courtyards. Manor rooms evoke a sense of being in the English countryside (although you're on busy road in a built-up upmarket residential neighborhood)—most of these have private balconies (ask for one with a sea and city view). Service is particularly slick and helpful, as you'd expect from such an intimate, tightly run manor house. Some of the city's best restaurants are a short drive away.

11 Sir Arthur Rd., Morningside. www.africanpridehotels.com. 📞 **031/303-9520.** Fax 031/303-2763. 10 units. R2,140–R3,014 double. AE, DC, MC, V. **Amenities:** Restaurant; lounge; 2 bars; library; pool; room service. *In room:* A/C, TV, hair dryer, massage (by arrangement), minibar, free Wi-Fi.

10

KWAZULU-NATAL | Durban

HANG WITH THE KIFF durbanites

Durban embraces quirk and laid-back fun in a way that happens nowhere else in South Africa. There's tremendous creative energy here and a definite sense that you can do whatever you want, without being judged or stared at for your enterprising individuality. This combination of creative flair and ebullient willingness to try means that ideas are quickly transformed into reality, and perhaps the reason the city's is creatively at least 15 months ahead of the rest of the country, as local S.A. designer Deon Chang recently argued. Durbanites are essentially different: Saunter along the beachfront and you'll get a feel for the diversity of cultures and individuality of spirit; strike up a conversation and you will find them open, with a down-to-earth sense of humor. If you find Cape Town a touch stuck up, you'll discover the antithesis in Durban, where laid back and *kiff* (cool) is the default position. You'll find surf culture fused with designer ballsiness—pick up a Holmes Brothers T-shirt (bearing slogans such as "Malema Don't Surf"), or scour the clothing factory shops along semi-industrial Stamford Hill Road for heaps of bargains on usually pricey surf gear, which is acceptable apparel just about anywhere in the city, and ideal for the sultry weather. To hang with the locals, check out the eateries and cafes on or near Helen Joseph (Davenport) Road, and definitely dip into **Corner Café** (see "Where to Eat," below). Dubbed a "kindergarten for adults," **UNIT 11 ★**, 190 Stamford Hill Rd. (𝒞 **072/970-2735;** www.unit11.co.za), is a converted warehouse with a low-key bar-cum-club vibe designed for after-work and nighttime schmoozing (for a decidedly younger crowd); table tennis and foosball tables provide more entertainment on top of live bands and entertainment events that avoid the mainstream. Finally, for a bit of late-night disco ball gazing, **Origin ★★★**, 9 Clarke Rd., Lower Glenwood (www.330.co.za), is the club of choice, with the best sound and several floors of diverse spaces in which to get your groove on—the owner, DJ Martin McHale, virtually invented the late-night electronic music scene in South Africa.

The Concierge Boutique Bungalows ★★ 𝄞 All urban-cool and designer-chic, Durban's most innovative hotel is tucked down a quiet side street, but close to the city's pulse. It was fashioned from eight heritage-listed bungalows—their street-facing 1920s facades retained and incorporated as plant-filled verandas that function as extended living areas spilling out of the slick, contemporary bedrooms. It's an inspired conversion, with quirky in-room detailing; a host of modern conveniences; and the daytime **Freedom Café,** partially fashioned out of a bright red shipping container—a splendid example of audacious recycling, as are the old park benches rescued from the beachfront. Room interiors are funky, and although some are quite small, this is made up for by access to leafy semiprivate outdoor terraces (though noisy neighbors can be tedious). Service, though, can be extremely laid back.

37–43 St. Mary's Ave., Greyville. www.the-concierge.co.za. 𝒞 **031/309-4434.** Fax 031/309-4453. 12 units. R1,450 double. AE, DC, MC, V. **Amenities:** Restaurant; bar; airport transfers (R350 one-way); concierge services; room service. *In room:* A/C and fan, TV, hairdryer, MP3 docking station, minibar, free Wi-Fi.

Essenwood Guest House ★★ 𝄞 If you don't enjoy the anonymity of a hotel and would like to experience what it's like to live in the most sought-after residential area in Durban, then this mansion in a leafy garden is ideal. A rose-tinted colonial homestead built in 1924 in a large tropical garden with a pool, this was originally the home of one of Durban's sugar barons. Paddy and John, themselves former sugar-cane farmers, restored it, furnished it with tasteful antiques and artworks, and opened it to guests. The spacious suites have views of the city and distant ocean; request one of the four with private, broad verandahs. Dinners can be served by prior arrangement, but the city center and Morningside's restaurants are a 5-minute drive away.

630 Stephen Dlamini (Essenwood) Rd., Berea 4001. www.essenwoodhouse.co.za. ©/fax **031/207-4547.** 7 units. R920–R990 double. Rate includes breakfast. AE, DC, MC, V. No children under 12. **Amenities:** Dining room with meals on request; pool. *In room:* A/C, TV, hair dryer (on request), minibar, Wi-Fi (R1 per minute).

Goble Palms Guest Lodge & Urban Retreat ★ 🎣 This gracious Edwardian revamp has very comfortable rooms and a plush "colonial-contemporary" look that's homey and luxurious without being fussy. Lionel and Leanne Gafney provide a wonderful, personal introduction to the city and their professionally run small hotel offers a cheerful retreat after a day of sightseeing, or after a long flight. Besides a breakfast terrace with sea views, there's a sociable pub, and a number of cozy lounges, and your hosts will summon spa treatments to your room, and make any bookings for meals or trips.

120 Goble Rd., Morningside 4001. www.goblepalms.co.za. © **031/312-2598.** R990 double, R1,090 superior double. Rates include breakfast. MC, V. **Amenities:** Breakfast room; lounges; bar; airport transfers (R350 one-way); pool. *In room:* A/C, TV, hair dryer, free Wi-Fi.

Quarters ★ Now part of a chain of similarly fashioned "boutique" hotels, the original Quarters comprises four Victorian houses set on a very busy intersection— the best reason to stay here is that some 20 restaurants lie within a 5km (3-mile) radius, many within walking distance. The relatively spacious rooms all have queen-size sleigh beds and a pleasant ambience; windows are also double-glazed to eliminate the constant noise, though this is scant protection from the sound of the person above flushing the toilet—ask for a room on one of the top floors. **Quarters on Avondale,** farther up Sandile Thusi (Argyle) Road, is a more luxurious affair, with executive suites, yet rooms still have the same bland decor and potential road noise.

101 Florida Rd., Durban 4001. www.quarters.co.za. © **031/303-5246.** Fax 031/303-5269. 23 units. R1,720 standard double; R1,780 superior double. Rates include breakfast. AE, DC, MC, V. Children accepted by prior arrangement only. **Amenities:** Restaurant; bar; room service. *In room:* A/C, TV, hair dryer, Wi-Fi (R30 per half hour).

Upton Hall ★★ With its partly crenellated 1930s facade and combination of stone and redbrick architecture, this new custom-built "urban castle" is located in an opulent part of town, with the best (and priciest) rooms offering great city views (including the Moses Mabhida Stadium) from private balconies. Even without benefit of a view, these are among the most luxurious and carefully designed rooms in the city, each one subtly themed: In the "Wildlife" room, animal references are understated (there's a Nguni cowhide-covered ottoman; not a zebra skin in sight), while "Beaches" offers an all-natural, tranquil atmosphere. Public spaces are vast and uncluttered with dark wood-paneled walls and a smart member's club atmosphere, which continues throughout a variety of indoor and outdoor dining spots.

16 Eastbourne Rd., Morningside, Durban. www.uptonhall.co.za. © **031/303-7987.** Fax 031/303-5897. 10 units. R2,770–R4,770 double. AE, DC, MC, V. **Amenities:** Restaurant; lounge; cigar bar; gym; pool; room service; wine cellar. *In room:* A/C, TV, hair dryer, heated towel rack, minibar, underfloor heating (in bathroom), free Wi-Fi.

UMHLANGA ROCKS & NORTH COAST

Given the location of Durban's new airport, now north of the city, and Zululand's reserves and coastline beckoning, it may be more convenient to base yourself here.

Oyster Box Hotel ★★★   Bang on the Umhlanga beach, with direct views and instant access, this is one of Durban's oldest hotels, successfully overhauled in 2009 (to a tune of half a billion rand) to become the trendiest, most luxurious hotel on the coast. It's still very much colonial-themed (even staff is in period costume) with much original architecture and detailing surviving (curving staircase, checkerboard floors, mosaic tiles), and a good selection of local art. However, they've also piled on the statues, chandeliers, and potted palms, which is a little over the top. Each room is unique; they're all very pretty, but the classic sea-facing units are very small. Spatially, it's rather convoluted (it's a heritage building after all) but you'll have fun discovering its many parts: Do visit the sexy new spa, with its Turkish hammam—like something from a Fellini dream sequence (or early James Bond movie). However, for this kind of money, you'd expect more consistency of service from staff.

2 Lighthouse Rd., Umhlanga Rocks. www.oysterbox.co.za. ℭ **031/514-5000.** Fax 031/514-5100. 86 units. R4,830–R4,960 classic and garden loft double, R5,340–R5,940 sea-facing double, R7,600–R9,660 sea-facing cabanas and family suites, R10,360–R13,450 sea-facing luxury and deluxe suites, R15,890 garden villa, R50,000 presidential suite. 1 child under 12 stays free if sharing with 2 adults, children 12–16 pay R400. Rates include breakfast. AE, DC, MC, V. **Amenities:** 3 restaurants; 3 bars; lounges; cinema; concierge; 2 heated pools; room service; spa; wine cellar with private dining. *In room:* A/C, TV/DVD, movie library, hair dryer, heated towel rack, minibar, MP3 docking station, plunge pool (in 3 suites and 8 villas), free Wi-Fi.

Teremok Marine ★★★   If you like well-judged opulence combined with a genuinely intimate atmosphere, this is our top guest house pick in Durban, offering very good value for your money. Carefully, imaginatively designed, this former home of a Russian émigré is run with such polish and personal care that you feel yourself instantly at home and relaxed. Despite nearby townhouses and apartments, you're ensconced within leafy gardens, and an ongoing soundtrack of Indian Ocean crashing on the nearby shore; you also have one of the prettiest little spas in town right on your doorstep. Each suite-proportioned room is laid out with flair, and personalized attention to detail. A chauffeured vehicle takes you to local restaurants, and although there isn't a full-on view of the beach, walking there is relatively easy—or a 2-minute car trip.

49 Marine Dr., Umhlanga Rocks. www.teremok.co.za. ℭ **031/561-5848.** Fax 031/561-5860. 8 units. R3,000 double. Rates include breakfast and laundry. AE, DC, MC, V. **Amenities:** Breakfast room; honesty bar; lounge; DVD library; pool; spa. *In room:* A/C and fan, TV/DVD, movie library, CD library, hair dryer, free Internet (cable supplied), MP3 docking station.

Where to Eat

Combine weather so benign you can dine outdoors year-round (except, perhaps, during the August winds); sea views; a stew of Victorian, Art Deco, and other, more eclectically hodgepodge (and occasionally ramshackle) architectural leanings (with blander concrete modernism taking over much of the North Coast); and a melting pot of cultural flavors, and you can see why Durban's dining scene is so interesting. The tendency here is toward relaxed, informal dining; locals congregate to stir up an atmosphere that is buoyant, vivacious, and frequently celebratory.

IN DURBAN

It's quite easy to navigate the local cafe and restaurant scene (avoiding the high prices and anonymity of starched hotel dining rooms), with much of it concentrated in the Glenwood-Berea-Morningside residential belt (the best are reviewed below). If you're up for cruising for a table, try sauntering along Morningside's Florida and Lilian Ngoyi (Windermere) roads. The relentlessly popular star of bustling Florida is **Spiga D'Oro** (reviewed below)—a serious Durban institution, it's worth a visit any time of day, if only to sip coffee and watch the migrating crowds. Florida is also where you can dine in one of Durban's prettiest heritage buildings, currently revamped as see-and-be-seen **Czar** (✆ 031/312-8001; dinner only, closed Sun) which does a wild assortment of dishes, mixing it up with sushi, dim sum, and steam-fried duck (served on Parmesan rösti). Asian-inspired, but with strong contemporary influences. If you're in the mood for steak along this stretch, **Butcher Boys,** 170 Florida Rd. (✆ **031/312-8248**), specializes in aged grain-fed beef.

In many ways better than Florida road, though, is **Helen Joseph (Davenport) Road** in Glenwood. Here you'll find great artisanal coffee and scrumptious Camembert and sundried-tomato muffins at **The Green Bean Coffee Roastery ★**, at no. 147 (✆ **031/201-8122**), which feels like someone's living room. It's a bit of a 1970s time machine, albeit with an up-to-date approach to dark-roasting their own three-bean Ethiopian blend; excellent baked goodies (Mel's milk tart is genius) and a very local vibe. Middle Eastern **Yossi's,** at no. 127 (✆ **031/201-0090**), is hugely popular, but, truth be told, it's really the warm vibe, open terrace, and chance to smoke a hookah that keep people coming back for more. (Don't miss the live jazz on Wed and Sun evenings.) Around the corner on Bulwer Road, **Earthmother Organic** (✆ **031/202-1527**) has a slightly hippie vibe, but don't be put you off—the food is deeply satisfying: organic, healthy salads, interesting combinations from their deli, and tempting baked goods are served in an overgrown garden. Also on Bulwer is the **Arts Cafe** (✆ **031/201-9969**), where you can eat from a light, cafe-style menu while sitting under spreading trees at the entrance to the KZNSA Gallery (which, incidentally, hosts inspired exhibitions). A supervised play area allows parents to relax while kids run around. If you'd like a more sophisticated approach to coffee and crumpets, check out the decadent high tea spread at **The Saint James on Venice,** 100 Venice Rd., Morningside (✆ **031/312-9488;** lunch and afternoon tea 11:30am–3pm).

Perhaps it's the year-round balmy weather, or the perennial casual atmosphere, but Durban has fewer fine-dining outlets than other cities. Among the best, **9th Avenue Bistro ★★★** (✆ **031/312-9134**), in the Avonmore Centre, not far from the buzz of Florida Road, is reportedly better than ever under new chef, Graham Nielsen. The menu remains exciting and experimental, and it changes often; however, we still prefer **Café 1999** and **Spice,** both reviewed below. *Note:* There's a crop of beach-front eateries destined to start up in a series of smart new spaces erected for the World Cup. At press time, however, these stood empty.

Café 1999 ★★★ MEDITERRANEAN With Marcelle Labuschagne in the kitchen and her partner, Sean Roberts, handling the front of house and plying wine and considerable charm on his countless fans, it's little wonder that 1999 is widely considered Durban's best bet for a special night out. It's high up on the Berea, and ill-positioned (facing a small parking lot), so it must be the modern, delicious take on

Mediterranean cooking that keeps pulling them in. Menu items are offered in "tidbit" (like artichokes baked with ricotta and basil on tomato coulis) or "bigbit" (perhaps seared tuna with sesame and ginger with fresh mussels) portions, so you can taste to your stomach's capacity; try their signature boned loin of lamb, or snack on ginger and lime prawns. If you can't decide, leave it to Sean.

Silvervause Centre, at Silverton and Vause rds., Berea. © **031/202-3406.** www.cafe1999.co.za. Reservations highly recommended. Main courses R75-R12. AE, DC, MC, V. Mon-Sat 12:30-2:30pm and Mon-Fri 6:30-10:30pm.

Corner Café ★ LIGHT FARE   You come here for the buzzy Durban vibe and the eco-obsessed owner, Judd. Given his predilection for all things tasty, local, and green, it follows that the food is almost always reliable (if, occasionally, on the small side). A chalkboard alerts you to the day's specials (usually a quichelike tart, or perhaps a fillet of freshly caught fish), and a small one-sheet clipboard menu, delivered by boho waiters, or Judd himself. It's a lively, open space dominated by a photographic mural that looks like a Google Earth portrait of suburban Durban. Random chairs and tables, a small sofa arrangement, displays by local artists, and jewelry for sale; there's even a barber out back. It's hard to resist the sociable main dining area, but there are a few tables outdoors if you crave the sun.

At Brand and Cromwell rds., Glenwood. © **031/201-0219.** www.thecornercafe.co.za. Mains R40-R65. MC, V. Mon-Sat 6am-5pm.

Market ★★ 🍴 INNOVATIVE   Just up from the Greyville Racecourse, this quiet, off-road, tree-shaded courtyard is a sublime city hideaway where tasty, market-fresh, unfussy food comes out of a tiny kitchen helmed by Melanie Shepherd. It's also very unpretentious (sesame lentil burgers, grilled haloumi and avocado on rye, fish cakes, grilled rump, duck confit with butterbean compote) with no distinction between starters and mains—you simply order what takes your fancy, and let your waiter know what should come first. Listen carefully for the day's specials—these are almost always worth ordering. There are great-sounding dishes for vegetarians, and a breakfast menu that's worth skipping the hotel buffet.

40 Gladys Mazibuko (Marriott) Rd., Berea. © **031/309-8581.** www.themarketrestaurant.co.za. Dinner items R40-R95. AE, DC, MC, V. Mon 7:30am-4:30pm; Tues-Sat 7:30am-11:30pm.

Spice ★★★ FUSION   In a comfy Edwardian home, culinary sorceress Linda Govender-Burger has a decidedly different take on what can be achieved with spices. In a marriage of East and West, oxtail is tweaked with cinnamon, a pear and leek soup fringed with cumin, and trout spiced with fennel. Results are inevitably delicious. Linda does a light lunch menu that works well in balmy Durban, and her scrumptious salads are inspired: How about slivers of roasted duck (infused with cumin and clove) with port-soaked oranges, and a Turkish fig dressing?

362 Lilian Ngoyi (Windermere) Rd., Windermere. © **031/303-6375.** Mains R78-R132. AE, DC, MC, V. Tues-Sun noon-3pm; Tues-Sat 6pm-late.

Spiga d'Oro ★ 🍴 ITALIAN   The one place in Durban that every local mentions among its favorites, Spiga is a popular family-owned Italian eatery known for languid breakfasts and shmoozy all-day sessions. During the day, it's limited to the mellow streetside cafe (where the walls are covered with graffiti by appreciative clientele—including two famous Bills: Clinton and Gates), but as evening hits, fairy lights ignite the Victorian-era cast-iron facade forming an electric petticoat at the edge of the busy Florida Road restaurant stretch. This is also when Spiga unlocks the doors to its

BUNNY chow 'N' ALL

Durban curry is an entirely unique food genre, which stands out as a signature cuisine among otherwise polyglot dining choices. Although its roots are obviously in India, and the taste for spicy, tongue-tingling sauces arrived with the indentured servants who came to work the sugar plantations, the local curry tastes quite different from what you'll eat in India. Essentially Durban curries employ far more chili—so be wary when offered "extra-hot." A popular Indian restaurant in an old Berea home, **Vintage,** 20 Windermere Rd. (*© **031/309-1328**), serves up the usual north and south Indian suspects, but to sample one or two distinctively Durban curries, rather head down the drag to **Indian Connection ★**, 485 Windermere (*© **031/312-1440;** www.indian-connection.com; daily 11am–3pm and 5:30pm–late). If you're truly adventurous, however, and looking for a down-home experience that will clue you in to the way Durbanites feast, there are a few very special, very affordable places where you'll get close to the city's social underbelly. **Gounden's** is tucked into a tatty, humorless room at the back of a panelbeater workshop on Eaton Rd., Umbilo: Besides real-deal Durban curries, many say it serves the city's best bunny chow, a local culinary invention that's sufficiently famous to have loaned its name to a restaurant in New York (www.bunnychowny.com). Basically, it's a hollowed out quarter (or half) loaf of bread (usually white) filled with curry. You use the loaf's innards to dunk in the sauce and slowly eat your way down, taking care not to tear a hole in the crust, eaten along with the contents. A big step up, but not without its own brand of lowbrow kitsch, is **Hotel Britannia,** 1299 Umgeni Rd. (*© **031/303-2266;** www.hotelbrits.co.za), Durban's oldest inn, now tucked behind a highway flyover in an insalubrious semi-industrial area. Step inside the air-conditioned cool with countless real Durbanites who've gathered here for a beer and a bunny.

additional dining spaces, with seating away from the sidewalk. The kitchen is experienced enough not to mess up: pizzas, pastas, and traditional Italian fare are usually spot on and crowd-pleasing.

200 Florida Rd., Morningside. *© **031/303-9511.** www.spigadoro.co.za. Mains R45–R85. AE, DC, MC, V. Daily 7am–late.

ON THE NORTH COAST

If you're in Umhlanga and can do without an ocean breeze, a good choice is still **Ile Maurice ★**, 9 McCausland Crescent (*© **031/561-7609;** Tues–Sun noon–3pm and 6:30–10:15pm, open Mon during Christmas season); the hands-on Mauvis family (still lovingly remembered by Durbanites for their former city restaurant, San Geran) has been offering a mix of traditional French and Mauritian cuisine and excellent seafood for decades; try the octopus or crayfish curry, or the memorable langoustine and lentil soup. With a far better location (and views), the **Ocean Terrace** offers every reason to try the curry buffet (see "Table with a Sea View, Please," box below); it's a good value (considering the opulence of the venue) and gives you the opportunity to examine the chichi decor of the revamped Oyster Box Hotel under pankah fans.

Umhlanga may be well geared to tourist tastes, but most Durbanite foodies swear that the best eateries are even farther up the coast, in Umdloti, Ballito, and beyond. At the end of a dirt road seemingly in the middle of nowhere (just across the highway

"TABLE WITH A sea VIEW, PLEASE"

The venue may take precedence over the food, but no one should leave Durban before ambling along the pier directly in front of uShaka Marine World and scoring a table (or bar stool) at the sublime **Moyo on the Pier,** which rises from the water just beyond the breakers. Looking a bit like a futuristic pagoda and dressed up in Afro-chic pinks, with plenty of clever accessories made from recycled bits and pieces, this is perhaps the ultimate spot for a sunset cocktail (pricey, but worth it). The selection of "African tapas" is forgettable but will stave off a hunger until dinnertime. And, if you don't fancy being in the city for sunset, grab a cocktail and a window seat at **The Lighthouse Bar ★★** at the Oyster Box Hotel; it's a flamboyant mix of glam-retro (lipstick red canvas upholstered bar chairs) and, of course, the eponymous lighthouse view.

Needless to say, any other sea-view dining venue is better scheduled for lunch; even in summer, the sun disappears relatively early on the east coast. A fine choice, in decadent surroundings,

is **The Ocean Terrace ★** (**℡ 031/514-5000;** daily 12:30–2:30pm and 6:30–10:30pm) at the Oyster Box; it's a good upmarket bistro-style eatery with a colonial-meets-North African look. Bag a table on the veranda overlooking the lighthouse; Oysters are, of course, always available, but the authentic Durban curry is the real crowd-pleaser. Next door, in the Beverly Hills Hotel, **Sugar Club ★★** (**℡ 031/561-2211;** daily 7–11am and 7–11pm), offers contemporary fine dining right next to the ocean. Downstairs, overlooking the sea and large swimming pool, is **Elements Café Bar** (**℡ 031/561-2211;** daily 11am–9pm), with an appealing all-white decor and a light, contemporary cafe menu.

Just 25 minutes north of Durban city center, in Umdloti (the seaside suburb just north of Umhlanga), is **Bean Bag Bahia,** 32 North Beach Rd. (**℡ 031/568-2229;** Mon–Fro 9am–10pm, Sat–Sun 8am–10pm). Floor-to-ceiling windows overlook the beach and provide a light-filled space with the freshness of salty sea air. The menu is inspired by the

from Ballito—yet away from its frenzied development), **Tin Roof ★** (**℡ 032/947-2548**) serves slightly experimental lunches and decadent-looking desserts in an airy space overlooking a nursery. Also in a nursery is **Sage Café ★**, Hybrid Living Centre, 1 Old Fort Rd., Umhlali (**℡ 032/525-5115;** www.hybridlivingcentre.co.za), one of the best daytime dining spots in the province, with a strong focus on fresh, organic ingredients and wholesome tastes. Light meals extend to bangers and mash, prawn and calamari pasta, and a fresh, zesty chicken, lemon, zucchini, and thyme risotto. Easy-drinking wines are available, and the venue is also designed with children in mind (there are sitters to look after kids while you eat or browse the deli). And for those really prepared to travel for a rollicking food experience, there's **The Prawn Shack** (see box), 110km (68 miles) north of Durban on Amatikulu Beach. It's literally a shack on the beach, and you don't have to guess what they specialize in.

Back nearer Umhlanga, in Mount Edgecombe, **Marco Paulo ★**, Shop 3, Accord House, 2 Golf Course Dr. (**℡ 031/502-2221**), is a bistro with Italian leanings; interesting cuts of meat, subtly creative pastas, and daily inventiveness make this another one where locals keep returning.

tastes of Brazil, but they also churn out pizza, decent coffee, and cocktails—good reason to head here at sunset. Locals know to grab a sea-facing table at **Bel Punto** ★★ (✆ **031/5682407**), a family-run Italian restaurant with proper homemade pasta and tiramisu: It's on the first floor of the Umdloti Centre, 1 South Beach Rd. (just right of the traffic circle as you arrive in the village).

But if you'd like to combine your table with a dip, the best sea-view dining lies farther north still. Around 30 minutes north of Durban city center, the **Salt Rock Hotel** (✆ **032/525-5025;** www.saltrockbeach.co.za) is by no means fancy, but this old, laidback beach hotel is an institution: Amid tropical grounds, waiters serve fresh curry all day on the terrace (try the crab and prawn curries, after a round of oysters). It's an easy stroll down to the beach and the tidal pool (great for kids), and for a fee you can wash off afterward in the hotel pool. However, if you're after the ultimate get-out-of-town dining excursion, head beyond the Tugela River mouth, to Zululand's Amatikulu Beach (around 170km/105½ from Durban), and spend the afternoon indulging a serious hunger (and thirst) at the **Prawn Shack** ★★ (✆ **084/737-6493;** www.shak.co.za; Sat–Sun lunch only; reservations essential). You'll be plied seafood during a multicourse feast that's packed with grilled prawns, prawn tails, prawn bunny chow, and chili prawn pasta. Line fish and rare beef are also served; you're welcomed with a caipirinha and baked Camembert for dessert. It's ultrarelaxed and very rustic—right on the beach, adjacent to an abandoned prawn factory. Rather than driving back to the city after you've stuffed yourself with prawns and cocktails, reserve one of the simple, personally decorated rooms at the **Hatchery** (www.thehatchery.co.za; ✆ **035/337-4969** or 084/959-8827), a laid-back inn fashioned from, yes, an old prawn hatchery—2km (1⅓ miles) from the restaurant. Accommodations (from R500 double) are quirky and right on the beach; there's a full kitchen, but you can hire a cook to look after you. Here, you're perfectly poised to start your adventure in Zululand.

ZULULAND

Cross the Tugela River (88km/55 miles north of Durban), traditionally the southern frontier of Zululand, and you soon feel as if you've entered a new country. Passing a largely rural population through KwaZulu-Natal's Big 5 reserves and coastal wetlands, you are now traveling the ancestral lands of the Zulu, and birthplace of our current president, Jacob Zuma.

Most visitors spend at least 2 days in or near **Hluhluwe-Umfolozi,** the province's largest reserve. Run by eZemvelo KwaZulu-Natal Wildlife, it is home to the Big 5 and has the most sought-after wilderness trails in the country. In addition, its proximity to Durban (less than a 3-hr. drive, on good roads) makes it one of South Africa's most accessible Big 5 game reserves, and its prolific game, varied vegetation, and top-class budget accommodations make for an experience to rival Kruger National Park.

If, however, your idea of the "wild life" is pausing in your pursuit of lions with a drink poured by your personal ranger, there are also a number of private reserves to cater to your every need. Lying north of Hluhluwe and close to (and, in the case of **Phinda,** part of) the province's vast wetland park, these luxurious private game reserves are close enough to the coast to add diving with dolphins, sharks, and a magical array of tropical fish to your Big 5 experience—the combination of big game, lagoon, and beach is, in fact, one of the benefits of choosing a safari in KwaZulu-Natal.

A World Heritage Site, **iSimangaliso Wetland Park** (previously Greater St Lucia Wetland Park, for which you may still see signage) is a top destination for divers, fishermen, and birders, as well as the rare loggerhead and leatherback turtles that have been returning to these beaches to breed every summer for thousands of years. Encompassing the foothills of the Lebombo Mountains, wetlands, forests, lakes, and the coastal coral reefs, the park is quite literally a paradise, but its proximity to Durban—and, indeed, Johannesburg—means you may have to share it with many others who similarly appreciate its natural bounty. If you're looking for a more exclusive experience (with access to parts that are still untouched and untamed), you're best off traveling farther north to **Mabibi, Rocktail Bay,** and **Kosi Bay**—indisputable highlights of this coast, where a handful of guests find themselves alone on a stretch of pristine beach and coastal forest that goes on for hundreds of miles.

Essentials

VISITOR INFORMATION   The best regional office to visit en route from Durban is **Eshowe Publicity** (© 035/474-1141; Mon–Thurs 7:30am–4pm, Fri till 3pm), on Hutchinson Street. For information on the Hluhluwe region, call the **Hluhluwe Tourism Association** (© 035/562-0353). For information on the **iSimangaliso Wetland Park,** call © 035/590-1633 (www.isimangaliso.com), or the **St Lucia Publicity Association** (© 035/590-1247). For specific information and reservations on the other provincial game reserves, contact **KZN Wildlife** (© 033/845-1000; www.kznwildlife.com).

GETTING THERE & AROUND   The N2 toll road leading north out of Durban traverses the Zululand hinterland; east lies the iSimangaliso Wetland Park, Phinda private game reserve, and the birding reserves (Ndumo and Mkuzi); west lies Hluhluwe and most of the Zulu museums and cultural villages. The quickest way to get to Zululand is to fly to Richard's Bay Airport, but it is more practical to fly to Durban and rent a car, as there is virtually no public transport in Zululand. You could also arrange a space on the Hluhluwe Shuttle with **Thompsons** (© 035/562-3002). (Private reserves can supply transfers from Richard's Bay or Durban airport.)

SAFETY   The very northern Zululand coast is a malarial area in the rainy summer season, and there is a medium to low risk in iSimangaliso Wetland Park, depending on the time of the year. For the most up-to-date advice, contact your doctor (also see chapter 13).

An Overview of the Best Zululand Reserves

Run by KZN Wildlife, **Hluhluwe-Umfolozi** is, at 96,453 hectares (238,824 acres), by far the province's largest Big 5 reserve and offers, like Kruger, an opportunity for those on a tight budget to stay in a reserve in basic accommodations. It is open to daytime visitors as well as overnight guests, which gives you the flexibility to base yourself in the **iSimangaliso Wetland Park,** where you are closer to both the ocean and the estuary, and to visit Hluhluwe as a day-tripper (although, since early morning and late afternoons are when most game action happens, this isn't really advisable—rather spend the night). Zululand's finest game preserve is the 23,000 hectares (56,800 acres) **Phinda,** affording access to a varied and beautiful terrain

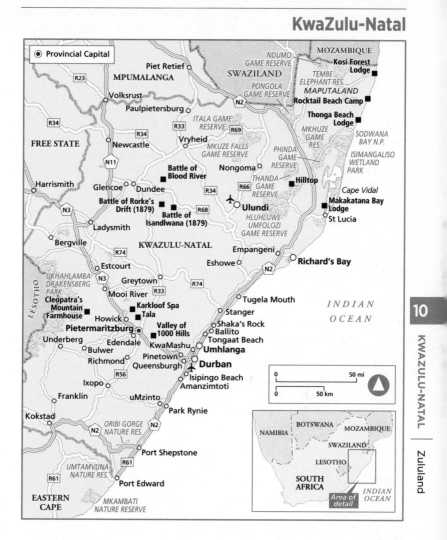

and—particularly in the case of their Forest and Vlei lodges—the most stylish bush accommodations in the province. Twenty kilometers (12 miles) north of Hluhluwe lies the 14,000-hectare (34,595-acre) **Thanda Private Game Reserve,** virtually across the road from Phinda. Modeled on the luxury lodges surrounding Kruger, the reserve—particularly if you opt for the tiny tented camp—provides a very exclusive bush experience, although the level of guiding can't really compete with Phinda. There's more laid-on luxury to be had at **Mkhuze Falls Private Game Reserve** (www.mkhuzefalls.com; ✆ 034/414-1018)—a Big 5 preserve comprising over 17,000 hectares (41,990 acres) with some of the best-value lodgings in the country; it's comfortable, but with a good dose of bush-style glam-kitsch (animal prints galore; elephant tusks around the headboard) that may not suit everyone. At R4,900 to

DISCOVERING ZULU history

The proud amaZulu have fascinated Westerners ever since the first party of British settlers gained permission to trade from the great Zulu king Shaka, known as "Africa's Napoleon" for his military genius. As king, he was to unite the amaZulu into the mightiest army in the Southern Hemisphere and develop new and lethal fighting implements and tactics, including the highly successful "horns of the bull" maneuver to outflank the enemy. In 1828, Shaka was murdered by his half-brothers Mhlangana and Dingaan, and Dingaan was crowned king.

Distrustful of the large number of "white wizards" settling in the region, Dingaan ordered the massacre of the Trekker party, led by Piet Retief, whom he had invited—unarmed—to a celebratory banquet at his royal *kraal* uMgungundlovu. (A kraal is a series of thatched beehive-shaped huts encircling a central, smaller kraal, or cattle enclosure.) Dingaan paid heavily for this treachery at the **Battle of Blood River**, in which the Zulu nation suffered such heavy casualties that it was to split the state for a generation. In 1840, Dingaan was killed by his brother Mpande, who succeeded him as king.

The amaZulu were reunited again under Mpande's eldest, Cetshwayo, who became king in 1873 after murdering a number of his siblings, and built a new royal kraal at Ulundi. Though by all accounts a reasonable man, Cetshwayo could not negotiate with the uncompromising English, who now wanted total control of southern Africa, with no pesky "savages" to destroy their imperialist advance on the goldfields. In 1878, the British ordered Cetshwayo to disband his army within 30 days, give up

Zululand's independence, and place himself under the supervision of an English commissioner. This totally unreasonable ultimatum, designed to ignite a war, resulted in the **Battle of Islandwana** and England's most crushing defeat. Nine months later, on July 4, 1879, 5,000 British redcoats under a vengeful Lord Chelmsford advanced on Ulundi and razed it to the ground. A captured King Cetshwayo was exiled to Cape Town and later England; he was reinstated as a puppet in 1883. This was to be the last Anglo-Zulu battle, the might of the Zulu empire finally broken.

Although as yet unsuccessful in its bid to become a World Heritage Site, the area that is today known as the **Emakhosini Ophathe Heritage Park** (or "Valley of the Kings") is of huge significance to the Zulu people, and is where Senzangakhona, the father of Shaka, Mpande and Dingaan, is buried. You can visit Dingaan's homestead at **uMgungundlovu** (or "Secret Place of the Great Elephant"), part of which has been reconstructed and features 200-year-old artifacts; there is also a memorial to Piet Retief and his 100-strong delegation (ⓒ **035/450-2254;** daily 9am–4pm). You can also visit a reconstruction of the royal kraal at **Ondini,** near Ulundi. To get here, take the R68 off the N2 to Eshowe, stopping to visit the **Zulu Historical Museum** and the **Vukani Collection** first (see reviews below), or to meet Graham Chennells at the George Hotel for his highly recommended tours of the region (see "Guided Tours," below). To reach uMgungundlovu, take the R34 to Vryheid and look for the turnoff on your left.

While Westerners head for the many cultural villages dotted throughout

R6,500 double, the five East African–style luxury tents are the best value. Nearby **Amakhosi Lodge** (www.amakhosi.com; ⓒ **034/414-1157**), in the 10,000-hectare (24,700-acre) **AmaZulu Private Game Reserve,** also offers good value, with all-inclusive river suites going for R4,400 to R7,200, depending on season.

Zululand, many urban Zulu parents bring their children to the **Vukani Collection,** housed at the **Fort Nongqayi Museum Village** ★★ (🕿 035/474-5274; www. eshowemuseums.org.za; R25 adults, R5 children; Mon–Fri 8am–4pm, Sat 9am–4pm, Sun 10am–4pm), in eShowe, to gain insight into the rituals, codes, and crafts of the past. This is the finest collection of Zulu traditional arts and crafts anywhere, and a visit here is essential for anyone interested in collecting or understanding Zulu art, particularly traditional basket ware (not least to browse the handpicked selection of art and basket ware in the museum shop). Another highlight of the collection are the pots made by master potter Nesta Nala (her work is sold in international galleries throughout the world; since her death, her pots have sold for increasingly vast sums). Nesta walked for miles to find just the right clay before grinding and mixing, then sunbaking her paper-thin shapes and firing them in a hole in the ground. Pots are finally rubbed with fat and ashes, applied with a river stone. Keep an eye out for another award-winner, Allina Ndebele, whose tapestries are inspired by Zulu myths and legends as told to her by her grandmother.

Besides the collection, there is the **Zulu History Museum** housed in the 1883 **Fort Nongqayi,** where the Natal "Native" Police were garrisoned. This museum traces the history of the fort and the virtual enslavement of the Zulu as a result of a poll tax; it also houses a good beadwork collection, dating from the 1920s, and a collection of John Dunn's furniture. The son of settlers, Dunn became King Cetshwayo's political advisor and was the only white man to become a true Zulu chief, embracing Zulu polygamy by taking 49 wives. (*Note:* Book ahead so that a guide can be arranged.)

GUIDED TOURS Ex-mayor of eShowe (and proprietor of local hang-out, the George Hotel), **Graham Chennells** ★★★ offers the most authentic and exhilarating opportunities to see contemporary Zulu life in Africa. *National Geographic* has commissioned no less than three film shoots of his tours. Guests are provided with a Zulu guide, who introduces them to friends in the broader community. On most weekends, Graham can arrange attendance at a Zulu wedding, a coming-of-age celebration, *sangoma* healing rituals, or traditional church services, where guests are treated as part of the extended family. Graham is also the best person to contact if you want to attend any of the special events and ceremonies that happen in Zululand: On February 23, Sangoma Khekheke's **Annual Snake Dance** is attended by 1,000 people. September also sees **King Shaka Day Celebrations** and the **Zulu King's Reed Dance**—here some 15,000 young women congregate to dance for King Goodwill Zwelithini. Most of October is taken up with the **Prophet Shembe's celebrations;** on Sundays some 30,000 people participate in prayer dancing. During the first week in December, the King's first **"Fruit Ceremony"** must be held before the reaping of crops can begin. For more information, go to www.eshowe. com, or call the George Hotel, 36 Main St., eShowe (🕿 035/474-4919 or 082/492-6918; www.wheretostay.co.za/georgehotel).

Finally, there are the beautiful marine reserves, where you can stay at **Thonga Beach Lodge** or **Rocktail Bay,** both of which offer a chance to explore the coastal dune forest, laze away the days snorkeling and scuba-diving in tropical waters, and perhaps witness one of nature's most primeval miracles. From October to February, the large leatherback turtle (weighing in at 600kg/1,320 lb.) and its smaller relative, the loggerhead turtle, travel thousands of miles, using ancient navigational techniques to return to the precise beach on which they were born, heaving themselves ashore to produce the next generation—a cycle some believe dates back more than 6,000 years. **Kosi Forest Lodge,** sister lodge of Thonga Beach Lodge, is the ideal base for exploring the Kosi Bay estuarine system, another Maputaland jewel. This intricate hub of wonder comprises swamp, dune, coastal, mangrove, and sand forests, including an extraordinary collection of tropical plants, animals, and birds, including the rare Palm Nut Vulture.

HLUHLUWE-UMFOLOZI GAME RESERVE ★★

Established in 1895, this is the oldest wildlife sanctuary in Africa and birthplace of the Wilderness Trail concept. Once separate reserves, Mluhluwe (pronounced Shloe-*shloe*-whee) and Umfolozi were united in 1989 to form the provinces' premier wildlife destination; it's the second-most-popular park after Kruger. A mere 5% the size of its Mpumalanga counterpart, the reserve is home to a large variety of wildlife, including the Big 5, cheetahs, hyenas, wild dogs, wildebeest, giraffes, hippos, zebras, and a large variety of antelopes. Certainly, this is one of the best places to spot rhino, particularly the white (from the Afrikaans-Dutch "wijd" or square-lipped) variety. Many consider its unique combination of forest, woodland, savanna, and grasslands, and its hot, humid, wet summers, the "real" Africa—well worth visiting as an alternative or addition to Kruger.

Treks along various **Wilderness Trails ★★★** are conducted by rangers from March to November in the 25,000-hectare (61,750-acre) Umfolozi wilderness, once the royal hunting grounds of King Shaka. Access to this area has only ever been permitted to those on foot, making this one of the most pristine reserves in the world. Book them well in advance (see "Hiking" under "Staying Active," earlier in this chapter).

VISITOR INFORMATION Open daily March through October from 6am to 6pm, and November through February from 5am to 7pm. There's a daily conservancy fee of R110 per adult, R55 per child. Guided 2- or 3-hour game drives (R270–R300 per adult, R135–R150 per child) take place in the early morning and again from late afternoon, when it is cooler and the animals tend to be more active; these are open to overnight guests only. Guided walks are R215 to R250 per person (no children under 13). For more information, call **Hilltop Camp** (✆ **035/562-0848**) or **Umfolozi Camp** (✆ **035/550-8477**).

GETTING THERE The reserve is about 280km (174 miles) north of Durban, with two entrances leading off the N2. The quickest way to get to Hilltop Camp is via Memorial Gate, 50km (31 miles) north of Mtubatuba (Hilltop is approximately 30 min. from here), but if you want to enter the park sooner, enter via Nyalazi Gate (turn off on the R618 at Mtubatuba). Adhering to the 40kmph (25-mph) speed limit, it's about a 50-minute drive to the camp. The third entrance, Cengeni Gate, is approached from the west, 30km (19 miles) from Ulundi. To drive from Cengeni to Hilltop, allow 3 hours.

Where to Stay & Eat

Of the two public rest camps in the park, **Mpila**—an unfenced camp in the Umfolozi section—is the best choice for an authentic, self-catering bush stayover. Accommodations are mostly basic, with shared kitchen facilities and bathrooms. You may want to ask about one of the two-bedroom cottages or tents (en suite, with electricity, but with shared kitchen). There is no restaurant; Mpila's shop provides basic provisions. At the other end of the spectrum, **Hilltop** (reviewed below), in the Hluhluwe section, was once rated among the best public camps in the country, but has become increasingly run down; it's still a good budget base (also for day forays to Mkuzi or Lake St Lucia, 2 hr. from Hilltop), and the lack of upkeep is balanced with wonderful proximity to nature.

Apart from Mpila and Hilltop a number of houses are available, which KZN Wildlife calls **bush lodges,** situated in secluded areas picked for their natural beauty. These are unfenced, necessitating the protection of an armed ranger for bush walks; most also have a resident cook (though you may have to provide ingredients; check beforehand), or you may choose full efficiency. These lodges (most of which sleep eight) are available only for exclusive bookings, making this option best for a group or family, or a couple prepared to pay a little extra for total privacy. In the Umfolozi section of the park, there are also eight two-bed units called **Nselweni Bush Lodge;** these go for R1,400 double. For more information on any of these, write to bookings@ kznwildlife.com, or call ✆ **033/845-1000.**

Hilltop Camp 🛶 Appropriately named, this camp commands lovely views of the surrounding hills and valleys, and offers a variety of accommodations options, though sadly all are looking a little frayed. Depending on numbers your best bet is one of the two-bed en-suite chalets (with kitchenette) and the four-bed chalets (with fully equipped kitchens). For some of the best locations, request nos. 10 to 14, 28 to 33, or 44 to 49. The shop sells basic provisions (frozen meat, fire lighters, liquor), but it's worth stocking up in Durban or dining at the restaurant. If you can afford a private reserve don't bother booking here, but we can't ignore that this is the best way to overnight in a Big 5 reserve in KwaZulu-Natal if you are on a budget.

Hluhluwe Game Reserve, entrances signposted off the N2. www.kznwildlife.com. ✆ **035/562-0255.** Fax 035/562-0113. Reservations ✆ **033/845-1000.** 69 units, some with shared bathroom. 2-bed chalet R1,280 double, 2-bed rondawel R640 double. 4 bed-chalet R2,250 for 4. AE, DC, M, V. **Amenities:** Restaurant; bar/lounge; babysitting; boat tours; fuel station; game drives; high-speed Internet (R10 per 15 min., when operational); pool. In room: Kitchenette or kitchen (in chalets), no phone.

PHINDA PRIVATE GAME RESERVE ★★★

Bordering the iSimangaliso Wetland Park and adjoining Mkhuze Game Reserve in the south, Phinda is home to the Big 5 and comprises 23,000 hectares (56,800 acres) encompassing seven distinct habitats, including sand forests, mountains, wetlands, and river valleys. The diversity of landscapes, the scale of the terrain, and the variety of animal sightings makes this among the very best wildlife preserves in the world, with 415 bird species to tick off. Wildlife numbers may not be as abundant as in, say, Sabi Sands adjoining Kruger (p. 340), but most visitors are here for the exceptional range of experiences available, and given a few days, you're likely to enjoy a rich mix of encounters, backed up by solid guiding and exquisite scenery. Based here, you also have the option of diversifying your safari experience with adventure-style excursions that might include diving the coral reefs at nearby Mabibi or Sodwana; flights over the surrounding Maputaland wilderness (including to Lake Sibaya, the largest freshwater lake in South Africa); deep-sea fishing; turtle-tracking; and canoeing and cruising the Mzinene River. You also have the chance to join your ranger for a walk through the bush, where you might find yourself trailing rhino, or picking up the tracks of predators, or the unexpectedly gentle-looking padlike "fingerprints" of elephant. Phinda also offers, unquestionably, the most stylish bush accommodations in KwaZulu-Natal.

Where to Stay & Eat

All the Phinda lodges are managed by &Beyond, specializing in luxury safaris and one of the best-known conservation outfits in the world; game drives and bush walks are top-class, always with the best-trained rangers in the business. To book any of these, contact ✆ **011/809-4300** or 021/532-5800, or explore the possibilities at www.phinda.com. In addition to those below, there are two private lodges discussed in the box, and a sixth lodge: Equally exclusive, but a bit more hippie, **Rock Camp** consists of six adobe-like chalets built into the mountainside, with private plunge pools overlooking a watering hole. This was scheduled for a relaunch with a newly refurbished look at press time; rates match those of Vlei Lodge (reviewed below). Transfers from Durban to Phinda cost R3,480 per vehicle by road, or R4,950 per person by air; from Richard's Bay airport, you'll pay R1,938 per vehicle, or R1,600 per person. *Note:* Phinda's rates include all meals, local beverages, and activities within the reserve.

Forest Lodge ★★★ When they launched in 1993, these Zen-like hand-built, glass-encased suites were lauded as the most stylish bedrooms in Africa. Spending a night in them is still electrifying. Located within a torchwood tree sand forest and constructed with minimal impact on the environment each suite is utterly private and the floor-to-ceiling glass and wraparound wooden decks put you in the bosom of the natural environment you came for. You'll regularly spot nyala and red duiker stealthily moving through the forest as you navigate the pathways to the dining area or pool.

16 units. High season R11,970 double, midseason R9,860 double, low season R7,270 double. Rates include all meals, most drinks and game-viewing activities. AE, DC, MC, V. **Amenities:** Dining area; bar; lounge; babysitting; pool; free Wi-Fi (unreliable). *In room:* A/C and fan, hair dryer, minibar.

Mountain Lodge ★★★ ☺ Not quite as flash as Forest—nor as intimate as Vlei or Rock—the oldest of the Phinda lodges underwent an overhaul in 2008; each suite has the usual &Beyond luxuries, but the view across the surrounding plains and the distant Lebombo Mountains from your private pool and al fresco shower on your terrace is what you'll really want to savor. Understandably, the complex has a more hotel-like atmosphere than the smaller lodges, and it's consequently the most child-friendly; not only are children especially well looked after here, but there are stone and thatch family-size chalets designed to help nervous children (or parents) relax. Once in your suite, the only intrusion you'll suffer is at the hands of naughty, playful monkeys.

20 units. High season R11,970 double, midseason R9,860 double, low season R7,270 double. AE, DC, MC, V. **Amenities:** Dining room; bar; babysitting; pool; room service; free Wi-Fi (unreliable). *In room:* A/C, hair dryer, minibar, plunge pool.

Private Mansions in the Bush

The latest addition to Phinda's accommodations is **Phinda Zuka Lodge ★★★**, a private, exclusive lodge in the conservancy's savanna-rich south; Zuka comprises four chalets, with dedicated use of your own pool, ranger and tracker, chef, and other staff; it's perfect for family gatherings and special-occasion safaris. Pricing is seasonal, from R20,790 to R33,570 per night. Meanwhile, the drop-dead-gorgeous and modern **Homestead ★★★**, a plush four-bedroom mansion, will set you back R36,750 to R49,000 for a night, with all the trimmings, including exclusive everything.

Vlei Lodge ★★★ In terms of privacy, gracious accommodations, and setting, Vlei (pronounced *Flay*) has got to be the pick of the Phinda lodges: a handful of glass-fronted modern timber dwellings raised on stilts under thatch and located a discreet distance from one another. Your private quarters (bigger than Forest) are plush—with massive four-poster bed and walk-in wardrobes—yet match the tranquil environs; each has a biggish private rim-flow plunge pool overlooking marsh and woodland; a totally different visual experience to the tree-surrounded setting at Forest Lodge. Vlei is also completely unfenced, so you get all kinds of animals wandering through, and the sense of being in the wilds is very real.

6 units. High season R13,050 double, midseason R11,000 double, low season R8,490 double. AE, DC, MC, V. **Amenities:** Dining room; bar; pool; free Wi-Fi. *In room:* A/C, hair dryer, minibar, plunge pool.

ISIMANGALISO WETLAND PARK ★★★

From the Mfolozi swamps in the south, this RAMSAR and World Heritage Site stretches 220km (136 miles) northward to Mozambique, incorporating the **St Lucia Game and Marine Reserves, False Bay Park, Cape Vidal, Sodwana Bay, Mkhuze Game Reserve, Lake Sibaya** and **Kosi Bay Nature Reserve.** Covering 332,000 hectares (820,390 acres), it encompasses the three most important wetlands in Africa, mangrove forests, the dry savanna and thornveld of the western shores, the vegetated sand dunes of the eastern shores, most of South Africa's remaining swamp forests (home to the rare Pel's fishing owl and palm nut vulture, as well as over 400 other bird species), and the offshore coral reefs. An intriguing fact is that this is the only place on the planet where the largest terrestrial mammal (elephant) and the oldest terrestrial mammal (rhino) share an ecosystem with the oldest known fish (coelacanth) and largest marine mammal (whale). "Biggest" and "oldest" boasts aside, there are around 526 bird species, 50 amphibians, 128 reptiles, 1,039 fish, as well as huge populations of dolphins. And despite the reach of modern technology, this is also an area—particularly in the far north—where you can still get a glimpse of semi-traditional communities operating outside the context of tourism, often a real insight into the country's vast social diversity.

For a tailor-made tour of the area (which can be combined with excursions into Hluhluwe-Umfolozi Game Reserve), contact **SHAKAbarker** (✆ **035/590-1162;** www.shakabarker.com), a two-man eco-tourism outfit with a variety of ideas of what can be done in and around the wetland.

SOUTHERN ISIMANGALISO: LAKE ST LUCIA TO SODWANA BAY

The most accessible aspect is of iSimangaliso is Lake St Lucia. A 38,882-hectare (96,039-acre) expanse of water dotted with islands, it supports an abundance of wildlife, including Nile crocodiles, hippos, rhinos, elephants, buffaloes, and giraffes, as well as a host of water birds, including pelican, flamingos, herons, fish eagles, kingfishers, geese, ducks, and storks. The lake is flanked on the west by typical bush-veld terrain and on the east by the highest forested dunes in the world. These, inci-dentally, contain large deposits of titanium and zirconium, and conservationists waged—and won—a long-running war with mining consortia to protect what are claimed to be 25,000-year-old sand dunes.

The easiest way to explore the lake is to catch a ride on the 85-seat *Santa Lucia* ★★ (bookings advisable; ✆ **035/590-1340**) for a 90-minute guided tour; there are four departures a day. If you're here on a Friday or Saturday, take the 4pm sundowner cruise and plunder the fully licensed bar onboard. The launch point is clearly marked

HOW TO AVOID BECOMING DINNER OR BEING MAULED BY A hippo

Always keep a distance of about 3m (9¾ ft.) from the water's edge. Remember that crocodiles can remain underwater for up to 2 hours in just a foot of water, so don't assume you're safe just because there's no sign of them. If you see a V-shape on the surface of the water moving toward shore, get away fast; if the critter actually gets hold of you, try to locate its eyes and stick your thumbs in as deep as they'll go. Better looking but equally dangerous, hippos are more widespread and said to be the animal responsible for the greatest number of deaths in Africa (although mosquitoes are the number-one killer)—this, despite being vegetarians. They're most dangerous at night when they're on land for grazing, using paths often shared by humans to reach riverbanks. Hippos don't like anyone getting in their way, and they are particularly unpredictable when accompanied by their young. If you find yourself between a hippo and its destination, get out of the way fast: They're far faster on their stumpy-looking legs than you might imagine; if there's a tree, climb it.

off the R618 east, which leads to St Lucia Village at the mouth of the St Lucia Estuary. If you fail to spot at least one of the estimated 2,000 Nile crocs that lurk in the lake, then head for the informative **Crocodile Centre ★★**, McKenzie Street (✆ **035/590-1387;** daily 7:30am–4:30pm). Of the literally hundreds of crocodile parks throughout the country, this is by far the best—and the only recognized crocodile research facility in South Africa. Arrive at 2pm on a Saturday for a snake presentation, followed by feeding time for the crocs at 3pm. The center houses all of the African species of crocodile, including dwarf and long-snouted crocodiles. In case you are still wondering, swimming in the lake is strictly prohibited.

There are three guided hiking options in St. Lucia. We recommend the **St Lucia Nature Trail,** which winds through coastal grassland and floodplains, with usually excellent forest bird sightings and small antelopes. The 8km (5-mile) route starts at the Crocodile Center and lasts 3 hours. The beach hike from Mission Rocks to Bat Cave and back (5km/3 miles) is also worthwhile.

The only other reason to land in the touristy St Lucia Village is because you're on your way to **Cape Vidal ★**, a worthwhile 2-hour trip north to the coast; see "Escape to Cape Vidal," below.

Last but not least of iSimangaliso's attractions is **Sodwana Bay ★**, South Africa's diving mecca. Here the warm Agulhas current brings in some 1,200 varieties of fish, apparently second in number only to Australia's Great Barrier Reef. This is the best place in the country to become a qualified diver, but if you just want to snorkel and bob around in the warm Indian Ocean, head for Jesser Point.

Where to Stay & Eat Around Lake St Lucia

St Lucia Village has a few B&Bs, small hotels and lodges, none of them very inspiring (call **St Lucia Tourism,** an informal bureau run by volunteers, at ✆ **035/590-1247** or 035/562-0353, or see for yourself by visiting www.kzn.org.za); the village of St Lucia itself is pretty tacky and mobbed by tourists. A far better option is to stay in one of the privately owned lodges on the western shore, immersed in natural surrounds. The best of these is the exclusive **Makakatana Bay Lodge** (reviewed below). With 12 thatched chalets, **Hluhluwe River Lodge** (www.hluhluwe.co.za; ✆ 035/562-0246) offers similar activities but without the deep-forest location or proximity to the lake. High season rates are R4,620 double, or R5,610 in a deluxe chalet, including all meals and one game drive into Hluhluwe-Umfolozi Game Reserve. If this price strikes you as steep, it's worth considering **Falaza Game Park,** a smart tented camp on the western dunes of False Bay (**www.falaza.co.za;** ✆ **035/562-2319;** from R1,620 double with breakfast, or R3,996 double with all meals and game drives included). Facilities include a spa, restaurant and pool, and each tent is well equipped, with a choice of shower or bathroom or both.

Makakatana Bay Lodge ★★   It's hard to imagine feeling any more tucked away within the forest than you do at this intimate and exclusive lodge. Connected by raised wooden walkways, the smart, pared-down forest suites are arranged with privacy in mind, creating a luxurious hideaway feel. From the rooms and the public lounge, you can walk (via boardwalks and some steps into the forest) to the western shore of Lake St Lucia. Wildlife—including hippos and the occasional leopard—moves through the lodge at night and the sounds of the forest's very active life is strikingly clear, especially after dark when you find yourself at one with the wilderness that envelops you. The wooden cabins are light-filled, with big sliding doors opening to wraparound verandas. Look up from your al fresco shower at night, and there's a canopy of stars. It's a mere 45 minutes to Hluhluwe-Umfolozi for a Big 5 safari, and a similar distance to Makakatana's own beach—the entire journey is a game drive. Sunset is best enjoyed lakeside, watching pods of hippos emerging from the water, accompanied by a gin and tonic and an attentive guide.

Lake St. Lucia, iSimangaliso Wetland Park. www.makakatana.co.za. ✆ **035/550-4189.** 6 units. Summer R6,500 double, R6,900 honeymoon suite; winter R5,200 double, R5,700 honeymoon suite. Rates include all meals and activities. AE, DC, MC, V. **Amenities:** Dining room; bar; beach safaris; boat safaris; canoeing; cultural excursions; game drives; Internet (limited free access in reception); snorkeling. *In room:* A/C, hair dryer, minibar.

NORTHERN ISIMANGALISO: MABIBI, ROCKTAIL BAY & KOSI BAY ★★★

Home of the Tonga, Tembe, and Mabudu peoples, KwaZulu-Natal's northeastern seaboard, marketed as the "Elephant Coast," is the most remote part of the province, and consequently the most unspoiled. Large tracts are accessible only on foot, horseback, canoe, or four-wheel-drive, and much of it is off the electrical mainframe (although this does not affect the lodgings discussed here). This inaccessibility has protected it from development, and the coastline is both wild and absolutely pristine. The entire coastline stretching from Mapelane in the south to Kosi Bay (on the Mozambique border) and extending 5km (3 miles) into the ocean is divided into two marine reserves protecting the coastal dune forest and hinterland, beaches, aquatic life, and coral reefs. A minimum 3-day stay is necessary to validate the effort it takes to get here and take advantage of all there is to do: sunbathing, snorkeling, fishing, bird-watching (60% of the birds in South Africa have been recorded here, including the palm nut vulture, one of the rarest birds in the country and curious in that it feeds on the eponymous palm fruit, in addition to meat), canoeing the lakes, sampling *ilala* palm wine, and getting to know the region's 7,000 species of flora.

South Africa's largest freshwater lake, **Lake Sibaya,** lies only 10km (6¼ miles) north of Sodwana; but if you're headed for Rocktail or Kosi Bay, this is a major detour by road, and there's nothing much to do here but bird-watch or canoe. This in itself may be a major benefit—besides, on the west side of Sibaya is **Mabibi,** one of the most remote and beautiful stretches of beach in Africa. Mabibi is served by the quite-lovely **Thonga Beach Lodge** (reviewed below), which offers sundowners at the lake's edge (typically accompanied by sightings of hippos and crocs) as well as early morning kayak trips—also on Sibaya. Thonga is also the setting-off point for boat trips to some excellent diving; there's also whale-spotting and snorkeling with dolphins.

Between Mabibi and the Mozambican border is the estuarine **Kosi Reserve,** which is about 15km (9¼ miles) northeast of Kwangwanase (formerly Kosi Bay town) via a rough dirt road; if you're staying at Kosi Forest Lodge (reviewed below), they'll arrange a 4X4 pickup in town where you can leave your car overnight. The Lodge sends you off on four-wheel-drive vehicles (with a local guide) to get to the estuary mouth (some 5km/3 miles from the camp), where one of the most impressive views in the country overlooks Kosi Bay's four interlinked lakes, which is laced with hand-woven basket-style Tonga fish traps—a sight unchanged for 7 centuries. Turning back, you can see each of Kosi's four lakes, extending inland for some 20km (12 miles). Don't miss the opportunity to join one of the pre-breakfast canoe trips through this network of mirror surface channels. Nowhere is Zululand's transition between tropical and subtropical more apparent than here; if you have the time and the will to visit, this true wilderness area is the ultimate escape from any daily routine, not to mention one of the most relaxing ways to end any vacation.

Where to Stay & Eat

Set right on a wild and unspoiled beach, **Thonga Beach Lodge** (reviewed below) is the ultimate choice for a romantic beachside battery reboot (the 40km/25-mile coast-line has been rated among the world's top beaches); it's also a top-drawer base for dive enthusiasts. An alternative to Thonga is **Rocktail Beach Camp ★★**, run by the most respected conservation company in Southern Africa, Wilderness Safaris (www.wilderness-adventures.com; *©* **011/257-5111;** R2,800 double including breakfast and dinner). Although the beach is at least a 20-minute walk from the camp and only a few of the rooms have sea views, set back as it is in the shade of the lush Sand Forest, the Maputaland Marine Reserve is just offshore, offering world-class diving and snorkeling. The camp is simple and unfussy but comfortable, consisting of 17 en-suite tented rooms (including family tents), a dining room, bar, and lounge with a wraparound veranda and swimming pool. If don't mind being away from the beach entirely, then consider **Kosi Forest Lodge** (reviewed below).

Thonga Beach Lodge ★★★ ☺ The ocean—roaring its persistent lullaby—is an ever-present part of your time at the most romantic beachcomber's retreat on the KZN coast. Set amid a dense coastal milkwood forest, with sweeping views over the secluded coral-sand beaches of Mabibi, it's remote and sufficiently Crusoe-like, without foregoing luxuries like a cocktail bar on the beach and a ridiculously cheap spa (although, mercifully, there's zero cellphone reception). Carefully constructed to ensure minimal environmental impact, the big thatched-bush suites provide absolute privacy—the beach, too, is vast and secluded. Sundowner trips take you to the edge of Lake Sibaya: you can hop on a kayak and paddle around the lake, or set off on the sea to spot dolphins and whales. Drawn largely from the local community (who are in fact the lodge's major shareholder), staff are enthusiastic and knowledgeable about the area, adding significantly to the level of authenticity.

Pickups from Coastal Cashew Factory. www.isibindiafrica.co.za. *©* **035/475-6000** through -6003, or 079/491-4422. Reservations *©* **035/474-7100.** 12 units. High season R5,980–R6,380 sea-view double, R5,260–R5,520 forest-view double; low season R5,500 sea-view double, R4,780 forest-view double. AE, MC, V. **Amenities:** Dining area; bar; lounge; babysitting; beach volleyball; birding; boat trips;

fly-fishing (deep-sea fishing by arrangement); internet (R30 per half hour; extremely slow); kayaking; pool; scuba diving; spa; 4X4 transfers from main road (R175 return). *In room:* A/C and fan, hair dryer, minibar.

Kosi Forest Lodge ★★   In one of the most pristine estuaries, the only private lodge in the Kosi Bay Nature Reserve is tucked away amid the coastal dune forest alongside the Siyadla River. Sand pathways lead through a dense, pretty forest to private wood cabins floating on stilts above a clearing in the forest floor. Each has a deck out front and romantic outdoor shower and sunken bath at the back; spend the day dangling in a hammock between the trees in front of your porch, or set off on one of a host of estuarine, beach, and wilderness activities, including guided canoe trips (an unforgettable way to explore the estuary's placid waters), raffia forest walks, and excursions to nearby beaches and reserves such as Tembe Elephant Park. There are also turtle nesting excursions (Nov–Jan), with dinner served on the beach.

Kosi Bay Nature Reserve, approx. 15km (9¼ miles) from KwaNgwanase. www.isibindiafrica.co.za. ☏ **035/592-9239** or 082/873-8874. Reservations ☏ **035/474-1473**. Fax 035/474-1490. 8 units. High season R3,980 double, low season R3,180 double. DC, MC, V. **Amenities:** Dining area; bar; lounge; boat cruises; birding; canoe trips; fishing; guided walks; 4X4 transfers (prearranged). *In room:* Fan, no phone.

THE MIDLANDS & DRAKENSBERG MOUNTAINS

The Drakensberg extends from just north of Hoedspruit in the Limpopo Province 1,000km (620 miles) south to the mountain kingdom of Lesotho, where a series of spectacular peaks some 240km (149 miles) long creates the western border of Kwa-Zulu-Natal. Known as uKhahlamba (Barrier of Spears) to the Zulus, they were renamed "Dragon Mountains" by the Trekkers seeking to cross them. Both are apt descriptions of South Africa's premier mountain wilderness—the second-largest range in Africa, venerated for centuries by the ancient San people, who have made it the world's largest open-air gallery, with more than 35,000 images painted at 600 sites.

The main range falls within **uKhahlamba-Drakensberg Park,** a 243,000-hect-are (600,210-acre) semicircle that forms the western boundary of the province. Of this, the northern and central sections are the most spectacular, with majestic peaks surrounding grassed valleys fed by crystal-clear streams and pools—a hiker's paradise. The lower slopes of the Drakensberg are also breathtaking yet allow for a gentler, easier hike. The entire region is home to some 290 species of birds and 48 species of mammals. You don't have to be a particularly fit walker to appreciate the San rock paintings, to spot rare raptors, or to simply enjoy the chance to breathe the air in the aptly named Champagne Valley or Cathedral Peak. To enjoy the benefits of this World Heritage Site, all you need is a couple of days, a car, and the following information.

If you want to add the sensation of adventure to your trip, take a look at one of the **canopy tours** offered in the region (see "Staying Active," earlier in this chapter).

Essentials

VISITOR INFORMATION   Much of the Berg, as locals call it, falls under the protection of **KZN Wildlife** (☏ **033/845-1000;** www.kznwildlife.com). If you're traveling to Cathedral Peak, take time to visit the informal bureau at **Thokozisa Centre,** off the R600, 13km (8 miles) from Winterton (☏ **036/488-1207;** www.cdic.co.za).

GETTING THERE   The only way to get to the Berg is by road (or helicopter). To get to the **KwaZulu-Natal Wildlife** properties, you will need to drive from Durban or Johannesburg. The excellent N3 toll road is the main artery off which a number of tributaries feed, depending on which area you are visiting. Signposting is clear and the roads are good, but beware of thick mist and summer thunderstorms.

GETTING AROUND   Due to the geography of the area, there are no connecting road systems, making long, circuitous routes necessary to move from one part of the Berg to the next. Depending on where you are coming from, it's best to base yourself in one or two areas: We recommend a night or two at either Royal Natal or Giant's Castle (with excellent hiking available in either), followed by a night (at least) at Cleopatra Mountain Farmhouse. If you're traveling with young kids, you might want to limit yourself to Cathedral Peak Hotel, where you can head for the hills, knowing full well the youngsters will be in good hands, and have plenty to do. If you'd prefer to have a guide take you around the area—exploring the Midland, heading into the mountains, or even exploring the nearby Battlefields region—contact **Ron Gold** (*✆ 083/556-4068*), who comes with years of experience.

On Foot   Walks range from a few hours to several days. Detailed maps are available at KZN Wildlife camps, which are also departure points for all of the best hikes. The most popular books are David Bristow's *Best Walks of the Drakensberg* and *Drakensberg Walks: 120 Graded Hikes and Trails in the Berg* (Struik), which are light enough to carry and available from most bookshops, on the Internet, and at the KZN Wildlife shops. Because winter snows and summer rainfalls can put a damper on hiking expeditions, the best times to explore the Berg are spring and autumn. (For more information, see "Hiking" under "Staying Active," earlier in this chapter.)

Meandering Through the Midlands

An hour west of Durban, just beyond Pietermaritzberg, is the start of the **Midlands Meander,** an area of undulating green hills interspersed with rivers and indigenous and commercial forests, numerous arts and crafts stops, and some of the best accommodation destinations in the province; it's a great way to start a trip to the Drakensberg. With its cooler climate, these hillsides are carpeted in flowers in spring, while crisp cold autumns turn the Midlands palette burnt orange and yellow. Its beauty has attracted creative types since the early 1800s, and it remains home to artisans and slow-food proponents, who live among small country inns between dairy farms. The Meander (*✆ 033/330-8195;* www.midlandsmeander.co.za) is South Africa's first, largest, and most popular art-and-crafts route. Weavers, potters, woodturners, leather workers, artists, metalworkers, box makers, herb growers, cheese makers, and beer brewers line the route (there's even a winery trying against the odds). There are nearly 200 hundred stops on four varying but converging routes, extending over some 80km (50 miles). It's a great way to shop, or simply to meet a vast array of crafters and artists (don't miss world-renowned **Ardmore Ceramics** in Caversham *✆ 033/234-4869*). The spectrum of nearby dining and lodging options runs from luxurious to rustic and from full-service to efficiency; many establishments are converted from old farmhouses or outbuildings. Outdoor activities include trout fishing, hiking, mountain biking, hot-air ballooning, and "canopy hopping." The 3-hour "canopy tour" (Africa's largest) through the **Karkloof Nature Reserve** (see "Staying Active," earlier in this chapter) is an exhilarating way to explore the province's largest mist-belt forest, with towering yellowwoods harboring endemic Butler butterflies and Marshall eagles.

The Drakensberg

Provincial Capital

Accommodation

Area of detail

WHERE TO STAY & EAT IN THE MIDLANDS

For a selection of places to stay in every imaginable category, check out the interactive map under the "Explore the Meander" tab at www.midlandsmeander.co.za.

Hartford House ★★★ ✦   Located on a century-old racehorse stud farm, this romantic colonial country estate is best known for its award-wining fine-dining, but the setting (vast lawns, towering trees, a private lake, fabulous formal gardens) and accommodations are good reason to stay awhile. Each suite is done out to a different style—there's lots of flair and imagination, not to mention a grand collection of furniture (old and new), and original artworks (spanning diverse genres). We particularly like the more private, idyllically situated Lake Suites, popular with dignitaries and royals from this continent. This is a plum spot for trout and bass fishing.

Summerhill stud farm, Hlatikulu Rd., around 8km (5 miles) from Mooi River. www.hartford.co.za. ✆ **033/263-2713.** Fax 033/263-2818. 15 units. R1,240 small double, R1,840–R2,100 veranda suite double, R2,300–R2,900 pool, garden and manor suite double, R3,120 lake suite double. Rates include breakfast. AE, DC, MC, V. No children under 12. **Amenities:** Restaurant; bar; lounge; fly-fishing; pool; spa; free Wi-Fi (in the main house). *In room:* TV, fireplace (in most), hair dryer, underfloor heating.

Karkloof Spa ★★★   Dreamed up by a self-confessed spa junkie, Africa's most luxurious holistic retreat, located in a 3,500 hectare (8,649 acre) reserve, is predictably expensive. However, where else do you have limitless treatments, with virtually one therapist to every room? The spa's focus is authentic Thai massage, but various therapists are available for serious detox and destress programs; yoga, Thai Chai, and Thai boxing are also available. There are no schedules, routines, or rules; you're encouraged to do as you please, according to your whims, as time simply disappears. Each villa is a slick sanctuary with views from a large balcony and your gigantic bed. The kitchen prepares world-class meals according to your dietary preferences, and there's a specialized raw food menu. Excellent guides point out black and white rhino, giraffe, buffalo, zebra, wildebeest, eland, and shyer creatures, such as black-back jackals, and there's an easy walkway hike along the Karkloof River terminating in a spectacular waterfall.

Otto's Bluff Rd., Cramond, Pietermaritzburg 3600. www.karkloofspa.com. ✆ **033/569-1321.** 16 units. R18,000 double. Rates include all meals, drinks (except French champagne), spa treatments, laundry, and activities. AE, DC, MC, V. **Amenities:** Restaurant; bar; lounges; bikes; fishing; game drives; guided walks; library; heated outdoor pool; room service; spa. *In room:* A/C, TV/DVD, butler, hair dryer, minibar, free Wi-Fi.

Exploring the Drakensberg

THE NORTHERN DRAKENSBERG   Falling within the 8,000-hectare (19,760-acre) **Royal Natal National Park,** the **Amphitheatre ★★★**—a dramatic wall of rock some 8km (5 miles) long, flanked by the Sentinel (3,165m/10,381 ft.) and Eastern Buttress (3,047m/9,994 ft.)—is the most awesome rock formation in the Drakensberg and the most photographed. This is where you'll find **Mont-aux-Sources,** so named by the French missionaries who visited the region in 1836, as the mountain acts as a watershed and the source for three major rivers: the Tugela, Vaal, and Orange. Seven kilometers (4¼ miles) from its source, the Tugela plunges 948m (3,109 ft.)—the second-highest series of falls in the world. The 6-hour **Tugela Gorge Walk,** in the Royal Natal National Park, will take you past the base of these falls, which afford excellent views of the Amphitheatre, or you can scale the summit. Like the rest of the Drakensberg, Royal Natal is ideal for hiking, with a superb network of graded walks catering to all levels of fitness and agility. Entrance to Royal

Natal (☎ **036/438-6303;** Apr–Sept 6am–6pm, Oct–Mar 5am–7pm) costs R30 per adult, R20 per child; gates close at 10pm if you are staying at **Thendele** (see "Where to Stay & Eat," below).

THE CENTRAL DRAKENSBERG   There are three distinct areas: the beautiful (3,004m/9,853-ft.) **Cathedral Peak ★★★** in the north, which has the easiest mountain to climb (a 9-hr. round-trip) and the best family hotel in the Drakensberg at its feet; the relatively populated **Champagne Valley,** where most of the Berg resorts are based, and the **Giant's Castle ★★★** area, a magnet for both hikers and those interested in San rock art. Situated in the northern section of Giant's Castle, **Injisuthi** camp (R840 double for a four-bed chalet) is cradled between the Injasuti (or "Little Tugela") and Delmhlwazini rivers at the head of the Injasuti Valley. This is a truly isolated wilderness, ideal for hikers, with breathtaking walks dominated by Cathkin Peak, Monk's Cowl, Champagne Castle, and Battle Cave. The (relatively luxurious) **Giant's Castle** camp, famous for its relatively easy access to San rock art, is a short walk away in the main caves museum, situated on a grassy plateau among the deep valleys running down from the face of the High Drakensberg. Both camps serve as the departure point for numerous trails, serviced by an extensive network of overnight huts and caves. Within the reserve, **Ndedema Gorge** contains almost 4,000 paintings at 17 sites, including **Sebaayeni Cave,** which has 1,146 paintings. The reserve is open daily (Apr–Sept 6am–6pm, Oct–Mar 5am–7pm; Giant's Castle admission R25 adult, R13 child; Injisuthi R20 adult, R10 child). Initially established to protect the eland, Africa's largest antelope, the Giant's Castle reserve is today one of the few places where you'll see the rare lammergeyer, or "bearded vulture," particularly in winter, when rangers feed the vultures in what is known as the **"vulture restaurant."** If you're in the area, check out the **Drakensberg Canopy Tour ★★★** (see "Staying Active" earlier in this chapter).

THE SOUTHERN DRAKENSBERG   Accessed by travelling the R103 (Midlands Meander) via the town of Nottingham Road, or the easier, less-scenic route via Bulwer, the south is less dramatic, with more of a pastoral setting. The alpine backdrop and rural peace is very restorative however, and there's a real sense of being in a slightly forgotten time. Trout anglers favor this region, with its abundance of crystal clear lakes and rivers, and the opportunities to hike in serene surrounds are practically endless—and there are some attractive places to stay. There are also several wildlife preserves, of which **Kamberg** and **Loteni,** home to reedbuck, blesbuck, eland, bushbuck and oribi, are worth a visit. In the Kamberg Valley, just 2 hours from Durban (mostly on good roads), **Cleopatra Mountain Farmhouse** (reviewed below) is a luxurious refuge after walking the uKhahlamba Drakensberg ranges; there's a wonderful circular trail through the Loteni Reserve to work off the calories picked up in Cleopatra's unforgettable restaurant.

Even more rural, the far southern Drakensberg region is served by the towns of Underberg, Himeville and Bulwer, where you can pick up basic provisions for hiking; the best place to stay in this less-visited part of the Berg is Himeville's **Moorcroft Manor Country House ★** (www.moorcroft.co.za; ☎ **033/702-1967;** from R1,250 double in summer) a real gem. And, if you're looking for an unusual cultural spin on the region, stop off at Himeville's museum which gives mainly information about the first white settlers who arrived in the 1890s.

However, for most, the absolute highlight of the southern Drakensberg is the **Sani Pass ★★★**: The highest road in South Africa, it leads all along the upper Mkomazana River to the border with Lesotho (2,874m/9,427 ft. above sea level), and includes no less than 14 hairpin bends on the way up. The last part of the unpaved stretch (behind the South African border post) is steep and rocky in the extreme and only manageable with a 4X4 vehicle, but there's big reward in the form of unforgettable views of the rugged alpine landscape. If you're keen to see a bit of **Lesotho** (a small, mountainous country that's entirely landlocked by South Africa), you can cross the border (open daily, 6am–6pm) and take lunch at the little restaurant on the other side; there's a Basotho cultural village to investigate, too. Far better than a quick stop would be to overnight in one of ten rondavels at the **Sani Top Chalet** (www.sani topchalet.co.za; ✆ **076/386-7021** or 033/702-1069; R1,200 double including dinner and breakfast; cheaper options also available), a generator-powered lodge with fireplaces, breathtaking views, cozy rooms, and the highest pub in Africa—it's 8km (5 miles) beyond the South African border post. In winter, it's occasionally possible to ski or snowboard up here (bring your own equipment), or you can hire a guide (R200 per day) and hike to **Thabana Ntlenyana** (3,482m/11,421 ft.), the highest point south of Kilimanjaro; you can also arrange to go exploring on a Basotho pony, and various cultural tours are available. If you don't have a 4X4, you can join a trip to the Pass with **Major Adventures** (www.majoradventures.com; R500 per person), which departs from the Underberg Hotel (in Underberg) at 9am (stopping at B&Bs for pickups along the way) and returns around 4pm—be sure to take your passport along for the border crossing. Note that winter night temperatures, especially in the southern Berg, can drop below 32°F (0°C).

WHERE TO STAY & EAT

Hikers who want to stay overnight in the mountains must book their huts and caves through the KZN Wildlife office closest to the trail (✆ **033/845-1000;** www.kzn wildlife.com); the camps below are the best bases for walking—hikes start literally from your front door. *Note:* Entry fees for the Drakensberg parks vary between R20 and R30 per adult and R10 to R13 per child.

Northern Drakensberg

Montusi Mountain Lodge ★★ ☺ If you don't mind being outside the park, this is the closest thing to luxury near Royal Natal, with the Amphitheatre escarpment visible from each of the free-standing suites (provided there's no haze). Set on 1,000 hectares (2,471 acres), Montusi is family-run and very comfortable—the clean, crisp design of each luxuriously furnished thatched cottage is offset by African art and enough genuine "Berg" influence to keep things real (book suite 9 for the best view). There's a great freeform pool surrounded by natural rocks, and a string of outdoor activities to keep energetic youngsters (and grown-ups) entertained; five hikes start from the property. It's not on the same scale as Cathedral Peak (below), so things are far more personal.

45km (28 miles) NW of Bergville, 18km (11 miles) from Royal Natal National Park. From Bergville, follow the R74 north for 28km (17 miles); then follow signs for Northern Berg, and then Montusi. www.montusi. co.za. ✆ **036/438-6243.** Fax 036/438-6566. 14 units. R2,600 double. Rates include breakfast and dinner. Children 2–12 sharing with 2 adults in 2-bedroom suite pay 50%. AE, DC, MC, V. **Amenities:** Restaurant; lounge; bar; bikes; fishing; hiking; horseback riding; quad biking; tennis court; pool; free Wi-Fi (in main building). *In room:* Fans, TV/DVD, gas fireplace, hair dryer, minifridge.

Thendele Hutted Camp ★ 🔥 Deep within the Royal Natal National Park in one of the most picturesque settings in the country, with a view of the Amphitheatre from every chalet, Thendele enjoys the best location of all the KZN Wildlife camps. Overlooked by the brooding sandstone cliffs of Dooley, among yellowwood forests and protea savanna, you'll often hear boulders rumbling in the Thukela River below after a fierce summer thunderstorm. For such a riveting, intimate relationship with nature, it's probably worth putting up with the tired decor (long scheduled for overhaul); the camp also has no restaurant. A shop keeps basic provisions (and alcohol), but for fresh supplies, stock up in Bergville or try the restaurant at the Orion Mountaux-Sources hotel, 20 minutes away (but return before 10pm, when gates close). Accommodations at Upper Camp are slightly more modern (but still in need of maintenance). For totally unobstructed views (and more comfort and space), book one of two six-bed cottages, or the totally private three-bedroom lodge; each comes with a personal cook.

Royal Natal National Park. www.kznwildlife.com. ✆ **036/438-6411.** Reservations ✆ **033/845-1000.** 29 units. R875 Lower Camp double, R995 Upper Camp double, R2,040 cottage (4 people), R3,300 lodge (6 people). AE, DC, MC, V. **Amenities:** Horseback riding; shop. *In room:* TV, kitchen, no phone.

Central Drakensberg

The cheaper alternative to **Cathedral Peak** (reviewed below) is KZN Wildlife-managed **Didima Camp** (from R840 double, depending on chalet type), the most "modern" of the official parks camps, with pool and tennis courts. An armada of reasonably outfitted chalets—shaped like upturned ships—floats across a Drakensberg foothill. Things are a bit forlorn and institutional, but there are majestic views, and each comes with a fireplace and satellite TV. Most are equipped for cooking, but there is also a restaurant, bar, and lounge in the main lodge. The **Didima Rock Art Centre** (daily 8am–1pm and 2–4pm; R50 adults, R25 children) is just down the drag if you want to learn more about San cave paintings.

For overnight stays in Champagne Valley, the old-fashioned **Champagne Castle Hotel** (www.champagnecastlehotel.co.za; ✆ **036/468-1063**), also located off the R600, is closest to the mountains and enjoys the best views, though it's nowhere as remote or charming as Cathedral Peak. Standard doubles start at R1,840 in season.

Cathedral Peak ★★ ☺ This is without a doubt the best big hotel option in the Drakensberg, situated in its own valley, at the foot of the mountains within the protected reserve. It offers great alpine views, comfortable rooms, and a very relaxed atmosphere. Even getting here is memorable—expect to slow to a halt for cattle cruising across the road, never mind the jaw-dropping views and photogenic mud huts dotting the countryside. Book a superior room (or suite if you can); they cost a bit more but they are worth it—patio doors open onto the gardens and more excellent mountain views. Trails start from the hotel, which provides maps or, for ease of mind, knowledgeable guides. The 11km (6.7-mile) Rainbow Gorge round-trip is recommended. Meals are huge buffets—don't miss the fresh-caught Drakensberg trout—and children have their own dining room, not to mention loads of activities to keep them busy.

uKhahlamba Drakensberg Park, 31km (19 miles) SW of Winterton. www.cathedralpeak.co.za. ✆ **036/488-1888.** Fax 036/488-1889. 104 units. R2,230–R2,490 deluxe double, R2,390–R2,650 superior double, R2,960–R3,250 executive/honeymoon suite, R4,570–R4,920 presidential suite. Rates include dinner, breakfast, and midmorning and afternoon tea. Children under 10 sharing with 2 adults pay R405–R665, children under 2 free. AE, DC, MC, V. **Amenities:** Dining room, 2 bars; archery; babysitting; badminton; bikes; bowling; children's games room; fishing; gym; 9-hole golf course; guided hikes; horseback riding; heated pool and paddling pool; quad bikes; squash court; 2 tennis courts; volleyball. *In room:* Fans, TV, hair dryer, minifridge, Wi-Fi (R100 per 24 hr.).

Giant's Castle Camp ★ Book a mountain-view chalet (not garden view) at this, KZN Wildlife's flagship mountain camp—many of the veranda-on-stilts enjoy sublime views (pick no. 39, 40, 43 or the honeymoon suite if possible). Besides close proximity to some of the best, most accessible examples of San cave art in the country, it's well maintained (although decor is rustic) and there's a fully licensed restaurant (with viewing deck) should you prefer not to cook. Provisions sold in the shop are basic. There's a mix of accommodation configurations, but if you're fussy or want the whole family under one (slightly more comfortable) roof, then go for the upmarket three-bedroom Rock Lodge, which enjoys the most private setting (and comes with its own chef).

Giant's Castle, 68km (42 miles) W of Mooi River, signposted off the N3. www.kznwildlife.com. © **036/353-3718.** Reservations © **033/845-1000.** 44 units. R840–R1,260 garden-view double, R960–R1,440 mountain-view double, R965 honeymoon suite, R2,400 6-bed mountain-view chalet, R3,300 6-bed lodge. AE, DC, MC, V. **Amenities:** Restaurant; bar; fishing; fuel station; hiking trails; Internet (for emergency use only); shop. *In room:* TV, fireplace (some), kitchen, no phone.

Southern Drakensberg: Kamberg Valley

Gourmands need no other ulterior motives to head straight to **Cleopatra Mountain Farmhouse**—the food is unforgettable, and the location and accommodations simply magical. For a more contemporary ambience, check out nearby **Qambathi.**

Cleopatra Mountain Farmhouse ★★★ Surrounded by mountains and burbling crystal-clear streams and waterfalls, the setting is as memorable as the stellar meals and the personally themed rooms. Décor is a quirky, imaginative blend of recycled antiques—Mouse Poynton, who designs everything herself, has a natural flair for eye-catching, unexpected arrangements. Mouse's husband, Richard, whose family established this farm back in 1936, is the epicurean genius who experiments and plays in the kitchen. Each night, your five-, six-, or seven-course seasonal meal is preambled with a stand-up performance in which Richard expounds upon the menu as you sip vintages from a carefully stocked underground cellar. Service is of the personable, understated, and attentive kind. It's a mere 20 minutes to Kamberg (Little Berg) for tours of Bushman rock art; and Giant's Castle is a 45-minute drive. Perfect.

Highmoor Rd., off Kamberg Rd., Kamberg Valley. www.cleomountain.com. © **033/267-7243** or via satellite 033/267-9900, -9902, or -9903. Fax 033/267-9901. 11 units. R3,190 double, R3,590–R3,790 suite, R3,990 cottage. Rates include breakfast, dinner, cheeseboard lunch, teas, coffees, and cake. MC, V. No children under 12. **Amenities:** Restaurant; bar; lounge; cooking courses; fishing; hiking trails; horseback riding; underground wine cellar. *In room* Fan, TV, fireplace (suites and cottages), hair dryer, minibar.

Qambathi Mountain Lodge ★★★ An immaculate makeover of an old gaol and post office, Qambathi brings cool contemporary glamour to a tranquil rural setting; you're right at the edge of the bush, with a vast game-trodden acreage to explore. Birds and baboons provide the soundtrack as sheep and cattle graze the adjacent farm, and delicious aromas emanate from the open-plan kitchen as superlative five-course dinners are prepared. It's designed on a very intimate scale—more a house with ample space than a hotel or inn, and you're treated as a personal guest. Decor is inspired by nature, with one-of-a-kind designs and organic materials. Many of the sitting areas are designed for two, so it's easy to find a private nook—although bedrooms are the kind you struggle to leave. Predinner fires and candles are lit on the deck; warmed by red wine, you stare up at a canopy of stars.

Qambathi Mountain Reserve, Kamberg, 30km (19 miles) from Rosetta. www.qambathi.co.za. © **033/267-7515** or 082/774-8164. Fax 033/267-7514. 5 units. R3,500 luxury double, R3,800 garden suite. Rates include dinner and breakfast. AE, DC, MC, V. 5% credit card surcharge. No children under 12. **Amenities:** Dining area; bar; lounge; bikes; horseback riding; small pool. *In room:* Hair dryer, underfloor heating.

THUNDERING WORLD WONDER: VICTORIA FALLS & VICINITY

W hen explorer David Livingstone first set eyes on Victoria Falls, its plumes of spray like cumulus clouds mushrooming upwards from a fissure in the earth, he remarked in awe that they must be "gazed upon by angels in their flight," and promptly named them for his queen. A century and a half later, the might of the British crown has waned, but the Zambezi River still pounds into the Batoka Gorge, drawing travelers to witness the thundering waters of the Zambezi plummeting 100m (328 ft.)—twice the height of Niagara.

Straddling the border between Zimbabwe and Zambia, Victoria Falls is justifiably called one of the Wonders of the Natural World, and spans almost 2km (1¼ miles), making it the largest show of its kind on Earth. The sight—and sound—of more than 9 million liters of water crashing down into the Batoka Gorge is a benign reminder of man's insignificance when faced with the power of nature, and one not easily forgotten. Even from afar the falls amaze: On a clear day, the roaring spray billows upwards for miles—seen from up to 80km (50 miles) away, it is as if the earth has a cauldron billowing clouds of smoke that finally dissipate high above the plains. It is this phenomenon that gave the falls its far more apt local name: *Mosi-Oa-Tunya*—literally, "The Smoke That Thunders."

People come here not only to immerse themselves in the spectacle of the falls, but also to partake in the varied adventure activities, from flinging themselves into the Batoka Gorge, to riding the world's most challenging commercially run rapids. Not for nothing has this area been dubbed the adrenaline capital of southern Africa.

If, however, your idea of the ideal Vic Falls trip is to get soaked under the Thundering Wonder (and make no mistake, you will get wet), then return to your lodge, kick back with a gin and tonic, and listen to hippos honk conversationally on the great Zambezi. Lodgings on both sides of the falls will provide this opportunity—and more.

ORIENTATION
Visitor Information

The **Zambia National Tourism Board** maintains an up-to-date website which is worth taking a look at (www.zambiatourism.com). To plan your trip on the Zimbabwean side, best to browse **www.gotovictoriafalls.com**, cohosted by all the tourist stakeholders in Victoria Falls. The drop-off in tourism numbers in the village has resulted in a wonderful team spirit, with all hotel staff, private operators, and other tourist stakeholders in the village bending over backwards to assist travelers planning a visit here; an atmosphere of appreciation prevails.

The largest Victoria Falls operator, specializing in the full spectrum of adventure activities, efficient transfers from the airport to both sides of the falls (as well as Botswana), and accommodation bookings for their own and other lodges, is **Wild Horizons** (www.wildhorizons.co.za; ✆ 263/13/44571, 44426, 42313, 42029 or 712/213-721). Wild Horizons is headquartered in Victoria Falls Village, Zimbabwe, but services visitors to both sides of the falls. Making use of their centralized booking facility gives you one point of contact for various reservations and should ensure smooth transfers. If you'd prefer to deal with an agent based on the Zambian side, the best agent, offering a similar range of services for similar prices (though activities on the Zambian side tend to be slightly more expensive), is **Safari Par Excellence** (www.safpar.com): Their office is at Zambezi Waterfront Lodge, off Mosi-Oa-Tunya Road, halfway between Livingstone and the Vic Falls bridge.

Getting There
BY PLANE

To get to Vic Falls you need to fly to Livingstone (Zambia) or Victoria Falls Village (Zimbabwe) via Johannesburg; it is not possible to fly direct from anywhere else in South Africa. (And too far and expensive to drive from S.A.) However it is a mere 90-minute drive from Kasane/Chobe destinations in Botswana.

TO ZAMBIA   With many more scheduled flights to Zambia, the majority of visitors are more likely to arrive on the Zambian side of the falls, at **Livingstone International Airport (LVI),** which is about 20 minutes from the falls. Not only do BA/Comair and SAA fly here daily, but budget airlines **1time** (www.1time.co.za) and **Kulula** (www.kulula.com) now also fly to Livingstone, at half the price of the big carriers (at press time around R1,800 round-trip to Jo'burg). If you've elected to stay in Vic Falls village, you can then transfer to the Zimbabwean side by road (about a 30-min. transfer; transfer cost is around $30); even with the additional visa fee for Zambia you will probably save money.

TO ZIMBABWE   Both SAA and BA/Comair fly once daily to **Victoria Falls International Airport;** Air Zimbabwe offers the same route and has been given a clean bill of health but we'd stick with the big carriers. Many hotels on this side offer a complimentary shuttle from the airport (about 10 min. from falls); if not, arrange this in advance (around $10). See chapter 13 for more.

BY TRAIN

It's billed as the most luxurious train in the world; certainly the **Rovos** ★★★ experience is hard to beat, rocked to sleep in your king-size bed as the world slips past beyond the large picture windows, having sampled a range of the finest South African wines (included in the price) and dined on gourmet meals in an Edwardian carriage. Board the train in Pretoria and spend the next 2 nights chugging north in the style one instantly becomes accustomed to (www.rovos.com; R14,850–R29,700 per person [depending on carriage], rates all inclusive for 2 nights/3 days). If you're up for a more extensive rail adventure, consider the **Shongololo Express** Southern Cross Adventure, a 16-day journey that travels leisurely between Victoria Falls and Johannesburg, making calls at destinations in Mozambique, Swaziland, Botswana, and Zambia (www.shongololo.com; R45,293–R61,480 per person for 15 nights [including breakfasts, dinners, and airport transfers; rates depending on carriage choice]).

Getting Around

The most convenient way to get around is to have your hotel or lodge arrange transfers (most of them offer a complimentary shuttle to the falls), or book a hotel within walking distance of the falls (the two best options on the Zimbabwean side are Victoria Falls Hotel and Ilala, while the Royal Livingstone and its cheaper sister, Zambian Sun, are within ambling distance on the Zambian side). If you do need any transfers, contact **Wild Horizons** (see "Visitor Information" above); their shuttles operate in both Zim and Zam, from 7:30am to 10:30pm, as well as offering a shuttle service to and from both airports, and regular departures to Kasane in Botswana.

Getting Beyond: Wilderness Air (ww.wilderness-air.com) offers a flying schedule to collaborate with the photographic safari season. Commencing in May, the schedule operates four times per week from Livingstone (five times per week from Lusaka). Travelers fly in air-conditioned C208 Cessna Caravans or a Cessna C210 (not air-conditioned) to camps in Zambia/Botswana.

> ### Country Codes
>
> **This chapter contains phone numbers for three countries. Phone numbers starting with 263 are in Zimbabwe, those starting with 260 are in Zambia, and those beginning with 27 are in South Africa. The Zimbabwean telephone exchange is temperamental. At certain times of the day, it is impossible to get through to any number; e-mail is far more reliable.**

BY BOAT ★★★

A number of companies run cruises on the calm, mesmerizing waters of the Upper Zambezi and at sunset, when the intense colors of the setting African sun are reflected in the swirling waters, this is an absolute must. If you're taking a commercial cruise (as opposed to one of the complimentary cruises offered by the Zambian lodges on the riverbanks, which are farther upstream where tranquillity prevails) you will however see more tourists than wildlife, but the atmosphere is laid back and friendly; however, some of the "booze cruises" offer unlimited liquor, which can result in unfortunate rowdy behavior; be warned and glide on by. The best boat by far is the **Ra-Ikane,** a small (max 14 guests) luxury cruise boat with period decor and memorabilia, and refined atmosphere. Tours last 3½ hours and depart daily at 4:30pm from

Ilala Hotel in Vic Falls town. Book through Wild Horizons. (Also see "Canoe Safaris," later in this chapter.)

BY TRAIN

Board a restored 1954 Class 14A steam locomotive, with dining cars and first-class coaches, operated by **Victoria Falls Steam Train Company** (www.steamtrain company.com)—and leave Zimbabwe's Victoria Falls to cross the Victoria Falls Bridge to Livingstone, Zambia (or vice versa). You can do the bridge run at sunset; they also offer "royal tea" or a Moonlight Dinner Run but cuisine standards don't match the rather hefty price tag. You'll also need to bring your passport, and be aware that rates don't cover visas (see "Visas" under "Fast Facts," below).

[Fast FACTS] VICTORIA FALLS & LIVINGSTONE

Business Hours Shops are generally open Monday through Saturday from 8am to 5pm. Activity centers and markets are open daily 6am to 6pm; many close only when the last traveler leaves.

Climate See "The Best Times to Come," above.

Crime With the stabilizing of the economic crisis that the dollarization of the Zimbabwean currency brought about, the Victoria Falls village has finally regained an air of optimism, and is quiet and safe. Hoteliers here are mindful of their vulnerable status in tourism, so there's tight security as well as a Tourism Police service (look out for the yellow jackets), with guards patrolling a broad area from 7am to 9pm daily. Bear in mind that Livingstone is a much larger town than Victoria Falls, and many people live here to cash in on tourists; be alert and don't walk around alone. The usual caveats apply: Avoid petty crime by not flashing valuables, and

stay in groups, particularly at night; also stay clear of deserted areas.

Currency Zimbabwe no longer has its own currency, so bring foreign currency: Dollars, pounds, euros, or South African rands are all accepted. On the Zambian side, you can buy *kwacha* (Zambian currency) at hotels, or use an ATM (either in Livingstone or at The Falls casino and entertainment center, near the border), but as U.S. dollars are the most preferred method of payment, it's easiest to carry these. Most prices can be quoted in U.S. dollars, but getting change on large notes is hard, so include some small dollar denominations (useful for tips as well). For more see "Money," in chapter 13.

Doctors In Livingstone: Contact Dr. Shafik's Clinic, 49 Akapelwa St. (© 260/213/32-1130). In Victoria Falls: Contact Dr. Fungayi at **Victoria Falls Surgery,** West Drive, off Park Way (© 263/13/ 43356; Mon–Fri

9:30am–5pm, Sat 9:30am– 5pm, Sun 9:30–5pm; after hours © 263/13/40529).

Drugstores Drugstores are called chemists or pharmacies. **In Livingstone: LF Moore Chemist** is also on Akapelwa Street (© 260/213/32-1640). In **Victoria Falls: Victoria Falls Pharmacy** is located in Phumula Centre, Park Way (© 263/13/44403; Mon– Fri 8am–6pm, Sat–Sun 8am–noon). A drugstore in the Kingdom Hotel is open daily.

Electricity Electricity in southern Africa runs on 220/230V, 50Hz AC, and sockets in Zimbabwe and Zambia take flat-pinned plugs. Pack an adapter/ voltage converter though most lodges will supply you with whatever you need.

Embassies & Consulates All offices are in the capital cities of Harare (Zimbabwe) and Lusaka (Zambia); if you have diplomatic problems, speak to your hotel manager and ask him to contact your country's local representative.

Emergencies Your hotel or lodge is your best bet for the safest medical and emergency care. Alternatively, contact **Medical Air Rescue Service,** a 24-hour emergency evacuation service (☎ **263/13/44764**). For an **ambulance,** call ☎ **44210;** for the **police,** call ☎ **44206;** to report a **fire,** call ☎ **44400;** for **general emergencies,** call ☎ **112** or 44206.

Health   Malaria If you are concerned, ask your physician about starting a course of antimalarial prophylaxics. If you suspect you have malaria, get to a doctor immediately for a test. For more information, see "Health," in chapter 13.

Language English is spoken in the tourist regions of Zimbabwe and Zambia.

Telephone Phone numbers in this chapter use codes for three countries. See "Country Codes," above. For tips on making

international and local calls, see "Telephones" in chapter 13.

Time Zone Both Zimbabwe and Zambia are 5 hours ahead of GMT and 7 hours ahead of Eastern Standard Time.

Tipping Naturally this is at your discretion, but if you are happy, tip $5 to $10 per day for communal staff. For guides, $5 to $10 per day per activity will be much appreciated.

Visas   Zambia: Single entry costs $50 (double entry is $80); a day-tripper visa costs $20. To check the latest fees see www.zambiaimmigration.gov.zm. **Zimbabwe:** Visa fees depend on nationality. For British nationals, a single entry costs $55 and $70 for double entry. Australians, New Zealanders, and Americans must pay $30; $45 for double-entry visa. Canadians, for some strange reason, pay $75. Double-check these figures if you intend to purchase a visa on

arrival: www.victoriafalls-guide.net.

Water Tap water is generally considered safe. You're often better off drinking the water provided—preferably purified rather than bottled—because local water is less processed and may be richer in mineral content than your stomach is used to.

Wildlife Keep your eye out for elephants and hippos when you're out walking, cycling, or canoeing. Do not block their routes—it's best not to turn around, but back away slowly. When driving on highways, keep a watchful eye out for animals emerging from the bush to cross the road. Baboons and monkeys are a nuisance on both sides of the falls. Never feed them; in fact, keep food out of sight and remember that—like all wild animals—they are unpredictable and potentially dangerous.

WHAT TO SEE & DO

The area is famous for its myriad adventure activities and excellent wildlife-viewing opportunities, but essentially the falls are the star of the show, thundering past you with all the power of a tsunami.

Soaking Up the Falls

There are two great vantage points, each in a national park and affording a different angle; it's worth covering both, but if you have time for only one, the better views by far are from the Zimbabwean side (though picturesque, you only see a very small section of the falls from the Zambian side). Note that you will almost certainly get wet: You can rent a raincoat for a few dollars or accept the inevitable and wear a swimsuit with sarong/shorts and T-shirt, and wear open shoes that will dry easily with nonslip soles. Your camera will need a waterproof bag; again these are available for rent if you don't own one. Note however that regardless of which side you visit, the views can be virtually obscured by the spray, particularly when water is high; it's still worth it just to feel the power, but to get a true sense of the extent of the falls you will need to take to the sky, preferably in a microlight.

One really worthwhile and unusual way to experience the falls is to book a trip to **Livingstone Island ★★★**, a tiny island at the lip of the falls. Only accessible from July to March, it is an unbelievable privilege to have lunch or high tea here, and you can even swim in a river pool (attached to a harness!) right on the edge of the falls. Cost is $65 to $120, depending on which time slot you book; max 16 people (14 if you book as a private group). The operation is run by class-act Tongabezi (see "Where to Stay," later in this chapter), but you can book with Wild Horizons.

Victoria Falls National Park ★★★ 📷 Victoria Falls National Park—which affords the best vantage of the falls—is a 2,340-hectare (5,780-acre) narrow strip that runs along the southern bank of the Zambezi River and protects the sensitive rainforest around the falls. It is walking distance from the village (simply follow Livingstone Way). You will almost certainly get drenched by the permanent spray, so rent a raincoat or umbrella at the entrance (or better still, just relish the experience and wear a costume with a T-shirt, and take a change of clothes). Definitely wear sandals that will dry easily and remember to put your camera in a waterproof bag. A clearly marked trail runs through the lush rainforest (look out for the aptly named flame lilies), with side trails leading to good viewing points of the falls. Head down the steep stairs to **Cataract View** for views of **Devil's Cataract ★★**; this is also where you'll find the unremarkable statue of David Livingstone. The final view point, nearest the falls bridge, is called **Danger Point**—here you can perch right on the edge of a cliff and peer down into the abyss (though again, when in full flood you'll see nothing but spray, which is exhilarating—particularly as the water truly does thunder—but a tad frustrating if you were hoping to see anything more than mist). When the moon is full, the park stays open later so that visitors can witness the lunar rainbow formed by the spray. Not only is it a beautiful sight, but the experience is untarnished by helicopters and microlights, which can be something of a nuisance during the day.

You don't really need a guide to visit the falls. Many unofficial guides stand near the entrances, but unless you want to learn more about the rainforests (in which case, hire a guide from a reputable company), chances are that they won't be able to show you anything other than the direction of the path, and will get in the way of your enjoyment and pace. However a guide will accompany you during full moon nights when the park stays open for visitors to see the lunar rainbows—utterly magical. This only happens when the water levels are high (Apr/May–June); during the dry season (Oct–Dec) there is usually not enough rising spray to create these "moonbows."

No phone. Admission $30. Daily 6am–6pm (later during full-moon nights, when entry is higher).

Mosi-oa-Tunya ★★ 📷 The Zambian side offers a different vantage point than its Zimbabwean counterpart, and the view is sometimes less obscured by spray, but you're only seeing a small part of the falls. Also, after a long, dry winter, water on this side can be reduced to a trickle, when views are nonexistent (particularly bad around Oct, but check with your hotel or host). However it's always pretty thrilling to cross the bridge to a vantage called Knife Edge, where you will stand suspended above the churning waters of Boiling Pot—a vicious rapid most rafters get to know a little too intimately. ***Warning:*** There are no fences on this side of the river, and it's easy to slip on the wet rocks attempting to get that extraspecial shot or glimpse. If you don't recover your footing, the chance of survival is nil.

Entrance off Livingstone Rd. No phone. Admission $10–$20. Year-round daily 6am–6pm.

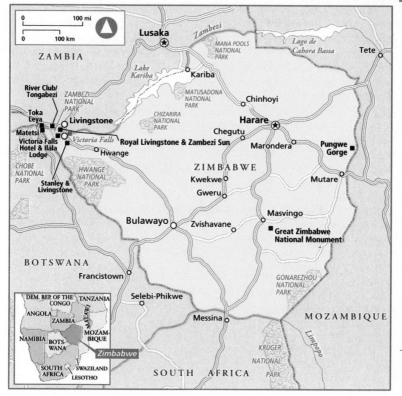

Viewing Wildlife

Given your proximity to Botswana, where the wildlife experience is incomparably more thrilling, Vic Falls should ideally be your last stop, with only a visit to the falls (by air and on foot) on the itinerary, with perhaps an adventure activity thrown in for good measure. However, if this is your only chance to go on safari, there are a number of tour operators who will arrange morning, afternoon, and night drives to Zambezi National Park, Mosi-Oa-Tunya Park, and Hwange, as well as full days in **Chobe, Botswana ★**; contact Wild Horizons (www.wildhorizons.co.za) or Safari Par Excellence (www.safpar.com). Safaris on foot, canoe or horseback are also available.

STAYING ACTIVE

All hotels will arrange reservations and give advice on the many activities on offer, most at no additional charge, though some do feel the need to add a small surcharge. If you're being careful with your budget and plan to do a lot, you can do all your bookings, transfers included, with **Wild Horizons** (www.wildhorizons.co.za) or **Saf Par** (www.safpar.com). **Adventure Zone** also has solid ethics. Note that the same activities paid for on the Zimbabwean side (Vic Falls Village) tend to be cheaper, as operators try to claw back their pole position as the best base to view the falls—a status enjoyed until Mugabe spoiled the party (now there's a conversation starter with locals). We include some of the more exhilarating for your perusal below:

BUNGEE JUMPING ★★ The checklists of most adventure-seekers aren't complete until they've done the heart-stopping 111m (364-ft.) bungee off the Vic Falls Bridge, stopping about 10m (33 ft.) from the boiling waters in the Batoka Gorge. Jumps take place daily (9am–1pm and 2–5pm); a solo jump costs $120 regardless of which side you are based ($145 for tandem).

ELEPHANT-BACK SAFARIS Lots of companies now offer elephant-back safaris, and it is suspected that some 50 elephants are held captive in the area. The growth of the activity has raised many controversial questions. The industry is under-regulated and, apart from the obvious animal welfare issues relating to concerns over training methods, and the environmental impact of keeping these animals captive, there is no obligation for commercial operators to provide for the lifetime care of these emotionally sensitive animals. Ascertain where the elephants have come from, how they are trained, where they are kept, and what the company's long-term plans are before you saddle up ($120).

GORGE SWING, ZIP LINE & FLYING FOX ★★★ Attached with a body harness to the world's highest commercial high wire, you step straight off the edge of the cliff and free fall into the Batoka Gorge. The Gorge Swing allows you to experience free-fall for 70m (230 ft.), before swinging you over the Zambezi as it churns its way down the gorge. This is the most terrifying jump in Vic Falls—best way to approach it is to warm up first with the Flying Fox, whereupon you more or less fly, fully harnessed to the cable slide lines above the Zambezi rapids at speeds of up to 105kmph (65 mph), or try the slightly more intimidating Zip Line. For the Flying Fox alone, the cost is $35; for the Zip Line it's $60; the Gorge Swing is $80; all three is $120. Or you could combine bungee with bridge swing/slide for $155.

FLYING OVER THE FALLS ★★★ 📷 The only way to get a real idea of the size of the falls is to take to the skies on a microlight flight—both are quieter than helicopter or fixed-wing flights, and you'll be sailing a great deal closer to nature. **Batoka Sky** (book through any of the adventure-activity operators above; flights leave from Livingstone) operates tricycle-style microlight flights from Zambia and charges $145 for 15 minutes. You can't take a camera (if you drop it, it may stop the engine below), so Batoka has a camera attached to the wheels; your pilot will take a photograph of you flying past the falls. Helicopter trips cost slightly more or less (usually about $10 less), depending on whom you book with.

GOLFING The 6,107m (20,358-ft.) **Elephant Hills Intercontinental** (📞 **263/13/44793**) course is at times just a stroke from the roaring Zambezi River, and the constant thundering presence of the falls—not to mention wildlife—makes this Gary Player–designed course one of the most interesting in Africa. Eighteen holes will run you around $55.

WALKING WITH LIONS 🖐 An activity now available on both sides of the falls, this is understandably tempting, but it remains highly criticized in conservation circles, which see no benefit whatsoever to the lions. Some suspect the cubs you encounter are released into private reserves where they become targets in "canned" hunts. However, it is a tempting photo-op—if you are interested you're looking at around $125 per person.

WHITE-WATER RAFTING ★★★ 🄾 This is the most exhilarating ride you'll ever have: An absolute must-do for adrenaline junkies. You need to be reasonably fit (not only to deal with the Class III to Class V rapids, but also for the 230m/754-ft. climb out of the gorge at the end of a tiring day, though you can be lifted out by helicopter for a substantial fee). You should also be a competent swimmer. Don't worry if you haven't done anything like it before—organizers offer dry-ground preparation before launching onto the water, and the safety and guiding standards are excellent. Operators pride themselves on offering the best commercially run rapids in the world; note that this does not prevent unforeseen disasters, with a few fatalities recorded every couple of years. The best time for rafting is when the water is low, from July to January; September and October are particularly good months. (From Apr–May, when the water is high, rafting is closed altogether.) The safest option is to get on a boat that has an oarsman who guides you along the safest path. The alternative, where everyone in the group has his or her own paddle, is much more fun, despite the fact that—or in large part because of it—you'll definitely end up in the water. River-boarding is the most hair-raising way to brave the rapids—alone, on a Boogie board, you literally surf the waves created by a selection of Class III to Class V rapids. Most river-rafting companies offer an optional half-day rafting, half-day boarding experience. One of the best river rafting companies, **Shearwater** (www.shearwater.com) are worth booking, but Wild Horizons or Saf Par will take care your with a reputable company (see above). Trips are offered from both the Zimbabwean and the Zambian side—Zambia has the added advantage of including a few extra rapids, and they also begin right beneath the falls; the benefit of being on the Zimbabwe side are the multirafting trips ★★★—after a full day rafting, overnighting on a sandy beach in the gorge is bliss—sure to be the highlight of your trip. Expect to pay $130 to $160 for a full day (depending on which side you start at). Prices include lunch, soft drinks, and all equipment.

WHERE TO STAY & EAT

There are basically two questions you need to ask yourself before booking your lodgings: Do I want to stay in Zimbabwe or in Zambia? Do I need to be within walking distance of the falls or stay relatively nearby but in tranquil, natural surroundings? Reasons to stay on the Zimbabwean side include great value for your money, a significant improvement in atmosphere since the dollarization of the economy, and the better views of the falls. In fact when the water levels of the Zambezi and falls subside (Aug to mid-Jan), there is often no water on the Zambian side of the falls at all, in which case you'd need to see them via microlight or helicopter, book a transfer to view them from the Zimbabwean side, or choose a hotel or lodge on that side. However, the major benefit of the best Zambian options is that they are all located on the banks of the Zambezi, a river that sees plenty of hippo and elephant action and has enormous pull, with views of riverine islands and the forested banks of the national park beyond—a romantic choice, regardless of water levels. Being walking distance from the falls has its uses, particularly if you're here for 1 night only, but the incessant helicopter noise can be an irritant, particularly if you've been spoiled by the wonders of being on safari.

In Zambia

The most convenient Zambian option is **Royal Livingstone** and sister hotel **Zambezi Sun,** which are right next to the falls, walking distance away. However, if you don't like large, impersonal hotels, and want peace and privacy, there are a number of lovely options farther upstream (the farther upstream the farther from the tourism activities on the water), all overlooking the Zambezi River. The best, all within 30 minutes of the falls, are reviewed below. Note that if you're watching your budget, it's worth considering **Waterberry Lodge** (www.waterberrylodge.com; $500 double; includes full board, sunset cruise, airport transfers), with seven simply furnished bungalows on the grassed riverbanks and gardens.

The River Club ★★★ A neighbor to Tongabezi (see below), this romantic retreat, its rooms built on stilts right on the Zambezi River, is the most overtly colonial of the Zambian lodges (it was in fact the inspiration for the Royal Livingstone), and one of our favorite lodges. Very much owner-run by Peter (who virtually hand-built the lodge, one of the first on the Zambezi, from scratch around an old farmhouse), the overall service standards are impeccable. Set amid lovely lawns, the main house is filled with period pieces and the atmosphere genteel yet informal. Meals are elegant affairs, with candlelit dinners often served in the gardens, after which you may choose to take a drink in the library, partake of a game of moonlit croquet, or flop into your huge bed, romantically swathed in mosquito nets, with the soothing sound of the river below. During the day, enjoy a rejuvenating riverside massage treatment, or laze around the gorgeous pool, located on the high bank of the river with great views of the dense bush beyond. Cuisine standards are high. It's located 30 minutes from the falls.

Bookings through S.A.: www.wilderness-safaris.com. ℂ **27/11/807-1800.** Lodge: 263/11/40-6563. Fax 27/11/883-0911. Or www.theriverclubafrica.com. 10 units (1 family unit). $1,060 double; rates include all meals and drinks except for premium-brand alcohol imports and laundry. Rates also include 5 house activities: Vic Falls tour; sunset river cruise; game drives; fishing; Livingstone tours and African village tour. MC, V. **Amenities:** Dining room; lounge; bush golf; canoeing; croquet; pétanque; snooker; sunset cruises; day trips (to Mosi-Oa-Tunya National Park, Livingstone and Railway Museum, croc farm); fishing; Internet; Wi-Fi; library; pool. *In room:* Hair dryer, fans, plunge pools (some).

Royal Livingstone ★★ & Zambezi Sun ☺ The single biggest reason to book into either of these is the proximity to the falls—the park entrance is 5 minutes walking distance, so you can visit as often as you want. It's also a good option if you like busy resort facilities—part of the Sun International hotel and entertainment complex, it incorporates the two hotels as well as **The Activity Centre,** an adult playground with a small casino, shops, eateries, offices, and banking facilities. The Zambezi Sun is pretty awful—often filled to capacity with tour groups, and very much a three-star resort hotel (from $552 double). If you want similar proximity but far more elegant surrounds the Royal Livingstone is worth the extra $150. It's large and also privy to package tours, but the decor and style here is in a class of its own. No expense has been spared in recreating opulent double volume public spaces with the graciousness the Edwardian/Victorian era; aside from the gentleman's-style club bar and luxurious lounge, there is a deck right on the river, which is a profoundly peaceful spot. Rooms however are bland and pokey; service is patchy. If you're on honeymoon you'd be much better off at more exclusive River Club or Tongabezi/Sindabezi.

Mosi-oa-Tunya Rd., P.O. Box 60151, Livingstone, Zambia. www.royal-livingstone-hotel.com or www.suninternational.com. ℂ **27/11/780/7810.** 173 units. Internet rate: $698 double, includes breakfast and park fees. Rack rate $785 double. Suite $1,898–$2,842, depending on size. Children pay 25% or 50% depending on age. AC, DC, MC, V. **Amenities:** 2 restaurants; activity center; sunset river deck; 2 pools. *In room:* A/C, TV, hair dryer, minibar (Livingstone only).

Toka Leya ★★★ ☺ This small tented camp is only about 10km (6¼ miles) upstream from the falls, yet—with only 12 tents, and no visible neighbors—as tranquil and exclusive a location as those farther upstream (though it is not as elevated, nor as groomed and luxurious as River Club or Tongabezi). We love sleeping under canvas, and the huge tents are supremely comfortable and elegantly furnished (one with double bedroom for families), with wildlife (elephants, hippo) often within view. The lounge-bar terrace is right on the river, as is the pool. Staff is laid back and contagiously happy; there are plenty of activities included in the rate and they make sure it all happens. Many of the guests are either on their way to or back from Wilderness Safari's Botswana camps, and the atmosphere is cosmopolitan and gregarious, as befits a camp this size (the inviting bar, with sunset views, is where everyone gathers to discuss their day). Cuisine average, though it's fun to have pizza if you've overdosed on the heavier meaty items that seem to still predominate.

Bookings through Wilderness Safaris. www.wilderness-safaris.com. ✆ **27/11/807-1800.** Lodge: 263/11/40-6563. Fax 27/11/883-0911. 10 units. $1,060 double; rates include all meals and drinks except for premium-brand alcohol imports. Rates also include Vic Falls tour, village tour, Livingstone tours and sunset cruises. MC, V. **Amenities:** Dining room; riverside lounge-bar; canoeing; sunset cruises; day trips (to Mosi-Oa-Tunya National Park, Livingstone museum and shops, Railway Museum, bridge tours; croc farm, and so on); Internet; Wi-Fi; pool. *In room:* Hair dryer, fans.

Tongabezi ★★★ Situated 20km (12 miles) upstream from the falls, overlooking a broad expanse of the Zambezi, romantic Tongabezi is a destination in its own right, with a range of luxurious accommodation options mostly open to the elements, various ways to make the most of the stunning river views, and superb cuisine. The thatched River Cottages, all with private verandas overlooking the river, are lovely (and closed off with walls and doors) but ideally you should try to reserve one of the huge, completely private and open River Houses—particularly the **Tree House,** which is carved out of the rock, with the mighty Zambezi River just meters from your bedroom. If you don't like the idea of being open to the elements, Nut House has slide and fold doors that open onto your private infinity plunge pool. There is also a brand-new family unit—with its own pool and walled compound; this is a great option for a family or friends traveling together. But for the ultimate in romance, a couple of nights at the satellite **Sindabezi Island Camp** ★★★ is a must for the more adventurous. Located on its own island (less than 10 min. by boat downstream), the five open-to-the-elements chalets are elevated into the riverbank, private and shaded by trees with en-suite bathrooms (hot water, flushing toilets) and wonderful river views. Dinner is served on raised decks and lit by candle and paraffin lamp—a truly romantic and 100% restorative experience—one of our favorite in Africa. Pity there's no pool, but you can always spend part of your day at Tongabezi.

Private Bag 31, Livingstone. www.tongabezi.com. ✆ **260/213/32-7450** or 260/213/32-4450. Fax 260/213/32-7484. Tongabezi 12 units. Sindabezi 5 units. Tongabezi river cottages $940–$1,130 double; Tongabezi houses $1,150–$1,550 double. Sindabezi $830–$1,080 double. Rates are fully inclusive of meals and drinks (excluding premium liquor), as well as boat trips, canoe trips, game drive and falls visit (park fees extra), local village, Livingstone museum and shopping. MC, V. Children under 7 by arrangement if not booking the new family unit; 7-14 sharing 50%. **Amenities:** Dining areas; bar; bird walks; bush/gorge walks; canoeing; fishing; game drives; library; pool; sunrise and sunset boat cruises; village tours visit to Zambian side of falls.

In Zimbabwe

If Ilala is full, Elephant Camp too pricey and Vic Falls Hotel too old-fashioned, the **Victoria Falls Safari Lodge** (10 min. from the falls) is more resortlike than the choice options reviewed below, but has lovely views of the surrounding bush, including a very productive waterhole, and friendly service (www.victoria-falls-safari-lodge.com; $400–$450 double for standard room).

Ilala Lodge ★★ 🏷 ☺ This gracious old dame, an easy 10-minute walk from the falls, is a Vic Falls stalwart, offering comfortable bedrooms, excellent service, and gardens that invite a second round of gin and tonics. It's relatively small (much more intimate than nearby Vic Falls Hotel) yet offers big hotel service: Its on-site sister-company, Zambezi Wildlife Safaris, is excellent and will arrange all activities, tours, and transfers. Palm Restaurant also has a good reputation, though it's a bit old-fashioned haute for some. With its shaped thatch roof, cane furniture, and lawns with views of the thick bush of the national park, it's one of the most comforting hotels: A timeless classic, well run, and the best value option on either side of the falls. The hotel is not completely fenced in, so don't be surprised if you hear the sounds of elephants and warthogs feeding outdoors at night.

411 Livingstone Way, Box 18, Victoria Falls. www.ilalalodge.com ☎ **263/13/44737,** 38, or 39. Fax 263/13/44740. 32 units. $286–$410 double. Rates include breakfast. Children under 12 pay $61 if sharing with parents; $72 if not. DC, MC, V. **Amenities:** Restaurant; bar/terrace; pool; room service; Wi-Fi. *In room:* TV, hair dryer.

The Elephant Camp ★★★ ☺ This luxurious new tented camp, a 15-minute drive from the falls, has a great view of the spray—distant enough here that they really do appear to be "clouds" billowing into the sky. It's an ephemeral view you won't tire of, most magnificent first thing in the morning (before the thermals reduce the size somewhat). Set on its own private reserve, with only nine privately located tents, the atmosphere here is very tranquil (not the best choice if you want action or people watching), and invites relaxation in your huge tent "suite," each with own comfortably furnished lounge area, plunge pool, four-poster bed, Victorian bath, indoor and outdoor showers, as well as essential luxuries (A/C and minibar). The kitchen produces superb meals, and you will be thoroughly spoiled by Jonathan, the gregarious, efficient manager, and his small but excellent team. A range of activities are included in the rate.

Reservations through Wild Horizons. www.wildhorizons.co.za. ☎ **263/13/44571.** 9 units. $650 double. Rates include all meals, drinks (excluding premium brands), airport transfers (VFA), 2 transfers to Victoria Falls town per day, laundry and Wild Horizons elephants meeting. Children 7–12 pay 50% of adult rate. No credit cards in camp. **Amenities:** Dining/lounge/bar terrace; pool. *In room:* A/C, hair dryer, minibar.

Victoria Falls Hotel ★★ ☺ 🏷 Located on sprawling grounds, this Edwardian colonial-era hotel (built in 1904, and much of it unchanged), is imbued with a great historical atmosphere, and the rates have never been better. Like Ilala it's also in a prime spot: within Victoria Falls National Park, overlooking the equally gracious Victoria Falls Bridge, and walking distance of the falls (follow a path through the gardens). A member of Leading Hotels of the World (though it's not luxurious in any contemporary sense), it was built for Cecil Rhodes's Cape-to-Cairo railway; today it's a reminder of the opulence of a bygone age, with columns, arched loggias, broad verandas, and chandeliers. The deluxe rooms and suites with views of the spray and bridge are definitely worth it; though note that rooms in original wings have bathrooms that will appear tiny to travelers used to modern en-suite room configurations. Enjoy drinks and high tea served on a generous, sweeping terrace with excellent views—a must even if you're not staying here. Service is well meaning but can be slow.

Mallet Dr., Box 10, Victoria Falls. www.victoriafallshotel.com ☎ **263/13/44751.** Fax 263/13/42354. 161 units. Standard room $250 double, deluxe room $300 double, suite $380. Rates include breakfast. AE, DC, MC, V. **Amenities:** 3 restaurants; 2 bars; various lounges; babysitting; chapel; Internet; library; playground; pool; room service; spa; tennis. *In room:* A/C, TV, hair dryer.

ORIGINAL EDEN: BOTSWANA

Botswana is home to one of the world's greatest natural phenomena: the largest inland delta in the world, a 15,000-sq.-km (5,850-sq.-mile) tranquil flood plain that fans out in the northwestern corner of the country, creating a paradise of palms, papyrus, and crystal-clear channels and deep lagoons. Set in a massive sea of desert sand, this fragile wonderland of waterways, islands, and forests is an oasis for wildlife drawn to its life-giving waters from the surrounding thirstland. For millennia, the Okavango Delta has reverberated to the primal sounds of nature: the twittering of birds and frogs; the rustling of reeds as wildebeest, hartebeest, buffalo, and zebra roam the islands; the splash of elephants wading across channels guarded by grunting hippos and silent crocs; and the hair-raising call of the predators that rule the night.

But it is not only animals and birds that are attracted to this huge, verdant oasis. With admirable prescience, the Botswana government has always operated a policy of low-volume, high-income tourism, thereby protecting southern Africa's premier wilderness destination from resort developers and large-scale package tourism. However, this exclusivity comes at a price—yet it doesn't stop people from flocking to claim one of the limited beds in one of the world's most game-rich and unspoiled wilderness areas. To service these visitors, a number of safari companies have been established in and around the delta, particularly in the Moremi Game Reserve, in the northeastern sector. It is both expensive and complicated to travel independently in Botswana so visitors are advised to contact one of these companies to arrange their itinerary; all those listed in this chapter are recommended. Most offer full-package vacations that cover the delta and environs and will organize everything for you from including flights and transfers to accommodations and a variety of game-viewing options.

Remember that if you do a whistle-stop visit, flying in 1 or even 2 nights and out the next day, you will be disappointed. The delta has its own unique moods and rhythms and a varying landscape: To experience these, you should plan to spend 4 nights here, preferably at two camps located in different habitats.

Aside from this, there is more to Botswana than the delta. To the northeast lies the **Chobe National Park,** a 12,000-sq.-km (4,680-sq.-mile) home to some 100,000 elephants. Lying between Chobe and the Okavango Delta are three bordering concessions, each offering far more exclusivity and terrain as beautiful as the delta: the 23,000-hectare (573,000-acre) **Kwando** reserve in the north; the 125,000-hectare (308,750-acre) **Linyanti** reserve in the east and, to the west of Linyanti, the 135,000-hectare (333,450-acre) **Selinda** reserve. Southward stretches the **Kalahari Desert,** with its spectacular **Makgadikgadi** and **Nxai Pans,** both of them protected by national parks, and the 5-million-hectare (12-million-acre) **Central Kalahari Game Reserve,** where the space is so vast that it is said you can hear the stars sing. Most safari companies include the Chobe area on their itineraries, but you would do well to also consider a 2-day sojourn taking in the stark, humbling beauty of the Kalahari and its pans.

But if you have time to explore only one area, make a trip to the delta your highest priority, not least because even this most pristine and popular wilderness area is under constant threat, and tourist numbers despite the high price tag provide credence to the conservationists' battle. A shortage of good grazing on adjacent lands makes the lush grass in the delta a standing temptation to stock farmers, especially in times of drought. Aside from this there is the ever-present pressure on dwindling water resources, not only from Botswana's thirsty diamond-mining industry but the ever-expanding town of Maun (principal jumping-off point for the delta), needs that must be balanced with the long-term need to protect this untamed African Eden, thus far unadulterated by our presence.

ORIENTATION
Visitor Information

Botswana's **Department of Tourism** has a new much improved website (www.botswanatourism.co.bw). Alternatively, contact one of the specialist safari operators listed later in the chapter directly.

Note: Should there be higher than average rainfall (as there was in 2011) the Okavango water levels can rise to such an extent that numerous areas of the Okavango Delta may become inaccessible later in the season when the floods peak, so it's worth dealing with one of the specialists recommended when planning your itinerary.

Getting There

BY PLANE   Air Botswana (www.airbotswana.co.bw) flies directly from Johannesburg to **Maun (MUB),** which is the starting point for most destinations in the Okavango Delta. Prices can vary greatly depending on the month you fly, but you're not going to get much change from R3,000 for a Jo'burg round-trip. Most operators will arrange for you to fly into Maun and then transfer you to your Delta camp by charter flight (see "Getting Around," below). To reach Chobe National Park and environs, you'll fly to **Kasane (BBK),** from where you can transfer by road; your operator or lodge should arrange this pickup. A more cost-effective route to Kasane is to fly into **Livingstone airport (LVI),** the Zambian airport close to Victoria Falls, and a mere 90-minute drive from Kasane; the road transfer will cost around $60. There are two budget airlines that fly to Livingstone (one-time round-trip to Jo'burg R1,800), so you could save quite a bit routing via Livingstone (and see the magnificent falls!). Spend the night at one of our recommended lodgings, then transfer by road to your Chobe lodgings: See the Victoria Falls chapter for more information on flights and transfers.

Botswana

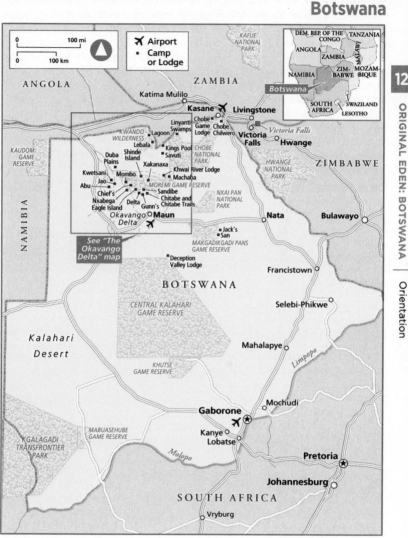

Getting Around

BY PLANE The region's large wilderness areas are mostly inaccessible by car, so flying is the most sensible way to get around, usually taking off from Maun. **Wilderness Air** (previously Sefofane; © 267/686-0778; www.sefofane.com) is the biggest; a well-run operator with superb safety record; you can query prices online with ease. Another reliable operator worth asking for a comparative quote if you are planning your own safari is **Mack Air** (© 267/686-0675; www.mackair.co.bw). It's certainly an exciting way to travel: Views are spectacular; the plane often has to buzz the airstrip to clear herds of grazing animals, and the "departure/arrivals" lounge may be a bench under a tree. Note that there may be an additional departure tax of $13; check with your agent or lodge if you need to carry this cash.

BY CAR   Traveling under your own steam at your own pace could be the adventure of a lifetime, but it will certainly affect your time as it takes a great deal of organization. You will need permits and a fully equipped four-wheel-drive and camping vehicle (which should cost around Pula 1,340 per day). For details, log on to **Maun Self Drive 4x4** (www.maunselfdrive4x4.com). The delta is huge, but because of variable water levels and private concessions, there are only four "regular" campsites available in the Moremi Wildlife Reserve; there are more in and around Chobe. Facilities are simple, providing drinkable water, showers (equipped with boilers), and rudimentary toilets. Both Maun and Kasane (612km/380 miles away) have large, well-stocked supermarkets.

WITH A PACKAGE TOUR   In Botswana, it really is worth using an established operator (recommendations to follow) to make your bookings and compare package prices before booking. Packages include, among other things, transport to the lodge or base camp; accommodations; food; most drinks; game-viewing, fishing, and photographic expeditions; professional guides; boat rental; and *mokoro* trips (sometimes you pay extra for park entry fees). See recommended operators under "Specialist Safaris & Operators," below.

WHEN TO GO   The **delta's** high season is predominantly during winter (June–Oct). Temperatures are cool enough that you'll have to pack in warm layers for the night, but game can be less concentrated because of the floods. October is an ideal month because game centers on dwindling water. During low season (Nov, Apr–May), temperatures are sweltering. Surprisingly healthy game populations move through the **Kalahari** year-round, but the desert comes to life with the summer rainfall (Dec–Apr), and thousands of plains game, such as springbok, gemsbok, and wildebeest, converge to feed on the grasses, with predators in close attendance.

[FastFACTS] BOTSWANA

Airport   See "Getting There" in this chapter and in chapter 13.

Banks   In Maun: Open Monday through Friday from 9am to 2.30pm (Wed noon), and Saturday from 8:15am to 10:45pm.

Doctor   If you need a doctor or dentist in Maun, the **Delta Medical Centre** is on the Tsheko-Tsheko road, which runs through the center of town (☏ **267/686-1411;** www.delta medicalcentre.org). Should you experience a medical emergency in the bush, the

operators and camps recommended below will take appropriate and immediate action.

Documents   See "Entry Requirements" and "Customs" in chapter 13.

Drugstore   Okavango Pharmacy (☏ **267/686-0043**) is also on Maun's main street, in the Lewis Building opposite Riley's garage complex.

Electricity   As in the rest of southern Africa, you'll need an adapter/voltage converter. Botswana uses 220/240V 15/13-amp

plug sockets. Plugs are two- and three-pin, round and flat. Remember that many bush camps do not have electricity but run on generators.

Embassies & Consulates   U.S. Embassy (☏ **267/395-3982;** the after-hours emergency telephone number is ☏ **267/395-7111**); the **British High Commission** (☏ **267/395-2841**); the **Canadian Consulate** (☏ **267/390-4411**); the **Irish Honorary Consul** (☏ **267/390-5807**). Note that the Australian and New

Zealand offices are in Pretoria, South Africa.

Language English is the official language and is widely spoken; Setswana is the national language, spoken by the Batswana people, who make up 50% of the population.

Safety Before you depart, consult your physician (or a travel-health specialist) about starting a course of antimalarial prophylactics. For more on malaria and safety in the bush, see chapter 13.

Taxes Sales tax is 10%, included in all prices quoted in this chapter, unless otherwise indicated.

Telephone & Internet Most camps communicate with Maun and each other via satellite radio and will transmit only emergency messages this way, rendering you unreachable for the duration of your stay. Few Botswana camps offer Internet access (and even if they do, cannot guarantee

the quality of the line), so let everyone know, and enjoy being marooned. *Note:* This chapter lists numbers for Botswana and South Africa, indicated by their country codes. Remember, Botswana has no regional or town codes.

To call southern Africa from another country: Dial the international access code (United States or Canada 011, United Kingdom or New Zealand 00, Australia 0011), plus the country code (**27** for South Africa, **263** for Zimbabwe, **267** for Botswana, and **260** for Zambia), plus the local number minus the 0 at the beginning of the city/area code. **To make an international call:** Dial 00, wait for a dial tone, then dial the country code (United States or Canada **1,** United Kingdom **44,** Australia **61,** New Zealand **64**), the area code, and the local number. **To make calls within Botswana:** Drop the 267

country code; there are no area codes.

Time Zone Botswana is 2 hours ahead of GMT, or 7 hours ahead of Eastern Standard Time.

Tipping Tipping at bush and delta camps is at guests' discretion, but a general rule of thumb is $5 to $10 per person per day (depending on length of stay), to be shared among the staff (look or ask for communal tipping box). Your guide is tipped separately, again at your discretion; the guideline is $10 to $20 per person per day, but the figure you pay is yours to decide.

Water Water in camp is drinkable, but most camps/lodges do supply plenty of bottled water. If there is a choice between purified water in reusable jugs or glass bottles, opt for these rather than the environmentally costly plastic bottled water.

SPECIALIST SAFARIS & OPERATORS

You'll have no trouble finding safari operators or packages. They run the gamut to suit a range of interests and pockets, from fly-in safaris to luxurious lodges, to all-hands-on-deck-type trips with nights spent under canvas.

Mobile vs. Fly-in Safaris

Certainly, the only way to appreciate the broad changes of scenery in Botswana is to plan a trip that encompasses the delta (in which you should try to visit both a "wet" (for mokoro trips) and "dry" (for game drives) camp, or one that combines these terrains), perhaps the greater Chobe Area, and a brief sojourn in the Kalahari. Note that Victoria Falls (see chapter 11) is an easy add-on, and hugely recommended if you have never been before (and just want to relax, with no scheduled activities). To cover this, you'll need to stay a minimum of 7 nights (preferably double that!). If you don't have enough time or don't like to move around that much, combine a 3-night Delta stay with 2 nights in the Kalahari for greatest contrast.

Most people with limited time opt for fly-in safaris, moving between camps to experience different landscapes within an hour, and usually with the same operator to ensure smooth transfers between camps (the exception being the Kalahari region, which many operators in the north do not cover; if you wish to add on a visit to this area, book a recommended operator in the north and then with Uncharted Africa, the best Kalahari outfit). Depending on your budget and what you want out of your trip, however, mobile safaris—the more traditional safari, in which you ride, walk, or canoe to your next camp—range from basic participation tours, during which you may be expected to erect your own tent (though this is increasingly rare), to the ultra-luxurious expeditions that require you to lift a finger only to summon another cold drink. Participants are transported in a suitably modified open-topped vehicle or a mokoro (the indigenous canoe) or modernized version, and they camp or lodge overnight at predetermined destinations. Usually the camps will be without electricity or the comforts of modern plumbing, but the experience of an authentic back-to-nature safari in this prime wilderness is unforgettably thrilling.

The following operators are mostly local to southern Africa. If you are using an international agent, chances are they will be using one of the following as their ground operator, so you may want to check that you're not saving money by booking direct. Also, if you are using an agent at home, make sure they are prepared to combine camps that are owned/operated by separate outfits if the itinerary demands it. For separate reviews of the top camps, see "Where to Stay & Eat," later in this chapter.

Tip: Another way to shop is to visit online travel agency www.africatravelresource. com. Their agents have personally inspected the accommodation scene and they provide honest online information on most lodges and camps in Botswana, and will create an itinerary to suit your budget.

African Bushcamps ★★★ 🌿 🎒 A small portfolio of owner-run semipermanent tented camps in Khwai (delta), Linyanti/Selinda, and Kalahari concession areas, as well as offering mobile tented camp expeditions, this is for the luxury camping seeker who is looking for the real deal: a simple, understated tented safari experience, similar to the original explorations of Africa, hosted by a couple that is passionate about both the bush and the guest experience. Great value for your money. www.african bushcamps.com

&Beyond ★★★ &Beyond (previously CC Africa) is, with Orient Express, the most stylish, luxurious safari outfit, known for the great design ethos of its camps. Operators are masters on how to escalate the guest experience into the realm of the unforgettable, while the exclusivity, privacy, and space of its suites are hard to beat. Service at their top camps is also top notch, with private butlers and the like. They also have a good selection of luxury camps in South and East Africa—booking at more than one you can negotiate discounts. &Beyond also offer a travel agent service to camps and hotels other than its own, so they can put together an itinerary anywhere to suit your budget. www.andbeyond.com.

Bush Ways Safaris ★ 🌿 This operator offers small and custom participation tours traveling overland through the country in an open Land Rover. Tours are themed around certain animals and best suited for more adventurous travelers who want an authentic camping experience in the wilds, with guests staying in small dome tents and evenings spent under stars around campfire. Several itineraries are available, taking in all parts of Botswana, including Chobe, the Delta, Makgadikgadi, and the Kalahari. www.bushways.com.

Footsteps in Africa ★★ ✔ ☺ Footsteps specializes in making Botswana affordable without compromising on comfort. You'll fly in with Delta Air, which it owns, and stay in moderate budget camps. These include the understandably popular Oddballs (offering overnight mokoro trips and camping on islands as side trips in season), Delta Camp (ideal for families, with four chalets sleeping three or four), and Mapula Lodge. They also have camps in up-and-coming Selinda concession, as well as a few options in Makgadikgadi/Kalahari. It's an unpretentious outfit, offering much more for your money than most; however it's a trade-only company so they will provide you with a relevant trade partner in your country. www.footsteps-in-africa.com.

Ker & Downey ★★★ Aside from its own concessions, this well-known tour operator has a super hand-picked property portfolio across southern Africa. With perhaps the best walking program (Footsteps) and mokoro (canoe) trails (see below) in the Delta, Ker & Downey expeditions are excellent value for those who want an authentic safari experience (fly-camping, but the comforts of staff). Agents will customize a very personal itinerary, depending on interest and budget; given their spread throughout southern Africa, you could do a grand journey across five countries, including semiurban and city destinations. (Wilderness Safaris, with a far greater spread of camps in southern Africa, is focused on wilderness areas.) www.kerdowney.com.

Kwando Safaris ★★ ✔ This small outfit is a relatively good value, with some of the best-located camps in Botswana and well spread from Kwara and Little Kwara in Delta area, and Lebala near Linyanti marshes, to their two camps in the Central Kalahari desert. It's more expensive than Footsteps, which is where you should look if you are watching your budget, but accommodation is more luxurious (though not up to Wilderness Safari standards). hwww.kwando.co.za.

Mike Penman's Wild Lifestyles ★★★ Voted 1 of the top 15 safari guides in the world by *Condé Nast Traveler,* Penman—who has produced and facilitated a number of wildlife documentaries—offers private, custom-made luxury tented safaris aimed particularly at people with an interest in photography or filmmaking. Tents usually house no more than four guests. For contact information, see "Photography & Film Safaris," below.

Moremi Safaris ★★★ Moremi owns a few camps (such as the excellent value Xakanaxa, reviewed below) but is an operator that will create an itinerary utilizing camps owned by others in order to best service the needs of the customer, such as a Wilderness Camp in the Delta with a Sanctuary lodge in Chobe. Or you can inquire into an elephant-back safari and they will recommend the three camps (Baines', Stanley's, and Abu) that offer this, and so on. They also cover Namibia, Zambia, Zimbabwe, South Africa, and Seychelles. www.moremi-safaris.com.

Orient Express Safaris ★★★ Orient Express needs no introduction. The well-heeled international globetrotter has a choice of three camps in Botswana: two in the delta (both incredible locations) and one in Chobe. In classic Orient Express style, all three offer top-of-the-range, unabashed luxury. &Beyond has perhaps the edge in terms of camp design and knowledge of the bush, but the staff training at Orient Express shines through, and Eagle Island Camp has perhaps the best bar in Africa. www.orient-express.com.

Penduka Safaris ★ Though it's based in Namibia, this trusted, reliable operator is one of the most established mobile safari companies in Botswana, offering fully catered and serviced yet rustic camping trips in campsites throughout most of southern Africa. www.pendukasafaris.com.

Sanctuary Retreats ★★   This top-end operator, a division of Abercrombie & Kent, offers a similar experience (at a similar price) as Wilderness Safaris. With just four lovely camps in northern Botswana (Baines', Stanley's, Chief's, and Chobe Chilwero, all reviewed below), they don't penetrate southern Africa like Wilderness Safaris does, but they can set up an itinerary that will take you from Botswana through Zambia to Tanzania and Kenya, with a side trip to Uganda to visit the gorillas. www.sanctuaryretreats.com.

Uncharted Africa Safari Co. ★★★   This is the foremost operator in Botswana's Kalahari region. Besides the luxurious HQ camp (Jack's Camp; see later in this chapter), you can ask for mobile expeditions into the desert, as well as trips north to the delta and Chobe—though that area is better serviced by Wilderness Safaris. If landscapes area as important to you as animals, I would urge you to include a sojourn at one of their desert camps, a personal favorite, into your Delta trip. www.unchartedafrica.com.

Wilderness Safaris ★★★   Wilderness Safaris has some of the best concessions in Botswana, and by far the most camps. Since launching the much-lauded Mombo Camp in mid-2000, the company has grown exponentially. Today they operate some 60 lodges and camps in southern Africa, producing enough revenue to conserve 2.7 million hectares of wilderness. Service and design is not quite as OTT as &Beyond's—with the exception of their pricey Premier Camps, the ethos is determinedly conservation. But this company has garnered immense respect within the industry, even among direct competitors. Given also their impeccable responsible tourism standards, it's a top choice.

Mokoro & Island Camping Expeditions

The cheapest and one of the most adventurous ways to enjoy the delta is to join a mokoro trip through the islands, accompanied by a poler with an intimate knowledge of these waters. **Oddballs** specializes in budget mokoro camping trips and also runs one of the best-known budget camps in the delta (for more, see "Where to Stay & Eat"). A little more pricey (but still way less per night than staying at one of the Delta's permanent camps, and a very exclusive, authentic experience), is Ker & Downey's **Kanana Mokoro Trail ★★★**, in the western part of the Delta. The trail camp is on a remote island and accommodates a maximum of four people in two twin bedded tents (both with bucket shower and bush toilet); besides the luxury of being alone on an island in paradise, the camp includes the services of five staff members: a personal chef, waiter, housekeeper, and mokoro guides ($470–$760 per person per night all inclusive, depending on season; www.kerdowney.com). Another great option is the 3-night **Selinda Canoe Trail ★★★**, departing every 3 days from (May–Oct). After being picked up from Selinda airstrip you are driven to a starting point on the Selinda spillway, paddling downstream, stopping whenever there is anything of interest on the banks or water, and overnighting in true wilderness areas. Nights are spent in fly camps (comprising dome tents with hot bucket showers and bush toilets) along the way. For more information on this trail contact Wilderness Safaris (www.wilderness-safaris-com).

Luxury River Safari

The **Zambezi Queen** ★★★ (www.zambeziqueen.com) is the newest addition to the luxury safari scene: A floating five-star hotel, with opulent interiors and superb service standards, operating on the Chobe river. This is ideal for a grand special event party (14 suites, sleeping max 28) or—with spacious suites, each with floor-to-ceiling windows for in-bed views of the action on the riverbanks—a romantic getaway for two. The entire upper deck is a cool, elegantly furnished lounge/bar/dinging/pool terrace, and the general atmosphere is one of low-key celebration, with plenty of opportunities to get to know your fellow "houseboat" guests. Choose between 2- or 3-night itinerary (from R7,350 double per night to R9,850 double per night, depending on season, for standard cabin. High season is May–Nov). The quickest way to get here is to fly to Kasane but you can also fly to Livingstone to view the Falls; the Zambezi Queen is berthed a mere 80km (50 miles) from Livingstone airport (see chapter 11 for more information).

Elephant-Back Safaris

For a discussion of the ethics of navigating your safari via animals, see p. 305.

Abu Camp ★★★ ☺   Randall Moore's pioneering camp, located in the 173,000ha Abu Concession, was the first the world to introduce fully fledged safaris on the back of a pachyderm, and it remains a great way to explore the Delta. Elephants cope equally well with water and sand, and they also get very close to other game; guests ride on comfortable, custom-made saddles. Accommodations comprise five extremely luxurious, custom-designed en-suite tents, furnished with mahogany sleigh beds in what is billed as "Afro-Bedouin" style. The more mod **Seba Camp,** overlooking a perennial lagoon, offers five additional en-suite tents and there is also a two-bedroom Villa for families, featured in *Travel + Leisure's* list of the 50 Most Romantic Places on Earth. The main drawbacks are the price (it has the dubious distinction of being the most expensive camp in Botswana) and the southwestern location (game on the eastern part of the Delta tends to be better). **Note:** For a less expensive elephant experience, book with Doug Groves at **Baines' Camp** (see "Where to Stay & Eat," below, or visit www.sanctuaryretreats.com). Or for a real money saver, book into **Macatoo** (below) and enjoy the same superb game-viewing, only from the back of a horse (at a tenth of the price).

Reservations: www.abucamp.co.za; www.sebacamp.co.za; or www.wilderness-safaris.com. © **267/686-1260.** Abu $5,248 double. AE, DC, MC, V. Abu camp is closed in wet season (mid-Dec to Feb). No children under 12.

Horse Safaris

African Horseback Safaris/Macatoo ★★★ 🏇   Also located in the scenically splendid Abu Concession, this is the top choice for both horse-riding enthusiasts and partners who are simply looking for an elegant camp with superb food and plenty of other (nonriding) ways of exploring the 200-hectare (500-acre) concession. Note that if you are going to be riding (there's a great selection of horses and tack) you will need to be reasonably fit (4–6 hr. spent in the saddle daily) and a competent, confident rider—you are in a true wilderness area, riding through rivers and amid predators, so horses are agile, and you need to be too. The safaris are based at the lovely **Macatoo Camp** ★★★, rated one of the most desirable camps in the entire delta by travelers, and excellent value too. The camp features walk-in, twin bedded tents furnished in vintage Africa style, each with their own en-suite shower and toilet. There is a comfortably furnished mess tent and a private pool. On 7-day safaris guests have the opportunity to experience the thrill of riding out to mobile fly-camps.

P.O. Box 20671. Maun, Botswana. www.africanhorseback.com. ℂ **267/686-1523.** £360–£450 per person per night, depending on season. AE, MC, V. Rates are all-inclusive except for tips and curio purchases. Children riders must be 12 and older, or choose not to ride.

Okavango Horse Safaris ★★★ These safaris are run in a private concession in the western delta area, bordering Moremi Game Reserve, and take you deep into the wetlands. Expect to spend between 4 and 6 hours a day in the saddle. Again, you will need to be a relatively experienced rider with the ability to gallop out of trouble. The tack is English style, and each saddle has a seat-saver for comfort. Trail riders move from **Kujwana Camp** (spacious safari tents with shower en suite and flush toilets) to **Mokolwane** (treehouses 2m/6½ ft.) off the ground with flush toilets and hot showers) to **Fly Camp** (spacious Meru tents with camp beds, bush toilets, and bucket showers). A maximum of eight riders can participate, and the safaris last between 5 and 10 days. Besides horse rides, guests are treated to game drives, bush walks, and mokoro trips, which helps keep activities varied and interesting. The camps are closed December through February.

Private Bag 23, Maun. www.okavangohorse.com. ℂ **267/686-1671.** Fax 267/686-1672. £380–£470 per person per night depending on season. Rates are all-inclusive. Transfers are £80–£195 per person return from Maun, depending on method of transportation. Single supplement (50%) for people unwilling to share. No credit card facilities. Children are accepted if they are strong, confident riders.

Cycling Safaris

MASHATU ★★ Radio-linked groups of cyclists set out at dawn and again at dusk on mountain bikes and overnight in wilderness camps. The focus is not so much on game tracking (at least not as much as the horseback safaris above, where the animals can take you over any kind of terrain) but more about enjoying the landscape; you will however encounter game that similarly enjoys the unencumbered traveling along dirt tracks. The most popular is the Mashatu 3-night, 4-day program, but bespoke cycling safaris can be created to suit the needs and skills of minimum four cyclists; spend an additional night at Mashatu Tented Camp and you can also enjoy a couple of game drives. For more information, call ℂ **27/11/442-2267** or 0861-SAFARI (723274) or log on to www.cyclemashatu.com.

Walking Safaris

FOOTSTEPS ACROSS THE DELTA ★★★ 🍴📷 It doesn't get more authentic than at this camp, the best for walking safaris in the Delta. Every day a small group of guests (could be just the two of you; never more than four) make their way by foot and/or mokoro. The emphasis is on enjoying the slow pace of the delta—the maximum distance each day is about 6km (3¾ miles), and you can travel light. Accommodations are in three twin-bedded en-suite tents (six maximum, though you may be fortunate enough to be just two); cuisine is exceptional, given the remoteness of the location. There's no electricity or flush toilets, but the experience is in many ways the ultimate in luxury for the right kind of person, and you can combine with a couple of nights' luxury at Ker & Downey's permanent camps. For more details, see Ker & Downey (www.kerdowney.com); Footsteps rate is $460 to $565 per person per night (all inclusive), depending on the season. To explore a different ecosystem in the highly rated Linyanti concession, look into **Linyanti Walking Safaris ★★★** (www.africanbushcamps.com); you are accommodated similarly, also with a maximum of four participants per safari; see accommodation review below.

Photography & Film Safaris

Mike Penman's Wild Lifestyles ★★★ These highly adventurous yet luxury tented safaris focus on learning about wildlife while affording you the best opportunities to capture the experience on film. Penman has been involved in conservation, photography, and filmmaking in Botswana for 18 years, producing his own documentaries and helping independent filmmakers and major TV networks. He personally conducts safaris into Moremi, the delta, Kalahari, Makgadikgadi, Nxai Pans, and Drotsky's Caves. Penman is known for his bold approach to lions and his ability to get right into the mix of things, placing you in a great position from which to capture the moment. Other, tamer photographic and birding safaris with professional guides are offered by Wilderness Safaris (see "Specialist Safaris & Operators," earlier in this chapter).

P.O. Box 250059, Maun, Botswana. www.wildlifestyles.com or www.mikepenman.com. (© **267/686-3664.** Fax 267/686-1045. Mobile safaris $450–$650 per person per day, depending on level of luxury required.

Cultural Safaris

If you're interested in Bushman or "San" culture, make sure you spend a few nights with **Uncharted Africa Safari Co.** in the Kalahari (see Jack's Camp, San Camp, and Planet Baobab, later in this chapter); one of the most exciting trips held once a year, personally led by Ralph Bousfield, is an 8-night initiation hunt, a rapidly disappearing Bushmen ritual. Uncharted will also, along with such operators as **Moremi Safaris & Tours,** organize a visit to the **Tsodilo Hills** (in the northwest, near the panhandle), where you can view some 3,000 rock paintings. The paintings are known for their fine clarity and wide variety, and trips can be made by air or four-wheel drive. There is also a traditional village in the foothills. An even more focused San experience is to be had at **Grasslands Bushman Lodge,** located on the western boundary of the Central Kalahari Game Reserve and operated by **Footsteps in Africa.** Activities encompass San clan activities (hunting, gathering, games, and ritual) with the San people who live there as well as game drives (both off-road and at night), an introduction to the predator conservation project, and horse-riding. For contact details for both, see "Specialist Safaris & Operators," earlier in this chapter.

THE OKAVANGO DELTA & MOREMI GAME RESERVE

For most, the highlight of southern Africa is a sojourn in the world's largest inland delta, and one of the most beautiful wildlife sanctuaries in Africa. Originating in Angola, the Okavango River flows southward for 1,300km (806 miles), finally spilling into the northwestern corner of Botswana and turning it into an aquatic paradise. Thanks to the same geological activity that caused the Great African Rift Valley, the delta is more or less contained by fault lines between which the crust has sunk and filled up with sediment. It is into this bowl that the Okavango River seeps and finally evaporates into the Kalahari Desert, rather than making its rightful way to the sea. The annual southward flow of water is precipitated by the rainy season in the north, which begins in the Angolan uplands between January and March, and usually arrives at its southernmost point—the delta—around June or July, when the water spreads out to form innumerable pools, channels, and lagoons. This in turn attracts huge herds of animals from the dry hinterland that come to the delta to quench their thirst, and still their hunger.

Where to Stay & Eat

The northeastern segment of the delta has been set aside as the **Moremi Game Reserve,** an 1,800-sq.-km (702-sq.-mile) expanse of wilderness extending across both wetland and dry terrain covering an estimated 20% of the delta. This, the most popular national park in Botswana, is both scenically exquisite and dense with exciting game (it's sometimes referred to as the predator capital of Africa), most of them quite habituated to humans. But being a national park, it also attracts its fair share of tourists, some of them on self-drive safaris from neighboring countries. So although you're paying top dollar, you may not feel as removed from civilization as you will in one of the private concessions that surround Moremi Game Reserve. (You will also not be allowed to drive off road in pursuit of tantalizing sightings.) The private reserves or concessions surrounding Moremi are southern Africa's most sought after; most contain only a couple of small, private safari camps and offer a greater variety of safari activities than the park as only camps outside the Moremi Game Reserve are allowed to have night game drives and walking safaris, or drive off designated roads to follow game. Concessions located in the south and east of the Delta tend to have a greater density and variety of game sightings (worth noting if your time is limited, but not a deal breaker). Rates are almost always quoted in dollars; please note that when a camp is marked with a good value sign, this is relative to what is offered by others—we realize that absolutely nothing here comes cheap. Finally, book as early as possible: These camps embody Botswana's prevailing tourism ethos of high end and low volume, so in peak season, when the waters are at their highest (usually mid-June to Oct, depending on camp), beds in popular camps are soon filled despite the heftier price tag.

IN MOREMI GAME PARK

Chief's Camp ★★★   This is one of the most luxurious camps in the heart of the delta, in the exclusive Mombo Concession (on the western side of Chief's Island, created by the seasonal floodwaters), with 52 different lions identified in a 9km (5½-mile) radius and almost daily leopard sightings (hence the Mombo area being known as predator capital of Africa); both white and black rhinos are also regular visitors to the area. One of the other reasons the camp is so popular is that it offers the experience of both a wet and dry camp: From June to October, when the floodwaters arrive, mokoro activities are available; this is also the time to book soothing spa treatments in the *sala* (pavilion) alongside the pool. Tents are very comfortable; each is furnished with large twin beds and comfortable armchairs, and features spacious, well-equipped bathrooms and private viewing decks sheltered by jackalberry and sausage trees. It all comes at quite a high price however; currently we think Eagle Island offers better value.

Reservations: Sanctuary Retreats. www.sanctuaryretreats.com. ℂ **27/11/438-4650.** Fax 27/11/787-7658. (see "Specialist Safaris & Operators," earlier in this chapter). 12 units. High season (mid-June to Oct) $3,990; Low season $3,140–$3,580. MC, V. No children under 9. **Amenities:** Dining area; bar; lounge; game drives; library; seasonal mokoro trips; pool; spa treatments; Wi-Fi. *In room:* Ceiling fan, hair dryer.

Mombo and Little Mombo ★★★   Located in Moremi in what is considered the number-one game-viewing area in the delta, Mombo has been host to numerous *National Geographic* and BBC shoots, and it is not unheard of to see as many as 12 mammal species without leaving your veranda. The camps (Little has only three rooms and its own kitchen, lounge, and plunge pool) are located on Mombo Island

The Okavango Delta

(just off the northwestern tip of Chief's Island), within a 45 000-hectare (111,150-acre) private concession deep within the Moremi Game Reserve. "Tents" are the size of small houses and use all-natural materials; suites are connected by a long walkway more than 1.8m (6 ft.) off the ground; this allows game to wander freely through the camp. Views, overlooking the floodplain, offer pretty much 24/7 wildlife channel. You certainly pay for the privilege of being here, and while the camps are pretty luxurious by Wilderness Safaris standards, this is not &Beyond. In fact, **Xigera ★★★**, the Wilderness Safari's Classic Camp also located within Moremi, has made serious inroads on Mombo's popularity, given the significant saving it offers for a similar "address."

Book through Wilderness Safaris (see "Specialist Safaris & Operators," earlier in this chapter). www.mombo.co.za or www.littlemombocamp.com. Mombo 9 units. Little Mombo 3 units. High season (June–Nov) $3,540; low season $2,940 double. Rates are all-inclusive. MC, V. No children under 8; July 1–Oct 31 age limit increases to 12. **Amenities:** Dining room; bar; lounge areas; game drives; 2 pools. *In room:* Hair dryer.

Xakanaxa Camp ★★ 🗡 One of three camps located on the large Xakanaxa lagoon, pretty Xakanaxa (pronounced Ka-*ka*-na-ka) is a relatively good value camp in

Moremi, offering arguably the best birding in the Delta (Oct–Dec particularly), guaranteed boating trips (the water flows here all year) and extensive nature drives into great game country (it's both a "wet" and "dry" camp). Some tents are perhaps a tad too close (you may have to put up with your loud neighbor recounting his day; ask for tents 1–3 which have most space around them), but they are very spacious walk-ins, with every comfort you could imagine, and lovely river views. It's not the most luxurious option in the delta, but a class act nevertheless. Note that as it is in Moremi reserve (as with the more expensive options above) you cannot go on night drives, game walks, or off-road; if this is important opt for Chitabe.

Book through Moremi Safaris & Tours. www.xakanaxa-camp.com. 12 units plus tour leader tent. 2 nights: high season (July–Oct) $3,790 double ($1,895 per night; shoulder season (Apr–June, Nov) $2,740 ($1,370 per night; low season (Dec–Mar) $2,440 double ($1,220 per night). Rates are all inclusive for the 2 days, including flights from Maun. Christmas and New Year surcharge. See website for 3- and 4-day specials. AE, DC, MC, V. **Amenities:** Dining and lounge areas; boat and mokoro trips; fire pit on waterside deck; game drives; plunge pool.

PRIVATE CONCESSIONS BORDERING MOREMI GAME PARK

Baines' Camp/Stanley's Camp ★★ 📷 On a concession south of Moremi, Baines' is a personal favorite, with only five guest chalets, each with four-poster beds that can be rolled out onto your deck so you can sleep under the stars—an unforgettable experience for those of us who long for an escape from nocturnal light pollution. Each suite is very privately situated, with terraces that look out onto the wilderness (ask for a view of the waterway) and spacious, well-laid-out bathrooms (no tubs, though). On arrival, you find yourself in a tranquil, tastefully decorated lounge built around a massive tree and overlooking a permanent waterway where noisy hippos play and wallow. Nearby, the more established **Stanley's Camp** offers eight tents at cheaper rates, with central mess tent, elegantly furnished in creams and tans (this is incidentally great value, on a par with Xakanaxa). Both properties offer the same activities, and one great drawing card is the **Elephant Experience ★★★**, a morning in which you spend some intimate time with three semi-habituated elephants, under the sensitive and expert guidance of Doug Groves.

Reservations: Sanctuary Retreats. www.sanctuaryretreats.com. 📞 **27/11/438-4650.** Fax 27/11/787-7658. 5 units. Baine's: high season (June 16–Oct) $2,270 double; low season (Nov–June 15) $1,420 double. Stanley's: high season (June 16–Oct) $1,810 double; low season (Nov–June 15) $1,190 double. All-inclusive, except for Elephant Experience (inquire direct). MC, V. No children under 12 at Baines; no children under 9 at Stanley's. **Amenities:** Dining area; bar; lounge; game drives; mokoro trips (seasonal); library; pool. In room: A/C, hair dryer, minibar.

Chitabe Camp and Chitabe Lediba ★★★ 🏆 😊 Wilderness Safari's most popular land-based Classic Camp is located in Chitabe, a 28,000-hectare (69,160-acre) concession in the southeast of the Delta (separated from Moremi only by the Gomoti Channel) and offering a great variety of habitats (a mix of Okavango and Kalahari, from palm-dotted floodplains and waterways to dry woodland). As only dry activities (day and night drives; nature walks) are offered here (expect to see high concentrations of predators), Chitabe is often combined with a few nights at water-based **Xigera ★★** (not reviewed but an excellent camp nevertheless) and **Selinda ★★★** (reviewed below), both superb Wilderness Safari Classic Camps. Chitabe is very exclusive, with only two camps, both built on an island; **Chitabe Lediba** is the more intimate, with only five en-suite tents (two with adjoining bedrooms suitable for families) with wooden floors and metal-framed four-poster beds under a canopy of trees. A few minutes away, in a similar setting, the **Chitabe** main camp is an eight-tented camp with tents built on wooden decks linked by raised wooden footbridges; service and guiding standards are excellent. Two elevated platforms can be used as sleep-out experiences for either camp. Guests staying for a few nights have the option of doing an overnight walking safari: On a **Chitabe Trail** ★★★, a max of four guests walk with an armed ranger, have their food cooked over an open fire, and spend the night sleeping under the stars in one of the camp's raised timber hides, swathed in mosquito nets—a recommended authentic bush experience.

Book through Wilderness Safaris (see "Specialist Safaris & Operators," earlier in this chapter). www.chitabe.com or www.chitabelediba.com. 8 and 5 units. High season (mid-June to Oct) $1,990 double; low season $1,300–$1,480. Rates for both are all-inclusive. MC, V. Children 8-12 permitted on game drives, but parents must book private game-drive vehicle. **Amenities:** Dining area; bar; lounge; bush walks; game drives (night and day); plunge pool. *In room:* Fans.

Duba Plains Camp ★★★   In the northernmost reaches of the delta, remote Duba used to be a find because of its superlative game-viewing yet "entry-level" pricing. It's now been discovered, though, so sadly there is now a surcharge; the camp itself is still a "classic" rather than "premier" Wilderness Safari but is the only camp in a 35,000-hectare (86,450-acre) private reserve, with sweeping grass plains, gin-clear freshwater pools, and palm islands—the real luxuries of the delta. Aside from the great sense of privacy (only six tents, each with wooden floors, fine linens, and a veranda overlooking the flood plains) there is the concession's famous lion and buffalo interactions: You'll see huge herds of buffalo (1,500–3,000), which, in turn, attract lions—sometimes up to 15 a day. Guests may choose among game drives, and walking safaris; mokoro trips are rare (dependent on floodwaters). Guiding standards are excellent, and rangers will go out of their way to track particular species.

Book through Wilderness Safaris (see "Specialist Safaris & Operators," earlier in this chapter). www.dubaplains.com. High season (mid-June to Oct) $2,190 double; low season $1,650–$1,880 double. Rates all-inclusive. MC, V. No children under 8. **Amenities:** Dining room; bar; game drives; library; pool on a raised terrace overlooking the plains. *In room:* Fan.

Eagle Island Camp ★★★ ◆   If you're looking for real luxury, classy decor, and a superlative location with both wet and dry activities, it doesn't get much better than this Orient Express camp. Made up of 12 luxury "tents," each with a private deck facing the lagoon (one with a private plunge pool, along with private guide and boat), is built on lush Xaxaba, a romantic island refuge. Accommodations are spread out for privacy, and the Fish Eagle Bar enjoys one of the best locations in Africa. Besides affording you all the luxury you'd expect from the Orient Express group, this is the ideal destination for birders. Set among the flood plains, Eagle Island enjoys a high concentration of fish eagles and other bird species, including kingfishers, herons, cormorants, pelicans, darters, and storks. Orient Express regularly transfers guests from here to **Khwai,** its semi-"dry" camp on the river in neighboring Moremi National Park, or, for real contrast, **Savute Elephant,** its Chobe camp; both are a 25-minute flight away. Relatively good value too.

Book through Orient Express Safaris. www.orient-express-safaris.co.za. ⓒ **011/481-6052** in South Africa. 12 units. High season (mid-June to Oct; Dec 21–Jan 2) $2,428 double. Low season $1,394 double. Rates are all-inclusive. AE, MC, V. No children under 12 except by prior arrangement. **Amenities:** Dining area; bar; airstrip; game drives; hiking; Internet; library; mokoro trips; heated pool; light-aircraft safaris. *In room:* A/C, hair dryer, intercom, minibar.

Jao Camp ★★★   Jao (rhymes with *ciao*) is one of Wilderness Safaris' top Premier camps (besting flagship Mombo, King's Pool, and Vumbura in the popularity stakes).

The Okavango Delta & Moremi Game Reserve

Offering both land and water experiences, as well as luxe facilities (a spa and a gym), it is located on an island in the northwest of the delta, on one of the finest concessions: 60,000 hectares (148,200 acres) of wilderness. Location aside, it is—in terms of style and luxury—one of the most gorgeous camps in the delta, designed by renowned architect Silvio Rech (of Ngorongoro Crater Lodge fame). Zen-like simplicity and airy elegance with natural materials neatly blend. The nine suite-tents are arranged along a long, raised wooden footbridge, ensuring privacy but long walks. Built on stilts alongside a lily-speckled waterway, each suite has a large private viewing deck, a *sala* for afternoon siestas, a beautiful open-air shower, and spacious living areas with open-plan en-suite bathrooms. All in all a more formal atmosphere given the price and the sprawling layout. It's worth noting that there are three "Classic" Wilderness Safaris camps in the Jao Concession, which could save you up to $630 a day, and you might possibly prefer the experience: **Kwetsani** (see below), as well as at **Jacana** (www.jacana.com), and the lovely **Tubu Tree Camp** (www.tubutreecamp. com), another five-tented camp offering more variety of habitat (wet activities May–Sept), and public facilities that include a pool. All three of these camps offer the same game-viewing at a greatly reduced price, and while not as spacious or luxurious as Premier Camps you will still want for absolutely nothing.

Book through Wilderness Safaris (see "Specialist Safaris & Operators," earlier in this chapter). www. jaocamp.com. High season (mid-June to Oct) $3,260 double; low season $2,190–$2,500 double. Rates are all-inclusive. MC, V. Children 8–12 permitted, but special arrangements must be made with management for private vehicles. **Amenities:** Dining area; bar; lounge; fishing; library; 2 pools; spa. *In room:* A/C, fans, hair dryer.

Khwai River Lodge ★★★   This is one of the oldest lodges in Botswana, opened in 1968 by Harry Selby (who, incidentally, worked for Philip Percival, immortalized by Hemingway as Pop in his *Green Hills of Africa*). Today it vies with Eagle Island as the Orient Express Group's most popular camp. It's gorgeous, with all the bells and whistles associated with Orient Express's luxurious approach to the bush safari—air-conditioned tents, a heated swimming pool, and a video library (and in one suite, a private plunge pool and indoor and outdoor bathrooms). The camp is slightly larger than Eagle Island, comprising 15 large twin-bedded tents, each with a private deck furnished with hammocks for comfortable viewing of the resident hippo and croc. The complex is built in the shade of indigenous leadwood and fig trees, and overlooks the Khwai River flood plain, where you are likely to see large numbers of elephants. Your chances of spotting lions, hyenas, wild dogs, and leopards are equally high. Due to popular demand, the spa has doubled in size.

Book through Orient Express Safaris (see "Specialist Safaris & Operators," earlier in this chapter). www. orient-express-safaris.co.za. 15 units. High season (mid-June to Oct; Dec 21–Jan 2) $2,428 double. Low season $1,394 double. Rates are all-inclusive. AE, MC, V. No children under 12 except by prior arrangement. **Amenities:** Dining room and lounge; bar; airstrip; boat and mokoro trips; game drives; heated pool; Internet; library; room service; VHS video and monitor. *In room:* A/C, fan, hair dryer, intercom, minibar.

Khwai Tented Camp ★★ 🗡 ☺   This tented camp is also located on the Khwai River, but here the similarity pretty much ends. Tiny and owner managed, this is not luxury on the scale of the similarly named Orient Express camp (no bedside tables or lamps or any of the almost hotel-like features of luxury tented camps), but it's an authentic safari, with comforts like flushing toilet (bucket showers only add to the sense of real camping), and high levels of service and professional guidance. It's also located in the Khwai community area, overlooking the reserve, so has the added benefits of walking and night drives, and proceeds directly benefit the local community. It's perhaps the best value option in the delta and, with only four tents, an intimate atmosphere prevails, perfect for a small group or family (though to share a tent with your kids look at their new Linyanti Ebony Bush Camp, see below). No pool is a small drawback.

Book through African Bush Camps. (see "Specialist Safaris & Operators," earlier in this chapter). www. africanbushcamps.com. High season (July–Oct) $1,380 double. Low season (Jan, Mar, Dec) $920 double. Children aged 7 to 15 pay 50% ($230) during low season; high season they pay full rate. Rates are all inclusive, but parents with young children will need private game vehicle, which is surcharged. No credit cards. **Amenities:** Dining/lounge area; game drives; night drives; game walks.

Kwetsani/Jacana/Tubu Tree Camps ★★★ 🦶

Also situated in the stunning Jao Concession area (to the northwest of Moremi Game Reserve), these three remote camps (all completely separate) each comprise only five tree house chalets built on stilts under thatched roofs and linked by raised walkways. Designed similarly to Jao (although far less ostentatiously), Kwetsani is much smaller and enjoys an intimate, relaxed atmosphere; dedicated guides make exploration of the varied terrain memorable, and besides mokoro and boat trips, night drives are available. Built on a heavily wooded island with mangosteen and fig trees, it is particularly beautiful from May to September, when the water levels are at their highest, but the game-viewing is best from October to April, when the flood plains are drier. Guests who want a "rougher" bush experience can book a night in an animal blind at nearby Jao camp. Aside from Jao and Kwetsani, there are also **Jacana Camp ★★★**—in a great island location overlooking the floodplains—and **Tubu Tree Camp ★★★**, also built on an island with equally beautiful views and stylish tents on stilts. (Note that all camps in the Jao concession belong to Wilderness Safaris.)

Book through Wilderness Safaris (see "Specialist Safaris & Operators," earlier in this chapter). www. wilderness-safaris.com. 5 units each. High season (mid-June to Oct) $1,990 double; low season $1,300–$1,480. Rates for both are all-inclusive. MC, V. Children 8–12 are permitted only if they are in a group with a private vehicle. **Amenities:** Dining area; bar; lounge; boat and mokoro trips; game drives; pool. In room: Fan.

Oddballs/Delta Camp ★★ 🦶 ☺

Located on Chief's Island, Oddballs Camp is a "wet" rustic camp (real tents) but offers the most affordable way to explore the delta. The emphasis is very much on relaxation, with great guides and a place to get your bare toes in the sand—ideal for lounging and watching the sun set over Chief's Island. Accommodations have improved over the years: still in dome tents on raised platforms, but now en-suite (with shower and flush toilet) and fully equipped for comfort. Nearby is the midlevel Odballs Enclave Camp, with just five tents; Delta Camp is the most luxurious Footsteps in Africa option on the Island, with seven reed and wood chalets. The mokoro camping trips are a highlight of the Footsteps in Africa experience though you need to book for 4 nights or more to enjoy these—you set off at dawn with your personal guide/mokoro poler and camp out on one of the islands; again all provisions and equipment are provided. One of the rare Botswana outfits that accepts kids of all ages.

Book through Footsteps in Africa. www.footsteps-in-africa.com. 14 units. High season (June–Oct) $680 double; low season $580 double. Rates include all meals and game activities (mokoro and walks). No credit cards in camp. **Amenities:** Dining/bar/lounge area; island walks; mokoro trips.

Vumbura Plains ★★ **& Little Vumbura** ★★★   In the northern part of the delta, bordering the area on which Duba is located, this superbly scenic private concession (pronounced *Voom*-boo-rah) comprises a 52,609-hectare (130,000-acre) wilderness; yet another offering a great variety of habitats—from palm-fringed waterways to open savanna and deep dry forest. With only two separate seven-roomed satellite camps, it is also very exclusive. Vumbura is probably the most contemporary Wilderness Safaris camp, appealing to a younger or simply more design-conscious market, with huge, minimalist spaces and squared configurations. Each of the privately situated rooms, connected via elevated timber walkways, has its own lounge as well as a private plunge pool and *sala* from which to enjoy the passing parade on the flood plains beyond. Personally, I'd head straight for its more realistically priced little sister, which offers the same game-viewing experience. If you don't mind sharing a plunge pool, **Little Vumbura** remains very exclusive, with only six tents and lovely public areas situated on a wooded island near the Plains camps, yet as a "Classic" rated camp offers great value.

Book through Wilderness Safaris (see "Specialist Safaris & Operators," earlier in this chapter). www. vumbura.com or www.littlevumbura.com. Vumbura Plains: high season (mid-June to Oct) $3,260 double; low season $2,190–$2,500 double. Little Vumbura: High season (mid-June to Oct) $2,190 double; low season $1,650–$1,880 double. Rates are all-inclusive. MC, V. Children 8–12 permitted, but special arrangements must be made with management for private vehicles. **Amenities:** Dining area; bar; lounge area; game drives; mokoro trips; pool. *In room:* Fans.

Nxabega Okavango Tented Camp ★★★ 🌶   This 8,000-hectare (19,800-acre) private concession on the western border of Moremi Game Reserve is currently &Beyond's most popular camp, so you can expect the trademarks of &Beyond (the best in Afro-chic style and luxury; attentive service; superb cuisine) along with a great location and currently very good pricing. It's a very scenic concession, offering real exclusivity (it encompasses only three camps, of which Nxabega is by far the most luxurious (the others are Ker & Downey's Kanana and the nine-unit Pom Pom Camp, both hours away). The camp itself has the feel of an elegant vintage gentlemen's club, with burnished teak, crisp white linen, parchment lampshades, and dressing tables with leather boxes—all very Hemingway meets Blixen. The 10 luxury en-suite tents, on raised wooden platforms with private verandas, are as comfortable as hotel rooms yet with the exhilaration of canvas (we always recommend tents over chalets on safari). But like Selinda (below), the real plus here is the relaxed atmosphere with great staff that get balance right between service and leaving you alone, and the overwhelming peace that comes from feeling as if you are a million miles from civilization.

Book through &Beyond (see "Specialist Safaris & Operators," earlier in this chapter). www.andbeyond africa.com. High season: mid-June to mid-Oct $2,020 double. Midseason: $1,530–$1,350. Low season: $900 double. Rates are all-inclusive. AE, DC, MC, V. Children welcome. **Amenities:** Dining room; lounge w/bar; airstrip; boat and mokoro trips; bush walks; game drives; interpretive center; pool. *In room:* Fan, hair dryer.

Sandibe Safari Lodge ★★   Bordering the southern edges of Chief's Island/ Moremi, the Santantadibe area is yet another that invites superlatives about the Delta, with all the benefits of being in a concession (off-road driving; walking safaris; night dives), and being &Beyond you know you are in for a treat: renowned for the quality of its guest experience, from surprising you with special spoils to the excellence of their guides. Sandibe offers exclusive access to 8,000 hectares (19,800 acres) plus an additional 19,000 shared hectares (66,700 acres), an area that includes permanent land and water activities. Eight African-style chalets have great outdoor showers, elegant fittings and furnishings, and large private decks with hammocks overlooking game-rich grassy plains. Food is equally good. However, it's not as relaxed or authentic as staying in the Nxabega, their tented camp (above); nor as cutting edge design-wise as their newer camps, Xudum and Xaranna (see below).

Book through &Beyond (see "Specialist Safaris & Operators," earlier in this chapter). www.andbeyond africa.com. High season: mid-June to mid-Oct $2,020. Midseason: $1,530–$1,350. Low season: $900 Rates are all-inclusive. DC, MC, V. Children welcome. **Amenities:** Dining/lounge area; bar; boat and mokoro trips; bush walks; game drives; massage; pool. *In room:* Hair dryer.

Shinde Island Camp ★★ East of Vumbura (see above), on a lush palm island in the heart of the northern delta, Shinde is surrounded by waterways that teem with birds and game, and offers both "wet" and "dry" activities. There are eight twin-bedded tents, each with viewing decks to watch game moving across the plains, but you can also rent a private section of Shinde known as **The Enclave:** Three tents are reserved for the use of a private party; the minimum stay here is 3 nights, and you get your own dining area, bar, lounge, and staff, including a top-notch guide. Shinde, Ker & Downey's flagship camp, is also the base headquarters for the nearby **Footsteps Across the Delta** ★★★ trail camp, the best walking safari option. *Note:* Offering the same basic facilities in a totally different setting, Ker & Downey's **Kanana Camp** ★★ (referred to as Shinde's watery sister) is situated in the southwestern part of the delta at the edge of the Xudum River; rates are slightly more affordable ($1,520 double in high season), and mokoro trips are offered from here into the Delta for two to four people; for these you camp out (with staff to look after you) on a remote island—idyllic. The revamped **Okuti** (same rate as Kanana) is one of the most interestingly designed camps in the delta (see the website for details).

Book through Ker & Downey (see "Specialist Safaris & Operators," earlier in this chapter). Shinde: 8 units. High season (July–Oct) $1,770 double; shoulder season (Apr–June and Nov) $1,190 double; low season (Jan–Mar) $920. DC, MC, V. No children under 10. **Amenities:** Dining area; bar; lounge/library; boat and mokoro trips; bush walks; fishing tackle; game drives; plunge pool.

Xudum and Xaranna ★★★ The most recent flagship camps from &Beyond, Xudum and Xaranna have both graced the pages of various international decor and gourmet magazines, and like Singita in S.A. and East Africa have heightened awareness of the modern interpretation of Afro-chic. Located on its own island in a private concession of some 25,000 hectares (61,800 acres) to the southeast of the Delta, Xaranna offers just nine beautifully furnished tents, each with a great view of the shimmering water that defines a stay here, private plunge pool, bathtub, and outdoor shower. Xudum, with nine split-level suites topped with thatched roofs and rooftop lookouts, is more earthbound and has a more permanent feel, but is equally modern, with private plunge pools and al fresco showers. The public spaces provide a surreal counterpoint of urban chic against a backdrop of paradise—together these are currently the most stylish camps in the Delta, but Nxabega offers better value.

Book through &Beyond (see "Specialist Safaris & Operators," earlier in this chapter). www.andbeyond africa.com. High season: mid-June to mid-Oct $2,950 double. Midseason: $1,840–$2,300. Low season: $1,740 Rates are all-inclusive. DC, MC, V. **Amenities:** Dining room/lounge; bar; boat and mokoro trips; bush walks; game drives; pool. *In room:* Hair dryer.

CHOBE & LINYANTI/SELINDA/ KWANDO REGION ★★★

The far northern region of Botswana comprises the **Chobe National Park** in the east and, lying between Chobe and the Okavango Delta, three bordering concessions: the 23,000-hectare (573,000-acre) **Kwando** reserve in the north (with just two camps); the 125,000-hectare (308,750-acre) **Linyanti** reserve in the east (bordering Chobe and comprising only four exclusive great-value camps), and, to the west of Linyanti, the 135,000-hectare (333,450-acre) **Selinda** reserve. The topography of these three concessions are essentially very similar, each with large tracts of (very boring) mopane woodland, but also featuring riparian forest and the open floodplains that accompany the permanently flowing waters of their rivers: a lush wonderland that is a huge draw for animals, making this as popular as the Delta to visitors who want to be immersed in a vast wilderness area, yet wish to share it with very few.

And it sure is a vast wilderness: Chobe National Park alone covers more than 11,000 sq. km (4,290 sq. miles) of northern Botswana, big enough to be home to some 100,000 elephants, traveling in what is believed to be the largest elephant herds in Africa, and moving freely into the concessions. In the dry season, the Chobe, Kwando, and Linyanti rivers are the only major source of water north of the Okavango, so game travels here from great distances (like elsewhere, private reserves are not fenced off from national parks, so animals migrate freely between them), which, in turn, ensures a large lion population. The area is also almost permanently atwitter with more than 460 species of birds. The Savuti area, in Linyanti's west-central region, was once submerged beneath an enormous inland sea and connected to the Okavango and Zambezi rivers; today it features a vast sea of open grassland and marshes. There is a fair number of permanently resident game here, including leopard, lion, and spotted hyena, but game numbers are greatly augmented at the beginning of the dry season, when large numbers of zebras and wildebeests move through the area from the west to the sweeter grasses on offer in the Mababe Depression to the south. While the Linyanti concession is bisected by the Savute Channel, Selinda is perhaps the plum concession, thanks to the **Selinda Spillway ★★★**: its waterways look very much like the Okavango Delta (most visitors cannot tell the difference), yet only a handful of guests to share the 135,000-hectare (333,450-acre) wilderness; it also usually has larger floodplains than Linyanti. The Spillway incidentally links the delta with the floodplains of the Linyanti Swamps and Kwando waterways, and in very wet years the waters flow in both directions! Aside from the quality of the game-viewing and exclusivity of the concession, Selinda is also home to one of our favorite camps in Africa (also named Selinda, owned by Wilderness Safaris; see below).

Where to Stay & Eat

Just a few minutes' drive from Kasane International Airport, Chobe National Park's 35km (22 miles) of river frontage is conveniently close to the Zimbabwe and Zambia borders, making Victoria Falls day trips possible (the falls are around a 90-min. drive from Kasane). As a result, it's quite a tourist-heavy area; also, as it's a national park, your guide cannot drive off road in pursuit of interesting sightings, nor can you go on night drives or game walks. We have reviewed the best options in the national park, but we recommend that you rather consider one of the lodges on waterways in private concessions reserves in and around the greater Chobe region. Many rate a stay in these concessions as high or higher than their stay in the delta: after all, this is almost 500,000 hectares for around 100 guests at any one time, making for one of the most genuine wilderness experiences in Africa. In addition to the options below there is now a floating luxury boutique hotel operating on the Chobe River: the **Zambezi Queen** ★★★ (see "Luxury River Safari," earlier in the chapter, for more on this super safari).

CHOBE NATIONAL PARK

Chobe Chilwero ★★   One of Botswana's most luxurious safari lodges, with the most sophisticated spa treatments in Botswana, this is a place for urban-style pampering while enjoying game sightings on the banks of the Chobe River. Chobe Chilwero is not strictly in the Chobe National Park but is just a few minutes from the main gates: Organized activities include game drives into the park, sunset boat cruises along the Chobe River (weather dependent), and day trips to Victoria Falls—this is also the place to stay if you want to include a trip to the falls without staying overnight there. Accommodations are in spacious, high thatch-roofed private cottages with massive bathrooms. A private garden and/or private balcony provide wonderful views over the Chobe River islands and flood plains as far as Namibia. A good option for the more nervous safari traveler, this is very much a mini-resort experience; personally we prefer things a little wilder.

Reservations: Sanctuary Retreats. www.sanctuaryretreats.com ℭ **27/11/438-4500.** Fax 27/11/787-7658. (see "Specialist Safaris & Operators," earlier in this chapter). 15 units. High season (June 16–Oct) $1,990 double; low season (Nov–June 15) $1,310 double. Rates are all-inclusive. MC, V. **Amenities:** Dining area; lounge; boat excursions; fishing; game drives; library; pool; spa; tours to Victoria Falls; wine cellar; Wi-Fi. *In room:* A/C, hair dryer.

Chobe Under Canvas ★★★ 🎒📷   If you like being pampered but relish the idea of "real" camping (not just sleeping under canvas but showering in water that's been perfumed by wood smoke), there is simply no better way to experience Chobe National Park than to book a few nights in one of these elegant tented camps. Inspired by their Serengeti operation, this has all the hallmarks of &Beyond: elegantly styled tents, comfortable beds and flushing toilets (but no running water), in carefully selected wilderness sites; excellent food (on tablecloths) and just superb service, including a private butler, yet still a truly authentic camp site (they have to move every 5 days), with all the informality that this implies. With only six tents, it's an exclusive way to get really close to the wilderness. *Note:* &Beyond also offer **Savute Under Canvas,** a similar experience, also within the park.

Book through &Beyond (see "Specialist Safaris & Operators," earlier in this chapter). High season (mid-June to mid-Oct $1,300. Midseason $990–$1,130. Low season $790. Rates are all-inclusive. DC, MC, V. **Amenities:** Dining/lounge area; bush walks; game drives.

Savute Elephant Camp ★★★   This distinguished Orient Express lodge—always our top-rated permanent camp within the national park (since been vindicated by its online popularity)—is located on the Savute channel before it enters Linyanti; beyond these waters lie arid Kalahari sandveld. It's accessible only by chartered light aircraft, so a stay here allows you to fully experience the magnetic pull of the Savute waters on the wildlife, particularly elephants, which are almost always in attendance. Expect the standard Orient Express luxury: accommodations in huge air-conditioned tents with large private viewing decks and outside showers, plus one suite with full indoor and outdoor bathroom and plunge pool. But remember: no off-road driving, no night drives, no game walks.

Book through Orient Express Safaris (see "Specialist Safaris & Operators," earlier in this chapter). 12 units. High season (mid-June to Oct; Dec 21–Jan 2) $2,428 double. Low season $1,394 double. Rates are all-inclusive. AE, MC, V. No children under 12 except by prior arrangement. **Amenities:** Dining and lounge areas; bar; airstrip; book and video library; game drives; heated pool; room service; VHS video and monitor. *In room:* A/C, fan, hair dryer, minibar.

LINYANTI & SELINDA CONCESSIONS

Kings Pool Camp ★★★   This is Wilderness Safaris' Premier Camp in the Linyanti private concession, located on the river, and probably the best option in the entire Chobe area. Each of the nine large suites, built on raised teak decks and covered in thatch, features the ultimate in luxury: a private plunge pool and *sala* (small pavilion) with wonderful views of the Kings Pool Lagoon. This waterway has great bird life and hippos, crocodiles, bushbucks, impalas, elephants, and sables. Activities are predominantly "dry" unless water levels allow: game drives, night drives, walks with a professional guide, and cruises along the Linyanti River in a double-decker boat (water levels permitting). Cheaper alternatives are Classic Camps that Wilderness Safari run in the Linyanti reserve: **Savuti Camp** (www.savuticamp.com), and the recommended **DumaTau ★★** (www.dumatau.com); both offering the same game-viewing for far less money.

Book through Wilderness Safaris (see "Specialist Safaris & Operators," earlier in this chapter). 9 units. High season (mid-June to Oct) $3,260 double; low season $2,280–$2,500. Rates are all-inclusive. MC, V. Children 8–12 are permitted with prior arrangement. **Amenities:** Restaurant; bar; lounge; pool.

Linyanti Bush & Ebony Camps ★★ 🍴 ☺   On the edge of the Linyati marshes, bordering the Chobe National Park, the Chobe Enclave sees huge concentrations of game in the winter months when water elsewhere is scarce, and these two intimate bush camps are a superb base. Personally run by owners Beks and Sophia, the tents offer understated luxury (flushing toilets; hot and cold running water) and superlative guides. Given the standard of game-viewing and accommodations (and the prices charged elsewhere), it also offers exceptional value. Located near enough to be booked as a large group, yet private enough to feel totally alone, the new Linyanti Ebony Camp is a great deal: just four tents, one of them a spacious family tent (with no age restriction), and the luxury of a small plunge pool. Note that if you're relatively fit, you should consider a 3-night **Linyanti Walking Safari**—a rudimentary but maximally authentic bush experience (a maximum of six guests sleep in mobile tents). (Should Linyanti be full, consider its seasonal **Saile Tented Camp,** a small, eight-bed camp on the same concession that affords a similarly exclusive and intimate experience, but slightly less luxury for slightly less money: $920–$1,380 double depending on season. African Bush Camps also has a camp in the delta, reviewed above, as well as one in the Kalahari, **Migration Camp.**)

Book through African Bush Camps (see "Specialist Safaris & Operators," earlier in this chapter). www. africanbushcamps.com. High season (July–Oct) $1,520 double. Low season (Jan, Mar, Dec) $990–$1190 double. Children aged 7 to 15 pay 50% ($230) during low season; high season they pay full rate. Rates are all inclusive, but parents with young children will need private game vehicle (surcharged). No credit cards. **Amenities:** Dining/bar/lounge/library area; boma/blind overlooking waterhole; game drives; game walks; plunge pool.

Selinda Camp ★★★ ✏️ This camp overlooks the Selinda Spillway, a waterway that spreads its way through arid topography to connect the delta to the Linyanti and Kwando wetlands; and very similar in topography to the delta. It's known for its incredible game experiences (including large numbers of predators, but rich in variety), but the service really sets this lovely camp apart. Managed by David and Alice, the atmosphere is of a team that thoroughly enjoys and understands the privilege of being here, and their enthusiasm is contagious. The nine en-suite tents are luxurious and private; activities run the full gamut: game drives, night drives, bush walks, and fishing. The surrounding grasslands make for superb game-viewing, and all tents enjoy a view of the spillway—one of very few sources of water in the area, making it a magnet for animals. It's far more exclusive than the delta, with the only other camp in this concession being Zarafa (www.wilderness-safaris.com), a four-tent Premier Camp (quite a bit pricier) overlooking the Zibalianja Lagoon.

Book through Wilderness Safaris (see "Specialist Safaris & Operators," earlier in this chapter). www.selindacamp.co.za. High season (mid-June to Oct) $1,990 double; low season $1,300–$1,480. Rates for both are all-inclusive. MC, V. No children under 8. **Amenities:** Dining area; lounge; bar; plunge pool. In room: Fan.

KWANDO CONCESSION

Kwando Lagoon & Lebala ★★ ☺ The remote Kwando concession sprawls over more than 232,000 hectares (573,040 acres), making it one of the largest privately run wildlife areas in Africa. Noted for its large herds of elephants, especially during the winter months, the area has some 80km (50 miles) of river frontage on its eastern boundary and attracts big numbers of large cats, buffaloes, kudus, and tsessebes as well. If you want to spot Africa's rarest predator, the wild dog, this is the place to come, especially around the middle of the year, when a pack returns to den here for 2 to 3 months (they've been returning to Kwando for 8 years now); the lions here are also famous for their spectacular kills. With more than 320 species of birds recorded, this area is understandably popular with birders. Thanks to specialist guides for families, it's popular with parents as well. Kwando Safaris runs two luxury tented camps on the Kwando River: **Lagoon** ★★ and **Lebala** ★★★—although they're just 30km (19 miles) apart, the area is so wild that the trip takes 2 hours. Both camps accommodate only 16 guests, in stilted en-suite safari tents with hot running water, flush toilets, and double basins. Lebala is more luxurious and features Victorian bathtubs and open-air showers. Both camps offer morning and night drives, as well as boat cruises and fishing expeditions to catch the famed tiger fish at Lagoon. A number of the guides are enthusiastic, award-winning photographers. Kwando also has two camps in the delta—**Kwara** ★★★ (eight rooms), on a forested island in the remote northern part; the smaller and more exclusive **Little Kwara** ★★★ (five rooms); a camp in the Kalahari, **Tau Pan** ★★; and one in Nxai Pan: **Nxai Camp** ★★ (just eight purpose-built desert rooms), which represents excellent value in the Kalahari. All camps have a pool.

Book through Kwando Safaris (see "Specialist Safaris & Operators," earlier in this chapter). www.kwando.co.za. Lagoon Camp 8 units. Lebala Camp 8 units. Lebala: High season (June–Oct) $1,930 double; shoulder season (Apr–May, Nov) $1,340; low season (Mar) $1,048. Lagoon: High season $1,750; shoulder season $1,240; low season $984. AE, DC, MC, V. Rates are all-inclusive. **Amenities:** Dining area; lounge; boat and mokoro trips; fishing; game drives; pool; guided walks.

THE DRY SOUTH: MAKGADIKGADI & NXAI PANS

The Kalahari, one of the longest unbroken stretches of sand in the world, reaches across the center of Botswana, north into Zaire, and south to the Orange River in South Africa. On its northern edge are the enormous complexes of the **Makgadikgadi Pans** and the relatively small but no less interesting **Nxai Pans,** characterized by ancient baobabs and large camelthorn trees. Game migrates between the two throughout the year. The Makgadikgadi is a vast (12,000-sq.-km/4,680-sq.-mile) game-filled expanse of flat, seasonally inundated land. There are two distinctly different seasons here: The dry season, lasting from April 15 to October 31 and the "wet" season, lasting from November 1 to April 14. During this latter period Makgadikgadi is best for game-viewing: When the pans fill with water after the rains, they host countless migratory birds, most notably huge flocks of flamingos. Most people associate the migration with East Africa, but here you'll also witness the last surviving migration of zebra and wildebeest in southern Africa, when some 30,000 animals, the majority being zebra, but also springboks, gemsboks (oryx), red hartebeests, move across the plains northward to Nxai.

But the Makgadikgadi Pans are equally splendid during the dry season (when prices in fact rise). This is when you can explore the salt pans on quad bikes, and experience what is perhaps the purest sensation of space: The horizons seem endless, and at night, above the pie-crust surface of the pans, the stars shine with a vibrancy found only in vast deserts.

Essentials

VISITOR INFORMATION The best safari operator here is **Uncharted Africa**— see "Specialist Safaris & Operators" earlier in this chapter, though **Wilderness Safaris, Kwando Safaris,** and **African Bush Camps** all have camps here too. For campsite reservations and more information, contact the **Department of Wildlife & National Parks** (www.botswanatourism.org).

GETTING THERE **By Plane** Your best bet is to fly to Maun and arrange a transfer with a tour company that arranges tours in the area (see "Getting Around," below), or deal directly with Uncharted Africa.

By Car It is not a good idea to venture onto the pans without a guide or a 4WD vehicle. You will find both in the towns of Gweta and Nata. These towns can be reached in 2 days from South Africa in a normal two-wheel-drive vehicle, and can be a useful stopover if you're driving to Maun.

GETTING AROUND **On a Guided Tour** For custom-made mobile tours in the pans, contact **Uncharted Africa Safari Co., Moremi Safaris & Tours, Bush Ways, Penduka,** or **Footsteps in Africa** (see "Specialist Safaris & Operators" earlier in this chapter, for contact details), or one of the other overland operators listed.

Where to Stay & Eat

Wilderness Safaris (see recommended specialist operators above) has a camp situated close to Deception Valley (a 3-hr. game drive transfer from the Deception Valley Lodge airstrip), near the northern border of the Central Kalahari Reserve. **Kalahari Plains Camps** comprises just six Meru-style en-suite tents, raised off the ground to catch the breeze and take in the sweeping views across the Kalahari and offers an excellent base from which to explore this vast, arid wilderness. It's not in the same league as Jack's Camp; however at $1,300 double per night, all-inclusive, it is a great option if you're watching your budget. Another good value new Kalahari entrant is **Migration Camp,** managed by African Bush Camps (see recommended specialist operators above), with a flat rate of $920 double all inclusive November to June (closed July–Oct).

Jack's Camp ★★★ 📷   Jack's Camp (voted number one favorite leisure hotel in Africa by *Condé Nast Traveler* readers in 2010) is *the* place to go to experience the Kalahari in style. Deep in the desert, at the edge of the world's largest salt pans, accommodations comprise 10 en-suite open-air safari tents, and styling is Bedouin-meets-Africa, with Persian rugs and teak furniture providing a counterpoint to the endless desert environs. If you grow bored of lolling about on antique rugs, you can head out for game drives, walking safaris with Bushmen trackers, or explorations of remote archaeological sites and geological features. December through April sees the spectacular migration of massive wildebeest and zebra herds, followed by hungry predators. Besides standard trips in custom 4WD vehicles, adventurous winter guests can take guided rides across the salt pans on quad bikes to **Kubu Island** ★★ and sleep for 2 nights under the stars amid the surreal desert boulders and baobabs (only mid-Apr to Oct), or experience "God's minimalism" at romantic **San Camp** ★★★. Count on outstanding staff, including qualified zoologists and biologists, Bushman trackers, and charming and well-trained local guides. All have been thoroughly trained by the very glamorous owner Ralph Bousfield (the camp is named for his father), whose 13-part Discovery Channel series has made him one of the most famous guides in Botswana. Note that the team also offers the most stylish mobile safari expeditions, including a sojourn in the delta, as well as a new family-friendly (and pocket-friendly) camp in Makgadikgadi, simply called **Camp Kalahari** ★.

Book through Uncharted Africa Safari Co. (see "Specialist Safaris & Operators," earlier in this chapter). www.unchartedafrica.com. Jack's Camp 10 units. High "dry" season (Apr 15–Oct) $2,550 double; low season (Jan–Apr 15); Nov–Dec $2,040 double 2 night minimum. San Camp $2,000 double. Camp Kalahari High season $1,122; low season $816. Kubu Expeditions $2,550/$2000/$1,222 depending on camp booking. Rates are all-inclusive. Only cash is accepted in camp. **Amenities:** Drinks tent; mess tent; tea tent; game drives; game/nature walks; library; museum; quad biking; cultural/historical tours.

Planet Baobab ★ 🥤 ☺   Imagine a giant anthill with a Planet Hollywood look-alike sign, a bar with a beer-bottle chandelier, and funkily decorated mud and grass huts in a grove of eight ancient baobab trees. Planet Baobab provides a fun base for younger budget travelers to explore the fascinating Makgadikgadi Pans. Guests can take guided walks with the San through the plants and trees of this fascinating area, or ride 4WD quad bikes over the salt pans during the dry season. Although you can opt to stay in a Bushman grass hut, you'll be better off in one of the traditional Bakalanga mud huts, which have private bathrooms. Meals are available, but you can also buy or bring your own provisions and make use of the shared kitchen. Planet Baobab is accessible by road; it's off the main road to Maun, 15 minutes from Gweta, but most visitors fly in.

Book through Uncharted Africa Safari Co. (see "Specialist Safaris & Operators," earlier in this chapter). 14 units. $140–$270 double; camping $38 per tent. Rates include breakfast. Other meals, drinks, and activities are extra. Ask about the various good-value itineraries. MC, V. **Amenities:** Dining area; bar; camping facilities; expeditions; communal kitchen; pool; quad biking; guided walks.

PLANNING YOUR TRIP TO SOUTHERN AFRICA

13

S outh Africa's major cities are generally smaller than those in Europe and the United States, but they offer comparable facilities, and make a comfortable starting point or base for your travels. Unless you're heading into really remote areas for an extended period of time, don't worry about packing for every eventuality: Anything you've forgotten can be bought here, credit cards are an accepted form of payment, and you're no more likely to be affected by water- or food-borne illnesses that you would be back home. You'll also find a relatively efficient tourism infrastructure, with plenty of services and facilities designed to help you make the most of your trip. Start by browsing the Web, or simply read through this chapter.

GETTING THERE

BY PLANE

Johannesburg's international airport, known as **OR Tambo International Airport** (JNB), and **Cape Town International** (CPT) are the major airport hubs in Southern Africa, though the new **Durban International** is starting to make inroads as international arrival point with big airlines like Air Emirates landing. That said, OR Tambo airport is the busiest in Africa, with direct connections into every regional airport, including those adjoining Kruger National Park (though its worth noting that quite a few lodges have their own airstrips), as well as to Durban in KwaZulu-Natal (a 3-hr. drive from the Zululand reserves), to Port Elizabeth, within easy driving distance (2–3 hr.) of the malaria-free Eastern Cape game reserves, Victoria Falls on both the Zimbabwean (Vic Falls airport) and Zambian (Livingstone airport) side and Botswana.

To add Botswana to a trip to South Africa, you will have to fly via Maun, gateway to the Okavango, or Kasane, gateway to Chobe. Note that Vic Falls can be reached by road from Kasane. This means you can fly from Johannesburg to Livingstone, the Zambian town nearest the falls (which two no-frills airlines fly to from Jo'burg), or to Victoria Falls Airport in Zimbabwe, then transfer onward to Chobe, Botswana via road—it's a mere 90-minute drive. For more details on getting there, see "Arriving" in each chapter.

FROM THE U.S. There are two airlines offering direct flights to South Africa: Star Alliance member **South African Airways** (**SAA;** ☏ **800/722-9675;** www. flysaa.com) departs from New York (JFK) and Washington Dulles (IAD). **Delta Air Lines** (☏ **800/221-1212;** www.delta.com) flies daily nonstop between Johannesburg and Atlanta. Flying indirect offers great savings however (at press time under R5,000): you can fly via a European capital with a European carrier such as Air France (stopping in Paris), Lufthansa (stopping in Frankfurt), KLM (stopping in Amsterdam), and so on, but the Middle Eastern carriers like Emirates often offer the best bargains. Don't book without looking at **British Airways** and **Virgin,** both stopping in London, with connection times usually no longer than an hour before flights continue on to Johannesburg or, better still, direct to Cape Town.

FROM THE UNITED KINGDOM This is an 11-hour (Jo'burg) to 11½-hour (Cape Town) flight, but with an hour-long time difference (2 hr. during daylight saving) and therefore no jet lag, which is just one reason why Cape Town has become home to so many European "swallows" who wing their way over to spend every southern summer here. **SAA** (☏ **0171/312-5005;** www.flysaa.com), **British Airways** (☏ **800/AIR-WAYS** [247-8297] or 0181/897-4000; www.british-airways.com), and **Virgin Air** (☏ **800/862-8621;** www.virgin-atlantic.com) offer direct flights to both Johannesburg and Cape Town. Alternatively, as above, check out any of the European carriers.

FROM AUSTRALIA & NEW ZEALAND Contact **SAA** (☏ **02/9223-4448**) or **Qantas** (☏ **13-13-13;** www.qantas.com.au). Qantas offers direct flights from Sydney to Johannesburg, and South African Airways offers direct flights from Perth. Flying time is approximately 14 to 15 hours from Sydney and 10 to 11 hours from Perth.

To Victoria Falls

The fastest way to get to **Victoria Falls** is to first fly to Johannesburg *or* Tambo, and then to either fly to **Livingstone International AIRPORT** (LVI), in Zambia, or **Victoria Falls International Airport** (VFA), in Zimbabwe; the flight takes under 2 hours. Contact either **SAA** (www.flysaa.com) or **British Airways/ComAir** (www. british-airways.com) for either routing. Good news for budget travelers (since the last edition) is that no-frills carriers 1time (www.1time.co.za) and Kulula (www.kulula. com) now also fly to Livingstone airport, at half the price of the big-name carriers. Note that Livingstone is not far (about 90 min. drive) by road from Kasane, in Botswana (Chobe area). From Kasane you can fly via **Air Botswana** (see below) or small plane (www.wilderness-air.com) to Maun.

To Botswana

To reach the Okavango Delta, you'll need to fly to Maun (MUB) via Johannesburg on **Air Botswana** (www.airbotswana.co.bw). Air Botswana also flies from Johannesburg to Kasane (ideal to reach the Chobe area), from Maun to Kasane, and from Kasane to Victoria Falls, though with a road transfer of only 90 minutes, with game-viewing en route, traveling by vehicle between Vic Falls and Kasane may be preferable (see how to reach Vic Falls, above).

In the unlikely event that you will want to visit Gaborone, the capital, **Air Botswana** also flies from Johannesburg to **Sir Seretse Khama International** (☏ **267/395-1921**), as do **SAA** and **British Airways.**

From Maun, you will board a light aircraft, chartered by the camp you have booked. Note that strict luggage restrictions currently apply: maximum 20kg (44 lb.) per person (including hand luggage and photographic equipment), packed in small 25x30x62cm (10x12x24 in.) soft bags. Charter prices vary, so be sure to compare the following companies' prices for the best deal: **Wilderness Air** (𝄐 **267/686-0778;** www.wilderness-air.com; previously Sefofane) is highly recommended, with a flawless track record; alternatively, there's **Mack Air** (𝄐 **267/686-0675;** www.mackair. co.bw), Kavango Air (www.kavangoair.com), and **Delta Air** (www.okavango.bw).

BY BOAT

Cape Town is featured on a number of luxury liner world-cruise itineraries, but getting here this way takes plenty of time (80 days from Cape Town to New York!) and money, and naturally, your experience of Southern Africa will be somewhat limited. However, if this has always been a dream vacation, book with the best, and take a look at **www.cunard.com** or **www.crystalcruises.com**.

GETTING AROUND

How you choose to get around depends largely on the length of your vacation, and what you want to see. Traveling in Zimbabwe, Zambia, and Botswana is straightforward—public transport is unreliable, roads ill-maintained (or virtually nonexistent), fuel supply potentially unreliable, and help can take a long time coming in the event of a road emergency. The most efficient way to get around in these countries is to fly directly to your intended destination, with all air and road transfers prearranged. However, hopping between two or three key destinations by plane in neighboring South Africa (or Namibia for that matter) is underutilizing your vacation time. With a well-maintained and -organized road system traversing arresting landscapes, a good range of car-rental companies, relatively affordable fuel costs, and—outside the cities—roads that are virtually empty of traffic, a combination of flight and road travel is the way to go if you are able to spend more than a week in South Africa (or are traveling in Namibia). The Western and Eastern Cape region, in particular, is a wonderful area to explore by car, with plenty of charming B&Bs, down-to-earth farm stays, and great-value guest lodges along the way. With a choice of malaria-free game reserves in the Eastern Cape, it makes logistical sense to go on safari here as a family. If you can afford the time, though, I'd recommend you fly north for your safari, either to the Kruger area, Madikwe (also malaria free), or the Okavango Delta. Or, if you've experienced these destinations on a prior trip, head east to the majestic mountains and lush subtropical game and coastal reserves of KwaZulu-Natal, relatively undiscovered by international tourists.

BY PLANE

If you have limited time to cover Africa's large distances, flying is definitely your best bet. Details for the domestic airlines servicing all the major cities in South Africa are as follows: **SA Express** and **SA Airlink** (both domestic subsidiaries of SAA; 𝄐 **27/11/978-1111;** www.flysaa.com) and **BAComair** (𝄐 **27/11/921-0222;** www.ba.com). Thankfully South Africa has its own budget airlines, often offering far lower fares on reliable fleets, though they do not service all domestic airports. These are **Kulula.com** (www.kulula.com), **1Time** (www.1time.co.za), and **Mango** (www. flymango.com). Check their prices against SAA however, particularly if you book well in advance. On busy routes SAA hold a few seats on flights at the same price (or even slightly lower) as their no-frills counterpart. As they have more flights you are safer should there be unexpected delays (though not necessarily) and there's the added advantage of complimentary drinks and a meal or snack, so naturally these seats get snapped up fast. All the lodges recommended in this book will arrange to charter a private flight directly into the reserve (or nearest airstrip) if time is limited; private airlines like Fed Air have regular daily flights into the reserves, which are not that expensive.

BY CAR

Given enough time, this is by far the best way to enjoy the rural beauty of South Africa, particularly the Western Cape where you can travel from Cape Town via Rte. 62 and the Garden Route to the Eastern Cape game reserves, a trip that will take 9 hours direct but makes for a comfortable 6- to 8-day (or longer) excursion on mostly semideserted roads, traveling through huge, meditative landscapes.

In urban centers, drivers comfortable traveling on the left side of the road are also better off renting a car to get around, because public transport in the cities is generally not geared toward tourists. Alternatively, use taxis while you are in the city and rent a car once you're ready to head out to the hills.

You'll need your driver's license to rent a car—your home driving license is good for 6 months—and most companies in South Africa stipulate that drivers should be a minimum of 21 years old (in Botswana, you must be 25 or older). You must have a letter of authority from the rental agency, and vehicles rented in South Africa may be taken into Botswana, Namibia, and Zimbabwe, though this requires 72 hours' notice, and additional insurance charges are applicable. You can leave the vehicle in these countries for a fee; in South Africa, you can hire a one-way rental car to any of the major cities.

All the major companies have branches in South Africa, including **Avis** (www.avis.com), **Hertz** (www.hertz.com), and **Budget** (www.budget.com). Also check out **Europcar,** but **Tempest Car Hire** (www.tempestcarhire.co.za) is a personal top choice, offering a combination of professional service, branches throughout the country (as well as in Namibia), and invariably the lowest rates. Note that it's best to prebook your vehicle, particularly if you're traveling during the peak season (Dec–Feb).

A Home on Wheels

Maui Motorhomes (www.maui.co.za) offer fully equipped camper vans and four-wheel-drive vehicles with pop-up tents on the rooftop (sleeping two or four), with a full listing of places to park it; they'll also pick you up in your vehicle from the airport. Essentially there are three types of motorhomes sleeping between two and five; rates vary, depending on the season and length of rental but you are looking at around R900 to R1,200 a day. **Britz Africa** (www.britz.co.za) and **SMH**

Carhire (www.smhcarhire.co.za) are two reputable companies offering a fleet of four-wheel-drive vehicles with rooftop tents (sleeping two or four in two easy-to-erect tents that are safely located above the vehicle), and equipped for serious camping (gas stove, chairs, and so on). This is a great road trip option, with the 4x4 vehicles ideal for touring off-the-beaten-track destinations. Also great for touring Namibia, where game is not always fenced.

CAR-RENTAL INSURANCE Before you drive off in a rental car, be sure you're adequately insured, covering such things as whether your policy extends to all persons who will be driving the rental car, how much liability is covered in case an outside party is injured in an accident, and whether the type of vehicle you are renting is included under your contract.

GASOLINE Fuel is referred to as "petrol" in South Africa and is available 24 hours a day in major centers. As of April 2011, 1 liter cost R10 (4 liters is approximately 1 gallon). For up-to-minute fuel prices visit www.aa.co.za/content/59/fuel-pricing. *Please note:* Gas stations are full-service, and you are expected to tip the attendant R5. Credit cards are not accepted as payment.

ROAD RULES South Africa has an excellent network of paved and dirt roads, with emergency services available along the major highways; you cannot rely on this sort of backup on road conditions in Zimbabwe, Zambia, or Botswana. Driving in all three countries is on the left side of the road—repeat the mantra "drive left, look right," and wear your seat belt at all times. Generally, the speed limit on national highways is 120kmph (74 mph), 100kmph (62 mph) on secondary rural roads, and 60kmph (37 mph) in urban areas. The **Automobile Association of South Africa (AA)** extends privileges to members of AAA in the United States and the Automobile Association in Britain. South African road condition information, route planning, toll information, distances, directions, and accommodations are available online (www.aa.co.za). For breakdowns, contact the local emergency number (© 083/843-22); however, if an international member has rented a vehicle, it is recommended that he or she confirms with the relevant car-rental company the procedures for dealing with an emergency or vehicle breakdown, and then use the emergency number provided by the car-rental company.

BY TRAIN

Nothing beats the romance of rail, and South Africa is blessed with two trains regularly included in the top-10 train trips in the world. There can be no better way to recover from jet lag than to fly to Johannesburg (arriving in the morning), and arranging for a transfer to Pretoria to board your railway coach (see below), and spend the next night or two being rocked south to Cape Town. If the journey is as important as the destination, splurge on a deluxe suite in the world-famous **Rovos Rail ★★★** (© 27/12/315-8242; www.rovos.co.za), though the longer-running **Blue Train** (© 27/12/334-8459; www.bluetrain.co.za) is not to be sneezed at. Both are billed as luxury hotels on wheels and predominantly run between Pretoria (the capital, near Johannesburg) and Cape Town. Of the two, Rovos Rail has the edge: It has the largest suites on wheels, the best en-suite bathrooms, beautiful dining rooms, great butler service, and an impressive wine list (included in the price, and a great introduction to South Africa's top wines). The Pretoria–Cape Town journey is a leisurely 2-night trip, while the Blue Train does it in 1 night. (*Tip:* I'd skip the Kimberley tour, a scheduled stop and tour on Rovos' Day 2, and stay cocooned in my suite.) Aside from the Pretoria–Cape Town run, there are a number of exciting routes, such as the 13-day journey to Tanzania or the 9-day journey to the Kruger, Durban, Garden Route, and Cape Town. It's expensive (R24,000–R48,000 for 3-day one-way trip between Pretoria and Cape Town, all-inclusive) but relative to the other great train journeys of the world, rather good value. For a full listing of departure days for this year and the following two, as well as times, schedules, and up-to-date rates, visit the website.

Aside from these luxury trips, there is **Premier Classe,** a kind of budget Blue Train, which travels between Johannesburg and Cape Town, and Johannesburg and Durban (✆ **087/802-6674;** http://shosholoza-meyl.co.za/premier_classe_timetable. html; R4,420 double and R2,020 double, respectively). However, it's worth knowing that travelers were left high and dry in 2010 when an internal dispute about rail maintenance stopped all Premier Classe trains from running. If you are a die-hard train enthusiast, it's definitely worth investigating, but make sure you have a backup plan.

BY BUS

The three established intercity bus companies are **Greyhound, Intercape,** and **Translux;** all offer unbeatable value when it comes to getting around the country, but it is a time-consuming business. Intercape is the largest privately owned intercity passenger transport service in Southern Africa, and probably the most luxurious. Book a ticket on its Sleeperline so you can recline and book your seat (try for the top front for the best view). Johannesburg to Cape Town takes approximately 19 hours (about 8 hr. less than the train).

An alternative to these is the 22-seater **Baz Bus,** which offers a flexible hop-on, hop-off scheme aimed at backpackers and covers almost the entire coastline, including some really off-the-beaten-track destinations, such as Port St Johns. It's not as comfortable as the intercity buses but a great way for budget travelers to explore the coast, areas around the Mpumalanga game reserves, Drakensberg, Swaziland, and Maputo, capital of neighboring Mozambique. You can purchase direct routes or 7-, 14-, and 21-day passes, which allow you to get on and hop off anywhere you wish for a fixed price.

○ **Baz Bus National** (✆ **27/21/439-2323;** www.bazbus.com; central reservations)
○ **Greyhound** (✆ **27/83/915-9500;** www.greyhound.co.za)
○ **Intercape** (✆ **08/61/287-287** or 27/21/380-4400 international; www.intercape. co.za)
○ **Translux** (✆ **08/61/589-282** or 27/11/774-3333; www.translux.co.za)

TIPS ON ACCOMMODATIONS

The choice of accommodations can make or break a holiday, so we take special pride in providing you with the best recommendations. The selection in this book covers a wide variety of budgets, but all share the common ability to delight—be it because of a fabulous location, special decor, authentic warmth, personal touches, and inspiring views (and, of course, some cover all these criteria). Should you require our assistance as travel planners to create a tailor-made itinerary based on your exacting requirements and including the essential with off-the-beaten-track experiences, we would be more than happy to assist; simply visit us at www.bestkept.co.za. We have personally inspected every lodging featured in this book, and many, many more that—for whatever reason—did not make the grade. We would love to make your trip to Southern Africa the most incredible experience—not only because we want you to have fun, to relax, to be pampered (as every holiday should promise), but because we want you to return home feeling serene and rejuvenated in ways that can only happen after you have spent time connecting with Africa's wildness—untamed, primal, magical.

In addition to this guide the following sites featuring property collections are highly recommended: Specializing in owner-managed establishments with real character, often in unusual locations, is the **Greenwood Guide to South Africa** (www. greenwoodguides.com). If you intend to spend a lengthy amount of time in South

Africa and cover a lot of ground, and if you like efficiency options off the beaten track or intimate places where you can interact with the owners and get a real sense of the local community, the Greenwood team's unerring eye for unusual and personal lodgings will stand you in good stead; we have yet to find a property we really didn't like that they recommended. **Portfolio** (www.portfoliocollection.com) brings out an attractive range, profiling the full spectrum of options across the country; all available online as well. If you stick to the Luxury and Great Comfort options (indicated by colored shields) in the B&B section, you're likely to be delighted with the good value they represent. Each review comes with at least one photograph—with more on their website. If a safari is the primary reason you're heading south, take a look at the excellent selection in **Classic Safari Camps of Africa** (www.classic safaricamps.com), though it's obviously not nearly as comprehensive as the recommendations you will find in this book. However, the selection is just a fraction of what's out there. If you want a luxury safari, interested in spending the night in a couple of camps, including a possible beach stop, you will certainly want to take a look at what **Wilderness Safaris** and **&Beyond** offer, both with camps in Kruger, Botswana, and Kwazulu Natal (www.wilderness-safaris.com and www.andbeyond. com). Wilderness Safaris has the best (and most) locations in Botswana; &Beyond has fewer properties but certainly has the edge in terms of design and general luxury of experience. &Beyond incidentally also offer a tour-booking service, covering a wide range of properties in addition to its own luxury safari destinations, which allows it to create itineraries to suit any budget.

With 16 properties in South Africa, **African Pride Hotels** (www.africanpride hotels.com) is the five-star offshoot of Africa's biggest hotel chain (Protea, a three- and four-star group aimed primarily at the corporate market); it's a young brand that's fast gaining momentum and placing emphasis on bling-luxury that'll most likely appeal to urban hipsters, or anyone looking for contemporary digs rather than the typical Laura Ashley look. The atmosphere is young, upbeat and playful; bedrooms are chic and public areas look like they're fashioned on trendy clubs. Some may find them brash and soulless, but there's no denying the effort put into the interiors of concrete-and-glass edifices such as 15 On Orange in Cape Town (p. 75).

If you want to try a deal like this, **Three Cities** (www.threecities.co.za) and **African Legacy Hotels** (www.africanlegacyhotels.co.za) are probably of the better hotel groups, offering sustained quality, though we generally prefer independently owned hotels (and Orient Express, naturally). Three Cities does however offer a wide variety, including safari destinations, in some of South Africa's best locations.

Note: South Africa has a great selection of efficiency options—good for families or for those wishing to prolong their stay—and, thanks to restaurant delivery services in most urban centers, you won't even have to cook. A number of companies offer what is referred to as the Villa Stay, most of them in Cape Town. **Icon Villas** (www.icape. co.za) offers a particularly good service, with a wide range of properties, from flats in the center of Cape Town to private villas on game lodges; but it is the hands-on management by proprietor Therese Botha, with her attention to detail, from quality of linen to great location, that gives them an edge. For rural budget options, browse the excellent Budget Getaways (**www.budget-getaways.co.za**), which covers the Western Cape. Alternatively go to **www.farmstay.co.za** for even more off-the-beaten-track options. Those looking at the most cost-effective way to travel should visit **www.homeexchange.com**. There are some superb South African homes listed here—many of them in the most sought-after areas in Cape Town, with views, pools, and ultraluxurious furnishings and fittings.

[FastFACTS] SOUTH AFRICA

Area Codes   The country code for South Africa is **27,** for Zambia **260,** for Zimbabwe **263,** for Botswana **267.** Metropole codes in South Africa: Cape Town is **021,** Johannesburg is **011,** Pretoria is **012,** Durban is **031,** Port Elizabeth is **041.**

Automobile Organizations   For South African road conditions and route planning, visit www.aa.co.za. For roadside assistance and breakdowns, dial ✆ **083/843-22.**

Business Hours   Generally business is conducted Monday to Friday from 9 or 10am to 5pm, and Saturday 9am to 1pm. Shops in malls are open every day, often till 8pm or later. Frustratingly (for locals at least) bank hours are shorter, most of them closing at 3:30 or 4pm on weekdays and 11pm on Saturdays.

Crime   See "Safety," below.

Customs   For information on what you can bring into Southern African countries, visit http://south-africa.visahq.com/customs. For information on what you're allowed to bring home, contact one of the following agencies:

U.S. Citizens   U.S. Customs & Border Protection (CBP), 1300 Pennsylvania Ave., NW, Washington, DC 20229 (✆ **877/287-8667;** www.cbp.gov).

Canadian Citizens   Canada Border Services Agency (✆ **800/461-9999** in Canada, or 204/983-3500; www.cbsa-asfc.gc.ca).

U.K. Citizens   HM Customs & Excise (✆ **0845/010-9000,** or 020/8929-0152 outside the U.K.; www.hmce.gov.uk).

Australian Citizens   Australian Customs Service (✆ **1300/363-263** or www.customs. gov.au).

New Zealand Citizens   New Zealand Customs, The Customhouse, 17–21 Whitmore St., Box 2218, Wellington (✆ **04/473-6099** or 0800/428-786; www.customs.govt.nz).

Disabled Travelers   While the legislation here is not the world's most sophisticated, it now demands that travelers with disabilities be taken into account. Great progress has been made at tourism facilities; many lodgings provide wheelchair-accessible and comfortable en-suite rooms. Plenty, however, are entirely unsuitable, and it may be easiest to join a tour provided by an operator that specializes in wheelchair travel and inspects every facility for your comfort. One such group is **www.rollingsa.co.za,** specializing in small group tours throughout South Africa; the reputable **www.flamingotours.co.za,** personally run by Capetonians Jeff and Pam Taylor (the latter a registered nurse), offers trips tailored to clients' specific needs, interests, and budget. The couple now also offers tours for blind and/or sight-impaired guests, as well as the deaf or hearing impaired. Adventure lovers should contact South African Bernard Goosen, who was an accountant until he climbed Kilimanjaro in a modified wheelchair, becoming the first person in the world to do so. Bernard now works full time on motivational and team building, as well as assisting individuals, both able and disabled, to fulfill their dreams, putting together specially designed outings with "off-road" wheelchairs (the latter available for rent). Contact him at bern@getmotivated.co.za, or call ✆ **27/83/648-7770.** If you plan to travel with friends or family rather than join a tour group, Johannesburg-based **Mobility One** (✆ **27/861-662-454** or 27/11/892-0638; www.mobilityone.co.za) rents various wheelchairs and scooters; they will deliver equipment to the airport or hotel for R350. For more local information, contact the **National Council for Persons with Physical Disabilities in South Africa** (www.ncppdsa.org.za; nationaloffice@ncppdsa.org.za).

Driving   See "Getting There & Getting Around," above.

Electricity   Electricity in South Africa, Botswana, and Zambia is 230 volts, alternating at 50 cycles per second. Electrical sockets in Zimbabwe usually supply at between 220 and 240 volts AC.

Embassies & Consulates **South Africa in the U.S.:** 3051 Massachusetts Ave. NW, Washington, DC 20008 (✆ **202/232-4400;** www.saembassy.org).

In Canada: 15 Sussex Dr., Ottawa, ON, K1M 1M8 (✆ **613/744-0330;** www.southafrica-canada.ca).

In the U.K.: South Africa House, Trafalgar Square, London WC2N 5DP (✆ **020/7451-7299;** http://southafrica.embassyhomepage.com.

In Australia: Corner State Circle and Rhodes Place, Yarralumla ACT 2600 (✆ **02/6272-7300;** www.sahc.org.au).

Zambia in the U.S.: 2419 Massachusetts Ave. NW, Washington, DC (✆ **202/265-9717;** www.zambiaembassy.org). **In the U.K.:** 2 Palace Gate, Kensington, London W8 5NG (✆ **020/7589-6655;** www.zambia.embassyhomepage.com).

Zimbabwe in the U.S.: 1608 New Hampshire NW, Washington, DC 20009 (✆ **202/332-7100;** www.zimbabwe-embassy.us).

In Canada: 332 Somerset St. West, Ottawa, ON, K2P 0J9 (✆ **613/421-2824;** ww.zimottawa.com).

In the U.K.: 429 Strand, London WC2R 0QE (✆ **020/7836-7755;** www.zimbabwe.embassyhomepage.com).

In Australia: 11 Culgoa Circuit, O'Malley ACT 2606 (✆ **02/6286-2281;** zimbabwe.visahq.com).

Botswana in the U.S.: 1531–1533 New Hampshire Ave. NW, Washington, DC 20036 (✆ **202/244-4990;** www.botswanaembassy.org).

In Canada: 30 Chinook Crescent, Ottawa, H2H 7EI (✆ **613/596-0166**).

In the U.K.: 6 Stratford Place, London W1C 1AY (✆ **020/7499-0031;** www.botswana.embassyhomepage.com).

In Australia: 52 Culgoa Circuit, O'Malley ACT 2606 (✆ **02/6290-7500;** http://botswana.visahq.com).

Embassies, high commissions, or consulates in South Africa (for full listing see www.southafrica.com/embassies): U.S. Embassy: 877 Pretorius St., Arcadia, in Pretoria (✆ **27/12/342-1048;** fax 27/12/342-5504; http://southafrica.usembassy.gov). Canadian Embassy: 1103 Arcadia St., Hatfield, Pretoria 0083 (✆ **27/12/422-3000**). U.K. Embassy: 255 Hill St., Arcadia 0002, Pretoria (✆ **27/12/483-1200;** www.ukinsouthafrica.fco.gov.uk) Australian Embassy: 292 Orient St., Arcadia, Pretoria 0083 (✆ **27/12/423-6000;** www.southafrica.embassy.gov.au).

Emergencies **South Africa:** ✆ **10177** ambulance, ✆ **10111** police and fire, ✆ **112** from cellphones.

In Zambia: ✆ **999** police, ✆ **991** medical, ✆ **993** fire; ✆ **112** from mobiles.

In Zimbabwe: ✆ **999** for police, medical emergency, and fire.

Family Travel South Africa is regarded as the most child-friendly country in Africa, with plenty of family accommodations options, well-stocked shops, sunshine, safe beaches, high hygiene standards, malaria-free game reserves, varied yet familiar cuisine, and babysitters on tap. Hotels and guest lodges usually provide discounts for children under 12, and children under age 2 sharing with parents are usually allowed to stay for free. Ages and discounts vary considerably, however, so it's best to check beforehand. South Africa also has a large number of excellent efficiency apartments, cottages, and luxury homes, increasingly referred to in the trade as "villas"—particularly in Cape Town where many foreign "swallows" only require their luxury homes for a few months of the year. This is often the cheapest way to purchase top-end comfort and luxury accommodation for families who want real space and privacy (and many of the villa agents also offer full concierge services to arrange chef, chauffer, au pair, spa treatments, tours, and so on). Take a look at "Tips on Accommodations," earlier in this chapter. Bear in mind that some lodges in private game reserves are loathe to accept children under 12, though this policy has seen a welcome reversal in the past few years, with many of the best now specifically welcoming children with child-friendly programs (these indicated with the "Kids" icon; see also our "Best Of" recommendations in chapter 1). Because immunizations are not recommended for those under 5, choose a malaria-free area if you are traveling with very young children. Again, there is something special about renting your own space, so don't rule out a self-drive budget safari in the Kruger, even as a precursor to a sojourn in a luxury lodge or camp where you will be provided with a vehicle and guide.

Gasoline (Petrol)   See "Getting Around," above.

Health   Visiting South Africa should pose no threat to your health: Hygiene is rarely a problem in tourist areas, tap water is safe, stomach upsets from food are rare, there are no weird tropical viruses, private hospitals are efficient and the staff is of the highest caliber, and medical assistance is generally always within a 10-minute to 2-hour drive. Procedures, particularly dental and plastic surgery, are so highly rated and relatively inexpensive that there is now a roaring trade in safari/surgery vacations. Still, there are a few things to watch out for, discussed below. Unless you're already covered by a health plan while you're abroad, it's probably a good idea to take out medical travel insurance, particularly if you're going to participate in adventure activities. Be sure to carry your identification card in your wallet. In the event of serious medical conditions in Botswana, Zambia, and Zimbabwe, every effort should be made to go to Johannesburg.

While you will find an excellent range of over-the-counter medicines in pharmacies, bring your own prescription medications as well as copies of your prescriptions, with the generic name, in case you lose your pills or run out. If you wear glasses or contact lenses, pack an extra pair.

Contact the **International Association for Medical Assistance to Travelers** (www.iamat. org) for up-to-date tips on travel health concerns, as well as lists of local, English-speaking doctors; of course, your local host or concierge will do same, and the reference is probably a great deal more reliable. You will find listings of clinics overseas at the **International Society of Travel Medicine** (www.istm.org), though, personally, I'd go straight to **www.netcare.co.za**, a collection of top private clinics throughout South Africa, with listings of all their specialists in every region on the website, the Netcare Hospital they practice from, and their direct telephone number. For travel-specific medical queries, I'd look no further than **www.travelclinic.co.za**, also with branches throughout South Africa.

If you need more reassurance, the United States **Centers for Disease Control and Prevention** (*©* **800/311-3435;** www.cdc.gov) provides up-to-date information on health hazards by region or country and offers tips on food safety. The website www.tripprep.com, sponsored by a consortium of travel-medicine practitioners, offers helpful advice on traveling abroad. Alternatively, remember the following:

AIDS: South Africa has more people living with AIDS than any other country in the world. If you're entering into sexual relations, use a condom. If you need medical treatment during your stay, there's no real risk that you'll contract the virus in the process. Even so, it's best to err on the side of caution and insist on treatment at a private hospital, if possible.

Bilharzia: Do not swim in dams, ponds, or rivers unless they are recommended as bilharzia free. Symptoms are difficult to detect at first—fatigue followed by abdominal pain and bloody urine or stools—but can be effectively treated.

Bugs, Bites & Other Wildlife Concerns: You are unlikely to encounter snakes—they are shy, and, with the exception of puff adders, tend to move off when they sense humans approaching. If you get bitten, stay calm—very few are fatal—and get to a hospital. Scorpions and spiders are similarly timid, and most are totally harmless. To avoid them, shake out clothing that's been lying on the ground, and be careful when gathering firewood. If you're hiking through the bush, beware of ticks; tick-bite fever is very unpleasant, though you should recover in 4 to 5 days. To remove ticks, smear Vaseline over them until they let go. Visitors to the national parks and reserves should always remember that they are in a wilderness area; even animals that look cute are wild and should not be approached (this includes baboons, which will sometimes vandalize cars in search of food). If you're on a self-drive safari, make sure you get out of your vehicle only at designated sites. While most rest camps in the national parks are fenced for your protection, this is not the case with lodges and camps situated in private reserves. Animals—including such dangerous ones as hippos, lions, and elephants—roam right through them. After dark, it's essential that you seek accompaniment to and from your room by a guide. Even when you're in a safari vehicle on a game drive, your ranger will caution you not to stand up, make sudden or loud noises, or otherwise draw attention to yourself. Occasionally, the ranger may leave the vehicle to track game on foot; always remain seated in the vehicle. It is probably unnecessary to point out that lions and crocodiles are dangerous; however, hippos kill more humans in Africa than any other mammal, and you should take this seriously. Hippos may look harmlessly ponderous, but they can move amazingly fast and are absolutely lethal when provoked. Even some of the smaller animals should be treated with a great deal of respect. The honey badger is the most tenacious of adversaries, and even lions keep their distance from them. And of course, the most serious bite comes from a tiny female, known as the Anophele (mosquito).

Cholera: Risk to travelers anywhere in Southern Africa is minimal, and the cholera vaccine is recommended for aid and refugee workers only.

Dietary Red Flags: Vegetarians and others with special dietary requirements visiting game lodges and camps must let their hosts know well in advance; in fact, it is worth alerting any establishment serving dinner and/or lunch that you have dietary requirements well in advance. Note that many South Africans who describe themselves as "vegetarians" eat fish or even chicken, so it's best to specify exactly what your requirements are. Outside the major cities, vegetarians may struggle to find restaurants that offer any kind of choice. Travelers with any kind of intolerance or allergy should impress upon servers the seriousness of their condition when inquiring about the ingredients in a particular dish.

Malaria: Parts of northern KwaZulu-Natal, Kruger National Park and surrounding reserves, Zimbabwe, and Botswana are all high-risk malaria zones (transmitted only by the female mosquito, who requires blood to develop her eggs), though some areas become low-risk in the dry winter months. Both Hluhluwe-Umfolozi (KwaZulu-Natal) and the Kruger are usually low-risk areas from May to September; swinging to high risk December to April (generally, this may mean no medication is necessary June–Aug, though other protective measures are advisable; see below). Please note that the malaria season depends on the rainfall during the previous summer. Always check with a travel clinic or your medical practitioner. You will most likely be prescribed Malarone (or Malanil, as it also known); it is the most effective (98%) and has the fewest side effects. You have to take it only 1 day before entering a malarial area and continue the course for only 7 days after you leave the area.

You'll find more useful information on **www.meditravel.co.za** and **www.malaria.org.za**, or call the 24-hour malaria hot line at ℂ **+27 (0)82 234 1800** to give detailed explanation on risk and advice on precautionary measures.

Sun: Remember that the sun doesn't have to be shining to burn you. Wear a broad-brimmed hat, and apply a high-factor sunscreen or total block—at least initially. Wear sunglasses that reduce both UVA and UVB rays substantially, and stay out of the sun between

11am and 3pm. Children should be kept well covered at the beach; it can take as little as 15 minutes for an infant's skin to develop third-degree burns. **Note:** Some recent research suggests that sun block in fact causes skin cancer, and that the only real preventative method of coping with the sun's rays is to stay out of them during the aforementioned peak hours—outside of those times, a dose of sunlight is quite healthy and in fact necessary.

Holidays   Banks, government offices, post offices, and most museums are closed on the following legal national holidays: January 1 (New Year's Day); March 21 (Human Rights Day); Good Friday, Easter Sunday and Monday; April 27 (Founders/Freedom Day); May 1 (Workers Day); June 16 (Soweto/Youth Day); August 9 (Women's Day); September 24 (Heritage Day); December 16 (Day of Reconciliation); Christmas Day; and December 26 (Boxing Day). For more information on holidays, see "South Africa Calendar of Events," in chapter 2.

Hospitals   See **www.netcare.co.za**, a collection of top private clinics throughout South Africa. See "Health," above.

Insurance   For information on traveler's insurance, trip-cancellation insurance, and medical insurance while traveling, see www.frommers.com/planning.

Internet Access   There are literally thousands of cybercafes throughout South Africa's urban areas. Increasingly, hotels and guesthouses throughout the region are offering (sometimes slow) Wi-Fi as a complimentary service. The entire V&A Waterfront Shopping Mall in Cape Town now offers free Wi-Fi, and you can check out the list of cafes and restaurants offering free Wi-Fi access by looking at who has joined www.redbutton.co.za, or SkyRove, or HipZone.

LGBT Travelers   South Africa's constitution outlaws any discrimination on the basis of sexual orientation, making it one of the most progressive in the world. Big cities are gay friendly, and Cape Town, often called the gay capital of Africa, was voted the second-largest gay capital in the world (see "The Great Gay EsCape," p. 134, for details on gay-friendly accommodations and nightlife). Gay Pages is South Africa's largest and longest-running directory for local gay and lesbians; to find out what they're up to, from ballroom dancing to finding an exclusive men's-only bar in seemingly staid Pretoria, visit **www.gaysouthafrica.org.za**. Alternatively, for a host of up-to-the-minute news, as well as such opportunities as SMS dating, look at **www.Q.co.za**, the gay news and resource site from the *Mail & Guardian* newspaper. For a tourist-orientated listing of gay-friendly places and events in Cape Town, including accommodations, adventure activities, tours, and entertainment, visit **www.capetown.tv**. Leaving Cape Town, the Western Cape is a great area to tour by car, with gay-run and gay-friendly lodgings in myriad little villages in the Winelands, coast, and Karoo (Barrydale has even been fondly nicknamed "Marydale"). Upmarket lodges and camps in private game reserves are equally accepting, so book a safari with any of the lodges listed in this guide. If you're looking for gay-friendly or gay-only establishments in more obscure destinations, augment your research with the limited but interesting selection on www.togs.co.za.

The same general level of acceptance is not true of countries bordering South Africa. Zimbabwean President Robert Mugabe is a virulent homophobe, and homosexuality is effectively a criminal offense, so be discreet if visiting here or Zambia (though the towns adjoining Victoria Falls are pretty international in their outlook). For more information, visit **The International Gay and Lesbian Travel Association** (www.iglta.org), the trade association for the gay and lesbian travel industry. It offers an online directory of gay- and lesbian-friendly travel businesses; go to its website and click on "Members."

Money   The **South African currency unit** is the **rand** (ZAR or R), with 100 cents making up R1. Notes come in R10, R20, R50, R100, and R200. Minted coins come in 1-, 2-, and 5-rand denominations, and 2, 5, 10, 20, and 50 cents—small change doesn't buy much;

gather and use for tips. Despite the relative stability of the economy and the size of its gold reserves, the rand value can fluctuate wildly. To give some idea: In 2007, the rand was hovering at R7 to $1 and R14 to £1; at the start of 2009, it was fluctuating between R9 and R11 to the $1 and hit highs of R18 to the £1. At press time it was back at around R7 to the $1 and R11 to £1, but do check before making calculations.

In 2011, the **pula,** official currency of **Botswana,** was hovering between P6.4 and P6.9 for $1. This has little effect on visitors though, as lodgings and camps quote and charge in U.S. dollars almost without exception. In Zambia, most lodgings do the same, quoting rates in dollars or euros, and even roadside hawkers prefer foreign currency. If you do pick up some local currency, you will find the **Zambian** currency unit is the **kwacha (K),** in denominations of 50, 100, 500, 1,000, 5,000, and 10,000, 20,000, and 50,000 kwacha notes.

Zimbabwe's hyperinflation—kicked off in the early 2000s by Mugabe's "land reform" policy, in which vast swathes of productive white-owned farmland were given to so-called war veterans and now lie fallow—led to a replacement of the Zim dollar with foreign currencies. This "dollarization" process was finally legalized in 2009 (by which time a trillion note could not even buy a loaf of bread, and its value against the U.S. dollar was cut in half every 2 days). The payment of goods and services in Zimbabwe is thus now only in foreign currencies, including the U.S. dollar, Euro, pound, South African rand, and Botswana pula, but the dollar remains the most popular.

THE VALUE OF LOCAL CURRENCIES VS. OTHER POPULAR CURRENCIES

	US$	C$	UK£	Euro (€)	AU$	NZ$
R1	$0.15	C$0.15	£0.09	€0.10	A$0.14	NZ$0.18
BWP1	$0.15	C$0.15	£0.09	€0.11	A$0.19	NZ$0.19

ATMs: ATMs (cashpoints) offering 24-hour service are located throughout South Africa, even in small towns. (Obviously, this does not apply to lodges in remote locations, such as nature reserves, with the exception of Skukuza Rest Camp in Kruger.) Be warned that while travelers can withdraw money (in local currency) from ATMs in Zambia, banks may lose their connections with the credit card exchanges, and you will find ATMs only in major towns in Botswana. Best to prepay the bulk of your trip, including transfers, and carry some foreign currency with you for tips and gifts, as popular foreign currencies are all welcomed in Zambia, Zimbabwe and Botswana.

Let your bank know that you are traveling; be sure to remember your PIN, and your daily withdrawal limit. Please be wary when drawing cash—don't be distracted by strangers, and make sure they keep their distance.

Credit Cards: For the most part, you'll find credit cards to be invaluable (but beware card skimming; see the box "Don't let your credit card out of your sight!"). Accepted by the vast majority of retailers in South Africa, credit cards requiring a PIN are also the safest, most convenient way to access local currency via ATMs.

Newspapers & Magazines The weekly *Mail & Guardian* (www.mg.co.za) is one of the most intelligent papers and comes out every Friday with a comprehensive entertainment section. Local papers include the *Star* or the *Sowetan* in Johannesburg, the *Cape Times* and *Argus* in Cape Town, the *Natal Mercury* in Durban, and the *Eastern Province Herald* in Port Elizabeth. *Business Day* is South Africa's (very slim but well-written) version of the *Wall Street Journal* or *Financial Times*. *Go!* (www.gomag.co.za) and *Getaway* (www.getaway.co.za) are monthly travel magazines that cover destinations throughout Africa and are well worth purchasing (or browsing) for cheap accommodations listings and up-to-date information; the latter has some superb photography to further tempt you.

Passports   See www.frommers.com/planning for information on how to obtain a passport.

For Residents of Australia: Contact the **Australian Passport Information Service** at ℭ **131-232,** or visit the government website at www.passports.gov.au.

For Residents of Canada: Contact the central **Passport Office,** Department of Foreign Affairs and International Trade, Ottawa, ON K1A 0G3 (ℭ **800/567-6868;** www.ppt.gc.ca).

For Residents of Ireland: Contact the **Passport Office,** Setanta Centre, Molesworth Street, Dublin 2 (ℭ **01/671-1633;** www.irlgov.ie/iveagh).

For Residents of New Zealand: Contact the **Passports Office** at ℭ **0800/225-050** in New Zealand, or 04/474-8100; or log on to www.passports.govt.nz.

For Residents of the United Kingdom: Visit your nearest passport office, major post office, or travel agency; contact the **United Kingdom Passport Service** at ℭ **0870/521-0410;** or search the website www.ukpa.gov.uk.

For Residents of the United States: To find your regional passport office, either check the U.S. Department of State's website or call the **National Passport Information Center** toll-free number (ℭ **877/487-2778**) for automated information.

Police   South Africa: ℭ **10111** or ℭ **112** from mobile phones (soon also from fixed-line phones).

Safety   Safety rules for travelers here are the same as elsewhere in the world, though the high incidence of crime warrants extra caution in southern African cities. However, by far the majority of cases occur in the suburbs, which are poorly policed, away from the main tourist destinations. The South African authorities make it a high priority to protect tourists; tourism police are deployed in several of the large towns, and the vast majority of visitors travel in South Africa without incident.

Take care, however: Criminals operate in many guises, and you'd be wise, for instance, not to accept unsolicited assistance with transport when arriving at the airport. As a general rule, always be aware of the people around you, whether you're walking down a busy city street or driving through a deserted suburb. If you sense danger, act on your instincts and cross the road, pop into a shop, or head for company. Don't flash expensive jewelry or fancy cameras; wear handbag straps across the neck and shoulder, and keep a good grip on items. Don't walk any of the major city-center streets after dark, especially if you're alone. Be on guard if you are alone on an empty beach or mountainside near urban areas; it's worth carrying a cellphone on you at all times, with emergency numbers (see "Useful Telephone Numbers," below) keyed in for easy access. Avoid no-go areas, such as Hillbrow, Jo'burg's notorious inner-city suburb, or visit only with a trusted guide or friend. Find out from your hotel or host how best to get where you're going and what's been happening on the streets recently. Finally, if you're confronted by an assailant, keep calm, don't make eye contact, don't resist in any way, and cooperate: Hand over whatever's requested, and you will survive shaken but unharmed.

With such widespread poverty, you will inevitably have to deal with beggars, some of them children. Money is often spent on alcohol or drugs; should you feel the need to make a difference, donate to a relevant charity (again, your host or concierge can advise). Some beggars offer services, such as watching your car while you shop or dine. This is an acceptable part of the informal economy. There is no need to feel intimidated, and how much you tip them is entirely personal, though with unemployment running as high as 40%, this is the best way to help the many who need the dignity of a sense of employment as much as your small change.

Safety on the Road: If you're used to civilized, law-abiding drivers, you'll find South African road manners leave a lot to be desired. Drunk driving can be a problem, so be extra aware of others, particularly when driving at night. When driving, keep your car doors locked, particularly in Johannesburg (it's a good idea to also lock your room, and don't open the door unless you're expecting someone or the person is known to you). Never leave valuables in clear view in your car, even when you are in it. Do not pick up hitchhikers, and if you're on a driving vacation, rent or keep a cellphone with you. Call the Automobile Association of South Africa (p. 444) should you break down. Call the police if you feel nervous and wish for an escort or company. If you are at a remote site or beach, be aware of who is there when you approach the spot, and don't leave your car if you don't feel safe. Trust your instincts. Also be aware of suspicious persons approaching you at a remote site; again, a cellphone, with the correct emergency numbers on speed dial, is recommended for peace of mind.

Discrimination: South Africa has come a long way since 1994 and, generally speaking, is home to some of the world's most politically sensitive communities. That said, you will still come across some die-hard racists and homophobes, usually (but by no means exclusively) outside of the urban areas. This should not be the case with any of our recommendations; if you encounter problems, let us know in writing and we'll investigate.

Senior Travel   South Africa is not a difficult destination for seniors to navigate. Driving on the "wrong" side of the road is probably the most intimidating prospect you'll have to face here. Admission prices to attractions are usually reduced for seniors (also known as "pensioners" in South Africa). Don't be shy about asking for discounts, and always carry some kind of identification that shows your date of birth. Accommodations discounts are unusual; national parks, for instance, may offer special rates, but these are for South African nationals only. Note that members of **AARP**, 601 E St. NW, Washington, DC 20049 (✆ **888/687-2277;** www.aarp.org), have access to a wide range of benefits, including *AARP: The Magazine* and a monthly newsletter; anyone over 50 can join. **Elderhostel** (✆ **877/426-8056;** www.elderhostel.org) is an excellent site, arranging study programs for those ages 55 and over, to all the countries listed in this guide; **ElderTreks** (✆ **800/741-7956;** www.eldertreks.com) does the same. **INTRAV** (✆ **800/456-8100;** www.intrav.com) is a high-end tour operator that caters to the mature, discerning traveler (not specifically seniors), with trips around the world that include guided safaris. In the U.K., **Saga** (www.saga.co.uk) leads the charge, offering a wide range of options for those over 50.

Smoking   Smoking is not permitted in public enclosed places. Some restaurants have partitioned areas for smokers.

Student Travel   If you're traveling internationally, you'd be wise to arm yourself with an **International Student Identity Card (ISIC),** which will offer savings on some entrance fees and has basic health and life insurance and a 24-hour help line. The card is available from **STA Travel** (📞 **800/781-4040** in North America; www.sta.com or www.statravel.com; or www.statravel.co.uk in the U.K.), the biggest student travel agency in the world, and the place to start looking for flights if you're a student. If you're no longer a student but are still under 26, you can get an **International Youth Travel Card (IYTC)** from the same people, which entitles you to some discounts (but not on museum admissions). **Travel CUTS** (📞 **800/667-2887** or 416/614-2887; www.travelcuts.com) offers similar services for both Canadian and U.S. residents. Irish students may prefer to turn to **USIT** (📞 **01/602-1600;** www.usitnow.ie), an Ireland-based specialist in student, youth, and independent travel.

South Africa has a large number of lodges and activities catering to the backpacker market—in Cape Town, contact **Africa Travel Centre** (📞 **27/21/423-5555;** www.backpackers.co.za), a recommended backpackers' resource near the center of town, with comfortable accommodations and an excellent travel desk aimed at the budget traveler.

Taxes   South Africa levies a 14% value-added tax (VAT) on most goods and services—make sure this is included in any quoted price (by law, items must be marked as clearly excluding VAT or having VAT included). Foreign visitors are not exempt for paying VAT on purchased goods. They may, however, claim back VAT paid on items taken out of the country when the total value exceeds R250. The refund may be lodged by presenting the tax invoice (make sure it has a VAT registration number on it) together with their passport to the VAT Refund Administrator's offices, which are situated at OR Tambo and Cape Town International Airports, as well as at visitor bureaus. Call 📞 **021/934-8675** to find locations and hours.

Telephones   There are five cellphone service providers—Cell C, MTN, Vodacom, 8ta, and Virgin Mobile—offering excellent coverage. Landline services are operated by a monopoly (Telkom); a second operator, Neotel, is in operation but with extremely limited service, and hardly noticeable to most people. Telkom public telephones use coins, phone cards, or Worldcall. Phone cards and Worldcall can be purchased at most retail stores, petrol stations, post offices and airports.

Avoid paying the massive markups on hotel telephone bills by bringing your own cell and purchasing a telephone number/SIM card for local calls. If you need to call home a lot, your best bet (certainly the cheapest) is of course, to use Skype. Herewith some background telephone tips regardless of how you choose to dial that number:

To call southern Africa from another country: Dial the international access code (United States or Canada 011, United Kingdom or New Zealand 00, Australia 0011) plus the **country code** (the country code for South Africa is 27; for Zimbabwe, it is 263; for Botswana, it is 267), plus the local region code (minus the 0) and the number.

To make an international call from South Africa: Dial 00, then the country code (U.S. or Canada 1, U.K. 44, Australia 61, New Zealand 64), the area code, and the local number.

To charge international calls from South Africa: Dial AT&T Direct (📞 0-800-99-0123), Sprint (📞 0800-99-0001), or MCI (📞 0800-99-0011).

To make a local call: If you have a number with the country code, you will need to drop the country code and add a zero (0) to the city code (except in Botswana, which has no city codes). In South Africa, you dial the city or region code (for example, 012 before every Cape Town number, or 011 before Gauteng numbers, 031 for Durban, and so on). Note also that if you are using a mobile phone, you always need to enter the network code before the telephone number; codes 082, 083, 084, 072, 073, 074, and 076 are all for cellphone numbers, and these codes must also not be dropped.

Looking for a number: In South Africa: Call directory assistance at 📞 **1023** for numbers in South Africa, and 📞 **0903** for international numbers. To track down a service, call 📞 **10118.** Be patient, speak slowly, and check spellings with your operator. Better still use the directory assistance offered by the cellphone network you signed up with; the biggest, Vodacom, answers to 110 and is far more efficient than Telkom.

Useful Telephone Numbers: In South Africa, call directory assistance at ℂ **1023** for numbers in South Africa and ℂ **0903** for international numbers when using a landline. (ℂ **110** if using a cellphone). **Computicket** (ℂ **083/915-8000;** www.computicket.co.za) is a free national booking service that covers cinema and concert seats, as well as inter-city bus tickets; payment can be made over the phone by credit card or online. Some events and services are booked exclusively through Webtickets (www.webtickets.co.za), a service which usually requires you to print out your tickets.

Time   Southern Africa is 2 hours ahead of GMT (that is, 7 hr. ahead of Eastern Standard Time).

Tipping   Add 10% to 20% to your restaurant bill, 10% to your taxi. Porters get around R5 per bag. There are no self-serve garages or gas stations; when filling up with fuel, tip the person around R5; this is also what you tip informal car guards (identified by their neon bib) who look after cars on the street. It's also worth leaving some money for the person cleaning your hotel room. Be generous if you feel the service warrants it—this is one of the best ways to alleviate the poverty you may find distressing.

Visas   **South Africa:** Aside from a valid passport, citizens of the United States, the E.U., the U.K., Canada, Australia, and New Zealand need only a return ticket for a 90-day stay in South Africa. Upon entering, you will automatically be given a free entry permit sticker. Visitors wanting to stay for a longer period will have to apply formally for a visa, as opposed to relying on the automatic entry permit. For more information, visit the South African Home Affairs Department website, **www.home-affairs.gov.za**.

Botswana: To enter Botswana, sufficient funds to finance your stay, as well as outgoing travel documents, are required. Holders of U.S., Commonwealth (S.A., Australian, and NZ), and most European passports (including U.K. and Irish) do not require visas.

Zimbabwe: Note that you may purchase a single-entry visa upon arrival (by far the easiest option). You will need cash (in dollars) as well as return tickets, and may need to prove sufficient funds to support your stay.

Should you wish to leave, even for a few hours, and then reenter Zimbabwe, you will need to buy a double entry visa upon arrival; it works out cheaper. (Note that multiple-entry visas cannot be obtained at the port of entry; you'll have to go to the town office, and it may take up to 7 working days. If you need a multiple-entry visa, visit the Zimbabwe Embassy in your country prior to departure.)

Visa fees depend on nationality. Most nationalities (including Americans, Australians, and New Zealanders) are charged $30 for a single entry (double entry $45). British and Irish nationals pay $55 for a single entry; $70 for double entry. Canadians pay $75. Make sure you have the right amount in dollars, and double-check these figures before departure with travel agent or visit www.victoriafalls-guide.net. Remember to take two passport photographs; you can print out and complete the application forms beforehand but this is not necessary. If you really want to you can obtain your visa in advance, but this will incur an additional fee; consult your travel agent in this regard or use Travel Document Systems. (For visa applications and physical addresses in New York, San Francisco, and Washington, D.C., visit www.traveldocs.com.)

Zambia: All nationalities are charged $50 for a single-entry visa and $80 for a double- or multiple-entry visa. Note that day visitors to the Zambian side of Victoria Falls from Zimbabwe can purchase a $20 **day-tripper visa** at the bridge (www.zambiaimmigration.gov.zm).

Visitor Information   **South Africa:** South African Tourism. Two excellent sites worth browsing before you leave are www.southafrica.net and www.southafrica.info.

In the U.S.: 500 Fifth Ave., 20th Floor, Ste. 2040, New York, NY 10110 (© 212/730-2929; info.us@southafrica.net). Brochure line © 800/593-1318.

In Canada: 4117 Lawrence Ave. E., Ste. 2, Ontario M1E 2S2 (© 0416/966-4059).

In the U.K.: 6 Alt Grove, London SW19 4DZ (© 02/8971-9350; info.uk@southafrica.net). Brochure line © 0870/1550044.

In Australia: 117 York St., Ste. 301, Level 3, Sydney, NSW 2000 (© 02-9261-5000; info@southafricantourism.com.au). Brochure line © 800/238-643.

Water   South African tap water is safe to drink in all cities and most rural areas. Always ask in game reserves. We love places that offer purified iced water in glass jugs or bottles rather than the environmentally polluting plastic bottles (in Durban, look out for Dew glass-bottled water, which is harvested from the atmosphere). If you care, do make a fuss at hotels and guesthouses where plastic bottles are provided as a matter of course—it's amazing what a little consciousness-raising feedback can do to make a difference. Please note that South Africa is drought sensitive so try not to waste water.

Weather   For up to 3 days ahead see www.weathersa.co.za or call © **082-162.**

Index